**If you have Windows 3.X,**
1. INSERT the disc in your CD-ROM drive.
2. Go to the Windows Program Manager.
3. SELECT File, then Run.
4. In the Run dialog box, TYPE D:\SETUP.EXE. (This assumes that your CD-ROM runs from the D drive; if it runs from another drive, enter that letter instead.)
5. CLICK on OK.
6. Follow the prompts by clicking on NEXT or YES.
7. Once Employment Guide is installed, DOUBLE-CLICK on its icon in the "BNA Libraries on CD" group to begin using the Guide.

## WHAT'S ON THE DISC:

**EMPLOYMENT GUIDE:** Here's where you'll find practical guidance on HR policies and procedures, including hiring, recordkeeping, wage and hour law, pay systems, payroll administration, benefits administration, retirement and pension benefits, and termination.

**EMPLOYMENT GUIDE INDEX:** This detailed index to the Employment Guide is one of the best ways to find information quickly. You'll soon find it invaluable.

**BULLETIN TO MANAGEMENT:** This weekly publication gives you newsworthy reporting of all subject areas covered in the Employment Guide. Your Employment Guide on CD contains the archives of Bulletin to Management.

## MOVING AROUND EMPLOYMENT GUIDE:

Links are the primary method of moving around the CD. You can double-click on an icon, button, or text link, to move to another part of the CD. After following a link, you can use the BACKTRACK button at the top of the screen to return to the previous screen.

## FINDING INFORMATION ON THE CD:

**MAIN MENU:** From the Main Menu, double-click on any of these icons to begin your research.

- Employment Guide
- Employment Guide Index
- Bulletin to Management...

 **EMPLOYMENT GUIDE INDEX:** This is the best place to begin your research. The entire Employment Guide can be accessed through the comprehensive list of index terms found in the Master Index. Double-click on any letter of the alphabet to go to that section of the Index. You can also enter word searches in the Index.

 **TABLE OF CONTENTS:** Once you have followed a link to an infobase, such as the Employment Guide, you can use the CONTENTS button at the top of the screen to view a "Table of Contents" for that infobase. Double-click on the Plus (+) or Minus (-) signs to open or close the "Chapters." When you find a topic of interest, double-click directly on the topic to open the chapter and begin reading. You can also enter word searches in the Table of Contents.

**SEARCHING:** Once you are in an infobase, click on the WORDS button at the top of the screen to begin a word search in the open infobase. Type a word or phrase, such as *overtime pay*, then click on the VIEW RESULTS button. Your search results will be displayed in CONTENTS format. When you find a topic of interest, double-click directly on the topic to open the chapter and begin reading. Use the NEXT button at the top of the screen to see where your search terms appear.

**STATE INFORMATION:** Once you are in the Guidebook, click on the STATE button at the top of the screen. You may type in the state(s) abbreviation or name as well as specific words to search within your selected state(s). Alternatively, you may enter a WORDS search in the Employment Guide Index for a complete listing of individual state coverage. Enter the Master Index, click on the WORDS button at the top of the screen, type in the state's full name, then click on View Results.

**GETTING STARTED:** Try this on-screen tutorial to better understand how to use Folio Views software and for tips on getting the most out of your CD subscription.

## SYSTEM RECOMMENDATIONS:

System recommendations include an IBM-compatible MS-DOS or Windows 95 PC with an 486 processor or better, MS-DOS 5.0 or higher, Windows 3.1 or higher, 8MB RAM, hard disk drive with at least 6MB free space, CD-ROM drive (double speed or better) with driver software, color monitor (VGA or better), and a printer (optional) with at least 2MB RAM. For optimum performance, a Pentium processor or better with 16MB RAM.

While this is the recommended configuration, the following system components may be substituted, with sacrifices in speed and performance: 80386 processor with 6MB RAM, running MS-DOS 3.2 or higher and Windows.

# Human Resource Management

## NINTH EDITION

## Robert L. Mathis
University of Nebraska at Omaha

## John H. Jackson
University of Wyoming

**South-Western College Publishing**
Thomson Learning™

Australia • Canada • Denmark • Japan • Mexico • New Zealand • Philippines
Puerto Rico • Singapore • South Africa • Spain • United Kingdom • United States

Publisher: Dave Shaut
Acquisitions Editor: Charles E. McCormick, Jr.
Developmental Editor: Judy O'Neill
Marketing Manager: Joseph A. Sabatino
Production Editor: Deanna R. Quinn
Media and Technology Editor: Kevin von Gillern
Media Production Editor: Robin K. Browning
Manufacturing Coordinator: Dana Began Schwartz
Internal Design: Ellen Pettengell Design
Cartoon Research: Feldman & Associates, Inc.
Photography Manager: Cary Benbow
Cover Design: Paul Neff Design
Cover Images: © 1999 Photodisc and © 1999 Artville
Production House and Compositor: D&G Limited, LLC
Printer: West Group

Printed in the United States of America
1  2  3  4  5  02  01  00  99

For more information contact South-Western College Publishing, 5101 Madison Road,
Cincinnati, Ohio, 45227 or find us on the Internet at http://www.swcollege.com

**For permission to use material from this text or product, contact us by**
• **telephone: 1-800-730-2214**
• **fax: 1-800-730-2215**
• **web: http://www.thomsonrights.com**

**Library of Congress Cataloging-in-Publication Data**
Mathis, Robert L.
    Human resource management / Robert L. Mathis, John H. Jackson --
9th ed.
        p.      cm.
    Includes bibliographical references (p. ) and indexes.
    ISBN 0-538-89004-5 (package)
    ISBN 0-538-89005-3 (book : hard : alk. paper)
    ISBN 0-538-89006-1 (CD)
    1. Personnel management.      I.   Jackson, John Harold.   II.   Title.
HF5549.M3349 2000
658.3--dc21                                                99-15314

This book is printed on acid-free paper.

# Contents in Brief

# Contents

## SECTION 2

# Staffing the Organization  139

# SECTION 3

# Training and Developing Human Resources 313

## SECTION 4

# Compensating Human Resources 413

## SECTION 5

# Employee and Labor Relations 527

# Preface

*❝The future has suddenly and dramatically become the present. ❞*
**R. Babson**

Organizations today face many challenges in the management of their human resources. Every week brings news media reports on organization downsizing, workforce diversity, shortages of skilled workers in many industries, and other concerns. The purpose of this book is to provide understanding of developments in the field of human resource (HR) management that managers will face in the new century.

The ninth edition of the book continues the successful tradition established in the past, but authors again have made many changes in this edition to address newly emerging issues and research and to reflect changes in the way HR management activities are being implemented. The goal is to build on past experiences and to continue as the leading HR management text. Authors sometimes do what is referred to as "a cosmetic revision," using the same basic content with some new design features to justify the need for a new edition. This approach is not acceptable to the authors of this book; consequently, every line and word of content from the previous edition has been reviewed, and major revisions have been made. We believe that the ninth edition is the most current, readable, and excellent HR text available.

There are a number of reasons for someone to read this book. Certainly not everyone who reads it will become an HR manager. In fact, most students who take HR courses will not even become HR generalists or specialists. But everyone who works in any organization will come in contact with HR management—both effective and ineffective. Those who become operating managers must be able to manage HR activities, because they can have major consequences for every organization. One continuing feature of the book is specifying the areas of contact between operating managers and the HR unit. Throughout the book these "interfaces" describe typical divisions of HR responsibilities, even though some variations oc-

cur depending on the size of the organization, its technology, history, and other factors.

Another important audience for the book is composed of practicing HR professionals. Previous editions of the book have aided hundreds of HR professionals to enhance their knowledge and to prepare for professional exams, so that they can become PHR or SPHR certified by the Human Resource Certification Institute (HRCI). This edition will continue to be valuable to HR professionals, and conscious efforts have been made by the authors to provide content coverage of the topics in the HRCI content outline, which is reproduced in Appendix A.

## In the Ninth Edition

This edition continues some features highly regarded in past editions, but some new ones have been added as well. A few of the latter are noted next.

### BNA Employment Guide (Student Edition)

An important addition to the ninth edition is the inclusion of the *BNA Employment Guide (Student Edition)* on CD-ROM (EMG). Produced by the Bureau of National Affairs, an industry leader in providing HR information to the HR professionals, the EMG contains current coverage of HR policies, compliance issues, forms, and details to supplement the text coverage. Also, a number of issues of the highly regarded *Bulletin to Management*, from BNA, a weekly update for HR professionals, have been included. To tie the BNA CD to text content throughout the book, most chapters contain specific BNA section notations as a margin feature. Each of the margin citations to the *BNA Employment Guide* directs readers to specific content on the CD relevant to the material being discussed at that point in the chapter.

## Internet

As the Internet has exploded in usage by HR professionals, a number of HR activities have been affected. To incorporate more Internet links, several features have been added or expanded. First, throughout the text the *Logging On* feature identifies websites that contain useful sources of HR information in specific content areas. Each of these items contains a specific World Wide Web address, and all were active at the publication time of this text. Second, the end of each chapter contains a feature, *Using the Internet*, which presents an exercise requiring students to use a designated Internet site to respond to typical HR situations or managerial requests. Finally, where appropriate, references from web addresses are cited in the chapter notes.

# Organization of the Ninth Edition

The organization of the ninth edition reflects significant changes from the previous edition. Key changes are noted next.

## Eighteen Chapters

In this edition there are 18 chapters, down from 20 in the previous edition. The material on HR information systems and assessing HR effectiveness has been integrated into Chapters 2 and 3, where HR planning and organizational competitiveness are discussed. Also, the content on union-management relations has been combined into one chapter.

## HR as Strategic Business Contributor

The need for HR professionals and the activities they direct to contribute to the strategic business success of organizations is stressed. This emphasis is introduced in the first three chapters, which have been revised significantly. The first chapter looks at three roles of HR management: *strategic, operational,* and *administrative,* and how HR activities must support these three roles. Chapter 2 addresses strategic human resource planning, and additional coverage of strategic HR forces has been included.

## HR's Contribution to Organizational Effectiveness and Global Success

A significantly revised Chapter 3 focuses on human resources as they affect organizational competitiveness. The chapter specifically discusses the impact that human resources have on productivity, quality, and service in organizations. The chapter considers productivity from individual, organizational, and national perspectives, and develops a model for evaluating the effectiveness of HR management in an organization. The global dimensions of competitiveness and HR management are examined in Chapter 4.

## Equal Employment and Affirmative Action

Major revisions have been made in Chapters 5 and 6 that cover equal employment opportunity (EEO). The authors believe that the issues of diversity and equal employment are closely linked, and Chapter 5 begins with a discussion of diversity and HR management's role with managing diversity. Then the legal framework for EEO is covered, along with both sides of the contentious debate on affirmative action. Chapter 5 adds material on managing diversity and on problems associated with diversity training. Also, the discussion of validity has been changed and the content of the affirmative action debate has been updated to reflect the most recent court decisions and other developments. The sixth chapter contains a detailed look at various aspects of implementing equal employment, such as sexual harassment, age discrimination, religious discrimination, and many others. The coverage of sexual harassment, as a result of recent U.S. Supreme Court decisions, has been revised and expanded.

## Staffing the Organization

Chapter 7, which covers job analysis, contains significant new content on the competency identification process for jobs and work. The traditional coverage of generating task-based job descriptions and job specifications has been changed also. Recruiting in tight labor markets is the focus of Chapter 8. The difficulties of recruiting scarce-skilled employees and new methods of attracting these individuals are discussed. Specifically, the chapter highlights the use of the Internet and flexible staffing approaches. The growing use of professional employer organizations and employee leasing are considered as other approaches to staffing organizational jobs. The well-regarded coverage on selection has been expanded to encompass the selection strategy choices that management must make. The coverage of psychological testing includes a review of material on the "Big Five" personality traits as predictors. The text identifies common selection interview questions by predictor area.

## Training and Developing Human Potential

Chapter 10 on training contains comprehensive coverage on employee orientation and major issues associated with training. Specific content addresses the effects of educational and skill deficiencies of U.S. workers and how employers are addressing those deficiencies. Chapter 11 looks at the means used to develop human resources. The dilemma of downsizing middle management over the last decade and the resulting current shortage of effective middle managers is examined. The chapter also discusses changes in jobs and the career implications of those changes.

## Performance Management

Chapter 12 expands the material on identifying and measuring employee performance. *Combination methods* for appraising performance are a part of the performance appraisal process discussions. The 360° approach and other means of feedback are integral in many performance management systems. The chapter emphasizes performance management and the role of the performance appraisal process in enhancing the performance of human resources in organizations.

## Compensating Human Resources

Compensation of human resources covers pay administration, incentives, and benefits. Information has been included on approaches such as broadbanding and competency-based pay to augment the detailed coverage of base compensation, pay-for-performance, and variable-pay programs that are presented in Chapters 13 and 14. New coverage of variable-pay plans of various types has been added. Also, changes in content have been made in Chapter 15, on benefits, in order to highlight the growing cost concerns facing HR professionals and organizations.

## Employee Relations

Employee relations has several aspects, including health, safety, and security. The well-regarded coverage in Chapter 16 of health, safety, and security has been continued, exploring such areas as hazard communications, personal protective equipment, bloodborne pathogens, and other OSHA compliance issues. A growing issue discussed is the need to prevent workplace violence, which sometimes is a result of domestic violence away from work situations. The various issues associated with employee rights and discipline, such as employment-at-will, privacy rights, and substance abuse have been expanded in Chapter 17. New coverage has been added on such emerging issues as electronic monitoring, privacy, and e-mail, and other employee-rights issues affected by technology.

## Union-Management Relations

Two previous chapters on labor-management relations and collective bargaining have been combined into one chapter, in order to focus on the changing role of unions in the U.S. economy. Caution was taken to retain the essential content while carefully pruning expendable detail. In addition, new material has been included on union efforts to target employers, and on international differences in labor relations systems. Also discussed are reasons for the decline of unions' share of the U.S. civilian workforce and management's strategic choice between cooperating and trying to stay nonunion.

# Chapter Features

Each chapter begins with specific learning objectives that have been identified for that chapter. Next, the *HR Transitions* feature contains an example of an HR problem, situation, or practice in an actual organization that illustrates some facet of that chapter's content. Each chapter also presents "HR Perspective" vignettes that highlight specific practices by employers, research studies on HR management topics, and/or ethical issues in HR management. Both the *BNA Employment Guide* and the *Logging On* features provide linkages to additional material beyond the text content.

Following a point-by-point summary, the review and discussions questions are linked to the opening learning objectives. Key terms and concepts are listed, and a "Using the Internet" exercise is included. At the end of every chapter is a case that presents a real-life problem or situation using actual organizations as examples. Finally, reference notes to sources cited in the chapter are given. Particular attention was given by the authors to including current references and research to keep the text as the one that competitors emulate.

# Supplements

## Student Resource Guide
### (ISBN 0-538-89009-6)

Designed from a student's perspective by William D. Kelly, SPHR, this useful study guide comes with all the tools necessary to maximize results in class and on exams. Chapter objectives, chapter summaries, chapter outlines, and study questions (including matching, true/false, idea completion, multiple choice, and essay questions) with an answer key are provided.

## HR Management Professional Review
### (ISBN 0-534-76811-3)

A Web-based learning companion, the HR Management Professional Review uses a question-and-feedback format to give individuals the opportunity to identify and review their professional knowledge of HR management content. The HR Management Professional Review provides a broad-based review of topics central to HR management that professionals must know. For individuals who will be taking tests over HR management content, a prologue of test-taking tips is included to ease exam anxiety and provide practical advice. Visit *www.itped.com* for more information.

## Videos (ISBNs 0-538-89013-4, 0-324-02397-9, 0-324-02398-7)

A diverse selection of custom-produced videos, part of South-Western College Publishing's BusinessLink video library, are available in three volumes to introduce topics, supplement lecture material, and stimulate discussion. Featuring companies such as Valassis

Communications, Hudson's, and Yahoo!, segments illustrate human resource issues providing insights into conducting performance appraisals, motivating for performance, interviewing, and more.

## Instructor's Manual
### (ISBN 0-538-89007-X)

The instructor's manual, prepared by Cary Thorp, University of Nebraska–Lincoln, represents one of the most exciting, professionally useful instructor's aids available. Comprehensive teaching materials, including chapter overviews, chapter outlines, instructor's notes, and suggested answers to end-of-chapter Review and Discussion Questions and Using the Internet exercises are provided for every chapter. A guide to the videos available for use in classes includes notes about how to introduce the videos to your students, points to consider when viewing various segments, and questions for discussion.

## Test Bank (ISBN 0-538-89008-8)

The test bank contains over 1,500 test questions prepared by Roger Dean, of Washington and Lee University. Multiple-choice , true/false, and essay questions are provided for every chapter. Answers are cross-referenced to pages in the textbook that pinpoint where relevant material in the text can be found. When the answer to a true/false question is false, feedback is provided to underscore the reason why.

The test bank is also available in a computerized Windows™-compatible format. Thomson Learning Testing Tools™ (ISBN 0-538-89012-6) is a fully integrated software suite of test creation, delivery, and classroom management tools. With Thompson Learning Testing Tools instructors can deliver testing activities on paper, via a local area network, or online. Explore *www.itped.com* for more information.

## Transparency Acetates
### (ISBN 0-538-89011-8)

Prepared by Cary Thorp, University of Nebraska–Lincoln, in conjunction with the instructor's manual, a full-color set of 120 transparency acetates is also available to instructors to enhance classroom presentations. All acetates are tied to the instructor's notes provided in the instructor's manual, prompting users about appropriate times to display them and giving them points to emphasize as they are discussed. Acetates include core diagrams from the text in addition to content that ranges beyond textbook coverage.

## Microsoft® PowerPoint® Presentation Slides (ISBN 0-538-89010-X)

A comprehensive set of full-color presentation graphics is available to supplement course content, in version 4.0 and 7.0 formats. All that is needed is Windows® to run the PowerPoint® viewer and an LCD panel for classroom display.

## Human Resource Management Web Site

At *mathis.swcollege.com* instructors and students will find useful tools and additional resources to enrich and extend textbook presentations. Instructors will find downloadable ancillary materials and additional cases that address various dimensions of text content in different organizational settings (selected especially for use with *Human Resource Management, Ninth Edition*, by Nicholas E. Dayan, SPHR, a practicing HR executive). Career advice, information about how to analyze cases, as well as quick links to important organizations and companies mentioned in the text, can be found at mathis.swcollege.com.

# Acknowledgments

Producing any book requires assistance from many others. The authors are especially grateful to those individuals who provided reviews and numerous helpful comments for the ninth edition. Including two reviewers who asked to remain anonymous, the following individuals did comprehensive reviews:

Larry Brandt — Nova Southeastern University

Derek E. Crews — Alderson-Broaddus College
Avis L. Johnson — University of Akron
Daniel Lybrook — Purdue University

Fraya Wagner-Marsh — Eastern Michigan University
Jonathan Monat — California State University at Long Beach
Donald P. Rogers, SPHR — Rollins College
Joy Schneer — Rider University
Cary Thorp — University of Nebraska–Lincoln

In addition, specific suggestions from Carl Thornton (General Motors Institute) were appreciated.

Finally, some leading HR professionals provided ideas and assistance. Appreciation is expressed to Nicholas Dayan, SPHR; William D. Kelly, SPHR; Michael R. Losey, SPHR; Jerry L. Sellentin, SPHR; and Raymond B. Weinberg, SPHR.

Those involved in changing messy scrawls into printed ideas deserve special recognition. At the top of that list is Jo Ann Mathis, whose guidance and prodding made this book better. Others who assisted with many critical details include Carolyn Foster and our copy editor, Chris Thillen. Special thanks for assistance with developing some special figures for the text go to Deann Mandel. Also, Julie Woodard did a superb job of identifying and compiling the Internet features found throughout the book.

The authors are especially appreciative to Charles McCormick, Jr., our South-Western College Publishing editor, for making the planning and transitions required for the edition less stressful than they could have been. We also appreciate the support and encouragement throughout the production process of Judy O'Neill and Deanna Quinn of South-Western College Publishing.

The authors are confident that this edition will continue to be the standard for the HR field. We believe that it is a relevant and interesting text for those learning more about HR management, and we are optimistic that those who use the book will agree.

Robert L. Mathis, SPHR — John H. Jackson
Omaha, Nebraska — Laramie, Wyoming

# About the Authors

## DR. ROBERT L. MATHIS

Dr. Robert Mathis is Professor of Management at the University of Nebraska at Omaha (UNO). Born and raised in Texas, he received a B.B.A. and M.B.A. from Texas Tech University and a Ph.D. in Management and Organization from the University of Colorado. At UNO he has received the University's "Excellence in Teaching" award.

Dr. Mathis has co-authored several books and has published numerous articles covering a variety of topics over the last 25 years. On the professional level, Dr. Mathis has held numerous national offices in the Society for Human Resource Management and in other professional organizations, including the Academy of Management. He also has served as President of the Human Resource Certification Institute (HRCI) and is certified as a Senior Professional in Human Resources (SPHR) by HRCI.

He has had extensive consulting experiences with organizations of all sizes in a variety of areas. Firms assisted have been in telecommunications, telemarketing, financial, manufacturing, retail, health-care, and utility industries. He has extensive specialized consulting experience in establishing or revising compensation plans for small- and medium-sized firms. Internationally, Dr. Mathis has consulting and training experience with organizations in Australia, Lithuania, Romania, Moldova, and Taiwan.

## DR. JOHN H. JACKSON

Dr. John H. Jackson is Professor of Management at the University of Wyoming. Born in Alaska, he received his B.B.A. and M.B.A. from Texas Tech University. He then worked in the telecommunications industry in human resources management for several years. After leaving that industry, he completed his doctoral studies at the University of Colorado and received his Ph.D. in Management and Organization.

During his academic career, Dr. Jackson has authored four other college texts and over 50 articles and papers, including those appearing in *Academy of Management Review, Journal of Management, Human Resources Management,* and *Human Resources Planning.* He has consulted widely with a variety of organizations on HR and management development matters. During the past several years, Dr. Jackson has served as an expert witness in a number of HR-related cases.

At the University of Wyoming he served two terms as Department Head in the Department of Management and Marketing. Dr. Jackson has received teaching awards at Wyoming and was one of the first to work with two-way interactive television for MBA students in the state. In addition, he designed one of the first classes in the nation on *Business Environment and Natural Resources.* In addition to teaching, Dr. Jackson is president of Silverwood Ranches, Inc.

# HR Management—Strategies and Environment

## CHAPTER 1

# Changing Nature of Human Resource Management

*After you have read this chapter, you should be able to:*

- Identify four major HR challenges currently facing organizations and managers.

- List and define each of the seven major categories of HR activities.

- Identify the three different roles of HR management.

- Discuss the three dimensions associated with HR management as a strategic business contributor.

- Explain why HR professionals and operating managers must view HR management as an interface.

- Discuss why ethical issues and professionalism affect HR management as a career field.

# HR Management Contributes to Organizational Success

More effective management of human resources (HR) increasingly is being seen as positively affecting performance in organizations, both large and small.

A joint venture between General Electric and a Japanese company, GE Fanuc is a manufacturer of factory automation and control products. Headquartered in Virginia with 1,500 employees, the HR department primarily performed administrative support activities. But when Donald Borwhat, Jr., took over as Senior Vice President of Human Resources, he and his staff began by restructuring and decentralizing the HR entity so that each functional area of the company has an HR manager assigned to it. The HR managers were expected to be key contributors to their areas by becoming knowledgeable about the business issues faced by their business functional units. Today, HR managers participate in developing business strategies and ensure that human resource dimensions are considered. For instance, the HR manager for manufacturing has HR responsibilities for 600 employees. In that role she contributes to workflow, production, scheduling, and other manufacturing decisions. It also means that she is more accessible to and has more credibility with manufacturing workers, most of whom are hourly workers.

Making the transition in HR management required going from seven to three levels of management, greatly expanding the use of cross-functional work teams, and significantly increasing training. To ease employee and managerial anxieties about the changes, GE Fanuc promised that no employees would lose their jobs. Managers and supervisors affected by the elimination of levels were offered promotions, transfers to other jobs in GE Fanuc, or early retirement buyouts. Additionally, employees were promised profit sharing, which has resulted in up to three weeks additional pay in profit sharing bonuses in some years.

The test of the change is in the results. GE Fanuc's revenue is up

women employees, who composed about three-fourths of the bank's workers. As a result, several years later about one-fourth of all managers and executives are women. Similar attention also was focused on other diverse groups of employees. So that all employees were given opportunities to grow and learn, the Bank of Montreal's Institute of Learning was established at a cost exceeding $50 million. The goal of providing five days of training and education to every employee each year has been met for several years.

To focus on performance, each department and every employee have

> *HR managers participate in developing strategies and ensure that human resource dimensions are considered.*

almost 18%. Over 40 work teams meet regularly to discuss work goals, track their performance against established measures, and discuss problems and issues. Employee turnover is also extremely low in most areas.

Transitions in HR management are also paying off in the Bank of Montreal, based in Montreal, Quebec. Emphasizing human resources has involved 35,000 employees in organizational success. This recognition meant focusing greater attention on the talents of diverse employees working at the bank. Specific efforts were made to expand opportunities for

performance targets and measures on such factors as customer service, return on equity, and profitability. Yearly, the scores from all measures are computed as indices, and then compiled into one figure to measure overall bank performance. Executives believe that their emphasis on HR activities has contributed significantly to the Bank of Montreal's achieving period profits for seven years in a row.

In summary, it is evident that the transition of HR management at GE Fanuc and at Bank of Montreal has enhanced organizational competitiveness and success.[1]

> ❝ *HR should be defined not by what it does, but by what it delivers.* ❞
> DAVID ULRICH

**Human Resource (HR) management**
The design of formal systems in an organization to ensure the effective and efficient use of human talent to accomplish the organizational goals.

As human resources have become viewed as more critical to organizational success, many organizations have realized that it is the *people* in an organization that can provide a competitive advantage.[2] Throughout the book it will be emphasized that the people as human resources contribute to and affect the competitive success of the organization. **Human Resource (HR) management** deals with the design of formal systems in an organization to ensure the effective and efficient use of human talent to accomplish organizational goals. In an organization, the management of human resources means that they must be recruited, compensated, trained, and developed.

# HR Management Challenges

The environment faced by HR management is a challenging one; changes are occurring rapidly across a wide range of issues. A study by the Hudson Institute, entitled *Workforce 2020,* has highlighted some of the most important workforce issues.[3] From that and other sources, it appears that the most prevalent challenges facing HR management are as follows:

- Economic and technological change
- Workforce availability and quality concerns
- Demographics and diversity issues
- Organizational restructuring

## Economic and Technological Change

Several economic changes have occurred that have altered employment and occupational patterns in the United States. A major change is the shift of jobs from manufacturing and agriculture to service industries and telecommunications. This shift has meant that some organizations have had to reduce the number of employees, while others have had to attract and retain employees with different capabilities than previously were needed. Additionally, pressures from global competitors have forced many U.S. firms to close facilities, adapt their management practices, and increase productivity and decrease labor costs in order to become more competitive. Finally, the explosive growth of information technology, particularly that linked to the Internet, has forced many changes throughout organizations of all types.

**OCCUPATIONAL SHIFTS** Projections of the growth and decline in jobs illustrates the economic and employment shifts currently occurring. Figure 1–1 indicates the occupations with the largest percentage growth anticipated between 1996 and 2006. It is interesting to note that in Figure 1–1 most of the fastest-growing occupations percentagewise are related to information technology or health care. The increase in the technology jobs is due to the rapid increase in the use of information technology, such as databases, system design and analysis, and desktop publishing. The health care jobs are growing as a result of the aging of the U.S. population and workforce, a factor discussed later.

**FIGURE 1–1** *The 10 Occupations with the Fastest Employment Growth, 1996–2006*

| Occupation | Employment | | Change, 1996–2006 | |
|---|---|---|---|---|
| | 1996 | 2006 | Number | Percent |
| Database administrators, computer support specialists, and all other computer scientists | 212 | 461 | 249 | 118 |
| Computer engineers | 216 | 451 | 235 | 109 |
| Systems analysts | 506 | 1,025 | 520 | 103 |
| Personal and home care aides | 202 | 374 | 171 | 85 |
| Physical and corrective therapy assistants and aides | 84 | 151 | 66 | 79 |
| Home health aides | 495 | 873 | 378 | 76 |
| Medical assistants | 225 | 391 | 166 | 74 |
| Desktop publishing specialists | 30 | 53 | 22 | 74 |
| Physical therapists | 115 | 196 | 81 | 71 |
| Occupational therapy assistants and aides | 16 | 26 | 11 | 69 |

*Numbers in Thousands of Jobs*

SOURCE: U.S. Department of Labor, Bureau of Labor Statistics, http://stats.bls.gov/ecopro.table6.htm

**GLOBAL COMPETITION** One major factor affecting these shifts is the globalization of economic forces. As seen the past few years, the collapse of Asian economies had significant effects on U.S.-based organizations. One estimate by U.S. government statisticians is that over 25% of all U.S. manufacturing workers hold jobs dependent on exporting goods to other countries. This is particularly true with more highly skilled, technical jobs in technology-driven industries. As a result, these export-driven jobs pay wages averaging 25% higher than most other manufacturing jobs.[4] On the other hand, the less-skilled manufacturing assembly jobs have been shifting from the higher-wage, developed economies in the United States and Western Europe to developing countries in Eastern Europe, China, Thailand, Mexico, and the Phillippines.

Due to the increase in information technology, global linkages are now more extensive and production and transportation can be coordinated worldwide. Therefore, the loss of manufacturing jobs in the United States has been replaced with jobs in information technology, financial services, health care, and retail services.

In summary, the U.S. economy has become a service economy, and that shift is expected to continue. Over 80% of U.S. jobs are in service industries, and most new jobs created by the year 2006 also will be in services. It is estimated that manufacturing jobs will represent only 12% to 15% of all U.S. jobs by that date.

## Workforce Availability and Quality

In many parts of the United States today, significant workforce shortages exist due to an inadequate supply of workers with the skills needed to perform the jobs being added. In the last several years news reports have regularly described tight labor markets with unemployment rates in some locales below 3%. Also, continuously there are reports by industries and companies facing shortages of qualified,

*LOGGING ON . . .*
**Workforce Composition**
Data on workforce composition and trends from the U.S. Department of Labor, Bureau of Labor Statistics are available at this site.

**http://stats.bls.gov./
sahome.html**

experienced workers. Jobs with extreme supply shortages for several years have included specialized information systems technicians, physical therapists, plumbers, air conditioning repair technicians, and many others. Consequently, HR professionals have faced greater pressures to recruit and train workers.

**WORKFORCE QUALITY DEFICIT** Many occupational groups and industries will require more educated workers in the coming years. The number of jobs requiring advanced knowledge is expected to grow at a much more rapid rate than the number of other jobs. This growth means that people without high school diplomas or appropriate college degrees increasingly will be at a disadvantage, as their employment opportunities are confined to the lowest-paying service jobs. In short, there is a growing gap between the knowledge and skills required by many jobs and those possessed by employees and applicants. Several different studies and projections all point to the likelihood that employers in many industries will have difficulties obtaining sufficiently educated and trained workers.

Estimates are that about half of the U.S. workforce (about 50 million workers) needs or will need new or enhanced workplace training to adapt to the myriad job and technological changes that are occurring. At the same time, many individuals who are obtaining higher education degrees are doing so in nontechnical or nonscientific fields rather than engineering or computer sciences, where the greatest gap between job growth and worker supply exists. On the lower end, far too many students graduating from U.S. high schools lack the basic mathematical, reasoning, and writing skills needed for many jobs.

Unless major efforts are made to improve educational systems, especially those serving minorities, employers will be unable to find enough qualified workers for the growing number of "knowledge jobs." A number of employers are addressing the deficiencies that many employees have in basic literacy and mathematical skills by administering basic skills assessments to employees. Then they conduct basic mathematics and English skills training classes at workplace sites for employees with deficiencies. Some employers also sponsor programs for employees and their family members to aid them in obtaining general equivalency diplomas. To address the skills deficiencies, HR management must do the following:

- Assess more accurately the knowledge and skills of existing employees, as well as the knowledge and skills needed for specific jobs.
- Make training for future jobs and skills available for employees at all levels, not just managers and professionals.
- Increase the usage of new training methods, such as interactive videos, individualized computer training, and via the Internet.
- Become active partners with public school systems to aid in upgrading the knowledge and skills of high school graduates.

**GROWTH IN CONTINGENT WORKFORCE** In the past, temporary workers were used for vacation relief, maternity leave, or workload peaks. Today "contingent workers" (temporary workers, independent contractors, leased employees, and part-timers) represent over 20% of the workforce. Many employers operate with a core group of regular employees with critical skills and then expand and contract the workforce through the use of contingent workers.

This practice requires determining staffing needs and deciding in advance which employees or positions should form the "core" and which should be more fluid. At one large firm, about 10% of the workforce is contingent now. The company sees using contingent employees as a way to stabilize the workforce. Instead of hiring regular workers when work piles up and then firing them when the work is finished, the company relies more on temporary workers and independent contractors. Productivity is measured in output per hour. Thus, if employees are paid only when they are working (as contingents are), overall productivity increases.

Another reason for the growth in contingent workers is the reduced legal liability faced by employers. As more and more employment-related lawsuits have been filed, some employers have become more wary about adding employees. Instead, by using contract workers supplied by others, they face fewer employment legal issues regarding selection, discrimination, benefits, discipline, and termination.

## Demographics and Diversity

The U.S. workforce has been changing dramatically. It is more diverse racially, women are in the labor force in much greater numbers than ever before, and the average age of the workforce is now considerably older than before. As a result of these demographic shifts, HR management in organizations has had to adapt to a more varied labor force both externally and internally. The three most prominent dimensions of the demographic shifts affecting organizations are highlighted next.

**RACIAL/ETHNIC DIVERSITY** Projections by the U.S. Bureau of Labor Statistics are that the racial/ethnic mix of the U.S. workforce will continue to shift. The white labor force is expected to decline from 80% of the workforce in 1986 to about 73% by 2006. As Figure 1–2 indicates, the Asian and Hispanic labor forces

**BNA**
**Using Contingent Workers**
**445.10**
Review the types of contingent workers and the legal issues associated with their use.

**FIGURE 1–2** *Racial/Ethnic Shifts in U.S. Labor Force, 1996–2006*

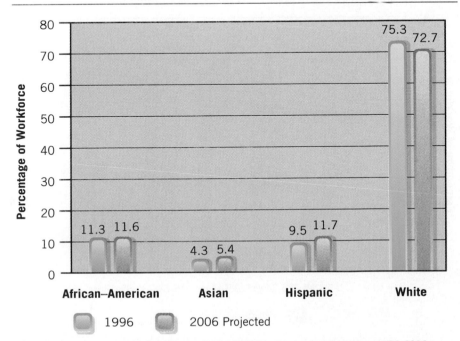

SOURCE: U.S. Department of Labor, Bureau of Labor Statistics, Employment Projections 1996–2006.

are expected to increase faster than the African-American labor force. This increase means that non-whites will compose about 28% of the U.S. labor force by 2006. Also, with 36% of all children under age 18 being non-white, the demographic shifts to greater racial/ethnic diversity are likely to continue. In addition, immigration of individuals into the United States is heavily weighted toward non-whites.

The importance of all these shifts is that HR professionals must ensure that diverse groups are managed and treated equitably in organizations. Also, HR professionals will have to develop diversity-oriented training so that all employees, regardless of background and heritage, can succeed in workplaces free from discrimination and inappropriate behaviors. It also means that more attention will have to be given to recruiting, staffing, and promoting individuals without regard to their racial/ethnic heritage, so that equal employment results for all.[5]

**AGING OF THE WORKFORCE** Most of the developed countries are experiencing an aging of their populations—including Australia, Japan, most European countries, and the United States. In the United States, the median age will continue to increase from about 31 years in 1986 to over 40 by 2006. This increase is due in part to people living longer and in part to a decrease in the number of younger people, particularly in the 16–24 age bracket. Figure 1–3 illustrates the percentage shifts in the U.S. workforce, with those over age 45 showing the greatest increase. In fact, it is projected that by 2020 about 20% of the U.S. population will be 65 or older, and that there will be as many people over 65 as there will be ages 20–35.[6]

**FIGURE 1–3** *Age Distribution of U.S. Civilian Labor Force, 1996–2006*

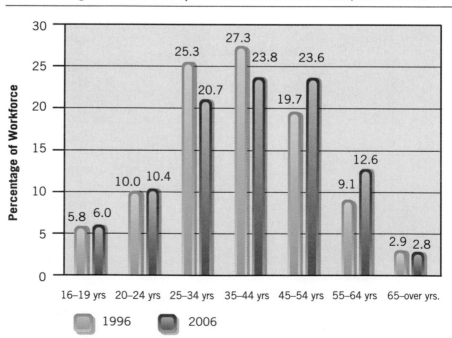

SOURCE: U.S. Department of Labor, Bureau of Labor Statistics, Employment Projections 1996–2006.

The aging of the population also is reflected in the occupational shifts noted previously. The growth in medically related jobs will be due primarily to providing care to older persons who will live longer and need greater medical care. Taken together, this aging issue means that HR professionals will continue to face significant staffing difficulties. Efforts to attract older workers through the use of part-time and flexible staffing will increase.[7] Also, as more older workers with a lifetime of experience and skills retire, HR will face significant challenges in replacing them with workers having the capabilities and work ethic that characterize many older workers.

For HR management, elder care will grow as a major HR issue. More workers will have primary care responsibilities for aging, elderly relatives, with over 22 million U.S. households having elder-care responsibilities. One estimate is that lost productivity due to workers having elder care responsibilities is at least $11 billion per year.[8] Even group benefit programs are changing, with long-term care insurance being added by an increasing number of employers. In these programs workers can allocate some of their "benefit dollars" to buy long-term care insurance at lower group rates.

**LOGGING ON . . .**
**ElderCare Web**
Contains reference materials and resources on elder care issues.

**http://www.ice.net/ ~kstevens/ELDERWEB.HTM**

**BALANCING WORK AND FAMILY**  For many workers in the United States, balancing the demands of family and work is a significant challenge. While this balancing has always been a concern, the growth in the number of working women and dual-career couples has resulted in greater tensions for many workers. According to data from the U.S. Census Bureau, families and households today can be described as follows:

- The "traditional family" represents only 10% or less of today's U.S. households.
- The number of households of married couples with no children living at home is growing and represents more households than those of married couples with children.
- Dual-career couples compose about 60% of all married couples, representing 30.3 million couples.
- Households headed by a single parent make up almost 30% of all families, with women heading most of these households.
- Single-parent households are less prevalent among whites than among other racial/ethnic groups.
- Seventy percent of all women with children under age six are in the workforce, and 60% of all women with children under age three are working.
- Both men and women are marrying at later ages, with the median age of first marriage for men about 27 and for women about 24.
- A majority of both men and women aged 18 to 24 still live with their parents or are considered dependents.

The decline of the traditional family and the increasing numbers of dual-career couples and working single parents place more stress on employees to balance family and work. For instance, many employees are less willing than in the past to accept relocations and transfers if it means sacrificing family or leisure time. Organizations that do get employees to relocate often must offer employment assistance for spouses. Such assistance can include contacting other employers, providing counseling and assistance in resume development, and hiring employment search firms to assist the relocated spouse. Additionally, balancing work and family concerns has particular career implications for women, because women more than men tend to interrupt careers for child rearing.

To respond to these concerns employers are facing growing pressures to provide "family-friendly" policies and benefits. The assistance given by employers ranges from maintaining references on child-care providers to establishing on-site child-care and elder-care facilities. Also, employers must have HR policies that comply with legislation requiring many employers with at least 50 workers to provide up to 12 weeks of unpaid parental/family leave, as noted in the Family and Medical Leave Act.

## Organizational Restructuring

Many organizations have restructured in the past few years in order to become more competitive. Also, mergers and acquisitions of firms in the same industries have been made to ensure global competitiveness. The "mega-mergers" in the banking, petroleum, and telecommunications industries have been very visible, but mergers and acquisitions of firms in many other industries have increased in recent years.

As part of the organizational changes, many organizations have "rightsized" either by (1) eliminating layers of managers, (2) closing facilities, (3) merging with other organizations, or (4) outplacing workers. A common transformation has been to flatten organizations by removing several layers of management and to improve productivity, quality, and service while also reducing costs. As a result, jobs are redesigned and people affected. One of the challenges that HR management faces with organizational restructuring is dealing with the human consequences of change. The human cost associated with downsizing has been much discussed in the popular press: a survivor's mentality for those who remain, unfulfilled cost savings estimates, loss of loyalty, and many people looking for new jobs.

Whereas many large firms have cut jobs by reducing their workforces, many smaller firms have continued to create jobs. This is particularly true in high-technology industries, such as software development. These entrepreneurial firms are faced with growth, while trying to attract sufficient workers with flexible capabilities and to conserve financial resources. More discussion on HR's role in organizational restructurings is found in Chapter 2, focusing on strategic HR planning. Consequently, in both large and small organizations the management of HR activities is crucial.

# HR Management Activities

The central focus for HR management must be on contributing to organizational success. As Figure 1–4 depicts, key to enhancing organizational performance is ensuring that human resources activities support organizational efforts focusing on *productivity, service,* and *quality.*

- *Productivity:*  As measured by the amount of output per employee, continuous improvement of productivity has become even more important as global competition has increased. The productivity of the human resources in an organization is affected significantly by management efforts, programs, and systems.
- *Quality:*  The quality of products and services delivered significantly affects organizational success over the long term. If an organization gains a reputa-

**FIGURE 1–4** *Management Activities*

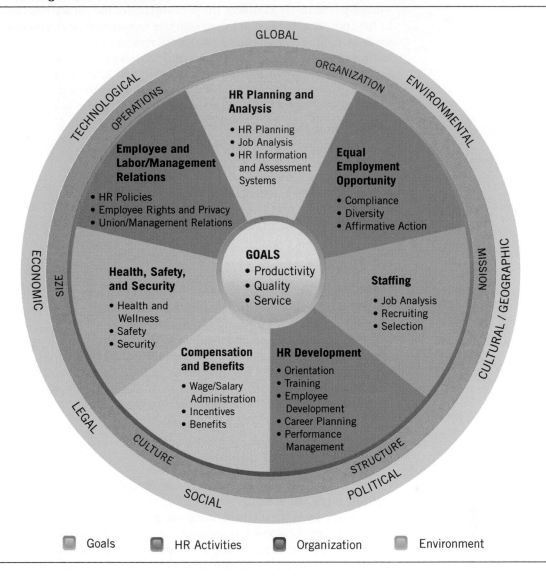

tion for providing poor-quality products and services, it reduces its organizational growth and performance. An emphasis on quality requires continuous changes aimed at improving work processes. That need opens the door for reengineering the organizational work done by people. Customer value received and satisfaction become the bases for judging success, along with more traditional HR measures of performance and efficiency.

- *Service:* Because people frequently produce the products or services offered by an organization, HR management considerations must be included when identifying service blockages and redesigning operational processes. Involving all employees, not just managers, in problem solving often requires changes in corporate culture, leadership styles, and HR policies and practices.

To accomplish these goals, HR management is composed of several groups of interlinked activities. However, the performance of the HR activities must be done in the context of the organization, which is represented by the inner rings in Figure 1–4. Additionally, all managers with HR responsibilities must consider external environmental forces—such as legal, political, economic, social, cultural, and technological ones—when addressing these activities. These external considerations are especially important when HR activities must be managed internationally, as discussed in Chapter 4. The HR activities for which a brief overview follows are:

- HR Planning and Analysis
- Equal Employment Opportunity
- Staffing
- HR Development
- Compensation and Benefits
- Health, Safety, and Security
- Employee and Labor/Management Relations

## HR Planning and Analysis

HR planning and analysis activities have several facets. Through *HR planning,* managers attempt to anticipate forces that will influence the future supply of and demand for employees. Having adequate *human resource information systems (HRIS)* to provide accurate and timely information for HR planning is crucial. The importance of human resources in organizational competitiveness must be addressed as well. As part of maintaining organizational competitiveness, HR analysis and assessment of *HR effectiveness* must occur. The internationalization of organizations has resulted in greater emphasis on *global HR management.* These topics are examined in Chapters 2, 3, and 4.

## Equal Employment Opportunity

*Compliance* with equal employment opportunity (EEO) laws and regulations affects all other HR activities and is integral to HR management. For instance, strategic HR plans must ensure sufficient availability of a *diversity* of individuals to meet *affirmative action* requirements. In addition, when recruiting, selecting, and training individuals, all managers must be aware of EEO requirements. The nature of EEO compliance is discussed in Chapters 5 and 6.

## Staffing

The aim of staffing is to provide an adequate supply of qualified individuals to fill the jobs in an organization. By studying what workers do, *job analysis* is the foundation for the staffing function. From this, *job descriptions* and *job specifications* can be prepared to *recruit* applicants for job openings. The *selection* process is concerned with choosing the most qualified individuals to fill jobs in the organization. Staffing activities are discussed in Chapters 7, 8, and 9.

## HR Development

Beginning with the *orientation* of new employees, HR training and development also includes *job-skill training.* As jobs evolve and change, ongoing *retraining* is necessary to accommodate technological changes. Encouraging *development* of all employees, including supervisors and managers, is necessary to prepare organizations for future challenges. *Career planning* identifies paths and activities for individual employees as they develop within the organization. Assessing how employees perform their jobs is the focus of *performance management*. Activities associated with HR development are examined in Chapters 10, 11, and 12.

## Compensation and Benefits

Compensation rewards people for performing organizational work through *pay, incentives,* and *benefits*. Employers must develop and refine their basic *wage and salary* systems. Also, *incentive programs* such as gainsharing and productivity rewards are growing in usage. The rapid increase in the costs of *benefits,* especially health-care benefits, will continue to be a major issue. Compensation and benefits activities are discussed in Chapters 13, 14, and 15.

## Health, Safety, and Security

The physical and mental health and safety of employees are vital concerns. The Occupational Safety and Health Act of 1970 (OSHA) has made organizations more responsive to *health and safety* concerns. The traditional concern for *safety* has focused on eliminating accidents and injuries at work. Additional concerns are *health* issues arising from hazardous work with certain chemicals and newer technologies. Through a broader focus on health, HR management can assist employees with substance abuse and other problems through *employee assistance programs* (EAP) in order to retain otherwise satisfactory employees. Employee *wellness programs* to promote good health and exercise are becoming more widespread.

Workplace *security* has grown in importance, in response to the increasing number of acts of workplace violence. HR management must ensure that managers and employees can work in a safe environment. Health, safety, and security activities are examined in Chapter 16.

## Employee and Labor/Management Relations

The relationship between managers and their employees must be handled effectively if both the employees and the organization are to prosper together. Whether or not some of the employees are represented by a union, *employee rights* must be addressed. It is important to develop, communicate, and update HR *policies and rules* so that managers and employees alike know what is expected. In some organizations, *union/management relations* must be addressed as well. Activities associated with employee and labor/management relations are discussed in Chapters 16, 17, and 18.

# HR Management in Transition

The field of HR management is undergoing transition because organizations themselves are changing. As a result, the terminology in the field is in transition. Traditionally called *personnel departments,* many of these entities have been renamed *human resource departments*. But more than the name has changed as HR management continues to be the "people" focus in organizations.

## HR as Employee Advocate

Traditionally, HR has been viewed as the "employee advocate" in organizations.[9] As the voice for employee concerns, HR professionals traditionally have been seen as "company morale officers" who do not understand the business realities of the organizations and do not contribute measurably to the strategic success of the business. Some have even suggested dismantling HR departments totally because they contribute little to the productivity and growth of organizations.[10]

Despite this view, HR plays a valuable role as the "champion" for employees and employee issues. One example is the stress that many employees feel when balancing work and family pressures. HR professionals must be the advocate for employees, recognizing that they have other lives besides work, and ensuring that organizational policies and practices consider these pressures. Otherwise, in many cases, the organization loses valuable human resources who do not want to continue working in a "family-unfriendly" environment. Closely related, HR professionals spend considerable time on HR "crisis management" dealing with employee problems that are both work and non-work related.[11]

Another facet of employee advocacy is to ensure that fair and equitable treatment is given to people regardless of their personal background or circumstances.[12] Some entity inside the organization must monitor employee situations and respond to employee complaints about unfair treatment or inappropriate actions. Otherwise, employers would face even more lawsuits and regulatory complaints than they do now.

As HR management has changed, it has become clear that there is a need for HR to balance being the advocate for employees and being a business contributor.[13] What this balancing means is that it is vital for HR professionals to represent employee issues and concerns in the organization. However, just being an effective employee advocate is not sufficient. Instead, the HR professionals must be strategic contributors, partners with operating managers, administratively efficient, and cost effective.

As Figure 1–5 depicts, HR management has three roles in organizations. The traditional administrative and operational roles of HR management have broadened to include more strategic facets. It should be emphasized that as HR roles shift to the right, the previous roles still must be met and the additional ones performed. Also, the continuum shows that the primary focus of HR as it becomes more strategic, changes to considerations with longer time horizons and the broader impact of HR decisions.

## Administrative Role of HR Management

The administrative role of HR management is heavily oriented to processing and record keeping. Maintaining employee files and HR-related databases, processing employee benefits claims, answering questions about tuition and/or sick leave policies, and compiling and submitting required state and federal government reports are all examples of the administrative nature of HR management. These activities must be performed efficiently and promptly.

However, this role resulted in HR management in some organizations getting the reputation of paper shufflers who primarily tell managers and employees what cannot be done. If limited to the administrative role, HR staff are seen primarily as clerical and lower-level administrative contributors to the organization.[14]

**FIGURE 1–5 *HR Management Roles***

| | Administrative | Operational | Strategic |
|---|---|---|---|
| **Focus** | Administrative processing and record keeping | Operational support | Organization-wide, global |
| **Timing** | Short term (less than 1 year) | Intermediate term (1–2 years) | Longer term (2–5 years) |
| **Typical Activities** | • Administering employee benefits<br>• Conducting new employee orientations<br>• Interpreting HR policies and procedures<br>• Preparing equal employment reports | • Managing compensation programs<br>• Recruiting and selecting for current openings<br>• Conducting safety training<br>• Resolving employee complaints | • Assessing workforce trends and issues<br>• Engaging in community workforce development planning<br>• Assisting in organizational restructuring and downsizing<br>• Advising on mergers or acquisitions<br>• Planning compensation strategies |

In some organizations these administrative functions are being outsourced to external providers, rather than being done inside the HR departments. Also, technology is being used to automate many of the administrative tasks. More about the outsourcing of HR administrative processes is discussed later in this chapter.

## Operational Role of HR Management

Operational activities are tactical in nature. Compliance with equal employment opportunity and other laws must be ensured, employment applications must be processed, current openings must be filled through interviews, supervisors must be trained, safety problems must be resolved, and wages and salaries must be administered. In short, a wide variety of the efforts performed typically are associated with coordinating the management of HR activities with the actions of managers and supervisors throughout the organization. This operational emphasis still exists in some organizations, partly because of individual limitations of HR staff members and partly because of top management's resistance to an expanded HR role.

Typically, the operational role requires HR professionals to identify and implement operational programs and policies in the organization. They are the major *implementors* of the HR portion of organizational strategic plans developed by top management, rather than being deeply involved in developing those strategic plans.

## Strategic Role of HR Management

Organizational human resources have grown as a strategic emphasis because effective use of people in the organization can provide a *competitive advantage,* both domestically and abroad. The strategic role of HR management emphasizes that the people in an organization are valuable resources representing significant organizational investments. For HR to play a strategic role it must focus on the longer-term implications of HR issues.[15] How changing workforce demographics and workforce shortages will affect the organization, and what means will be used to address the shortages over time, are illustrations of the strategic role. The importance of this role has been the subject of extensive discussion recently in the field, and those discussions have emphasized the need for HR management to become a greater strategic contributor to the success of organizations.

# HR Management as Strategic Business Contributor

One of the most important shifts in the emphasis of HR management in the past few years has been the recognition of HR as a strategic business contributor. Even organizations that are not-for-profit, such as governmental or social service entities, must manage their human resources as being valuable and in a "business-oriented" manner. Based upon the research and writings of a number of scholars, including David Ulrich of the University of Michigan, the importance of HR being a *strategic business partner* has been stressed.[16] This emphasis has several facets to it.

## Enhancing Organizational Performance

Organizational performance can be seen in how effectively the products or services of the organization are delivered to the customers. The human resources in organizations are the ones who design, produce, and deliver those services. Therefore, one goal of HR management is to establish activities that contribute to superior organizational performance.[17] Only by doing so can HR professionals justify the claim that they contribute to the strategic success of the organization.

**INVOLVEMENT IN STRATEGIC PLANNING** Integral to being a strategic partner is for HR to have "a seat at the table" when organizational strategic planning is being done. Strategically, then, human resources must be viewed in the same context as the financial, technological, and other resources that are managed in organizations. For instance, the strategic planning team at one consumer retailer was considering setting strategic goals to expand the number of stores by 25% and move geographically into new areas. The HR executive provided information on workforce availability and typical pay rates for each of the areas and recommended that the plans be scaled back due to tight labor markets for hiring employees at pay rates consistent with the financial plans being considered. This illustration of HR professionals participating in strategic planning is being seen more frequently in organizations today than in the past.

**DECISION MAKING ON MERGERS, ACQUISITIONS, AND DOWNSIZING** In many industries today, organizations are merging with or acquiring other firms. One prime illustration is the banking and financial services industry, in which combinations of banks have resulted in changes at Bank of America, Wells Fargo, Nations Bank, First Union, and others large and small. The merger of Chrysler and

Daimler-Benz has had significant implications for the automobile industry. Many other examples could be cited as well.

In all of these mergers and acquisitions there are numerous HR issues associated with combined organizational cultures and operations. If they are viewed as strategic contributors, HR professionals will participate in the discussions prior to top management making final decisions. For example, in a firm with 1,000 employees, the Vice-President of Human Resources spends one week in any firm that is proposed for merger or acquisition to determine if the "corporate cultures" of the two entities are compatible. Two potential acquisitions that were viable financially were not made because he determined that the organizations would not mesh well and that some talented employees in both organizations probably would quit. But according to one survey of 88 companies, this level of involvement by HR professionals is unusual. That study found that less than one-third of those involved in mergers surveyed have adequately considered HR issues.[18]

**REDESIGNING ORGANIZATIONS AND WORK PROCESSES** It is well established in the strategic planning process that organization structure follows strategic planning. The implication of this concept is that changes in the organization structure and how work is divided into jobs should become the vehicles for the organization to drive toward its strategic plans and goals.

A complete understanding of strategic sources of competitive advantages for human resources must include analyses of the internal strengths and weaknesses of the human resources in an organization. Those in HR management must be the ones working with operating executives and managers to revise the organization and its components. Ulrich likens this need to that of being an organizational architect. He suggests that HR managers should function much as architects do when redesigning existing buildings.[19] In this role HR professionals prepare new ways to align the organization and its work with the strategic thrust of each business unit.

**ENSURING FINANCIAL ACCOUNTABILITY FOR HR RESULTS** A final part of the HR management link to organizational performance is to demonstrate on a continuing basis that HR activities and efforts contribute to the financial results of the organization.[20] Traditionally, HR was seen as activity-oriented, focusing on what was done, rather than what financial costs and benefits resulted from HR efforts. For instance, in one firm the HR director reported every month to senior management how many people were hired and how many had left the organization. However, the senior managers were becoming increasingly concerned about how long employment openings were vacant and the high turnover rate in customer service jobs. A new HR director was hired who conducted a study that documented the cost of losing customer service representatives. The HR director then requested funds to raise wages for customer service representatives and also implemented an incentive program for those employees. Also, a new customer service training program was developed. After one year the HR director was able to document net benefits of $150,000 in reduction of turnover and lower hiring costs for customer service representatives.

In the past HR professionals justified their existence by counting activities and tasks performed. To be strategic contributors, HR professionals must measure what their activities produce as organizational results, specifically as a return on the investments in human resources.[21] HR management that focuses on high-performance work practices has been linked to better financial performance of the organization.[22]

This shift to being a strategic business contributor requires that all HR activities be examined and justified as producing results and value for the organization. Figure 1–6 indicates the HR priorities according to a recent survey of HR executives. For instance, training must be justified by the increase in capabilities of employees and the value that training produces in greater organizational results. In summary, HR must justify its existence as an organizational contributor, and not just a cost center.

## Expanding Human Capital

**Human capital**
The total *value* of human resources to the organization.

Another goal for those focusing on HR management, as well as operating executives and managers, is to enhance the human capital of the organization. **Human capital** is the total *value* of human resources to the organization. Also sometimes referred to as *intellectual capital,* it is composed of the people in the organization and what capabilities they have and can utilize in their jobs.

A critical part of expanding human capital is to utilize the talents of all people inside the organization and to bring in the best from the diverse population outside. Due to the shifting demographics in the workforce, HR management must be built to maximize the capabilities of all the diverse human resources. Thus, HR professionals must be those who ensure that all people, regardless of their life circumstances or backgrounds, are provided opportunities to develop their capabilities.

**ATTRACTING AND RETAINING HUMAN RESOURCES** As strategic business contributors, HR professionals must ensure an adequate supply of people with the capabilities needed to fill organizational jobs. Various experts on human capital have predicted a skills shortage for U.S. organizations that would hurt their competitive edge unless more investment is made in human capital. If that trend spreads as predicted, being able to attract people to the organization with the requisite capabilities currently requires more planning and creative implementation than in the past. For instance, at a computer software firm, growth is being limited by shortages of programmers and systems analysts. The company plans to open a new facility in another state so that a different labor market can be tapped, and the HR director heads up the site-selection team.

**FIGURE 1–6** *Human Resource Priorities*

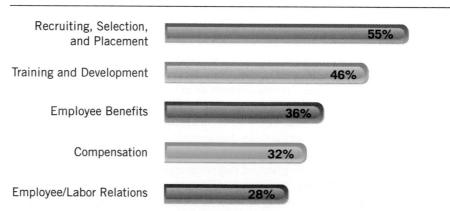

| | |
|---|---|
| Recruiting, Selection, and Placement | 55% |
| Training and Development | 46% |
| Employee Benefits | 36% |
| Compensation | 32% |
| Employee/Labor Relations | 28% |

SOURCE: Reprinted with permission from *Bulletin to Management (BNA Policy and Practice Series)* Vol. 49, No. 4, Pt. II, Pp. 1 (January 29, 1998) Copyright 1998 by The Bureau of National Affairs, Inc. (800-372-1033) <http://www.bna.com>

## HR PERSPECTIVE

# Workforce Availability—Tight Now and Getting Worse

Michael Ottenweller can tell you about the tight labor market—first-hand. His family-owned metal fabrication business in Fort Wayne, Indiana, has turned down contracts with Caterpillar ranging in value from $3 to $6 million. He had no choice—he simply could not find enough workers to do the jobs. In fact, throughout the midwestern United States the low unemployment rate has resulted in many job openings going unfilled. Consequently, some slowing of economic growth has begun.

To find clear evidence that a workforce shortage exists, one need go no farther than many shopping malls, grocery stores, or other retail stores. The jobs available in the retail industry typically pay less and are less exciting than jobs in some other industries. As a result, retail employees are being recruited by high-technology firms offering more

money, better benefits, and different work. The void in staffing retail businesses can be painfully apparent to customers who have to wait for service or who find clerks with little knowledge of merchandise.

But perhaps no segment of the economy has felt the workforce shortage more than the trucking industry. The amount of truck freight is growing rapidly and is projected to continue to increase through 2004. The industry needs from 300,000 to 500,000 new drivers each year. Turnover rates range from 80% to 200%. In many trucking firms drivers regularly jump to competitors for more money. Working conditions such as spending up to 14 days on the road, sleeping in a truck, and rarely being home do not appeal to many workers. It is estimated that 50,000 truckers leave the industry each year and 300,000 switch jobs within the

industry. Increasingly tight deadlines, only five hours of sleep per night, and employer monitoring of rigs on the road by satellite make drivers less satisfied with jobs that used to appeal to freedom-loving "knights of the road." With the increased demand for drivers has come the inevitable upward pressure on wages. Starting annual salaries average $34,000 and many companies pay $55,000 or above for experienced drivers. Special retention bonuses, safety incentives, and other strategies are being used to attract and retain drivers.

In many other industries availability of sufficient workers with the necessary capabilities and experience is a problem as well. Based on current population and workforce projections, the worker shortages appear likely to grow in future years.[23]

As the HR Perspective indicates, in many geographic locations in the United States and in many occupations, it is difficult to find sufficient qualified workers with the necessary capabilities. Truck drivers, welders, computer software engineers, legal assistants, and many others are just some jobs for which difficulty in recruiting has occurred. In many geographic locales in the United States, the official unemployment rate has been below 3%, which creates more staffing pressures.

To meet the staffing challenges, HR professionals are using a greater number of options. Traditionally, work was done by people who were employees. Increasingly today, work is done by independent contract workers, consultants, temporary workers, and others who are not employees of organizations. Developing policies, negotiating contracts, evaluating staffing suppliers, and monitoring work performance of these non-employees requires a broader role than when all workers are employees.

But recruiting and selecting new employees is only part of the challenge. The HR activities in organizations must be revised in order to retain employees. For every employee who does not leave the organization for a new job elsewhere, that is one less employee who has to be recruited from outside. Therefore, significant emphasis is being placed on keeping existing employees and providing growth opportunities for them.

**DEVELOPING HUMAN RESOURCE CAPABILITIES** The human capital in organizations is valuable because of the capabilities that the people have. As part of the strategic role, HR managers are often seen as responsible for expanding the capabilities of the human resources in an organization. Currently, considerable emphasis is being focused on the competencies that the employees in the organization have and will need for the organization to grow in the future.

HR management must lead in developing the competencies that employees have in several ways. First, the needed capabilities must be identified and linked to the work done in the organization. This identification often requires active cooperation between HR professionals and operating managers. Next, the capabilities of each employee much be assessed. This approach requires that the competencies and depth of those competencies be identified. For example, in a firm with 100 employees, the HR director is developing career plans and succession charts to determine if the firm has sufficient human resources to operate and manage the 70% growth it expects over the upcoming four years.

Once the comparison of the "gap" between capabilities needed in the organization and those existing in employees is identified, then training and development activities must be designed. The focus throughout is providing guidance to employees and creating awareness of career growth possibilities within the organization. For many individuals, continuing to enhance their capabilities and knowing that there are growth opportunities in the organization may lead to greater job satisfaction and longer employment with that organization.

**IDENTIFYING AND REWARDING PERFORMANCE** The formal reward systems in organizations must be aligned with the strategic goals for the organization. It is important that the human capital in organizations be rewarded competitively for their capabilities. Currently, many organizations are emphasizing compensation based on individual, team, and organizational performance.

If performance is going to be emphasized, then the means of identifying employee performance must be developed or reviewed. This is particularly true when employees work in teams or if their supervisors and managers are located elsewhere.

Once employee performance has been measured, it must be linked to compensation programs. Unlike traditional compensation programs that provide "cost-of-living" or other across-the-board pay increases, HR is having to develop and implement more performance-oriented reward programs. In this regard they are having to serve as agents of change because of the increasing complexity of compensation issues.[24]

Base pay for many jobs and fields has increased faster due to worker shortages than pay structures have increased in organizations. This imbalance has affected employee retention, and has required HR professionals to develop more and different compensation programs tailored to the demands of different employee groups and business unit realities.[25]

There has been a significant increase in variable pay programs, such as gain-sharing, team-based incentives, and others. These programs link rewards directly to organizational performance goals, so that the compensation system is integrally linked to the strategic objectives and results of the organization. Benefit programs also have had to become more varied and cost-effective as well.

# Delivering Cost-Effective Compliance Systems

The third part of HR management being a strategic business contributor is to deliver HR services and activities in a cost-effective manner that ensures compliance with applicable laws and regulations. Figure 1–7 indicates that there has been a mismatch between the way HR professionals have allocated their efforts and what contributes value for the organization. Based on a study of HR's role in organizations, the study results show that the greatest amount of time and costs of HR management are concentrated at the administrative level. However, HR management adds the greatest value at the strategic level, and the administrative activities produce a limited value for the organization. Two aspects that must be considered in this area are legal compliance and administrative systems.

**ENSURING LEGAL COMPLIANCE** Over the past thirty years numerous laws and regulations have been enacted at national, state, and local levels. Every year these regulations have been expanded due to regulatory actions and judicial decisions. As a result, considerable time and effort must be spent by HR professionals and other managers in organizations ensuring that compliance with HR-related laws and regulations occurs. Just to name a few, consider the following areas that must be managed daily by HR staff members.

- Equal employment
- Sexual harassment prevention
- Health benefit portability
- Pension compliance reporting
- Family/medical leaves
- Safety and health management
- Union contract grievances
- Disability accommodations

The role of HR is to ensure that the organization and its managers and employees know of these regulations, and that HR management reduces the legal liabilities and complies with the myriad regulations. With more and more people willing to file lawsuits, and more government enforcement agencies inspecting HR practices in organizations, it is crucial that HR management be done in ways that reduce the legal exposures faced by the organization.

*LOGGING ON . . .*
**Employment Laws Assistance for Workers and Small Business (elaws)**
Contains an interactive system to help employers and employees understand and comply with numerous employment laws enforced by U.S. Department of Labor.

**http://www.dol.gov/elaws/**

FIGURE 1–7 *Cost of HR vs. Value Added of HR*

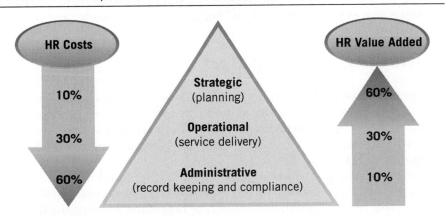

SOURCE: Lyle M. Spencer, *Reengineering Human Resources* (New York: © John Wiley & Sons 1995), 16. Reprinted by permission of John Wiley & Sons, Inc.

**DEMONSTRATING ADMINISTRATIVE EFFICIENCY** A final part of HR management is to deliver HR services and activities in a cost-effective and timely manner. Many HR professionals are aware that there is too much "administrivia" affecting HR. One study of senior-level HR executives found that 59% of their time is spent on administrative matters, and only 6% is spent on strategic issues with the remainder being operational in nature. But the HR executives indicated that they would rather spend only 6% on administration and 92% on strategy.[26] Three trends in this area are currently affecting HR delivery systems.

First is the growing use of information systems to replace the manual record keeping and processing of HR data. There are numerous federal, state, and local laws requiring that organizations keep many different records on employees. The requirements are so varied that it is difficult to identify exactly what should be kept and for how long. Generally records relating to employment, work schedules, wages, performance appraisals, merit and seniority systems, and affirmative action programs should be kept by all employers who are subject to provisions of the Fair Labor Standards Act (FLSA). Other records may be required on issues related to EEO, OSHA, or the Age Discrimination Act. The most commonly required retention time for such records is three years. Throughout the book, details on the most important laws and regulations are presented in appropriate content sections.

Second, rather than HR information being centrally processed and controlled, it has been more dispersed, so that managers and employees can access HR data themselves. The distribution of HR information has changed dramatically as a result of the widespread usage of e-mail, the Internet, distributed information processing, and other technology. However, with wider access has come the need for greater security to protect employee privacy of certain types of data and to preserve the integrity of the data from improper alteration.

A third trend is the growing use of outsourcing of HR activities. Increasingly, HR departmental functions are being examined to determine if outside providers can perform them more efficiently and at lower cost than when done internally. Figure 1–8 indicates the HR activities for which outsourcing has occurred or is likely to occur. Not reflected in those figures is the large number of employers that have outsourced payroll administration, which is often done by HR or accounting staff members.

In summary, HR professionals must cost-justify their existence and administratively deliver HR activities efficiently and responsively. Otherwise, HR management is seen as a cost center that does not produce results for the organization.

# Managing HR Activities

Managers and supervisors throughout organizations are responsible for the effective use of all the resources available to them. Therefore, effective management of the human resources is integral to any manager's job, whether as a hospital head nurse, assistant manager in a retail store, director of engineering, or president of a nonprofit agency.

Moreover, cooperation among people who specialize in HR and other managers is critical to organizational success, especially when global operations are involved.[27] This cooperation requires contact, or **interface,** between the HR unit and managers within the organization. These points of contact represent the "boundaries" that determine who does what in the various HR activities. In

**Interfaces**
Areas of contact between the HR unit and managers within the organization.

**FIGURE 1–8** *Prevalance of HR Outsourcing*

EAP/Wellness Programs — 62% / 12%

Pension Administration — 51% / 11%

Background/Reference Checks — 39% / 19%

Benefits Administration — 33% / 18%

Employee Surveys — 33% / 14%

Training and Development — 19% / 17%

Pre-employment Testing — 15% / 10%

Currently Outsourcing

Recruiting — 12% / 11%

Considering Outsourcing

SOURCE: Aon Consulting: "HR . . . Today and Tomorrow," Supplement to *HR Magazine*, August 1997, 5. Reprinted with the permission of *HR Magazine* published by the Society for Human Resource Management, Alexandria, VA.

organizations, decisions must be made to manage "people-related" activities; they cannot be left to chance.

Figure 1–9 illustrates how some of the responsibilities in the process of selection interviewing might be divided between the HR unit and other managers. A possible division of HR responsibilities is outlined throughout the book, illustrating HR responsibilities in a particular area and who typically performs what portion of them. These are not attempts to indicate "the one way" all organizations should perform HR activities but are simply illustrations of how these activities can be divided. For example, in one medium-sized bank, all new non-management employees are hired by the HR department. In another equally successful company, applicants are screened by the HR department, but the new employees actually are selected by the supervisors for whom they will work.

In smaller organizations without separate HR departments, cooperation among managers at different levels and in different departments also is essential if HR activities are to be performed well. For instance, in a small distribution firm hiring a new sales representative, the sales manager coordinates with the office supervisor, who may place a recruiting ad in a local newspaper, respond to telephone inquiries about the job from interested applicants, and conduct a telephone screening interview.

FIGURE 1–9 *Typical Selection Interviewing Interface between HR Unit and Other Managers*

| HR Unit | Managers |
|---|---|
| • Develops legal, effective interviewing techniques<br>• Trains managers in conducting selection interviews<br>• Conducts interviews and testing<br>• Sends top three applicants to managers for final interview<br>• Checks references<br>• Does final interviewing and hiring for certain job classifications | • Advise HR of job openings<br>• Decide whether to do own final interviewing<br>• Receive interview training from HR unit<br>• Do final interviewing and hiring where appropriate<br>• Review reference information<br>• Provide feedback to HR unit on hiring/rejection decisions |

## Evolution of HR Management

Before 1900, improving the working life of individuals was a major concern of reformers. Some employees attempted to start unions or strike for improved conditions. However, HR management as a specialized function in organizations began its formal emergence shortly before 1900. Before that time, most hiring, firing, training, and pay-adjustment decisions were made by individual supervisors. Also, the scientific management studies conducted by Frederick W. Taylor and others, beginning in 1885, helped management identify ways to make work more efficient and less fatiguing, thus increasing worker productivity.

As organizations grew larger, many managerial functions such as purchasing and personnel began to be performed by specialists. The growth of organizations also led to the establishment of the first personnel departments about 1910. Work by individuals such as Frank and Lillian Gilbreth dealt with task design and efficiency. The Hawthorne Studies, conducted by Elton Mayo in the mid-1920s, revealed the impact of work groups on individual workers. Ultimately, these studies led to the development and use of employee counseling and testing in industry.

**1930s TO 1950s** In the 1930s, the passage of several major labor laws, such as the National Labor Relations Act of 1935, led to the growth of unions. The importance of collective bargaining and union/management relations following the labor unions' rise to power in the 1940s and 1950s expanded the responsibilities of the personnel area in many organizations, especially those in manufacturing, utilities, and transportation. Such work as keeping payroll and retirement records, arranging stockholder visits, managing school relations, and organizing company picnics was often the major role of personnel departments. The role of the HR department in the organization as a staff function to support operational (line) departments expanded during this period, and line/staff issues grew to influence HR departments in the following decades.

**1960s TO 1980s** Increased legal requirements and constraints arising from the social legislation of the 1960s and 1970s forced dramatic changes in the HR departments of most organizations. HR departments had to become much more professional and more concerned about the legal ramifications of policies and practices. Also, organizations took a new look at employee involvement and quality of work as a result of concerns about the impact of automation and job design on worker productivity.

During the 1980s, the strategic role of HR management became essential as organizations reduced staff, closed plants, or "restructured." Outplacing employees and retraining the rest became prime concerns of HR departments. Containing the costs of health-care benefits also grew in importance.[28]

**1990s** During the 1990s, organizational restructuring continued. A study of HR executives involved in reengineering the HR management in their companies found that the traditional HR function began shifting its emphases.[29] As Figure 1–10 indicates, the HR managers of the future will need to be more strategic and proactive.

Changing demographics and increasing shortages of workers with the needed capabilities have grown in importance. Related to the demographic shifts, HR management has had to address the issues and implications of workforce diversity. Both the outsourcing of HR activities and the computerization of the administrative aspects of HR activities, even in small firms, have received attention as well. Finally, growth in issues involving employee rights, such as drug testing and smoking restrictions, are affecting how HR activities are managed.

**FIGURE 1–10** *Shifts in HR Management*

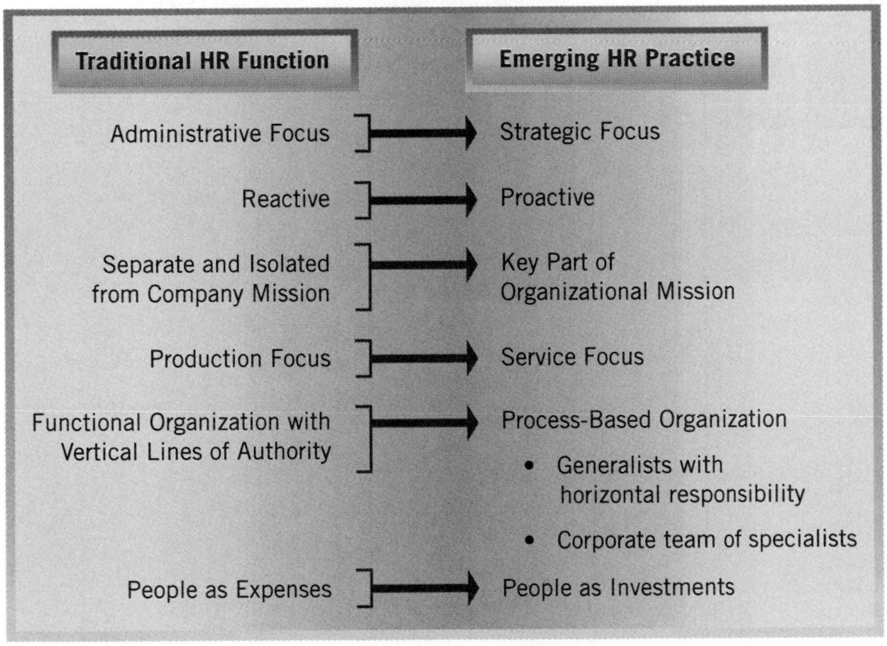

SOURCE: *HR 21: Human Resources for the Next Century* (Washington, DC: Watson, Wyatt Worldwide.) Used with permission.

**FIGURE 1–11** *Sample HR Unit Structure*

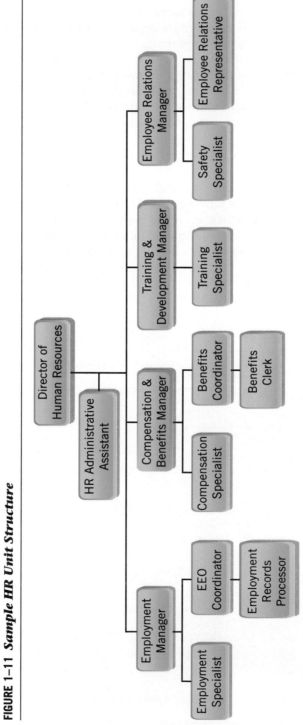

# Organizing the HR Unit

HR management as an organizational function traditionally was viewed as a *staff* function. Staff functions provide advisory, control, or support services to the *line* functions. Line functions are those portions of the organization directly concerned with operations resulting in products or services. Line authority gives people the right to make decisions regarding their part of the workflow; however, traditional staff authority only gives people the right to advise the line managers who will make the decisions.

Two different organizational arrangements that include an HR department are common. In one structure the HR function reports directly to the CEO, which is likely to result in greater status and access to the strategy-making process in organizations. Another structure that is still frequently found has the head of the HR unit reporting to the Vice President of Finance/Administration. This structure often leads to HR being focused more on operational and administrative issues.

Within the HR unit, it is common to structure jobs around the major HR activities. Figure 1–11 shows a typical HR department organization for a firm with no workers represented by unions.

A wide variety of jobs can be performed in HR departments. As a firm grows large enough to need someone to focus primarily on HR activities, the role of the **HR generalist** emerges—that is, a person who has responsibility for performing a variety of HR activities. Further growth leads to adding **HR specialists** who have in-depth knowledge and expertise in a limited area. Intensive knowledge of an activity such as benefits, testing, training, or affirmative action compliance typifies the work of HR specialists.

**HR generalist**
A person with responsibility for performing a variety of HR activities.

**HR specialist**
A person with in-depth knowledge and expertise in a limited area of HR.

**HR MANAGEMENT COSTS** As an organization grows, so does the need for a separate HR department, especially in today's climate of increasing emphasis on human resources. As might be expected, the number of HR-unit employees needed to serve 800 employees is not significantly different from the number needed to serve 2,800 employees. The same activities simply must be provided for more people. Consequently, the cost per employee of having an HR department is greater in organizations with fewer than 250 employees, as Figure 1–12 shows.

Two HR management trends are evident today in a growing number of organizations. One is the decentralization of HR activities and the other is outsourcing of HR activities.

**DECENTRALIZING HR ACTIVITIES** How HR activities are coordinated and structured varies considerably from organization to organization. Many organizations have centralized HR departments, whereas these departments are decentralized throughout other organizations.

*Centralization* and *decentralization* are the end points on a continuum. Organizations are seldom totally centralized or decentralized. The degree to which authority to make HR decisions is concentrated or dispersed determines the amount of decentralization that exists. With centralization, HR decision-making authority/responsibility is concentrated upward in the organization; whereas with decentralization HR decision-making authority/responsibility is distributed downward throughout the organization. How large an HR staff is or should be, or the extent of centralized or decentralized HR decision-making in organizations, is determined by many factors: culture of the organization, management style of the executives, geographic location, industry patterns, extent of unionization, and others.

**FIGURE 1–12** *Costs of the HR Function*

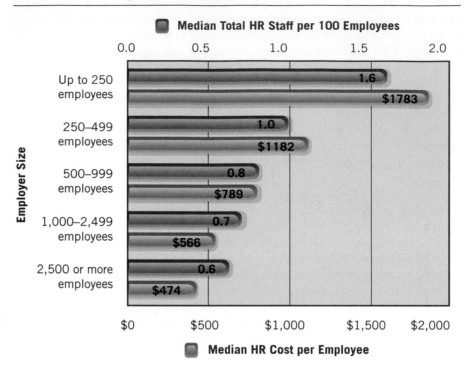

SOURCE: Adapted from *Bulletin to Management (BNA Policy and Practice Series)*, Vol. 49, No. 24, Pt II (June 18, 1998) Copyright 1998 by The Bureau of National Affairs, Inc. (800-372-1033) <http://www.bna.com>

What is occurring in some organizations is that HR activities are being aligned more with the specific business needs of individual operating entities and subsidiaries. The result is the shrinking of the staff in a centralized HR department for an entire organization. For instance, a financial services company has six different subsidiaries. Each subsidiary has its own HR director and HR staff; and compensation, training, and employment are all handled by the HR professionals in each of the strategic business units. The only centralized HR activities are benefits design and administration, human resource information systems design and administration, and equal employment compliance reporting and monitoring. In this way the HR central and administrative functions can be centralized for efficiency, while also allowing each business unit to develop and tailor its HR practices to its own needs.

Even smaller organizations are decentralizing HR activities. In one hospital with about 800 employees, four HR representatives are designated for different sections of the hospital. These individuals are the primary contact for all HR needs of managers and employees in the various hospital departments. The only centralized HR functions are those mentioned earlier. The Vice President of Human Resources serves primarily as a strategist with the CEO and other senior-level managers. As a result of this shift, the hospital has had to train the HR professionals who specialized in an HR function such as employment to become HR generalists. In this way the HR "partnership" with operating managers has become stronger.

## HR PERSPECTIVE
# Research on HR Outsourcing

Outsourcing of HR management activities has grown in recent years. In a research study published in *Human Resource Planning*, Scott Lever surveyed HR executives to identify HR outsourcing trends and reasons that outsourcing decisions were made. The 69 HR professionals surveyed who were using outsourcing were primarily in light manufacturing and service industry firms. The greatest amounts of outsourcing were in the areas of payroll, benefits, recruiting, and training. However, there was limited outsourcing of compensation activities.

The primary reasons given for outsourcing some HR activities were to outsource processes in which the organization had limited internal investments in systems and where there was significant variation in workload levels during the year. Those factors were especially evident in the outsourcing of payroll and benefits. For outsourcing of training and recruiting, the primary reasons were to respond to rapidly changing needs and provide special technical expertise.

Overall, outsourcing was seen by the HR executives surveyed as being beneficial to tapping external expertise in areas where HR practices and challenges are shifting rapidly. Also, being able to use outsourcing to obtain skilled assistance in training and recruiting was especially noted. Finally, the degree to which human resource information systems (HRIS) are outsourced was found to be a concern if they were not coordinated well with other HR activities, whether performed inside or outsourced.[30]

**OUTSOURCING HR ACTIVITIES** In a growing number of organizations, various HR activities are being outsourced to outside providers and consultants. The HR Perspective discusses research done on HR outsourcing.

Outsourcing some HR activities can be beneficial for organizations for several reasons. First, the contractor is likely to maintain more current systems and processes, so that the employer does not have to keep buying new items, such as computer software, programs, and hardware.[31] Also, many contractors have special expertise that is unavailable to HR managers in smaller organizations, whose time and experience both may be limited. A major benefit is to reduce HR payroll costs and shift activities to the outsourcing contractor. This shift means that the HR department has fewer people and more flexibility in changing its structure and operations as organizational changes require.[32]

But outsourcing HR activities has some disadvantages also. First, the success of outsourcing rests in the competence of the outside vendor. Having a contract that identifies what will be done and what continuing support will be provided is crucial. Obviously, selecting an outsider who fails to provide good services or results reflects negatively on the HR staff in the organization. Second, some concerns exist about "losing control" by utilizing outsourcing. When data are available from and services are provided by an outsider, the HR staff may feel less important and more anxious because they do not have as much access and control. This concern can be partially addressed by clearly identifying the outsourcing relationship.[33] In addition, sometimes outsourcing may cost more than providing some HR activities in-house, particularly if the contract is not clear on a variety of factors. In summary, there definitely are risks associated with outsourcing, but there are distinct advantages as well. Detailed analyses should be done by HR managers before outsourcing occurs, followed by periodic evaluations.[34]

*LOGGING ON . . .*
**Outsourcing**
General information on starting a company outsourcing program is available from the Outsourcing Institute at

**http://www.outsourcing.com**

## Ethics and HR Management

As the issues faced by HR managers have increased in number and complexity, so have the pressures and challenges of acting ethically. Ethical issues pose fundamental questions about fairness, justice, truthfulness, and social responsibility. Concerns have been raised about the ethical standards used by managers and employees, particularly those in business organizations.

It appears that the concerns are well-founded, if the results of one study of 1,300 employees and managers in multiple industries is an indication. About 48% of those surveyed admit engaging in unethical behavior at work. Some of the most frequently mentioned items were cheating on expense accounts, paying or accepting bribes and kickbacks, forging signatures, and lying about sick leave.[35]

**BNA**

**Ethics Policy 1432.20.20**
Many organizations have ethics policies. Review the information on types of ethics policies and then compare the ethics policy for an employer you can access.

**WHAT IS ETHICAL BEHAVIOR?**   Ethics deals with what "ought" to be done. For the HR manager, there are ethical ways in which the manager *ought* to act relative to a given human resource issue. However, determining specific actions is not always easy. Ethical issues in management, including HR issues, often have five dimensions:[36]

- *Extended consequences:*   Ethical decisions have consequences beyond the decisions themselves. Closing a plant and moving it to another location to avoid unionization of a workforce has an impact on the affected workers, their families, the community, and other businesses.
- *Multiple alternatives:*   Various alternatives exist in most decision-making situations, so the issue may involve how far to "bend" rules. For example, deciding how much flexibility to offer employees with family problems, while denying other employees similar flexibility, may require considering various alternatives.
- *Mixed outcomes:*   Decisions with ethical dimensions often involve weighing some beneficial outcomes against some negative ones. For example, preserving the jobs of some workers in a plant might require eliminating the jobs of others. The result would be a mix of negative and positive outcomes for the organization and the affected employees.
- *Uncertain consequences:*   The consequences of decisions with ethical dimensions often are not known. Should employees' personal lifestyles or family situations eliminate them from promotion even though they clearly are the most qualified candidates?
- *Personal effects:*   Ethical decisions often affect the personal lives of employees, their families, and others. Allowing foreign customers to dictate that they will not have a female or minority sales representative call on them may help with the business relationship short term, but what are the effects on the employees denied career opportunities?

**RESPONDING TO ETHICAL SITUATIONS**   To respond to situations with ethical elements, the following guides are suggested for thought:[37]

- Does the behavior or result achieved comply with all *applicable laws, regulations,* and *government codes?*
- Does the behavior or result achieved comply with all *organizational standards* of ethical behavior?
- Does the behavior or result achieved comply with *professional standards* of ethical behavior?

## HR PERSPECTIVE
# SHRM Code of Ethics

As a member of the Society for Human Resource Management (SHRM), I pledge myself to:

- Maintain the highest standards of professional and personal conduct.
- Strive for personal growth in the field of human resource management.
- Support the Society's goals and objectives for developing the human resource management profession.
- Encourage my employer to make the fair and equitable treatment of all employees a primary concern.
- Strive to make my employer profitable both in monetary terms and through the support and encouragement of effective employment practices.
- Instill in the employees and the public a sense of confidence about the conduct and intentions of my employer.
- Maintain loyalty to my employer and pursue its objectives in ways that are consistent with the public interest.
- Uphold all laws and regulations relating to my employer's activities.
- Refrain from using my official positions, either regular or volunteer, to secure special privilege, gain or benefit for myself.
- Maintain the confidentiality of privileged information.
- Improve public understanding of the role of human resource management.

This Code of Ethics for members of the Society for Human Resource Management has been adopted to promote and maintain the highest standards of personal conduct and professional standards among its members. Adherence to this code is required for membership in the Society and serves to assure public confidence in the integrity and service of human resource management professionals.

Source: Society for Human Resource Management, used with permission.

What the preceding three points make clear is that just complying with the laws does not guarantee ethical behavior. Laws and regulations cannot cover every situation that HR professionals and employees will face. Instead, people must be guided by values and personal behavior "codes," but employers have a role to play through HR management.[38] A code of ethics adopted for HR professionals by the Society for Human Resource Management (SHRM) is reproduced in the accompanying HR Perspective.

**ETHICAL ISSUES IN HR MANAGEMENT** HR professionals regularly are faced with ethical issues.[39] According to a study by SHRM and the Ethics Resource Center, a majority of the HR professionals surveyed indicated that they had seen unethical workplace conduct in the previous year. The most common unethical incidents by employees were lying to supervisors, employee drug or alcohol abuse, and falsification of records. Almost half of the HR professionals also indicated that their organization had pressured them to compromise their own ethical standards in order to meet financial, scheduling, or other operational goals.[40]

With HR management in an international environment, other ethical pressures arise. Such practices as gift giving and hiring vary in other countries, and some of those practices would not be accepted as ethical in the United States. Consequently, all managers, including HR managers, must deal with ethical issues and be sensitive to how they interplay with HR activities. One way to address ethical issues in organizations is to conduct training of executives, managers, and employees. Training of managers and employees in ethics compliance has been found to reduce the incidence of ethical problems.[41]

The complete study of ethics is philosophical, complex, and beyond the scope of this book. The intent here is to highlight ethical aspects of HR management. Various ethical issues in HR management are highlighted throughout the text as well.

# HR Management Competencies and Careers

As HR management has become more and more complex, greater demands are placed on individuals who make the HR field their career specialty. Although most readers of this book will not become HR managers, it is important that they know about the competencies required for those choosing HR as a career field.

Changes in the HR field are leading to changes in the competencies and capabilities of individuals concentrating on HR management. The development of broader competencies by HR professionals will ensure that HR management plays a strategic role in organizational success. One study by SHRM found that HR professionals must have core competencies, level-specific competencies, and role-specific competencies.[42] Based on these and other studies and surveys, it appears that three sets of capabilities are important for HR professionals:

- Knowledge of business and organization
- Influence and change management
- Specific HR knowledge and expertise

## Knowledge of Business and Organization

HR professionals must have knowledge of the organization and its strategies if they are to contribute strategically. This knowledge also means that they must have understanding of the financial, technological, and other facets of the industry and the organization.[43] As illustration, in some organizations the top HR executive jobs are being filled by individuals who have been successful operations managers, but have never worked in HR. The thinking behind such a move is that good strategic business managers can rely on the HR specialists reporting to them, while bringing a performance-oriented, strategic view of HR management to the top of the organization. In other organizations, top HR managers have come up through HR specialities, and have demonstrated that they understand broader business and strategic realities, not just HR management functional issues.

## Influence and Change Management

Another key capability that HR professionals need is to be able to influence others and guide changes in organizations. Given the myriad HR-related changes affecting today's organizations, HR professionals must be able to influence others. One study at Eli Lilly and Company found that influencing through relationship building, leadership, and effective communication are important HR competencies.[44]

## Specific HR Knowledge and Expertise

The idea that "liking to work with people" is the major qualification necessary for success in HR is one of the greatest myths about the field. It ignores the technical knowledge and education needed. Depending on the job, HR professionals may need considerable knowledge about tax laws, finance, statistics, or computers. In all cases, they need extensive knowledge about equal employment opportunity regulations and wage/hour regulations. The body of knowledge of the HR field, as used by the Human Resource Certification Institute (HRCI), is contained in Appendix A. This outline reveals the breadth and depth of knowledge necessary for HR professionals. Additionally, those who want to succeed in the field must update their knowledge continually. Reading HR publications, such as those listed in Appendix C, is one way to do this.

**PROFESSIONAL INVOLVEMENT** The broad range of issues faced by HR professionals has made involvement in professional associations and organizations important. For HR generalists, the largest organization is the Society for Human Resource Management (SHRM). Public-sector HR professionals tend to be concentrated in the International Personal Management Association (IPMA). Other major functional specialty HR organizations exist, such as the International Association for Human Resource Information Management (IHRIM), the American Compensation Association (ACA), and the American Society for Training and Development (ASTD). A listing of major HR-related associations and organizations is contained in Appendix B.

**LOGGING ON . . .**
**SHRM**
This site contains HR News On-Line and information on all of the services and products available through the Society for Human Resource Management.

**http://www.shrm.org**

**CERTIFICATION** One of the characteristics of a professional field is having a means to certify the knowledge and competence of members of the profession. The C.P.A. for accountants and the C.L.U. for life insurance underwriters are well-known examples. The most well-known certification program for HR generalists is administered by the Human Resource Certification Institute (HRCI), which is affiliated with SHRM. The program has seen significant growth in the number of those certified in the 1990s. Over 12,000 HR professionals annually sit for the HRCI exam now, compared with 3,000 in the early 1990s. Currently over 30,000 HRCI certified individuals are active in the HR field.[45]

Increasingly, employers hiring or promoting HR professionals are requesting certification as a "plus." One survey of HR professionals found that about two-thirds of them felt that HR certification gave them more credibility with corporate peers and senior managers.[46] Certification by HRCI is available at two levels; and both levels have education and experience requirements.

Additional certification programs exist for both specialists and generalists sponsored by other organizations. For specialists, here are some of the most well-known programs:

- Certified Compensation Professional (CCP), sponsored by the American Compensation Association
- Certified Employee Benefits Specialist (CEBS), sponsored by the International Foundation of Employee Benefits Plans
- Certified Benefits Professional (CBP), sponsored by the American Compensation Association
- Certified Safety Professional (CSP), sponsored by the Board of Certified Safety Professionals
- Occupational Health and Safety Technologist (OHST), given by the American Board of Industrial Hygiene and the Board of Certified Safety Professionals

# Summary

- HR management is concerned with formal systems in organizations to ensure the effective and efficient use of human talent to accomplish organizational goals.
- HR challenges faced by managers and organizations include economic and technological changes, workforce availability and quality concerns, demographics and diversity, and organizational restructuring.
- HR management activities can be grouped as follows: HR planning and analysis, equal employment opportunity compliance, staffing, HR development, compensation and benefits, health, safety and security, and employee and labor/management relations.
- HR management must perform three roles: administrative, operational, and strategic.
- It is important for HR management to be a strategic business contributor in organizations.

- To enhance organizational performance, HR management must be involved in strategic plans and decision making, participate in redesigning organizations and work processes, and demonstrate financial accountability for results.
- Expanding human capital requires HR management to develop means to attract and retain human resources, develop their capabilities, and identify and reward performance.
- Decentralization and outsourcing are being utilized more frequently in the management of HR units than they were in past years.
- Ethical behavior is crucial in HR management, and a number of HR ethical issues are regularly being faced by HR professionals.
- HR as a career field requires maintaining current knowledge in HR management.
- Professional certification has grown in importance for HR generalists and specialists.

# Review and Discussion Questions

1. How have some of the HR challenges listed in the chapter affected organizations at which you have worked?
2. What are the seven major sets of HR activities, and what activities fall within each set?
3. Why is it important for HR management to evolve from the administrative and operational roles to the strategic one?
4. To be a strategic business contributor, HR management must enhance organizational performance, expand human capital, and be cost-effective. Discuss how HR professionals must balance the competing demands made on them.
5. Discuss the following statement: "In many ways, all managers are and must be HR managers."
6. What do you see as the most interesting part of HR as a career field?

# Terms to Know

| | |
|---|---|
| HR generalist   27 | Human Resource (HR) |
| HR specialist   27 |    management   4 |
| human capital   18 | interfaces   22 |

# Using the Internet

## Outsourcing

Assume that you are the HR Manager for a large company. Department managers are requesting information on outsourcing non-core functions in their departments. Prepare a general memo to all department managers. In this memo, include what outsourcing is, the benefits of outsourcing , and the three phases involved in the outsourcing process.

Log onto the web site mentioned earlier in this chapter (see "Outsourcing HR Activities") to assist you with writing this memo. The site is from the Outsourcing Institute at:
**http://www.outsourcing.com**.

# CASE

## Remedy for HR Management

HR management is contributing to the success of both large and small organizations. One smaller organization, Remedy Corporation of Mountain View, California, has seen management of human resources as contributing to its business success. Based in California's Silicon Valley, Remedy provides internal help desks for computer networks and databases. Customers contact Remedy for assistance with network computing problems. Started in 1990 by three high-technology experts, Remedy currently has almost $40 million in annual revenue.

When the founders started the company, they established as one basic value that working at Remedy should be enjoyable as well as profitable. That belief has helped create a company culture today that gives Remedy competitive advantages when recruiting and retaining workers in the challenging labor market of Silicon Valley.

Because recruiting of employees to handle growth at Remedy is so crucial, the HR unit has used various unique approaches. For instance, they rent mini cars at local tracks and invite promising job applicants to drive the cars. An aggressive employee referral program pays employees up to $5,000 for referring new hires who stay with the firm. In another effort, Remedy had its executives wearing animal costumes as part of a "jungle" recruiting campaign.

All of these "fun" programs have a more important

business purpose: to demonstrate that people are important at Remedy. The HR unit prides itself on prompt feedback to potential employees. In one recent program, managers washed the cars of their employees to indicate their appreciation for employees' efforts at the company.

But traditionalists would ask if all this fun pays off. Remedy's answer is an unqualified *yes*. Over 40% of all Remedy's new employees came from the employee referral program. The firm's cost to hire each new employee is about $2,000 less than the industry average. Even more important, those hired stay longer with Remedy, as indicated by its retention rate of 42 months compared to the Silicon Valley average of 20 months. Also, employee turnover is about 8% annually—significantly below the industry average. It is obvious that Remedy's approach to HR management is paying off, both in an enjoyable company culture and in contributing to organizational success.[47]

### Questions

1. What is your view about "fun at work" being used as a specific part of HR management?
2. Compare the approach to HR management at Remedy to that at a current or previous job you have had.

# Notes

1. Adapted from Gillian Flynn, "Workforce 2000 Begins Here," *Workforce,* May 1997, 78–84; and Gillian Flynn, "Bank of Montreal Invests in Its Workers," *Workforce,* December 1997, 30–38.

2. Lynda Gratton, "The New Rules of HR Strategy," *HR Focus,* June 1998, 13–14.

3. Richard W. Judy and Carol D'Amico, *Workforce 2020: Work and Workers in the 21st Century* (Indianapolis: Hudson Institute, 1997).

4. Peter Morici, "Export Our Way to Prosperity," *Foreign Policy,* Winter 1995–1996, 3.

5. Marc Adams, "Building a Rainbow, One Stripe at a Time," *HR Magazine,* August 1998, 72–79.

6. Judy and D'Amico, *Workforce 2020,* 5.

7. Rick Garnitz, "Aging Workforce Poses an HR challenge," *ACA News,* March 1999, 20–21; and Carol Patton, "Golden Solutions," *Human Resource Executive,* August 1998, 63–65.

8. "DOL Offers Advice on Eldercare Programs," *HR Policies & Practices Update,* May 30, 1998, 3–4.

9. "HR's Role in Transformation of Work Debated by HR Executives," *Human Resources Report,* April 20, 1998, 418.

10. Thomas A. Stewart, "Taking On the Last Bureaucracy," *Fortune,* January 15, 1996, 105–106.

11. Allan Halcrow, "Survey Shows HR in Transition," *Workforce,* June 1998, 73–80.

12. Bruce R. Ellig, "Is the Human Resource Function Neglecting the Employees?" *Human Resource Management,* Spring 1997, 91–95.

13. Jennifer Laabs, "Why HR Can't Win Today," *Workforce,* May 1998, 63–74.

14. Robert Galford, "Why Doesn't This HR Department Get Any Respect?" *Harvard Business Review,* March-April, 1998, 24–26.

15. Lin Grensing-Pophal, "Taking Your Seat at the Table," *HR Magazine,* March 1999, 90–94; and Andrew R. McIlvane, "Window of Opportunity," *Human Resource Executive,* June 5, 1998, 36–38.

16. Dave Ulrich, *Human Resource Champions* (Boston: Harvard Business School Press, 1997).

17. Louis R. Forbringer and Carol Oeth, "Human Resources at Mercantile Bancorporation, Inc.," *Human Resource Management,* Summer 1998, 177–189.

18. "The Missing M & A Link," *The Wall Street Journal,* October 7, 1997, A1.

19. Dave Ulrich, "A New Mandate for Human Resources," *Harvard Business Review,* January-February 1998, 124–134.

20. Shari Caudron, "The CEO Needs You: Are You Delivering?" *Workforce,* June 1997, 63–68.

21. Linda Davidson, "Measure What You Bring to the Bottom Line," *Workforce,* September 1998, 34–40.

22. Mark Huselid, "The Impact of Human Resource Management Practices on Turnover, Productivity, and Corporate Financial Performance," *Academy of Management Journal,* 38 (1995), 635–672.

23. Adapted from Michael M. Phillips, "Midwest's Headache: Not Enough Workers," *The Wall Street Journal,* April 27, 1998, A1; Margaret W. Pressler, "Retail Industry Shops to Find Scarce Employees," *The Denver Post,* April 19, 1998, 7A; Chris Woodward, "Driver Shortage Makes Truckers King of the Road," *USA Today,* March 25, 1997, G1; and Anna W. Mathews, "Wanted: 400,000 Long Distance Truck Drivers," *The Wall Street Journal,* September 11, 1997, B1.

24. Barbara Parus, "Designing a Total Rewards Program to Retain Critical Talent in the New Millenium," *ACA News,* February 1999, 20–23.

25. Cathy Gedvilas, "Rewarding the 'New Breed' Information Workers," *ACA News,* July/August 1998, 30–35.

26. "Administrative Woes," *Human Resource Executive,* January 1998, 82.

27. "Global Competition Encourages Partnership Between HR and Line Management, Study Says," *HR Policies & Practices Update,* April 18, 1998. 4.

28. Mindy W. Toran, "Rolling with the Changes," *Human Resource Executive,* June 5, 1998, 39–41.

29. *HR 21: Human Resources for the Next Century* (Washington, DC: Watson, Wyatt Worldwide, 1995).

30. Adapted from Scott Lever, "An Analysis of Managerial Motivations Behind Outsourcing Practice in Human Resources," *Human Resource Planning* 20, 2 (1997), 37–48.

31. Len Strazewski, "Double Duty," *Human Resource Executive,* July 1998, 35–38.

32. Carla Johnson, "Changing Shapes," *HR Magazine,* March, 1999, 40–48.

33. "The Ongoings of Outsourcing," *Outsourcing Guide,* August 1998, 2–5.

34. Howard R. Mitchell III, "A Moving Issue: To Outsource or Not to Outsource," *HR Magazine,* May 1998, 59–68.

35. Del Jones, "48% of Workers Admit to Unethical or Illegal Acts," *USA Today,* April 4, 1997, 1A.

36. Based on information in Larue T. Hosmer, *The Ethics of Management* (Homewood, IL: Richard D. Irwin, 1987), 12–14.

37. Robert D. Gatewood and Archie B. Carrell, "Assessment of Ethical Performance of Organization Members: A Conceptual Framework," *Academy of Management Review* 16 (1991), 667–690.

38. Gary R. Weaver, Linda Klebe Trevino, and Philip L. Cochran, "Corporate Ethics Systems," *Academy of Management Journal* 42 (1999), 41–57; and Craig Dreilinger, "Get Real (And Ethics Will Follow)," *Workforce,* August 1998, 101–102.

39. "HR Staff Feeling, Seeing Ethics Pressure," *Bulletin to Management,* February 12, 1998, 41.

40. *The Business Ethics Survey* (Alexandria, VA: Society for Human Resources Management, 1998).

41. Andrew R. McIlvane, "Work Ethics," *Human Resource Executive,* August 1998, 30–34.

42. Stephen C. Schoonover, *HR Competencies for the Year 2000* (Alexandria, VA: SHRM Foundation, 1998).

43. Kevin Barksdale, "Why We Should Update HR Education," *Journal of Management Education* 22 (1998), 526–530.

44. Debra L. McDaniel, "A Competency Model for Human Resources," in David D. Dubois, *The Competency Case Book* (Amherst, MA: HRD Press, 1998), 121–156.

45. Linda Micco, "Ranks of Certified HR Professionals are Swelling Rapidly," *HR News,* June 15, 1998, 14.

46. "Certification Lends HR Greater Credibility," *Workforce,* April 1998, 23.

47. Adapted from Gillian Flynn, "Remedy Cures for Work Doldrums," *Workforce,* February 1998, 38–42.

# CHAPTER 2
# Strategic Human Resource Planning

*After you have read this chapter, you should be able to:*

- Discuss why human resources can be a core competency for organizations.

- Explain how organizational culture and industry life-cycle stages affect HR strategies and activities.

- Define HR planning and outline the HR planning process.

- Discuss why external environmental scanning is an important part of HR planning and what factors must be considered.

- Explain how an internal assessment of current jobs and skills is vital to HR planning.

- Identify what a human resource information system (HRIS) is and why it is useful when doing HR planning.

- Identify factors to be considered in forecasting the supply and demand for human resources in an organization.

- Discuss several ways to manage a surplus of human resources.

## HR TRANSITIONS

# Welfare to Work

To fill many jobs, particularly those requiring lower knowledge, skills, and abilities, HR managers increasingly are having to use people who are out of work—those on welfare—and many success stories are being told.

The tight labor market has not been the only factor motivating HR managers to hire welfare workers. A major impetus has been the Personal Responsibility and Welfare Reconciliation Act of 1996. This act required that by September 1997, 25% of individuals receiving welfare assistance be employed or in work training programs. The percentage increases each year to 50% by September 2002. To attain these targets, many employers are "encouraged" to hire welfare recipients through tax incentives and wage-subsidy programs during the early tenure of workers formerly on welfare.

What some employers initially saw as a "social responsibility" has evolved into a source of workers to fill jobs, enabling organizations to expand their workforces in order to meet business objectives. One study by the Welfare to Work Partnership, composed of over 5,000 member companies, found that in one year 135,000 welfare recipients had been hired by U.S. companies. The study also reported that over one million welfare recipients had stopped receiving welfare benefits because of getting jobs, entering work training programs, or being dropped from welfare.

Employers who participate in welfare-to-work programs have found that many welfare recipients wanted to work but had inadequate education, skills, or work habits. Consequently,

both government and employer-sponsored programs have been established to assist the welfare-to-work transition. In Tulsa, Oklahoma, Zebco—a leading manufacturer of fishing equipment—and the Metropolitan Tulsa Chamber of Commerce developed a program to teach welfare recipients workplace skills. During the six-month program, individuals attend classroom training four hours daily to learn both educational skills and how to get and hold jobs. Typical topics covered in this training program, as well as in programs elsewhere, include the importance of being on time, what transportation arrangements exist, how to find child-care providers, how to

dress for work, and how to interview. Interestingly, because a number of welfare recipients are single mothers, some private-sector child-care providers have had success hiring women on welfare as day-care workers. Despite the relatively low wages paid in the child-care industry, about two-thirds of the former welfare recipients are still employed after one year. About 80% of those who completed the Tulsa program are still working.

Here are some other success stories:

- *Sprint Corporation:* About 85% of the former welfare recipients were

still employed as telephone operators after six months, compared with only 33% of the non-welfare recipients hired into the same job at the same time.

- *United Airlines:* Over 500 of the 760 former welfare recipients hired were still with the airline a year later.
- *Giant Foods:* Over 100 welfare recipients had been hired as cashiers, pharmacy clerks, baker's assistants, and etc., and about 80% were still employed after the 90-day introductory period.
- *Marriott Corporation:* A leader in welfare-to-work programs, Marriott has hired several thousand welfare

*Employers who participate in welfare-to-work programs have found that many welfare recipients wanted to work but had inadequate education, skills, or work habits.*

recipients. Their success is measured by the fact that almost 70% are still with Marriott.

All of these examples illustrate that additional sources for a sufficient supply of human resources are being tapped by employers as part of meeting their HR planning needs. The examples also illustrate that a broad range of HR activities, but especially training, must be seen as integral to organizations in obtaining the human resources needed for the future.[1]

> **❝** *Plan Ahead: it wasn't raining when Noah built the ark.* **❞**
>
> RICHARD CUSHING

This chapter deals with planning for the human resources that the organization will need in the future. The opening discussion of using welfare-to-work programs as a future source of human resources is one means. But any description of HR planning must begin on a level one step higher—with the overall strategic plan of the organization. **Strategic planning** can be defined as the process of identifying organizational objectives and the actions needed to achieve those objectives. It involves analyzing such areas as finance, marketing, and human resources to determine the capacities of the organization to meet its objectives.

The process of strategic planning can be thought of as circular in nature. As Figure 2–1 shows, the process begins with identifying and recognizing the philosophy and mission of the organization. This first step addresses the most fundamental questions about the organization:

- Why does the organization exist?
- What unique contribution does it make?
- What are the underlying values and motivations of owners and key managers?

Once the philosophy and mission of the organization are identified, the next requirement is to scan the environment. This scanning is especially important when rapid changes are occurring, such as in the last several years. HR managers also need the results of environmental scanning. For example, some questions might be: What recruiting approaches are competitors currently using to attract

**Strategic planning**
The process of identifying organizational objectives and the actions needed to achieve those objectives.

**FIGURE 2–1** *Strategic Planning Process*

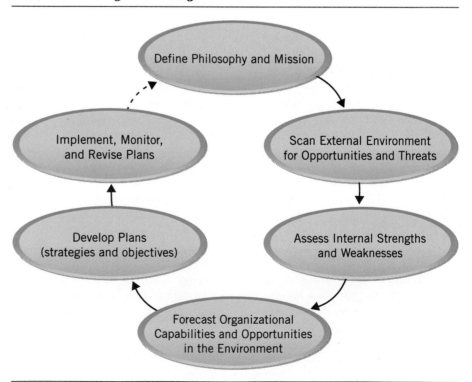

scarce specialties? How are competitors using welfare-to-work programs? Will a new product under development require a production process using an expanded number of workers with different knowledge and skills? Answers to these questions illustrate that HR managers must be able to predict what capabilities employees will have to implement the business strategy. Workforce patterns and conditions, social values and lifestyles, and technological developments are some external factors to consider.

After external forces are examined, an internal assessment is made of what the organization *can* do before a decision is reached on what it *should* do. Internal strengths and weaknesses must be identified in light of the philosophy and culture of the organization. Factors such as current workforce skills, retirement patterns, and demographic profiles of current employees are items that relate to human resource capabilities. Next comes forecasting organizational capabilities and future opportunities in the environment to match organizational objectives and strategies.

The development of strategies and objectives often is based on a **SWOT analysis,** which examines the *strengths* and *weaknesses* of the organizations internally and the *opportunities* and *threats* externally. The purpose of the SWOT analysis is to develop strategies that align organizational strengths with opportunities externally, to identify internal weaknesses to be addressed, and to acknowledge threats that could affect organizational success.

**SWOT analysis**
examines the *strengths* and *weaknesses* of the organizations internally and the *opportunities* and *threats* externally.

Finally, specific plans are developed to identify how strategies will be implemented. Details of the plans become the basis for implementation and later adjustments. Like all plans, they must be monitored, adjusted, and updated continually. The strategic planning process is circular, since the environment is always changing and a specific step in the process must be repeated continually.

# Organizational Strategy and Human Resources

The development of specific business strategies must be based on the areas of strength that an organization has. Referred to as *core competencies* by Hamel and Prahalad, they are the foundation for creating the competitive advantage for an organization.[2] A **core competency** is a unique capability in the organization that creates high value and that differentiates the organization from its competition.

**Core competency**
A unique capability in the organization that creates high value and that differentiates the organization from its competition.

## Human Resources as a Core Competency

Certainly, many organizations have voiced the idea that their human resources differentiate them from their competitors. Organizations as widely diverse as Federal Express, Nordstrom's Department Stores, and Gateway Computers have focused on human resources as having special strategic value for the organization. The significance of human resources as a core competency was confirmed in a study of 293 U.S. firms. The study found that HR management effectiveness positively affected organizational productivity, financial performance, and stock market value.[3]

Some ways that human resources become a core competency are through attracting and retaining employees with unique professional and technical capabilities, investing in training and development of those employees, and compensating them in ways that keep them competitive with their counterparts in other organizations. The value of human resources was demonstrated several years ago, when United Parcel Service workers went on strike. In offices around the country, customers had concerns that the brown-shirted UPS drivers, whom customers often knew by their first names, were not working. Fortunately for UPS, its drivers, and their customers, the strike was settled relatively quickly. Another illustration is what happened in the banking industry with the many mergers and acquisitions. Smaller, community-oriented banks have picked up numerous small- and medium-sized commercial loan customers because they emphasize that "you can talk to the same person," rather than having to call an automated service center in another state.

## Resource-Based Organizational Strategies

There has been growing recognition that human resources contribute to sustaining a competitive advantage for organizations. Jay Barney and others have focused on four factors that are important to organizational strategic accomplishments.[4] Those factors, called the VRIO framework, are related to human resources as follows:

- *Value:*  Human resources that can create value are those that can respond to external threats and opportunities. Having this ability means that employees can make decisions and be innovative when faced with environmental changes.
- *Rareness:*  The special capabilities of people in the organization provide it significant advantages. Especially important is that the human resources in an organization be provided training and development to enhance their capabilities, so that they are continually seen as "the best" by customers and industry colleagues. This rareness also helps in attracting and retaining employees with scarce and unique knowledge, skills, and abilities. Reducing employee turnover is certainly important in preserving the rareness of human resources.
- *Imitability:*  Human resources have a special strategic value when they cannot be easily imitated by others. Southwest Airlines, Disney, and Marriott Corporation each have created images with customers and competitors that they are different and better at customer service. Any competitors trying to copy the HR management "culture" created in these organizations would have to significantly change many organizational and HR aspects.
- *Organization:*  The human resources must be organized in order for an entity to take advantage of the competitive advantages just noted. This means that the human resources must be able to work effectively together, and have HR policies and programs managed in ways that support the people working in the organization.

Using a VRIO framework as the foundation for HR management means that people are truly seen as assets, not as expenses. It also means that the culture of organizations must be considered when developing organizational and HR strategies.

## Organizational Culture and HR Strategy

**Organizational culture**
A pattern of shared values and beliefs giving members of an organization meaning and providing them with rules for behavior.

**Organizational culture** is a pattern of shared values and beliefs giving members of an organization meaning and providing them with rules for behavior. These values are inherent in the ways organizations and their members view themselves, define opportunities, and plan strategies. Much as personality shapes an individual, organizational culture shapes its members' responses and defines what an organization can or is willing to do.

The culture of an organization is seen in the norms of expected behaviors, values, philosophies, rituals, and symbols used by its employees. Culture evolves over a period of time. Only if an organization has a history in which people have shared experiences for years does a culture stabilize. A relatively new firm, such as a business existing for less than two years, probably has not developed a stabilized culture.

Managers must consider the culture of the organization because otherwise excellent strategies can be negated by a culture that is incompatible with the strategies. Further, it is the culture of the organization, as viewed by the people in it, that affects the attraction and retention of competent employees.[5] Numerous examples can be given of key technical, professional, and administrative employees leaving firms because of corporate cultures that seem to devalue people and create barriers to the use of individual capabilities. In contrast, by creating a culture that values people highly, some corporations have been very successful at attracting, training, and retaining former welfare recipients.

The culture of an organization also affects the way external forces are viewed. In one culture, external events are seen as threatening, whereas another culture views risks and changes as challenges requiring immediate responses. The latter type of culture can be a source of competitive advantage, especially if it is unique and hard to duplicate. This is especially true as an organization evolves through the life cycle in an industry.

## Organization/Industry Life-Cycle Stages and HR Strategy

As noted, organizations go through evolutionary life cycles, and the stage in which an organization finds itself in an industry affects the human resource strategies it should use. For example, the HR needs of a small, three-year-old high-technology software firm will be different from those of Netscape or America Online. The relationship between the life cycle of an organization and HR management activities is profiled in Figure 2–2.[6]

**EMBRYONIC** At the embryonic stage a high-risk, entrepreneurial spirit pervades the organization. Because the founders often operate with limited financial resources, base pay often is modest. When skills are needed, the organization recruits and hires individuals who already have the necessary capabilities. Training and development are done on an as-needed basis.

**GROWTH** During the growth stage, the organization needs investments to expand facilities, marketing, and human resources to take advantage of the demand for its products and services. Often, backlog and scheduling problems indicate that the organization has grown faster than its ability to handle the demand. Extensive efforts are made to recruit employees to handle the expanded workload. It is also important to have HR plans, and planning processes, rather than just reacting to immediate pressures. Compensation practices have to become more market-competitive in order to attract sufficient employees with the necessary capabilities. Communicating with those employees about career opportunities affects their retention, so career planning efforts and HR development efforts to support them are expanded.

**SHAKEOUTS** In the shakeout stage the industry reacts to rapid growth, and not all firms will continue to exist. Some will be bought out by other larger competitors; others will fade from the industry. The explosive growth in Internet businesses

**FIGURE 2–2  *Industry Life Cycle and HR Management***

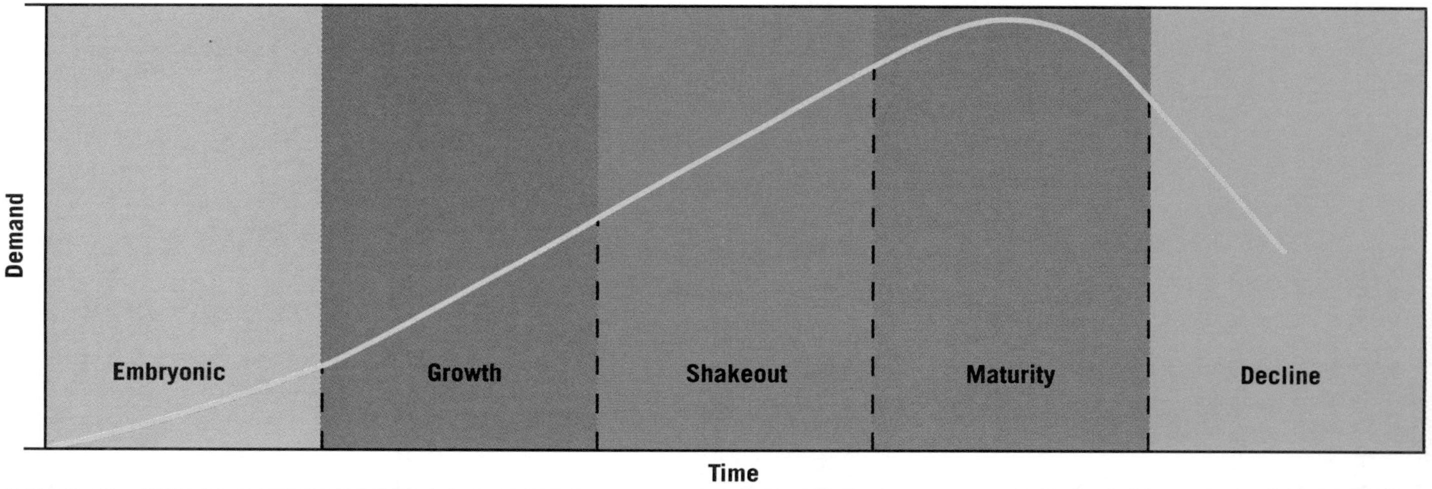

| HR Activities | Embryonic | Growth | Shakeout | Maturity | Decline |
|---|---|---|---|---|---|
| **Staffing** | Recruit and retain highly capable people. | Respond to escalating need for qualified workers in numerous fields. | Internal movement and job shifts as organizational restructuring occurs. | Retaining key performers while limited advancement opportunities exist. | Retaining key employees while eliminating some jobs and creating others. |
| **Compensation** | Lower base pay with some broad-based, longer-term incentives for risk-taking employees, and limited benefits. | Mid-market competitive pay, increased use of annual performance incentives, and expanded benefits. | Control compensation expenses while maintaining market-competitive pay, short- and longer-term incentives. | Higher base wages, expanded annual incentives, lucrative executive stock options, and comprehensive benefit plans. | Tight cost control and pay reduction. Short-term cash and long-term stock and scaled-back benefits. |
| **HR Development** | Limited training and development using external resources. | Identification of competencies and career growth needs and addition of some internal HR development resources. | Review of employee capabilities and HR development needs for high-potential, scarce-skilled employees using external and internal resources. | Extensive internal training and development programs and use of "big-name" external training resources. | Retraining and career transition planning through external training and development activities. |

and the consolidations of Internet providers by such firms as America Online, Microsoft, and Yahoo illustrate how shakeouts occur. Regarding HR management in a shakeout industry, competition to retain human resources is important, especially while restructuring and reducing the number of jobs to control costs. Compensation costs must be monitored, but a balance is required in order to retain key employees using short- and longer-term incentives. HR development is focused on high-potential, scarce-skilled employees who are seen as ones who will ensure that the organization is a major player following the shakeout.

**MATURITY** In the maturity stage, the organization and its culture are stabilized. Size and success enable the organization to develop even more formalized plans, policies, and procedures. Often, organizational politics flourish and HR activities expand. Compensation programs become a major focus for HR efforts, and they are expanded to reward executives as well. Extensive HR development occurs, coordinated by an internal training staff.

**DECLINE** The organization in the decline stage faces resistance to change. Numerous examples can be cited in the manufacturing sectors of the U.S. economy. Manufacturing firms have had to reduce their workforces, close plants, and use their accumulated profits from the past to diversify into other industries. During the decline stage, employers try certain HR practices such as productivity-enhancement and cost-reduction programs. Unionized workers resist the decline by demanding no pay cuts and greater job-security provisions in their contracts. Nevertheless, employers are compelled to reduce their workforces through attrition, early retirement incentives, and major facility closings.

## Linking Organizational Strategies and HR Plans

Strategic planning must include planning for human resources to carry out the rest of the plan. Figure 2–3 shows the relationship among the variables that

**FIGURE 2–3  *Factors That Determine HR Plans***

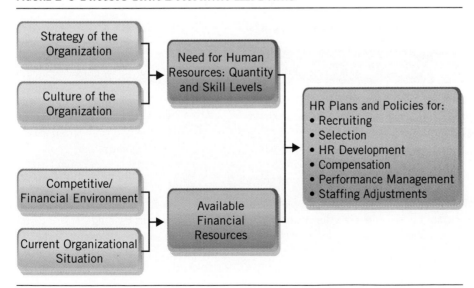

*LOGGING ON . . .*
**The Human Resource Professionals Gateway to the Internet**
This site contains Human Resource Management information to aid organizations with strategic HR planning issues.

**http://www.teleport.com/ ~erwilson/**

ultimately determine the HR plans an organization will develop. Business strategy affects strategies and activities in the HR area. For example, several years ago, a large bank began planning to become one of the top financial institutions in the country. Two parts of its strategic plan were (1) to adopt a global focus and (2) to improve service. HR plans to support global goals included integrating compensation and benefits systems and hiring policies for international operations and domestic operations. Service improvement plans hinged on well-trained, capable first-level employees. But an HR diagnosis turned up basic skills deficiencies in employees. As a result of HR planning, a series of programs designed to remedy basic skills problems in the workforce was developed. The coordination of company-wide strategic planning and strategic HR planning was successful in this case because HR plans supported corporate strategic plans.

There are many possible approaches to understanding the strategies that an organization may choose.[7] To illustrate the relationship between strategy and HR, two basic business strategies can be identified: *cost-leadership* and *differentiation*.[8] Figure 2–4 compares HR needs under each strategy and suggests the HR approaches that may be most appropriate.[9] The first strategy may be appropriate in a relatively stable business environment. It approaches competition on the basis of low price and high quality of product or service. The differential strategy is more appropriate in a more dynamic environment characterized by rapid change (such as the computer software industry). It requires continually finding new products and new markets. The two categories may not be mutually exclusive, because it is possible for an organization to pursue one strategy in one product or service area and a different one with others.

The cost-leadership strategy requires an organization to "build" its own employees to fit its specialized needs. This approach requires a longer HR planning horizon. When specific skills are found to be needed for a new market or product, it may be more difficult to internally develop them quickly. However, with a differentiation strategy, responsiveness means that HR planning is likely to have a shorter time frame, and greater use of external sources will be used to staff the organization. The HR Perspective discusses a study that examined the involvement of HR executives when determining organizational strategies and core competencies.

**FIGURE 2–4** *Linkage of Organizational and HR Strategies*

| Organizational Strategy | Strategic Focus | HR Strategy | HR Activities |
|---|---|---|---|
| **Cost-Leadership** | • Efficiency<br>• Stability<br>• Cost control | • Long HR planning horizon<br>• Build skills in existing employee<br>• Job and employee specialization for production and control | • Promote from within<br>• Extensive training<br>• Hire and train for specific capabilities |
| **Differentiation** | • Growth<br>• Innovation<br>• Decentralization | • Shorter HR planning horizon<br>• Hire the HR capabilities needed<br>• Broader, more flexible jobs and employees | • External staffing<br>• Less training<br>• Hire and train for broad competencies |

HR PERSPECTIVE

# Research on Human Resources as a Core Competency and Organizational Strategy

A group of researchers (Wright, McMahan, McCormick, and Sherman) conducted a study of the effect of organizational strategy, core competencies, and HR executive involvement on both organizational and HR management performance in some petrochemical refineries. As reported in *Human Resource Management*, the researchers mailed surveys to all petrochemical refineries in the United States and received responses from 86 of them.

The surveys asked about each refinery's organizational strategy, as reflected in the product mix produced and the refinery's financial performance. The surveys also asked petrochemical HR executives to evaluate employee skills and motivations and indicate the involvement of HR executives in the strategic management of their firms.

The study results showed that HR involvement in strategic decision making is more positive when the refinery was following a product innovation strategy instead of one emphasizing cost control. Interestingly, the relationship between HR executives and the effectiveness of HR activities was higher where skilled employees were seen as being a core competency of he refinery.

Using both of these findings, the researchers suggest that when an organizational strategy of differentiation and innovation is being followed, then human resources are a core competency supporting that strategy. In those situations, HR executives are more involved as strategic decision-makers, thus allowing them to ensure that human resources are viewed as a "core" strength of the organization. However, when human resources are seen as costs to be constricted when a cost-control strategy is being followed, then HR executives are not as heavily involved in organizational strategic decision making.[10]

# Human Resource Planning

The competitive organizational strategy of the firm as a whole becomes the basis for **human resource (HR) planning,** which is the process of analyzing and identifying the need for and availability of human resources so that the organization can meet its objectives. This section discusses HR planning responsibilities, the importance of HR planning in small and entrepreneurial organizations, and the HR planning process.

**Human resource (HR) planning**
The process of analyzing and identifying the need for and availability of human resources so that the organization can meet its objectives.

## HR Planning Responsibilities

In most organizations that do HR planning, the top HR executive and subordinate staff specialists have most of the responsibilities for this planning. However, as Figure 2–5 indicates, other managers must provide data for the HR specialists to analyze. In turn, those managers need to receive data from the HR unit. Because top managers are responsible for overall strategic planning, they usually ask the HR unit to project the human resources needed to implement overall organizational goals.

## HR Planning in Evolving Small and Entrepreneurial Organizations

HR management and ultimately HR planning are critical in small and entrepreneurial organizations. "People problems" are among the most frustrating ones faced by small-business owners and entrepreneurs.

**FIGURE 2–5 *Typical HR Planning Responsibilities***

| HR Unit | Managers |
|---|---|
| • Participates in strategic planning process for overall organization<br>• Identifies HR strategies<br>• Designs HR planning data systems<br>• Compiles and analyzes data from managers on staffing needs<br>• Implements HR plan as approved by top management | • Identify supply-and-demand needs for each division/department<br>• Review/discuss HR planning information with HR specialists<br>• Integrate HR plan with departmental plans<br>• Monitor HR plan to identify changes needed<br>• Review employee succession plans associated with HR plan |

**EVOLUTION OF HR ACTIVITIES**    At the beginning of a small business's existence, only very basic HR activities must be performed. Compensation and government-mandated benefits must be paid. As the organization evolves, more employees must be recruited and selected. Also, some orientation and on-the-job training are necessary, though they are often done haphazardly.

The evolution of the business proceeds through several stages. The focus of each stage reflects the needs of the organization at the time. In the initial stage, the organization first hires an HR clerk, then possibly an HR administrator. As the organization grows, it may add more HR professionals, often including an employment or benefits specialist. With further growth, other specialists, such as trainers, may be needed. From this point, additional clerical and specialist employees can be added, and separate functional departments (employment, compensation, benefits, and training) can evolve.

**SMALL BUSINESS AND FAMILY ISSUES**    One factor often affecting the planning of HR activities in small firms is family considerations. Particular difficulties arise when a growing business is passed on from one generation to another, resulting in a mix of family and nonfamily employees. Some family members may use employees as "pawns" in disagreements with other family members in the firm. Also, nonfamily employees may see different HR policies and rules being used for family members than for them.

Key to the successful transition of a business from one generation to another is having a clearly identified HR plan. Crucial in small businesses is incorporating the role of key nonfamily members with HR planning efforts. Often, nonfamily members have important capabilities and expertise that family members do not possess. Therefore, planning for the attraction and retention of these "outsiders" may be vital to the future success of smaller organizations. One survey of over 3,000 small businesses found that management succession was one of the top challenges faced by family-owned firms.[11] It even may be that the nonfamily members will assume top management leadership roles, with some or all family members who are owners serving on the Board of Directors, but not being active managers in the firm. Additionally, nonfamily executives may be the intermediaries who focus on the needs of the business when family-member conflicts arise. Small businesses, depending on how small they are, may use the HR planning that follows, but in very small organizations the process is much more intuitive and often done entirely by the top executives, who often are family members.

## HR Planning Process

The steps in the HR planning process are shown in Figure 2–6. Notice that the HR planning process begins with considering the organizational objectives and strategies. Then both external and internal assessments of HR needs and supply sources must be done and forecasts developed. Key to assessing internal human resources is having solid information, which is accessible through a human resource information system (HRIS).

Once the assessments are complete, forecasts must be developed to identify the mismatch between HR supply and HR demand. HR strategies and plans to address the imbalance, both short and long term, must be developed.

**HR strategies** are the means used to aid the organization in anticipating and managing the supply and demand for human resources. These HR strategies provide overall direction for how HR activities will be developed and managed. Finally, specific HR plans are developed to provide more specific direction for the management of HR activities.

**HR strategies**
The means used to aid the organization in anticipating and managing the supply and demand for human resources.

**FIGURE 2–6** *HR Planning Process*

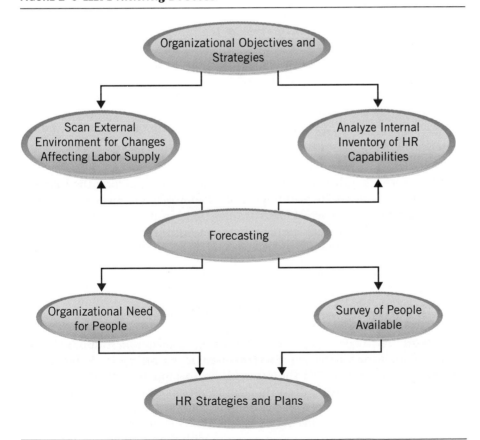

**DEVELOPING THE HR PLAN** The HR plan must be guided by longer-term plans. For example, in planning for human resources, an organization must consider the allocation of people to jobs over long periods of time—not just for the next month or even the next year. This allocation requires knowledge of any foreseen expansions or reductions in operations and any technological changes that may affect the organization. On the basis of such analyses, plans can be made for shifting employees within the organization, laying off or otherwise cutting back the number of employees, or retraining present employees. Factors to consider include the current level of employee knowledge, skills, and abilities in an organization and the expected vacancies resulting from retirement, promotion, transfer, sick leave, or discharge.

In summary, the HR plan provides a road map for the future, identifying where employees are likely to be obtained, when employees will be needed, and what training and development employees must have. Through *succession planning,* employee *career paths* can be tailored to individual needs that are consistent with organizational requirements. Succession plans are discussed in more detail in Chapter 11.

Further, the compensation system has to fit with the performance appraisal system, which must fit with HR development decisions, and so on. In summary, the different HR activities must be aligned with the general business strategy, as well as the overall HR strategy, in order to support business goals.

**EVALUATING HR PLANNING** If HR planning is done well, the following benefits should result:

- Upper management has a better view of the human resource dimensions of business decisions.
- HR costs may be lower because management can anticipate imbalances before they become unmanageable and expensive.
- More time is available to locate talent because needs are anticipated and identified before the actual staffing is required.
- Better opportunities exist to include women and minority groups in future growth plans.
- Development of managers can be better planned.

To the extent that these results can be measured, they can form the basis for evaluating the success of HR planning. Another approach is to measure projected levels of demand against actual levels at some point in the future. But the most telling evidence of successful HR planning is an organization in which the human resources are consistently aligned with the needs of the business over a period of time.

# Scanning the External Environment

**Environmental scanning**
The process of studying the environment of the organization to pinpoint opportunities and threats.

At the heart of strategic planning is the knowledge gained from scanning the external environment for changes. **Environmental scanning** is the process of studying the environment of the organization to pinpoint opportunities and threats. Scanning especially affects HR planning because each organization must draw from the same labor market that supplies all other employers. Indeed, one measure of organizational effectiveness is the ability of an organization to compete for a sufficient supply of human resources with the appropriate capabilities.

Many factors can influence the supply of labor available to an employer. Some of the more significant environmental factors are identified in Figure 2–7. They include government influences; economic, geographic, and competitive conditions; workforce composition; and work patterns.

## Government Influences

A major element that affects labor supply is the government. Today, managers are confronted with an expanding and often bewildering array of government rules as regulation of HR activities has steadily increased. As a result, HR planning must be done by individuals who understand the legal requirements of various government regulations.

Government trade policies and restrictions can affect HR planning. Under a *closed-import policy,* foreign firms may establish more American-based manufacturing operations using American labor. An *open-import policy,* on the other hand, creates an entirely different economic labor environment.

Tax legislation at local, state, and federal levels also affects HR planning. Pension provisions and Social Security legislation may change retirement patterns and funding options. Elimination or expansion of tax benefits for job-training expenses might alter some job-training activities associated with workforce expansions. Employee benefits may be affected significantly by tax law changes. Tax credits for employee day care and financial aid for education may affect employer

**FIGURE 2–7** *External Environmental Factors Affecting Labor Supply for an Organization*

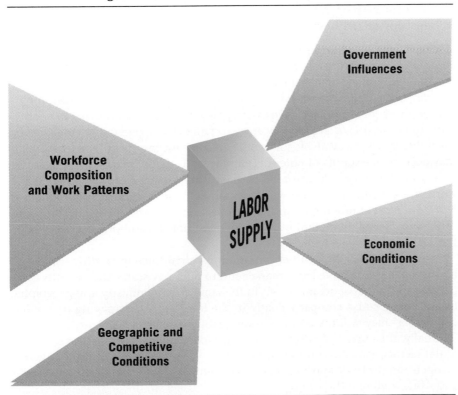

practices in recruiting and retaining workers. In summary, an organization must consider a wide variety of government policies, regulations, and laws when doing HR planning.

## Economic Conditions

The general business cycle of recessions and booms also affects HR planning. Such factors as interest rates, inflation, and economic growth help determine the availability of workers and figure into organizational plans and objectives. Decisions on wages, overtime, and hiring or laying off workers all hinge on economic conditions. For example, suppose economic conditions lead to a decrease in the unemployment rate. There is a considerable difference between finding qualified applicants in a 3% unemployment market and in a 7% unemployment market. In the 3% unemployment market, significantly fewer qualified applicants are likely to be available for any kind of position. Those who are available may be less employable because they are less educated, less skilled, or unwilling to work. As the unemployment rate rises, the number of qualified people looking for work increases, making it easier to fill jobs.

## Geographic and Competitive Concerns

Employers must consider the following geographic and competitive concerns in making HR plans:

- Net migration into the area
- Other employers in the area
- Employee resistance to geographic relocation
- Direct competitors in the area
- Impact of international competition on the area

The *net migration* into a particular region is important. For example, in the past decade, the population of U.S. cities in the South, Southwest, and West have grown rapidly and provided a ready source of labor.

*Other employers* in a geographic region can greatly expand or diminish the labor supply. If, for example, a large military facility is closing or moving to another geographic location, a large supply of good civilian labor, previously employed by the military, may be available for a while. In contrast, the opening of a new plant may decrease the supply of potential employees in a labor market for some time.

Within the last decade, there has been growing reluctance on the part of many workers, especially those with working spouses, to accept *geographic relocation* as a precondition of moving up in the organization. This trend has forced organizations to change their employee development policies and practices, as well as their HR plans.

*Direct competitors* are another important external force in staffing. Failure to consider the competitive labor market and to offer pay scales and benefits competitive with those of organizations in the same general industry and geographic location may cost a company dearly in the long run. Underpaying or "undercompeting" may result in a much lower-quality workforce.

Finally, the impact of *international competition,* as well as numerous other external factors, must be considered as part of environmental scanning. A global competition for labor appears to be developing as global competitors shift jobs and workers around the world.

## Workforce Composition and Work Patterns

Changes in the composition of the workforce, combined with the use of varied work patterns, have created workplaces and organizations that are very different from those of a decade ago. As noted in Chapter 1, demographic shifts have resulted in greater workforce diversity. Many organizations are addressing concerns about having sufficient workers with the necessary capabilities, and have turned to such sources as welfare-to-work programs. The use of outsourcing and contingent workers also must be considered as part of human resource planning. As Figure 2–8 indicates, part-time employees are used in various ways. Working patterns and arrangements are also shifting, and these shifts must be considered during HR planning.

**ALTERNATIVE WORK SCHEDULES** The traditional work schedule, in which employees work full time, 8 hours a day, 5 days a week at the employer's place of operations, is in transition. Organizations have been experimenting with many different possibilities for change: the 4-day, 40-hour week; the 4-day, 32-hour week; the 3-day week; and flexible scheduling. Many employers have adopted some flexibility in work schedules and locations. Changes of this nature must be considered in HR planning. These alternative work schedules allow organizations to make better use of workers by matching work demands to work hours. Workers also are better able to balance their work and family responsibilities.

One type of schedule redesign is **flextime,** in which employees work a set number of hours per day but vary starting and ending times. The traditional starting and ending times of the 8-hour work shift can vary up to one or more hours at the beginning and end of the normal workday. Flextime allows management to relax some of the traditional "time clock" control of employees. Generally, use of flextime has resulted in higher employee morale and reduced absenteeism and

*LOGGING ON . . .*
**Workforce Online**
This site offers a forum for organizations to obtain product information, legal tips, and current human resource news information. A research tool is also available at this site.

**http://www.workforceonline. com**

**Flextime**
A scheduling arrangement in which employees work a set number of hours per day but vary starting and ending times.

**FIGURE 2–8** *Part-time Worker Usage by Type*

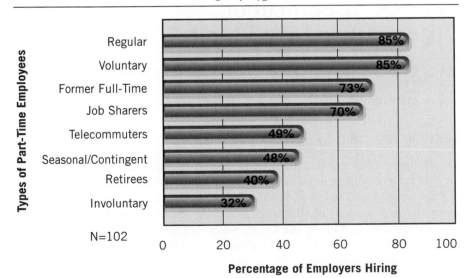

SOURCE: Adapted from "Part-time Employment" (New York: The Conference Board), vol. 6. No. 1.

**Compressed workweek**
Workweek in which a full
week's work is
accomplished in fewer
than five days.

*BNA 605.40.20-30*
**Flextime and Compressed
Workweek**
The nature of flextime and
compressed workweeks
must be coordinated with
overtime pay requirements.
Review these requirements
and compare them to alternative work patterns in
your previous employment
situations.

employee turnover. However, some problems must be addressed when flextime is used, particularly if unionized workers are involved.[12]

Another way to change work patterns is with the **compressed workweek,** in which a full week's work is accomplished in fewer than five days. Compression simply alters the number of hours per day per employee, usually resulting in longer working times each day and a decreased number of days worked per week.

**ALTERNATIVE WORK ARRANGEMENTS** A growing number of employers are allowing workers to use widely different working arrangements. Some employees work partly at home and partly at an office, and share office space with other "office nomads." According to data from governmental statistics for a recent year, over 21 million U.S. workers worked at home for some or all of the time.[13]

*Telecommuting* is the process of going to work via electronic computing and telecommunications equipment. Many U.S. employers have telecommuting employees or are experimenting with them, including such firms as American Express, Travelers Insurance, and J.C. Penney Co. Other types of nontraditional work arrangements have been labeled in various ways.

Although it does not deal with working hours, another work arrangement is *hoteling,* in which workers check in with an office concierge, carry their own nameplates with them, and are assigned to work cubicles or small offices. A worker uses the assigned office for a day or more, but other workers may use the same office in later days and weeks.

Other employees have *virtual offices,* which means that their offices are wherever they are, whenever they are there. An office could be a customer's project room, an airport conference room, a work suite in a hotel resort, a business-class seat on an international airline flight, or even a rental car.

The shift to such arrangements means that work is done anywhere, anytime, and that people are judged more on results than on "putting in time." Greater trust, less direct supervision, and more self-scheduling are all job characteristics of those with virtual offices and other less traditional arrangements.

# Internal Assessment of Organizational Workforce

Analyzing the jobs that will need to be done and the skills of people currently available to do them is the next part of HR planning. The needs of the organization must be compared against the labor supply available.

## Auditing Jobs and Skills

The starting point for evaluating internal strengths and weaknesses is an audit of the jobs currently being done in the organization. This internal assessment helps to position an organization to develop or maintain a competitive advantage.[14] A comprehensive analysis of all current jobs provides a basis for forecasting what jobs will need to be done in the future. Much of the data to answer these questions should be available from existing staffing and organizational databases. The following questions are addressed during the internal assessment:

- What jobs now exist?
- How many individuals are performing each job?

- What are the reporting relationships of jobs?
- How essential is each job?
- What jobs will be needed to implement the organizational strategy?
- What are the characteristics of anticipated jobs?

## Organizational Capabilities Inventory

As those doing HR planning gain an understanding of current jobs and the new jobs that will be necessary to carry out organizational plans, they can make a detailed audit of current employees and their capabilities. The basic source of data on employees is the HR records in the organization. By utilizing different databases in an HRIS, it is possible to identify the employees' capabilities, knowledge, and skills. Planners can use these inventories to determine long-range needs for recruiting, selection, and HR development. Also, that information can be the basis for determining which additional capabilities will be needed in the future workforce that may not currently exist, but will be needed.[15]

**COMPONENTS OF ORGANIZATIONAL CAPABILITIES INVENTORY** This inventory of organizational capabilities often consists of:

- Individual employee demographics (age, length of service in the organization, time in present job)
- Individual career progression (jobs held, time in each job, promotions or other job changes, pay rates)
- Individual performance data (work accomplishment, growth in skills)

These three types of information can be expanded to include:

- Education and training
- Mobility and geographic preference
- Specific aptitudes, abilities, and interests
- Areas of interest and internal promotion ladders
- Promotability ratings
- Anticipated retirement

All the information that goes into an employee's skills inventory affects the employee's career. Therefore, the data and their use must meet the same standards of job-relatedness and nondiscrimination as those used when the employee was initially hired. Furthermore, security of such information is important to ensure that sensitive information is available only to those who have specific use for it.

**USING ORGANIZATIONAL INVENTORY DATA** Data on individual employees can be aggregated into a profile of the current organizational workforce. This profile reveals many of the current strengths and deficiencies. The absence of some specialized expertise, such as advanced computer skills, may affect the ability of an organization to take advantage of new technological developments. Likewise, if a large group of experienced employees are all in the same age bracket, their eventual retirement will lead to high turnover and a major void in the organization. For example, in one case, eight skilled line workers in a small rural electric utility were due to retire within a three-year period. Yet it takes seven years of apprenticeship and on-the-job training for a person to be qualified for a senior skilled job within the utility.

Other areas often profiled include turnover, mobility restrictions of current workers, and specialized job qualifications. A number of these factors are ones over which the organization has little control. Some employees will die, leave the firm, retire, or otherwise contribute to a reduction in the current employee force. It can be helpful to plot charts giving an overview of the employee situation for each department in an organization, suggesting where external candidates might be needed to fill future positions. Similarly, the chart may indicate where there is a reservoir of trained people that the employer can tap to meet future conditions. Increasingly, employers are making use of a computerized human resource information system (HRIS) to compile such records.

# Human Resource Information Systems (HRIS)

**Human resource information system (HRIS)**
An integrated system designed to provide information used in HR decision making.

Computers have simplified the task of analyzing vast amounts of data, and they can be invaluable aids in HR management, from payroll processing to record retention. With computer hardware, software, and databases, organizations can keep records and information better, as well as retrieve them with greater ease. A **human resource information system (HRIS)** is an integrated system designed to provide information used in HR decision making. Although an HRIS does not have to be computerized, most are.

## Purposes of an HRIS

An HRIS serves two major purposes in organizations. One relates to administrative and operational efficiency, the other to effectiveness. The first purpose of an HRIS is to improve the efficiency with which data on employees and HR activities is compiled. Many HR activities can be performed more efficiently and with less paperwork if automated. When on-line data input is used, fewer forms must be stored, and less manual record keeping is necessary. Much of the reengineering of HR activities has focused on identifying the flow of HR data and how the data can be retrieved more efficiently for authorized users. Workflow, automation of some HR activities, and automation of HR record keeping are key to improving HR operations by making workflow more efficient.

The second purpose of an HRIS is more strategic and related to HR planning. Having accessible data enables HR planning and managerial decision making to be based to a greater degree on information rather than relying on managerial perception and intuition. For example, instead of manually doing a turnover analysis by department, length of service, and educational background, a specialist can quickly compile such a report by using an HRIS and various sorting and analysis functions.

HR management has grown in strategic value in many organizations; accordingly, there has been an increased emphasis on obtaining and using HRIS data for strategic planning and human resource forecasting, which focus on broader HR effectiveness over time.

## Uses of an HRIS

An HRIS has many uses in an organization. The most basic is the automation of payroll and benefit activities. With an HRIS, employees' time records are entered into the system, and the appropriate deductions and other individual adjustments are reflected in the final paychecks. As a result of HRIS development and implementation in many organizations, several payroll functions are being transferred from accounting departments to HR departments. Another common use of HRIS is EEO/affirmative action tracking. Beyond these basic activities, many other HR activities can be affected by the use of an HRIS, as Figure 2–9 illustrates.

## Establishing an HRIS

The explosion of information technology has changed the nature of HR information usage. Just a few years ago, most HR information had to be compiled and maintained on mainframe computers. Today, many different types of information technology are being integrated and used so that HR professionals can access HR-related data and communicate it to other managers and executives.

**CHOOSING AN HRIS** It is crucial when establishing an HRIS that the system be able to support the HR strategies of the organization. This requires analyses of the

*LOGGING ON . . .*
**Human Resources
Microsystems**
Details on the latest in HR information systems are available on this site for organizations to view.

**http://www.hrms.com**

**FIGURE 2–9** *Uses of a Human Resource Information System (HRIS)*

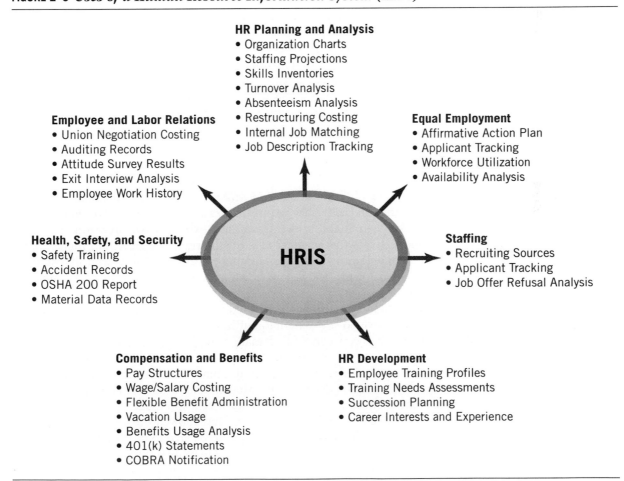

**HR Planning and Analysis**
• Organization Charts
• Staffing Projections
• Skills Inventories
• Turnover Analysis
• Absenteeism Analysis
• Restructuring Costing
• Internal Job Matching
• Job Description Tracking

**Employee and Labor Relations**
• Union Negotiation Costing
• Auditing Records
• Attitude Survey Results
• Exit Interview Analysis
• Employee Work History

**Equal Employment**
• Affirmative Action Plan
• Applicant Tracking
• Workforce Utilization
• Availability Analysis

**Health, Safety, and Security**
• Safety Training
• Accident Records
• OSHA 200 Report
• Material Data Records

**HRIS**

**Staffing**
• Recruiting Sources
• Applicant Tracking
• Job Offer Refusal Analysis

**Compensation and Benefits**
• Pay Structures
• Wage/Salary Costing
• Flexible Benefit Administration
• Vacation Usage
• Benefits Usage Analysis
• 401(k) Statements
• COBRA Notification

**HR Development**
• Employee Training Profiles
• Training Needs Assessments
• Succession Planning
• Career Interests and Experience

uses of HR information, both in the HR unit and throughout the organization. Too often, the decisions about an HRIS are made based primarily on cost factors, rather than on how well the HRIS supports HR decision making.

## DESIGNING AND IMPLEMENTING AN HRIS

To design an effective HRIS, experts advise starting with questions about the data to be included:

- What information is available, and what information is needed about people in the organization?
- To what uses will the information be put?
- In what format should the output be presented to fit with other company records?
- Who needs the information?
- When and how often is it needed?

Answers to these questions help pinpoint the necessary hardware and software. Experts recommend that a *project team* be established and extensive planning be done. This team often includes representatives from several departments in the organization, including the HR and management information/data processing areas. The team serves as a steering committee to review user needs, identify desired capabilities of the system, solicit and examine bids from software and hardware vendors, and identify the implementation process required to install the system. By involving a cross-section of managers and others, the organization attempts to ensure that the HRIS fulfills its potential, is accepted by users, and is implemented in an organized manner.[16]

Many different types of software systems are available to provide human resource information. Some HRIS software systems use mainframe computers and represent significant costs for purchase and installation. Other HR software systems can be run on personal computers and through local area or wide area networks in organizations. Growing use is being made of the Internet as a base for HR information systems.

**ACCESSING THE HRIS VIA INTRANETS AND EXTRANETS** The dramatic increase in the use of the Internet is raising possibilities and concerns for HR professionals, particularly when establishing intranets and extranets. An **intranet** is an organizational network that operates over the Internet. The growth in the use of HR intranets for obtaining and disseminating HR information is seen in a study of about 50 global firms, about 45% of whom are using global intranets, up from 27% in just one year.[17]

An **extranet** is an Internet-linked network that allows employees access to information provided by external entities. For instance, with an extranet, employees can access benefit information maintained by a third-party benefits administrator.[18] In another situation employees can access their payroll information from a payroll service provider and submit their travel requests to an external travel-service provider. For both extranets and intranets, security is important to prevent unauthorized or inappropriate access and usage.[19]

Use of web-based information systems has allowed the firm's HR unit to become more administratively efficient and to be able to deal with more strategic and longer-term HR planning issues.[20] Firms have used these web-based HRIS options in four primary ways:[21]

*BNA 1210.20.30. 10-20*

**E-mail and Intranets**
An overview of electronic communication means and the advantage and issues associated with them are described.

**Intranet**
An organizational network that operates over the Internet.

**Extranet**
An Internet-linked network that allows employees access to information provided by external entities.

- *Bulletin boards:*   Information on personnel policies, job posting, and training materials can be accessed by employees globally.
- *Data access:*   Linked to databases, an extranet or intranet allows employees themselves to access benefit information such as sick leave usage, 401(k) balances, and so on, freeing up time for HR staff members who previously spent considerable time answering routine employee inquiries.
- *Employee self-service:*   Many intranet uses incorporate employee self-service options whereby employees can access and update their own personnel records, change or enroll in employee benefits plans, and respond to employment opportunities in other locations. Obviously, maintaining security is critical when the employee self-service option is available.[22]
- *Extended linkage:*   Integrating extranets and intranets allows the databases of vendors of HR services and an employer to be linked so that data can be exchanged electronically. Also, employees can communicate directly from throughout the world to submit and retrieve personnel details.

**TRAINING**   Training those who will be using an HRIS is critical to the successful implementation of an HRIS. This training takes place at several levels. First, everyone in the organization concerned with data on employees has to be trained to use new recording forms compatible with the input requirements of the system. In addition, HR staff members and HR executives must be trained on the system. Support and instruction from hardware and software vendors also are important in order for the organization to realize the full benefits of the system. One study of HRIS successes found that the presence of in-house training was linked with greater user satisfaction with an HRIS.[23]

**ENSURING SECURITY AND PRIVACY**   Two other issues of concern are *security* and *privacy*. Controls must be built into the system to restrict indiscriminate access to HRIS data on employees. For instance, health insurance claims might identify someone who has undergone psychiatric counseling or treatment for alcoholism, and access to such information must be limited. Likewise, performance appraisal ratings on employees must be guarded.

# Forecasting

The information gathered from external environmental scanning and assessment of internal strengths and weaknesses is used to predict or *forecast* HR supply and demand in light of organizational objectives and strategies. **Forecasting** uses information from the past and present to identify expected future conditions. Projections for the future are, of course, subject to error. Changes in the conditions on which the projections are based might even completely invalidate them, which is the chance forecasters take. Usually, though, experienced people are able to forecast with enough accuracy to benefit organizational long-range planning.

Approaches to forecasting human resources range from a manager's best guess to a rigorous and complex computer simulation. Simple assumptions may be sufficient in certain instances, but complex models may be necessary for others. It is beyond the scope of this text to discuss in detail the numerous methods of forecasting available, but a few of the more prominent ones will be highlighted.

Despite the availability of sophisticated mathematical models and techniques, forecasting is still a combination of quantitative method and subjective judg-

**Forecasting**
Identifying expected future conditions based on information from the past and present.

ment. The facts must be evaluated and weighed by knowledgeable individuals, such as managers and HR experts, who use the mathematical models as a tool rather than relying on them blindly.

## Forecasting Periods

HR forecasting should be done over three planning periods: short range, intermediate, and long range. The most commonly used planning period is *short range,* usually a period of six months to one year. This level of planning is routine in many organizations because very few assumptions about the future are necessary for such short-range plans. These short-range forecasts offer the best estimates of the immediate HR needs of an organization. Intermediate and long-range forecasting are much more difficult processes. *Intermediate* plans usually project one to five years into the future, and *long-range* plans extend beyond five years.

## Forecasting the Need for Human Resources (Demand)

The main emphasis in HR forecasting to date has been on forecasting organizational need for human resources, or HR demand. Forecasts of demand may be either judgmental or mathematical. Figure 2–10 summarizes judgmental and mathematical approaches to forecasting HR demand. Even when mathematical methods are used, human judgments are also needed to confirm the conclusion of the mathematical models.

The demand for employees can be calculated on an organization-wide basis and/or calculated based on the needs of individual units in the organization. For example, to forecast that the firm needs 125 new employees next year might mean less than to forecast that it needs 25 new people in sales and customer service, 45 in production, 20 in accounting, 5 in HR, and 30 in the warehouse. This unit breakdown obviously allows for more consideration of the specific skills needed than the aggregate method does.

Forecasting human resources can be done using two frameworks. One approach considers specific openings that are likely to occur and uses that as the basis for planning. The openings (or demands) are created when employees leave a position because of promotions, transfers, and terminations. The analysis always begins with the top positions in the organization, because from those there can be no promotions to a higher level.

Based on this analysis, decision rules (or "fill rates") are developed for each job or level. For example, a decision rule for a financial institution might state that 50% of branch supervisor openings will be filled through promotions from customer service tellers, 25% through promotions from personal bankers, and 25% from new hires. But forecasters must be aware of chain effects throughout the organization, because as people are promoted, their previous positions become available. Continuing our example, forecasts for the need for customer service tellers and personal bankers would also have to be developed. The overall purpose of this analysis is to develop a forecast of the needs for human resources by number and type for the forecasted period.

## Forecasting Availability of Human Resources (Supply)

Once the need for human resources has been forecasted, then their availability must be identified. Forecasting the availability of human resources considers both

**FIGURE 2–10** *Methods for Forecasting HR Demand*

## Judgmental Methods

**Estimates** can be either top-down or bottom-up, but essentially people who are in a position to know are asked, "How many people will you need next year?"

**Rules of thumb** rely on general guidelines applied to a specific situation within the organization. For example, a guideline of "one operations manager per five reporting supervisors" aids in forecasting the number of supervisors needed in a division. However, it is important to adapt the guidelines to recognize widely varying departmental needs.

**The Delphi technique** uses input from a group of experts. The experts' opinions are sought using separate questionnaires on what forecasted situations will be. These expert opinions are then combined and returned to the experts for a second anonymous opinion. The process continues through several rounds until the experts essentially agree on a judgment. For example, this approach was used to forecast effects of technology on HR management and staffing needs.

**The nominal group technique,** unlike the Delphi technique, requires experts to meet face to face. Their ideals are usually generated independently at first, discussed as a group, and then compiled as a report.

## Mathematical Methods

**Statistical regression analysis** makes a statistical comparison of past relationships among various factors. For example, a statistical relationship between gross sales and number of employees in a retail chain may be useful in forecasting the number of employees that will be needed if the retailer's sales increase 30%.

**Simulation models** are representations of real situations in abstract form. For example, an econometric model forecasting the growth in software usage would lead to forecasting the need for software developers. Numerous simulation techniques are available, but surveys reveal that the more complex simulation techniques are used by relatively few firms.

**Productivity ratios** calculate the average number of units produced per employee. These averages can be applied to sales forecasts to determine the number of employees needed. For example, a firm could forecast the number of needed sales representatives using these ratios.

**Staffing ratios** can be used to estimate indirect labor. For example, if the company usually uses one clerical person for every 25 production employees, that ratio can be used to help estimate the need for clerical people.

---

*external* and *internal* supplies. Although the internal supply may be easier to calculate, it is important to calculate the external supply as accurately as possible.

**EXTERNAL SUPPLY** The external supply of potential employees available to the organization needs to be estimated. Extensive use of government labor force population estimates, trends in the industry, and many more complex and interrelated factors must be considered. Here are some of the factors that may be considered:

- Net migration into and out of the area
- Individuals entering and leaving the workforce
- Individuals graduating from schools and colleges
- Changing workforce composition and patterns
- Economic forecasts for the next few years
- Technological developments and shifts

- Actions of competing employers
- Government regulations and pressures
- Factors affecting persons entering and leaving the workforce

**INTERNAL SUPPLY** Figure 2–11 shows in general terms how the internal supply can be calculated. Estimating internal supply considers that employees move from their current jobs into others through promotions, lateral moves, and terminations. Also, it considers that the internal supply is influenced by training and development programs, transfer and promotion policies, and retirement policies, among other factors.

Internally, *succession analysis* is one method used to forecast the supply of people for certain positions. It relies on *replacement charts,* which are succession plans developed to identify potential personnel changes, select backup candidates, promote individuals, and keep track of attribution (resignations, retirements) for each department in an organization.

A *transition matrix,* or *Markov matrix,* can be used to model the internal flow of human resources. These matrices simply show as probabilities the average rate of historical movement from one job to another. Figure 2–12 presents a very simple transition matrix. For a line worker, for example, there is a 20% probability of being gone in 12 months, a 0% probability of promotion to manager, a 15% probability of promotion to supervisor, and a 65% probability of being a line worker this time next year. Such transition matrices form the bases for computer simulations of the internal flow of people through a large organization over time.

**COMPILING THE HR PLAN** With all the data collected and forecasts done, an organization has the information it needs to develop an HR plan. Such a plan can be extremely sophisticated or rather rudimentary. Regardless of its degree of com-

**FIGURE 2–11** *Estimating Internal Labor Supply for a Given Unit*

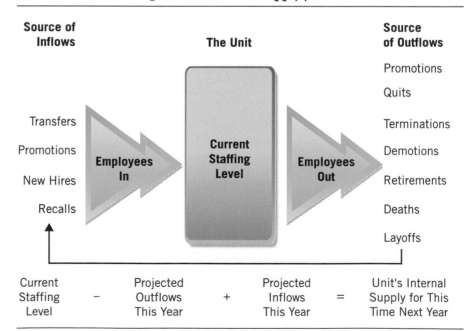

**FIGURE 2–12** *Transition Matrix for Twelve-Month Period*

|  | Exit | Manager | Supervisor | Line Worker |
|---|---|---|---|---|
| Manager | .15 | .85 | .00 | .00 |
| Supervisor | .10 | .15 | .70 | .05 |
| Line Worker | .20 | .00 | .15 | .65 |

plexity, the ultimate purpose of the plan is to enable managers in the organization to match the available supply of labor with the forecasted demands in light of the strategies of the firm. If the necessary skill level does not exist in the present workforce, employees may need to be trained in the new skill, or outside recruiting may need to be undertaken. Likewise, if the plan reveals that the firm employs too many people for its needs, a human resource surplus exists.

# Managing a Human Resource Surplus

All efforts involved in HR planning will be futile unless management takes action to implement the plans. Managerial actions vary depending on whether a surplus or a shortage of workers has been forecast. Consideration will be given here to managing a surplus of employees, since dealing with a shortage is considered later, in the recruiting and training chapters (Chapters 8 and 10). A surplus of workers can be managed within an HR plan in a variety of ways. But regardless of the means, the actions are difficult because they require that some employees be removed from the organization and workforce reductions are necessary.

## Workforce Reductions and the WARN Act

In this era of mergers, acquisitions, and downsizing, many workers have been laid off or had their jobs eliminated due to closing of selected offices, plants, and operations. To provide employees with sufficient notice, a federal law was passed, the Worker Adjustment and Retraining Notification (WARN) Act. This act requires employers to give a 60-day notice before a layoff or facility closing involving more than 50 pepole. However, part-time employees working fewer than 20 hours per week do not count toward the 50 employees. Also, seasonal employees do not have to receive WARN notification. The WARN Act also imposes stiff fines on employers who do not follow the required process and give proper notice.

## Downsizing

During the past decade in the United States, a large number of firms initiated aggressive programs to downsize their workforces. **Downsizing** is reducing the size of an organizational workforce. To avoid the negative terminology, some firms have called it "rightsizing." But the end result is that many people lose their jobs.

**CAUSES OF DOWNSIZING** There are two major reasons why organizations with a surplus of workers have instituted downsizing. First, many organizations have

*BNA 3640.30*
**The WARN ACT**
Details of when the act applies, how notification of facilities closings must be given, who receives notification, and penalties for non-compliance are reviewed in this section.

**Downsizing**
Reducing the size of an organizational workforce.

not competed effectively with foreign and domestic competition. With higher cost structures and lower productivity rates, many of these firms have had lower financial performance and have not adapted to rapid changes in their industries. Consequently, due to both competitive pressures and intense scrutiny by financial investors, corporations have had to take aggressive actions to improve organizational results. Cutting back the number of employees is one approach that demonstrates that management is trying to produce better results.

Another cause for downsizing has been the proliferation of mergers in many industries. One only has to look at the financial or telecommunications industry to see the consolidation in the number of firms. While some mergers are between two huge firms, such as British Petroleum and Amoco, or Norwest and Wells-Fargo banks, others have been smaller mergers, such as the merger of two local hospitals. But a common result of most mergers and acquisitions is that there is an excess of employees once the firms have been combined. Because much of the rationale for combinations is financial, eliminating employees with overlapping responsibilities is a primary concern. The wave of merger and acquisition activity in the United States has often left the new, combined companies with redundant departments, plants and people.[24]

In both causes for downsizing, there often is an undercurrent of change that management believes to be necessary. By restructuring the organization, management hopes to realign it to achieve strategic objectives. In some firms that have downsized, more jobs have been created than jobs eliminated; but often the new jobs are filled by employees with different capabilities and in different organizational areas from those in the old jobs.

**CONSEQUENCES OF DOWNSIZING** Despite the extensive usage of downsizing throughout many industries and organizations, there are significant questions about the longer-term value of downsizing. In some companies organizational performance has not improved significantly, although operating expenses decline in the short term. Only 43% of the firms in a study by the American Management Association (AMA) had an increase in operating profits as an immediate result of organizational restructurings, and only 30% had an increase in worker productivity. For instance, both Kodak Corporation and Apple Computer have cut thousands of workers in the past few years, and both firms are continuing to lose money or lag their competitors in profitability.[25] In the case of Kodak and many downsized firms, despite eliminating many workers, the final number of employees changed very little, but the disruption in the organization has caused significant problems. What these firms and others have found is that just cutting payroll expenses does not produce profits and strengthen growth if the firm's products, services, and productivity are flawed.

In some downsizings, so many employees in critical areas have been eliminated—or have chosen to leave—that customer service and productivity have declined. In the telecommunications industry, so many of the craft and technical workers of Bell Atlantic accepted a company buyout offer that the remaining installation and repair technicians could not keep up with customer service demands and work orders. At AT&T about 20% more managers elected to leave the firm than was anticipated, which reduced the managerial depth needed to handle the dynamic environmental facing AT&T.[26]

Corporations that are closing facilities or eliminating departments may need to offer financial transition arrangements. A **transition stay bonus** is extra payment for employees whose jobs are being eliminated, thereby motivating

**Transition stay bonus**
Extra payment for those employees whose jobs are being eliminated, thereby motivating them to remain with the organization for a period of time.

them to remain with the organization for a period of time. Figure 2–13 shows the nature of these bonus payments, according to a survey of over 800 firms.

Just as critical is the impact of job elimination on the remaining employees. The AMA survey found that in 69% of the surveyed firms, employee morale declined in the short term and 28% of the firms had longer-term declines in employee morale. Additionally, resignations and employee turnover all increased substantially in the year following the downsizing.[27] These consequences are crucial challenges to be addressed by HR management when organizational restructurings occur.

**MANAGING SURVIVORS OF DOWNSIZING** A common myth is that those who are still around after downsizing in any of its many forms are so glad to have a job that they pose no problems to the organization. However, some observers draw an analogy between those who survive downsizing and those who survive wartime but experience guilt because they were spared while their friends were not. The result is that the performance of the survivors and the communications throughout the organization may be affected.[28]

The first major *reduction in force (RIF)* of workers ever undertaken in a firm is often a major jolt to the employees' view of the company. Bitterness, anger, disbelief, and shock all are common reactions. For those who survive the cuts, the paternalistic culture and image of the firm as a "lifetime" employer often is gone forever. Survivors need information about why the actions had to be taken, and what the future holds for them personally. The more that employees are involved in the regrouping, the more likely the transition is to be smooth. Managers, too, find downsizing situations very stressful and react negatively to having to be the bearers of bad news.[29]

**FIGURE 2–13** *Transition Stay Bonus Policies*

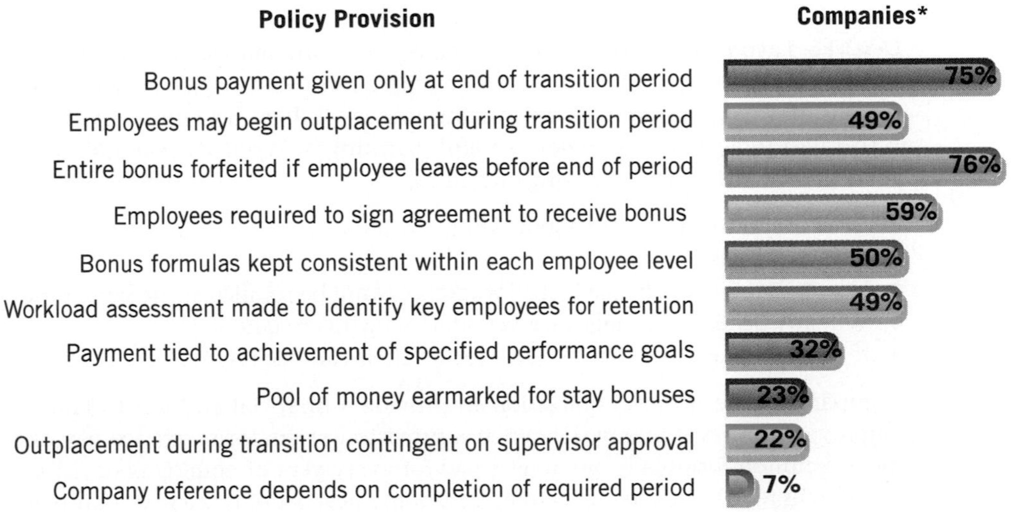

| Policy Provision | Companies* |
|---|---|
| Bonus payment given only at end of transition period | 75% |
| Employees may begin outplacement during transition period | 49% |
| Entire bonus forfeited if employee leaves before end of period | 76% |
| Employees required to sign agreement to receive bonus | 59% |
| Bonus formulas kept consistent within each employee level | 50% |
| Workload assessment made to identify key employees for retention | 49% |
| Payment tied to achievement of specified performance goals | 32% |
| Pool of money earmarked for stay bonuses | 23% |
| Outplacement during transition contingent on supervisor approval | 22% |
| Company reference depends on completion of required period | 7% |

* Sample includes both U.S. and Canadian firms.

SOURCE: *Retaining Employees During Critical Organizational Transitions* (Philadelphia: Right Management Consultants, 1997).

## Downsizing Approaches

Downsizing has inspired various innovative ways of removing people from the payroll, sometimes on a massive scale. Several alternatives can be used when downsizing must occur: Attrition, early retirement buyouts, and layoffs are the most common.

**ATTRITION AND HIRING FREEZES** *Attrition* occurs when individuals who quit, die, or retire are not replaced. With this approach, no one is cut out of a job, but those who remain must handle the same workload with fewer people. Unless turnover is high, attrition will eliminate only a relatively small number of employees. Therefore, employers may use a method that combines attrition with a freeze on hiring. This method is usually received with better employee understanding than many of the other methods.

**EARLY RETIREMENT BUYOUTS** Early retirement is a means of encouraging more senior workers to leave the organization early. As an incentive, employers make additional payments to employees so that they will not be penalized too much economically until their pensions and Social Security benefits take effect. Such voluntary termination programs, or buyouts, entice employees to quit with financial incentives. They are widely viewed as ways to accomplish workforce reduction without resorting to layoffs and individual firings.[30]

Buyouts appeal to employers because they can reduce payroll costs significantly over time. Although there are some up-front costs, the organization does not incur the continuing payroll costs. One hospital saved $2 for every $1 spent on early retirees. As noted, early retirement buyouts are viewed as a more humane way to reduce staff than terminating long-service, loyal employees. In addition, as long as buyouts are truly voluntary, the organization is less exposed to age discrimination suits.[31] Employees whom the company wishes would stay as well as those it wishes would leave can take advantage of the buyout. Consequently, some individuals whom the employer would rather retain often are among those who take a buyout.

*BNA 3640.10.10-20*
**Layoffs**
When layoffs occur, they can either be permanent or temporary. Review the differences in them and list some of the legal issues that affect employers.

**LAYOFFS** Layoffs occur when employees are put on unpaid leaves of absence. If business improves for the employer, then employees can be called back to work. Layoffs may be an appropriate downsizing strategy if there is a temporary downturn in an industry. Nevertheless, careful planning of layoffs is essential. Managers must consider the following questions:

- How are decisions made about whom to lay off, using seniority or performance records?
- How will call-backs be made if all workers cannot be recalled at the same time?
- Will any benefits coverage be given workers who are laid off?
- If workers take other jobs, do they forfeit their call-back rights?

Companies have no legal obligation to provide a financial cushion to laid-off employees; however, many do. When a provision exists for severance pay, the most common formula is one week's pay for every year of employment. Larger companies tend to be more generous. Loss of medical benefits is a major problem for laid-off employees. But under a federal law (COBRA), displaced workers can retain their medical group coverage for up to 18 months, and up to 36 months for dependents, if they pay the premiums themselves.

## Outplacement Services

**Outplacement** is a group of services provided to displaced employees to give them support and assistance. It is most often used with those involuntarily removed because of performance problems or elimination of jobs. A variety of services may be available to displaced employees. Outplacement services typically include personal career counseling, resume preparation and typing services, interviewing workshops, and referral assistance. Such services are generally provided by outside firms that specialize in outplacement assistance. Special severance pay arrangements also may be used. As Figure 2–14 indicates, firms commonly provide additional severance benefits and continue medical benefit coverage for a period of time at the same company-paid level as before. Other aids include retraining for different jobs, establishing on-site career centers, and contacting other employers for job placement opportunities.

In summary, a decade of experience with downsizing has led to some wisdom on how to deal with it if necessary.

- *Investigate alternatives to downsizing:*  Given the potential problems of downsizing, alternatives should be seriously considered first.
- *Involve those people necessary for success in the planning for downsizing:*  This involvement frequently is not done; those who have to make the downsizing operation work often are not involved in its planning.
- *Develop a comprehensive communications plan:*  Employees are entitled to advance notice so they can make plans.
- *Nurture the survivors:*  Remaining employees may be confused about their future careers. These and other concerns obviously can have negative effects.
- *Outplacement pays off:*  Helping separated employees find new work is good for the people and the reputation of the organization.

**Outplacement**
A group of services provided to displaced employees to give them support and assistance.

**FIGURE 2–14** *Outplacement Assistance by Company*

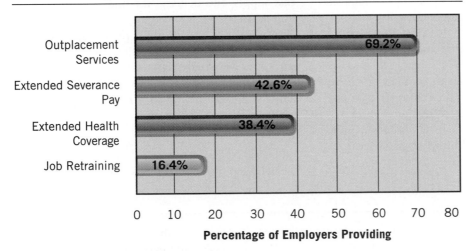

SOURCE: American Management Association, 1997.

# Summary

- HR planning is tied to the broader process of strategic planning, beginning with identifying the philosophy and mission of the organization.
- Human resources can provide a core competency for the organization, which may represent unique capabilities of the organization.
- Human resources can be part of resource-based organizational strategies if they have value, rareness, difficult imitability, and organization.
- HR strategies are affected by the culture of the organization and the life-cycle stages of the industry and the organization.
- Different organizational strategies require different approaches to HR planning.
- HR planning involves analyzing and identifying the future needs for and availability of human resources for the organization. The HR unit has major responsibilities in HR planning, but managers must provide supportive information and input.
- The HR planning process must be linked to organizational objectives and strategies.
- When developing HR plans, it is important for managers to scan the external environment to identify the effects of governmental influences,

economic conditions, geographic and competitive concerns, and workforce composition and patterns.
- Assessment of internal strengths and weaknesses as a part of HR planning requires that current jobs and employee capabilities be audited and organizational capabilities be inventoried.
- An HRIS is an integrated system designed to improve the efficiency with which HR data is compiled and to make HR records more useful to management as a source of information.
- An HRIS offers a wide range of HR uses, with payroll, benefits administration, and EEO/affirmative action tracking being the most prevalent.
- The growth of web-based HRIS options means that training and security issues must be addressed.
- Information on past and present conditions is used to identify expected future conditions and forecast the supply and demand for human resources. This process can be carried out with a variety of methods and for differing periods of time.
- Management of HR surpluses may require downsizing and outplacement. Attrition and early retirement are commonly used.

# Review and Discussion Questions

1. Describe some examples in your work experience of human resources being valuable, rare, hard to imitate, and well-organized.
2. Discuss how business strategy and HR practices vary in different industry life-cycle stages.
3. What is HR planning, and why must HR planning be seen as a process flowing from the organizational strategic plan?
4. Assume you have to develop an HR plan for a local bank. What specific external factors would be important for you to consider? Why?
5. At a computer software firm, how would you audit the current jobs and capabilities of employees?

6. Describe the advantages and disadvantages of employees using a web-based HRIS.
7. Why are the time frame and methods used to forecast supply and demand for human resources so important?
8. Assume that as a result of HR planning, a hospital identifies a shortage of physical therapists but a surplus of administrative workers. Discuss the actions that might be taken to address these problems, and explain why they must be approached carefully.

# Terms to Know

| | | |
|---|---|---|
| compressed workweek   54 | environmental scanning   50 | forecasting   59 |
| core competency   41 | extranet   58 | HR strategies   49 |
| downsizing   63 | flextime   53 | |

# Using the Internet

## Downsizing

The CEO and Senior Vice Presidents have called a special meeting to discuss and then evaluate a possible organizational downsizing. As the Senior HR Manager, you have been asked to develop alternatives to terminations and layoffs. Prepare a handout listing three alternatives to layoffs that would be beneficial to the organization.

Log on to the following web site:
**http://worksearch.gc.ca/hrooffice**
select English, and then select British Columbia to find the information.

## CASE

## Merging Incompatible Organizational Cultures

As the number of mergers and acquisitions has continued to rise, it has become evident that merging two different organizational cultures is not easy. Also, many anticipated benefits of the mergers are not realized because of different organizational and human resource cultures. According to one national estimate, 70% of all mergers and acquisitions do not meet expectations, and just 15% of all combinations achieve their stated financial objectives.

One example from the health-care industry illustrates the problems. Two large home-health-care organizations, both headquartered in southern California, had been fierce competitors. Homedco and Abbey Healthcare Group decided that rather than continuing to compete, they could strengthen their market positions by merging to create one large firm, Apria Healthcare Group. Together, they planned to expand their home health services nationwide as the effects of managed care spread.

Yet three years later the stock value of Apria had declined by 25%, and earnings fell. How far Apria declined was soon evident; when efforts began to find another company to take over the firm, few buyers were interested. What happened was primarily due to operational problems caused by the merger. Those issues had not been resolved because of internal conflict between the ex-Homedco and Abbey Healthcare executives and employees. Ultimately, the Board of Directors, which was evenly split, accepted the need to remove Timothy Aitken, former CEO of Abbey Healthcare, and have Jeremy Jones from Homedco as CEO.

It was obvious from the beginning that the organizational cultures were very different. Whereas Homedco had a more formalized structure with more centralized decision making, Abbey Healthcare had very decentralized decision making, and branch managers had significant authority. Also, merging computer and billing systems by using the Abbey Healthcare system meant that employees from Homedco had to be trained, which did not happen fast enough. As a result, numerous billing errors and the resulting complaints and phone calls from unhappy customers overwhelmed Apria customer service departments.

To save costs and eliminate duplication of jobs, about 14% of the employees in the combined company lost jobs. But the greatest number of those cut were former Abbey employees. For those remaining, it appeared that most Homedco managers were not affected as much as the Abbey Healthcare managers. For instance, only 6 of the 21 regional managers were formerly with Abbey Healthcare, which caused most of the best-performing Abbey sales representatives to quit. Even changing some basic HR policies caused problems. For example, when Homedco HR policies were extended into Abbey offices, a new dress code and time-recording procedures irritated many former Abbey workers. A significant number of them left in the first year. The level of conflict was so severe that employees from one firm referred to those from the other company as "idiots" and refused to return phone calls from employees with the other firm. Finally, both Aitken and Jones left the firm, and a new executive team has been struggling to rebuild Apria. Instead of being a healthy merger, it turned into the "merger from hell."

Unfortunately, this situation is not unusual; similar conflicting cultures have diminished the effective-ness of mergers by firms in other industries as well. One instance is a merger of two financial institutions, Society Corporation and Key Corporation (KeyCorp). Since the merger, the combined firm has grown only half as fast as other banks its size and has cut 5,000 employees. In this case, as well as the Apria one, it is evident that human resource issues and organizational culture incompatibilities can destroy the value of mergers that appear to be logical from a broad business strategy perspective.[32]

## Questions

1. Describe how analyses of human resource issues should have been done prior to the Apria merger.
2. Given the problems both KeyCorp and Apria have, what actions could be taken to begin creating better organizational cultures?

# Notes

1. Based on "Welfare-to-Work: A Good Start," *Business Week,* June 1, 1998, 102–106; "Welfare Recipients Stay on the Job Longer," *Omaha World-Herald,* May 27, 1998, A1, 10; Bill Leonard, "Welfare to Work: Filling a Tall Order," *HR Magazine,* May 1998, 78–87; and http://www.tulsachamber.com.
2. Gary Hamel and C.K. Prahalad, *Competing for Future* (Cambridge, MA: Harvard Business School Press, 1994), 227.
3. Mark A. Huselid, Susan E. Jackson, and Randall S. Schuler, "Technical and Strategic Human Resource Management Effectiveness as Determinants of Firm Performance," *Academy of Management Journal,* 40(1997), 171–188.
4. Jay B. Barney and Patrick M. Wright, "On Becoming a Strategic Partner: The Role of Human Resources in Gaining Competitive Advantage," *Human Resource Management,* Spring 1998, 31–46.
5. Russell W. Coff, "Human Assets and Management Dilemmas: Coping with Hazards on the Road to Resource-Based Theory," *Academy of Management Review,* 22(1997), 374–402.
6. The authors acknowledge that the development of concepts in Figure 2–2 are based on ideas suggested by Kathryn D. McKee, SPHR, CCP; Charles W. L. Hill and Gareth R. Jones, *Strategic Management* (Boston: Houghton Mifflin, 1998), 92–96; and Thomas A. Kochan and Thomas A. Barocci, *Human Resource Management and Industrial Relations* (Chicago: Scott, Foresman, 1985), 105.
7. Jay B. Barney, *Gaining and Sustaining Competitive Advantage* (Reading, MA: Addison-Wesley, 1997), Chapter 1.
8. Michael E. Porter, *Competitive Strategy: Techniques for Analyzing Industries and Competitors* (New York: Free Press, 1980).
9. Figure 2–4, as adapted, is based on ideas suggested in S. Ragburam and R. Arvey, "Business Strategy Links with Staffing and Training Practices," *Human Resource Planning* 17(1994), 58.
10. Adapted from Patrick M. Wright, Gary C. McMahan, Baline McCormick, and W. Scott Sherman, "Strategy, Core Competence, and HR Involvement as Determinants of HR Effectiveness and Refinery Performance," *Human Resource Management,* Spring 1998, 17–29.
11. Sharon Nelton, "Major Shifts in Leadership Lie Ahead," *Nation's Business,* June 1997, 56–57.
12. John D. Owen, "Flextime: Some Problems and Solutions," *Industrial and Labor Relations Review* 50(1997), 152–160.
13. "More Than 21 Million Worked at Home," *Bulletin to Management,* April 2, 1998, 101.
14. W. Jack Duncan, Peter M. Ginter, and Linda E. Swayne, "Competitive Advantage and Internal Organizational Assessment," *Academy of Management Executive,* August 1998, 6–16.
15. Timothy P. Summers and Suzanne B. Summers, "Strategic Skills Analysis for Selection and Development," *Human Resource Planning,* 20(1997), 14–19.
16. Susan Wolfe, "HRIS Usability: Why You Can't Afford to Ignore It," *IHRIM.Link,* January 1998, 44–52.
17. "Companies Making Strides on the Intranet Front," *HR Policies & Practices,* January 9, 1998, 1–2.
18. Mike Frost, "Extranets: A Big Boon—Especially for Small Companies," *HR Magazine,* January 1998, 31–35.

19. Samuel Greengard, "10 Ways to Protect Intranet Data," *Workforce,* September 1998, 78–81.

20. Tom Starner, "Being Direct," *Human Resource Executive,* March 4, 1999, 44–48; and Michelle Neely Martinez, "Intranets Boost HR to More Strategic, Future-Based Levels," *HR International Update,* February 1998, 1–3.

21. "Self Service HR: 4 Ways to Cash in on the Next Big HRIS Application," *Managing HR Information Systems,* September 1998, 1, 13–14, available at http://www.ioma.com.

22. Joel R. Lapointe, "A Method for Selecting the Right Employee Self-Service Situation," *HR Magazine,* August 1997, 37–42.

23. Victor Y. Haines and Andre Petit, "Conditions for Successful Human Resource Information Systems," *Human Resource Management,* Summer 1997, 261–275.

24. Carolyn Hirschman, "Time for a Change," *HR Magazine,* August 1998, 81–87.

25. Eric R. Quinones, "Massive Staff Cutbacks No Guarantee of Profits," *The Denver Post,* February 9, 1998, 3C.

26. Aaron Bernstein, "Oops, That's Too Much Downsizing," *Business Week,* June 8, 1998, 38; John J. Keller, "AT&T Buyout Package Attracts More Managers Than Expected," *The Wall Street Journal,* June 4, 1998, B6.

27. "Corporate Job Creation, Job Elimination, and Downsizing," 1997 Survey, American Management Association, 1–8.

28. Alex M. Susskind, Vernon D. Miller, and J. David Johnson, "Downsizing and Structural Holes," *Communication Research* 25(1998), 30–65.

29. Robert Folger and Daniel P. Skarlicki, "When Tough Times Make Tough Bosses: Managerial Distancing as a Function of Layoff Blame," *Academy of Management Journal,* 41(1998), 79–87.

30. Julie Cook, "Some Way Out," *Human Resource Executive,* September 1998, 1, 34–38.

31. Sue C. Erwin, Angus H. Macauley, and Jim O'Stuckey, "Tips to Help Employers Avoid Legal Claims for Downsizing," *Legal Report,* Summer 1997, 1–4.

32. Adapted from Rhonda L. Rundle, "Home Health Rivals Try Merger of Equals, Get Merger from Hell," *The Wall Street Journal,* February 26, 1998, A1; "The Perfect Blend," *Human Resource Executive,* May 19, 1998; 19–21; and Matt Murray, "KeyCorp Fails to Prove It Can Unlock Promise of Merger of Equals," *The Wall Street Journal,* August 25, 1998, A1

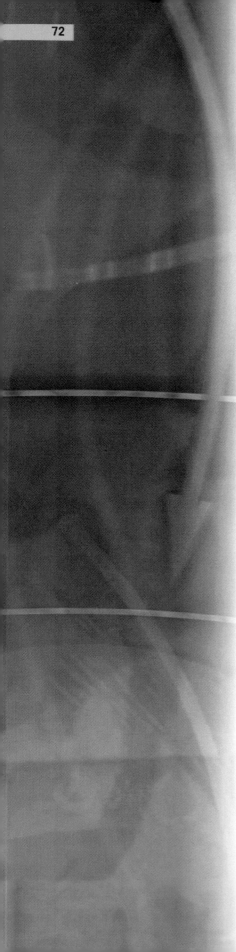

# CHAPTER 3

# Individuals, Jobs, and Effective HR Management

*After you have read this chapter, you should be able to:*

- Identify three areas where HR departments should set performance goals.

- Describe your current job using the job characteristics model.

- Discuss advantages and disadvantages of work teams.

- Compare and contrast ways of dealing with turnover and absenteeism.

- Enumerate ways to collect data for evaluating HR performance.

- Summarize the process of evaluating HR performance.

# Effective HR: Linking Individuals and Jobs Successfully

The kinds of Human Resources systems and practices that organizations develop differ to some extent. They evolve in response to different circumstances, but it is becoming clear that HR management does affect an organization's effectiveness and ability to compete. Three examples are given here to show how the relationships among individuals, jobs, and effective HR management can affect an organization.

*Plastics Lumber Company:* In Akron, Ohio, Alan Robbins started a small factory that converts old milk and soda bottles to fake lumber used in picnic tables, fences, etc. His major problems have been with his employees. He intentionally put his factory in a downtown location and hired local residents. When he began, he was lax and friendly—he would break out cold beers for everyone at the end of a shift, or grant employees personal loans. A turning point came when Mr. Robbins had to fire two workers for fighting on the work floor. One was roaming the factory looking for the other with an iron bar in his hand. Both men filed for unemployment compensation, and filed racial discrimination complaints. Mr. Robbins realized his laissez-faire approach to HR was not going to work. Other tough issues involving alcohol and drugs at work also emerged. In one month, he had to fire four of his 50 employees for cocaine and other substance abuse problems. Absenteeism is a constant problem. So is the threat of lawsuits and injury claims, as well as discrimination and unemployment claims. In response Mr. Robbins has built elaborate HR defenses against such problems and says he no longer

trusts his employees as much as he once did. His solution is an HR system built around a thick employment manual outlining what will be tolerated and what will not.

*Northwest Airlines:* Northwest's customer service and labor problems have gone from bad to the worst among major airlines. Northwest had the highest number of customer complaints, the most delayed flights, and second worst performance on mishandled bags. The airline recognized the problems, but the situation worsened as General Motors and Chrysler announced they were shifting some of

their business travel to a Northwest rival. The automakers were unhappy with high fares, delays, and cancellations by Northwest. The FAA is investigating an unusually high number of mechanical problems, and union employees had a strike. In looking at Northwest Airlines, the CEO of Continental Airlines observed, "They know they have some service issues." He further noted, "A successful company can't be at war with its own employees."

*Chrysler Corporation's Windsor Van Plant:* When 33-year-old James Bonini was named manager of the big van plant in Windsor, Ontario, virtually everyone was surprised. He was young and inexperienced for the big job in one of the least-automated plants—with hundreds of manual jobs. He was selected because his boss wanted to

shake up Chrysler's manufacturing plants, where managers thought they were drill sergeants, workers were dissatisfied, and quality problems were abundant.

Mr. Bonini made mistakes and was met with skepticism. But his common-sense management approach finally succeeded in changing the culture of the plant and attitudes of many employees. En route to that outcome, he took actions that had not been used before—and that paid off. He met with all the workers in small groups; interestingly, many workers had never even met a plant manager.

> *"A successful company can't be at war with its own employees."*

Bonini and his staff redesigned about 70% of the assembly operations and redesigned jobs to improve ergonomics, cost, and quality. His concern for his people showed up in incidents as minor as dealing with worker complaints about restrooms to changing telephone policy after a worker did not get a call in time to get to his dying wife's bedside. Bonini and his managers used worker teams to help draft standard operating procedures, and those teams made meaningful changes in the way workers did their jobs each day.

The plant's approach to individuals and their jobs was changed—a feat acknowledged positively by even the most hard-bitten skeptics. Workers and managers both had changed the way they viewed and did their jobs.[1]

> ❝ *The perception used to be that Human Resources thought about the happiness of employees. . . . Now we realize the overriding concern is the yield from employees.* ❞
>
> JEAN COYLE

This chapter focuses on *individuals:* their relationship with their employers and their motivation. It also looks at the *jobs* they do and the ways of measuring the effectiveness of HR management in dealing with individuals and their jobs. Throughout the chapter, important HR output variables are considered: productivity, quality, service, satisfaction, and turnover and absenteeism.

Individuals are both valuable and perverse commodities for the managers who rely on them to accomplish work. In some organizations the people and the innovative ideas they generate are really the "product" that the firm produces. In others, depending on the job design, people may be a necessary but much smaller part of the overall effort, because machines do most of the work.

What is the actual monetary value of an individual to an organization? Employers who compete on the basis of their employees' capabilities know the importance of people to the success of the organization. However, the exact monetary value of a skilled workforce may be difficult to identify. An organization may have created a workforce that works harder or smarter than competitors; or one that generates many new ideas and is continually learning new ways and finding better methods. There may be no formula to put a precise dollar amount on such favorable values and activities, but when a company is sold, such attributes of the workforce bring a premium price.[2]

Just as the quality of the workforce can be a competitive advantage, it can also be a liability. When very few employees know how to do their jobs, when people are constantly leaving the organization, and when those workers who remain refuse to change or work more effectively, the human resources are a competitive problem that puts the organization at a disadvantage. Simply having an effective strategy and good products or services does not guarantee success for an organization if the individual employees do not implement that strategy or produce organizational products or services efficiently.[3]

# Individual Employee Performance

Many factors can affect the performance of individual employees—their abilities, motivations, the support they receive, the nature of the work they are doing, and their relationship with the organization. The Human Resources unit in an organization exists in part to analyze and help correct problems in these areas.[4] Exactly what the role of the HR unit in an organization "should be" depends upon what upper management expects. As with any management function, HR management activities should be evaluated and reengineered as necessary so that they can contribute to the competitive performance of the organization and individuals at work.

In many organizations the performance depends largely on the performance of individual employees. There are many ways to think about the kind of performance required of employees for the organization to be successful; but here, we will consider three key elements: productivity, quality, and service.

# Productivity

The more productive an organization, the better its competitive advantage, because its costs to produce a unit of output are lower. Better productivity does not necessarily mean more is produced; perhaps fewer people (or less money or time) were used to produce the same amount. A useful way to measure the productivity of a workforce is the total cost of people per unit of output. In its most basic sense, **productivity** is a measure of the quantity and quality of work done, considering the cost of the resources it took to do the work. It is also useful to view productivity as a ratio between input and output. This ratio indicates the *value added* by an organization or in an economy.

**GLOBAL COMPETITIVENESS AND PRODUCTIVITY** At the national level, productivity is of concern for several reasons. First, high productivity leads to higher standards of living, as shown by the greater ability of a country to pay for what its citizens want. Next, increases in national wage levels (the cost of paying employees) without increases in national productivity lead to inflation, which results in an increase in costs and a decrease in purchasing power. Finally, lower rates of productivity make for higher labor costs and a less competitive position for a nation's products in the world marketplace.

**ORGANIZATIONS AND PRODUCTIVITY** Productivity at the organization level ultimately affects profitability and competitiveness in a for-profit organization and total costs in a not-for-profit organization. Decisions made about the value of an organization often are based on the productivity of which it is capable.[5]

Perhaps none of the resources used for productivity in organizations are so closely scrutinized as human resources. Many of the activities undertaken in an HR system deal with individual or organizational productivity. Pay, appraisal systems, training, selection, job design, and compensation are HR activities concerned very directly with productivity.[6]

Another useful way to measure organizational HR productivity is by considering **unit labor cost,** or the total labor cost per unit of output, which is computed by dividing the average cost of workers by their average levels of output. Using the unit labor cost, it can be seen that a company paying relatively high wages still can be economically competitive if it can also achieve an offsetting high productivity level.

**Productivity**
A measure of the quantity and quality of work done, considering the cost of the resources it took to do the work.

**Unit labor cost**
The total labor cost per unit of output, which is the average cost of workers divided by their average levels of output.

Dilbert reprinted by permission of United Feature Syndicate, Inc.

**INDIVIDUAL PRODUCTIVITY** How a given individual performs depends on three factors: ability to do the work, level of effort, and support given that person. Figure 3–1 illustrates these three factors. The relationship of these factors, widely acknowledged in management literature, is that *performance* (P) is the result of *ability* (A) times *effort* (E) times *support* (S) (P = A × E × S). Performance is diminished if *any* of these factors are reduced or absent.

Recruiting and selection are directly connected to the first factor, innate ability, which involves choosing the person with the right talents and interests for a given job. The second factor—the effort expended by an individual—is influenced by many HR issues, such as motivation, incentives, and job design. Organizational support, the third factor, includes training, equipment provided, knowledge of expectations, and perhaps a productive team situation. HR activities involved here include training and development and performance appraisal.

**INCREASING PRODUCTIVITY** U.S. firms have been on a decade-long crusade to improve organizational productivity. Much of the productivity improvement efforts have focused on the workforce.[7] The early stages included downsizing, reengineering jobs, increasing computer usage, and working employees harder. These approaches have done as much good as possible in some firms. Some ideas for the next step in productivity improvement include:

- *Outsource:*  Contract with someone else to perform activities previously done by employees of the organization. For instance, if UPS can deliver products at a lower cost than a manufacturing company can internally, then the firm could outsource shipping to UPS.
- *Make workers more efficient with capital equipment:*  A study of productivity in four countries found that in each country the less spent on equipment per worker, the less output per worker.[8]
- *Replace workers with equipment:*  Certain jobs are not well done by humans. The jobs may be mindless, physically difficult, etc. For example, a ditch usually is better dug by a person operating a backhoe than by a person with a shovel.
- *Help workers work better:*  Replace outmoded methods and rules, or find better ways of training people to work more efficiently.
- *Redesign the work:*  Some work can be redesigned to make it faster, easier, and possibly even more rewarding to employees. Such changes generally improve productivity.

**FIGURE 3–1 *Components of Individual Productivity***

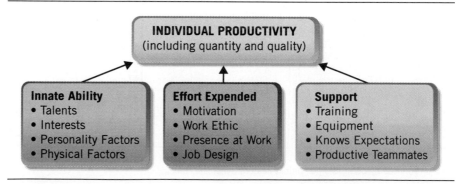

The need for productivity improvement will never end. With global competition there will always be a need to produce more at less cost, which entails working both harder and smarter in many situations.[9]

## Quality Production

*Quality* of production also must be considered as part of productivity, because one alternative might be to produce more but at a lower quality. At one time, American goods suffered as a result of this trade-off. W. Edwards Deming, an American quality expert, argued that getting the job done right the *first time*—through pride in craftsmanship, excellent training, and an unwillingness to tolerate delays, defects, and mistakes—is important to quality production.

Organizations throughout the world are proceeding on the quality front in many different ways, ranging from general training of workers on improving and maintaining quality to better engineering of products prior to manufacturing. One way in which organizations have focused on quality is by using international quality standards.

**ISO 9000** A set of quality standards called the ISO 9000 standards has been derived by the International Standards Organization in Geneva, Switzerland. These standards cover everything from training to purchasing and are being implemented widely in European countries. Companies that meet the standards are awarded a certificate. The purpose of the ISO 9000 certification is to show that an organization has documented its management processes and procedures and has a trained staff so that customers can be confident that organizational goods and services will be consistent in quality.

**TOTAL QUALITY MANAGEMENT (TQM)** Many organizations that have made major improvements in the quality of their operations have recognized that a broad-based quality effort has been needed. **Total Quality Management (TQM)** is a comprehensive management process focusing on the continuous improvement of organizational activities to enhance the quality of the goods and services supplied. TQM programs have become quite popular as organizations strive to improve their productivity and quality.

At the heart of TQM is the concept that it is *customer focused,* which means that every organizational activity should be evaluated and analyzed to determine if it contributes to meeting customers' needs and expectations. Another characteristic of TQM is the importance of *employee involvement.* Often, quality improvement teams of other group efforts are used to ensure that all employees understand the importance of quality and how their efforts affect quality. *Benchmarking* is another facet of TQM, in which quality efforts are measured and compared with measures both for the industry and for other organizations. It is hoped that providing measurement information on quality will help to make continuous improvements in quality a part of the organizational culture.

For some organizations, the promises of TQM have been realized; but for others, TQM became a short-term program that later was dropped. A nation-wide study of over 1,000 executives and managers found that only 45% of the organizations that had implemented TQM thought their programs had been successful.[10] However, some observers contend that quality concerns have

*LOGGING ON . . .*
**Total Quality Management**
This web site provides an excellent example of the total quality management principles and visions of one town and the success of the plan.

**http://www.ci.hickory.nc.us/ TQM/tqm.htm**

**Total Quality Management (TQM)**
A comprehensive management process focusing on the continuous improvement of organizational activities to enhance the quality of the goods and services supplied.

become much more basic to the way work is done. They argue it is a widespread philosophy caused by competitive pressures. The idea of continuous improvement has indeed been built into the approaches of many producers of goods and services.[11]

## Service

Delivering high-quality customer service is another important outcome that affects organizational competitive performance. High quality and productivity are both important in the third aspect of performance considered here—*customer service*. Service begins with product design and includes interaction with customers, ultimately providing a satisfactory meeting of customers' needs. Some firms do not produce products, only services. The U.S. economy is estimated to be composed of over 75% service jobs including retail, banking, travel, government, etc., where service is the basis for competition.

Overall, customer satisfaction has declined in the United States and other countries. The American Customer Satisfaction Index revealed that in many U.S. industries, customers are growing more dissatisfied with the customer service they receive.[12] However, if their expectations are met, customers are likely to be more satisfied, make favorable comments to others, and/or become repeat customers. Consequently, organizations working to enhance their competitiveness must work to enhance service.[13]

Service excellence is difficult to define, but people know it when they see it. In many organizations, service quality is affected significantly by individual employees who interact with customers.[14] The dimensions of service are depicted in Figure 3–2. Employing organizations have used many approaches attempting to improve productivity, quality, and service. In the process of doing so, the relationship between the organization and individual employees has been changed in many cases.[15]

**FIGURE 3–2 *Customer Service Dimensions***

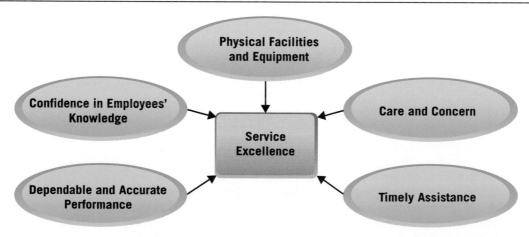

## Individual/Organizational Relationships

At one time loyalty and long service with one company were considered an appropriate individual/organizational relationship. Recently, changes have been noted in both loyalty and length of service, with employees leaving more frequently. Several factors are driving the changes, including the following:[16]

- Mergers and acquisitions
- Self-employment and contingent work
- Outsourcing jobs
- Loss of employment security
- Less management job tenure
- Altered "psychological contracts"

Surveys show that workers have grown more skeptical about their chances to share equitably in the success of the organizations that they helped create.[17] While some 60% or more of workers report they are satisfied with their jobs, only about half would recommend their employer as a good place to work and only 35% trust top management.[18] As a result, faith in management and belief in workplace reciprocity has eroded.

The idea of reciprocity seems to be a very significant issue in these changes. **Reciprocity** means to "give in return" and is basic to human feelings of fair treatment. When organizations merge, lay off large numbers of employees, outsource work, and use large numbers of temporary and part-time workers, employees see no reason to give their loyalty in return for this loss of job security.[19] These issues are illustrated in the HR Perspective that follows on the next page.

**Reciprocity**
A feeling of obligation to "give in return" or reciprocate good treatment.

## Importance of Employee/Organizational Relationships

It can be argued (and it is) that the relationship between an employer and employee really does not affect performance. The employer exchanges pay for the performance of specified work, and that is all that is necessary. As in a legal agreement, one party contracts for specific services of the other party. Recent research suggests that employees perform better when they work in a situation with mutual investment, or even overinvestment by the employer, than they do in a legal agreement situation.[20] The implication is that the employee-organizational relationship *does matter* and should be chosen carefully. Many employees seem to respond favorably in performance and attitude when organizations are willing to commit to a mutual relationship.

Such a commitment might include traditional benefits, rewards for longevity, flexible schedules, communication with supervisors, and work-life balance. These observations suggest that despite all the changes in workplaces, many employers still want committed workers willing to solve difficult problems. Many employees still want security and stability, interesting work, a supervisor they respect, and competitive pay and benefits.[21]

## The Psychological Contract

The long-term economic health of most organizations depends on the efforts of employees with the appropriate knowledge, skills, and abilities. One concept that has been useful in discussing employees' relationship with the organization is that of a **psychological contract,** which refers to the unwritten expectations

**Psychological contract**
The unwritten expectations that employees and employers have about the nature of their work relationships.

# Conflicts between "Flexible" Workforce and Employee Relationships

The Lamson & Sessions Co. plastics factory in Bowling Green, Ohio, is a case study of the relationship problems between an organization and its employees. Matters are also complicated by the relations among different groups of workers. There are five categories of employees: *full-time regular, temporaries, independent contractors, summer employees,* and *part-time employees.* Having different categories of employees offers Lamson & Sessions greater flexibility to adjust to demand for its product. Some of the less time-intensive jobs appeal to single mothers and college students.

Each group of workers views their jobs—and each other—differently. The plant came to this situation by hiring regular full-time employees when it started. But as the plant grew, only temporaries were added so the firm could preview their capabilities before hiring them. Temps do not get the same benefits as the regular employees, and regular employees get to vote on whether temps can become regular employees. Temps get $6.50/hr. while regular operators get $11.19/hr., plus benefits.

As a result, the situation leads to a "them vs. us" mentality. Turnover among new temp employees, many of whom dislike their jobs, is as high as 40% a month. However, turnover among regular workers is only about 1% per year. About half of the temps leaving each month are told to leave because of poor productivity or attendance. Quality is not a big issue, according to the plant manager, because the work of the temps is double-checked. Also, the full-time regular employees must constantly teach new temps how to perform the jobs. Temps say they dislike the open-ended nature of their work and the lack of commitment shown them by the company and other workers.

Independent contractors create less disturbance. For example, one contractor, the mother of two small children, carts home boxes of parts, assembles them, and brings them back a week later, earning $100 each time. She is not allowed inside the plant but does not care, and does not feel excluded.

Plant managers note that tension is inevitable when employers need mixes of different types of workers to remain flexible and competitive. They also note that management must be flexible as well. But regular workers speak in derogatory terms about temps, temps feel abused, and part-timers often leave during difficult times, leaving the rest of the remaining workers to do more work. The relationship between the company and its employees is certainly "flexible," but problematic.[22]

that employees and employers have about the nature of their work relationships. Because the psychological contract is individual and subjective in nature, it focuses on expectations about "fairness" that may not be defined clearly by employees.

Both tangible items (such as wages, benefits, employee productivity, and attendance) and intangible items (such as loyalty, fair treatment, and job security) are encompassed by psychological contracts between employers and employees. Many employers may attempt to detail their expectations through employee handbooks and policy manuals, but those materials are only part of the total "contractual" relationship.

**TRADITIONAL PSYCHOLOGICAL CONTRACT** In the "good old days," employees exchanged their efforts and capabilities for a secure job that offered rising wages, comprehensive benefits, and career progression within the organization. But as organizations have downsized and cut workers who have given long and loyal service, a growing number of employees question whether they should be loyal to their employers.[23] The transformation in the psychological contract mirrors an evolution in which organizations have moved from employing individuals just to perform tasks, to employing individuals expected to produce results.[24] Rather than just paying them to follow orders and put in time, increasingly employers are expecting employees to utilize their skills and capabilities to accomplish organizational results. According to one expert, the new psychological contract rewards employees for contributing to organizational success in the competitive marketplace for goods and services.

**LOYALTY** Studies suggest that employees *do* believe in these unwritten agreements or psychological contracts, and hope their employers will keep their sides of the agreement.[25] When employers do not, employees feel a minimal necessity to contribute to the organizational productivity because they no longer trust the company. Thus, employees' loyalty has been affected negatively.[26] Not everyone feels that a decline in employee loyalty is a problem.[27] However, more employers are finding that in tight labor markets turnover of key people occurs more frequently when employee loyalty is low, and they have concluded that a loyal and committed workforce is important.[28]

Perhaps loyalty is necessary, but it should be based on a new psychological contract with the following expectations:[29]

| **Employers provide:** | **Employees contribute:** |
| --- | --- |
| • Competitive compensation | • Continuous skill improvement |
| • Benefits tailored to the workforce | • Reasonable time with organization |
| • Flexibility to balance work and home life | • Extra effort when needed |

The remainder of this chapter uses the conceptual model shown in Figure 3–3. This model shows the linkages, beginning with individual and job characteristics, that lead to job satisfaction, organizational commitment, and affect the

**FIGURE 3–3 *Model of Individual/Organizational Performance***

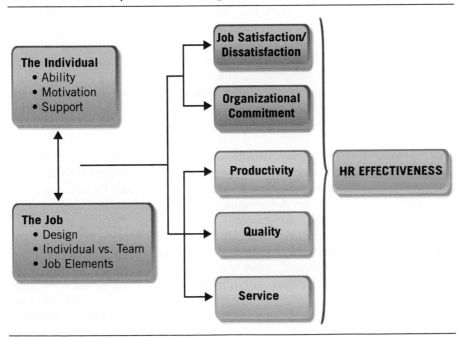

organizational outcomes—productivity, quality, and service—already discussed. All five output variables can be used to measure HR effectiveness.

# Individual Motivation

**Motivation**

The desire within a person causing that person to act.

The performance that employers look for in individuals rests on ability, motivation, and the support individuals receive; however, motivation is often the missing variable.[30] **Motivation** is the desire within a person causing that person to act. People usually act for one reason: to reach a goal. Thus, motivation is a goal-directed drive, and it seldom occurs in a void. The words *need, want, desire,* and *drive* are all similar to *motive,* from which the word *motivation* is derived. Understanding motivation is important because performance, reaction to compensation, and other HR concerns are related to motivation.

Approaches to understanding motivation differ because many individual theorists have developed their own views and theories. They approach motivation from different starting points, with different ideas in mind, and from different backgrounds. No one approach is considered to be the "ultimate." Each approach has contributed to the understanding of human motivation.

## Content Theories of Motivation

Content theories of motivation are concerned with the needs that people are attempting to satisfy. The most well-known theories are highlighted briefly next.

**LOGGING ON . . .**
**Personality and Motivation**
Research on individual differences in personality and motivation as it affects performance in the workplace is offered on this web site.

**http://pmc.psych.nwu.edu/ revelle/publications/ broadbent/broad.html**

**MASLOW'S HIERARCHY OF NEEDS** One theory of human motivation that has received a great deal of exposure in the past was developed by Abraham Maslow. In this theory, Maslow classified human needs into five categories that ascend in a definite order. Until the more basic needs are adequately fulfilled, a person will not strive to meet higher needs. Maslow's well-known hierarchy is composed of (1) physiological needs, (2) safety and security needs, (3) belonging and love needs, (4) esteem needs, and (5) self-actualization needs.

An assumption often made by those using Maslow's hierarchy is that workers in modern, technologically advanced societies basically have satisfied their physiological, safety, and belonging needs. Therefore, they will be motivated by the needs for self-esteem, esteem of others, and then self-actualization. Consequently, conditions to satisfy these needs should be present at work; the job itself should be meaningful and motivating.[31]

**HERZBERG'S MOTIVATION/HYGIENE THEORY** Frederick Herzberg's motivation/hygiene theory assumes that one group of factors, *motivators,* accounts for high levels of motivation. Another group of factors, *hygiene,* or maintenance factors, can cause discontent with work. Figure 3–4 compares Herzberg's motivators and hygiene factors with Maslow's needs of hierarchy.

The implication of Herzberg's research for management and HR practices is that although managers must carefully consider hygiene factors in order to avoid employee dissatisfaction, even if all these maintenance needs are addressed, people may not be motivated to work harder. Only motivators cause employees to exert more effort and thereby attain more productivity, and this theory suggests that managers should utilize the motivators as tools to enhance employee performance.

**FIGURE 3–4** *Maslow's and Herzberg's Ideas Compared*

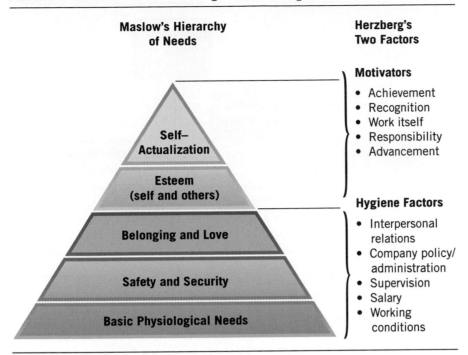

## Process Theories of Motivation

Process theories suggest that a variety of factors may prove to be motivating, depending on the needs of the individual, the situation the individual is in, and the rewards the individual expects for the work done. Theorists who hold to this view do not attempt to fit people into a single category, but rather accept human differences.

One process theory by Lyman Porter and E.E. Lawler focuses on the value a person places on a goal as well as the person's perceptions of workplace *equity,* or fairness, as factors that influence his or her job behavior. In a work situation, *perception* is the way an individual views the job. Figure 3–5 contains a simplified Porter and Lawler model, which indicates that motivation is influenced by people's expectations. If expectations are not met, people may feel that they have been unfairly treated and consequently become dissatisfied.

Using the Porter and Lawler model, suppose that a salesclerk is motivated to expend effort on her job. From this job she expects to receive two types of rewards: intrinsic (internal) and extrinsic (external). For this salesclerk, intrinsic rewards could include a feeling of accomplishment, a feeling of recognition, or other motivators. Extrinsic rewards might be such items as pay, benefits, good working conditions, and other hygiene factors. The salesclerk compares her performance with what she expected and evaluates it in light of both types of rewards she receives. She then reaches some level of job satisfaction or dissatisfaction. Once this level is reached, it is difficult to determine what she will do. If she is dissatisfied, she might put forth less effort in the future, she might

**FIGURE 3–5** *Porter and Lawler Motivation Model*

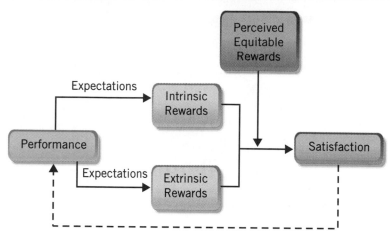

SOURCE: Adapted from Edward E. Lawler III and Lyman W. Porter, "The Effect of Performance on Job Satisfaction," *Industrial Relations* 7 (1966).

work harder to get the rewards she wants, or she might just accept her dissatisfaction. If she is highly satisfied, it does not always mean she will work harder. She may even slack off a bit, saying, "I got what I wanted."[32]

The essence of the Porter and Lawler view of motivation is perception. In addition, as the feedback loop in Figure 3–5 indicates, performance leads to satisfaction rather than satisfaction leading to performance.

# Job Design

Individual responses to jobs vary. A job may be motivating to one person but not to someone else. Also, depending on how jobs are designed, they may provide more or less opportunity for employees to satisfy their job-related needs. For example, a sales job may furnish a good opportunity to satisfy social needs, whereas a training assignment may satisfy a person's need to be an expert in a certain area. A job that gives little latitude may not satisfy an individual's need to be creative or innovative. Therefore, managers and employees alike are finding that understanding the characteristics of jobs requires broader perspectives than it did in the past.[33]

**Job design**

Organizing tasks, duties, and responsibilities into a productive unit of work.

Designing or redesigning jobs encompasses many factors. **Job design** refers to organizing tasks, duties, and responsibilities into a productive unit of work. It involves the content of jobs and the effect of jobs on employees. Identifying the components of a given job is an integral part of job design. More attention is being paid to job design for three major reasons:

● Job design can influence *performance* in certain jobs, especially those where employee motivation can make a substantial difference. Lower costs through reduced turnover and absenteeism also are related to good job design.
● Job design can affect *job satisfaction*. Because people are more satisfied with certain job configurations than with others, it is important to be able to identify what makes a "good" job.

- Job design can affect both *physical and mental health.* Problems such as hearing loss, backache, and leg pain sometimes can be traced directly to job design, as can stress and related high blood pressure and heart disease.

Not everyone would be happy as a physician, as an engineer, or as a dishwasher. But certain people like and do well at each of those jobs. The person/job fit is a simple but important concept that involves matching characteristics of people with characteristics of jobs. Obviously, if a person does not fit a job, either the person can be changed or replaced, or the job can be altered. In the past, it was much more common to make the round person fit the square job. However, successfully "reshaping" people is not easy to do. By redesigning jobs, the person/job fit can be improved more easily. Jobs may be designed properly when they are first established or "reengineered" later.

## Nature of Job Design

Identifying the components of a given job is an integral part of job design. Designing or redesigning jobs encompasses many factors, and a number of different techniques are available to the manager. Job design has been equated with job enrichment, a technique developed by Frederick Herzberg, but job design is much broader than job enrichment alone.

**JOB ENLARGEMENT AND JOB ENRICHMENT**  Attempts to alleviate some of the problems encountered in excessive job simplification fall under the general headings of job enlargement and job enrichment. **Job enlargement** involves broadening the scope of a job by expanding the number of different tasks to be performed. **Job enrichment** is increasing the depth of a job by adding responsibility for planning, organizing, controlling, and evaluating the job.[34]

A manager might enrich a job by promoting variety, requiring more skill and responsibility, providing more autonomy, and adding opportunities for personal growth. Giving an employee more planning and controlling responsibilities over the tasks to be done also enriches. However, simply adding more similar tasks does not enrich the job. Some examples of such actions that enrich a job include:

- Giving a person an entire job rather than just a piece of the work.
- Giving more freedom and authority so the employee can perform the job as he or she sees fit.
- Increasing a person's accountability for work by reducing external control.
- Expanding assignments so employees can learn to do new tasks and develop new areas of expertise.
- Giving feedback reports directly to employees rather than to management only.

**JOB ROTATION**  The technique known as **job rotation** can be a way to break the monotony of an otherwise routine job with little scope by shifting a person from job to job. For example, one week on the auto assembly line, John Williams attaches doors to the rest of the body assembly. The next week he attaches bumpers. The third week he puts in seat assemblies, then rotates back to doors again the following week. Job rotation need not be done on a weekly basis. John could spend one-third of a day on each job or one entire day, instead of a week, on each job. It has been argued, however, that rotation does little in the long run to solve the problem of employee boredom. Rotating a person from one boring

**Job enlargement**
Broadening the scope of a job by expanding the number of different tasks to be performed.

**Job enrichment**
Increasing the depth of a job by adding employee responsibility for planning, organizing, controlling, and evaluating the job.

**Job rotation**
The process of shifting a person from job to job.

job to another may help somewhat initially, but the jobs are still perceived to be boring. The advantage is that job rotation does develop an employee who can do many different jobs.

## Job Characteristics

The job-characteristics model by Hackman and Oldham identifies five important design characteristics of jobs. Figure 3–6 shows that *skill variety, task identity,* and *task significance* affect meaningfulness of work. *Autonomy* stimulates responsibility, and *feedback* provides knowledge of results. Following is a description of each characteristic.

**Skill variety**
The extent to which the work requires several different activities for successful completion.

**SKILL VARIETY** The extent to which the work requires several different activities for successful completion indicates its **skill variety.** For example, low skill variety exists when an assembly-line worker performs the same two tasks repetitively. The more skills involved, the more meaningful the work.

Skill variety can be enhanced in several ways. Job rotation can break the monotony of an otherwise routine job with little scope by shifting a person from job to job. Job enlargement may as well.

**Task identity**
The extent to which the job includes a "whole" identifiable unit of work that is carried out from start to finish and that results in a visible outcome.

**TASK IDENTITY** The extent to which the job includes a "whole" identifiable unit of work that is carried out from start to finish and that results in a visible outcome is its **task identity.** For example, one corporation changed its customer service processes so that when a customer calls with a problem, one employee, called a Customer Care Advocate, handles most or all facets of the problem from maintenance to repair. As a result, more than 40% of customer problems are resolved by one person while the customer is still on the line. Previously, less than

**FIGURE 3–6 *Job-Characteristics Model***

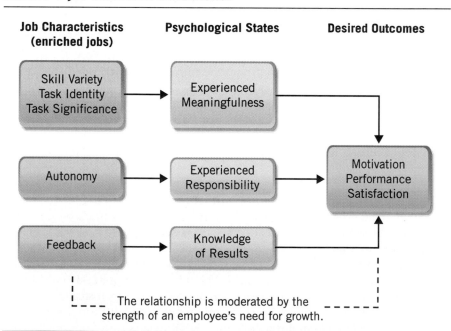

1% of the customer problems were resolved immediately because the customer service representative had to complete paperwork and forward it to operations, which then followed a number of separate steps using different people to resolve problems. In the current system, the Customer Care Advocate can identify more closely with solving a customer's problem.

**TASK SIGNIFICANCE** The amount of impact the job has on other people indicates its **task significance.** A job is more meaningful if it is important to other people for some reason. For instance, a soldier may experience more fulfillment when defending his or her country from a real threat than when merely training to stay ready in case such a threat arises. In the earlier example, the Customer Care Advocate's task has significance because it affects customers considerably.

**AUTONOMY** The extent of individual freedom and discretion in the work and its scheduling indicates **autonomy.** More autonomy leads to a greater feeling of personal responsibility for the work. Efforts to increase autonomy may lead to what was characterized as job enrichment by Frederick Herzberg. Examples of actions that increase autonomy include giving more freedom and authority so the employee can perform the job as he or she sees fit and increasing an employee's accountability for work by reducing external control.

**FEEDBACK** The amount of information employees receive about how well or how poorly they have performed is **feedback.** The advantage of feedback is that it helps employees to understand the effectiveness of their performance and contributes to their overall knowledge about the work. At one firm, feedback reports from customers who contact the company with problems are given directly to the employees who handle the customers' complaints, instead of being given only to the department manager.

## Consequences of Job Design

Jobs designed to take advantage of these important job characteristics are more likely to be positively received by employees. Such characteristics help distinguish between "good" and "bad" jobs. Many approaches to enhancing productivity and quality reflect efforts to expand some of the job characteristics.[35]

Because of the effects of job design on performance, employee satisfaction, health, and many other factors, many organizations are changing or have already changed the design of some jobs. A broader approach is reengineering work and jobs.

## Changes in Job Design: "Reengineering" Jobs

One movement that has affected the design and characteristics of jobs and work is reengineering. **Reengineering** is rethinking and redesigning work to improve cost, service, and speed. The reengineering process may include such techniques as creating work teams, training employees in multiple skills so they can do multiple jobs, pushing decision making as far down the organizational hierarchy as possible, and reorganizing operations and offices to simplify and speed work.[36]

The thrust of reengineering is not downsizing or restructuring the organization but focusing on the flow of work and how jobs themselves need to change

**Task significance**
The amount of impact the job has on other people.

**Autonomy**
The extent of individual freedom and discretion in the work and its scheduling.

**Feedback**
The amount of information received about how well or how poorly one has performed.

**Reengineering**
Rethinking and redesigning work to improve cost, service, and speed.

to improve the processes associated with work.[37] Reengineering assumes that the ultimate focus of all organizational work should be the customer, and it attempts to generate dramatic improvement in organizational productivity, quality, and service. As a result, many jobs are changed, and greater use of technology is made, particularly of information systems and computers.

## Using Teams in Jobs

Typically, a job is thought of as something done by one person. However, where it is appropriate, jobs may be designed for teams. In an attempt to make jobs more meaningful and to take advantage of the increased productivity and commitment that can follow, more organizations are using teams of employees instead of individuals for jobs. Some firms have gone as far as dropping the terms *workers* and *employees,* replacing them with *teammates, crew members, cast members,* and others that emphasize teamwork.

**Special-purpose team**
An organizational team that is formed to address specific problems and may continue to work together to improve work processes or the quality of products and services.

**SPECIAL-PURPOSE TEAMS AND QUALITY CIRCLES** Several types of teams are used in organizations today that function outside the scope of members' normal jobs and meet from time to time. One is the **special-purpose team,** which is formed to address specific problems and may continue to work together to improve work processes or the quality of products and services. Often, these teams are a mixture of employees, supervisors, and managers. Another kind of team is the **quality circle,** a small group of employees who monitor productivity and quality and suggest solutions to problems. In many organizations, these problem-solving teams are part of Total Quality Management (TQM) efforts. Care must be taken that such teams do not violate federal labor laws. In a number of court cases, teams selected by and dominated by managers have been ruled to violate provisions of the National Labor Relations Act.

**Quality circle**
A small group of employees who monitor productivity and quality and suggest solutions to problems.

**Production cells**
Groupings of workers who produce entire products or components of products.

**PRODUCTION CELLS** Another way work is restructured is through the use of production cells. As used in a number of manufacturing operations, **production cells** are groupings of workers who produce entire products or components of products. As many as fifty employees and as few as two can be grouped into a production cell, and each cell has all necessary machines and equipment. The cells ultimately replace the assembly line as the primary means of production.

**Self-directed work team**
An organizational team composed of individuals who are assigned a cluster of tasks, duties, and responsibilities to be accomplished.

**SELF-DIRECTED WORK TEAMS** The **self-directed work team** is composed of individuals who are assigned a cluster of tasks, duties, and responsibilities to be accomplished. Unlike special-purpose teams, these teams become the regular entities in which team members work.

An interesting challenge for self-directed work teams involves the emergence or development of team leaders. This role is different from the traditional role played by supervisors or managers. Rather than directing and giving orders, the team leader becomes a facilitator to assist the team, mediate and resolve conflicts among team members, and interact with other teams and managers in other parts of the organization. Shared leadership may be necessary; here, team members rotate leadership for different phases of projects in which special expertise may be beneficial.[38] Certain characteristics have been identified for the successful use of self-directed work teams in the United States:[39]

- *Teams value and endorse dissent:* The effective use of self-directed work teams requires that conflict and dissent be recognized and addressed. Contrary to what some might believe, suppressing dissent and conflict to preserve harmony ultimately becomes destructive to the effective operations of the team.
- *Teams use "shamrock" structures and have some variation in membership:* As Figure 3–7 shows, a **shamrock team** is composed of a core of members, resource experts who join the team as appropriate, and part-time/temporary members as needed. As identified by Charles Handy, the presence of core members provides stability, but the infusion of the resource experts and part-time/temporary members provides renewal and change to the team.
- *Teams have authority to make decisions:* For self-directed work teams to be effective, they must be allowed to function with sufficient authority to make decisions about team activities and operations. As transition to self-directed work teams occurs, significant efforts are necessary to define the areas and scope of authority of the teams as well as their goals.

**Shamrock team**

An organizational team composed of a core of members, resource experts who join the team as appropriate, and part-time/temporary members as needed.

**FIGURE 3–7 *Shamrock Team***

## Advantages and Disadvantages of Team Jobs

Teams have been popular job redesigns for much of the last two decades. Improved productivity, greater employee involvement, more widespread employee learning, and greater employee ownership of problems are among the potential benefits.[40] Some organizations have found favorable results with *transnational* teams as the challenges of managing across borders becomes more common and complex.[41] Even *virtual teams* linked primarily through advanced technology can contribute despite geographical dispersion of essential employees. Virtual teams also can easily take advantage of previously unavailable expertise.[42]

But not everyone has been pleased with teams as a part of job design. In some cases employers find that teams work better with employees who are "group oriented." Further, much work does not really need a team, and peer pressure may lead to unethical behavior.[43] Many companies have used teamwork without much thought. Too often, teamwork can be a buzzword or "feel-good" device that may actually get in the way of good decisions. Further, compensating individual team members so that they see themselves as a team rather than just a group of individuals is often a problem.[44] The HR Perspective on the next page relates how Levi Strauss Company has used teams in redesigned jobs.

# Job Satisfaction and Organizational Commitment

In its most basic sense, **job satisfaction** is a positive emotional state resulting from evaluating one's job experiences. Job *dis*satisfaction occurs when these expectations are not met. For example, if an employee expects clean and safe working conditions on the job, then the employee is likely to be dissatisfied if the workplace is dirty and dangerous.

Job satisfaction has many dimensions. Commonly noted facets are satisfaction with the work itself, wages, recognition, rapport with supervisors and coworkers, and chance for advancement. Each dimension contributes to an individual's overall feeling of satisfaction with the job itself, but the "job" is defined differently by different people.[45]

**Job satisfaction**

A positive emotional state resulting from evaluating one's job experiences.

# At Levi Strauss, Teams Are a Problem

Levi Strauss redesigned the assembly-line work at its U.S. plants in an effort to cut the costs associated with repetitive stress injuries. It further hoped to be able to continue doing the work in U.S. plants instead of moving significant production overseas. Levi Strauss had stayed with its U.S. manufacturing operations long after competitors had moved significant production offshore.

The company abandoned its old piecework system, in which a worker repeatedly performed a simple, single task (like sewing seams or attaching zippers) and was paid according to how much work he or she accomplished. In the team system, groups of 10 to 35 workers would be paid as part of a team according to the number of pants the group produced. Workers could rotate to different tasks, helping relieve monotony and reducing repetitive stress injuries.

However, the new team production system led not to more produc-tivity, but to a quagmire of lower production, infighting, and stress. Threats and insults became more common. Friendships dissolved as faster workers tried to get rid of slower ones. The quantity of pants produced per hour worked dropped the next year to 77% of pre-team levels. Since then, productivity has gradually improved, but it is still only 93% of the original level. Additionally, labor cost per pair of pants was up 25%. Just as critical, wages of top performers fell. For example, one skilled woman saw her hourly pay drop from $8.75 to $7.00 per hour because of slow teammates. But the slower employees saw their pay increase—eliminating savings for Levi Strauss. Unit labor cost to stitch a pair of "Dockers" pants rose from $5.00 to $7.50.

The basic problem was the nature of the work. Speed of production relates directly to workers' skills and stamina in a series of grueling, repetitive motions necessary to stitch the fabric. Top performers, on seeing pay shrink, decided not to work so hard. "You feel cheated because you are making less so why give them 120%" one noted. When a team member was absent or slow, the rest of the team had to make up for the lack of production, which made better-performing workers angry that they had to carry poorer performers. Dividing up the work of absent team members led to trouble as well. Team members were merciless to injured or absent teammates, causing resentment and turnover. Management noted that teams often created a tremendous amount of peer pressure, and that peer pressure was not always healthy.

Ultimately, Levi Strauss laid off 6,000 employees—one-third of its domestic workforce. Unofficially, much of the approach is being scrapped as managers try to improve productivity. Even so, one long-term employee notes, "I hate teams. Levi's is not the place it used to be."[46]

The number of people who are dissatisfied with their jobs nationally varies with the unemployment rate. Higher unemployment rates usually mean more dissatisfied workers because it is more difficult to change jobs, and people stay longer on jobs they do not like. Those workers who are mostly satisfied with their jobs vary from 60 to 85 percent of the total. These numbers are similar to those found in Europe when employees are asked about satisfaction with their jobs.[47] Individual managers seem to have a greater impact on employee satisfaction than the company itself.[48]

There is no simple formula for predicting a worker's satisfaction. Furthermore, the relationship between productivity and job satisfaction is not entirely clear. The critical factor is what employees expect from their jobs and what they are receiving as rewards from their jobs. Although job satisfaction itself is interesting and important, perhaps the "bottom line" is the impact that job satisfaction has on organizational commitment, which affects the goals of productivity, quality, and service.

If employees are committed to an organization, they are more likely to be more productive. **Organizational commitment** is the degree to which employees believe in and accept organizational goals and desire to remain with the organization. Research has revealed that job satisfaction and organizational commitment tend to influence each other. What this finding suggests is that people who are relatively satisfied with their jobs will be somewhat more committed to the organization and also that people who are relatively committed to the organization are more likely to have greater job satisfaction.

A logical extension of organizational commitment focuses specifically on continuance commitment factors, which suggests that decisions to remain with or leave an organization ultimately are reflected in employee absenteeism and turnover statistics. Individuals who are not as satisfied with their jobs or who are not as committed to the organization are more likely to withdraw from the organization, either occasionally through absenteeism or permanently through turnover.

**Organizational commitment**
The degree to which employees believe in and accept organizational goals and desire to remain with the organization.

## Absenteeism

Absenteeism is expensive, as seen in estimates that absenteeism nationally costs $505 per employee per year.[49] Being absent from work may seem like a small matter to an employee. But if a manager needs 12 people in a unit to get the work done, and 4 of the 12 are absent most of the time, the unit's work will probably not get done, or additional workers will have to be hired. Nationally, 7.2 days per employee are lost to absenteeism each year.[50]

**TYPES OF ABSENTEEISM** Employees can be absent from work for several reasons. Figure 3–8 depicts the reasons for unscheduled absences. Clearly, some absenteeism is unavoidable. People do get sick and have family issues such as sick children that make it impossible for them to attend work. This is usually referred to

**FIGURE 3–8** *Reasons for Unscheduled Absences*

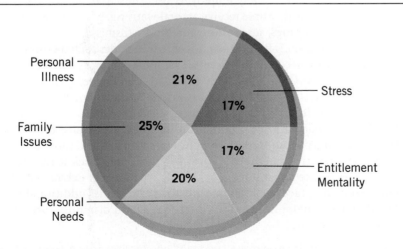

SOURCE: Data from CCH Survey of over 400 firms, as presented in "Why Workers Don't Show Up," *Business Week*, November 16, 1998, 8.

as *involuntary* absenteeism. However, much absenteeism is avoidable; it is called *voluntary* absenteeism. Often, a relatively small number of individuals in the workplace are responsible for a disproportionate share of the total absenteeism in an organization.

Because illness, death in the family, and other personal reasons for absences are unavoidable and understandable, many employers have sick-leave policies that allow employees a certain number of paid absent days per year. Absenteeism tends to be highest in governmental agencies, utilities, and manufacturing firms. Absenteeism is lowest in retail/wholesale firms, possibly because those industries use a large percentage of part-time workers.

**MEASURING ABSENTEEISM** Controlling or reducing absenteeism must begin with continuous monitoring of the absenteeism statistics in work units. Such monitoring helps managers pinpoint employees who are frequently absent and the departments that have excessive absenteeism.

Various methods of measuring or computing absenteeism exist. One formula for computing absenteeism rates, suggested by the U.S. Department of Labor, is as follows:

$$\frac{\text{Number of person-days lost through job absence during period}}{(\text{Average number of employees}) \times (\text{Number of work days})} \times 100$$

(This rate also can be based on number of hours instead of number of days.)

**BNA:**

**Absenteeism**

Review the policy considerations at 1459.10.10–1459.10.30. Then compare these considerations to an absenteeism policy in an actual employee handbook.

**CONTROLLING ABSENTEEISM** Controlling voluntary absenteeism is easier if managers understand its causes more clearly. However, there are a variety of thoughts on reducing voluntary absenteeism. Organizational policies on absenteeism should be stated clearly in an employee handbook and stressed by supervisors and managers. The policies and rules an organization uses to govern absenteeism may provide a clue to the effectiveness of its control. Studies indicate that absence rates are highly related to the policies used to control absenteeism.[51]

Absenteeism control options fall into three categories: (1) discipline, (2) positive reinforcement, and (3) a combination of both. A brief look at each follows.

- *Disciplinary approach:* Many employers use a disciplinary approach. People who are absent the first time receive an oral warning, but subsequent absences bring written warnings, suspension, and finally dismissal.[52]
- *Positive reinforcement:* Positive reinforcement includes such methods as giving employees cash, recognition, time off, or other rewards for meeting attendance standards. Offering rewards for good attendance, giving bonuses for missing fewer than a certain number of days, and "buying back" unused sick leave are all positive methods of reducing absenteeism.
- *Combination approach:* Combination approaches ideally reward desired behaviors and punish undesired behaviors. One of the most effective absenteeism control methods is to provide paid sick-leave banks for employees to use up to some level. Once that level is exhausted, then the employees may face the loss of some pay if they miss additional work unless they have major illnesses in which long-term disability insurance coverage would begin.

Another method is known as a *"no-fault" absenteeism* policy. Here, the reasons for absences do not matter, but the employees must manage their time rather than having managers make decisions about excused and unexcused absences.

Once absenteeism exceeds normal limits, then disciplinary action up to and including termination of employment can occur.

Some firms have extended their policies to provide a *paid time-off* (PTO) program in which vacation time, holidays, and sick leave for each employee are combined into a PTO account. Employees use days from their accounts at their discretion for illness, personal time, or vacation. If employees run out of days in their accounts, then they are not paid for any additional days missed. The PTO programs generally have reduced absenteeism, particularly one-day absences, but overall, time away from work often increases because employees use all of "their" time off by taking unused days as vacation days.

## Turnover

Like absenteeism, turnover is related to job dissatisfaction.[53] **Turnover** occurs when employees leave an organization and have to be replaced. Excessive turnover can be a very costly problem, one with a major impact on productivity. One firm had a turnover rate of more than 120% per year! It cost the company $1.5 million a year in lost productivity, increased training time, increased employee selection time, lost work efficiency, and other indirect costs. But cost is not the only reason turnover is important. Lengthy training times, interrupted schedules, additional overtime, mistakes, and not having knowledgeable employees in place are some of the frustrations associated with excessive turnover. Turnover rates average about 16% per year for all companies, but 21% per year for computer companies.[54] Computer companies average higher turnover because their employees have many opportunities to change jobs in a "hot" industry.

**Turnover**
Process in which employees leave the organization and have to be replaced.

**TYPES OF TURNOVER** Turnover often is classified as voluntary or involuntary. The *involuntary turnover* occurs when an employee is fired. *Voluntary turnover* occurs when an employee leaves by choice and can be caused by many factors. Causes include lack of challenge, better opportunity elsewhere, pay, supervision, geography, and pressure. Certainly, not all turnover is negative. Some workforce losses are quite desirable, especially if those workers who leave are lower-performing, less reliable individuals.

**MEASURING TURNOVER** The turnover rate for an organization can be computed in different ways. The following formula from the U.S. Department of Labor is widely used. (*Separation* means leaving the organization.)

$$\frac{\text{Number of employee separations during the month}}{\text{(Total number of employees at midmonth)}} \times 100$$

Common turnover figures range from almost zero to over 100% per year, and normal turnover rates vary among industries. Organizations that require entry-level employees to have few skills are likely to have higher turnover rates among those employees than among managerial personnel. As a result, it is important that turnover rates be computed by work units. For instance, one organization had a companywide turnover rate that was not severe—but 80% of the turnover occurred within one department. This imbalance indicated that some action was needed to resolve problems in that unit.

**CONTROLLING TURNOVER** Turnover can be controlled in several ways. During the *recruiting* process, the job should be outlined and a realistic preview of the job pre-

***LOGGING ON . . .***
**Turnover Analysis**
A sample summary analysis and score sheet of a high turnover position is available for viewing. This sample contains the factors used to measure the job.

**http://www.achievementtec.com/15.htm**

sented, so that the reality of the job matches the expectations of the new employee. A good way to eliminate voluntary turnover is to *improve selection* and to better match applicants to jobs. By fine-tuning the selection process and hiring people who will not have disciplinary problems and low performance, employers can reduce involuntary turnover.

Good *employee orientation* also helps reduce turnover, because employees who are properly inducted into the company and are well-trained tend to be less likely to leave. *Compensation* also is important. A fair and equitable pay system can help prevent turnover. Inadequate rewards may lead to voluntary turnover, especially with employees such as salespeople, whose compensation is tied directly to their performance. *Career planning* and *internal promotion* can help an organization keep employees, because if individuals believe they have no opportunities for career advancement, they may leave the organization.

Finally, turnover may be linked to personal factors that the organization cannot control. This is particularly true with part-time workers. Here are some of the many reasons employees quit that cannot be controlled by the organization: (1) the employee moves out of the geographic area, (2) the employee decides to stay home for family reasons, (3) the employee's spouse is transferred, or (4) a student employee graduates from college.

Even though some turnover is inevitable, organizations must take steps to control turnover, particularly that caused by organizational factors such as poor supervision, inadequate training, and inconsistent policies. HR activities should be examined as part of the turnover control efforts.

# Assessing HR Effectiveness

Productivity, quality, service, absenteeism, and turnover are all measurable—and they are related to the way activities are performed in an organization. Yet, there is a long-standing myth that one cannot really measure what the HR function does.[55] That myth has hurt HR departments in some cases, because it suggests that any value added by HR efforts is somehow "mystical" or "magical." None of that is true; HR—like marketing, legal, or finance—must be evaluated based on the value it adds to the organization. Defining and measuring HR effectiveness is not as straightforward as it might be in some more easily quantifiable areas, but it can be done.[56]

**Effectiveness**

The extent to which goals have been met.

**Efficiency**

The degree to which operations are done in an economical manner.

**Effectiveness** for organizations is often defined as the extent to which goals have been met. **Efficiency** is the degree to which operations are done in an economical manner. Efficiency can also be thought of as cost per unit of output. To be effective, organizations must be able to achieve their goals, but must reach them using limited resources efficiently. For example, providing on-site child care for all employees might help an employer to achieve an effectiveness goal of reducing turnover, but it could be too expensive (reducing efficiency of expenditures) for that employer to implement.

Other departments, managers, and employees are the main "customers" for HR services. If those services are lacking, too expensive, or of poor quality, then the organization may have to consider outsourcing some HR activities.

The HR department is an organization within an organization. What it does (or does not do) affects the entire organizational system. To function effectively, HR needs a clear vision of what it does and whom it serves. That perspective should unify the HR staff and provide a basis for making decisions. HR can position itself as a partner in an organization, but only by demonstrating to the rest of the organization that there are real links between what HR activities contribute and organizational results. To demonstrate to the rest of the organization that the HR unit is a partner with a positive influence on the bottom line of the business, HR professionals must be prepared to measure the results of HR activities. Then the HR unit must communicate that information to the rest of the organization. Measurement is a key to demonstrating the success of the HR activities.[57] Figure 3–9 shows a general approach to evaluating the efficiency and effectiveness of HR activities.

**FIGURE 3–9** *Overview of the Evaluation Process for HR*

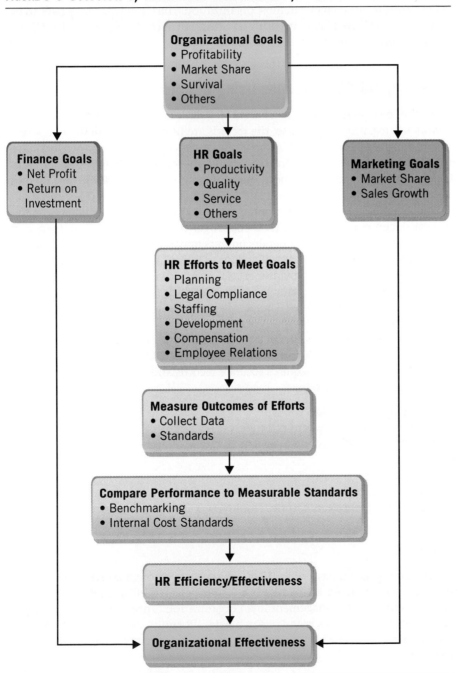

## HR Evaluation Model

The contribution of the HR unit's efforts to organizational effectiveness and the efficiency of the department's activities should both be measured. Studies of large and medium-sized firms in the United States have found relationships between the best HR practices and reduced turnover and increased employee productivity. Further, those practices enhanced profitability and market value of the firms studied. A high-quality, highly motivated workforce is hard for competition to replicate, which is an advantage that improves organizational effectiveness.[58]

Data to evaluate performance can come from several sources. Some of those sources are already available in most organizations, but some data may have to be collected. Considered here are using existing HR records, an HR audit, HR research for assessment, and exit interviews.

## Assessing HR Effectiveness Using Records

With the proliferation of government regulations, the number of required records has expanded. Of course, the records are useful only if they are kept current and properly organized. Managers who must cope with the paperwork have not always accepted such record-keeping requirements easily. Also, many managers feel that HR records can be a source of trouble because they can be used to question past managerial actions.

Another view of HR record-keeping activities is that HR records serve as important documentation should legal challenges occur. Disciplinary actions, past performance appraisals, and other documents may provide the necessary "proof" that employers need to defend their actions as job related and nondiscriminatory. Records and data also can provide a crucial source of information to audit or assess the effectiveness of any unit, and they provide the basis for research into possible causes of HR problems. The HR Perspective reports on a study of the effectiveness.

Jac Fitz-Enz, who studies HR effectiveness, has suggested some diagnostic measures from records to check the effectiveness of the HR function. Note how each of the following measures requires accurate records and a comprehensive human resource information system:

- HR expense per employee
- Compensation as a percent of expenses
- HR department expense as a percent of total expenses
- Cost of hires
- Turnover rate
- Absence rate
- Workers compensation cost per employee

## HR Audit

**HR audit**
A formal research effort that evaluates the current state of HR management in an organization.

One general means for assessing HR effectiveness is through an HR audit, similar to a financial audit. An **HR audit** is a formal research effort that evaluates the current status of HR management in an organization. Through the development and use of statistical reports and research data, HR audits attempt to evaluate how well HR activities have been performed, so that management can identify what needs to be improved.[60]

# Research on HR Effectiveness

Huselid, Jackson, and Schuler studied the effect of HR managers' capabilities on HR effectiveness. They then looked at the impact of HR's effectiveness on financial performance at 293 firms. In this study, two aspects of effectiveness were examined. *Technical effectiveness* for HR departments was defined as the extent to which the department successfully handled recruiting, selection, performance management, training, and administration of compensation and benefits. *Strategic effectiveness* was defined as designing and implementing a set of internally consis-

tent policies and practices to ensure that the company's human capital contributes to the achievement of its business objectives.

The researchers found that the level of *technical HR effectiveness* was higher than levels of *strategic HR effectiveness.* Effective HR management was related to improved financial performance as measured by employee productivity, cash flow, and market value of the firm.

The researchers concluded that technical HR competence contributes to a competitive advantage for smaller firms and for global firms

competing in countries with unsophisticated HR practices. But for most large U.S. firms, improvements to strategic HR activities have the greatest potential for financial gains.

The authors of this study further suggest that the technical skills of HR staff are important because they provide for movement into the strategic effectiveness necessary to make HR a financial contributor to organizational success. In other words, the basic *technical* HR activities must be performed well for the HR department to become more effective strategically.[59]

An HR audit begins with a determination by management of the objectives it wants to achieve in the HR area. The audit compares the actual state of HR activities with these objectives, as the sample audit in Figure 3–10 does.

## Using HR Research for Assessment

**HR research** is the analysis of data to determine the effectiveness of past and present HR practices. Research in general can be categorized as *primary* or *secondary*. In **primary research,** data is gathered firsthand for the specific project being conducted. Attitude surveys, questionnaires, interviews, and experiments are all primary research methods. **Secondary research** makes use of research already done by others and reported in books, articles in professional journals, or other sources.

Individuals who plan to do primary research should decide first what they wish to study. Examples of primary research topics are causes of nursing employee turnover, employee attitudes about flextime, and the relationship of preemployment physical exams to workers' compensation claims.

HR practitioners do primary research when they conduct a pay survey on computer system jobs in other companies in their geographic area or a study of turnover costs and reasons that employees in technical jobs leave more frequently during the first 24 to 30 months of employment. Thus, primary research has very specific applications to resolving actual HR problems in particular organizations. Examples of primary research can be found in the *Academy of Management Journal, Personnel Psychology,* and the other research-oriented journals listed in Appendix C. The research studies described in these journals can offer HR

**HR research**
The analysis of data from HR records to determine the effectiveness of past and present HR practices.

**Primary research**
Research method in which data is gathered firsthand for the specific project being conducted.

**Secondary research**
Research method using data already gathered by others and reported in books, articles in professional journals, or other sources.

**FIGURE 3–10** *Sample HR Audit Checklist*

---

This HR management audit allows you to rate the extent to which an organization has basic HR activities in place and how well they are being performed. In deciding upon your rating, consider also how other managers and employees would rate the activities. The total score provides a guide for actions that will improve HR activities in your organization.

*Instructions:* For each of the items listed below, rate your organization using the following scale:

| | |
|---|---|
| VERY GOOD (complete, current, and done well) | 3 points |
| ADEQUATE (needs only some updating) | 2 points |
| WEAK (needs major improvements/changes) | 1 point |
| BASICALLY NONEXISTENT | 0 points |

- - - - - - - - - - - - - - - - - - - - - - - - - - - - - - - - - - - - - - - - - - - - - - -

**I. LEGAL COMPLIANCE**

_____ **1.** Equal employment opportunity (EEO) requirements

_____ **2.** Immigration reform

_____ **3.** Health and safety (OSHA)

_____ **4.** Wage and hour laws (FLSA)

_____ **5.** Employment-at-will statements

_____ **6.** Privacy protection

_____ **7.** ERISA reporting/compliance

_____ **8.** Family/medical leave (FMLA)

**II. OBTAINING HUMAN RESOURCES**

_____ **9.** Current job descriptions and specifications

_____ **10.** HR supply-and-demand estimates (for 3 years)

_____ **11.** Recruiting process and procedures

_____ **12.** Job-related selection interviews

_____ **13.** Physical exam procedures

**III. MAINTAINING HUMAN RESOURCES**

_____ **14.** Formal wage/salary system

_____ **15.** Current benefits programs/options

_____ **16.** Employee recognition programs

_____ **17.** Employee handbook/personnel policy manual

_____ **18.** Absenteeism and turnover control

_____ **19.** Grievance resolution process

_____ **20.** HR record-keeping/information systems

**IV. DEVELOPING HUMAN RESOURCES**

_____ **21.** New employee orientation program

_____ **22.** Job skills training programs

_____ **23.** Employee development programs

_____ **24.** Job-related performance appraisal

_____ **25.** Appraisal feedback training of managers

_____ **TOTAL POINTS**

- - - - - - - - - - - - - - - - - - - - - - - - - - - - - - - - - - - - - - - - - - - - - - -

**HR Audit Scoring**

Evaluate the score on the HR audit as follows:

**60–75** HR activities are complete, effective, and probably meeting most legal compliance requirements.

**45–59** HR activities are being performed adequately, but they are not as complete or effective as they should be. Also, it is likely that some potential legal risks exist.

**30–44** Major HR problems exist, and significant attention needs to be devoted to adding and changing the HR activities in the organization.

**Below 30** Serious potential legal liabilities exist, and it is likely that significant HR problems are not being addressed.

SOURCE: Developed by Robert L. Mathis, Mathis & Associates, L.L.C., 1429 North 131st Avenue Circle, Omaha, Nebraska, 68154. All rights reserved. No part of this audit may be reproduced in any form or by any means, without written permission from Mathis & Associates.

---

professionals guidance on factors affecting HR problems and the impact of management approaches to HR issues.

The following sections describe some primary methods often used in HR research: experiments and pilot projects, employee attitude surveys, and exit interviews.

**Experiment**
Research to determine how factors respond when changes are made in one or more variables, or conditions.

**EXPERIMENTS AND PILOT PROJECTS** Experiments and pilot projects can provide useful HR insights. An **experiment** involves studying how factors respond when changes are made in one or more variables, or conditions. For instance, to test the impact of flextime scheduling on employee turnover, a firm might allow flexible scheduling in one department on a pilot basis. If the turnover rate of the employees in that department drops in comparison with the turnover in other departments still working set schedules, then the experimental pilot project may indicate that flexible scheduling can reduce turnover. Next, the firm might extend the use of flexible scheduling to other departments.

**EMPLOYEE ATTITUDE SURVEYS** Employee opinions can be used to diagnose specific problem areas, identify employee needs or preferences, and reveal areas in which HR activities are well received or are viewed negatively. For example, questionnaires may be sent to employees to collect ideas for revising a performance appraisal system. Another common use of a questionnaire is to determine if employees are satisfied with their benefits programs.

Questionnaires can be distributed by supervisors or the HR unit, given out with employee paychecks, or mailed to employees' homes. More accurate information usually is obtained if employees can provide their input anonymously. New ways to obtain employee survey information include electronic mail (e-mail) surveys and interactive telephone surveys using touch-tone responses.

The **attitude survey** focuses on employees' feelings and beliefs about their jobs and the organization. By serving as a sounding board to allow employees to air their views about their jobs, their supervisors, their coworkers, and organizational policies and practices, these surveys can be starting points for improving productivity. Some employers conduct attitude surveys on a regularly scheduled basis (such as every year), while others do so intermittently. As the use of e-mail has spread, more organizations have begun conducting attitude surveys electronically.

Attitude surveys can be custom-designed to address specific issues and concerns in an organization. But only surveys that are valid and reliable can measure attitudes accurately. Often a "research" survey developed in-house is poorly structured, asks questions in a confusing manner, or leads employees to respond in ways that will give "favorable" results.

By asking employees to respond candidly to an attitude survey, management is building up employees' expectations that action will be taken on the concerns identified. Therefore, a crucial part of conducting an attitude survey is to provide feedback to those who participated in it. It is especially important that even negative survey results be communicated to avoid fostering the appearance of hiding the results or placing blame. Generally, it is recommended that employee feedback be done through meetings with managers, supervisors, and employees; often this is done in small groups to encourage interaction and discussion. That approach is consistent with the most common reason for conducting an attitude survey—to diagnose strengths and weaknesses so that actions can be taken to improve the HR activities in an organization.

**EXIT INTERVIEWS** One widely used type of interview is the **exit interview,** in which those who are leaving the organization are asked to identify the reasons for their departure. This information can be used to correct problems so that others will not leave. HR specialists rather than supervisors usually conduct exit interviews, and a skilled HR interviewer can gain useful information. A wide range of issues can be examined in exit interviews, including reasons for leaving, supervision, pay, training, and the best-liked and least-liked aspects of the job.

**LOGGING ON . . .**
**Employee Attitude Surveys**
CVR Center for Values Research, Inc., provides information on employee attitude surveys, including the statements that are measured and the roles played by management for assessing and administering a successful survey.

**http://www.cvrdallas.com/ index.htm**

**Attitude survey**
A special type of survey that focuses on employees' feelings and beliefs about their jobs and the organization.

**Exit interview**
An interview in which those leaving the organization are asked to identify the reasons for their departure.

Most employers who do exit interviews use standard questions so the information is in a format that allows summarizing and reporting to management for assessment.

Departing employees may be reluctant to divulge their real reasons for leaving because they may wish to return to the company some day. Also, they may fear that candid responses will hinder their chances of receiving favorable references. One major reason employees commonly give for leaving their jobs is an offer for more pay elsewhere. However, the pay increase may not be the only factor. To uncover other reasons, it may be more useful to contact the departing employee a month or so after departure. Also, former employees may be more willing to provide information on questionnaires mailed to their homes or in telephone conversations conducted some time after they have left the organization.

# HR Performance and Benchmarking

When information on HR performance has been gathered, it must be compared to a standard. A standard is a model or measure against which something is compared to determine its performance. For example, it is meaningless to know that organizational turnover rate is 75% if it is not known what the turnover rates at comparable organizations might be. One approach to assessing HR effectiveness is **benchmarking,** which compares specific measures of performance against data on those measures in other "best practices" organizations.

**Benchmarking**
Comparing specific measures of performance against data on those measures in other "best practices" organizations.

HR professionals attempting to benchmark try to locate organizations that do certain activities very well and thus become the "benchmarks." One means for obtaining benchmarking data is through telephone calls, which then may be followed up with questionnaires and site visits to benchmarking partners. The most commonly benchmarked performance measures in HR management are:[61]

- Total compensation as a percentage of net income before taxes
- Percent of management positions filled internally
- Dollar sales per employee
- Benefits as a percentage of payroll cost

## Professional Organizations as Information Sources for Benchmarking

HR specialists can gain information and insights from managers and specialists in other organizations by participating in professional groups. The most prominent professional organizations are the Society for Human Resource Management (SHRM) and the International Personnel Management Association (IPMA). These organizations publish professional journals and newsletters, conduct annual meetings and conferences, and offer many other services, often through local chapters. SHRM is composed primarily of private-sector HR professionals, whereas members of IPMA primarily are HR managers from local, state, and federal government agencies.

Professional HR journals and publications of professional organizations are a useful communication link among managers, HR specialists, researchers, and other practitioners. Appendix C contains a list of publications that often contain HR management information.

*LOGGING ON . . .*
**Association for Human Resource Management (AHRM)**
Sixteen different links to HR associations can be accessed through this website.

**http://www.ahrm.org**

Surveys done by various professional organizations can also provide useful perspectives. Some organizations, such as the Bureau of National Affairs and the Conference Board, sponsor surveys on HR practices in various communities, states, and regions. The results are distributed to participating organizations.

Finally, private management consulting firms and local colleges and universities can assist in HR research. These outside researchers may be more knowledgeable and unbiased than people inside the organization. Consultants skilled in questionnaire design and data analysis can give expert advice on HR research.

## Doing the Benchmarking Analysis

A useful way to analyze HR involves calculating ratios. The ratios can be calculated and compared from year to year, providing information about changes in HR operations. For example, one suggested series of ratios and measures to consider is shown in Figure 3–11.

Effectiveness is best determined by comparing ratio measures with benchmarked national statistics. The comparisons should be tracked internally over time. For instance, the Society for Human Resource Management (SHRM) and the Saratoga Institute have developed benchmarks based on data from over 500

**FIGURE 3–11** *HR Ratios and Measures for Assessment*

| HR FUNCTION | USEFUL RATIOS | |
|---|---|---|
| • **Selection** | $\dfrac{\text{Long-term vacancies}}{\text{Total jobs}}$ | $\dfrac{\text{Vacancies filled internally}}{\text{Total vacancies}}$ |
| | $\dfrac{\text{Time to fill vacancy}}{\text{Total vacancies}}$ | $\dfrac{\text{Offers accepted}}{\text{Offers extended}}$ |
| • **Training** | $\dfrac{\text{Number of days training}}{\text{Number of employees}}$ | $\dfrac{\text{Total training budget}}{\text{Total vacancies}}$ |
| • **Compensation** | $\dfrac{\text{Total compensation costs}}{\text{Total revenue}}$ | $\dfrac{\text{Basic salary cost}}{\text{Total compensation cost}}$ |
| • **Employee relations** | $\dfrac{\text{Resignations}}{\text{Total employees per year}}$ | $\dfrac{\text{Length of service}}{\text{Total employees}}$ |
| | $\dfrac{\text{Absences}}{\text{Days worked per months}}$ | $\dfrac{\text{Total managers}}{\text{Total employees}}$ |
| • **Overall HR** | $\dfrac{\text{Part-time employees}}{\text{Total employees}}$ | $\dfrac{\text{HR professionals}}{\text{Total employees}}$ |

companies, presented by industry and by organizational size. The Saratoga Institute in Santa Clara, California, surveys employers annually and compiles information that allows individual employers to compare HR costs against national figures.

---

Here is an example of how HR costing models can be developed. The following equations show how to compute interviewing costs.

$$C/I = \frac{ST + MT}{I}$$

where:

C/I  =  cost of interviewing
ST  =  total staff time spent interviewing (interviewer's hourly rate × hours)
MT  =  management time spent interviewing (manager's hourly rate × hours)
I  =  number of applicants interviewed

An example helps to illustrate use of the formula. Assume that an employment interview specialist is paid $12 an hour and interviews eight applicants for a job for an hour each. Following the personal interview, the applicants are interviewed by a department manager paid $20 an hour for 30 minutes each. The interview costs would be:

$$\frac{\overset{ST}{\overbrace{(\$12 \times 8 \text{ hours})}} + \overset{MT}{\overbrace{(\$20 \times 4 \text{ hours})}}}{8 \text{ interviews}} = \frac{\$96 + \$80}{8} = \frac{\$176}{8} = \$22 \text{ per applicant}$$

What this equation might indicate is the benefit of reducing the number of applicants interviewed by using better employment screening devices. Obviously, the costs of those screening items, such as a paper-and-pencil test, must be included when total selection costs are calculated.

SOURCE: Adapted from Jac Fitz-Enz, *How to Measure Human Resource Management,* 2nd ed. (New York: McGraw-Hill, 1995), 61–63.

---

**RETURN ON INVESTMENT (ROI) AND ECONOMIC VALUE ADDED (EVA)** Return on investment (ROI) and economic value added (EVA) are two related approaches to measuring the contribution and cost of HR. Both calculations are a bit complex, so they are just highlighted here.

**Return on investment (ROI)** can show the value of expenditures for HR activities. It can also be used to show how long it will take for the activities to pay for themselves. The following formula can be used to calculate the ROI for a new HR activity:

**Return on investment (ROI)**

Calculation showing the value of expenditures for HR activities.

$$(A - B) - C + D = ROI$$

where:

A  =  current operating costs for the time period
B  =  operating costs for a new or enhanced system for the time period
C  =  one-time cost of acquisition and implementation
D  =  value of gains from productivity improvements for the time period

**Economic value added (EVA)** is a firm's net operating profit after the cost of capital is deducted. Cost of capital is the minimum rate of return demanded by shareholders. When a company is making more than the cost of capital, it is creating wealth for shareholders. An EVA approach requires that all policies, procedures, measures, and methods use cost of capital as a benchmark against which their return is judged. Human resource decisions can be subjected to the same analyses. Both of these methods are useful, and specific information on them is available from other sources.

**Economic value added (EVA)**
A firm's net operating profit after the cost of capital is deducted.

**UTILITY OR COST/BENEFIT ANALYSES**  In **utility analysis,** economic or other statistical models are built to identify the costs and benefits associated with specific HR activities. These models generally contain equations that identify the relevant factors influencing the HR activity under study. According to Jac Fitz-Enz—a pioneer in measuring HR effectiveness—formulas and measures should be derived from a listing of activities and the variables associated with those activities. An example that quantifies selection interviewing costs follows.

Continuing efforts to cost-justify expenditures will require HR professionals to be versed in research and assessment approaches and methods. To face the challenges outlined throughout this text, effective HR management will be essential in organizations both in the United States and globally.

**Utility analysis**
Analysis in which economic or other statistical models are built to identify the costs and benefits associated with specific HR activities.

# Summary

- Productivity at national, organizational, and individual levels is critical for organizational success.
- Total Quality Management (TQM) is a comprehensive management process focusing on the continuous improvement of organizational activities to enhance the quality of the goods and services supplied. But the success of TQM has been mixed.
- Service is critical to meeting customer expectations, and HR must support service through selection, training, and other activities.
- A psychological contract contains the unwritten expectations that employees and employers have about the nature of their work relationships. Those contracts are being transformed in different organizations.
- Motivation deals with "whys" of human behavior, and employers want motivated employees.
- Various theories of motivation have been developed. Maslow's hierarchy of needs and Herzberg's motivation/hygiene theory are widely known content theories.

- Job design is organizing tasks, duties, and responsibilities into a productive unit of work.
- The job-characteristics model suggests that five characteristics of jobs (skill variety, task identity, task significance, autonomy, and feedback from the organization) affect motivation, performance, and satisfaction.
- Teams increasingly are being used in organizations. Special-purpose teams, production cells, and self-directed work teams have all been used successfully.
- Self-directed work teams are more successful when dissent is valued, membership is flexible, and teams have decision-making authority.
- Job satisfaction affects commitment to the organization, which in turn affects the rates of absenteeism and turnover.
- Absenteeism is expensive, but it can be controlled by discipline, positive reinforcement, or some combination of the two.
- Turnover has been studied extensively and appears to be strongly related to certain external, work-related, and personal factors.

- HR departments must set goals and measure effectiveness.
- Research on HR activities answers questions with facts, not guesswork.
- Primary researchers gather data directly on issues, whereas secondary researchers use research done by others and reported elsewhere.
- Research information can be gathered from several sources, including experiments, pilot projects, various types of surveys, and exit interviews.

- Systematic programs of HR research are used to assess the overall effectiveness of HR activities.
- Benchmarking allows an organization to compare its practices against "best practices" in different organizations.
- Professional organizations provide useful sources of information on HR activities.
- HR audits can be used to gather comprehensive information on how well HR activities in an organization are being performed.

## Review and Discussion Questions

1. Discuss why productivity in an organization depends to a large extent on individual productivity.
2. Discuss the advantages and disadvantages of self-directed work teams.
3. Discuss the concept of organizational commitment to jobs you have had.
4. How would you conduct HR research on turnover and absenteeism problems in a bank?
5. Using the HR audit checklist, rate an organization where you have worked.
6. Why is assessing and measuring the effectiveness and efficiency of HR programs so important?

## Terms to Know

attitude survey   99
autonomy   87
benchmarking   100
economic value added (EVA)
    103
effectiveness   94
efficiency   94
exit interview   99
experiment   98
feedback   87
HR audit   96
HR research   97
job design   84

job enlargement   85
job enrichment   85
job rotation   85
job satisfaction   89
motivation   82
organizational commitment   91
primary research   97
production cells   88
productivity   75
psychological contract   79
quality circle   88
reciprocity   79
reengineering   87

return on investment (ROI)   102
secondary research   97
self-directed work team   88
shamrock team   89
skill variety   86
special-purpose team   88
task identity   86
task significance   87
Total Quality Management (TQM)
    77
turnover   93
unit labor cost   75
utility analysis   103

## Using the Internet

## Self-Directed Work Teams and Their Development

As the HR manager you have been informed by the top level of management that teams will be implemented for the production floor. They have asked you to meet with the supervisors to devise a plan of action to develop the teams and ensure their success. To prepare for your meeting with the production supervisors use the following website on self-directed work teams, and investigate the success of the Allstate nine-step charter process for developing teams. Then, detail the steps for the meeting.
**http://users.ids.net/~brim/sdwtt.html**

# CASE

# Benchmarking HR at Goodyear

Goodyear Tire and Rubber Company, like most businesses, has seen massive change and has tried to focus on finding new and better ways to get work done. As part of that search, the company has used benchmarking to help identify the "best practices" for all facets of its operations, including human resources. By measuring itself and comparing the measurements against those of other companies, Goodyear has managed to find more efficient ways to get work done.

The idea behind benchmarking is that it is possible to examine the best practices of other organizations and make changes in operations based on what is learned. More than 70% of the Fortune 500 companies use benchmarking regularly. A benefit of benchmarking is that it forces companies to focus on the specific factors that lead to success or failure.

When Goodyear begins a benchmarking project, it spends up to three months planning. There are major discussions about what the firm hopes to accomplish. Those who are participants receive training in the process. From the highly focused questions that are developed by the benchmark team come answers about specific practices and results. Developing these questions and answers may require conducting interviews in person or over the phone, bringing in an academic to design a scientific study to examine a problem, or using outside consultants to gather information. But obtaining information about Goodyear's practices and those of the other company (or companies) is the key thrust. Communicating information so that comparisons can be made and new ideas generated is the basis for benchmarking.

Recently, when the company—as part of the broader benchmarking process—examined compensation strategies, it put together an internal team with individuals from many departments. The team developed questions and studied topics such as variable pay, the pay for top performers, and the role of training in compensation. Team members first determined what the company needed to learn and then created an agenda to gather the information. After conducting interviews and gathering data from many other sources, the team compared notes on the practices of various successful companies. Then it made its recommendations for changes at Goodyear.

When HR began to benchmark its own practices, it examined a wide range of issues. Leadership development, succession planning, benefits, safety, and compensation were all benchmarked. The company wanted to tie employee compensation to individual performance and the firm's goals of improving customer service and shareholder satisfaction.

After about six months of examining several *Fortune* 100 companies, Goodyear's HR staff made several changes, including altering the way the company approached its compensation program. It concluded that to remain competitive and provide better customer service, it needed to better define the employee performance appraisal process and tie that activity to Goodyear's business objectives. That link meant clearly communicating what each position was expected to contribute and what its responsibilities were. As a result, part of the Chairman's compensation is now "at risk," depending on the company's financial performance.

The HR Director has summarized Goodyear's use of benchmarking as a way to evaluate the success of company practices and to assess effectiveness. He says, "If your goal is continuous improvement, your company will always want to learn what other companies are doing. And it is important for HR to be aligned with the corporate strategy and be recognized as a valuable resource for change."[62]

## Questions

1. Explain how benchmarking HR relates to productivity, service, and quality at Goodyear.
2. How could the results from benchmarking be used for making organizational change at Goodyear?

# Notes

1. Adapted from Tim Aeppel, "Personnel Disorders Sap a Factory Owner of His Early Idealism," *The Wall Street Journal,* January 14, 1998, A1; Donna Rosato, "Northwest's Poor Service Sullies Deal," *USA Today,* June 15, 1998, 6B; and Gabriella Stern, "How a Young Manager Shook Up the Culture at Old Chrysler Plant," *The Wall Street Journal,* April 21, 1997, A1.

2. "Determining the Value of Human Resources," *ViewPoint on Value,* (Omaha, NE: Blackman and Associates), July/August 1998, 4.

3. David P. Norton, "Aligning Strategy and Performance with the Balanced Scorecard," *ACA Journal,* Autumn 1997, 18–26.

4. David Ulrich, "A New Mandate for Human Resources," *Harvard Business Review,* January-February 1998, 124.

5. Bernard Wysocki Jr., "Why an Acquisition? Often It's the People," *The Wall Street Journal,* October 6, 1997, A1; Erick Schonfield, "Have the Urge to Merge?", *Fortune,* March 31, 1997, 114.

6. Keith Whitefield and Michael Poole, "Organizing Employment for High Performance," *Organization Studies,* Winter 1997, 745.

7. M.J. Mandel, "You Ain't Seen Nothing Yet," *Business Week,* August 31, 1998, 60–61.

8. Frederick D. Buzzie, "Plain Talk about Productivity," *Across the Board,* January 1997, 43–47.

9. Joseph Weber, "The Year of the Deal," *Business Week,* July 13, 1998, 52–53.

10. Bob Cardy, "What Happened to Quality?", *Human Resource Division News,* Summer 1998, 14–15.

11. Zahir Irani and John Sharp, "Integrating Continuous Improvement and Innovation into a Corporate Culture," *Technovation,* vol. 17, no. 4, 199–206.

12. Del Jones, "Buyers Get No Satisfaction," *USA Today,* January 22, 1997, 1B.

13. Thomas A. Stewart, "A Satisfied Customer Isn't Enough," *Fortune,* July 21, 1997, 112.

14. "Service with a Smile," *The Economist,* April 25, 1998, 63; Hal Lancaster, "Giving Good Service, Never an Easy Task, Is Getting Harder," *The Wall Street Journal,* June 9, 1998, B1.

15. John M. Hannon, "Leveraging HRM to Enrich Competitive Intelligence, *Human Resource Management,* 36 (1997), 409.

16. Joseph Coates, "Emerging HR Issues for the Twenty-First Century," *Employment Relations Today,* Winter 1997, 1; Dallas Salisbury, "The Changing Employment Contract," *Compensation and Benefits Review,* January-February 1997, 78.

17. "Workers Expect to Share the Wealth," *Bulletin to Management—Data Graph,* October 16, 1997, 332.

18. Maggie Jackson, "Bosses Take a Beating," *Omaha World-Herald,* September 7, 1997, G1.

19. Ann Vincola and Nancy Mobley, "Performance Management through a Work/Life Lens," *HR Focus,* February 1998, 9.

20. This discussion is based on Ann Tsoi, Jane Pearce, Lyman Porter, and Angela Tripoli, "Alternative Approaches to the Employee-Organization Relationship: Does Investment in Employees Pay Off?", *Academy of Management Journal,* 40 (1997), 1089–1121.

21. Hal Lancaster, "Will Hiring a Full Stuff Be the Next Fashion in Management?", *The Wall Street Journal,* April 28, 1998, B1; Sue Shellenbarger, "Employers Are Finding It Doesn't Cost Much to Keep a Staff Happy," *The Wall Street Journal,* July 22, 1998, B1.

22. Tim Aeppel, "Life at the Factory," *The Wall Street Journal,* March 18, 1997, 1.

23. James H. Carbone, "Loyalty: Subversive Doctrine?", *Academy of Management Executive,* August 1997, 80–87.

24. Barbara Parus, "A New Deal to Attract and Retain Talent in the Virtual Workplace," *ACA News,* March 1999, 29–23; and Emily Thornton, "More Cracks in the Social Contract," *Business Week,* October 27, 1997, 70E, 20.

25. Charley Braun, "Organizational Infidelity," *Academy of Management Executive,* November 1997, 11.

26. "A Man of Flint," *The Economist,* June 20, 1998, 79.

27. Alan Webber, "Best Firms Don't Need Employee Loyalty," *USA Today,* July 22, 1998, 11A.

28. Joseph White and Jo Ann Lublin, "Some Companies Try to Rebuild Loyalty," *The Wall Street Journal,* September 27, 1996, B1.

29. "Worker Loyalty: Not What It Used to Be?", *Bulletin to Management,* June 25, 1998, 1.

30. R.D. Jeffords, H.E. Bresee, C.D. Parsons, "Motivating Top Performers," *Internal Auditing,* Fall 1997, 52–56.

31. Thomas Petzinger Jr., "The Front Lines," *The Wall Street Journal,* April 25, 1997, B1.

32. Roberta Maynard, "How to Motivate Low Wage Workers," *Nation's Business,* May 1997, 35.

33. Peter Cappelli, "Rethinking the Nature of Work: A Look at the Research Evidence," *Compensation and Benefits Review,* July-August 1997, 50–60.

34. Pascal Zachary, "The New Search for Meaning in 'Meaningless' Work," *The Wall Street Journal,* January 9, 1997, B1.

35. Joan Rentsch and Robert Steel, "Testing the Durability of Job Characteristics as Predictors of Absenteeism over a Six-Year Period," *Personnel Psychology,* 51 (1998), 165.

36. Dan Danbom, "Hate Your Job? These Are Even Worse," *Denver Post,* June 7, 1998, 6J.

37. Thomas Petzinger Jr., "A Plant Manager Keeps Reinventing His Production Line," *The Wall Street Journal,* September 19, 1997, B1.

38. Gareth R. Jones and Jennifer M. George, "The Experience and Evolution of Trust: Implications for Cooperation and Teamwork," *Academy of Management Review,* 23 (1998), 531.

39. John R. Hollenbeck, et al., "Extending the Multilevel Theory of Team Decision Making," *Academy of Management Journal,* 41 (1998), 269.

40. Thomas Petzinger, Jr., "The Front Lines," *The Wall Street Journal,* October 17, 1997, B1.

41. Scott A. Snell, et al., "Designing and Supporting Transnational Teams," *Human Resource Management,* 37 (1998), 147–158.

42. "Anthony Townsend, Samuel DeMarie, and Anthony Hendrickson, "Virtual Teams; Technology and the Workplace of the Future," *Academy of Management Executive,* August 1998, 17.

43. Tim Aeppel, "Missing the Boss," *The Wall Street Journal,* September 8, 1997, A1; Allan B. Drexler and Russ Forrester, "Teamwork—Not Necessarily the Answer," *HR Magazine,* January 1998, 55; Stephanie Armour, "Office Ethics: Teams Make It Hard to Tattle," *USA Today,* February 17, 1998, 6B.

44. Perry Pascarella, "Compensating Teams," *Across the Board,* February 1997, 16.

45. Hal Lancaster, "Needy or Greedy? How Money Fits Into Job Satisfaction," *The Wall Street Journal,* June 30, 1998, B1.

46. Ralph King Jr., "Teams Therapy," *The Wall Street Journal,* May 20, 1998, 1.

47. Jeanne Peck, "Times Are Good, So Why Are We Whining?", *Denver Post,* April 19, 1998, B1; Robert Taylor, "Europe's Unhappy World of Work," *Financial Times,* May 16, 1997, 1.

48. It's the Manager, Stupid," *The Economist,* August 8, 1998, 54.

49. "Worker Absenteeism Still on the Rise," *Benefits & Compensation Solutions,* December 1995, 8.

50. David Cotter and Cecil Williams, "Managing Health-Related Absences," *Compensation and Benefits Review,* May-June 1997, 58.

51. Jessica P. Vistnes, "Gender Differences in Days Lost from Work Due to Illness," *Industrial and Labor Relations Review,* 50 (1997), 304.

52. M. Michael Markowich, "When Is Excessive Absenteeism Grounds for Disciplinary Action?", *ACA News,* July/August 1998, 36.

53. Rodger W. Griffeth, et al., "Comparative Tests of Multivariate Models of Recruiting Source Effects," *Journal of Management,* 23 (1997), 19.

54. Bill Gates, "Internet a Rich Source of Medical Information," *Omaha World-Herald,* March 15, 1998, 2M.

55. Jen Condoding, "Echos from the Line: HR Lacks Strategic Initiative," *HR Focus,* July 1997, 1.

56. Sharon A. Lobel and Leslie Faught, "Forty Methods for Proving the Value of Work/Life Interventions," *Compensation and Benefits Review,* November-December 1996, 50.

57. Mark Smith and Susan Marinakis, "Measuring HR Value Added from the Outside In," *Employment Relations Today,* Autumn 1997, 59.

58. Wayne Cascio, Clifford Young, and James Morris, "Financial Consequences of Employment-Change Decisions in Major U.S. Corporations," *Academy of Management Journal,* 40 (1997), 1175.

59. Mark Huselid, Susan Jackson, and Randall Schulder, "Technical and Strategic Human Resource Management Effectiveness as Determinates of Firm Performance," *Academy of Management Journal,* 40 (1997), 171.

60. Mark Spoginardi, "Conducting a Human Resources Audit—A Primer," *Employee Relations Law Journal,* 23 (1997), 105.

61. "Compose Your Company to These Performance-Management Benchmarks," *IOMA's Pay for Performance Report,* January 1998, 1.

62. Adapted from Samuel Greengard, "Discover Best Practices," *Personnel Journal,* November 1995, 62–73.

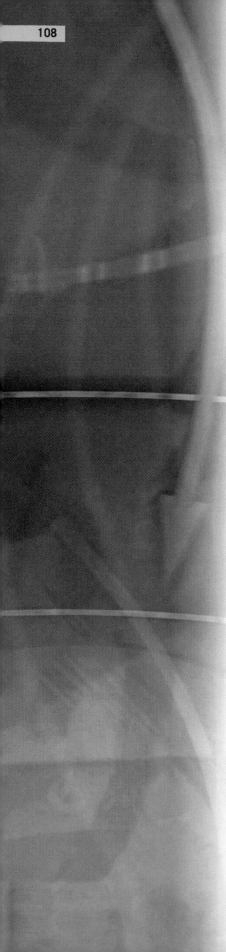

# CHAPTER 4
# Global Human Resource Management

**After you have read this chapter, you should be able to:**

- Discuss the major factors influencing global HR management.

- Define *culture* and explain how national cultures can be classified.

- List and define several types of international employees.

- Explain why staffing activities are more complex for international jobs than for domestic ones.

- Discuss three aspects of international training and development.

- Identify basic international compensation practices.

- Describe several international health, safety, and security concerns.

## HR TRANSITIONS

# Mercedes-Benz Builds World-Class Vehicles in Alabama

Building Mercedes vehicles in Alabama may have seemed somewhat unusual a few years ago, but not any longer. Certainly, when Mercedes-Benz announced that it had selected Alabama as the site for building its "M" class sports utility vehicles, many skeptics wondered how successful that plant would be. Along with other car manufacturers such as Toyota, Nissan, and BMW, all of which have established manufacturing plants in the United States, Mercedes followed the growing trend—also seen in other industries—of foreign-owned corporations establishing operations in the United States. Now one of the most notable successes in combining foreign firms and U.S. workers can be seen at Mercedes-Benz and its Vance, Alabama, plant.

Central Alabama is hardly where one would have expected Mercedes to build a new plant. Vance, Alabama (population 400), is an hour's drive from Birmingham, and now has a 1-million-square-feet plant for building Mercedes M class vehicles. Mercedes chose to build in Vance for several reasons. First, wage rates and overall labor costs in the U.S. are significantly lower compared to German wage and benefit costs. Second, the U.S. is the largest market for sport utility vehicles. Third, the State of Alabama offered Mercedes incentives valued at $250 million, including $90 million in training assistance. Finally, there was a supply of quality workers, who could be trained to build the M class vehicles.

When Mercedes started taking applications for workers, the state of Alabama provided employment screening assistance. Over 40,000 Alabamians applied for the 650 jobs the plant would fill at start-up. Virtually none of the applicants had previous experience building cars. Andreas Renschler, a German sent to head up the M class plant, referred to the plant as a "learning field" both for workers and Mercedes. In choosing workers, Mercedes focused on adaptability and the ability of individuals to work in teams. For Mercedes, the firm could try new and more flexible production methods that were not typical in its German plants.

Once selected, approximately 160 Alabama workers went to Germany to work at Mercedes plants as part of their training. There they learned production tasks from specially selected German workers and supervisors. As more Alabama workers were trained in Germany, it ultimately became less necessary to send the remaining new hires to Germany, so 70 Germans were sent to Alabama to work for two years as trainers at the training facilities in Alabama. In preparation for these interchanges, two weeks of language and culture training were given to those traveling to Germany or Alabama.

The Mercedes M class management team was international in nature also. Renschler hired a Canadian with experience at Toyota and an American who had worked at General Motors and Nissan plants in the United States.

Five years later, the plant and the M class vehicles are a huge success. About 80,000 vehicles are being produced annually, and the plant cannot keep up with the demand. The quality of vehicles produced in the Alabama plant has equaled or exceeded the quality of other vehicles produced in Germany over much longer periods of time. As a result, the Alabama plant is being expanded and more workers are being added. With all of these successes, probably the best indicator that Alabama workers are building world-class vehicles is this: Because of the high demand for the M class vehicles in Europe and worldwide, Mercedes has had to convert a plant in Austria to produce M class vehicles. Mercedes is sending Alabama workers to train Austrian workers in the production methods and working approaches used in Alabama. Truly Alabama workers and Mercedes have become global in nature.[1]

> *One of the most notable successes in combining foreign firms and U.S. workers can be seen at Mercedes-Benz and its Vance, Alabama, plant.*

*66 You develop long-lasting company power by developing local people. 99*

YUICHI KATO

The internationalization of business has proceeded at a rapid pace as the world has become a global economy. Many U.S. firms receive a substantial portion of their profits and sales from outside the United States, and estimates are that the largest 100 U.S. multinational firms have foreign sales of more than $500 billion in one year. For firms such as Colgate and Coca-Cola, foreign sales and profits account for over 60% of total sales and profits. Other U.S. firms have substantial operations in other countries as well.[2]

Globalization has had a major impact on HR management,[3] and has raised a number of issues noted in earlier chapters. But additional issues have included:

● How should a company staff plants around the world with a mix of parent-country nationals, host-country nationals, or third-country nationals?
● How will these employees be recruited, selected, trained, compensated, and managed?
● What characteristics of the countries being considered affect the HR decisions that must be made?

# A Survey of Business Issues Worldwide

The impact of global competition can be seen in many U.S. industries. The automobile, steel, and electronics industries have closed unproductive facilities or reduced employment because of competition from firms in Japan, Taiwan, Korea, Germany, and other countries. At the same time, as the opening discussion of Mercedes in Alabama illustrates, foreign-owned firms have been investing in plants and creating jobs in the United States. The growth in employment resulting from foreign investments has helped to replace some of the jobs lost at U.S. firms due to downsizing.

An international agreement, the General Agreement on Tariffs and Trade (GATT), was signed to provide general guidelines on trade practices among nations, but a number of provisions in GATT affect HR practices in the various countries, including the United States. The brief look at the various areas of the world that follows illustrates some of those HR issues, as well as the changing nature of international economic linkages.

## North America

The United States, Canada, and Mexico have recognized the importance of world trade by eliminating barriers and working more closely together, starting in North America.[4] One aspect of this cooperation is that U.S. firms, as well as companies from other nations such as Japan, South Korea, and Taiwan, have taken advantage of the lower Mexican wage rates to establish operations in Mexico. The signing of the North American Free Trade Agreement (NAFTA) expanded trade opportunities among Canada, the United States, and Mexico. But NAFTA also placed restrictions on employers to ensure that their HR practices in Mexico met certain standards. The Commission on Labor Cooperation (CLC) was established as part of NAFTA to review complaints filed in the United States, Canada, or Mex-

**LOGGING ON . . .**
**ECA International Global Partners in Human Resources**
This global human resource network provides expatriate remuneration survey reports for 68 countries and publications dealing with human resource management issues.

**http://www.ecaltd.com**

ico regarding occupational safety and health, child labor, benefits, and labor-management relations.

## Latin America

One highlight of recent years in Latin America is the resurgence of the economies of the largest countries, specifically Brazil, Argentina, and Chile. Economic austerity programs in those countries have reduced their inflation rates to more normal levels. Expanding populations created by relatively high birthrates have led to those countries being seen as attractive for foreign investment, and many multinational organizations based in the United States, Asian countries, and European nations have expanded operations through joint ventures with host-country firms.[5]

## Asia

In Asia, Japan's economy has been maturing, and Japanese society has been changing because of a rapidly aging population. Also, younger Japanese are becoming more "westernized" and are buying more imported goods. Gradually the Japanese government has had to open up its markets and make changes in its economy in response to pressure from the United States and other countries.

Economic relations between foreign firms and firms in such Asian countries as Taiwan, South Korea, Singapore, and Malaysia have become more complex, and their exports have increased dramatically. The rapid growth of the economies in those Asian countries, as well as in Indonesia, Thailand, and Vietnam, has led more foreign firms to establish manufacturing facilities there and to increase trade opportunities.

Two other Asian countries, India and China, have huge populations. Consequently, a growing number of foreign firms are establishing operations in those nations.[6] But the difficulty of attracting foreign managers and professionals to these countries and the costs of providing for them have created a shortage of qualified human resources in both India and China.

## Europe

Changes in Europe, after the disintegration of the USSR into 14 independent states, include opening to international commerce the economies of Eastern European countries. This change has given U.S.-based and other firms dramatically expanded opportunities to sell products and services. Also, the ample supply of workers available in those countries, whose wage rates are relatively low, means that labor-intensive manufacturing facilities can be established to tap the available labor pools.[7]

In Western Europe, efforts to create a unified European economic market have led to cross-country mergers of firms and greater cooperation by European governments. The creation of the Euro, a unified currency, is reshaping European economies also. At the same time, some national governmental efforts may have the effect of limiting the import of U.S.- and Japanese-made goods to participating European countries. Therefore, U.S. and Asian firms have added offices and production facilities in Europe to avoid potential trade restrictions.

The stagnation of the economies and high costs imposed on employers in Western European countries such as Germany and France have led to double-digit unemployment rates. As a result, many European-headquartered organizations have shifted production to new plants in the United States and other countries, as the Mercedes-Benz plant in Alabama illustrates.

## Africa

In many parts of Africa, opportunities for international operations are inhibited by civil strife and corrupt governments. Also, the infrastructure in many countries is inadequate. A more positive outlook exists for the country of South Africa since its discredited apartheid policy was repealed. As a result, foreign firms are entering South Africa and establishing operations and joint ventures. But race relations still must be considered by HR professionals in global organizations operating in South Africa.

# Factors Affecting Global HR Management

Managing human resources in different cultures, economies, and legal systems presents some challenges. However, when well done, HR management pays dividends. A seven-year study in Britain of over 100 foreign companies showed that good HR management, as well as other factors, accounted for more of the variance in profitability and productivity than did technology, or research and development.[8]

The most common obstacles to effective HR management are cross-cultural adaptation, different organizational/workforce values, differences in management style, and management turnover. Doing business globally requires that adaptations be made to reflect these factors. It is crucial that such concerns be seen as interrelated by managers and professionals as they do business and establish operations globally. Figure 4–1 depicts the general considerations for HR managers with global responsibilities. Each of those factors will be examined briefly.

## Legal and Political Factors

The nature and stability of political systems vary from country to country. U.S. firms are accustomed to a relatively stable political system, and the same is true in many of the other developed countries in Europe. Although presidents, prime ministers, premiers, governors, senators, and representatives may change, the legal systems are well-established, and global firms can depend on continuity and consistency.

However, in many other nations, the legal and political systems are turbulent. Some governments regularly are overthrown by military coups. Others are ruled by dictators and despots who use their power to require international firms to buy goods and services from host-country firms owned or controlled by the rulers or the rulers' families. In some parts of the world, one-party rule has led to pervasive corruption, while in others there are so many parties that governments change constantly. Also, legal systems vary in character and stability, with business contracts sometimes becoming unenforceable because of internal political factors.

International firms may have to decide strategically when to comply with certain laws and regulations and when to ignore them because of operational or political reasons. Another issue involves ethics. Because of restrictions imposed

**FIGURE 4–1** *Considerations Affecting Global HR Management*

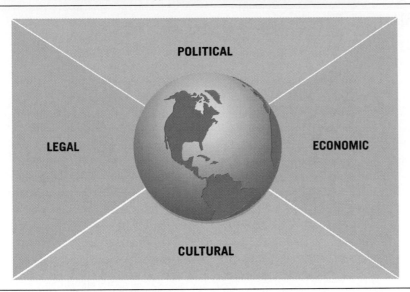

on U.S.-based firms through the Foreign Corrupt Practices Act (FCPA), a fine line exists between paying "agent fees," which is legal, and bribery, which is illegal.

HR regulations and laws vary among countries in character and detail. In many Western European countries, laws on labor unions and employment make it difficult to reduce the number of workers because required payments to former employees can be very high, as the HR Perspective on the next page indicates. Equal employment legislation exists to varying degrees.

In some countries, laws address issues such as employment discrimination and sexual harassment. In others, because of religious or ethical differences, employment discrimination may be an accepted practice.

All of these factors reveal that it is crucial for HR professionals to conduct a comprehensive review of the political environment and employment-related laws before beginning operations in a country. The role and nature of labor unions should be a part of that review.

## Economic Factors

Economic factors affect the other three factors in Figure 4–1. Different countries have different economic systems. Some even still operate with a modified version of communism, which has essentially failed. For example, in China communism is the official economic approach. But as the government attempts to move to a more mixed model, it is using unemployment and layoffs to reduce government enterprises bloated with too many workers.[9]

Many lesser-developed nations are receptive to foreign investment in order to create jobs for their growing populations. Global firms often obtain significantly cheaper labor rates in these countries than they do in Western Europe, Japan, and the United States. However, whether firms can realize significant profits in developing nations may be determined by currency fluctuations and restrictions on transfer of earnings.

# The Legal and Political Environment of Unemployment in Europe

Europe cannot seem to shake its chronic unemployment. The unemployment rate has ranged from almost 20% in Spain to over 10% in France–but it averages about 12%. Joblessness is much higher in Europe than in the United States or Japan. The accompanying chart shows the percent employed recently compared to the base year of 1980. While the United States has created many new jobs, Europe has created very few.

Forecasts are that even with an improvement in the economy and employment, unemployment at over 10% will continue in European Union (EU) countries. Why?

Economists disagree about many matters, but not about unemployment. Generally they agree that labor markets need to be flexible, but in European countries they are relatively rigid. Very generous unemployment benefits, high minimum wages, strong unions, and unique

(by U.S. standards) laws dissuade employers from hiring more employees. For example, in Spain, a permanent employee who is fired can get 45 days' pay times the number of years he has been with the company. It is a large liability, so few firms create more permanent jobs. Similar legislation in other countries tends to keep those who have jobs at work, but the effect of the protective legislation keeps employers from creating more jobs. Economists tell us that in the long run, without such laws, firms that cut costs and become more productive create more jobs because productive industries tend to expand.

The pressure of world competition that is forcing painful reform is not popular in Europe. Many Europeans are crying "enough," and questioning how quickly the European economies can transform themselves into the Anglo-Saxon model of capitalism. That formula— high productivity, low jobless rates, and a minimal social safety net—is not typical in most Western European countries. For example, a recent French poll found that two-thirds of the French people prefer their rich benefits and high unemployment to America's approach of lower unemployment and limited social welfare benefits. Of course, elected politicians tend to follow the wishes of their constituents, bringing political and legal factors together—in this case, resulting in an average of 12% unemployment.[10]

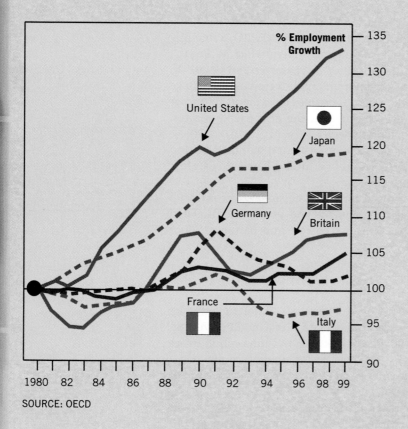

SOURCE: OECD

Also, political instability can lead to situations in which the assets of foreign firms are seized. In addition, nations with weak economies may not be able to invest in maintaining and upgrading the necessary elements of their infrastructures, such as roads, electric power, schools, and telecommunications. The absence of good infrastructures may make it more difficult to convince managers from the United States or Japan to take assignments overseas.

Economic conditions vary greatly. For example, Figure 4–2 shows the relative *cost of living* for major cities in the world. Cost of living is a major economic consideration for global corporations.

In many developed countries, especially in Europe, unemployment has grown, but employment restrictions and wage levels remain high. Consequently, many European firms are transferring jobs to lower-wage countries, as Mercedes-Benz did at its Alabama plant. In addition, both personal and corporate tax rates are quite high. These factors all must be evaluated as part of the process of deciding whether to begin or purchase operations in foreign countries.

## Cultural Factors

Cultural forces represent another important concern affecting international HR management. The culture of organizations was discussed earlier in the text, and

*LOGGING ON . . .*
**The Online Development Center of Basil Rouskas Associates, Inc.— International HR Issues**
An international directory of HR professionals is listed at this website to assist HR professionals with international issues. Other related websites are also listed for expatriates and travelers.

**http://www.basilrouskas. com/international.htm**

**FIGURE 4–2** *Cost-of-Living Comparison in Major World Cities*

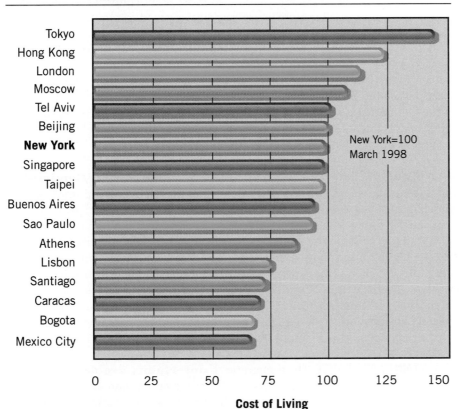

New York=100
March 1998

Cost of Living

SOURCE: European Information Union, 1998.

## Culture

**Culture**
The societal forces affecting the values, beliefs, and actions of a distinct group of people.

of course, national cultures also exist. **Culture** is composed of the societal forces affecting the values, beliefs, and actions of a distinct group of people. Cultural differences certainly exist between nations, but significant cultural differences exist within countries also. One only has to look at the conflicts caused by religion or ethnicity in Central Europe and other parts of the world to see the importance of culture on international organizations. Getting individuals from different ethnic or tribal backgrounds working together may be difficult in some parts of the world. Culture can lead to ethical differences among countries. The HR Perspective on the next page gives several examples.

One widely used way to classify and compare cultures has been developed by Geert Hofstede, a Dutch scholar and researcher. Hofstede conducted research on over 100,000 IBM employees in 53 countries, and he identified five dimensions useful in identifying and comparing culture. A review of each of those dimensions follows.[11]

**Power distance**
Dimension of culture that refers to the inequality among the people of a nation.

**POWER DISTANCE**  The dimension of **power distance** refers to the inequality among the people of a nation. In countries such as Germany, the Netherlands, and the United States, there is a smaller power distance—which means there is less inequality—than in such countries as France, Indonesia, Russia, and China. As power distance increases, there are greater status and authority differences between superiors and subordinates.

One way in which differences on this dimension affect HR activities is that the reactions to management authority differ among cultures. A more autocratic approach to managing is more common in most other countries, while in the United States there is a bit more use of participatory management.

**Individualism**
Dimension of culture that refers to the extent to which people in a country prefer to act as individuals instead of members of groups.

**INDIVIDUALISM**  Another dimension of culture identified by Hofstede is **individualism,** which is the extent to which people in a country prefer to act as individuals instead of members of groups. On this dimension, people in Asian countries tend to be less individualistic and more group-oriented, whereas those in the United States score the highest in individualism. An implication of these differences is that more collective action and less individual competition is likely in those countries that deemphasize individualism.

**Masculinity/Femininity**
Dimension of cultures that refers to the degree to which "masculine" values prevail over "feminine" values.

**MASCULINITY/FEMININITY**  The cultural dimension **masculinity/femininity** refers to the degree to which "masculine" values prevail over "feminine" values. Masculine values identified by Hofstede were assertiveness, performance orientation, success, and competitiveness, whereas feminine values included quality of life, close personal relationships, and caring. Respondents from Japan had the highest masculinity scores, while those from the Netherlands had more femininity-oriented values. Differences on this dimension may be tied to the role of women in the culture. Considering the different roles of women and what is "acceptable" for women in the United States, Saudi Arabia, Japan, and Mexico suggests how this dimension might affect the assignment of women expatriates to managerial jobs in the various countries.

**Uncertainty avoidance**
Dimension of culture that refers to the preference of people in a country for structured rather than unstructured situations.

**UNCERTAINTY AVOIDANCE**  The dimension of **uncertainty avoidance** refers to the preference of people in a country for structured rather than unstructured situations. A structured situation is one in which rules can be established and there are clear guides on how people are expected to act. Nations high on this factor, such as Japan, France, and Russia, tend to be more resistant to change and more

## HR PERSPECTIVE
# Cultural and Ethical Differences

Why do negotiators from some countries get loud, angry, emotional, and gesture wildly in business negotiations, while others sit quietly, smile, and make sure they get what they want? It is, in many cases, differences in culture. Culture is in one sense a shared set of meanings, values, and common views on relations with other people, right and wrong, etc. These differences lead to different ideas as to what constitutes ethical business behavior. For example:

- In one Eastern European country, obtaining a new telephone line in less than three months requires making a cash payment, referred to as an "expediting charge" (a bribe in most places), to the local manager of the telephone office. All parties to the deal know that the manager will retain the cash, but a telephone is essential for doing business internationally.
- Foreign firms wishing to do business in one Asian Pacific country must hire a "business representative" in order to obtain appropriate licenses and operating permits. In this country, it is well known that the two best representatives are relatives of the head of the country. It also is common to give the representative 10%–20% ownership in the business as a "gift" for promptly completing the licensing process.

A U.S.-based firm engaged in such practices could be violating the Foreign Corrupt Practices Act (FCPA), which prohibits U.S. firms from engaging in bribery and other practices in foreign countries that would be illegal in the United States. Competing firms from other countries are not bound by similar restrictions. However, the law reflects the U.S. culture's view on the ethics of bribery.

Specifically relating to HR management, another major concern is the use of child labor and prison labor. According to one estimate, over 80 million children under age 18 are working in factories and fields for international companies. In some countries, people convicted of "political crimes" are forced to work in factories that manufacture goods to be sold to U.S. and European firms. In those countries, prison labor also competes with other labor sources at lower wage rates.

When stories of these situations have been publicized, customer boycotts and news media coverage have focused unfavorable attention on the companies involved. To counter such concerns, firms such as Levi Strauss and Starbuck's Coffee, among others, have established minimum standards that must be met by all operations of their subcontractors and suppliers. Unfortunately, other firms have not been as aggressive.[12]

rigid. In contrast, people in places such as Hong Kong, the United States, and Indonesia tend to have more "business energy" and to be more flexible.

A logical use of differences on this factor is to anticipate how people in different countries will react to changes instituted in organizations. In more flexible cultures, what is less certain may be more intriguing and challenging, which may lead to greater entrepreneurship and risk taking than in the more "rigid" countries.

**LONG-TERM ORIENTATION** The dimension of **long-term orientation** refers to values people hold that emphasize the future, as opposed to short-term values, which focus on the present and the past. Long-term values include thrift and persistence, while short-term values include respecting tradition and fulfilling social obligations. People scoring the highest on long-term orientation were China and Hong Kong, while people in Russia, the United States, and France tended to have more short-term orientation.

Differences in many other facets of culture could be discussed. But it is enough to recognize that international HR managers and professionals must recognize that cultural dimensions differ from country to country and even within coun-

**Long-term orientation**
Dimension of culture that refers to values people hold that emphasize the future, as opposed to short-term values focusing on the present and the past.

tries. Therefore, the HR activities appropriate in one culture or country may have to be altered to fit appropriately into another culture or country.

## Types of Global Organizations

A growing number of organizations that operate within only one country are recognizing that they must change and develop a more international perspective.[13] Organizations may pass through three stages as they broaden out into the world, as shown in Figure 4–3. A discussion of each stage follows.

**Importing and exporting**
The phase of international interaction in which an organization begins selling and buying goods and services with organizations in other countries.

**IMPORTING AND EXPORTING** The first phase of international interaction consists of **importing and exporting.** Here, an organization begins selling and buying goods and services with organizations in other countries. Most of the international contacts are made by the sales and marketing staff and a limited number of other executives who negotiate contracts. Generally, HR activities are not affected except for travel policies for those going abroad.

**FIGURE 4–3** *Transition to Global Organization*

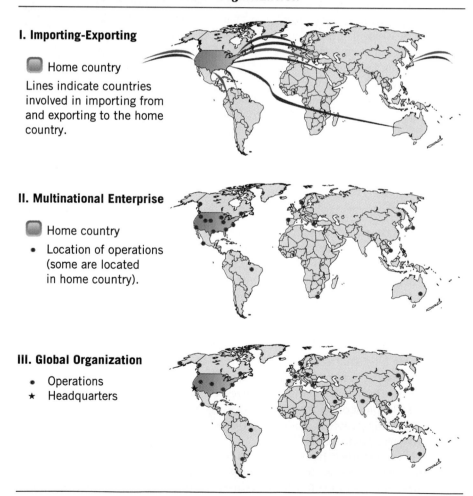

**I. Importing-Exporting**

🔲 Home country
Lines indicate countries involved in importing from and exporting to the home country.

**II. Multinational Enterprise**

🔲 Home country
• Location of operations (some are located in home country).

**III. Global Organization**
• Operations
★ Headquarters

**MULTINATIONAL ENTERPRISES** As firms develop and expand, they identify opportunities to begin operating in other countries. A **multinational enterprise (MNE)** is one in which organizational units are located in foreign countries. Typically these units provide goods and services for the geographic areas surrounding the countries where operations exist. Key management positions in the foreign operations are filled with employees from the home country of the corporation. As the MNE expands, it hires workers from the countries in which it has operations. HR practices for employees sent from corporate headquarters must be developed so that these employees and their dependents may continue their economic lifestyles while stationed outside the home country. Ways to link these individuals to the parent company are also critical, especially if the international job assignment is two to three years long. There are likely to be laws and regulations differing from those in the home country that must be considered. As a result, the HR professionals in the parent organization must become knowledgeable about each country in which the MNE operates and know how staffing, training, compensation, health and safety, and labor relations must be adapted.[14]

**Multinational enterprise (MNE)**
An organization with units located in foreign countries.

**GLOBAL ORGANIZATION** The MNE can be thought of as an *international* firm, in that it operates in various countries but each foreign business unit is operated separately. In contrast, a **global organization** has corporate units in a number of countries that are integrated to operate as one organization worldwide. An MNE may evolve into a global organization as operations in various countries become more integrated.

**Global organization**
An organization that has corporate units in a number of countries that are integrated to operate as one organization worldwide.

Another example of making the transition from MNE to global organization involves Ford Motor Co. in the early 1990s. Ford started shifting from having a separate, relatively autonomous unit on each continent to operating as a global firm. One facet of Ford's approach illustrates the shift. Previously, Ford had its major design centers in the United States, and centers elsewhere adapted U.S.-designed vehicles to market needs in various countries. If separate Ford vehicles were developed, they often differed in model name and style. Under the global approach, Ford is merging design facilities and people from all over the world. In centers located in several countries, designers, engineers, and production specialists will work in teams to develop cars. Ford plans to develop a common "platform" and model for what it hopes will become a "world car" that can be produced and sold throughout the world. It will differ in different countries only in having the steering wheel and the instrumentation on the right for such countries as Great Britain and Australia.

HR management in truly global organizations moves people, especially key managers and professionals, throughout the world. Individuals who speak several languages fluently are highly valued, and they will move among divisions and countries as they assume more responsibilities and experience career growth. As much as possible, international HR management must be viewed strategically in these organizations.[15] Global HR policies and activities are developed, but decentralization of decision making to subsidiary units and operations in other countries is necessary in order for country-specific adjustments to be made.[16]

## Managing Internationally

Are good domestic managers going to make good managers in another country? How is management on a day-to-day basis different internationally? The specific

***LOGGING ON . . .***
**HR Global Network**
This site contains archives and resources on the latest new ideas in global HR and training. A list of resources and archives for academic knowledge is also provided to assist HR professionals in global management.

**http://www.mcb.co.uk/hr/**

answers to these questions depend on the countries involved. However, some observations from those who have managed in multiple countries can be useful.

Managing globally means dealing with eclectic staffs and teams, understanding foreign competition, and studying the politics, culture, and operating style in different markets. Global managers apparently must handle more complexity, relate well to very diverse groups, learn to listen rather than talk, and be comfortable with the observation "I have no idea what will happen today."[17] Clearly understanding their own company objectives and administrative approach is important as well.[18]

Differences in successful managers can be great across countries. For example, the successful head of a major Chinese appliance manufacturer approaches management and leadership much differently than would be tolerated in the United States. He assesses employees' performance each month and adjusts pay monthly—up or down. Poor employees are humiliated. The slowest worker on each shift must explain his problems in public. Managers who fail to reach goals are named in the company paper, and must volunteer for a pay cut.[19]

Protocol, dress, greetings, and even business cards are potentially cultural differences that can work against the unattentive manager.[20] Dealing with gender issues among countries can be a problem as well, as the HR Perspective shows.

Despite somewhat different challenges for global managers than those faced by domestic managers, the need for international managerial talent is increasing. Finding and selecting good expatriates (including managers) is the next topic.

# International Staffing

Staffing (or finding, choosing and placing) good employees is difficult even at home. However, it becomes more difficult in other countries. For example, until recently in Russia, very few Russians had resumes available to give to prospective employers with vacant positions. Consequently, recruiting is often done only by word of mouth. Only recently have more sophisticated methods—such as structured interviews, testing or work samples—been used on a limited basis. More systematic selection is becoming necessary in Russia and many of the former Soviet-bloc countries as younger, more highly educated candidates are being needed by international firms.[21]

Deciding on the mix of local employees, employees from the home country, and even people from third countries that will best meet organizational goals is a challenge.[22] In staffing an overseas operation, cost is a major factor to be considered. The cost of establishing a manager or professional in another country can run as high as $1 million for a three-year job assignment. The actual costs for placing a key manager outside the United States often are twice the manager's annual salary. For instance, if the manager is going to Japan, the costs may be even higher when housing costs, schooling subsidies, and tax equalization payment are calculated. Further, if a manager or professional executive quits an international assignment prematurely or insists on a transfer home, associated costs can equal or exceed the annual salary. "Failure" rates for managers sent to other countries run as high as 45%.[23]

# The Female Factor

Even though slightly more than half of the world population is female, in some countries being female presents some special problems in dealing with local males about business issues.

For example, in Pakistan a female pilot for a major international carrier made radio contact with ground control personnel who were so astonished to hear a woman they refused to speak to her. Consequently, the male copilot had to take over the landing. Many American women wonder if they must start all over again overseas after attaining success in the United States. Their bosses often have similar concerns, especially in male-dominated cultures of the Middle East, Latin America, and Asia. The fear is that women will not be taken seriously and therefore are unable to represent the company's interests effectively.

Male chauvinism is still a fact of life in many other countries as well.

For example, in Poland, most of the business persons one will meet are male. In such a male-dominated society, admonishing Polish businessmen for their sexist attitudes, real or perceived, does not help change those attitudes or advance women's business efforts.

The female factor may have its greatest impact in some Islamic countries. The role of women in much of the Islamic world is different from that in the United States, though not uniformly so. For example, in Egypt only 9% of women are in paid employment, and only about 10% of managers are female. In very conservative countries such as Iran and Saudi Arabia, even shaking hands with a woman can cause extreme embarrassment. Just getting into Saudi Arabia is difficult for a woman who is unaccompanied by a husband or close relative, because the government will not issue her a visa. Once in Saudi Arabia, a woman will find that people are segregated

by gender and a woman must be escorted in public. She may not drive, and taxi drivers will not pick up unaccompanied female customers.

Although small mistakes in etiquette are usually forgiven in most countries, some social customs regarding females elicit strong emotional reactions if ignored. For instance, proper dress is very important for women working abroad. Longer skirts and higher necklines are good rules of thumb. In Asia, modest and gentle behavior is the expectation for females. Also, in many places the friendly, open smiles of U.S. women business professionals may be seen as an invitation for a more personal relationship. As a result, U.S. businesswomen should learn that it is best to err on the side of formality when doing business in many countries.[24]

Factors that are most likely to be causes of concern for an employee sent overseas are shown in Figure 4–4. The figure shows that only roughly two-thirds to three-fourths of employees sent to another country are satisfied with the way the top five support needs are being met.

To meet these needs, organizations are outsourcing various functions, citing gains in cost effectiveness, expertise, and efficiency. Several respondents to a survey on the subject suggested that outsourcing certain HR functions to international experts may be a long-term trend.[25]

## Types of International Employees

International employees can be placed in three different classifications.

- An **expatriate** is an employee working in a unit or plant who is not a citizen of the country in which the unit or plant is located but is a citizen of the country in which the organization is headquartered.

**Expatriate**
An employee working in a unit or plant who is not a citizen of the country in which the unit or plant is located, but is a citizen of the country in which the organization is headquartered.

**FIGURE 4–4** *Concerns in International Assignments*

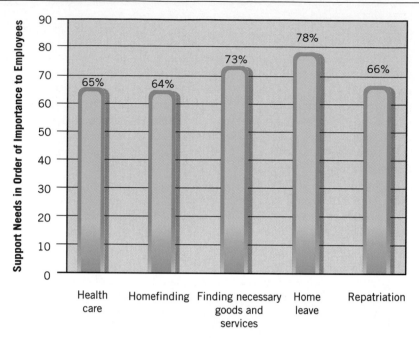

SOURCE: *1997 International Assignee Research Project,* Berlitz International, HFS Mobility Services, SHRM International HR, 1997, 3.

**Host-country national**

An employee working in a unit or plant who is a citizen of the country in which the unit or plant is located, but where the unit or plant is operated by an organization headquartered in another country.

**Third-country national**

An employee who is a citizen of one country, working in a second country, and employed by an organization headquartered in a third country.

- A **host-country national** is an employee working in a unit or plant who is a citizen of the country in which the unit or plant is located, but where the unit or plant is operated by an organization headquartered in another country.
- A **third-country national** is a citizen of one country, working in a second country, and employed by an organization headquartered in a third country.

Each of these individuals presents some unique HR management challenges. Because in a given situation each is a citizen of a different country, different tax laws and other factors apply. HR professionals have to be knowledgeable about the laws and customs of each country. They must establish appropriate payroll and record-keeping procedures, among other activities, to ensure compliance with varying regulations and requirements.

**EXPATRIATES** Many MNEs use expatriates to ensure that foreign operations are linked effectively with the parent corporations. Generally, expatriates also are used to develop international capabilities within an organization. Experienced expatriates can provide a pool of talent that can be tapped as the organization expands its operations more broadly into even more countries. Japanese-owned firms with operations in the United States have rotated Japanese managers through U.S. operations in order to expand the knowledge of U.S. business practices in the Japanese firms.

Several types of expatriates may be differentiated by job assignment, because not all individuals who decide to work as expatriates are similar in the assignments undertaken.

- *Volunteer expatriates:*   These are persons who want to work abroad for a period of time because of career or self-development interests. Often, these expatriates volunteer for shorter-term assignments of less than a year so that they can experience other cultures and travel to desired parts of the world.
- *Traditional expatriates:*   These are professionals and managers assigned to work in foreign operations for one to three years. They then rotate back to the parent corporation in the home country.
- *Career development expatriates:*   These individuals are placed in foreign jobs to develop the international management capabilities of the firm. They may serve one to three "tours" in different countries, so that they can develop a broader understanding of international operations.
- *Global expatriates:*   The broadcast category comprises those individuals who move from one country to another. Often, they prefer to work internationally rather than in the home country.

*BNA 445.30.20-445.30.30*
**Hiring Foreign Nationals**
This section provides an overview of the U.S. Visa requirements for non-U.S. citizens hired by U.S. employers.

American managers are developing a reputation as being somewhat more versatile and adaptable, perhaps because of leading a more diverse workforce at home. Their management education is often very good as well—both from formal business schools and in-house training programs.[26] Whirlpool, GTE, Quaker Oats, and others are using retired American managers to staff hard-to-fill temporary international jobs. They find it is faster and less expensive than relocating a regular expatriate, who would normally expect to stay three years or more.[27]

**HOST-COUNTRY NATIONALS**   Using host-country nationals is important for several reasons. It is important if the organization wants to establish clearly that it is making a commitment to the host country and not just setting up a foreign operation. Host-country nationals often know the culture, politics, laws, and business customs better than an outsider would. Also, tapping into the informal "power" network may be important. In one Southeast Asian country, foreign companies have learned that a firm's problems are resolved more quickly if a family member of that country's president is a consultant to the firm or a member of its management. But U.S. firms must take care that the individuals used actually perform work for the company; the "salary" must not be a disguised bribe paid in order to obtain contracts. Otherwise, the firms could be in violation of the FCPA addressing foreign corrupt practices. Another reason to use host-country nationals is to provide employment in the country. In many lesser-developed countries, compensation levels are significantly lower than in the United States, so U.S. firms can gain cost advantages by using host-country nationals to staff many jobs.

Recruiting the first group of local employees can be a challenge. The initial group helps create a culture for that organization—for better or worse. Yet, the opportunity for serious errors is great. For example, many countries have very different employment laws, which may make it difficult to dismiss an employee. In countries where there is a shortage of qualified candidates, good potential employees may be lost if not approached correctly. To accomplish successful hiring of host-country nationals, many firms form partnerships with local companies to help with hiring.[28]

**THIRD-COUNTRY NATIONALS**   Using third-country nationals emphasizes that a truly global approach is being taken. Often, these individuals are used to handle responsibilities throughout a continent or region. For instance, a major U.S.-based electronics company has its European headquarters in Brussels, Belgium.

While most employees on the clerical staff are Belgians, only about 20% of the professionals and managers are from Belgium. Most of the rest, except for five U.S. expatriates, are from other Western European countries.

It is unusual to find third-country nationals in a new multinational enterprise (MNE). These are usually staffed with qualified nationals and expatriates. Third-country nationals are often first hired when a company has several foreign operations and decides to open another. The choice is often between transferring another expatriate from headquarters or transferring an employee from another overseas operation. Third-country nationals are more common in MNEs with headquarters in North America than in other regions.[29]

**TRANSNATIONAL PROJECT TEAMS**  There has been a dramatic increase in the number and variety of multicultural or "transnational" teams. These teams may be temporary or somewhat permanent and are formed to solve a specific problem or to handle ongoing activities. They often include headquarters representatives, host-country nationals, and third-country nationals. They are useful not only as potentially valuable business units but also as development vehicles for leaders. Eastman Kodak formed a transnational team based in London to launch its photo CD at the same time in several European countries. The team dealt with complex strategic issues across geographic and cultural barriers.[30]

## Selection for International Assignments

The selection process for an international assignment should provide a realistic picture of the life, work, and culture to which the employee may be sent. HR managers should prepare a comprehensive description of the job to be done. This description especially should note responsibilities that would be unusual in the home nation, including negotiating with public officials; interpreting local work codes; and responding to ethical, moral, and personal issues such as religious prohibitions and personal freedoms. Figure 4–5 shows the most frequently cited key competencies for expatriates. Most of these competencies can be categorized as either cultural adaptability or communication skills. The following discussion examines those ideas.

**CULTURAL ADAPTABILITY**  Most staffing "failures" among those placed in foreign assignments occur because of cultural adjustment problems, not because of difficulties with the jobs or inadequate technical skills. Organizational support for the employees is particularly important for successful cultural adjustment. Once employees have been selected for international assignments, continuing organizational support for the employees is crucial. The intention of expatriates to quit and their commitment to their organizations are affected by how they view the support given to them by their employers.

Throughout the selection process, especially in the selection interviews, it is crucial to assess the potential employee's ability to accept and adapt to different customs, management practices, laws, religious values, and infrastructure conditions. For example, in Nigeria the local telephone system is so inefficient that overseas calls can be made more easily than crosstown calls, especially in Lagos, the capital city. A U.S. citizen who is accustomed to the convenience and reliability of the U.S. telephone system may become impatient and angry when confronted with such delays.

**FIGURE 4–5** *Global Skills and Competencies for Successful Expatriates*

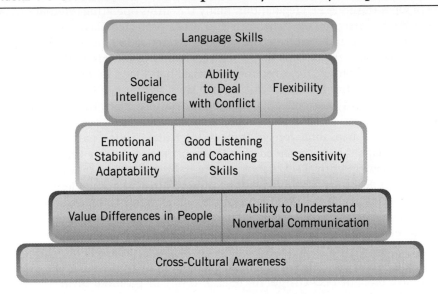

SOURCE: Adapted from Michael L. Wheeler, "Global Diversity," *Business Week,* December 1, 1997, 37.

**COMMUNICATION SKILLS** One of the most basic skills needed by expatriate employees is the ability to communicate orally and in writing in the host-country language. Inability to communicate adequately in the language may significantly inhibit the success of an expatriate. Numerous firms with international operations select individuals based on their technical and managerial capabilities and then have the selected individuals take foreign language training. Intensive 10-day courses offered by Berlitz and other schools teach basic foreign language skills.

But in any language there is more to communication than simply vocabulary. Greetings, gestures, pace, and proximity all are different in various countries.[31] Basic values about other people and interacting with them are at least as important as speaking the language.

**FAMILY FACTORS** The preferences and attitudes of spouses and other family members also are major staffing considerations. Two of the most common reasons for turning down international assignments are family considerations and spouses' careers.[32] Nearly three-fourths of expatriates are married, and most are male. Of the expatriates who are married, only about 13% are not accompanied on overseas assignments by their spouse.[33]

With the growth in dual-career couples, the difficulty of transferring international employees is likely to increase, particularly given work-permit restrictions common in many countries. Some international firms have begun career services to assist spouses in getting jobs with other international firms.

**EQUAL EMPLOYMENT OPPORTUNITY (EEO) CONCERNS** The assignment of women and members of racial/ethnic minorities to international posts involves legal issues, because these individuals may be protected by U.S. Equal Employment Opportunity (EEO) regulations. Many U.S. firms operating internationally have limited assignments of women and other protected-class individuals in deference to cultural concerns. The Civil Rights Act of 1991 extended coverage of EEO laws and regulations to U.S. citizens working internationally for U.S.-controlled companies. However, the act states that if laws in a foreign country require actions that conflict with U.S. EEO laws, the foreign laws will apply. If no laws exist, only customs or cultural considerations, then the U.S. EEO laws will apply.

In a related area, some foreign firms in the United States, particularly those owned by Japan, have "reserved" top-level positions for those from the home country. Consequently, EEO charges have been brought against these firms. Previous court decisions have ruled that because of a treaty between Japan and the United States, Japanese subsidiaries can give preference to Japanese over U.S. citizens.

However, it should be noted that most other EEO regulations and laws do apply to foreign-owned firms. In a closely related area, women have brought sexual harassment charges against foreign managers, and other protected-class individuals have brought EEO charges for refusal to hire or promote them.[34] In those cases, courts have treated the foreign-owned firms just as they would U.S.-owned employers.

# International Training and Development

Just as in any organization—global in scope or not—training and development are key factors for HR success. For the global firm these activities are just as important, but for incoming expatriates, host-country nationals, and third-country nationals, training and development is crucial. The training needs of a German expatriate assigned to the United States for the first time might be very different than the needs of an employee working for the company as a factory assembler in Mexico, but both need training to be effective.[35] For example, when companies first began to put down roots in Mexico on the U.S./Mexican border, there was little incentive to train employees who were seen simply as a source of cheap labor. But employee turnover rates ran over 20% a month in many places, and employers found that the gains in labor costs were offset with shoddy quality. Training quickly became an important part of turning the HR catastrophe around. Greatly improved productivity has resulted from programs of continuous training, skills improvement, vocational training, and employees training other employees.[36]

Figure 4–6 shows three different kinds of training and development activities for global employees. Not all apply to every type of international employee, but all are important.

## Pre-Departure Orientation and Training

The orientation and training that expatriates and their families receive before departure have a major impact on the success of the overseas assignment. Three areas affect the cross-cultural adjustment process: (a) work adjustment, (b) interaction adjustment, and (c) general adjustment. Permeating all of those

**FIGURE 4–6** *International Training and Development*

areas is the need for training in foreign language and culture familiarization. Many firms have formal training programs for expatriates and their families, and this training has been found to have a positive effect on cross-cultural adjustment.[38]

Individuals selected to work outside the United States for MNEs need answers to many specific questions about their host countries. Such areas as political and historical forces, geographic and climatic conditions, and general living conditions are topics frequently covered in the orientation and training sessions on the culture of the host country. Expatriates and their families also must receive detailed, country-specific training on customs in the host country. Such knowledge will greatly ease their way in dealing with host-country counterparts. Training in such customs and practices also should be part of the training programs for individuals who will not live outside the home country but will travel to other countries for business purposes.

A related issue is the promotion and transfer of foreign citizens to positions in the United States. As more global organizations start or expand U.S. operations, more cross-cultural training will be necessary for international employees relocated to the United States. For example, many Japanese firms operating in the United States have training programs to prepare Japanese for the food, customs, and other practices of U.S. life. The acceptance of a foreign boss by U.S. workers is another concern. These issues point to the importance of training and development for international adjustment.

Once global employees arrive in the host country, they will need assistance in "settling in." Arrangements should be made for someone to meet them and assist them. Obtaining housing, establishing bank accounts, obtaining driver's licenses, arranging for admissions to schools for dependent children, and establishing a medical provider relationship are all basics when relocating to a new city, internationally or not. But differences in culture, language, and laws may complicate these activities in a foreign country. The sooner the expatriates and their families can establish a "normal" life, the better the adjustment will be, and the less likely that expatriate failure will occur.

## Continuing Employee Training/Development

Career planning and continued involvement of expatriates in corporate employee development activities are essential. One of the greatest deterrents to accepting foreign assignments is employees' concern that they will be "out of sight, out of mind." If they do not have direct and regular contact with others at the corporate headquarters, many expatriates experience anxiety about their continued career progression. Therefore, the international experiences of expatriates must be seen as beneficial to the employer and to the expatriate's career.[37]

One way to overcome problems in this area is for firms to invite the expatriates back for regular interaction and development programs with other company managers and professionals. Another useful approach is to establish a mentoring system. In this system, an expatriate is matched with a corporate executive in the headquarters. This executive talks with the expatriate frequently, ensures that the expatriate's name is submitted during promotion and development discussions at the headquarters, and resolves any headquarters-based problems experienced by the expatriate.[39]

Opportunities for continuing education represent another way for international employees to continue their development. In some of the more developed European countries, foreign executives and professionals may enroll in Master of Business Administration (MBA) programs at well-respected universities. By obtaining an MBA while on the international assignment, the expatriate keeps up with those with similar jobs in the home country who pursue advanced degrees while working full time.

## Repatriation Training and Development

**Repatriation**
The process of bringing expatriates home.

The process of bringing expatriates home is called **repatriation.** Some major difficulties can arise when it is time to bring expatriates home. For example, the special compensation packages often available to expatriates are dropped, which means that the expatriates experience a net decrease in total income, even if they receive promotions and pay increases. In addition to concerns about personal finances, repatriated employees must readjust to a closer working and reporting relationship with other corporate employees. Often, expatriates have a greater degree of flexibility, autonomy, and independent decision making than do their counterparts in the United States.

Expatriates often must also be reacclimatized to U.S. lifestyles, transportation services, and other cultural practices, especially if they have been living in less-developed countries.[40] For example, the wife of a U.S. expatriate was accustomed to bargaining for lower prices when she shopped in the foreign country. During the first week after her return to the United States, she tried to bargain with the checkout cashier at a supermarket before she realized that she was back in a place where this practice was not normal.

# International Compensation

Organizations with employees in many different countries face some special compensation pressures. Variations in laws, living costs, tax policies, and other factors all must be considered in establishing the compensation for expatriate managers and professionals. Even fluctuations in the value of the U.S. dollar must be tracked and adjustments made as the dollar rises or falls in relation to currency rates in other countries. Add to all of these concerns the need to compensate employees for the costs of housing, schooling of children, and yearly transportation home for themselves and their family members. When all these different issues are considered, it is evident that international compensation is extremely complex. Typical components of an international compensation package for expatriates are shown in Figure 4–7. Several approaches to international compensation are discussed next.

## Balance-Sheet Approach

Many multinational firms have compensation programs that use the balance-sheet approach. The **balance-sheet approach** provides international employees with a compensation package that equalizes cost differences between the international assignment and the same assignment in the home country of the individual or the corporation. The balance-sheet approach is based on some key assumptions, which are discussed next.[41]

**HOME-COUNTRY REFERENCE POINT** The compensation package is developed to keep global employees at a level appropriate to their jobs in relation to similar jobs in the home country. Special benefits or allowances are provided to allow the global employees to maintain a standard of living at least equivalent to what they would have in the home country.

**Balance-sheet approach**
An approach to international compensation that provides international employees with a compensation package that equalizes cost differences between the international assignment and the same assignment in the home country of the individual or the corporation.

**FIGURE 4–7** *Typical Expatriate Compensation Components*

**Tax equalization plan**
Compensation plan used to protect expatriates from negative tax consequences.

**LIMITED DURATION OF GLOBAL ASSIGNMENT** Another basic premise of the balance-sheet approach is that expatriate employees generally have international assignments lasting two to three years. The international compensation package is designed to keep the expatriates "whole" for a few years until they can be reintegrated into the home-country compensation program. Thus, the "temporary" compensation package for the international assignment must be structured to make it easy for the repatriated employee to reenter the domestic compensation and benefits programs. Also, it is assumed that the international employee will retire in the home country, so pension and other retirement benefits will be home-country-based.

## Global Market Approach

Increasingly, global organizations have recognized that attracting, retaining, and motivating managers with global capabilities requires taking a broader perspective than just sending expatriates overseas. As mentioned earlier, in many large multinational enterprises, key executives have worked in several countries and may be of many different nationalities. These executives are moved from one part of the world to another and to corporate headquarters wherever the firms are based. It appears that there is a high demand for these global managers, and they almost form their own "global market" for compensation purposes.

Unlike the balance-sheet approach, a global market approach to compensation requires that the international assignment be viewed as continual, not just temporary, though the assignment may take the employee to different countries for differing lengths of time. This approach is much more comprehensive in that the core components, such as insurance benefits and relocation expenses, are present regardless of the country to which the employee is assigned. But pegging the appropriate pay level, considering rates in the host country, home country, and/or headquarters country, becomes more complex. Further, the acceptability of distributing compensation unequally based on performance varies from country to country.[42] Therefore, global compensation requires greater flexibility, more detailed analyses, and greater administrative effort. Some factors affecting executive compensation include the "cultural distance" from headquarters and how much responsibility and autonomy the subsidiary incurs.

## Tax Concerns

Many international compensation plans attempt to protect expatriates from negative tax consequences by using a **tax equalization plan.** Under this plan, the company adjusts an employee's base income downward by the amount of estimated U.S. tax to be paid for the year. Thus, the employee pays only the foreign-country tax. The intent of the tax equalization plan is to ensure that expatriates will not pay any more or less in taxes than if they had stayed in the United States.

# Global Employee Relations Issues

Several issues related to employee relations are often concerns in international situations. *Health and safety issues* may be of concern to employees overseas, and *security* has become a very difficult issue in certain areas of the world. The nature of *labor unions* and labor laws can be an important variable for managers from other countries when dealing with host-country national employees. Finally, *maintaining the expatriate employee* in an international position given the potential difficulties deserves attention.

## Global Health and Safety

Safety and health laws and regulations vary from country to country, ranging from virtually nonexistent to more stringent than in the United States. The importance placed on workplace safety varies among different countries.

With more and more expatriates working internationally, especially in some of the less-developed countries, significant health and safety issues are arising, and addressing these issues is part of the HR role.[43] For instance, in many parts of the former Soviet Union, medical facilities are more primitive, treatment is not as available, and pharmaceuticals are less easily obtained. U.S. expatriates traveling to such countries as Turkmenistan and Tajikistan commonly take antibiotics, other medications, and syringes and needles with them in case they need them. Similar practices are recommended for those traveling or working in some African and lesser-developed Asian countries, including China.

Another consideration is provision of emergency evacuation services. For instance, how to evacuate and care for an expatriate employee who sustains internal injuries in a car accident in the Ukraine or Sierra Leone may be a major issue. Many global firms purchase coverage for their international employees from an organization that provides emergency services, such as International SOS, Global Assistance Network, or U.S. Assist. To use such a service, an employer pays a membership fee per employee, and all employee travelers are given emergency contact numbers. If an emergency arises, the emergency services company will dispatch physicians or even transport employees by chartered aircraft. If adequate medical assistance can be obtained locally, the emergency services company maintains a referral list and will make arrangements for the expatriate to receive treatment. Legal counsel in foreign countries, emergency cash for medical expenses, and assistance in retrieving lost documents or having them reissued also are provided by emergency services firms.

## International Security and Terrorism

As more U.S. firms operate internationally, the threat of terrorist actions against those firms and the employees working for them increases. U.S. citizens are especially vulnerable to extortions, kidnapping, bombing, physical harassment, and other terrorist activities. In a three-month period in a recent year, several hundred terrorist acts were aimed at businesses and businesspeople. Many of these acts targeted company facilities and offices. Nevertheless, individual employees and their families living abroad must constantly be aware of security issues.[44]

Countries vary in the extent to which they are likely to see violence at the workplace. Figure 4–8 shows the share of workers reporting violence on the job in different countries.

It should be noted, of course, that not all violence occurs at work. Kidnapping, murder, home invasion, robberies, and car-jackings are relatively frequent in some places.[45] People who appear affluent are targets, and in some countries a person can appear ostentatiously wealthy simply by wearing eyeglasses.[46] Many firms provide bodyguards who escort executives everywhere. Different routes of

*LOGGING ON . . .*
**Travel Advisories**
U.S. State Department Warnings and Consider Advisory Sheets are distributed by St. Olaf College (Minnesota) of all countries at

**http://www.stolaf.edu/ network/travelisories.html**

**FIGURE 4–8** *Violence at Work Globally*

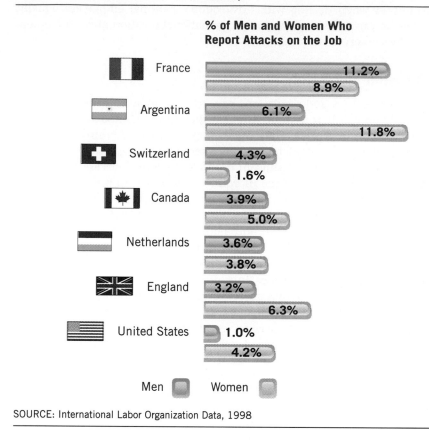

% of Men and Women Who Report Attacks on the Job

France — 11.2% / 8.9%
Argentina — 6.1% / 11.8%
Switzerland — 4.3% / 1.6%
Canada — 3.9% / 5.0%
Netherlands — 3.6% / 3.8%
England — 3.2% / 6.3%
United States — 1.0% / 4.2%

Men ☐ Women ☐

SOURCE: International Labor Organization Data, 1998

travel are used, so that "normal" patterns of movement are difficult for terrorists to identify. Family members of employees also receive training in security. Children are told to avoid wearing sweatshirts with U.S. logos and to be discreet when meeting friends. In a number of countries schools for children of U.S. expatriates have instituted tight security measures, including sign-in procedures for visitors, guards for the grounds, and improved security fences and surveillance equipment.[47]

Firms themselves are taking other actions. For example, one U.S. firm removed its large signs from facilities in a Latin American country. Removal of signs identifying offices and facilities reduces the visibility of the firm and thus reduces its potential as a target for terrorist acts. Many international firms screen entry by all employees, and many use metal detectors to scan all packages, briefcases, and other items. Physical barriers, such as iron security fences, concrete barricades, bulletproof glass, and electronic surveillance devices, are common in offices.

## Global Labor-Management Relations

The strength and nature of unions different from country to country. In some countries, unions either do not exist at all or are relatively weak. Such is the case in China and a number of African countries. In other countries, unions are extremely strong and are closely tied to political parties.[48] This is the case in

# Research on Expatriate Withdrawal from International Assignments

Margaret Shaffer and David Harrison conducted research using a sample of over 600 expatriates living in 45 countries to determine reasons behind their decisions to quit their international assignments. Using their research, as reported in *Personnel Psychology*, the authors of the study built a model to predict turnover among expatriates.

The picture that emerged from the research was consistent with what turnover research in the United States has found: Work-related factors of *job satisfaction* and *organiza-*

*tional commitment* were significant predictors of expatriate withdrawal. The researchers also found that factors including non-work satisfaction and several family variables—spouse adjustment, spouse satisfaction, and living conditions—were important.

The researchers concluded that international Human Resources management efforts must address *non-work factors*, including those associated with the foreign environment and with the expatriate's family, in order to reduce turnover of

expatriates. They also concluded that family issues have a strong impact on satisfaction and adjustment throughout the entire duration of the overseas assignment, and expatriate retention can be improved by initiating HR management strategies that focus on them. Additionally, researchers identified listing of family-related practices that international employers should consider using.[49]

---

some European countries. In still other countries, such as the United States and Great Britain, unions have declined in influence and membership during the last decade.

Some countries require that firms have union or worker representatives on their boards of directors. This practice is very common in European countries, where it is called **co-determination.** But signs of change in Europe are beginning to emerge.[50] Predictions are that in the next decade unions will have less power in Europe as competition worldwide forces change.[51] However, union militancy is increasing in some lesser-developed countries, such as Brazil, Mexico, Poland, and Romania.

Differences from country to country in how collective bargaining occurs also are quite noticeable. In the United States, local unions bargain with individual employers to set wages and working conditions. In Australia, unions argue their cases before arbitration tribunals. In Scandinavia, national agreements with associations of employers are the norm. In France and Germany, industry-wide or region-wide agreements are common. In Japan, local unions do the bargaining but combine at some point to determine national wage patterns. In spite of these differences, unions appear to have somewhat similar effects internationally in most situations regarding employment and provision of benefits.

**Co-determination**
A practice whereby union or worker representatives are given positions on a company's board of directors.

## Maintaining the Expatriate Employee

Problems associated with expatriate assignments have been noted throughout the chapter. Some interesting research on expatriates' psychological withdrawal from international assignments is reflected in the HR Perspective. Those problems are well-documented but not always dealt with very well by employers who need to send employees overseas. Yet, international strategies are threatened with ineffectiveness when those who are offered such international assignments refuse them or take them unwillingly.

Whether the problem is with the family, salaries, loss of visibility in the company, living conditions, danger, or whatever, the loss of good employees with international experience is a big issue for some organizations. For example, one executive noted that after spending three years of hard work overseas—generating millions of dollars in profit for the company—when it was time to come home, suddenly his supervisors were saying, "Where will we send him?" "What will he do?" "What will we pay him?" "Why won't he stay overseas?" Another notes that when his three years were over and he needed to come back to the United States because of his children's ages, his superiors quickly turned the discussion toward another three years abroad. In the end he became discouraged and gave up 18 years with the company to move to another firm in the United States.[52]

Behind the hype and the horror stories, there is one valid generalization about foreign assignments: They can pay professional and personal dividends, but they carry some real risks.[53] The organizations that help their expatriates deal with the risks—and choose the right people for those very challenging assignments—ultimately share in the benefits with their successful employees.

# Summary

- International HR activities must be adapted to reflect what is appropriate in different countries.
- Global HR management is most influenced by legal, political, economic, and cultural factors.
- Culture is composed of the societal forces affecting the values, beliefs, and actions of a distinct group of people.
- One scheme for classifying national cultures considers power distance, individualism, masculinity/femininity, uncertainty avoidance, and long-term orientation.
- Organizations doing business internationally may evolve from organizations engaged in importing and exporting activities, to multinational enterprises, to global organizations.
- Staffing international jobs can be costly, and selection criteria must include a wide range of skills,

abilities, and family factors in addition to the required business knowledge and experience.
- Training and development activities for international employees focus on pre-departure orientation and training, continued employee development, and readjustment training for repatriates.
- Compensation practices for international employees are much more complex than those for domestic employees, because many more factors must be considered.
- Global organizations must be concerned about the health, safety, and security of their employees.
- Labor-management relations vary from country to country.

# Review and Discussion Questions

1. Discuss the following statement: "Shifts in the types of jobs and the industries in which jobs are gained or lost reflect global competition and other economic shifts that are occurring in the United States."
2. Select a country and identify how you believe it would stand on Hofstede's five dimensions of culture.
3. What are some advantages and disadvantages associated with using expatriate managers instead of host-country nationals?

4. Assume you have been asked to consider a job in a foreign country with a U.S.-based corporation. Develop a list of questions and issues that the corporation should address with you before you make your decision.
5. Assuming you accepted a foreign job, what should the content of the pre-departure training be for you and your family?

6. Discuss the following statement: Global compensation packages should keep expatriates even with what they would receive at home, but not allow them to get rich.
7. Suppose an expatriate employee is to work in Bulgaria for two years. What health, safety, and security issues should be addressed?

## Terms to Know

balance-sheet approach   129
co-determination   133
culture   116
expatriate   121
global organization   119
host-country national   122

importing and exporting   118
individualism   116
long-term orientation   117
masculinity/femininity   116
multinational enterprise (MNE)
   119

power distance   116
repatriation   128
tax equalization plan   130
third-country national   122
uncertainty avoidance   116

# Using the Internet

## Training Your Workforce for Global Business Negotiations

With the globalization of the marketplace, your company has decided to explore some international business opportunities. They have informed you, the HR manager, that they are sending a team to Colombia to negotiate a business agreement. It is your responsibility to train the team on some of the customs and negotiating tactics that are acceptable in Colombia. Use the website **http://www.getcustoms.com** to obtain the information. Access the passport database, choose Colombia, and go to Colombia's business practices. Then identify five negotiating tactics to share with the team.

## CASE

## McDonald's Global HR

One of the best-known companies worldwide is McDonald's Corporation. The fast-food chain, with its symbol of the golden arches, has spread from the United States into 91 countries. With over 18,000 restaurants worldwide, McDonald's serves 33 million people each day. International sales are an important part of McDonald's business, and over 50% of the company's operating income results from sales outside the United States. To generate these sales, McDonald's employs over one million people, and by 2000, McDonald's had grown to over two million employees.

Operating in so many different countries means that McDonald's has had to adapt its products, services, and HR practices to legal, political, economic, and cultural factors in each one of those countries. A few examples illustrate how adaptations have been made. In some countries, such as India, beef is not acceptable as a food to a major part of the population, so McDonald's uses lamb or mutton. To appeal to

Japanese customers, McDonald's has developed teriyaki burgers. Separate dining rooms for men and women have been constructed in McDonald's restaurants in some Middle Eastern countries.

HR practices also have had to be adapted. Before beginning operations in a different country, HR professionals at McDonald's research the country and determine how HR activities must be adjusted. One method of obtaining information is to contact HR professionals from other U.S. firms operating in the country and ask them questions about laws, political factors, and cultural issues. In addition, the firm conducts an analysis using a detailed outline to ensure that all relevant information has been gathered. Data gathered might include what employment restrictions exist on ages of employees and hours of work, what benefits must be offered to full-time and part-time employees (if part-time work is allowed), and other operational requirements. For instance, in some of the former communist countries in Eastern Europe, employers provide locker rooms and showers for their employees. These facilities are necessary because shower facilities, and even consistent water supplies, are unavailable in many homes, particularly in more rural areas around major cities. Also, public transportation must be evaluated to ensure that employees have adequate means to travel to work.

Once a decision has been made to begin operations in a new country, the employment process must begin. Often, McDonald's is seen as a desirable employer, particularly when its first restaurant is being opened in a country. For instance, in Russia, 27,000 people initially applied to work at the first Moscow McDonald's, which currently has over 1,500 employees. Because customer service is so important to McDonald's, recruiting and selection activities focus on obtaining employees with customer service skills. For worker positions such as counter representative

and cashier, the focus is to identify individuals who will be friendly, customer-service-oriented employees. A "trial" process whereby some applicants work for a few days on a conditional basis may be used to ensure that these individuals will represent McDonald's appropriately and will work well with other employees.

For store managers, the company uses a selection profile emphasizing leadership skills, high work expectations, and management abilities appropriate to a fast-paced restaurant environment. Once applicant screening and interviews have been completed, individuals are asked to work for up to a week in a restaurant. During that time, both the applicants and the company representatives evaluate one another to see if the job "fit" is appropriate. After the first group of store managers and assistant managers are selected, future managers and assistant managers are chosen using internal promotions based on job performance.

Once the restaurants are staffed, training becomes crucial to acquaint new employees with their jobs and the McDonald's philosophy of customer service and quality. McDonald's has taken its Hamburger University curriculum from the United States and translated it into 22 different languages to use in training centers throughout the world. Once training has been done for trainers and managers, they then conduct training for all employees selected to work at McDonald's locations in the foreign countries.[54]

## Questions

1. Identify cultural factors that might be important in a training program for food handlers at McDonald's in Saudi Arabia.
2. Rather than focusing on the differences, what similarities do you expect exist among McDonald's customers and employees in both the United States and abroad?

# Notes

1. Based on information provided by Linda Paulmeno, Director of Communications, Mercedes-Benz U.S. at Alabama Business Conference, January 1999; David Stamps, "Mercedes-Benz Sows a Learning Field," *Training*, June 1997, 27; and Bill Vlasic, "In Alabama, the Soul of a New Mercedes?" *Business Week*, March 31, 1997, 70.
2. Patricia Kranz, "A New Breed of Blue Chips," *Business Week*, July 7, 1997, 52–95.
3. William G. Sanders and Mason A. Carpenter, "Internationalization and Firm Governance," *Academy of Management Journal* 41 (1998), 158.
4. Jeffrey Garken, "Why the Global Economy Is Here to Stay," *Business Week*, March 23, 1998, 21.
5. "A Survey of Business in Latin America," *The Economist*, December 6, 1997 (special section P1–26).
6. "Pay as You Learn," *The Economist*, May 10, 1997, 32.
7. "Employment Trends," *Manpower Argus*, June 1998, 1–11.
8. Maurreen Minehan, "New Research Shows Investment in People Outperforms Investment in Technology," *Worldlink*, July 1998, 1.

9. Kathy Chen, "Endurance Test," *The Wall Street Journal*, April 30, 1998, R14.

10. Skip Kaltenheuser, "A Little Dab Will Do You?", *World Trade*, January 1999, 58–62; "Portrait of a Changing Europe," *Business Week*, April 27, 1998, 92; "OECD Employment Outlook," *Financial Times*, June 23, 1998, 7; "Can Europe Get Back to Work," *The Economist*, August 8, 1998, 61; "Europe Hits a Brick Wall," *The Economist*, April 5, 1997, 21; and Carl Edmondson, "A Continent at the Breaking Point," *Business Week*, February 24, 1997, 50.

11. Based on information in Geert Hofstede, "Business Cultures," *The UNESCO Courier*, April 1994, 12–17; and Geert Hofstede, "Cultural Constraints in Management Theories," *Academy of Management Executive*, February 1993, 81–94.

12. Andrea Charman, "Going Global? What about Your Cultural Strategy," *Purchasing Today*, September 1998, 43–45.

13. Charlene Marmer Solomon, "Brace for Change," *Global Workforce*, January 1999, 6–10.

14. Tatiana Kostova and Srilata Zaheer, "Organizational Legitimacy Under Conditions of Complexity: The Case of Multinational Enterprises," *Academy of Management Review* 24 (1999), 64–81; and Ruth Thaler-Carter, "Portrait of an International Human Resources Professional," *International HR Update*, December 1997, 1.

15. Allan Bird, Sully Taylor, and Schon Beechler, "A Typology of International Human Resources Management in Japanese Multinational Corporations: Organizational Implications," *Human Resource Management*, Summer 1998, 159–172.

16. Alfred J. Walker, "The Global HR Model," *HR Focus*, April 1998, S9–S11.

17. Hal Lancaster, "Learning to Manage in a Global Workplace," *The Wall Street Journal*, June 2, 1998, B1.

18. David Molnar and G. Michael Lowe, "Seven Keys to International Management," *HR Focus*, May 1997, 11; and John Fadel and Mark Petti, "International HR Policies," *Workforce*, April 1997, 529.

19. "China and the Chaebol," *The Economist*, December 20, 1997, 97.

20. Richard Gesteland, "Do's and Taboos," *The Rotarian*, April 1998, 26–29.

21. Donald M. Bostwick, "Human Resource Management Practices in Post-Soviet Russia," *International Focus* (SHRM), 1998, 2.

22. Shari Caudron, "World Class Executives," *Industry Week*, December 1, 1997, 60.

23. Victoria Griffith, "Move Me, Move My Spouse," *Financial Times*, April 28, 1997, 16.

24. Based on Helen Trickett, "Covering New Ground," *Business Traveler*, April 1997, 33; and Shelda Hodge, "The Female Factor," *Purchasing Today*, July 1997, 38–39.

25. Windham International, *1996 Survey on HR Program Outsourcing* (New York: Windham International, 1996), 25–26.

26. Del Jones, "Versatility, Training Give Edge to Americans Abroad," *USA Today*, January 26, 1997, 1B.

27. Jo Ann S. Lublin, "Companies Send Intrepid Retirees to Work Abroad," *The Wall Street Journal*, March 2, 1998, B1.

28. Valerie Frazee, "How to Hire Locally," *Global Workforce*, July 1998, 19.

29. Calvin Reynolds, "Strategic Employment of Third-Country Nationals," *Human Resource Planning*, March 1998, 33.

30. Paul Iles and P.K. Hayers, "Managing Diversity in Transnational Project Teams," *Journal of Managerial Psychology* 12, (1998), 95.

31. T. Russell Walker, "Where the Rubber Meets the Road," *Global Workforce*, January 1999, 14–15.

32. Julie Cook, "Lending an Ear," *Human Resource Executive*, February 1999, 54–56.

33. *Global Relocation Trends* (New York: Windham International, 1997), 9.

34. Pepi Sappal, "Sometimes It's Hard to Be a Woman," *HR World*, January/February 1999, 21–24.

35. Charlene Solomon, "Destination USA," *Workforce*, April 1997, S18.

36. Joel Millman, "High Tech Jobs Transfer to Mexico with Surprising Speed," *The Wall Street Journal*, April 9, 1998, A18.

37. "Focus: Global Training," *BNA Workforce Strategies*, November 24, 1997, WS63–66.

38. Valerie Frazee, "Send Your Expats Prepared for Success," *Global Workforce*, March 1999, 6–8.

39. Widget Finn, "Someone to Watch Over You," *HR World*, January/February 1999, 27–29.

40. Reyer Swaak, "Repatriation: A Weak Link in Global HR," *HR Focus*, April 1997, 29.

41. Valerie Frazee, "Is the Balance Sheet Right for your Expatriates?", *Global Workforce*, September 1998, 19.

42. May Mukuda, "Moving Toward Globalization," *ACA Journal* (Winter 1997), 57.

43. Thomas H. Valk, "Global EAPs Help Expatriates Succeed," *SHRM/AOOP Working Mind Series*, April 1998, 1.

44. Julie Cook, "Spanning the Globe," *Human Resource Executive*, June 5, 1998, 57.

45. Samuel Greengard, "Mission Possible: Protecting Employees Abroad," *Workforce*, August 1997, 30.

46. Vanessa Houlder, "Your Money or Your Life," *Financial Times*, June 30, 1998, 12.

47. Lori Lincoln, "Wanted: American Money," *Business Traveler*, April 1997, 17.

48. Michael Schuman, "Korean Unions Step Up Fight on Layoffs," *The Wall Street Journal*, February 11, 1998, A18.

49. Margaret Schaffer and David Harrison, "Expatriates' Psychological Withdrawal from International Assignments," *Personnel Psychology* (1998), 87.

50. Helene Cooper and Tom Kamm, "Loosening Up," *The Wall Street Journal*, June 4, 1998, A1.

51. William Erikson, "Workplace Earthquake?", *Business Week*, April 17, 1998, 106.

52. Cynthia Kemper, "Glamor of Overseas Work Fades with 'Ex Pat' Stigma," *Denver Post*, September 7, 1997, E6.

53. John S. McClenahen, "To Go or Not To Go?", *Industry Week*, January 20, 1997, 33.

54. Adapted from Robert Grossman, "HR in Asia," *HR Magazine*, July 1997, 104; and Charlene M. Solomon, "Big Mac's McGlobal HR Secrets," *Personnel Journal* (April 1996), 47–54.

# SECTION 2
# Staffing the Organization

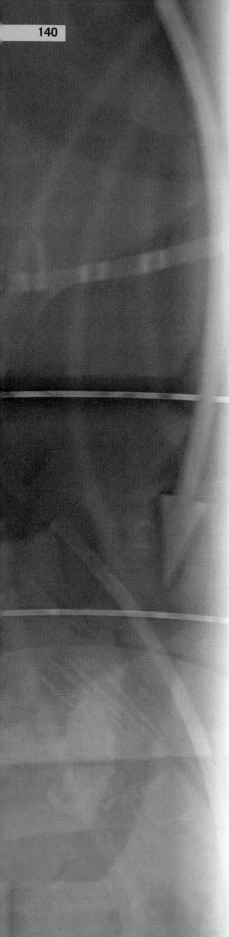

# CHAPTER 5
# Diversity and Equal Employment Opportunity

*After you have read this chapter, you should be able to:*

- Define *diversity management,* and discuss what it encompasses.

- Differentiate among diversity management, equal employment opportunity (EEO), and affirmative action.

- Discuss several arguments supporting and opposing affirmative action.

- Explain how to identify when illegal discrimination occurs, and define five basic EEO concepts.

- Discuss the key provisions of the Civil Rights Act of 1964, Title VII, and the Civil Rights Act of 1991.

- Discuss the two general approaches that can be used to comply with the 1978 Uniform Guidelines on Employee Selection Procedures.

- Define *validity* and *reliability,* and explain three approaches to validating employment requirements.

# Diversity and Law Enforcement

Law enforcement takes place in many venues and with all citizens regardless of background. Yet law enforcement officers as a group do not reflect the diversity of the citizenry. For years, police work was seen mostly as men's work—and white men filled most officer's jobs. Increasingly it has become clear that having a more diverse group of law enforcement officers has some real advantages, yet making the transition to that more diverse workforce has presented some challenges.

Recently, a suspect was handcuffed in front of his three young children and became agitated, demanding an apology. The male deputy who handcuffed him was not in the mood for debate, and the atmosphere grew very tense. Fifteen-year police veteran Cheryl Peck stepped in and calmly pointed out, "Look, we don't know you. We don't know what your intentions are." Peck's words and female presence evidently reduced tensions. The results were the same—the suspect was taken into custody—but the circumstances were different (and less threatening) thanks to the female officer's presence.

Local law enforcement agencies began hiring women in the early 1970s. They still employ fewer women than men, but the number of women is growing. A survey of 800 police departments throughout the United States found that about 12% of nearly 600,000 officers are female.

Early on, some female officers noted an "overprotective" attitude on the part of their male colleagues. Other observers have noted that departments are much more professional with a mix of male and female officers.

"Some of the guys could get pretty raunchy—with women there they had to

quit. But that is the way it should be," Peck notes. Further, a shift to community policing requires that officers reflect the makeup of the community, and that in turn requires adding more women officers. Additionally, a number of law enforcement officials believe women possess superior interpersonal skills and want to recruit more.

But despite the benefits, changing the diversity mix of law enforcement agencies reflects the same challenges of doing so in other sectors of U.S. industry. One controversy focuses on the tests required to become officers. About 83% of law enforcement departments require applicants to pass a test on reading, writing, and

*It has become clear that having a more diverse group of law enforcement officers has some real advantages.*

reasoning—the so-called cognitive skills. Because the Federal Department of Justice was concerned that cognitive tests keep out more racial minority applicants than whites, it designed a new police exam that focuses on personality variables instead. The only remaining cognitive section was a reading test. To pass, applicants had to score only as well as the bottom 1% of current officers. Many argued that the test was "watered down." They pointed out that if police forces cannot test for intellectual skills, they will end up with recruits who cannot learn, write crime reports, or do well in court when confronted by defense lawyers.

Whether or not the test is a valid one for recruiting good police officers, other controversies have surfaced

around its use. For example, in Suffolk County, New York, where African Americans make up 4.8% of the county and Hispanic Americans 6.6%, their representation on the police force was only 2.2% and 4.6% respectively. The county devised a plan to improve those numbers, under pressure from the U.S. Justice Department. Forty-three new African American and Hispanic American cadets were assured officer's jobs if they earned junior college criminal justice degrees and passed an entrance exam. While completing their degrees, these promising applicants worked part-time as unpaid police clerks. Most also enrolled in a prep course designed to

help them with the exam. In the course the instructor offered test questions and some "preferred answers" on the test. Consequently, all of the candidates passed the test. However, controversy flared about "cheating," fairness, and reverse discrimination. Further, the New York supreme court ruled that Suffolk County did not explore sufficient alternatives before recruiting on the basis of skin color. The candidates, caught in the middle, felt they were being penalized because the county had devised a faulty program.

Even with its advantages, diversity is sometimes controversial and difficult to achieve. The Police Commissioner in Suffolk County says that he wants more diversity, but admits "I'm not sure how we get there."[1]

> 66 *The notion that diversity had a business imperative and gave us a strategic advantage came later.* 99
>
> JOHN BRYAN

Differences among people at work are both a managerial plus and minus. It has been clear for many years from classic studies done in social psychology that groups made up of very different people are more creative and more able to see all sides of an issue. But groups often do not choose to be diverse in makeup, and do not always get along as well as groups made up of more similar members.

People have many dimensions—age, gender, race, color, and religion are only a few. The concept of **diversity** recognizes the differences among people.

**Diversity**
Differences among people.

# The Nature of Diversity

The existence of diversity is apparent in most organizations. As suggested in a number of studies, diversity has both positive and negative consequences. On the positive side, it provides organizations opportunities to tap a broader, more diverse set of people, ideas, and experiences. Diversity is particularly valuable in a business organization because it often reflects the diversity of customers and the marketplace. By capitalizing on the diversity internally, business organizations may be able to adapt better to the subtle differences in various customer markets.

On the negative side, diversity may initially lead to increased tensions and conflicts in the workplace. In some organizations, people who are part of well-established groups with relatively similar backgrounds and racial or ethnic heritages have demonstrated reluctance to accept people who are "different." Fortunately, outright hostility and physical resistance have occurred in relatively few work situations. But tensions have increased in other circumstances as diversity efforts have been instituted in work settings. Communication difficulties and conflicts between workers may occur more often in organizations having greater diversity of people. Consequently, organizations must be *proactive* not only in addressing diversity concerns by existing employees but also in supporting individuals with different backgrounds and heritages.

Probably the worst response to diversity is to ignore it. Because of its many dimensions, the concept of diversity should be viewed broadly (see Figure 5–1). Any of these dimensions can create conflicts between people at work, but they can also bring the advantages of different ideas and viewpoints, which is why organizations address diversity as a strategic human resource issue.

**LOGGING ON . . .**
**The Diversity Forum**
This website provides extensive links to companies committed to diversity, job opportunities, diversity resources, and research capabilities.

**http://www.diversityforum. com/**

## Demographics and Diversity

Diversity is seen in demographic differences in the workforce.[2] The shifting makeup of the U.S. population accounts for today's increased workforce diversity as many organizations hire from a more diverse pool of potential workers.

Organizations have been seeing the effects of these demographics trends for several years. A more detailed look at some of the key changes follows. According to the U.S. Department of Labor:

● Total workforce growth will be slower between 1996 and 2006 than in previous decades.

**FIGURE 5-1** *Dimensions of Diversity*

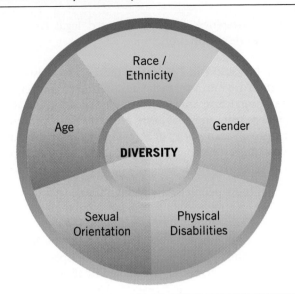

- Only one-third of the entrants to the workforce between 1990 and 2005 will be white males.
- Women will constitute a greater proportion of the labor force than in the past, and 63% of all U.S. women will be in the workforce by 2005.
- Minority racial and ethnic groups will account for a growing percentage of the overall labor force. Immigrants will expand this growth.
- The average age of the U.S. population will increase, and more workers who retire from full-time jobs will work part-time.
- As a result of these and other shifts, employers in a variety of industries will face shortages of qualified workers.

**WOMEN IN THE WORKFORCE** The influx of women into the workforce has major social and economic consequences. It is projected that 63% of all women of working age, and over 80% of women from 25 to 40 years old, will be working or looking for work by 2000. This increase will mean that women will make up 47% of the total workforce by 2005. Further, about half of all currently working women are single, separated, divorced, widowed, or otherwise single heads of households. Consequently, they are "primary" income earners, not co-income providers.

One major consequence of having an increased percentage of women in the workforce is that balancing work and family issues will continue to grow in importance. Also, as more women enter the workforce, greater diversity will be found in organizations. Some other implications for HR management of more women working include the following:

- Greater flexibility in work patterns and schedules to accommodate women with family responsibilities, part-time work interests, or other pressures.
- More variety in benefits programs and HR policies, including child-care assistance and parental-leave programs.

- Job placement assistance for working spouses whose mates are offered relocation transfers.
- Greater employer awareness of gender-related legal issues such as sexual harassment and sex discrimination.[3]

**RACIAL AND ETHNIC DIVERSITY IN THE WORKFORCE** The fastest-growing segments of the U.S. population are minority racial and ethnic groups, especially Hispanic Americans, African Americans, and Asian Americans. By 2000, about 30% of the U.S. population will be from such minority groups. Already, "minority" individuals make up a majority in many cities of at least 100,000 population in California, Texas, and Florida. Some of the changes in racial and ethnic groups are as follows:

- The population of Asian Americans is expected to jump fivefold from 1990 to 2050, with half of these people being foreign born.
- The number of African Americans in the labor force grew twice as fast as the number of whites from 1990 to 2000.
- Hispanic Americans will be the largest minority group by 2010. Projections are that about 20% of the U.S. population will be Hispanic by 2020, with the number of Hispanic Americans having tripled by then.

Much of the growth in the various racial and ethnic groups is due to immigration from other countries. Approximately 700,000 immigrants are arriving annually in the United States. As Figure 5–2 shows, immigrants come into the country as temporary workers, visitors, students, illegals, or in other situations.

During the 1950s most immigrants were Europeans, whereas in the 1990s, Hispanics and Asians predominated. Today, about one-third of immigrants have less than a high school education, while about one-fourth are college graduates. Increasingly, people with advanced degrees in science and engineering being hired by U.S. firms are foreign born.[4]

Possible implications of the increase in racial and ethnic cultural diversity are as follows:

- The potential for work-related conflicts among various racial and ethnic groups could increase.

**FIGURE 5–2** *Status of Immigrants in the United States*

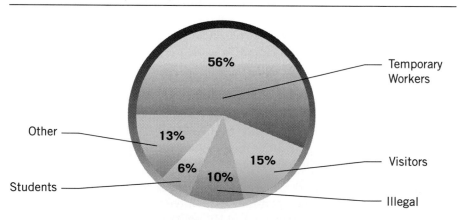

SOURCE: U.S. Department of Labor, Bureau of Labor Statistics, 1999.

- Extensive employer-sponsored cultural awareness and diversity training may be required to defuse conflicts and promote multicultural understanding.
- Training in communication skills for those with English as a second language will increase, and job training will have to accommodate the different language abilities of a multicultural workforce.
- Employees skilled in more than one language will be vital, particularly in service industries in certain geographic locales.
- Greater cultural diversity in dress, customs, and lifestyles will be seen in workplaces.

**AGING OF THE WORKFORCE** Most of the developed countries—including Australia, Japan, most European countries, and the United States—are experiencing an aging of their populations. For the United States, the median age will be 39 in 2000—up from 31.5 just 15 years earlier. This increase is due partly to people living longer and partly to a decrease in the number of young people, particularly in the 16–24 age bracket. Little growth in this age group is projected until after 2005.

A major implication of this age shift is that employers such as hotels, fast-food chains, and retailers will continue to face significant staffing difficulties. Many employers are attracting older persons to return to the workforce through the use of part-time and other scheduling options. According to the U.S. Bureau of Labor Statistics, the number of workers aged 55 to 64 holding part-time jobs has been increasing. Many of these older workers are people who lost their jobs in organizational restructurings or who took early retirement buyout packages.

A change in Social Security regulations allows individuals over age 65 to earn more per year without affecting their Social Security payments. As a result, it is likely that the number of older workers interested in working part-time will increase, and that they will work more hours than previously.

Implications of the shifting age of the U.S. workforce include the following:[5]

- Retirement will change in character as organizations and older workers choose phased retirements, early retirement buyouts, and part-time work.
- Service industries will actively recruit senior workers for many jobs.
- Retirement benefits will increase in importance, particularly pension and health-care coverage for retirees.
- Fewer promotion opportunities will exist for midcareer baby boomers and the baby busters below them in experience.
- Baby boomers will have more "multiple" careers as they leave organizations (voluntarily or through organizational restructurings) and/or as they start their own businesses.

**INDIVIDUALS WITH DISABILITIES IN THE WORKFORCE** Another group adding diversity to the workforce is composed of individuals with disabilities. With the passage of the Americans with Disabilities Act (ADA), employers were reminded of their responsibilities for employing individuals with disabilities. At least 43 million Americans with disabilities are covered by the ADA. The disabilities of this group are shown in Figure 5–3. Estimates are that up to 10 million of these individuals could be added to the workforce if appropriate accommodations were made. The number of individuals with disabilities is expected to continue growing as the workforce ages. Also, people with AIDS or other life-threatening illnesses are considered disabled, and their numbers are expected to increase. The ADA is discussed further in Chapter 6.

**FIGURE 5–3** *Disabled Population in the United States*

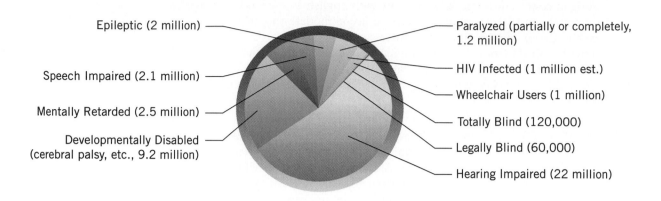

Epileptic (2 million)

Speech Impaired (2.1 million)

Mentally Retarded (2.5 million)

Developmentally Disabled
(cerebral palsy, etc., 9.2 million)

Paralyzed (partially or completely,
1.2 million)

HIV Infected (1 million est.)

Wheelchair Users (1 million)

Totally Blind (120,000)

Legally Blind (60,000)

Hearing Impaired (22 million)

SOURCE: Office of Special Education and Rehabilitative Services, Centers for Disease Control.

Implications of greater employment of individuals with disabilities include the following:

● Employers must define more precisely what are the essential tasks in jobs and what knowledge, skills, and abilities are needed to perform each job.
● Accommodating individuals with disabilities will become more common by providing more flexible work schedules, altering facilities, and purchasing special equipment.
● Nondisabled workers will be trained in ways to work with coworkers with disabilities.
● Employment-related health and medical examination requirements will be revised to avoid discriminating against individuals with disabilities.

**INDIVIDUALS WITH DIFFERING SEXUAL ORIENTATIONS IN THE WORKFORCE** As if demographic diversity did not place pressure enough on managers and organizations, individuals in the workforce today have widely varying lifestyles that can have work-related consequences. A growing number of employers are facing legislative efforts to protect individuals with differing sexual orientations from employment discrimination, though at present, only a few cities and states have passed such laws. In addition, there are growing concerns about balancing employee privacy rights with legitimate employer requirements.

Some implications of these issues include the following:

● The potential for workplace conflicts is heightened as people with different lifestyles and sexual orientations work together. Training to reduce such conflicts will be necessary.
● Access to employee records will be limited, and the types of information kept must be reviewed.
● Generally, managers must recognize that they should not attempt to "control" off-the-job behavior of employees unless it has a direct, negative effect on the organization. Even then, difficulties may exist.

## Best Companies for African, Asian, and Hispanic Americans

Many organizations make "politically correct" statements about diversity, but which firms do something about it? What do they do, and how well does it work? *Fortune* magazine considered these questions and listed the 50 best companies for three racial minority groups. The article concludes that there are common characteristics involved in being a "good" company for people of color:

- The racial and gender mix of management (especially senior management)
- Whether the company hires, promotes, and retains minorities
- Open discussion of delicate race matters

- Manager's bonuses tied to performance in diversity issues

But even the best firms are by no means perfect. Many of the 50 companies rated best for racial minorities and women have been sued for discrimination at some point and paid the settlements when they lost cases. However, it is interesting to note that none of the companies seem concerned about quotas, even though numbers are often used to measure diversity. Members of racial minority groups represent 14% of the officials and managers at the 50 companies—higher than the 12.4% nationally.

The result has been that the 50 best companies outperformed the

Standard and Poor's in average return on investment (ROI) over both a 3- and 5-year period: 125% to 112% ROI for 3 years and 201% to 171% for 5 years. The top 10 companies in this "diversity elite" are:[6]

- Pacific Enterprises (California)
- Applied Materials (California)
- Advantica (South Carolina)
- Bank America (California)
- Fannie Mae (Washington, DC)
- Marriott International (Maryland)
- Edison International (California)
- Computer Associates (New York)
- Ryder System (Florida)
- Pitney Bowes (Connecticut)

# Managing Diversity

As organizations become more aware of both the advantages and inevitability of diversity in the workplace, they are finding that the advantages do not happen automatically—sensible management of diversity is necessary. (See the HR Perspective.) For example, failure to manage the potential difficulties associated with diversity can lead to the following problems:[7]

- *Higher turnover costs:* The turnover rate for African Americans in the United States is 40% higher than for whites, and women turn over twice as often as men. The lack of opportunity for career growth is a primary reason why professionals and managers in these groups leave their jobs.
- *Higher absenteeism costs:* Similarly, absenteeism is often higher for women and for minority-group men. This costly absenteeism is related to many minority individuals feeling that they are not being valued by the organization. For women workers who are mothers, the lack of work/family balance also has significant effects on absenteeism.
- *Lawsuits:* Employee plaintiffs win two-thirds of the discrimination lawsuits filed. The average jury award is $600,000. Failure to train and monitor managers' behaviors in this area can be quite expensive.
- *Failure to compete well for talent:* Recruiting and retaining diverse employees is more difficult. Companies cited as the best places to work for women and minorities tend to be more successful in attracting and retaining the best employees in these labor market segments.

**LOGGING ON . . .**
**The Eastern Point Approach to Managing Diversity**
This is an example of one company's approach to managing a diverse workforce, which has resulted in increased performance and productivity.

http://www.eastpt.com/divers.htm

● *Reduced organizational performance:* The often-mentioned potential business advantages of diversity—better marketplace understanding, creativity and problem solving, and global effectiveness—simply do not happen unless the diverse workforce is given the opportunity and means to contribute to these goals.

## Common Components of Diversity Management Efforts

There are many different sources of advice and opinions about how to approach the challenges of diversity in an organization. Figure 5–4 summarizes the most commonly cited components of diversity management efforts. For diversity to succeed, it should be approached from the standpoint of its advantages. Training, diversity committees, promotion, and mentoring are all common means for achieving the positive benefits from diversity. Establishing management accountability for diversity can take many forms.[8] Tying bonuses to performance in diversity is a powerful approach. Many organizations, including Allstate Insurance Company, also survey employees on how well their managers are doing on diversity—and the resulting index determines 25% of each manager's bonus.[9]

## Prevalence of Diversity Programs

Larger organizations are more likely to have diversity programs. Roughly three-fourths of the *Fortune* 500 companies have diversity programs, and another 8%

**FIGURE 5–4** *Major Components of Successful Diversity Management*

were planning to implement programs, according to a survey by the Society for Human Resource Management. However, only about 50% of the firms have a mechanism in place to measure the impact of the programs.

Smaller companies have diversity programs as well, but only about one-third of the smaller companies have such programs. Diversity training is most commonly found in companies with diversity programs. Approximately 90% of the larger organizations surveyed include diversity training, with middle managers being most often trained. However, for several reasons (discussed next) the effectiveness of diversity training is uncertain.[10]

## Diversity Training

Diversity training seeks to eliminate infringements on legal rights, and to minimize discrimination, harassment, and lawsuits. Approaches to such training vary but often include at least three components.

- *Legal awareness:* Focuses on the legal implications of discrimination. Diversity training typically addresses federal and state laws and regulations on equal employment, and examines consequences of violations of those laws and regulations.
- *Cultural awareness:* Attempts to deal with stereotypes, typically through discussion and exercises. The desired outcome is for all participants to see the others as valuable human beings.
- *Sensitivity training:* Aims at "sensitizing" people to the differences among them and how their words and behaviors are seen by others. Some training includes exercises containing examples of harassing and other behaviors. These exercises are designed to show white males how discrimination feels.

Although diversity training is designed to correct problems, in many cases it appears to have made them worse. In both public- and private-sector organizations, very mixed reviews about the effectiveness of diversity training suggest that either the programs or their implementations are suspect.[11] Common complaints are:

- Diversity training tends to draw attention to differences, building walls rather than breaking them down.
- Diversity training without other initiatives (such as accountability) becomes meaningless.
- The diversity training is viewed as "politically correct," which is an idea that lacks credibility for a significant proportion of the workforce.
- Diversity training is seen as focused on "blaming" majority individuals for past wrongs by those with an "axe to grind."[12]

Some argue that diversity training has failed, pointing out that it does not reduce discrimination and harassment complaints, often produces divisive effects, and does not teach the necessary behaviors for getting along in a diverse workplace. This last point, focusing on behaviors, seems to hold the most promise for making diversity training more effective. One statement capturing this focus said, "Employers are not liable for the beliefs of their employees. But employers *are* responsible for the illegal behavior and conduct of their employees."[13] Teaching appropriate behaviors and skills in relationships with others is more likely to produce satisfactory results than focusing just on attitudes and beliefs among diverse employees.

# Diversity, Equal Employment, and Affirmative Action

It is very easy to note that diversity exists, and most people recognize that there are differences between themselves and others. However, acceptance of diversity is another matter when the rights of an individual are affected because of such differences. The debate about differences and how they should be handled in employment situations has led to various effects. To assist in identifying the issues involved in workplace diversity, it is critical that terminology often used generally and incorrectly be clarified.

Figure 5–5 shows that diversity management is the highest level at which organizations have addressed diversity issues. To review, diversity management is concerned with developing organizational initiatives that value all people equally, regardless of their differences. In managing diversity, efforts are made by both the organization and the individuals in it to adapt to and accept the importance of diversity.

As the figure shows, organizations can also address diversity issues in more restricted ways: equal employment opportunity and affirmative action. These levels are discussed next.

## Equal Employment Opportunity

**Equal employment opportunity (EEO)**

The concept that individuals should have equal treatment in all employment-related actions.

**Equal employment opportunity (EEO)** is a broad concept holding that individuals should have equal treatment in all employment-related actions. Individuals who are covered under equal employment laws are protected from illegal discrimination, which occurs when individuals having a common characteristic are discriminated against based on that characteristic. Various laws have been passed to protect individuals who share certain characteristics, such as race, age, or gender. Those having the designated characteristics are referred to as a protected class or as members of a protected group. A **protected class** is composed of individuals who fall within a group identified for protection under equal employment laws and regulations. Many of the protected classes historically have been subjected to illegal discrimination. The following bases for protection have been identified by various federal laws:

**Protected class**

Those individuals who fall within a group identified for protection under equal employment laws and regulations.

- Race, ethnic origin, color (African Americans, Hispanic Americans, Native Americans, Asian Americans)
- Gender (women, including those who are pregnant)
- Age (individuals over 40)
- Individuals with disabilities (physical or mental)
- Military experience (Vietnam-era veterans)
- Religion (special beliefs and practices)

For instance, suppose a firm that is attempting to comply with EEO regulations has relatively few Hispanic managers. To increase the number of Hispanics, the firm will take steps to recruit and interview Hispanics who meet the minimum qualifications for the management jobs. Notice that what the firm is providing is equal employment opportunity for *qualified* individuals to be considered for employment. To remedy areas in which it appears that individuals in protected classes have not had equal employment opportunities, some employers have developed affirmative action policies.

**FIGURE 5–5** *Diversity Management, Equal Employment Opportunity, and Affirmative Action*

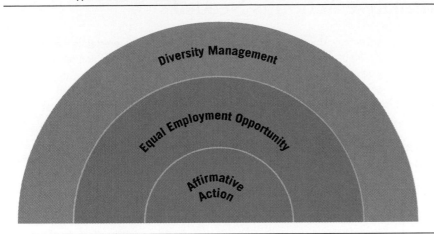

## Affirmative Action

**Affirmative action** occurs when employers identify problem areas, set goals, and take positive steps to guarantee equal employment opportunities for people in a protected class. Affirmative action focuses on hiring, training, and promoting of protected-class members where they are *underrepresented* in an organization in relation to their availability in the labor markets from which recruiting occurs. Sometimes employers have instituted affirmative action voluntarily, but many times employers have been required to do so because they are government contractors having over 50 employees and over $50,000 in government contracts annually.

**AFFIRMATIVE ACTION AND REVERSE DISCRIMINATION** When equal employment opportunity regulations are discussed, probably the most volatile issues concern the view that affirmative action leads to *quotas, preferential selection,* and *reverse discrimination.* At the heart of the conflict is the employers' role in selecting, training, and promoting protected-class members when they are underrepresented in various jobs in an organization. Those who are not members of any protected class have claimed that there is discrimination in reverse. This **reverse discrimination** may exist when a person is denied an opportunity because of preferences given to a member of a protected class who may be less qualified. Specifically, some critics charge that white males are at a disadvantage today, even though they traditionally have held many of the better jobs. These critics say that white males are having to "pay for the sins of their fathers."

It has been stated by some that the use of affirmative action to remedy underrepresentation of protected-class members is really a form of *quotas,* or "hiring by the numbers." However, the Civil Rights Act of 1991 specifically prohibits the use of quotas. It also sets limits on when affirmative action plans can be challenged by individuals who are not members of a protected class. Some phrases used to convey that affirmative action goals are not quotas include "relative numbers," "appropriately represented," "representative sample," and "balanced workforce."

Along with the economic restructuring of many organizations has come a growing backlash against affirmative action.[14] As noted, some see it as an unfair

### Affirmative action
A process in which employers identify problem areas, set goals, and take positive steps to guarantee equal employment opportunities for people in a protected class.

### Reverse discrimination
A condition that may exist when a person is denied an opportunity because of preferences given to protected-class individuals who may be less qualified.

# HR PERSPECTIVE

# Debate: Why Affirmative Action Is Needed

Supporters have offered many reasons why affirmative action is necessary and important. Some common reasons are given here.

1. **Affirmative action is needed to overcome past injustices or eliminate the effects of those injustices.** Proponents of affirmative action believe it is necessary because of the historical inequities that have existed in the United States. In particular, women and racial minorities have long been subjected to unfair employment treatment by being relegated to lower positions (such as clerical and low-paying jobs), not being considered qualified, and being discriminated against for promotions. Without affirmative action, the inequities will continue to exist for individuals who are not white males.

2. **Women and minorities have taken the brunt of the inequality in the past; but now more equality can be created, even if temporary injustice to some may result.** White males in particular may be disadvantaged temporarily in order for affirmative action to create broader opportunities for all—the greatest good. Proponents argue that there must be programs to ensure that women and minorities be considered for employment opportunities so that they can be competitive with males and nonminorities. An often-cited example is that in a running contest, someone running against a well-trained athlete starts at a disadvantage. Women and minorities have had such a dis-

advantage. Consequently, for a period of time, they should be given a head start in order to ensure that a truly competitive contest occurs.

3. **Raising the employment level of women and minorities will benefit U.S. society in the long run.** Statistics consistently indicate that the greatest percentage of those in lower socioeconomic groups belong to minority groups. If affirmative action assists these minorities, then it is a means to address socioeconomic disparities. Without affirmative action, proponents believe that a larger percentage of the U.S. population will be consigned to being permanently economically disadvantaged. When economic levels are low, other social ills proliferate, such as single-parent families, crime, drug use, and educational disparities. Ultimately, then, a vicious circle of desperation will continue unless special efforts are made to provide access to better jobs for all individuals.

4. **Properly used, affirmative action does not discriminate against males or nonminorities.** An affirmative action plan should help remedy a situation in which disproportionately few women and minorities are employed compared with their numbers in the labor markets from which they are drawn. The plan should have a deadline for accomplishing its long-term goals. All individuals must meet the basic qualifications for jobs. Once all of these

job criteria are established, qualified women or minorities should be chosen. In this way, those not selected are discriminated against only in the sense that they did not get the jobs.

Proponents of affirmative action also stress that affirmative action involves not *quotas* but *goals*. The difference is that quotas are specific, required numbers, whereas goals are targets for "good faith" efforts to ensure that protected-class individuals truly are given consideration when employment-related decisions are made.

5. **Affirmative action promotes long-term civility and tolerance through forced interaction.** The United States is a diverse country facing social integration issues, and change is occurring rapidly. In order to staff their jobs, employers will have to tap the talents of the diverse members of the U.S. labor force and to find ways for all inhabitants to work together effectively. When women and minorities are placed in widely varying work environments and males and nonminorities interact and work with them, there will be greater understanding among the diverse peoples in the United States. Additionally, women and minorities who are given opportunities can become role models who will make preferences in the future unnecessary. Thus, if successful, affirmative action ultimately may no longer be necessary.

# HR PERSPECTIVE
# Debate: Why Affirmative Action Should Be Eliminated

While proponents argue in favor of affirmative action, opponents argue against it. They offer the following reasons why affirmative action should be eliminated.

1. **Creating preferences for women and minorities results in reverse discrimination.** Those opposed to affirmative action believe that discriminating *for* someone means discriminating *against* someone else. If equality is the ultimate aim, then discriminating for or against anyone on any basis other than the knowledge, skills, and abilities needed to perform jobs is wrong. Equal employment opportunity means that people should compete for jobs according to their qualifications. If any factor such as gender or race is considered in addition to qualifications, then there is discrimination in reverse, which is counter to creating a truly equal society.

2. **Affirmative action results in greater polarization and separatism along gender and racial lines.** The opponents of affirmative action believe that affirmative action establishes two groups: women and minorities who are in protected classes, and everyone else. For any job, a person will clearly fall into one group or the other. In reality, according to affirmative action classification efforts, women may or may not fall into the "special" category, depending on whether there has been disparate impact on them. Thus, affirmative action may be applicable to some groups but not to others in various employment situations. Regardless of the basis for classification, affirmative action results in males and nonminorities being affected negatively because of their gender or race. Consequently, they become bitter against the protected groups, leading to greater racism or prejudice.

3. **Affirmative action stigmatizes those it is designed to help.** The opponents of affirmative action cite examples wherein less-qualified women and minorities were given jobs or promotions over more-qualified males and nonminorities. When protected-class individuals perform poorly in jobs because they do not have the knowledge, skills, and abilities needed, the result is to reinforce gender or racial stereotypes.

Because affirmative action has come to be viewed by some people as placing unqualified women and minorities in jobs, it reinforces the beliefs held by some that women and minorities could not succeed on their own efforts. Thus, any women or minority members who have responsible positions are there only because of who they are, not because of what they can do and have done.

4. **Affirmative action penalizes individuals (males and nonminorities) even though they have not been guilty of practicing discrimination.** Opponents argue that affirmative action is unfair to "innocent victims"—males and nonminorities. These innocent victims had nothing to do with past discrimination or disparate impact and were not even present at the time. Thus, the opponents of affirmative action wonder why these individuals should have to pay for the remediation of these discriminatory actions.

5. **Preferences through affirmative action lead to conflicts between protected groups.** In this argument, opponents cite examples that illustrate how using preferences for one underrepresented racial minority group has led to discrimination against women or members of another racial minority group when these groups were adequately represented. Conflicts between African American organizations and Asian American organizations are one example. Another is the situation in which Hispanic Americans have sued employers because African Americans were overrepresented.

Closely related is the difficulty of "classifying" people at all. While gender is a bit clearer, melding of races and backgrounds has made racial/ethnic classification difficult. If someone has parents and grandparents from three different ethnic groups, it is difficult to determine how the person should be classified. Thus, focusing on someone's racial/ethnic background may lead to multiple or inaccurate classifications. This process points out the difficulties of classifying people in any way other than by their qualifications and abilities, according to those opposed to affirmative action.

quota system rather than sound HR management. Proponents of affirmative action maintain that it is a proactive way for employers to ensure that protected-class members have equal opportunity in all aspects of employment, and that it is indeed sound management. The accompanying HR Perspective provides both viewpoints.[15]

**COURT DECISIONS AND LEGISLATION ON AFFIRMATIVE ACTION** Increasingly, court decisions and legislative efforts have focused on restricting the use of affirmative action. California's Civil Rights Initiative stipulated that the State of California:

> Shall not discriminate against or grant preferential treatment to any individual or group on the basis of race, sex, color, ethnicity, or national origin in the operation of public employment, public education, or public contracting.

More evidence comes from a federal court decision regarding admission standards at the University of Texas Law School. The university used separate admissions committees to evaluate minority and nonminority applicants. The suit was brought by Cheryl Hopwood and three other students who were denied admission to the law school, even though they had test scores and grade point averages significantly higher than those of a majority of African Americans and Hispanic Americans who were admitted. Clarifying an earlier case, *Bakke v. University of California,* the Fifth Circuit Court of Appeals in *Hopwood v. State of Texas* ruled:[16]

> The use of race in admissions for diversity in higher education contradicts, rather than furthers, the aims of equal protection. Diversity fosters, rather than minimizes, the use of race. It treats minorities as a group, rather than as individuals. It may further remedial purposes, but just as likely, may promote improper racial stereotypes, thus fueling racial hostility.

Finally, a federal court in Washington voided a government requirement that radio and television stations must seek minority job applicants. The Federal Communications Commission (FCC) had required stations to go out and find minority and female applicants, which resulted in the broadcasting companies granting special hiring preferences to minorities. The judge noted, "We do not think it matters whether a government hiring program imposes hard quotas, soft quotas, or goals. Any of these techniques induces an employer to hire with an eye toward meeting the numerical target. As such they can and surely will result in individuals being granted a preference because of their race."[17]

That clear statement illustrates the idea that affirmative action as a concept is under attack by courts and employers, as well as by males and nonminorities. Whether that trend continues will depend on future changes in the makeup of the U.S. Supreme Court and the results of presidential and congressional elections.

The authors of this text believe that whether one supports or opposes affirmative action, it is important to understand why its supporters believe that it is needed and why its opponents believe it should be discontinued. Because the "final" status of affirmative action has not been determined, we have presented the arguments on both sides of the debate without advocating one of the positions.[18]

# Civil Rights Acts of 1964 and 1991

Numerous federal, state, and local laws address equal employment opportunity concerns. As the chart in Figure 5–6 indicates, some laws have a general civil

**FIGURE 5–6** *Major Federal Equal Employment Opportunity Laws and Regulations*

| Act | Year | Provisions |
| --- | --- | --- |
| Equal Pay Act | 1963 | Requires equal pay for men and women performing substantially the same work |
| Title VII, Civil Rights Act of 1964 | 1964 | Prohibits discrimination in employment on basis of race, color, religion, sex, or national origin |
| Executive Orders 11246 and 11375 | 1965 1967 | Require federal contractors and subcontractors to eliminate employment discrimination and prior discrimination through affirmative action |
| Age Discrimination in Employment Act (as amended in 1978 and 1986) | 1967 | Prohibits discrimination against persons over age 40 and restricts mandatory retirement requirements, except where age is a bona fide occupational qualification |
| Executive Order 11478 | 1969 | Prohibits discrimination in the U.S. Postal Service and in the various government agencies on the basis of race, color, religion, sex, national origin, handicap, or age |
| Vocational Rehabilitation Act Rehabilitation Act of 1974 | 1973 1974 | Prohibit employers with federal contracts over $2,500 from discriminating against individuals with disabilities |
| Vietnam-Era Veterans Readjustment Act | 1974 | Prohibits discrimination against Vietnam-era veterans by federal contractors and the U.S. government and requires affirmative action |
| Pregnancy Discrimination Act | 1978 | Prohibits discrimination against women affected by pregnancy, childbirth, or related medical conditions; requires that they be treated as all other employees for employment-related purposes, including benefits |
| Immigration Reform and Control Act | 1986 1990 1996 | Establishes penalties for employers who knowingly hire illegal aliens; prohibits employment discrimination on the basis of national origin or citizenship |
| Americans with Disabilities Act | 1990 | Requires employer accommodation of individuals with disabilities |
| Older Workers Benefit Protection Act of 1990 | 1990 | Prohibits age-based discrimination in early retirement and other benefits plans |
| Civil Rights Act of 1991 | 1991 | Overturns several past Supreme Court decisions and changes damage claims provisions |
| Congressional Accountability Act | 1995 | Extends EEO and Civil Rights Act provisions to U.S. congressional staff |

rights emphasis, while others address specific EEO issues and concerns. At this point, it is important to discuss two major broad-based civil rights acts that encompass many areas. In Chapter 6, specific acts and priorities will be discussed.

Even if an organization has no regard for the principles of EEO, it must follow federal, state, and local EEO laws and regulations to avoid costly penalties. Whether violations of such laws occur intentionally, accidentally, or through ignorance, many employers have learned the hard way that they may be required to pay back wages, reinstate individuals to their jobs, reimburse attorneys' fees, and possibly pay punitive damages. Even if not guilty, the employer still will have considerable costs in HR staff and managerial time involved and legal fees. Therefore, it is financially prudent to establish an organizational culture in which compliance with EEO laws and regulations is expected.

## Civil Rights Act of 1964, Title VII

Although the first civil rights act was passed in 1866, it was not until the passage of the Civil Rights Act of 1964 that the keystone of antidiscrimination legislation was put into place. The Civil Rights Act of 1964 was passed in part to bring about equality in all employment-related decisions. As is often the case, the law contains ambiguous provisions giving considerable leeway to agencies that enforce the law. The Equal Employment Opportunity Commission (EEOC) was established to enforce the provisions of Title VII, the portion of the act that deals with employment.

**PROVISIONS OF TITLE VII** In Title VII, Section 703(a) of the act it states:[19]

It shall be unlawful employment practice for an employer: (1) to fail or refuse to hire or to discharge any individual, or otherwise to discriminate against any individual with respect to his compensation, terms, conditions, or privileges of employment, because of such individual's race, color, religion, sex, or national origin; or (2) to limit, segregate, or classify his employees in any way which would deprive or tend to deprive any individual of employment opportunities or otherwise adversely affect his status as an employee because of such individual's race, color, religion, sex, or national origin.

**WHO IS COVERED?** Title VII, as amended by the Equal Employment Opportunity Act of 1972, covers most employers in the United States. Any organization meeting one of the criteria in the following list is subject to rules and regulations that specific government agencies set up to administer the act:

- All private employers of 15 or more persons who are employed 20 or more weeks per year
- All educational institutions, public and private
- State and local governments
- Public and private employment agencies
- Labor unions with 15 or more members
- Joint (labor/management) committees for apprenticeships and training[20]

## Civil Rights Act of 1991

The major purpose for passing the Civil Rights Act of 1991 was to overturn or modify seven U.S. Supreme Court decisions handed down during the 1988–1990 period. Those decisions made it more difficult for individuals filing discrimination charges to win their cases. Also, the 1991 act amended other federal laws, including Title VII of the 1964 Civil Rights Act and Section 1981 of the Civil Rights Act of 1866. The major effects of the 1991 act are discussed next.

Supreme Court decisions made it more difficult for protected-class individuals to use statistics to show that illegal discrimination had occurred. The 1991 act reversed those rulings, relying on earlier reasoning in the *Griggs v. Duke Power* decision. The Civil Rights Act of 1991 requires employers to show that an employment practice is *job-related for the position* and is consistent with *business necessity.* The act did clarify that the plaintiffs bringing the discrimination charges must identify the particular employer practice being challenged.

**DISCRIMINATORY INTENT**  The Civil Rights Act of 1991 overturned several court decisions that had made it more difficult for plaintiffs to bring suits based on intentional discrimination. Under the 1991 act, the plaintiff charging intentional discrimination must show only that protected-class status played *some factor.* For employers, this means that an individual's race, color, religion, sex, or national origin *must play no factor* in the challenged employment practice.

**COMPENSATORY AND PUNITIVE DAMAGES AND JURY TRIALS**  The 1991 act allows victims of discrimination on the basis of sex, religion, or disability to receive both compensatory and punitive damages in cases of intentional discrimination. Under the 1991 act, compensatory damages do not include back pay or interest on that pay, additional pay, or other damages authorized by Title VII of the 1964 Civil Rights Act. Compensatory damages typically include payments for emotional pain and suffering, loss of enjoyment of life, mental anguish, or inconvenience. However, limits were set on the amount of compensatory and punitive damages, extending from a cap of $50,000 for employers with 100 or fewer employees to a cap of $300,000 for those with over 500 employees.

Additionally, the 1991 act allows jury trials to determine the liability for and the amount of compensatory and punitive damages, subject to the caps just mentioned. Prior to passage of this act, decisions in these cases were made by judges. Generally, this provision is viewed as a victory for people who bring discrimination suits against their employers, because juries tend to more often find for individuals than for employers.

**OTHER PROVISIONS OF THE 1991 ACT**  The Civil Rights Act of 1991 contained some sections that addressed a variety of other issues. More detailed discussions of most issues appear later in this chapter or in Chapter 6. Briefly, some of the issues and the provisions of the act are as follows:

- *Race norming:*  The act prohibited adjustment of employment test scores or use of alternative scoring mechanisms on the basis of the race or gender of test takers. The concern addressed by this provision is the use of different passing or cut-off scores for protected-class members than for those individuals in nonprotected classes.
- *International employees:*  The act extended coverage of U.S. EEO laws to U.S. citizens working abroad, except where local laws or customs conflict.
- *Government employee rights:*  Responding to criticism that some government employees were being excluded from EEO law coverage, Congress extended such coverage to employees of the Senate, presidential appointments, and previously excluded state government employees.

**EFFECTS OF THE CIVIL RIGHTS ACT OF 1991**  By overturning some U.S. Supreme Court decisions, the 1991 act negated many of the more "employer-friendly" decisions made by the Supreme Court from 1988 to 1990. Allowing jury trials and compensatory and punitive damages in cases involving allegations of intentional discrimination means that the costs of being found guilty of illegal discrimination have increased significantly. The number of EEO complaints filed likely will continue to increase because of some of the provisions of the 1991 act. Consequently, more than ever before, employers must make sure their actions are job related and based on business necessity.

# Enforcement Agencies

Government agencies at several levels have powers to investigate illegal discriminatory practices. At the state and local levels, various commissions have enforcement authority. At the federal level, the two most prominent agencies are the Equal Employment Opportunity Commission (EEOC) and the Office of Federal Contract Compliance Programs (OFCCP).[21]

## Equal Employment Opportunity Commission (EEOC)

The EEOC, created by the Civil Rights Act of 1964, is responsible for enforcing the employment-related provisions of the act. The agency initiates investigations, responds to complaints, and develops guidelines to enforce various laws. The EEOC has enforcement authority for charges brought under the following federal laws:

- Civil Rights Act of 1964, Title VII
- Civil Rights Act of 1991
- Equal Pay Act
- Pregnancy Discrimination Act
- Age Discrimination in Employment Act
- Americans with Disabilities Act
- Vocational Rehabilitation Act

The EEOC has been given expanded powers several times since 1964 and is the major agency involved with employment discrimination. Over the years, the EEOC has been given the responsibility to investigate equal pay violations, age discrimination, and discrimination based on disability.

An independent regulatory agency, the EEOC is composed of five members appointed by the President and confirmed by the Senate. No more than three members of the commission can be from the same political party, and members serve for seven years. In addition, the EEOC has a staff of lawyers and compliance officers who do investigative and follow-up work for the commission. For an example of one EEOC enforcement activity, see the HR Perspective on testers.

## Office of Federal Contract Compliance Programs (OFCCP)

While the EEOC is an independent agency, the OFCCP is part of the Department of Labor, established by executive order to ensure that federal contractors and subcontractors have nondiscriminatory practices. A major thrust of OFCCP efforts is to require that federal contractors and subcontractors take affirmative action to overcome the effects of prior discriminatory practices. Affirmative action plans are discussed in detail in the next chapter.

## Enforcement Philosophies and Efforts

Since 1964, the various U.S. presidential administrations have viewed EEO and affirmative action enforcement efforts from different philosophical perspectives. Often the thrust and aggressiveness of enforcement efforts have varied depend-

**LOGGING ON . . .**
**U.S. Equal Employment Opportunity Commission**
The commission's website provides information about its purpose, facts about employment discrimination, enforcement statistics, and details on technical assistance programs.

**http://www.eeoc.gov**

**BNA: 1892**
**EEOC and OFCCP Offices**
A directory of the local offices of the EEOC and OFCCP are contained in this section.

## HR PERSPECTIVE

# "Testers"

Beginning several years ago, the EEOC started using "matched-pair" testers who posed as consumers, or applicants for jobs to determine whether employers would discriminate in their treatments of the individuals. One tester might be white and the other African American, for instance. The two individuals apply for a job and then compare their treatment. These testers can then testify in court as to their differential treatment if necessary. Unlike abstract statistical arguments about whether there is evidence of different treatment for different races with a certain employer, this testing has a direct, concrete kind of impact.

Testing has been used previously in housing discrimination, but its status in employment cases was doubtful until the advent of amendments to the Civil Rights Act and a district court ruling supporting the right of testers to give testimony about their treatment in civil rights cases seeking damages. Critics say the technique is like "entrapment" on the criminal side, and that it sets up fake encounters and is intrusive. Further, critics charge that it is unrealistic for testers to apply for jobs, thereby initiating the employment process with no intention of working for that employer.

The use of testers has outraged employers, whose argument is that because the testers are not truly applicants, they should not be able to file charges. As a result of pressure from U.S. congressional representatives, the EEOC for one year reversed its stand on the use of testers in discrimination cases. Controlled by Republicans, the House Appropriations Committee threatened to withhold $37 million requested from the EEOC budget request. However, if the composition of the U.S. Congress changes, it is likely that the EEOC will resume use of testers.

Interestingly, some employers are seeking to use the technique themselves as an "audit" of their own HR employees. These firms would rather find out about and correct problems themselves, before an outside group does tests.[22]

ing on whether a Republican or Democratic president and Congress were in office. The purpose of pointing this out is not to suggest who is right or wrong but rather to emphasize that laws are enforced by agencies staffed by presidential appointees. Differing degrees of activism and emphasis result, depending on the philosophical beliefs and priorities held by a particular administration.

## State and Local Enforcement Agencies

In addition to federal laws and orders, many states and municipalities have passed their own laws prohibiting discrimination on a variety of bases. Often, these laws are modeled after federal laws; however, state and local laws sometimes provide greater remedies, require different actions, or prohibit discrimination in areas beyond those addressed by federal law. As a result, state and local enforcement bodies have been established to enforce EEO compliance. Fortunately, the three levels of agencies generally coordinate their activities to avoid multiple investigations of the same EEO complaints.

*BNA: 1895*
**Equal Employment Agencies**
A history of state and local agencies is contained here. Identify the agencies and their locations that are closest to you.

# Interpretations of EEO Laws and Regulations

Laws establishing the legal basis for equal employment opportunity generally have been written broadly. Consequently, only through application to specific organizational situations can one see how the laws affect employers.

**FIGURE 5–7** *Average EEO Awards in Discrimination Cases*

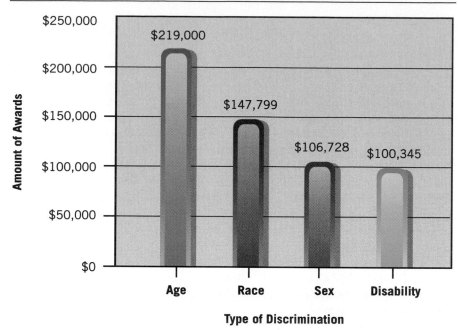

SOURCE: Based on data in Sheldon Steinhauser, "Age Bias," *HR Magazine*, July 1998, 87.

The broad nature of the laws has led enforcement agencies to develop guidelines and to enforce the acts as they deem appropriate. However, agency rulings and the language of those rulings have caused confusion and have been interpreted differently by employers. Interpretation of ambiguous provisions in the laws also shifts as the membership of the agencies changes.

The court system is left to resolve the disputes and issue interpretations of the laws. The courts, especially the lower courts, have issued conflicting rulings and interpretations. The ultimate interpretation often has rested on decisions by the U.S. Supreme Court, although Supreme Court rulings, too, have been interpreted differently.

Thus, equal employment opportunity is an evolving concept that often is confusing. However, for employers equal employment violations are costly, as Figure 5–7 indicates.

## When Does Illegal Discrimination Occur?

Equal employment laws and regulations address concerns about discrimination in employment practices. The word *discrimination* simply means that differences among items or people are recognized. Thus, discrimination involves choosing among alternatives. For example, employers must discriminate (choose) among applicants for a job on the basis of job requirements and candidates' qualifications. However, discrimination can be illegal in employment-related situations in which either: (1) different standards are used to judge different individuals, or (2) the same standard is used, but it is not related to the individuals' jobs.

When deciding if and when illegal discrimination has occurred, courts and regulatory agencies have had to consider the following issues:

- Disparate treatment
- Disparate impact
- Business necessity and job relatedness

- Bona fide occupational qualification
- Burden of proof
- Retaliation

**DISPARATE TREATMENT AND DISPARATE IMPACT** It would seem that the motives or intentions of the employer might enter into the determination of whether discrimination has occurred—but they do not. It is the outcome of the employer's actions, not the intent, that will be considered by the regulatory agencies or courts when deciding if illegal discrimination has occurred. Two concepts used to activate this principle are *disparate treatment* and *disparate impact.*

**Disparate treatment** occurs when protected-class members are treated differently from others. For example, if female applicants must take a special skills test not given to male applicants, then disparate treatment may be occurring. If disparate treatment has occurred, the courts generally have said that intentional discrimination exists.

**Disparate impact** occurs when there is substantial underrepresentation of protected-class members as a result of employment decisions that work to their disadvantage. The landmark case that established the importance of disparate impact as a legal foundation of EEO law is *Griggs v. Duke Power* (1971).[23] The decision of the U.S. Supreme Court established two major points:

- It is not enough to show a lack of discriminatory intent if the employment tool results in a disparate impact that discriminates against one group more than another or continues a past pattern of discrimination.
- The employer has the burden of proving that an employment requirement is directly job related as a "business necessity." Consequently, the intelligence test and high school diploma requirements of Duke Power were ruled not to be related to the job.

**BUSINESS NECESSITY AND JOB RELATEDNESS** A **business necessity** is a practice necessary for safe and efficient organizational operations. Business necessity has been the subject of numerous court decisions. Educational requirements often are based on business necessity. However, an employer who requires a minimum level of education, such as a high school diploma, must be able to defend the requirement as essential to the performance of the job. For instance, equating a degree or diploma with the possession of math or reading abilities is considered questionable. Having a general requirement for a degree cannot always be justified on the basis of the need for a certain level of ability. All requirements must be *job related,* or proven necessary for job performance. Determining and defending the job relatedness of employment requirements through validation procedures is discussed later in this chapter.

**BONA FIDE OCCUPATIONAL QUALIFICATION (BFOQ)** Title VII of the 1964 Civil Rights Act specifically states that employers may discriminate on the basis of sex, religion, or national origin if the characteristic can be justified as a "bona fide occupational qualification reasonably necessary to the normal operation of the particular business or enterprise."[24] Thus, a **bona fide occupational qualification (BFOQ)** is a legitimate reason why an employer can exclude persons on otherwise illegal bases of consideration. What constitutes a BFOQ has been subject to different interpretations in various courts across the country.

---

**Disparate treatment**
Situation that exists when protected-class members are treated differently from others.

**Disparate impact**
Situation that exists when there is a substantial underrepresentation of protected-class members as a result of employment decisions that work to their disadvantage.

**Business necessity**
A practice necessary for safe and efficient organizational operations.

**Bona fide occupational qualification (BFOQ)**
A characteristic providing a legitimate reason why an employer can exclude persons on otherwise illegal bases of consideration.

**BURDEN OF PROOF** Another legal issue that arises when discrimination is alleged is the determination of which party has the *burden of proof.* At issue is what individuals who are filing suit against employers must prove in order to establish that illegal discrimination has occurred.

Based on the evolution of court decisions, current laws and regulations state that the plaintiff charging discrimination (1) must be a protected-class member and (2) must prove that disparate impact or disparate treatment existed. Once a court rules that a *prima facie* (preliminary) case has been made, the burden of proof shifts to the employer. The employer then must show that the bases for making employment-related decisions were specifically job related and consistent with considerations of business necessity.

**Retaliation**
Punitive actions taken by employers against individuals who exercise their legal rights.

**RETALIATION** Employers are prohibited by EEO laws from retaliating against individuals who file discrimination charges. **Retaliation** occurs when employers take punitive actions against individuals who exercise their legal rights. For example, an employer was ruled to have engaged in retaliation when an employee who filed a discrimination charge was assigned undesirable hours and his work schedule was changed frequently. Various laws, including Title VII of the Civil Rights Act of 1964, protect individuals who have (1) made a charge, testified, assisted, or participated in any investigation, proceeding, or hearing" or (2) "opposed any practice made unlawful.

To implement the provisions of the Civil Rights Act of 1964 and the interpretations of it based on court decisions, the EEOC and other federal agencies developed their own compliance guidelines and regulations, each agency having a slightly different set of rules and expectations. Finally, in 1978, the major government agencies involved agreed on a set of uniform guidelines.

# Uniform Guidelines on Employee Selection Procedures

The Uniform Guidelines on Employee Selection Procedures apply to the federal EEOC, the U.S. Department of Labor's OFCCP, the U.S. Department of Justice, and the federal Office of Personnel Management. The guidelines provide a framework used to determine if employers are adhering to federal laws on discrimination. These guidelines affect virtually all phases of HR management because they apply to employment procedures, including but not limited to the following:

- Hiring (qualifications required, application blanks, interviews, tests)
- Promotions (qualifications, selection process)
- Recruiting (advertising, availability of announcements)
- Demotion (why made, punishments given)
- Performance appraisals (methods used, links to promotions and pay)
- Training (access to training programs, development efforts)
- Labor union membership requirements (apprenticeship programs, work assignments)
- Licensing and certification requirements (job requirements tied to job qualifications)

The guidelines apply to most employment-related decisions, not just to the initial hiring process. Two major means of compliance are identified by the guidelines: (1) no disparate impact and (2) job-related validation.

## No Disparate Impact Approach

Generally, regarding discrimination in organizations, the most important issue is the *effect* of employment policies and procedures, regardless of the *intent*. *Disparate impact* occurs whenever there is a substantial underrepresentation of protected-class members in employment decisions. The Uniform Guidelines identify one approach in the following statement: "These guidelines do not require a user to conduct validity studies of selection procedures where no adverse impact results."[25]

Under the guidelines, disparate impact is determined with the **4/5ths rule.** If the selection rate for any protected group is less than 80% (4/5ths) of the selection rate for the majority group or less than 80% of the group's representation in the relevant labor market, discrimination exists. Thus, the guidelines have attempted to define discrimination in statistical terms. Disparate impact can be checked both internally and externally.

**INTERNAL** Checking disparate impact internally compares the treatment received by protected-class members with that received by nonprotected-group members. As shown in Figure 5–8, the Standard Company interviewed both men and women for jobs. Of the men who applied, 40% were hired; of the women who applied, 25% were hired. The selection rate for women is less than 80% (4/5ths) of the selection rate for men (40% × 4/5 = 32%). Consequently, Standard Company's employment process does have "disparate impact."

**4/5ths Rule**

Rule stating that discrimination generally is considered to occur if the selection rate for a protected group is less than 80% of the group's representation in the relevant labor market or less than 80% of the selection rate for the majority group.

**FIGURE 5–8** *Internal Disparate Impact at Standard Company*

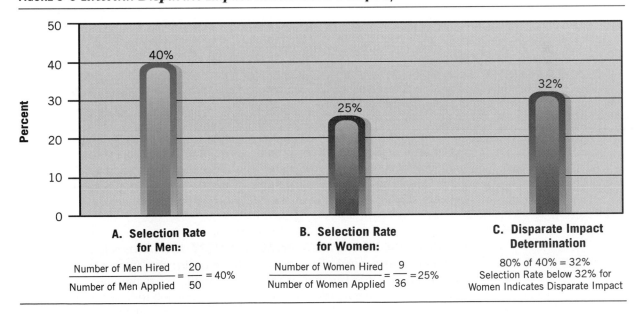

HR activities for which internal disparate impact can be checked internally most frequently include:

- Candidates selected for interviews of those recruited
- Performance appraisal ratings as they affect pay increases
- Promotions, demotions, and terminations
- Pass rates for various selection tests

**EXTERNAL** Employers can check for disparate impact externally by comparing the percentage of employed workers in a protected class in the organization with the percentage of protected-class members in the relevant labor market. The relevant labor market consists of the areas where the firm recruits workers, not just where those employed live. External comparisons can also consider the percentage of protected-class members who are recruited and who apply for jobs to ensure that the employer has drawn a "representative sample" from the relevant labor market. Although employers are not required to maintain exact proportionate equality, they must be "close." Courts have applied statistical analyses to determine if any disparities that exist are too high.

To illustrate, assume the following situation. In the Valleyville area, Hispanic Americans make up 15% of those in the job market. RJ Company is a firm with 500 employees, 50 of whom are Hispanic. Disparate impact is determined as follows if the 4/5ths rule is applied:

Percent of Hispanics in the labor market (15%)

$\times$ 4/5ths rule (.8)

Disparate-impact level (12%)

15%

$\times$.8

12%

*Comparison:*

RJ Co. has 50/500 = 10% Hispanics.

Disparate-impact level = 12% Hispanics.

Therefore, disparate impact exists because fewer than 12% of the firm's employees are Hispanic.

The preceding example illustrates one way external disparate impact can be determined. In reality, statistical comparisons for disparate-impact determination may use more complex methods. Note also that external disparate-impact charges make up a very small number of EEOC cases. Instead, most cases deal with the disparate impact of internal employment practices.

**EFFECT OF THE NO DISPARATE IMPACT STRATEGY** The 4/5ths rule is a yardstick that employers can use to determine if there is disparate impact on protected-class members. However, to meet the 4/5ths compliance requirement, employers must have no disparate impact at any level or in any job for any protected class. (The next chapter contains more details.) Consequently, using this strategy is not really as easy or risk-free as it may appear. Instead, employers may want to turn to another compliance approach: validating that their employment decisions are based on job-related factors.

## Job-Related Validation Approach

Under the job-related validation approach the employment practices that must be valid include such practices and tests as job descriptions, educational requirements, experience requirements, work skills, application forms, interviews, written tests, and performance appraisals. Virtually every factor used to make employment-related decisions—recruiting, selection, promotion, termination, discipline, and performance appraisal—must be shown to be specifically job related. Hence, the concept of validity affects many of the common tools used to make HR decisions.

**Validity** is simply the extent to which a test actually measures what it says it measures. The concept relates to inferences made from tests. It may be valid to infer that college admission test scores predict college academic performance. However, it is probably invalid to infer that those same test scores predict athletic performance. As applied to employment settings, a test is any employment procedure used as the basis for making an employment-related decision. For a general intelligence test to be valid, it must actually measure intelligence, not just vocabulary. An employment test that is valid must measure the person's ability to perform the job for which he or she is being hired. Validity is discussed in detail in the next section.

**Validity**
The extent to which a test actually measures what it says it measures.

The ideal condition for employment-related tests is to be both valid and reliable. **Reliability** refers to the consistency with which a test measures an item. For a test to be reliable, an individual's score should be about the same every time the individual takes that test (allowing for the effects of practice). Unless a test measures a trait consistently (or reliably), it is of little value in predicting job performance.

**Reliability**
The consistency with which a test measures an item.

Reliability can be measured by several different statistical methodologies. The most frequent ones are test-retest, alternate forms, and internal-consistency estimates. A more detailed methodological discussion is beyond the scope of this text; those interested can consult appropriate statistical references.[26]

# Validity and Equal Employment

If a charge of discrimination is brought against an employer on the basis of disparate impact, a *prima facie* case has been established. The employer then must be able to demonstrate that its employment procedures are valid, which means to demonstrate that they relate to the job and the requirements of the job. A key element in establishing job-relatedness is to conduct a *job analysis* to identify the *knowledge, skills,* and *abilities (KSAs)* and other characteristics needed to perform a job satisfactorily. A detailed examination of the job provides the foundation for linking the KSAs to job requirements and job performance. Chapter 7 discusses job analysis in more detail. Both the Civil Rights Act of 1964, as interpreted by the *Griggs v. Duke Power* decision, and the Civil Rights Act of 1991 emphasize the importance of job relatedness in establishing validity.

Using an invalid instrument to select, place, or promote an employee has never been a good management practice, regardless of its legality. Management also should be concerned with using valid instruments from the standpoint of operational efficiency. Using invalid tests may result in screening out individuals who might have been satisfactory performers and hiring less satisfactory workers instead. In one sense, then, current requirements have done management a favor by forcing employers to do what they should have been doing previously—using job-related employment procedures.

The 1978 uniform selection guidelines recognize validation strategies measuring three types of validity:

- Content validity
- Criterion-related validity (concurrent and predictive)
- Construct validity

## Content Validity

**Content validity**

Validity measured by use of a logical, nonstatistical method to identify the KSAs and other characteristics necessary to perform a job.

**Content validity** is a logical, nonstatistical method used to identify the KSAs and other characteristics necessary to perform a job. A test has content validity if it reflects an actual sample of the work done on the job in question. For example, an arithmetic test for a retail cashier should contain problems that typically would be faced by cashiers on the job. Content validity is especially useful if the workforce is not large enough to allow other, more statistical approaches.

A content validity study begins with a comprehensive job analysis to identify what is done on a job and what KSAs are used. Then managers, supervisors, and HR specialists must identify the most important KSAs needed for the job. Finally, a test is devised to determine if individuals have the necessary KSAs. The test may be an interview question about previous supervisory experience, or an ability test in which someone types a letter using a word-processing software program, or a knowledge test about consumer credit regulations.

Many practitioners and specialists see content validity as a common-sense way to validate staffing requirements that is more realistic than statistically oriented methods. Consequently, content validity approaches are growing in use.

## Criterion-Related Validity

**Criterion-related validity**

Validity measured by a procedure that uses a test as the predictor of how well an individual will perform on the job.

Employment tests of any kind attempt to predict how well an individual will perform on the job. In measuring **criterion-related validity,** a test is the *predictor* and the desired KSAs and measures for job performance are the *criterion variables*. Job analysis determines as exactly as possible what KSAs and behaviors are needed for each task in the job. Tests (predictors) are then devised and used to measure different dimensions of the criterion-related variables. Examples of "tests" are: (1) having a college degree, (2) scoring a required number of words per minute on a typing test, or (3) having five years of banking experience. These predictors are then validated against criteria used to measure job performance, such as performance appraisals, sales records, and absenteeism rates. If the predictors satisfactorily predict job performance behavior, they are legally acceptable and useful.

**Correlation coefficient**

An index number giving the relationship between a predictor and a criterion variable.

A simple analogy is to think of two circles, one labeled *predictor* and the other *criterion variable*. The criterion-related approach to validity attempts to see how much the two circles overlap. The more overlap, the better the performance of the predictor. The degree of overlap is described by a **correlation coefficient,** which is an index number giving the relationship between a predictor and a criterion variable. These coefficients can range from $-1.0$ to $+1.0$. A correlation coefficient of +.99 indicates that the test is almost an exact predictor, whereas a +.02 correlation coefficient indicates that the test is a very poor predictor.

There are two different approaches to criterion-related validity. *Concurrent validity* represents an "at-the-same-time" approach, while *predictive validity* represents a "before-the-fact" approach.

**CONCURRENT VALIDITY** *Concurrent* means "at the same time." As shown in Figure 5–9, when an employer measures **concurrent validity,** a test is given to current employees and the scores are correlated with their performance ratings, determined by such measures as accident rates, absenteeism records, and supervisory performance appraisals. A high correlation suggests that the test can differentiate between the better-performing employees and those with poor performance records.

A drawback of the concurrent validity approach is that employees who have not performed satisfactorily are probably no longer with the firm and therefore cannot be tested, while extremely good employees may have been promoted or may have left the organization for better jobs. Furthermore, an unknown is how people who were not hired would have performed if given opportunities to do so. Thus, the firm does not really have a full range of people to test. Also, the test takers may not be motivated to perform well on the test because they already have jobs. Any learning that has taken place on the job may influence test scores, presenting another problem. Applicants taking the test without the benefit of on-the-job experience might score low on the test but might be able to learn to do the job well. As a result of these problems, a researcher might conclude that a test is valid when it is not, or might discard a test because the data indicate that it is invalid when, in fact, it is valid. In either case, the organization has lost because of poor research.

**Concurrent validity**
Validity measured when an employer tests current employees and correlates the scores with their performance ratings.

**FIGURE 5–9** *Concurrent Validity*

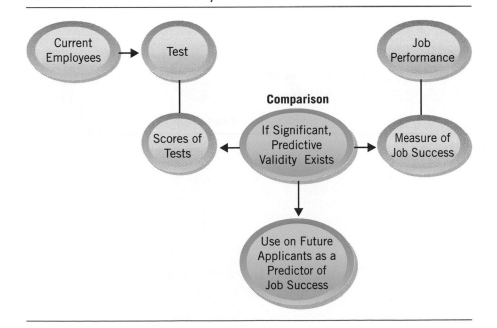

**Predictive validity**
Validity measured when test results of applicants are compared with subsequent job performance.

**PREDICTIVE VALIDITY** To measure **predictive validity,** test results of applicants are compared with their subsequent job performance. The following example illustrates how a predictive validity study might be designed. A retail chain, Eastern Discount, wants to establish the predictive validity of requiring one year of cashiering experience, a test it plans to use in hiring cashiers. Obviously, the retail outlet wants to use the test that will do the best job of separating those who will do well from those who will not. Eastern Discount first hires 30 people, regardless of cashiering experience or other criteria that might be directly related to experience. Some time later (perhaps after one year), the performance of these same employees is compared. Success on the job is measured by such yardsticks as absenteeism, accidents, errors, and performance appraisals. If those employees who had one year of experience at the time when they were hired demonstrate better performance than those without such experience, as demonstrated by statistical comparisons, then the experience requirement is considered a valid predictor of performance and may be used in hiring future employees (see Figure 5–10).

In the past, predictive validity has been preferred by the EEOC because it is presumed to give the strongest tie to job performance. However, predictive validity requires (1) a fairly large number of people (usually at least 30) and (2) a time gap between the test and the performance (usually one year). As a result, predictive validity is not useful in many situations. Because of these and other problems, other types of validity often are used.

## Construct Validity

**Construct validity**
Validity showing a relationship between an abstract characteristic and job performance.

**Construct validity** shows a relationship between an abstract characteristic inferred from research and job performance. Researchers who study behavior have

**FIGURE 5–10** *Predictive Validity*

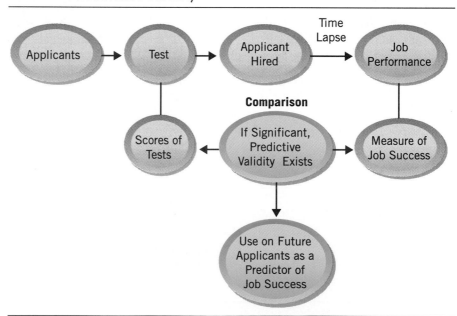

given various personality characteristics names such as *introversion, aggression,* and *dominance.* These are called *constructs.* Other common constructs for which tests have been devised are creativity, leadership potential, and interpersonal sensitivity. Because a hypothetical construct is used as a predictor in establishing this type of validity, personality tests and tests that measure other such constructs are more likely to be questioned for their legality and usefulness than other measures of validity. Consequently, construct validity is used less frequently in employment selection than the other types of validity.

## Validity Generalization

**Validity generalization** is the extension of the validity of a test with different groups, similar jobs, or other organizations. Rather than viewing the validity of a test as being limited to a specific situation and usage, one views the test as a valid predictor in other situations as well. Those advocating validity generalization believe that variances in the validity of a test are attributable to the statistical and research methods used; this means that it should not be necessary to perform a separate validation study for every usage of an employment test. Proponents particularly believe validity generalization exists for general ability tests.

**Validity generalization**
The extension of the validity of a test to different groups, similar jobs, or other organizations.

Although the approach is controversial, it has been adopted by the U.S. Employment Service, a federal agency, for the General Aptitude Test Battery (GATB). Also, it has been adopted for use throughout the United States in many state and local job service offices. As more and more such jobs services adopt the approach, more detailed records of results will be available. Anyone interested in learning more about the GATB and validity generalization should contact a state job service office in a specific locale to find out how it is used.

# Summary

- Diversity, which recognizes differences among people, is growing as an HR issue.
- Organizations have a demographically more diverse workforce than in the past, and continuing changes are expected.
- Major demographic shifts include the increasing number and percentage of women working, growth in minority racial and ethnic groups, and the aging of the workforce. Other changes involve the need to provide accommodations for individuals with disabilities and to adapt to workers with different sexual orientations.
- Diversity management is concerned with advancing organizational initiatives that value all people equally regardless of their differences.
- Effective management of diversity often means that it must be differentiated from affirmative action.
- Diversity training has had limited success, possibly because it too often has focused on beliefs rather than behaviors.

- Equal employment opportunity (EEO) is a broad concept holding that individuals should have equal treatment in all employment-related actions.
- Protected classes are composed of individuals identified for protection under equal employment laws and regulations.
- Affirmative action requires employers to identify problem areas in the employment of protected-class members and to set goals and take steps to overcome those problems.
- The question of whether affirmative action leads to reverse discrimination has been intensely litigated, and the debate continues today.
- EEO is part of effective management for two reasons: (1) it focuses on using the talents of all human resources; (2) the costs of being found guilty of illegal discrimination can be substantial.
- Disparate treatment occurs when protected-class members are treated differently from others, whether or not there is discriminatory intent.

- Disparate impact occurs when employment decisions work to the disadvantage of members of protected classes, whether or not there is discriminatory intent.
- Employers must be able to defend their management practices based on bona fide occupational qualifications (BFOQ), business necessity, and job relatedness.
- Retaliation occurs when an employer takes punitive actions against individuals who exercise their legal rights, and it is illegal under various laws.
- The 1964 Civil Rights Act, Title VII, was the first significant equal employment law. The Civil Rights Act of 1991 altered or expanded on the 1964 provisions by overturning several U.S. Supreme Court decisions.
- The Civil Rights Act of 1991 addressed a variety of issues, such as disparate impact, discriminatory intent, compensatory and punitive damages, jury trials, and EEO rights of international employees.
- The Equal Employment Opportunity Commission (EEOC) and the Office of Federal Contract Compliance Programs (OFCCP) are the major federal equal employment enforcement agencies.
- The 1978 Uniform Guidelines on Employee Selection Procedures are used by enforcement agencies to examine recruiting, hiring, promotion, and many other employment practices.
- Under the 1978 guidelines, two alternative compliance approaches are identified: (1) no disparate impact and (2) job-related validation.
- Job-related validation requires that tests measure what they are supposed to measure (validity) in a consistent manner (reliability).
- Disparate impact can be determined through the use of the 4/5ths rule.
- There are three types of validity: content, criterion-related, and construct.
- The content-validity approach is growing in use because it shows the job relatedness of a measure by using a sample of the actual work to be performed.
- The two criterion-related strategies measure concurrent validity and predictive validity. Whereas predictive validity involves a "before-the-fact" measure, concurrent validity involves a comparison of tests and criteria measures available at the same time.
- Construct validity involves the relationship between a measure of an abstract characteristic, such as intelligence, and job performance.

# Review and Discussion Questions

1. Discuss the following statement: "U.S. organizations must adjust to diversity if they are to manage the workforce of the present and future."
2. Explain why diversity management represents a much broader approach to workforce diversity than providing equal employment opportunity or affirmative action.
3. Regarding the affirmative action debate, why do you support or oppose affirmative action?
4. If you were asked by an employer to review an employment decision to determine if discrimination had occurred, what factors would you consider, and how would you evaluate them?
5. Why is the Civil Rights Act of 1991 such a significant law?
6. Why is the job-related validation approach considered more business-oriented than the no disparate impact approach in complying with the 1978 Uniform Guidelines on Employee Selection Procedures?
7. Explain what validity is and why the content validity approach is growing in use compared with the criterion-related and construct validity approaches.

# Terms to Know

# Using the Internet

## Defining and Managing Workplace Diversity

Imagine that you are the training and development manager at a company with a very diverse workforce. Some tension among employees has been noticed by the senior-level staff. They believe the organization is in need of some diversity training and have asked you to develop the program. They have posed several questions to you.

Using the following website, answer their questions.
**http://www.aphis.usda.gov/mb/wfd/**

1. Name five items contributing to diversity not including gender, sex, or national origin.
2. Give examples of the four layers of diversity.
3. What can we do to take full advantage of diversity in organizations?

# CASE

## Hooters

Hooters is a company that has staffed its restaurants with attractive women, known as Hooters Girls. The uniforms of the Hooters Girls consist of short shorts, tank tops or half-shirts, and suntan-colored hose. In approximately 150 Hooters restaurants, the food staff was virtually all female, and males tended to be hired into kitchen, cook, or "back-room" jobs. Many women's groups criticized the "blatant sexist" appeal used at Hooters restaurants to attract and entertain customers.

Meanwhile, employment practices at Hooters caused enough concern that the EEOC began an intensive investigation of Hooters. The EEOC concluded that Hooters was violating EEO laws and regulations by refusing to hire men as wait staff, bartenders, and hosts. Hooters and the EEOC held initial discussions in which the EEOC demanded the following:

- Hooters would establish a fund estimated at over $22 million for men who had been denied employment. Any male who claimed to have applied for one of the "female-designated" jobs would be entitled to up to $10,000.
- Hooters would run newspaper ads inviting males to file claims and encouraging them to apply at Hooters.
- Hooters henceforth would be guilty of violating EEO laws anytime the number of men hired fell below 40% of the total hiring rate.
- Hooters would discontinue using the Hooters Girls in advertising, to avoid discouraging males from applying for jobs.
- Hooters would provide sensitivity training to teach Hooters employees how to be more sensitive to men's needs.

Hooters rejected the EEOC demands and ran full-page ads in many newspapers showing a burly, mustached man—wearing a blond wig, tank top, short shorts, and tennis shoes. In one hand the man was holding a plate of chicken wings, and in the other a sign saying, "Washington—Get a Grip." Specifically in response to the EEOC, Hooters' legal counsel stated that "The business of Hooters is predominantly the provision of entertainment, diversion, and amusement based on the sex appeal of the Hooters Girls." Hooters felt the EEOC was being so unreasonable that it decided to take the offensive.

Ultimately, the EEOC's position was rejected. Therefore, Hooters was allowed to continue hiring attractive young women for its waitstaff and other customer-contact jobs.[27]

## Questions

1. Make the argument that selecting only attractive women is a violation of EEO.
2. When is an approach like Hooters' aggressive response to the EEOC's demands likely to be effective, and when might it backfire?

# Notes

1. Adapted from Dennis Huspeni, "Women's Perspective Helps Force," *The Denver Post,* June 17, 1998, B1; David Price, "Police Need Brains Not Personality," *USA Today,* July 30, 1998, 13A; Paul M. Barrett, "Legal Limbo," *The Wall Street Journal,* October 12, 1998, A1; and Kevin Johnson, "Survey: Women Muscled Out by Bias, Harassment," *USA Today,* November 28, 1998, 1A.
2. Throughout the following section, various statistics on workforce composition and trends are taken from U.S. Department of Labor, Bureau of Labor Statistics, and Census Bureau data widely reported in various reference and news media reports. For additional details, consult http://stats.bls.gov.
3. Brenda Paik Sunoo, "Initiatives for Women Boost Retention," *Workforce,* November 1998, 97; and Tara Parker-Pope, "Inside P&G, a Pitch to Keep Women Employees," *The Wall Street Journal,* September 9, 1998, B1.
4. Howard Gleckman, "High Tech Talent: Don't Bolt the Golden Door," *Business Week* March 16, 1998, 30.
5. Rick Garnitz, "Aging Work Force Poses an HR Challenge," *ACA News,* March 1999, 20–24.

6. Adapted from Roy Johnson, "The 50 Best Companies for Asians, Blacks, and Hispanics," *Fortune,* August 3, 1998, 94–122.
7. The following list is adapted from Gail Robinson and Kathleen Dechant, "Building a Business Case for Diversity," *Academy of Management Executive,* August 1997, 21.
8. Patricia Digh, "The Next Challenge: Holding People Accountable," *HR Magazine,* October 1998, 63–69.
9. Leon Wynter, "Allstate Rates Managers on Handling Diversity," *The Wall Street Journal,* October 1, 1997, B1.
10. "SHRM Releases New Survey on Diversity Programs," *Mosaics,* July/August 1998, 1.
11. Norma M. Rucucci, "Cultural Diversity Programs to Prepare for Work Force 2000: What's Gone Wrong?", *Public Personnel Management,* Spring 1997, 35–41; and Gillian Flynn, "The Harsh Reality of Diversity Programs," *Workforce,* December 1998, 26–35.
12. Kathryn F. Clark, "Breaking Barriers," *Human Resource Executive,* September 1998, 39–44.
13. Helen Hemophill and Ray Haines, *Discrimination, Harassment, and the Failure of Diversity Training* (Westport, CT: Quorum Books), 1997.

14. Gillian Flynn, "White Males See Diversity's Other Side," *Workforce,* February 1999, 52–55.
15. The authors acknowledge the assistance of Christina Harjehausen in structuring the content of the debate on affirmative action.
16. *Bakke v. the University of California,* 109 S.Ct. (1978); and *Hopwood v. State of Texas,* 78 F. 3d 932 (1996).
17. Steven A. Holmes, "FCC Rule on Hiring Minorities Tossed Out," *The Denver Post,* April 15, 1998, 1A.
18. For a summary of the political issues on affirmative action, see Clint Bolick, "A Middle Ground on Affirmative Action," *The Wall Street Journal,* January 6, 1998, A18.
19. Civil Rights Act of 1964, Title VII, sec. 703a.
20. U.S. Equal Employment Opportunity Commission, *Affirmative Action and Equal Employment* (Washington, DC: U.S. Government Printing Office, 1974), 12–13.
21. Leon G. Wynter, "Business and Race," *The Wall Street Journal,* July 1, 1998, B1.
22. Based on Linda Micco, "EEOC Under Congressional Pressure, Suspends Use of Testers," *HR News,* September 1998, 15; and Rochelle Sharp, "EEOC Backs Away from Filing Race-Bias Suit in Face of Congressional Opposition to Testers,"

*The Wall Street Journal,* June 24, 1998, A4.

23. *Griggs v. Duke Power Co.,* 401 U.S. 424 (1971).

24. Civil Rights Act of 1964, Title VII, sec. 703c.

25. "Adoption by Four Agencies of Uniform Guidelines on Employee Selection Procedures (1978)," *Federal Register,* August 15, 1978, Part IV, 38295–38309.

26. For a discussion of statistical methodological details related to employment selection, see Robert D. Gatewood and Hubert S. Feild, *Human Resource Selection,* 4th ed. (Chicago: Dryden Press, 1998), 111–209.

27. Based on R.J. Barro, "So You Want to Hire Beautiful: Well Why Not?", *Business Week,* March 16, 1998, 18; *Hooters of America vs. Phillips 1998,* USAPP Lexis 20137, 9th Cir., March 12, 1998; Del Jones, "Feds Want Chain to Hire 'Hooters Guys,'" *USA Today,* November 15, 1995, 1B; J. Bovard, "The EEOC's War on Hooters," *The Wall Street Journal,* November 17, 1995, A15; and "EEOC Dropping Sex-Bias Inquiry of Hooters Chain," *Albuquerque Journal,* May 2, 1996, A1.

# CHAPTER 6
# Implementing Equal Employment

*After you have read this chapter, you should be able to:*

- Discuss the two types of sexual harassment and how employers should respond to complaints.

- Give examples of two sex-based discrimination issues besides sexual harassment.

- Identify two age discrimination issues.

- Discuss the major requirements of the Americans with Disabilities Act.

- Describe two bases of EEO discrimination in addition to those listed above.

- Identify typical EEO record-keeping requirements and those records used in the EEO investigative process.

- Discuss the contents of an affirmative action plan (AAP).

# The Costs of Discrimination

Over the past several decades since passage of the Civil Rights Act of 1964, numerous employers have been found guilty of illegal employment discrimination. Whether based on age, sex, race, disability, or other factors, both large and small employers have paid for their illegal human resource actions. But employers continue to engage in discriminatory practices that lead to large fines and settlements, sometimes through ignorance and sometimes intentionally. Some examples illustrate that employment discrimination is expensive.

## Sex Discrimination and Sexual Harassment

*Smith-Barney,* a Wall Street brokerage firm, agreed to spend $15 million over four years to increase diversity in the firm. As part of the settlement of a lawsuit, the firm agreed over a three-year time period to raise the percentage of female brokers in its training classes to 33% of the total, and to have 25% of its investment banker training classes composed of females. At the time, only 14.5% of the 15,000 Smith-Barney brokers were women.

*Mitsubishi Motors* paid $34 million to settle a class-action sexual harassment lawsuit filed by 350 current and former female employees. This settlement was the largest class-action settlement ever paid for sexual harassment charges brought by the EEOC. Separately, the firm also agreed to pay $9.5 million to 27 current and former employees.

*Rustic Inn Crabhouse,* a Fort Lauderdale restaurant, was found to have discriminated against three women who were pregnant. The restaurant had a policy of shifting waitresses to lower-paying cashier and hostess jobs after their fifth month of pregnancy, based upon trying to protect pregnant women from lifting and carrying heavy food trays. Rejecting that policy, a federal jury awarded the three women almost $800,000. The firm announced that it was appealing the decision.

## Racial/Ethnic Discrimination

*Tempel Steel Co.,* based in Niles, Illinois, settled a race bias case on behalf of African Americans who had applied for or who could show that they would have applied for jobs at the firm. Only 70 of the firm's 1,000 workers were African Americans. The case involved Tempel's recruiting practices, in which job advertisements were placed in Polish- and German-language newspapers where few African Americans would see them. Therefore, the recruiting continued a past pattern of discrimination. In addition to paying $4 million total to the victims of past discrimination, the firm was required to file reports on its hiring practices for four years and pay $500,000 to set up a training program to help African American employees qualify for the higher-skilled, higher-paying jobs in the two factories in the Chicago area.

An African American laywer at a national law firm's Washington, D.C., office was awarded $2.5 million for race discrimination. He alleged that even though he was given good performance reviews, he was paid $3,000 less per year than others, was not considered for partnership on the same schedule, and was dismissed from the firm due to his race.

## Age Discrimination

*First Union,* a large financial institution based in Charlotte, North Carolina, settled an age discrimination lawsuit by agreeing to pay $58.5 million. The 239 workers in the case, all over age 40, lost their jobs when smaller banks were bought by First Union. The lawsuit charged that in many situations the plaintiffs were replaced by younger, less-experienced workers who were paid lower salaries.

> *Whether based on age, sex, race, disability, or other factors, both large and small employers have paid for their illegal discriminatory actions.*

*First America,* an Iowa-based telemarketing firm, was ordered by a federal jury to pay over $300,000 to a 62-year-old sales representative. The sales rep was not promoted, despite a satisfactory work record, so he filed a lawsuit. Also, the sales rep charged that once he filed the lawsuit, the firm refused to pay him some sales commissions, which was a form of retaliation prohibited by EEOC regulations.

All of these cases emphasize that illegal employment discrimination can represent significant costs. Therefore, employers of all sizes must be familiar with EEO laws and regulations and ensure that their practices are nondiscriminatory.[1]

> ❝ *Our equality lies in the right for each of us to grow to our full capacity whatever it is.* ❞
>
> PEARL BUCK

As the examples in the opening discussion indicate, the days are past when employers can manage their workforces in any manner they wish. Federal, state, and local laws prohibit unfair discrimination against individuals on a variety of bases. One purpose of this chapter is to discuss the range of issues that have been addressed by Equal Employment Opportunity (EEO) laws, regulations, and court decisions. The other purpose is to review what employers should do to comply with the regulations and requirements of various EEO enforcement agencies. Because race discrimination is still the most prevalent form of employment discrimination, a look at this area is next.

# Discrimination Based on Race, National Origin, and Citizenship

The original purpose of the Civil Rights Act of 1964 was to address race discrimination. This area continues to be important today, and employers must be aware of practices that may be discriminatory on the basis of race. Further, the EEOC and the affirmative action requirements of the Office of Federal Contract Compliance Programs (OFCCP) specifically designate race as an area for investigation and reporting.

Race is often a factor in discrimination on the basis of national origin. What are the rights of people from other countries, especially those illegally in the United States, with regard to employment and equality? Illegal aliens often are called *undocumented workers* because they do not have the appropriate permits and documents from the Immigration and Naturalization Service. The passage of the Immigration Reform and Control Acts (IRCA) and later revisions to it have clarified issues regarding employment of immigrants.

## Immigration Reform and Control Acts (IRCA)

To deal with problems arising from the continued flow of immigrants to the United States, the IRCA was passed in 1986 and has been revised in later years. The IRCA makes it illegal for an employer to discriminate in recruiting, hiring, or terminating based on an individual's national origin or citizenship. Many employers were avoiding the recruitment and hiring of individuals who were "foreign looking" or who spoke with an accent, fearing they might be undocumented workers. Hispanic leaders voiced concern about the discriminatory effects of this practice on Hispanic Americans.

A revision of the act attempted to address this issue by prohibiting employers from using disparate treatment, such as requiring more documentation from some prospective employees than from others. In addition, the IRCA requires that employers who knowingly hire illegal aliens be penalized.

**HIGH-TECHNOLOGY AND SKILLED WORKER VISAS** Recent revisions to the IRCA changed some of the restrictions on the entry of immigrants to work in U.S. organizations, particularly those organizations with high-technology and other "scarce-

## HR PERSPECTIVE

# Bilingual Employees and "English-Only" Requirements

As the diversity of the workforce has increased, more employees have language skills beyond English. Interestingly, some employers have attempted to restrict the use of foreign languages, while other employers have recognized that bilingual employees have valuable skills.

### "English-Only" Requirements

A number of employers have policies requiring that employees speak only English at work. Employers with these policies contend that the policies are necessary for valid business purposes. For instance, a manufacturer has a requirement that all employees working with dangerous chemicals use English in order to communicate hazardous situations to other workers and to be able to read chemical labels. The EEOC has issued guidelines clearly stating that employers may require workers to speak only English at certain times or in certain situations, but the business necessity of the requirements must be justified.

Some cases that have created more difficulties for employees involve retailers requiring that sales employees speak only English. Such policies generally have been enforced for use when waiting on customers. However, requiring employees to speak only English in situations not requiring customer contact has been ruled to be more questionable. Also, questions asked during the selection process about an applicant's language skills should be limited to situations in which workers will have job-related reasons for using a foreign language. The employer is restricted to making such inquiries only for jobs that make use of the foreign language.

The prudent use of English-only rules can be seen at 3Com Corporation in Illinois. Among its 1,200 employees, over 20 different languages are spoken. Employees of 3Com are required to speak English in group settings on the job, but may use other languages in nonwork situations. The company also offers courses on English as a second language for employees wishing to improve their English skills.

### Bilingual Employees

Some employers with a diverse customer base have found it beneficial to have bilingual employees. For instance, some teleservicing firms have identified employees with Spanish-speaking skills, so that calls from Spanish-language customers can be directed to the bilingual representatives. Also, a number of airlines have bilingual flight attendants on international flights. Those individuals often wear pins with the flag of the country whose language they speak, so that foreign-language customers can contact someone speaking their languages.

However, one issue with bilingual employees is whether they should receive extra pay for having the additional language capabilities and using them at work. Some employers do not pay bilingual employees extra, believing that paying for the jobs being done is more appropriate than paying individuals for language skills that are used infrequently on the job. Other employers pay "language premiums" if employees must speak to customers in another language. For instance, MCI-World Com pays workers in some locations a 10% bonus if they are required to use a foreign language a majority of the time with customers. Delta Airlines pays bilingual flight attendants extra hourly pay on international routes.

As both employees and customers of more companies become more diverse, English-language and bilingual policies are likely to be issues. It seems that the difficulties of deciding when English-only is a business necessity, and when bilingual language skills are advantageous, will be faced by employers in all types of industries.[2]

---

skill" areas. The number of immigrants allowed legal entry was increased, and categories for entry visas were revised.[3] As the HR Perspective indicates, foreign-language skills have created issues with many employers.

**EMPLOYER DOCUMENTATION REQUIREMENTS**  Under the acts just described, employers are required to examine identification documents for new employees, who also must sign verification forms about their eligibility to work legally in the United States. Employers must ask for proof of identity, such as a driver's license with a picture, Social Security card, birth certificate, immigration permit, or other documents. The required I–9 form must be completed by all new employees within 72 hours.

### Conviction and Arrest Records

Court decisions consistently have ruled that using records of arrests, rather than records of convictions, has a disparate impact on some racial and ethnic minority groups protected by Title VII. An arrest, unlike a conviction, does not imply guilt. Statistics indicate that in some geographic areas, more members of some minority groups are arrested than nonminorities.

Generally, courts have held that conviction records may be used in determining employability if the offense is job related. For example, a bank could use an applicant's conviction for embezzlement as a valid basis for rejection. Some courts have held that only job-related convictions occurring within the most recent five to seven years may be considered. Consequently, employers inquiring about convictions often add a phrase such as "indication of a conviction will not be an absolute bar to employment."

# Gender Discrimination and Sexual Harassment

Title VII of the Civil Rights Act of 1964 prohibits discrimination in employment on the basis of gender. Other laws and regulations are aimed at eliminating such discrimination in specific areas. This section begins with a discussion of sexual harassment and then discusses other forms of gender-based discrimination.

The Equal Employment Opportunity Commission (EEOC) has issued guidelines designed to curtail sexual harassment. A variety of definitions of sexual harassment exist, but generally **sexual harassment** refers to actions that are sexually directed, are unwanted, and subject the worker to adverse employment conditions or create a hostile work environment. Sexual harassment can occur between a boss and a subordinate, among coworkers, and when nonemployees have business contacts with employees.

**Sexual harassment**
Actions that are sexually directed, are unwanted, and subject the worker to adverse employment conditions or create a hostile work environment.

Because of the increased awareness of sexual harassment resulting from events such as those involving President Clinton, employers and individuals affected by sexual harassment are less tolerant of it. However, as more men and women work together, more voluntary relationships based on affection and romance develop.

### Workplace Relationships and Romances

As more and more men and women work together in teams and on projects, more employers are becoming concerned about personal relationships between employees. Could permitting such relationships lead to liability for sexual harassment claims when relationships end?

The appeal of workplace relationships was succinctly described by a 28-year-old single male information systems specialist: "When you're working 50 to 60 hours per week, the only place to meet women is at work." When work-based friendships lead to romance and off-the-job sexual relationships, managers and employers face a dilemma: Do they monitor for and protect the firm from potential sexual harassment complaints, thereby "meddling" in employees' private, off-the-job lives? Or do they simply ignore such relationships and the potential problems they present?

The greatest concerns are romantic relationships between supervisors and subordinates, because the harassment of subordinates by supervisors is the most frequent type of sexual harassment situation. Though many companies prohibit relatives from having direct-reporting relationships, extending this policy to people who are dating raises resistance from those involved, who may believe that what they do after work is none of their employers' concern.

Some experts even suggest that romantically involved employees who have a supervisor-subordinate relationship be required to sign a written agreement releasing the employer from any current or future claim of sexual harassment. Employment attorneys generally recommend that the HR manager remind both parties in workplace romances of the company policy on sexual harassment and encourage either party to contact the HR department should the relationship cool and become one involving unwanted and unwelcome attentions. Also, the HR manager always should document that such conversations occurred.[4]

## Types of Sexual Harassment

The victims of sexual harassment are more likely to bring charges and take legal actions against employers and harassing individuals than they were in the past. According to EEOC statistics, well over 90% of the sexual harassment charges filed have involved harassment of women by men. However, some sexual harassment cases have been filed by men against women managers and supervisors and for same-sex harassment.

Two types of sexual harassment are defined as follows.

- *Quid pro quo* harassment occurs when an employer or supervisor links specific employment outcomes to the individuals' granting sexual favors.
- *Hostile environment* harassment occurs when the harassment has the effect of unreasonably interfering with work performance or psychological well-being or when intimidating or offensive working conditions are created.

**Cathy**

**QUID PRO QUO** Linking any condition of employment—including pay raises, promotions, assignments of work and work hours, performance appraisals, meetings, disciplinary actions, and many others—to the granting of sexual favors can be the basis for a charge of *quid pro quo* (meaning "something for something") harassment. Certainly, harassment by supervisors and managers who expect sexual favors as a condition for a raise or promotion is inappropriate behavior in a work environment. This view has been supported in a wide variety of cases.

**HOSTILE ENVIRONMENT** The second type of sexual harassment involves the creation of a hostile work environment. In *Harris v. Forklift Systems, Inc.,* the U.S. Supreme Court ruled that in determining if a hostile environment exists, the following factors should be considered.[5]

- Whether the conduct was physically threatening or humiliating, rather than just offensive
- Whether the conduct interfered unreasonably with an employee's work performance
- Whether the conduct affected the employee's psychological well-being

Numerous cases in which sexual harassment has been found illustrate that what is harmless joking or teasing in the eyes of one person may be offensive and hostile behavior in the eyes of another. Commenting on dress or appearance, telling jokes that are suggestive or sexual in nature, allowing centerfold posters to be on display, or making continual requests to get together after work can lead to the creation of a hostile work environment.

## Changing Legal Standards on Sexual Harassment

In 1998, the U.S. Supreme Court issued rulings in three different cases in which charges of sexual harassment were brought by different individuals working for different employers.[6] Grouping these cases together, the U.S. Supreme Court issued decisions that significantly clarified both the legal aspects of when sexual harassment occurs and what actions employers should take to reduce their liabilities if sexual harassment claims are filed. A look at the implications of the three cases follows.

**DEFINITION OF SEXUAL HARASSMENT** First, the three decisions make it clear that sexual harassment, whether quid pro quo or hostile environment, or whether with different or same-sex individuals, is illegal. The courts will look at the conduct and actions of both the employer's representatives and the complainants.

**TANGIBLE EMPLOYMENT ACTIONS** As Figure 6–1 indicates, if the employee suffered any tangible employment action (such as being denied raises, being terminated, or being refused access to training) because of the sexual harassment, then the employers are liable. However, even if the employee suffered no tangible employment action, and the employer has not produced an affirmative defense, then employer liability still exists.[7]

**AFFIRMATIVE DEFENSE AND REASONABLE CARE** Only if the employer can produce evidence of an affirmative defense in which the employer took *reasonable care* to prohibit sexual harassment does the employer have the possibility of avoiding liability.

**FIGURE 6–1** *Sexual Harassment Liability Determination*

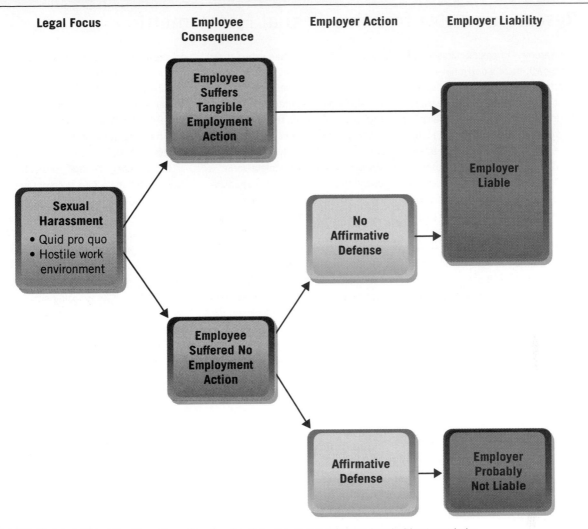

SOURCE: Virginia Collins, SilverStone Consulting, Omaha, Nebraska. May not be reproduced without permission.

Components of ensuring reasonable care include the following:

- Establishing a sexual harassment policy
- Communicating the policy regularly
- Training all employees, especially supervisors and managers, on avoiding sexual harassment
- Investigating and taking action when complaints are voiced

## Employer Responses to Sexual Harassment Complaints

Employers generally are held responsible for sexual harassment unless they take appropriate action in response to complaints. Also, employers are held responsible if they knew (or should have known) of the conduct and failed to stop it.

# Research on Confronting Sexual Harassment

As awareness of sexual harassment has grown, more women have reported incidents of sexual harassment to both internal organizational representatives and governmental enforcement agencies. To add some research on women's decisions to report or confront sexual harassment, Adams-Roy and Barling conducted a study that was published in the *Journal of Organizational Behavior*.

The authors conducted a survey of 800 women in seven different Canadian organizations. The wide range of organizations included employees at a hospital, a manufacturing plant, one prison, three military bases, and a real estate agency. Almost 18% of the women surveyed indicated that they had experienced sexual harassment at work some time in the past. Then the research questionnaire inquired about actions that the individuals took, if any, to report the incident or confront the harasser. Additionally, the individuals were asked to complete some questions inquiring about organizational and interaction justice.

Using all of this data, the analyses done by the researchers found that individual perceptions of the fairness of organizational policies about sexual harassment affected reporting or confronting sexual harassment at work. But most surprising, those who had reported sexual harassment by following formal policies and procedures had poorer perceptions of organizational justice. The researchers suggest that these results indicate that the women who utilized the formal processes likely were disappointed with the resolution of their complaints.

In summary, the study indicates that just having a formal complaint process and using it is not enough. The outcome of the process must be seen as just; otherwise, the process is viewed negatively. Therefore, both having a process and having it operate in a manner seen as fair are necessary for employees facing sexual harassment to believe that their treatment is just.[9]

**SEXUAL HARASSMENT POLICY AND COMPLAINT PROCESS** The U.S. Supreme Court decisions make it clear that every employer should have a policy on sexual harassment that addresses such issues as the following:

- Instructions on how to report complaints, including how to bypass a supervisor if he or she is involved in the harassment
- Assurances of confidentiality and protection against retaliation by those against whom the complaint is filed
- A guarantee of prompt investigation
- A statement that disciplinary action will be taken against sexual harassers, up to and including termination of employment

It is important that all employers, even small ones, have specific sexual harassment complaint procedures and policies that allow a complainant to bypass a supervisor if the harasser is the supervisor.[8] If such a complaint process exists and it is not used by the complainant, the employer has a better standing in refuting sexual harassment claims. The HR Perspective discusses a research study on using complaint processes to confront sexual harassment.

**COMMUNICATION OF SEXUAL HARASSMENT POLICY** All employees, especially supervisors and managers, should be informed that sexual harassment will not be tolerated in an organization. To create such an awareness, communications to all employees should highlight the employer's policy on sexual harassment and the importance of creating and maintaining a work environment free of sexual harassment. The communications should be ongoing to reinforce to all employees that sexual harassment will not be tolerated and will be dealt with severely.

**TRAINING OF MANAGERS, SUPERVISORS, AND EMPLOYEES** Training of all employees, especially supervisors and managers, is recommended. The training should identify what constitutes sexual harassment and alert employees to the types of behaviors that create problems. Analyses of the Supreme Court decisions by legal experts consistently stress that all employers should hold sexual harassment training regularly.[10] For smaller employers without formal training programs, this training can be developed by training and human resource consultants, legal counsel, local college human resource professors, or others. But regardless of organizational size, specific training on sexual harassment should be done regularly in all companies.

**INVESTIGATION AND ACTION** Once management has knowledge of sexual harassment, the investigation process should begin. Often, to provide objectivity, an HR staff member, a key senior manager, and/or outside legal counsel will lead the investigation. The procedures to be followed should be identified at the time the sexual harassment policy is developed, and all steps taken during the investigation should be documented. It is crucial to ensure that the complainant is not subjected to any further harassment or to retaliation for filing the complaint.

Prompt action by the employer to investigate sexual harassment complaints and then to punish the identified harassers aid an employer's defense. In summary, if harassment situations are taken seriously by employers, the ultimate outcomes are more likely to be favorable for them.

## Pregnancy Discrimination

The Pregnancy Discrimination Act (PDA) of 1978 was passed as an amendment to the Civil Rights Act of 1964. Its major provision was that any employer with 15 or more employees had to treat maternity leave the same as other personal or medical leaves. Closely related to the PDA is the Family and Medical Leave Act (FMLA) of 1993, which requires that individuals be given up to 12 weeks of family leave without pay and also requires that those taking family leave be allowed to return to jobs (see Chapter 15 for details). The FMLA applies to both men and women.

In court cases filed by pregnant workers alleging illegal discrimination, it generally has been ruled that the PDA requires employers to treat pregnant employees the same as nonpregnant employees with similar abilities or inabilities. Therefore, if a nonpregnant employees with a bad back is accommodated by not having to lift some file boxes, then a pregnant employee who has been advised by a physician to avoid heavy lifting must be accommodated in the same manner.[11]

## Compensation Issues and Sex Discrimination

A number of concerns have been raised about employer compensation practices that discriminate on the basis of sex. At issue in several compensation practices is the extent to which men and women are treated differently, with women most frequently receiving lower compensation or benefits. Equal pay, pay equity, and benefits coverage are three prominent issues.

**EQUAL PAY** The Equal Pay Act, enacted in 1963, requires employers to pay similar wage rates for similar work without regard to gender. Tasks performed only intermittently or infrequently do not make jobs different enough to justify significantly different wages. Differences in pay may be allowed because of (1) differences in seniority, (2) differences in performance, (3) differences in quality and/or quantity of production, and (4) factors other than sex, such as skill, effort, and working conditions.

The importance of considering job responsibilities and skills under equal pay can be seen in a case involving a female vice president of an insurance company who was paid less than the five other vice presidents, all of whom were male. The court decision ruled against the woman because the employer was able to show that her job had substantially different tasks that were not as crucial to company operations. Also, the court noted that the skills needed to do her job were not as great as those associated with the vice presidential jobs held by the males.[12]

**Pay equity**

Similarity in pay for jobs requiring comparable levels of knowledge, skill, and ability, even where actual job duties differ significantly.

**PAY EQUITY** According to the concept of **pay equity,** the pay for jobs requiring comparable levels of knowledge, skill, and ability should be similar even if actual duties differ significantly. This concept has also been called *comparable worth* when earlier cases were addressed. The Equal Pay Act applies to jobs that are substantially the same, whereas pay equity applies to jobs that are *valued* similarly in the organization, whether or not they are the same.

A major reason for the development of the pay equity idea is the continuing gap between the earnings of women and men. For instance, in 1959, the average pay of full-time women workers was 59% of that of full-time men workers. By the late 1990s, the gap had shrunk to about 76%.[13] More in-depth data show that the education and age of women workers affects the size of the gaps. As Figure 6–2 indicates, the pay of younger female college graduates consistently is higher than that of older female graduates. Even greater disparity exists when pay for lower-skilled, less-educated women is compared with pay for lower-skilled, less-educated men.

As discussed in more detail in Chapter 13 on compensation, a number of state and local government employers have mandated pay equity for public-sector employees through legislation. Some Canadian provinces have enacted similar laws. But except where state laws have mandated pay equity, U.S. federal courts generally have ruled that the existence of pay differences between jobs held by women and jobs held by men is not sufficient to prove that illegal discrimination has occurred.

**PAYCHECK FAIRNESS ACT OF 1999** To address the continuing gap between men's and women's wages, in 1999 President Clinton proposed new legislation, called the Paycheck Fairness Act. This legislation would allow women to sue employers for unlimited damages, in addition to the back pay available under such laws. Also, the act would provide the EEOC more enforcement workers to handle equal pay and cases related to pay equity. As of the writing of this text, this bill has not been passed into law.

**BENEFITS COVERAGE** A final area of sex-based differences in compensation relates to benefits coverage. One concern has been labeled "unisex" pension coverage. The *Arizona Governing Committee v. Norris* decision held that an employer's deferred compensation plan violated Title VII because female employees received

**FIGURE 6–2** *Women's Earnings as a Percentage of Men's, By Degree and Major*

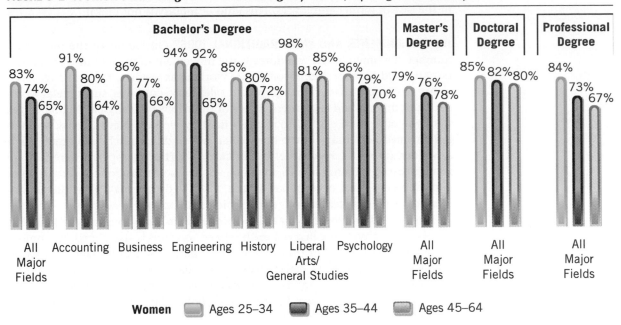

SOURCE: Adapted with permission from *Bulletin to Management (BNA Policy and Practice Series)*, Vol. 49, No. 25, Pp. 197 (June 25, 1998) by the Bureau of National Affairs, Inc. (800-372-1033) <http://www.bna.com>

lower monthly benefits payments than men received on retirement, despite the fact that women contributed equally to the plan.[14] Regardless of longevity differences, men and women who contribute equally to pension plans must receive equal monthly payments.

## Sex Discrimination in Jobs and Careers

The selection and promotion criteria that employers use can discriminate against women. Some cases have found that women were not allowed to enter certain jobs or job fields. Particularly problematic is the use of marital or family status as a basis for not selecting women.

**NEPOTISM** Many employers have policies that restrict or prohibit **nepotism,** the practice of allowing relatives to work for the same employer. Other firms require only that relatives not work directly for or with each other or be placed in a position where potential collusion or conflicts could occur. The policies most frequently cover spouses, brothers, sisters, mothers, fathers, sons, and daughters. Generally, employer anti-nepotism policies have been upheld by courts, in spite of the concern that they tend to discriminate against women more than men (because women tend to be denied employment or leave employers more often as a result of marriage to other employees).

However, inquiries about previous names (not maiden names) under which an applicant may have worked may be necessary in order to check reference infor-

**Nepotism**
Practice of allowing relatives to work for the same employer.

mation with former employers, educational institutions, or employers' own files, in the case of former employees. This kind of inquiry is not illegal.

**JOB ASSIGNMENTS AND "NONTRADITIONAL JOBS"** One result of the increasing number of women in the workforce is the movement of women into jobs traditionally held by men. More women are working as welders, railroad engineers, utility repair specialists, farm equipment sales representatives, sheet metal workers, truck drivers, and carpenters. Many of these jobs typically pay higher wages than the office and clerical jobs often held by women. Nevertheless, women hold a small percentage of the blue-collar jobs traditionally held by men, such as welder, carpenter, mechanic, and bricklayer.[15] Thus, it appears there still are gender-based groupings of jobs, in which women hold most jobs of certain types and men hold most other types of jobs. Clearly, discrimination in the assignment of women to certain jobs and job fields still exists.

The right of employers to reassign women from hazardous jobs to jobs that may be lower paying because of health-related concerns is another issue. Employers' fears about higher health-insurance costs, and even possible lawsuits involving such problems as birth defects caused by damage sustained during pregnancy, have led some employers to institute *reproductive and fetal protection policies*. However, the U.S. Supreme Court has ruled such policies are illegal. Also, having different job conditions for men and women usually is held to be discriminatory.

**Glass ceiling**
Discriminatory practices that have prevented women and other protected-class members from advancing to executive-level jobs.

**THE "GLASS CEILING"** For years, women's groups have alleged that women encounter a "glass ceiling" in the workplace. The **glass ceiling** refers to discriminatory practices that have prevented women and other protected-class members from advancing to executive-level jobs. The extent of the problem is seen in the fact that white males compose 43% of the workforce but hold 95% of all senior management positions. In the nation's largest corporations, only a few women are CEOs, and women compose less than 10% of the executive vice presidents in larger firms. Figure 6–3 shows the percentages of women and minority managers by industry segment. Statistics reveal that women tend to have better opportunities to progress in smaller firms and, of course, when they start their own businesses. Also, in computer-related fields, women are increasing their representation in management, particularly in data processing service and software development firms.[16]

The Glass Ceiling Act of 1991 was passed in conjuction with the Civil Rights Act of 1991. A Glass Ceiling Commission was established to conduct a study on how to shatter the glass ceiling encountered by women and other protected-class members. Key recommendations in the commission's report included the following:[17]

- Employers should include diversity goals in strategic business plans, and managers should be accountable for meeting these goals.
- Affirmative action should be used to encourage firms to recruit more widely and give promotion opportunities to more diverse individuals.
- Women and minorities should be prepared for senior positions by the use of mentoring, training, and other programs.
- Federal government agencies should refine data collection requirements to avoid "double counting" of minority women, so that true statistics and measures of progress can be obtained.
- Increased government enforcement efforts are needed, as well as more funding and staffing of agencies such as the EEOC.

**FIGURE 6–3** *Percentages of Women and Minority Managers, by Industry Segment*

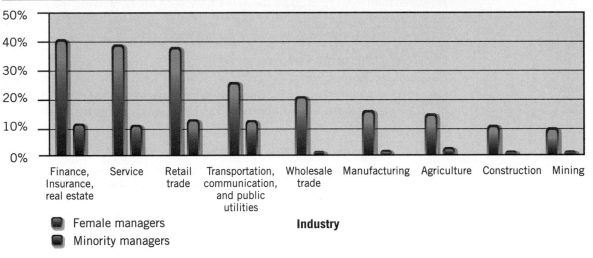

Female managers
Minority managers

**Industry**

SOURCE: U.S. Government, Federal Glass Ceiling Commission Report, 1995, as updated.

**"GLASS WALLS" AND "GLASS ELEVATORS"** A related problem is that women have tended to advance to senior management in a limited number of functional areas, such as human resources and corporate communications. Because jobs in these "supporting" areas tend to pay less than jobs in sales, marketing, operations, or finance, the overall impact is to reduce women's career progression and income. Limits that keep women from progressing only in certain fields have been referred to as "glass walls" or "glass elevators." Some firms have established formal mentoring programs in order to break down glass walls.

# Age Discrimination

For many years, race and sex discrimination cases overshadowed those dealing with age discrimination. Starting with passage of the 1978 amendments to the Age Discrimination in Employment Act (ADEA) of 1967, a dramatic increase in age discrimination suits occurred. However, in recent years, age discrimination still has followed race and sex discrimination as the basis for complaints filed with the EEOC.

## Age Discrimination in Employment Act (ADEA)

The Age Discriminaton in Employment Act of 1967, amended in 1978 and 1986, makes it illegal for an employer to discriminate in compensation, terms, conditions, or privileges of employment because of an individual's age. The later amendments first raised the minimum mandatory retirement age to 70 and then eliminated it completely. The ADEA applies to all individuals above the age of 40 working for employers having 20 or more workers. However, the act does not apply if age is a job-related occupational qualification.

Prohibitions against age discrimination do not apply when an individual is disciplined or discharged for good cause, such as poor job performance. Older

**LOGGING ON . . .**
**Administration on Aging**
This is an on-line Internet and e-mail resource on aging. This site provides information in its directory on associations, educational programs, government agencies and organizations, new sources, and current research.

**http://www.aoa.dhhs.gov/
aoa/pages/jpostlst.html**

workers who are poor performers can be terminated, just as anyone else can be. However, numerous suits under the ADEA have been filed involving workers over 40 who were forced to take "voluntary retirement" when organizational restructuring or workforce reduction programs were implemented.

**"OVERQUALIFIED" OLDER EMPLOYEES**  One issue that has led to age discrimination charges is labeling older workers as "overqualified" for jobs or promotions. In a number of cases, courts have ruled that the term *overqualified* may have been used as a code word for workers being too old, thus causing them not to be considered for employment.[18]

**AGE DISCRIMINATION AND WORKFORCE REDUCTIONS**  In the past decade, early retirement programs and organizational downsizing have been used by many employers to reduce their employment costs. Illegal age discrimination sometimes occurs in the process when an individual over the age of 40 is forced into retirement or is denied employment or promotion on the basis of age. If disparate impact or treatment for those over 40 exists, age discrimination occurs.

Ensuring that age discrimination—or any kind of illegal discrimination—does not affect employment decisions requires that documentation of performance be completed by supervisors and managers. In the case of older employees, care must be taken that references to age ("good old Fred" or "need younger blood") in conversations are not used with older employees. As mentioned, terminations based on documented performance deficiencies not related to age are perfectly legal.

However, employers should be careful about what they document and say. In one case, Westinghouse Electric abolished a number of jobs held by individuals over 40. A year after the terminations, a Westinghouse executive wrote a memo describing older employees as "blockers" who prevented young managers from being promoted. A 52-year-old former Westinghouse employee sued for age discrimination, and the U.S. Supreme Court ruled against Westinghouse because the memo reflected a "cumulative management attitude" about older workers. The terminated employee was awarded almost $250,000.[19]

## Older Workers Benefit Protection Act (OWBPA)

*BNA: 1805.60.60.10*
**OWBPA Waivers**
Details on the provisions for waivers and older worker rights in early retirement buyouts and workforce reductions can be reviewed here.

The Older Workers Benefit Protection Act (OWBPA) of 1990 was passed to amend the ADEA to ensure that equal treatment for older workers occurs in early retirement or severance situations. Many early retirement and downsizing efforts by employers target older workers by hoping to entice them to choose early retirement buyouts and enhanced severance packages. In exchange, employers often require the workers to sign waivers indicating that by accepting the retirement incentives, the workers waive their rights to sue the employers for age discrimination.

The OWBPA specifies that employees considering an early retirement buyout enhancement must:

- Receive copies of any waiver of their rights to sue for age discrimination.
- Be given sufficient time to consider the buyout offer, most frequently up to 45 days if they must sign a waiver of age discrimination rights.
- Be able to revoke their retirement agreement within seven days of signing the waiver.

These and other provisions of the OWBPA have provided guidelines to employers, as well as protection for older workers, when early retirement buyout and downsizing programs are used.

**FIGURE 6–4** *Major Sections of the Americans with Disabilities Act*

| Title I | Title II | Title III | Title IV | Title V |
|---|---|---|---|---|
| **Employment Provisions** | **Public Participation and Service** | **Public Access** | **Telecommunications** | **Administration and Enforcement** |
| Prohibits employment-related discrimination against persons with disabilities | Prohibits discrimination related to participation of disabled persons in government programs and for public transportation | Ensures accessibility of public and commercial facilities | Requires provision of telecommunications capabilities and television closed captions for persons with hearing and speech disabilities | Describes administrative and enforcement provisions and lists who is not covered by ADA |

# Americans with Disabilities Act (ADA)

The passage of the Americans with Disabilities Act (ADA) in 1990 represented an expansion in the scope and impact of laws and regulations on discrimination against individuals with disabilities. All employers with 15 or more employees are covered by the provisions of the ADA, which are enforced by the EEOC. The ADA was built upon the Vocational Rehabilitation Act of 1973 and the Rehabilitation Act of 1974, both of which applied only to federal contractors.

The ADA affects more than just employment matters, as Figure 6–4 shows, and it applies to private employers, employment agencies, labor unions, and state and local governments. The ADA contains the following requirements dealing with employment:

- Discrimination is prohibited against individuals with disabilities who can perform the *essential job functions,* a standard that is somewhat vague.
- A covered employer must have *reasonable accommodation* for persons with disabilities, so that they can function as employees, unless *undue hardship* would be placed on the employer.
- Preemployment medical examinations are prohibited except after an employment offer is made, conditional upon individuals passing a physical examination.
- Federal contractors and subcontractors with contracts valued at more than $2,500 must take affirmative action to hire qualified disabled individuals.

## Discrimination Against Individuals with Disabilities

Employers looking for workers with the knowledge, skills, and abilities to perform jobs often have neglected a significant source of good, dedicated people—individuals with physical or mental disabilities. According to U.S. government estimates, almost 50 million Americans have some sort of disability. Many of them between the ages of 16 and 64 are unemployed but would like to work if given appropriate opportunities. When individuals with disabilities are hired and placed in jobs that match their capabilities, they often succeed.

The number of complaints filed under the ADA has skyrocketed in recent years. According to statistics from the EEOC, over 40,000 disability discrimination complaints were filed in the first several years the act was in effect. Over half of those complaints had to do with discharge of employees with disabilities or employees who became disabled. Another 25% dealt with failure to provide reasonable accommodation.[20]

## Who Is Disabled?

**Disabled person**

Someone who has a physical or mental impairment that substantially limits that person in some major life activities, who has a record of such an impairment, or who is regarded as having such an impairment.

As defined by the ADA, a **disabled person** is someone who has a physical or mental impairment that substantially limits that person in some major life activities, who has a record of such an impairment, or who is regarded as having such an impairment. Persons who qualify for protection under the act include those who have obvious disabilities such as the absence of a limb, sight or hearing impairments, or other physical disabilities. Individuals with less visible disabilities classified as disabled under the ADA include persons with life-threatening diseases (AIDS, cancer, leukemia), rehabilitated drug users and alcoholics, and persons with major muscular limitations or breathing difficulties. People with various mental disabilities or impairments also qualify under the ADA. Regulations exclude current users of illegal drugs, people with sexual behavior disorders, and compulsive gamblers from being classified as disabled.[21]

**EEOC GUIDELINES ON DISABILITIES** To provide better guidance to those covered by the ADA, the EEOC issued additional clarifications of its guidelines, including the following:

- *Impairment* was defined as a physiological disorder affecting one or more body systems or a mental/psychological disorder. Specifically *excluded* are
  - Environmental, cultural, and economic disadvantages
  - Homosexuality and bisexuality
  - Normal deviation in height and weight
  - Normal personality traits (rudeness, quick temper, arrogance, etc.)
  - Pregnancy
  - Physical characteristics
- *Thinking, concentrating,* and *interacting with other people* were included as *major life activities*. Individuals impaired in one of these areas are covered by the ADA.
- A *substantial limitation* was clarified to mean a limitation in life activities other than working.

In spite of the EEOC guidelines, there is still some confusion as to who is disabled. For example, some court decisions and laws have protected individuals perceived as impaired to a degree that their employment is affected. Thus, even individuals with facial disfigurements may qualify for protection against employer discrimination. Other court decisions have found individuals who have high blood pressure, epilepsy, allergies, obesity, and color blindness to be disabled. Figure 6–5 indicates the most frequently cited impairments in ADA cases filed with the EEOC.

**MENTAL DISABILITIES** A growing area of concern under the ADA is individuals with mental disabilities. A mental illness is often more difficult to diagnose than a physical disability. In an attempt to add clarification, the EEOC has released explanatory guidelines; but the situations are still confusing. In one case, an employee claimed that mental stress due to a negative performance review meant

**FIGURE 6–5** *ADA Most Frequently Identified Impairments*

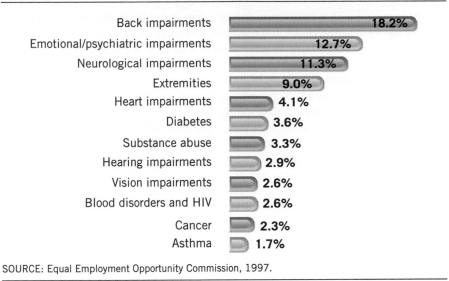

SOURCE: Equal Employment Opportunity Commission, 1997.

that she had a disability. Fortunately for employers, a U.S. Court of Appeals ruled against the employee.[22]

Deciding whether job pressures can create a disability covered under the ADA has been the subject of several court cases. Generally, employers have prevailed when mental disability charges have been brought against employers.[23]

**LIFE-THREATENING ILLNESSES** In recent years, the types of disabilities covered by various local, state, and federal acts prohibiting discrimination have been expanded. For example, a U.S. Supreme Court case held that an employer cannot discriminate against an individual whom the employer believes may have a contagious disease. The case involved an individual who had a relapse of tuberculosis and was discharged from her job as a schoolteacher because her employer feared her illness might be contagious.[24]

The most feared contagious disease is acquired immunodeficiency syndrome (AIDS). The disease was almost unknown in 1980, but it currently is estimated that a million people in the United States either have AIDS or are classified as HIV-positive.[25] A recent U.S. Supreme Court decision ruled that individuals infected with human immunodeficiency virus (HIV), not just those with AIDS, have a disability covered by the ADA.[26]

Unfortunately, employers and employees often react with fear about working with an AIDS victim. Nevertheless, if an employer does have an employee with a life-threatening illness, educating other employees is more appropriate than terminating the victim's employment. A medical leave of absence (without pay if that is the general policy) can be used to assist the AIDS-afflicted employee during medical treatments. Other employees should be told to keep medical records of affected persons confidential. Also, employees who indicate that they will not work with an AIDS victim should be told that their refusal to work is not protected by law, and that they could be subject to disciplinary action up to and including discharge.

## Essential Job Functions

**Essential job functions**
The fundamental job duties of the employment position that an individual with a disability holds or desires.

The ADA requires that employers identify the **essential job functions**—the fundamental job duties of the employment position that an individual with a disability holds or desires. These functions do not include marginal functions of the position.

The essential functions should be identified in written job descriptions that indicate the amount of time spent performing various functions and their criticality. Most employers have interpreted this provision to mean that they should develop and maintain current and comprehensive job descriptions for all jobs. These job descriptions should list the job functions in the order of "essentiality." Also, the job specification statements that identify the qualifications required of those in the jobs should specify the exact knowledge, skills, abilities, and physical demands involved. For example, hearing, seeing, speaking, climbing, lifting, and stooping should be mentioned when those actions are necessary in performing specific jobs.

## Reasonable Accommodation

**Reasonable accommodation**
A modification or adjustment to a job or work environment that enables a qualified individual with a disability to have equal employment opportunity.

A **reasonable accommodation** is a modification or adjustment to a job or work environment that enables a qualified individual with a disability to have equal employment opportunity. Employers are required to provide reasonable accommodation for individuals with disabilities to ensure that illegal discrimination does not occur.

There are several areas of reasonable accommodation. First, architectural barriers should not prohibit disabled individuals' *access to work areas or rest rooms.* A second area of reasonable accommodation is the *assignment of work tasks.* Satisfying this requirement may mean modifying jobs, work schedules, equipment, or work area layouts. Some examples include teaching sign language to a supervisor so that a deaf person can be employed, modifying work schedules to assist disabled workers, and having another worker perform minor duties. Also, employers can provide *special equipment,* such as visually enhanced computers or speech synthesizers for those with vision impairments.[27] Figure 6–6 shows some means commonly used by employers to provide reasonable accommodations. In summary, there are few specific rules on which an employer can rely in this area, because the courts consider every situation on its own merits.

## Undue Hardship

**Undue hardship**
Condition created when making a reasonable accommodation for individuals with disabilities that imposes significant difficulty or expense on an employer.

Reasonable accommodation is restricted to actions that do not place an "undue hardship" on an employer. An action places **undue hardship** on an employer if it imposes significant difficulty or expense. The ADA offers only general guidelines on when an accommodation becomes unreasonable and places undue hardship on an employer. More information on reasonable accommodations is given in Chapter 7, on job analysis and design.

Initially, employers were very concerned about facing extensive costs for remodeling facilities or making other accommodations, because some accommodations can be expensive. However, a study of compliance efforts done by the U.S. General Accounting Office found that over 50% of all accommodations cost employers nothing, while another 30% cost less than $500.[28]

**FIGURE 6–6** *Common Means of Reasonable Accommodation*

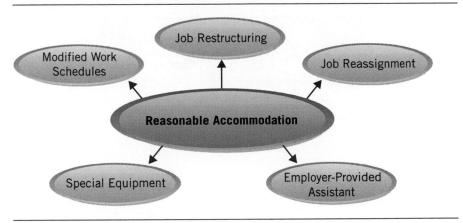

# Other Bases of Discrimination

There are several other bases of discrimination that various laws have identified as illegal. Religious discrimination is an area in which a growing number of issues are having to be addressed by employers.

## Religious Discrimination

Title VII of the Civil Rights Act identifies discrimination on the basis of religion as illegal. However, religious schools and institutions can use religion as a bona fide occupational qualification (BFOQ) for employment practices on a limited scale. As Figure 6–7 depicts, three major facets must be considered by employers with employee religious issues at work. The extent of religious discrimination is seen in a 99% increase in charges of illegal religious discrimination being filed with the EEOC in a recent year, totaling about 1,700. Another sign of the growing concern about religion is the development of religious guidelines for U.S. government employees issued in 1997. A bill to extend the guidelines to all employers has been proposed as well. The Workplace Religious Freedom Act explicitly spells out employer requirements to accommodate employees' religious practices. However, that bill has not yet been passed into law.

**WORK SCHEDULES AND REASONABLE ACCOMMODATION** Many religions have days of worship other than Sunday, which is typical in many U.S. religious denominations. Also, holidays other than Christmas are observed by individuals of the Jewish, Muslim, and other faiths.[29] As the workforce has become more diversified, all of these differences are affecting employers' holiday time-off and work-scheduling policies.

A major guide in this area was established by the U.S. Supreme Court in *TWA v. Hardison*. In that case, the Supreme Court ruled that an employer is required to make *reasonable accommodation* of an employee's religious beliefs. Because TWA had done so, the ruling denied Hardison's discrimination charges.[30]

**FIGURE 6–7** *Religious Issues at Work*

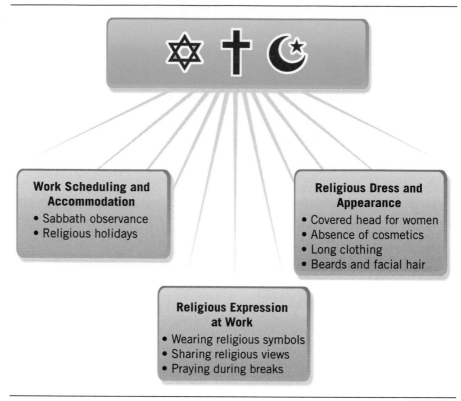

The impact of that decision can be seen in a recent case involving an employee who wished to make a religious pilgrimage in October. However, the retailer for whom the individual worked had a policy prohibiting employee vacations between October and January, due to the heavy holiday customer demands. A U.S. Court of Appeals ruled for the employer, finding that the employer's policy had a business purpose and that the employee could have taken the trip at a different time.[31] Both this case and others indicate that employers are advised to offer alternative work schedules, make use of compensatory time off, or otherwise adjust to employees' religious beliefs. Once reasonable accommodation efforts have been made, employers are considered to have abided by the law.[32]

**EXPRESSION OF RELIGIOUS BELIEFS** Another issue relates to *religious expression.* In the last several years, there have been several cases in which employees have sued employers for prohibiting them from expressing their religious beliefs at work. In one case, a Muslim employee filed a complaint that the employer would not let him pray during his work breaks, and that coworkers harassed him and wiped their shoes on his prayer rug. A state discrimination agency ruled for the employee.[33] In other cases, employers have had to take action because of the complaints by other workers that employees were aggressively "pushing" their religious views at work.

**RELIGIOUS DRESS AND APPEARANCE** Another potential area for conflict between employer policies and employees' religious practices is in the area of dress and appearance. Some religions have standards about the appropriate attire for women.

Also, some religions expect men to have beards and facial hair. For instance, a woman was fired for violating a retailer's dress standards by wearing a *hijab,* a head scarf worn by many Muslim women. After she filed a compaint outside the organization, the corporate office of the retailer requested that the woman be re-instated and granted her back pay for two weeks.[34] However, if the clothing rep-resents a safety hazard, such as wearing of long clothing around machinery, then employers generally have been able to enforce their requirements.

## Discrimination and Appearance

In addition to appearance issues related to religion, several EEO cases have been filed concerning the physical appearance of employees. Court decisions consis-tently have allowed employers to have dress codes as long as they are applied uni-formly. However, requiring a dress code for women but not for men has been ruled to constitute disparate treatment; therefore, it would be discriminatory. Most of the dress standards contested have required workers to dress in a conser-vative manner.

**HEIGHT/WEIGHT RESTRICTIONS** Many times, height/weight restrictions have been used to discriminate against women or other protected groups. For example, the state of Alabama violated Title VII in setting height and weight restrictions for correctional counselors. The restrictions (5 feet 2 inches and 120 pounds) would have excluded 41.14% of the female population of the country, but less than 1% of the men. The Supreme Court found that the state's attempt to justify the re-quirements as essential for job-related strength failed for lack of evidence. The Court suggested that if strength was the quality sought, the state should have adopted a strength requirement.[35]

Individuals also have brought cases claiming employment discrimination based on obesity or on unattractive appearance. Employers have lost many of the cases because of their inability to prove any direct job-related value in their re-quirements. In other cases, some courts have ruled that under the Americans with Disabilities Act (ADA), obese individuals may qualify as having a covered disability when they are perceived and treated as if they have a disability.

**HAIR AND GROOMING** Some employers have policies regarding the length of hair, facial hair, and other grooming standards. In one case, four men were fired for re-fusing to cut their long hair. The men claimed that they were being discriminated against because women workers were allowed to have longer hair. A U.S. Court of Appeals ruled that employer policies prohibiting long hair on male employees, but not female employees, are allowed.[36]

Cases also have addressed the issue of facial hair for men. Because African American men are more likely than white males to suffer from a skin disease that is worsened by shaving, they have filed suits challenging policies prohibiting beards or long sideburns. Generally, courts have ruled for employers in these cases, unless religious issues are involved.

## Sexual Orientation and Gay Rights

Recent battles over revising policies for nonheterosexuals in the U.S. military services illustrate the depth of emotions that accompany discussions of "gay rights." Some states and cities have passed laws prohibiting discrimination based

**LOGGING ON . . .**
**American Federation of Teachers—Human Rights and Community Relations**
This website provides information on conferences, conventions, news developments, resource materials, civil and human rights issues, and related sites regarding sexual orientation.

http://www.aft.org/humanrights/issues.htm

on sexual orientation or lifestyle. Even the issue of benefits coverage for "domestic partners," whether heterosexual or homosexual, has been the subject of state and city legislation. However, at the federal level no laws of a similar nature have been passed. Whether gay men and lesbians have rights under the equal protection amendment to the U.S. Constitution has not been decided by the U.S. Supreme Court.

Regarding transsexuals (individuals who have had sex-change surgery), court cases and the EEOC have ruled that sex discrimination under Title VII applies to a person's gender at birth. Thus, it does not apply to the new gender of those who have had gender-altering operations. Transvestites and individuals with other sexual behavior disorders are specifically excluded from being considered as disabled under the Americans with Disabilities Act of 1990.

## Veterans' Employment Rights

The employment rights of military veterans and reservists have been addressed several times. The two most important laws are highlighted next.

**VIETNAM-ERA VETERANS READJUSTMENT ACT OF 1974** Concern about the readjustment and absorption of Vietnam-era veterans into the workforce led to the passage of the Vietnam-Era Veterans Readjustment Act. The act requires that affirmative action in hiring and advancing Vietnam-era veterans be undertaken by federal contractors and subcontractors having contracts of $10,000 or more.

**UNIFORMED SERVICES EMPLOYMENT AND REEMPLOYMENT RIGHTS ACT OF 1994** Under the Uniformed Services Employment and Reemployment Rights Act of 1994, employees are required to notify their employers of military service obligations. Employees serving in the military must be provided leaves of absence and have reemployment rights for up to five years. Other provisions protect the right to benefits of employees called to military duty.[37]

## Seniority and Discrimination

Conflict between EEO regulations and organizational practices that give preference to employees on the basis of seniority represent another problem area. Employers, especially those with union contracts, frequently make layoff, promotion, and internal transfer decisions by giving employees with longer service first consideration. However, the use of seniority often means that there is disparate impact on protected-class members, who may be the workers most recently hired. The result of this system is that protected-class members who have obtained jobs through an affirmative action program are at a disadvantage because of their low levels of seniority. They may find themselves "last hired, first fired" or "last hired, last promoted." In some cases, the courts have held that a valid seniority system does *not* violate rights based on sex or race. In other cases, gender and racial considerations have been given precedence over seniority.

# EEO Compliance

Employers must comply with EEO regulations and guidelines. To do so, management should have an EEO policy statement and maintain all required EEO-related records.

## EEO Policy Statement

It is crucial that all employers have a written EEO policy statement. This policy should be widely disseminated throughout the organization. The policy can be communicated by posting it on bulletin boards, printing it in employee handbooks, reproducing it in organizational newsletters, and reinforcing it in training programs. The contents of the policy should clearly state the organizational commitment to equal employment. Particularly important is to incorporate the listing of the appropriate protected classes in the policy statement.[38]

*BNA: 410.40.50*
**EEO Policy Statement**
A sample EEO policy statement can be found at this location. Review it and compare it to the EEO policy statement in an actual employee handbook.

## EEO Records

All employers with 15 or more employees are required to keep certain records that can be requested by the Equal Employment Opportunity Commission (EEOC). If the organization meets certain criteria, then reports and investigations by the Office of Federal Contract Compliance Programs (OFCCP) also must be addressed. Under various laws, employers also are required to post an "officially approved notice" in a prominent place where employees can see it. This notice states that the employer is an equal opportunity employer and does not discriminate.

**EEO RECORDS RETENTION** All employment records must be maintained as required by the EEOC, and employer information reports must be filed with the federal government. Further, any personnel or employment record made or kept by the employer must be maintained for review by the EEOC. Such records include application forms and records concerning hiring, promotion, demotion, transfer, layoff, termination, rates of pay or other terms of compensation, and selection for training and apprenticeship. Even application forms or test papers completed by unsuccessful applicants may be requested. The length of time documents must be kept varies, but generally three years is recommended as a minimum.

Keeping good records, whether required by the government or not, is simply a good HR practice. Complete records are necessary for an employer to respond when a charge of discrimination is made and a compliance investigation begins.

**ANNUAL REPORTING FORM** The basic report that must be filed with the EEOC is the annual report form EEO–1 (see Appendix E). The following employers must file this report:

- All employers with 100 or more employees, except state and local governments
- Subsidiaries of other companies where total employees equal 100
- Federal contractors with at least 50 employees and contracts of $50,000 or more
- Financial institutions in which government funds are held or saving bonds are issued

The annual report must be filed by March 31 for the preceding year. The form requires employment data by job category, classified according to various protected classes.

**APPLICANT FLOW DATA** Under EEO laws and regulations, employers may be required to show that they do not discriminate in the recruiting and selection of members of protected classes. For instance, the number of women who applied

**FIGURE 6–8** *Applicant Flow Data Form*

# EQUAL EMPLOYMENT DATA COLLECTION FORM

The following statistical information is required for compliance with federal laws assuring equal employment opportunity without regard to race, color, sex, national origin, religion, age or disability, as well as the Vietnam-era readjustment act. The information requested is voluntary and will remain separate from your application for employment.

A  MONTH  DAY  YEAR   APPLICATION DATE

B  ☐☐☐ ☐☐ ☐☐☐☐  APPLICANT SOCIAL SECURITY NUMBER

C  ☐  FIRST INITIAL          D  ☐  MIDDLE INITIAL

D  ☐☐☐☐☐☐☐☐☐☐☐☐☐☐☐☐  LAST NAME

F  STREET   ☐☐☐☐☐☐☐☐☐☐☐☐☐☐☐☐☐☐☐☐☐☐  ADDRESS

G  CITY ☐☐☐☐☐☐☐☐☐☐☐☐  STATE (first 2 letters) ☐☐  ZIP ☐☐☐☐☐

H  ☐  1/ EEO CODES          EEO CODES 1/

| | |
|---|---|
| A—White Male | F— Hispanic Female (Spanish Orgin) |
| B—White Female | G—American Indian/Alaskan Native Male |
| C—Black Male | H—American Indian/Alaskan Native Female |
| D—Black Female | I— Asian or Pacific Islander Male |
| E—Hispanic Male (Spanish Orgin) | J— Asian or Pacific Islander Female |

MONTH  DAY  YEAR   BIRTH DATE

J  ☐  DO YOU HAVE A DISABILITY—Impairment which substantially limits one or more of your life activities?

K  ☐  ARE YOU A DISABLED VETERAN— 30% V.A. Compensation or discharged because of disability incurred in line of duty

L  ☐  ARE YOU A VIETNAM ERA VETERAN— 180 days Active Duty between Aug. 15, 1964 & May 7, 1975

JOB YOUR HAVE APPLIED FOR _____

LOCATION APPLICATION IS MADE FOR _____

(City or Town)                                     State

TO BE COMPLETED BY OFFICE ACCEPTING APPLICATION

☐  DIVISION

DEPT. APPLICATION IS MADE FOR

HR STAFF USE ONLY

☐☐☐☐☐☐☐☐☐☐

☐☐☐☐        ☐

M  ☐  REFERRAL SOURCE

A—Walk in/Write in
B—Ad Response
C—State Employment Agency
D—College Placement Office
E—Minority Referral Agency
F—Internet
G—Private Employment Agency

Applicant's Signature

and the number hired may be compared with the selection rate for men to determine if adverse impact exists. The fact that protected-class identification is not available in employer records is not considered a valid excuse for failure to provide the data required.

Because collection of racial data on application blanks and other preemployment records is not permitted, the EEOC allows employers to use a "visual" survey or a separate *applicant flow form* that is not used in the selection process. An example of such a form is shown in Figure 6–8. Notice that this form is filled out voluntarily by the applicant, and that the data must be maintained separately from all selection-related materials. These analyses may be useful in showing that an employer has underutilized a protected class because of an inadequate applicant flow of protected-class members, in spite of special efforts to recruit them.

## EEOC Compliance Investigation Process

When a discrimination complaint is received by the EEOC or a similar agency, it must be processed. Figure 6–9 indicates the number of complaints in a recent year by type of discrimination. To handle a growing number of complaints, the EEOC has instituted a system that categorizes complaints into three categories: *priority, needing further investigation,* and *immediate dismissal.*[39] If the EEOC decides to pursue a complaint, it uses the process outlined here.

**COMPLIANCE INVESTIGATIVE STAGES** In a typical situation, a complaint goes through several stages before the compliance process is completed. First, the charges

**LOGGING ON . . .**
**The U.S. Equal Employment Opportunity Commission— Enforcement Statistics**
The EEOC website gives access to statistics regarding the Equal Pay Act, ADA, Age Discrimination Act, and the Civil Rights Act.

http://www.eeoc.gov/stats/

**FIGURE 6–9** *Recent Year Charge Statistics from EEOC*

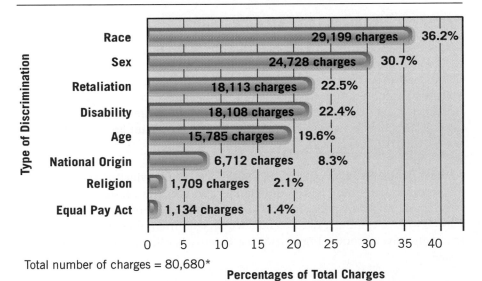

Total number of charges = 80,680*

**Percentages of Total Charges**

*Number for total charges reflects the number of individual charge filings. Because individuals often file charges claiming multiple types of discrimination, the number of total charges may be less than the total of the eight types of discrimination.

SOURCE: U.S. Equal Employment Opportunity Commission, 1998
(http://www.eeoc.gov/stats/charges.html).

are filed by an individual, a group of individuals, or their representative. A charge must be filed within 180 days of when the alleged discriminatory action occurred. Then the EEOC staff reviews the specifics of the charges to determine if it has *jurisdiction,* which means that the agency is authorized to investigate that type of charge. If jurisdiction exists, a notice of the charge must be served on the employer within 10 days after the filing, and the employer is asked to respond. Following the charge notification, the EEOC's major thurst turns to investigating the complaint.

If the charge is found to be valid, the next stage involves mediation efforts by the agency and the employer. If the employer agrees that discrimination has occurred and accepts the proposed settlement, then the employer posts a notice of relief within the company and takes the agreed-on actions. This notice indicates that the employer has reached an agreement on a discrimination charge and reiterates the employer's commitment to avoid future discriminatory actions.

**Right-to-sue letter**
A letter issued by the EEOC that notifies a complainant that he or she has 90 days in which to file a personal suit in federal court.

**INDIVIDUAL RIGHT TO SUE** If the employer objects to the charge and rejects conciliation, the EEOC can file suit or issue a **right-to-sue letter** to the complainant. The letter notifies the person that he or she has 90 days in which to file a personal suit in federal court. Thus, if the EEOC decides that it will not bring suit on behalf of the complainant, the individual has the right to bring suit. The suit usually is brought in the U.S. District Court having jurisdiction in the area.

**LITIGATION** In the court litigation stage, a legal trial takes place in the appropriate state or federal court. At that point, both sides retain lawyers and rely on the court to render a decision. The Civil Rights Act of 1991 provides for jury trials in most EEO cases. If either party disagrees with the court ruling, either can file appeals with a higher court. The U.S. Supreme Court becomes the ultimate adjudication body.

## Employer Responses to EEO Complaints

Many problems and expenses associated with EEO complaints can be controlled by employers who vigorously investigate their employees' discrimination complaints before they are taken to outside agencies. An internal employee complaint system and prompt, thorough respones to problem situations are essential tools in reducing EEO charges and in remedying illegal discriminatory actions. The general steps in effectively responding to an EEO complaint are outlined in Figure 6–10 and discussed next.

**REVIEW CLAIM AND EMPLOYEE'S PERSONNEL FILE** By reviewing the claim, the HR staff can determine which individuals and agencies are handling the investigation. Also, any personnel files on the employees involved should be reviewed to determine the nature and adequacy of internal documentation. For many employers, contacting outside legal counsel at this point also may be advisable.

**TAKE NO RETALIATORY ACTION** It is crucial that no retaliatory actions, even snide remarks, be used against individuals filing EEO complaints.[40] The HR staff should also notify relevant managers and supervisors of the complaint, instructing them to refrain from any retaliatory actions, such as changing job assignments or work schedules unnecessarily. However, appropriate disciplinary action that is work related still can be administered.

**FIGURE 6–10** *Stages in Responding to EEO Complaints*

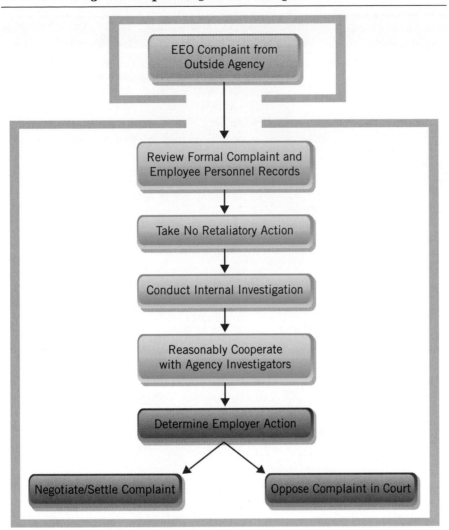

**CONDUCT INTERNAL INVESTIGATION** A thorough internal investigation of the facts and circumstances of the claim should be conducted. Some firms use outside legal counsel to conduct these investigations in order to obtain a more objective view. Once the investigative data have been obtained, then a decision about the strength or weakness of the employer's case should be determined. If the case is weak, possible settlement discussions may begin with the enforcement agency representatives. However, if the employer believes that a strong case exists, then the employer likely will draft a response to the claim that states the relevant facts and reasons why the employer does not believe the complaint is valid.

**REASONABLY COOPERATE WITH AGENCY INVESTIGATORS** It is highly recommended that the agency investigators be treated professionally, rather than as

**FIGURE 6–11** *Guidelines to Lawful and Unlawful Preemployment Inquiries*

| Subject of Inquiry | It May Not Be Discriminatory To Inquire About: | It May Be Discriminatory To Inquire About: |
| --- | --- | --- |
| 1. Name | a. Whether applicant has ever worked under a different name | a. The original name of an applicant whose name has been legally changed. <br> b. The ethnic association of applicant's name |
| 2. Age | a. If applicant is over the age of 18 <br> b. If applicant is under the age of 18 or 21 if job related (i.e., selling liquor in retail store) | a. Date of birth <br> b. Date of high school graduation |
| 3. Residence | a. Applicant's place of residence; length of applicant's residence in state and/or city where employer is located | a. Previous addresses <br> b. Birthplace of applicant or applicant's parents |
| 4. Race or Color | | a. Applicant's race or color of applicant's skin |
| 5. National Origin and Ancestry | | a. Applicant's lineage, ancestry, national origin, parentage, or nationality <br> b. Nationality of applicant's parents or spouse |
| 6. Sex and Family Composition | | a. Sex of applicant <br> b. Dependents of applicant <br> c. Marital status <br> d. Child-care arrangements |
| 7. Creed or Religion | | a. Applicant's religious affiliation <br> b. Church, parish, or holidays observed |
| 8. Citizenship | a. Whether the applicant is a citizen of the United States <br> b. Whether the applicant is in the country on a visa that permits him or her to work or is a citizen | a. Whether applicant is a citizen of a country other than the United States |
| 9. Language | a. Language applicant speaks and/or writes fluently, if job related | a. Applicant's native tongue; language commonly used at home |
| 10. References | a. Names of persons willing to provide professional and/or character references for applicant | a. Name of applicant's pastor or religious leader |

"the enemy." Berating the investigator, creating unncessary procedural demands, or refusing to allow access to requested documentation (within reason) serve only to antagonize the investigator. However, cooperating does not mean agreeing with all requests by the agency investigators, whether related to the existing charge or not.

**DETERMINE WHETHER TO NEGOTIATE, SETTLE, OR OPPOSE COMPLAINT** Once the agency investigation has been completed, the employer will be notified of the results. Also, the remedies proposed by the agency investigators will be identified. At that point, the HR staff, outside legal counsel, and senior managers often meet

**FIGURE 6–11** *Guidelines to Lawful and Unlawful Preemployment Inquiries (continued)*

| Subject of Inquiry | It May Not Be Discriminatory To Inquire About: | It May Be Discriminatory To Inquire About: |
|---|---|---|
| 11. Relatives | a. Names of relatives already employed by the employer | a. Name and/or address of any relative of applicant <br> b. Whom to contact in case of emergency |
| 12. Organizations | a. Applicant's membership in any professional, service, or trade organization | a. All clubs or social organizations to which applicant belongs |
| 13. Arrest Record and Convictions | a. Convictions, if related to job performance (disclaimer should accompany) | a. Number and kinds of arrests <br> b. Convictions unless related to job performance |
| 14. Photographs | | a. Photograph with application, with resume, or before hiring |
| 15. Height and Weight | | a. Any inquiry into height and weight of applicant except where a BFOQ |
| 16. Physical Limitations | a. Whether applicant has the ability to perform job-related functions with or without accommodation | a. The nature or severity of an illness or the individual's physical condition <br> b. Whether applicant has ever filed workers' compensation claim <br> c. Any recent or past operations or surgery and dates |
| 17. Education | a. Training applicant has received if related to the job under consideration <br> b. Highest level of education attained, if validated that having certain educational background (e.g., high school diploma or college degree) is necessary to perform the specific job | |
| 18. Military | a. What branch of the military applicant served in <br> b. Type of education or training received in military <br> c. Rank at discharge | a. Type of military discharge |
| 19. Financial Status | | a. Applicant's debts or assets <br> b. Garnishments |

SOURCE: Developed by Robert L. Mathis, Mathis & Associates, L.L.C., 1429 North 131st Avenue Circle, Omaha, NE 68154. All rights reserved. No part of this may be reproduced, in any form or by any means, without written permission from Mathis & Associates.

to decide whether to settle the complaint, negotiate different terms of the settlement, or to oppose the charges and begin court proceedings.

## Preemployment vs. After-Hire Inquiries

Figure 6–11 lists preemployment inquiries and identifies whether they may or may not be discriminatory. All those preemployment inquiries labeled in the figure as "may be discriminatory" have been so designated because of findings in a variety of court cases. Those labeled "may not be discriminatory" are practices

*BNA:485.10.10–*
*485.10.20*
**Job Offers and Acceptance and Rejection Letters**
Information on making job offers and contents of job offer letters are contained here.

that are legal, but only if they reflect a business necessity or are job related for the specific job under review.

Once an employer tells an applicant he or she is hired (the "point of hire"), inquiries that were prohibited earlier may be made. After hiring, medical examination forms, group insurance cards, and other enrollment cards containing inquiries related directly or indirectly to sex, age, or other bases may be requested. Photographs or evidence of race, religion, or national origin also may be requested after hire for legal and necessary purposes, but not before. Such data should be maintained in a separate personnel records system in order to avoid their use in making appraisal, discipline, termination, or promotion decisions.

# Affirmative Action Plans (AAPs)

Throughout the last 30 years, employers with federal contracts and other government entities have had to address additional areas of potential discrimination. Several acts and regulations have been issued that apply specifically to government contractors. These acts and regulations specify a minimum number of employees and size of government contracts. The requirements primarily come from federal Executive Orders 11246, 11375, and 11478. Many states have similar requirements for firms with state government contracts.

## Executive Orders 11246, 11375, and 11478

**Executive order**
An order issued by the President of the United States to provide direction to government departments on a specific issue or area.

Numerous executive orders have been issued that require employers holding federal government contracts not to discriminate on the basis of race, color, religion, national origin, or sex. An **executive order** is issued by the President of the United States to provide direction to government departments on a specific issue or area.

During the 1960s, by executive order, the Office of Federal Contract Compliance Programs (OFCCP) in the U.S. Department of Labor was established and given responsibility for enforcing nondiscrimination in government contracts. Under Executive Order 11246, issued in 1965, amended by Executive Order 11375 in 1967, and updated by Executive Order 11478 in 1979, the Secretary of Labor was given the power to cancel the contract of a noncomplying contractor or blacklist a noncomplying employer from future government contracts. These orders and additional equal employment acts have required employers to take affirmative action to overcome the effects of past discriminatory practices.

## Who Must Have an Affirmative Action Plan?

Even though affirmative action as a concept has been challenged in court, as described in Chapter 5, most federal government contractors still are required to have affirmative action plans (AAPs). Generally, an employer with at least 50 employees and over $50,000 in government contracts must have a formal, written affirmative action plan. A government contractor with fewer than 50 employees and contracts totaling more than $50,000 can be required to have an AAP if it has been found guilty of discrimination by the EEOC or other agencies. The contract size can vary depending on the protected group and the various laws on which the regulations rest.

FIGURE 6–12 *Components of an Affirmative Action Plan*

**I. INTERNAL BACKGROUND REVIEW**

**EEO and AAP Policy Statements**
- Accountability
- Dissemination
- Program components

**Workforce Analysis**
- Department analysis
- Job title/salary analysis
- Lines of progression analysis

**EEO and AAP Policy Statements**
- Job group definition
- Titles by job group
- Salaries by job group

**II. ANALYSES AND COMPARISONS**

**Availability Analysis—Externally**
- Eight-factor analysis
- By job group

**Utilization Analysis—Internally**
- Disparate impact calculation

**III. ACTIONS AND REPORTING**

**Goals and Timetables**
- Actions to reduce underutilization and concentration
- Time lines

**Internal Auditing and Reporting**
- Frequency
- Corrective action

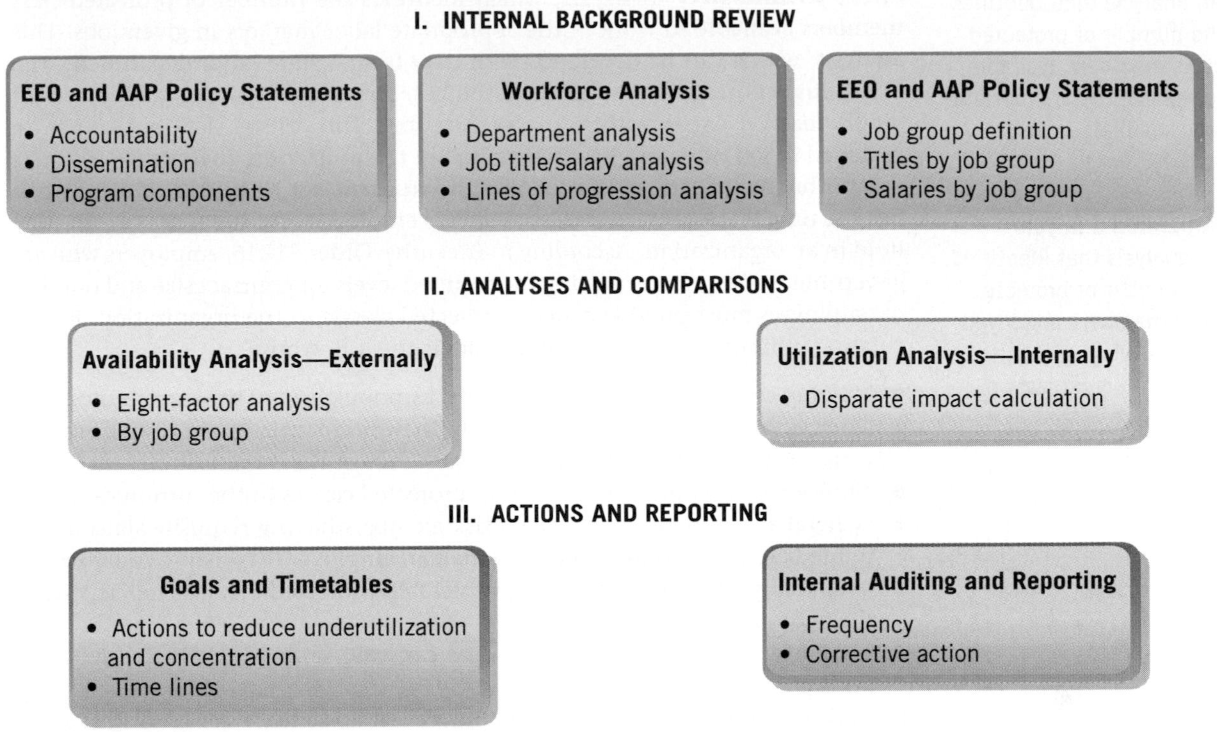

Courts have noted that any employer that is not a government contractor may have a *voluntary* AAP, although the employer *must* have such a plan if it wishes to be a government contractor. Where an employer that is not a government contractor has a required AAP, a court has ordered the employer to have an AAP as a result of past discriminatory practices and violations of laws.

## Contents of an Affirmative Action Plan

The contents of an AAP and the policies flowing from it must be available for review by managers and supervisors within the organization. Plans vary in length; some are long and require extensive staff time to prepare. Figure 6–12 depicts the phases in the development of an AAP.[41]

**INTERNAL BACKGROUND REVIEW** In this phase, the EEO and AAP *policy statements* are presented, including the employer's commitment to equal employment and affirmative action. Then the *workforce analysis* is done by detailing the makeup of the workforce as seen on an organization chart and by depicting departmental groupings, job titles and salaries, and the lines of progression. This analysis details the status of employees by gender, race, and other bases. The final part of the internal background review is to prepare a *job group analysis*. Unlike the workforce analysis, in which data are classified by organizational unit, the job group analysis looks at similar jobs throughout the organization, regardless of department. For instance, EEO *demographic* data on incumbents in all engineering jobs will be reported, regardless of departments. For instance, an electric utility may have eight levels of engineers in twelve different operating divisions.

**Availability analysis**
An analysis that identifies the number of protected-class members available to work in the appropriate labor markets in given jobs.

**Utilization analysis**
An analysis that identifies the number of protected-class members employed and the types of jobs they hold in an organization.

**ANALYSES AND COMPARISONS** Two different types of analyses are done. The first one is **availability analysis,** which identifies the number of protected-class members available to work in the appropriate labor markets in given jobs. This analysis, which can be developed with data from a state labor department, the U.S. Census Bureau, as well as other sources, serves as a basis for determining if *underutilization* exists within an organization. The census data also must be matched to job titles and job groups used in the utilization analysis.

Another major section of an AAP is the **utilization analysis,** which identifies the number of protected-class members employed and the types of jobs they hold in an organization. According to Executive Order 11246, employers who are government contractors meeting the required levels for contract size and number of employees must provide data on protected classes in the organization. In calculating utilization, the employer considers the following:

- Number of protected-class members in the population of the surrounding area
- Number of protected-class members in the workforce in the surrounding area compared with number in the total workforce of the organization
- Number of unemployed members of protected classes in the surrounding area
- General availability of protected-class members having requisite skills in the immediate area and in an area in which an employer reasonably could recruit
- Availability of promotable and transferable protected-class members within the organization
- Existence of training institutions that can train individuals in the requisite skills
- Realistic amount of training an employer can do to make all job classes available to protected-class members

Fortunately for many employers, much of the data on the population and workforce in the surrounding area is available in computerized form, so availability analysis and underutilization calculations can be done more easily. However, an employer still must maintain an accurate profile of the internal workforce.

**LOGGING ON . . .**
**AAP Software**
An example of a firm specializing in HR software management systems is available here. This firm offers a software program to assist employers in writing their affimative action plans.

**http://www.criterioninc.com/ Home.htm**

**ACTION AND REPORTING** Once all of the data have been analyzed and compared, then *underutilization* statistics must be calculated by comparing the workforce analyses with the utilization analysis. It is useful to think of this stage as comparing to see if the internal workforce is a "representative sampling" of the available external labor force from which employees are hired. One of several means of determining underutilization is the 4/5ths rule. Recall that the 4/5ths rule states that discrimination generally is considered to occur if the rate for a protected group is less than 80% of the group's representation in the relevant labor market, or less than 80% of the selection rate for the majority group.

Using the underutilization data, goals and timetables for reducing the underutilization of protected-class individuals must then be identified. Actions that will be taken to recruit, hire, promote, and train more protected-class individuals are described. The implementation of an AAP must be built on a commitment to affirmative action. The commitment must begin at the top of the organization. A crucial factor is the appointment of an affirmative action officer to monitor the plan.

Once a plan is developed, it should be distributed and explained to all managers and supervisors. It is particularly important that everyone involved in the employment process review the plan and receive training on its content. Also, the AAP must be updated and reviewed each year to reflect changes in the utilization and availability of protected-class members. If an audit of an AAP is done by the OFCCP, the employer must be prepared to provide additional details and documentation.

## Summary

- Discrimination on the basis of national origin still is illegal, but the Immigration Reform and Control Act has affected how many employers inquire about and verify citizenship.
- Sexual harassment takes two forms: (a) quid pro quo and (b) hostile environment.
- Employers should have policies on sexual harassment, have identifiable complaint procedures, train all employees on what constitutes sexual harassment, promptly investigate complaints, and take action when sexual harassment is found to have occurred.
- Sex discrimination can include any of the following: unequal job assignment, sexual harassment, pregnancy discrimination, or unequal compensation for similar jobs.
- Age discrimination, especially in the form of forced retirements and terminations, is a growing problem.

- The definition of who is disabled has been expanding in recent years.
- The Americans with Disabilities Act requires that most employers identify the essential functions of jobs, and make reasonable accommodation for individuals with disabilities, unless undue hardship results.
- Reasonable accommodation is a strategy that can be used to deal with religious discrimination situations.
- Implementation of equal employment opportunity requires appropriate record keeping, such as completing the annual report (EEO–1) and keeping applicant flow data.
- Many employers are required to develop affirmative action plans (AAPs) that identify problem areas in the employment of protected-class members and initiate goals and steps to overcome those problems.

## Review and Discussion Questions

1. Give examples that you have experienced or observed of the two types of sexual harassment in employment situations.
2. Based on your experiences, identify examples of sex discrimination in job conditions, sexual stereotyping, and pregnancy discrimination.
3. Why are age discrimination issues growing in importance?
4. The Americans with Disabilities Act contains several key terms. Define each: (a) *essential job function,* (b) *reasonable accommodation,* and (c) *undue hardship.*

5. Respond to the following comment made by the president of a company: "It's getting so that you can't ask anybody anything personal, because there are so many protected classes."
6. Discuss the following question: "How can I report protected-class statistics to the EEOC when I cannot ask about them on my application blank?"
7. Describe how to perform availability analyses and compute underutilization for an affirmative action plan.

## Terms to Know

| | | |
|---|---|---|
| availability analysis  206 | glass ceiling  186 | right-to-sue letter  200 |
| disabled person  190 | nepotism  185 | sexual harassment  178 |
| essential job functions  192 | pay equity  184 | undue hardship  192 |
| executive order  204 | reasonable accommodation  192 | utilization analysis  206 |

# Using the Internet

## Americans with Disabilities Act Regulations

As the HR manager, it is your job to ensure compliance with the Americans with Disabilities Act regulations. The division managers have recently brought forward some questions regarding compliance with this act. Answer the following questions for them so they might assist you in ensuring compliance.

1. What are the guidelines required legally for an individual to be protected by the Americans with Disabilities Act?

2. What organizations are affected by the employment provisions of the ADA? How are they affected by public accommodations?

3. Summarize what the final rule on Title III means for employers.

Use the following website to assit you:
**http://janweb.icdi.wvu.edu/kinder/**

# CASE

## Denny's Deals with Discrimination

Denny's a national restaurant chain with over 500 locations, faced a crisis in the mid 1990s due to discriminatory practices. For a number of years, African Americans and the National Association for the Advancement of Colored People (NAACP) had charged that African American customers were discriminated against in various ways. Finally, the NAACP and the U.S. Justice Department filed lawsuits against Denny's for illegal discrimination.

Denny's is owned by Flagstar Companies, a conglomerate with a number of subsidiaries. Flagstar signed an agreement with the NAACP to take aggressive action against racism at Denny's. Terms of the agreement included the following:

- A payment of $45 million was made to settle two class-action lawsuits brought under civil rights laws.
- Flagstar promised to increase the number of minority franchisees to 53 by 1997.
- Denny's agreed to purchase over $50 million worth of goods and services from minority-owned firms, representing about 12% of total supply purchases.
- Flagstar agreed to increase the percentage of minorities among employees, managers, and corporate staff. The firm indicated that almost half of its

new management positions would be staffed with African Americans by 2000.
- A toll-free number was established at Denny's corporate headquarters to be used by customers to report service problems, including discrimination. The number is displayed in Denny's restaurants. Complaints are investigated by a lawyer independent of the company.

All of these actions helped Denny's deal with some of its discriminatory practices. But the major change was to replace virtually all of the top management at Denny's. The current management team is headed by James Adamson, chairman and CEO of Flagstar. The team includes several women and minorities. Previously, the Denny's executive group had been almost exclusively white males.

To change the organizational culture throughout Denny's, a diversity training program was developed, and participation in it is mandatory for managers. Also, a portion of bonus payments to managers is now based on results in reducing customer complaints, including those relating to discrimination.

Several years later, Denny's took steps to make its commitment to equality even more evident. Denny's instituted a major TV advertising campaign featuring race and minority issues. In each ad, a minority teenager talks about race by stating, "Noticing a person's color doesn't make you a racist. Acting like it matters does."

In summary, Adamson recognized that continuing efforts are needed for Denny's to convince customers and employees, both nonminorities and minorities, that it believes in equal opportunity for all. For several years Adamson has had a very clear message for employees, managers, and franchises: "If you discriminate, you're history!"[42]

## Questions

1. Discuss why the previous absence of equal employment opportunity at Denny's showed ineffective management of human resources.
2. How likely is it that Denny's treatment of African Americans would have changed without legal intervention? Support your answer.
3. What are the advantages and disadvantages of Denny's approach to taking affirmative action to remedy its past problems with discrimination?

# Notes

1. "Record $34 Million for Sex Harassment," *Fair Employment Practices,* June 25, 1998, 73–74; "$86,257 Awarded in Discrimination Suit," *Omaha World-Herald,* February 1998, 4B; M.A. Jacobs, "Law Firm Loses Race Discrimination Case," *The Wall Street Journal,* March 25, 1996, B8; Patrick McGeehan, "Smith Barney Diversity Plan Represents a Major Leap for Women on Wall Street, *The Wall Street Journal,* November 19, 1997, B17; Stephanie Armour, "Age-Bias Case Sounds Warning," *USA Today,* October 24, 1997, B1; "Merrill Lynch Is Told to Pay $1.8 Million in Discrimination Case," *The Wall Street Journal,* January 22, 1997, B14; and "Iowan Awarded $300,000 in Age-Bias Lawsuit," *Omaha World-Herald,* May 16, 1998, A19.
2. Based on "Operating a Multilingual Workplace," *Bulletin to Management,* June 25, 1998, 200; Ann Davis, "English-Only Rules Spur Workers to Speak Legalese," *The Wall Street Journal,* November 23, 1997, B1+; and "Choice Words," *Human Resource Executive,* June 5, 1998, 95–97.
3. "Visa Quotas Are Increased for Foreign Professionals," *Human Resource Executive,* February 1999, 9; and Michael Maggio, "Understanding H-1B Specialty Workers," *Legal Report,* Summer 1998, 7–12.
4. Charles A. Pierce and Herman Aquinis, "Bridging the Gap between Romantic Relationships and Sexual Harassment in Organizations," *Journal of Organizational Behavior* 18 (1997), 197–200.
5. *Harris v. Forklift Systems, Inc.,* 114 S.Ct. 367 (1993).
6. *Burlington Industries v. Ellerth,* U.S. S.Ct. No. 97–569, June 26, 1998; *Faragher v. Boca Raton,* U.S. S.Ct. No. 97–282, June 26, 1998; and *Oncale v. Sundowner Offshore Services,* U.S. S.Ct. No. 96–568, March 4, 1998.
7. Jennifer Laabs, "What You're Liable for Now," *Workforce,* October 1998, 34–42.
8. Michael Barrier, "Sexual Harassment," *Nation's Business,* December 1998, 14–19.
9. Based on Jane Adams-Roy and Julian Barling, "Predicting the Decision to Confront or Report Sexual Harassment," *Journal of Organizational Behavior* 19 (1998), 329–336.
10. Gilbert Casellas and Irene L. Hill, "Sexual Harassment: Preventing and Avoiding Liability," *Legal Report,* Fall 1998, 1–5.
11. James A. Burns, Jr., "Accommodating Pregnant Employees," *Employee Relations Law Journal* 23 (1997), 139–144.
12. *Stopka v. Alliance of American Insurers,* CA7, No. 97–1974, April 1, 1998; and Sue Schellenbarger, "Pregnant Workers Clash with Employers Over Job Inflexibility," *The Wall Street Journal,* February 10, 1999, B1.
13. U.S. Bureau of the Census, 1998; Diana F. Furchtgott-Roth and Christine Stolba, "Comparable Worth Makes a Comeback," *The Wall Street Journal,* February 4, 1999, A22.
14. *Arizona Governing Committee v. Norris,* 103 S.Ct. 3492 (1983).
15. Diana Kunde, "Women Build Careers in Construction Trades," *Omaha World-Herald,* January 24, 1999, 1G.
16. U.S. Equal Employment Opportunity Commission, 1998.
17. Glass Ceiling Commission, *A Solid Investment: Making Use of the Nation's Human Capital* (Washington, DC: U.S. Department of Labor, 1995).
18. Timothy D. Schellhardt, "Jury to Consider If 'Overqualified' Signals Age Bias," *The Wall Street Journal,* July 27, 1998, B1, B8.
19. *Westinghouse Electric Corp v. Ryder,* U.S. S.Ct. No. 97–1070, February 23, 1998.
20. Based on data compiled by the federal Equal Employment Opportunity Commission, 1998.
21. Definitions used in this discussion of the Americans with Disabilities Act are those contained either in the act itself or in the *Technical Assistance Manual* issued by the EEOC; and Robert W. Thompson, "Justices May Clarify Definition of ADA-Covered Disabilities," *HR News,* February 1999, 9–10.
22. Francis A. McMorris, "Employee's Transfer Plea Rejected in Another Disabilities Act Ruling," *The Wall Street Journal,* January 21, 1997, B9.
23. Timothy Bland, "ADA: The Law Meets Medicine," *HR Magazine,* January 1999, 99–104; and Ann

Davis, "Courts Reject Many Mental-Disability Claims," *The Wall Street Journal,* July 22, 1997, B1, B6.

24. *School Board of Nassau County, Florida v. Airline,* 107 S.C. 1123 (1987).

25. Peter J. Petesch, "The ADA, HIV, and Risk Management Strategies," *Legal Report,* Summer 1998, 1–6.

26. *Bragdon v. Abbott,* U.S. S.Ct. No. 97–156, June 25, 1998.

27. Carolyn Hirschman, "Reasonable Accommodations at a Reasonable Cost," *HR Magazine,* July 1997, 85–88.

28. Barbara Gamble McGill, "ADA Accommodations Do Not Have to Break the Bank," *HR Magazine,* July 1997, 85–88.

29. For a discussion of various religions and their observance schedules, see Patricia Digh, "Religion In the Workplace," *HR Magazine,* December 1998, 85–91.

30. *Trans World Airlines v. Hardison,* 432 U.S. 63 (1977).

31. Jodi Spiegel Arthur, "Religious Rights Not Violated, Court Says," *Human Resource Executive,* June 5, 1998, 22.

32. Ronald A. Lindsay and Elizabeth H. Bach, "Religious Discrimination," http://www.shrm.org/docs/whitepapers/61214.htm, 1997.

33. Jessica Guynn, "Another Y2K Worry: Messiahs in the Workplace," *Omaha World-Herald,* February 7, 1999, 1G; and Stephanie Armour, "Conflict Grows between Bosses, Devout Workers," *USA Today,* November 21, 1997, 1B–2B.

34. "Companies Feel Push to Accommodate Employees' Religious Beliefs," *HR Policies and Practices Update,* September 19, 1997, 1–2.

35. *Dothard v. Rawlinson,* 433 U.S. 321 (1977).

36. *Harper v. Blockbuster Entertainment Corp.,* CA11, No. 96–2461–CV–DLG, April 29, 1998.

37. Public Law 103-353, October 13, 1944.

38. Jonathan Segal, "EEO Policies: Walking the Razor's Edge," *HR Magazine,* December 1997, 109–116.

39. Bill Leonard, "A New Era at the EEOC," *HR Magazine,* February 1999, 55–62; and Linda Micco, "EEOC Cuts Number of Pending Cases in Half Over Three Years," *HR News,* September 1998, 9.

40. Stephanie Armour and Barbara Hansen, "Flood of 'Retaliation' Cases Surfacing in U.S. Workplace," *USA Today,* February 10, 1999, 1A.

41. In structuring the components of AAPs, the authors acknowledge the assistance of Raymond B. Weinberg, SPHR, CCP; and Kathleen Shotkoski, PHR; of SilverStone Consulting, Omaha, NE.

42. Based on Bruce Horovitz, "Denny's Airs Anti-Racism Ads," *USA Today,* January 12, 1999, B1; F. Rice, "Denny's Changes Its Spots," *Fortune,* May 13, 1996, 133–142; and N. Harris, "A New Denny's—Diner by Diner," *Business Week,* March 25, 1996, 166–168.

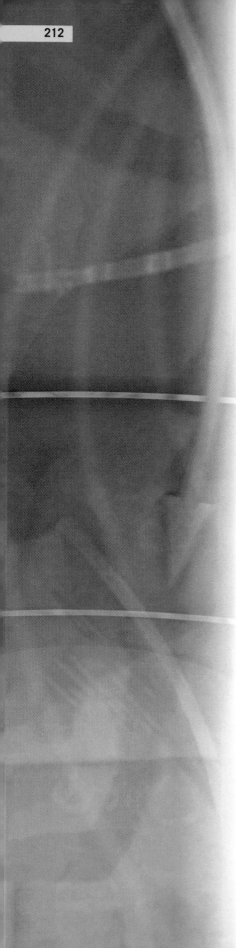

# CHAPTER 7

# Analyzing and Identifying Jobs

**After you have read this chapter, you should be able to:**

- Discuss why job analysis is changing as organizations change.

- Compare task-based job analysis with the competency approach of job analysis.

- Develop an organization chart using job families.

- Identify how job analysis information is used in four other HR activities.

- Explain how job analysis has both legal and behavioral aspects.

- List and explain four job analysis methods.

- Identify the five steps in conducting a job analysis.

- Write a job description and the job specifications for it.

# Decline of Secretaries, Growth of Administrative Coordinators

The changing nature of jobs is seen in many organizations and industries, especially those facing major changes due to external forces, such as financial services and telecommunications. But even in more stable industries, one of the most traditional jobs appears to be changing—that known in many organizations as *secretary* and/or *administrative assistant.*

Statistics from the U.S. government illustrate clearly that secretarial jobs are declining. For example, in 1983, secretary was the most common job for women, composing 8.7% of the jobs held by women in the civilian workforce. By the late 1990s, only 5.3% of the women working in the civilian labor force were secretaries, making it the fourth most common job for women. The three most common jobs for women had become sales, teaching, and food preparation. Further, the number of secretaries in the late '90s—3.2 million—was a decrease of 700,000 from 1983. This statistic is even more significant when considering the rapid growth in jobs and organizations that has occurred in the United States since 1983.

The traditional secretarial job has several common tasks associated with it. A look at typical secretarial tasks and duties, along with how they are done today, illustrates how the secretary job has changed.

*Typing correspondence:* Instead of giving handwritten correspondence to secretaries, many managers compose and transmit their own memos, letters, and reports via e-mail.

*Scheduling:* With the advent of computer scheduling systems, a growing number of organizations have all individuals' schedules on network sys-

tems, and meetings can be scheduled electronically.

*Voice mail:* The explosive growth of voice mail means that the message-taking function of secretaries has declined. For employees who are away from their desks frequently, messages can be retrieved while traveling or upon returning to the desk without human interface.

*Copying and filing:* Rather than employing secretaries as generalists who perform a variety of tasks, firms have created office services centers. These centers include specialized high-speed equipment for mass copy-

ing. Specialized technicians complete much of the copying, report building, and other production activities.

Some firms have eliminated most of the secretarial jobs. As an extreme example, the Chairman of a U.S. investment firm with 600 employees eliminated 85 secretarial jobs. All managers and executives now handle their own correspondence using e-mail and software, make and return their phone calls, and maintain their own schedules. For employees who were "technology deficient," the firm offered training classes. Some executives had to learn to type; others needed classes on sending and receiving e-mail messages and faxes, designing documents, learning presentation software, and using the company's voice mail system.

Interestingly, the company's productivity initially dipped some, but then returned to the same levels. One side effect was that managers started prioritizing their activities more and letting nonessential tasks drift, because those "make-work" tasks could no longer be delegated to secretaries. Some of the former secretaries lost their jobs, while some others transferred to different jobs in the firm where they could use their capabilities differently.

While most organizations do not take such an extreme approach, many organizations have examined the work

> *Many organizations have examined the work process and tasks performed by secretaries and decided that fewer secretaries are needed.*

processes and tasks performed by secretaries and decided that fewer secretaries are needed. The office support functions that must be performed have transformed the traditional secretarial job into that of the *administrative coordinator* or *executive assistant.* The differences between these jobs in terms of responsibility, authority, and organizational input are considerable. These coordinative jobs are often performed for more than one boss.

Yet, it is important to remember that in many organizations there is still considerable need for clerical and administrative support. Secretaries still compose about 17% of all office support staff. But even in these jobs, it likely will be important for organizations to continue analyzing and tracking the changing nature of secretarial jobs.[1]

> ❝ *Many organizations are today well along the path toward being "de-jobbed."* ❞
>
> WILLIAM BRIDGES

A primary focus of HR management is on the jobs and work performed by individuals in the organization. Because organizations are changing and jobs must fit so many different situations, managers and employees alike are finding that designing and analyzing jobs requires greater attention than in the past. As the opening discussion indicates, such changes are affecting secretarial jobs, as well as others.

Much current interest in analyzing jobs results from the importance assigned to the activity by federal and state courts. The legal defensibility of an employer's recruiting and selection procedures, performance appraisal system, employee disciplinary actions, and pay practices rests in part on the foundation of job analysis. In a number of court cases, employers have lost because their HR processes and practices were not viewed by judges or juries as sufficiently job related. Fundamentally, it is important to document that HR activities and the decisions resulting from them are clearly job-related and relatively consistent over time.

Additionally, analyzing and understanding the work done in the organization must be based on facts and data, not just personal perceptions of managers, supervisors, and employees. It has become evident in many organizations that analyzing both the way work is done and what employees do in their jobs is vital to maintaining organizational competitiveness.

# Nature of Job Analysis

**Job analysis**

A systematic way to gather and analyze information about the content and the human requirements of jobs, and the context in which jobs are performed.

The most basic building block of HR management, **job analysis,** is a systematic way to gather and analyze information about the content and human requirement of jobs, and the context in which jobs are performed. Job analysis usually involves collecting information on the characteristics of a job that differentiate it from other jobs. Information that can be helpful in making the distinction includes the following:

- Work activities and behaviors
- Interactions with others
- Performance standards
- Financial and budgeting impact
- Machines and equipment used
- Working conditions
- Supervision given and received
- Knowledge, skills, and abilities needed

## What Is a Job?

**Job**

A grouping of similar positions having common tasks, duties, and responsibilities.

**Position**

A job performed by one person.

Although the terms *job* and *position* are often used interchangeably, there is a slight difference in emphasis. A **job** is a grouping of common tasks, duties, and responsibilities. A **position** is a job performed by one person. Thus, if there are two persons operating word processing equipment, there are two positions (one for each person) but just one job (word processing operator).

## Differentiating between Job Analysis and Job Design

It is useful to clarify the differences between job design and job analysis. Job design is broader in nature and has as its primary thrust meshing the productivity needs of the organization with the needs of the individuals performing the various jobs. Increasingly, a key aim for job design is to provide individuals meaningful work that fits effectively into the flow of the organization. It is concerned with changing, simplifying, enlarging, enriching, or otherwise making jobs such that the efforts of each worker fit together better with other jobs.

Job analysis has a much narrower focus in that it is a formal system for gathering data about what people are doing in their jobs. The information generated by job analysis may be useful in redesigning jobs, but its primary purpose is to get a clear understanding of what is done on a job and what capabilities are needed to do a job as it has been designed. Documents that capture the elements identified during a job analysis are job descriptions and job specifications.

# Job Analysis and the Changing Nature of Jobs

Increasingly, commentators and writers are discussing the idea that the nature of jobs and work is changing so much that the concept of a "job" may be obsolete for many people. For instance, in some high-technology industries employees work in cross-functional project teams and shift from project to project. The focus in these industries is less on performing specific tasks and duties and more on fulfilling responsibilities and attaining results. For example, a project team of eight employees developing software to allow various credit cards to be used with ATMs worldwide will work on many different tasks, some individually and some with other team members. When that project is finished those employees will move to other projects, possibly with other employers. Such shifts may happen several times per year. Therefore, the basis for recruiting, selecting, and compensating these individuals is their competence and skills, not what they do.[2] Even the job of managers changes in such situations, for they must serve their project teams as facilitators, gatherers of resources, and removers of roadblocks.

However, in many industries that use lower-skilled workers, traditional jobs continue to exist. Studying these jobs and their work consequences is relatively easy because of the repetitiveness of the work and the limited number of tasks each worker performs.

Clearly, studying the two different types of jobs—the lower-skilled ones and highly technical ones—requires different approaches. Many of the typical processes associated with identifying job descriptions are still relevant with the lower-skilled, task-based jobs. However, for fast-moving organizations in high-technology industries, a job description is becoming an obsolete concept. Employees in these "virtual jobs" must be able to function without job descriptions and without the traditional parameters that are still useful with less changeable jobs.[3]

## Work Analysis

**Work analysis** studies the workflow, activities, context, and output of a job. This analysis can be conducted on a department, business process, or individual level. At one level, the industrial engineering approach of time and motion studies is useful in work analysis. At another level the linkage of what is done in one department may be looked at in relation to work activities performed

**Work analysis**
Studying the workflow, activities, context, and output of a job.

in another area. For instance, in an electric utility if a customer calls with a service outage problem, it is typical for a customer service representative to take the information and enter it into a database. Then in the operations department, a dispatcher may access the database to schedule a line technician to repair the problem. The customer would be called back and notified about the timing of the repair. The line technician also must receive instructions from a supervisor, who gets the information on workload and locations from the dispatcher.

A work analysis identified that there were too many steps involving too many different jobs in this process. Therefore, the utility implemented a new customer information system and combined the dispatching function with customer service. The redesign permitted the customer service representatives to access workload information and schedule the line technicians as part of the initial consumer phone calls, except in unusual situations. The redesign of jobs required redefining the jobs, tasks, duties, and responsibilities of several jobs. To implement the new jobs required training the customer service representatives in dispatching and moving dispatchers into the customer service department and training them in all facets of customer service. The result was a more responsive workflow, more efficient scheduling of line technicians, and broadening of the jobs of the customer service representatives.

This example illustrates that analyzing work activities and processes may require looking at what capabilities individuals need as well as what they do. That certainly would be true as office support jobs, such as the secretarial job, are examined. Increasingly, it is being recognized that jobs can be analyzed on the basis of both tasks and competencies.

## Task-Based Job Analysis

**Task**
A distinct, identifiable work activity composed of motions.

**Duty**
A larger work segment composed of several tasks that are performed by an individual.

**Job responsibilities**
Obligations to perform certain tasks and duties.

Analyzing jobs based upon what is done on the job focuses on the tasks, duties, and responsibilities performed in a job. A **task** is a distinct, identifiable work activity composed of motions, whereas a **duty** is a larger work segment composed of several tasks that are performed by an individual. Because both tasks and duties describe activities, it is not always easy or necessary to distinguish between the two. For example, if one of the employment supervisor's duties is to interview applicants, one task associated with that duty would be asking questions. **Job responsibilities** are obligations to perform certain tasks and duties.

For jobs that remain task-based, many standard phases of the job analysis process can continue. As indicated in the phases of traditional job analysis that are outlined later in the chapter, extensive effort is made to clarify what specifically is done on a job. Development of job descriptions identifies what is done and lists job functions.

## Competency Approach to Job Analysis

There is a growing interest in focusing on the competencies that individuals need in order to perform jobs, rather than on the tasks, duties, and responsibilities composing a job. This shift emphasizes that it is the capabilities that people have that truly influence organizational performance. As E.E. Lawler suggests, instead of thinking of individuals having jobs that are relatively stable and can be written up into typical job descriptions, it may be more relevant to focus on the competen-

**FIGURE 7–1** *Conceptual Model of Competencies*

cies used.[4] **Competencies** are basic characteristics that can be linked to enhanced performance by individuals or teams of individuals. The groupings of competencies, as Figure 7–1 indicates, may include knowledge, skills, and abilities.

**VISIBLE AND HIDDEN COMPETENCIES** Figure 7–1 illustrates that there are both hidden and visible competencies. Knowledge, being more visible, is recognized by many employers in matching individuals to jobs. With skills, although some are evident such as skill in constructing financial spreadsheets, others such as negotiating skills, may be less identifiable. But it is the "hidden" competencies of abilities, which may be more valuable, that can enhance performance. For example, the abilities to conceptualize strategic relationships and to resolve interpersonal conflicts are more difficult to identify and assess.

A growing number of organizations are using some facets of competency analysis. A survey of over 200 organizations sponsored by the American Compensation Association (ACA) asked about the major reasons that firms have used the competency approach. The three primary reasons given were (1) communicating valued behaviors throughout the organization; (2) raising the competency levels of the organization; and (3) emphasizing the capabilities of people to enhance organizational competitive advantage.[5]

Many earlier efforts to use competencies have been *job-based,* meaning that competencies are identified in the context of specific jobs. In this way the competency approach is a logical extension of traditional job analysis activities. However, some organizations are taking the competency approach to another level by focusing on *role-based* competencies. This shift has been accentuated by the growing use of work teams, whereby individuals move among tasks and jobs. Some of the roles might be leader, supporter, tactician, technical expert, administrator, or others. Through competency analysis, the competencies needed for individuals playing different roles in work teams can be identified. Then selection criteria, development activities, and other HR efforts must be revised to focus on the different sets of competencies needed for the various roles.

**COMPETENCY ANALYSIS METHODOLOGY** Unlike the traditional approach to analyzing jobs, which identifies the tasks, duties, knowledge, and skills associated with a job, the competency approach considers how the knowledge and skills are used. The competency approach also attempts to identify the hidden factors that are often critical to superior performance. For instance, many supervisors talk

**Competencies**
Basic characteristics that can be linked to enhanced performance by individuals or teams.

about employees' attitudes, but they have difficulty identifying what they mean by *attitude*. The competency approach uses some methodologies to help supervisors identify examples of what they mean by attitude and how those factors affect performance.

Several methodologies are available and being used to determine competencies, with *behavioral event interviews* being commonly found. This process involves the following steps:[6]

1. A team of senior managers identifies future performance results areas critical to the business and strategic plans of the organization. These concepts may be broader than those used in the past.
2. Panel groups are assembled, composed of individuals knowledgeable about the jobs in the company. This group can include both high- and low-performing employees, supervisors, managers, trainers, and others.
3. A facilitator from HR or an outside consultant interviews the panel members to get specific examples of job behaviors and actual occurrences on the jobs. During the interview the individuals are also asked about their thoughts and feelings during each of the described events.
4. Using the behavioral events, the facilitator develops detailed descriptions of each of the competencies. This descriptive phase provides clarity and specifics so that employees, supervisors, managers, and others in the organization have a clearer understanding of the competencies associated with jobs.
5. The competencies are rated and levels needed to meet them are identified. Then the competencies are specified for each of the jobs.
6. Finally, standards of performance are identified and tied to the jobs. Appropriate selection screening, training, and compensation processes focusing on competencies must be developed and implemented.

Examples of the competencies used in organizations vary widely. In one survey of 10 companies, the following were most common.[7]

- Customer focus
- Team orientation
- Technical expertise
- Results orientation
- Leadership
- Innovation
- Adaptability

## HR Activities and Competency Analysis

The competency approach focuses on linking business strategies to individual performance efforts. It also encourages employees to develop competencies that may be used in diverse work situations, rather than being boxed into a job. Development of employees focuses on enhancing their competencies, rather than preparing them for moving to jobs. In this way they can develop capabilities useful throughout the organization as it changes and evolves. The competency approach affects HR activities, particularly those following.[8]

- *Selection and placement:*  Once the competencies needed in jobs have been identified, selection and placement activities must be revised to focus on assessing the competencies of individuals.
- *HR development:*  Training and development efforts must be revised to stress a full range of competencies, rather than being narrowly focused on job skills and knowledge. The hidden competencies are more behaviorally based and require more varied approaches than have been common in many training

efforts. Also, in assessing training needs and evaluating the meeting of those needs, the focus must be on abilities, not just knowledge and skills. Career development also must focus on competency growth and opportunities both within and outside the organization.

- *Compensation and performance management:* Shifting from a task-based pay system to a competency-based pay system requires significant efforts. Assessing performance by measuring results and competencies, especially if work teams are used, is a daunting challenge—especially if the organization is highly structured. Rewarding individuals for demonstrating competencies, particularly those that are less evident and more behavioral, leads to significantly different compensation structures.[9] The ACA survey mentioned earlier found that competency-based compensation is the least common use of competency approaches in organizations.[10] More on competency-based pay programs appears in Chapter 13.

The difficulties with competency analysis are centered around the major shift in focus from tasks and duties to competencies. Shifting to competencies may lead to broadening jobs to allow more flexibility, greater cross-training, introduction and use of work teams, revising individually focused performance management and pay systems, and changing training efforts to focus on competency development. Yet, this shift to broaden jobs and competencies may not be compatible with the typical formal structures and job-focused activities in many organizations.

Ultimately, it may be that job analysis will shift in order to address the changing nature of broader and looser jobs in some areas, while continuing to be relevant in those areas where jobs remain task-based. Because the task-based approach is much more common, the remainder of this chapter concentrates on the traditional job analysis process.

# Organizational Components and Job Analysis

Effective HR management demands that job analysis be the foundation for a number of other HR activities.[11] The process of analyzing jobs in organizations requires planning of several factors. As Figure 7–2 indicates, some of the considerations are how it is to be done, who provides data, and who conducts and uses the data so that job descriptions and job specifications can be prepared and reviewed. Once those decisions are made, then several results are linked to a wide range of HR activities. The most fundamental use of job analysis is to provide the information necessary to develop job descriptions and specifications.

## Job Analysis Responsibilities

Most methods of job analysis require that a knowledgeable person describe what goes on in the job or make a series of judgments about specific activities required to do the job. Such information can be provided by the employee doing the job, the supervisor, and/or a trained job analyst. Each source is useful, but each has drawbacks. The supervisor seems to be the best source of information on what *should be* done, but employees often know more about what actually *is* done. However, both may lack the knowledge needed to complete a job

**FIGURE 7–2** *Decisions in the Job Analysis Process*

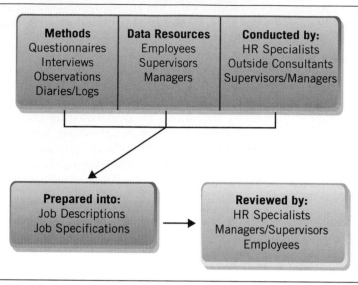

analysis and draw the appropriate conclusions from it. Thus, job analysis requires a high degree of coordination and cooperation between the HR unit and operating managers.

The responsibility for job analysis depends on who can best perform various aspects of the process. Figure 7–3 shows a typical division of responsibilities in organizations that have an HR unit. In small organizations, managers have to perform all the work activities identified in Figure 7–3. In larger companies, the HR unit supervises the process to maintain its integrity and writes the job descriptions and specifications for uniformity. The managers review the efforts of the HR unit to ensure accuracy and completeness. They also may request reanalysis when jobs change significantly.

**FIGURE 7–3** *Typical Job Analysis Responsibilities*

| HR Unit | Managers |
|---------|----------|
| ● Prepares and coordinates job analysis procedures | ● Complete or assist in completing job analysis information |
| ● Writes job descriptions and specifications for review by managers | ● Review and maintain accuracy of job descriptions/job specifications |
| ● Revises and periodically reviews job descriptions and specifications | ● May request new job analysis as jobs change |
| ● Reviews managerial input to ensure accuracy | ● Identify performance standards based on job analysis information |
| ● May seek assistance from outside experts for difficult or unusual analyses | |

# Job Descriptions and Job Specifications

In most cases, the job description and job specifications are combined into one document that contains several different sections. An overview of each section follows next.

**JOB DESCRIPTIONS** A **job description** indicates the tasks, duties, and responsibilities of a job. It identifies what is done, why it is done, where it is done, and briefly, how it is done.

**Performance standards** should flow directly from a job description, telling what the job accomplishes and how performance is measured in key areas of the job description. The reason for including the performance standards is clear. If employees know what is expected and how performance is to be measured, they have a much better chance of performing satisfactorily. Figure 7–4 shows a job description duty statement and some performance standards used for a customer response representative in a telecommunications firm.

Unfortunately, performance standards often are omitted from job descriptions. Even if performance standards have been identified and matched to job descriptions, they may not be known by employees if the job descriptions are not provided to employees but used only as tools by the HR department and managers. Such an approach limits the value of job descriptions.

**JOB SPECIFICATIONS** While the job description describes activities to be done, it is **job specifications** that list the knowledge, skills, and abilities an individual needs to perform a job satisfactorily. Knowledge, skills, and abilities (KSAs) include education, experience, work skill requirements, personal abilities, and mental and physical requirements. Job specifications for a data entry operator might include a required educational level, a certain number of months of experience, a typing ability of 60 words per minute, a high degree of visual concentration, and ability to work under time pressure. It is important to note that accurate job specifications identify what KSAs a person needs to do the job, not necessarily what qualifications the current employee possesses.

# Developing Job Families and Organization Charts

Once all jobs in the organization have been identified, it is often helpful for communicating with employees to group the jobs into job families and display them on an organization chart. There are various ways of identifying and grouping job families.

**JOB FAMILIES** A **job family** is a grouping of jobs having similar characteristics. In identifying job families, significant emphasis is placed on measuring the similarity of jobs. For instance, at one insurance company the HR director decided that jobs requiring specialized technical knowledge, skills, and abilities related to information systems (IS) should be viewed as a separate job family, regardless of the geographic locations of those jobs. Due to the nature of information systems jobs, attracting and retaining IS professionals was difficult, and special compensation programs were needed to match the compensation packages given by competing employers.

**ORGANIZATION CHARTS** In many organizations, organization charts are developed. An **organization chart** depicts the relationships among jobs in an organization. Organization charts have traditionally been hierarchical, showing

**Job description**
Identification of the tasks, duties, and responsibilities of a job.

**Performance standards**
Indicators of what the job accomplishes and how performance is measured.

**Job specifications**
List the knowledge, skills, and abilities (KSAs) an individual needs to do the job satisfactorily.

**Job family**
A grouping of jobs having similar characteristics.

**Organization chart**
A depiction of the relationships among jobs in an organization

**FIGURE 7–4** *Sample Job Duty Statements and Performance Standards*

**Job Title:** Customer Response Representative
**Supervisor:** Customer Response Supervisor

| Duty | Performance Standards |
|---|---|
| Discusses nonpayment of bills with customers and notifies them of nonpayment disconnecting of service. | • Flags accounts within two days that are not to be disconnected according to discussions with Local Manager.<br>• Mails notices to cable television customers so they will be received at least five days prior to disconnection date.<br>• Determines which accounts require credit deposit, based on prior payment history.<br>• Calmly discusses the nonpayment status of the account, along with options for reconnection with customers.<br>• Disconnects and reconnects long distance calling cards for nonpayments with 100% accuracy. |
| Receives and records trouble reports from customers on mechanized trouble-reporting system for telephone or proper form for cable television. Dispatches reports to appropriate personnel. | • Completes all required trouble information on the trouble-reporting system accurately with no more than five errors annually.<br>• Dispatches trouble ticket information to voice mail with 100% accuracy.<br>• Tests line if needed or as requested by technician for telephone troubles. |

the reporting relationships for authority and responsibilities. In most organizations, the charts can help clarify who reports to whom. In developing typical organization charts, such as the one shown in Figure 7–5, there are some general considerations:

1. *Focus of chart:* Label the chart to identify the scope of the chart, whether for a department, division, region, or the company as a whole.
2. *Simplicity:* Keep the chart as simple as possible, emphasizing primary lines of authority.
3. *Titles:* Use job titles, describing the job level and function, in each box on the chart. For example, the title of Director may not be sufficient. Where possible, indicate the area of responsibility, such as Director of Administration. Broader titles, such as General Manager or Secretary, need no further clarification.
4. *Incumbents:* Do not develop organization charts around existing people in the organization. First identify the functions, and then add names of incumbents to the charts.
5. *Jobs:* Depict the jobs in organizational units as rectangular boxes.
6. *Levels:* Use vertical placement to depict the relative position of jobs at different levels in the organization. Use horizontal placement to show jobs having similar levels of authority in the organization.
7. *Authority:* Show direct lines of authority with solid lines, drawn vertically and horizontally as appropriate. For indirect or functional authority, use dotted lines.

**FIGURE 7–5** *Telecommunications Firm Organization Chart*

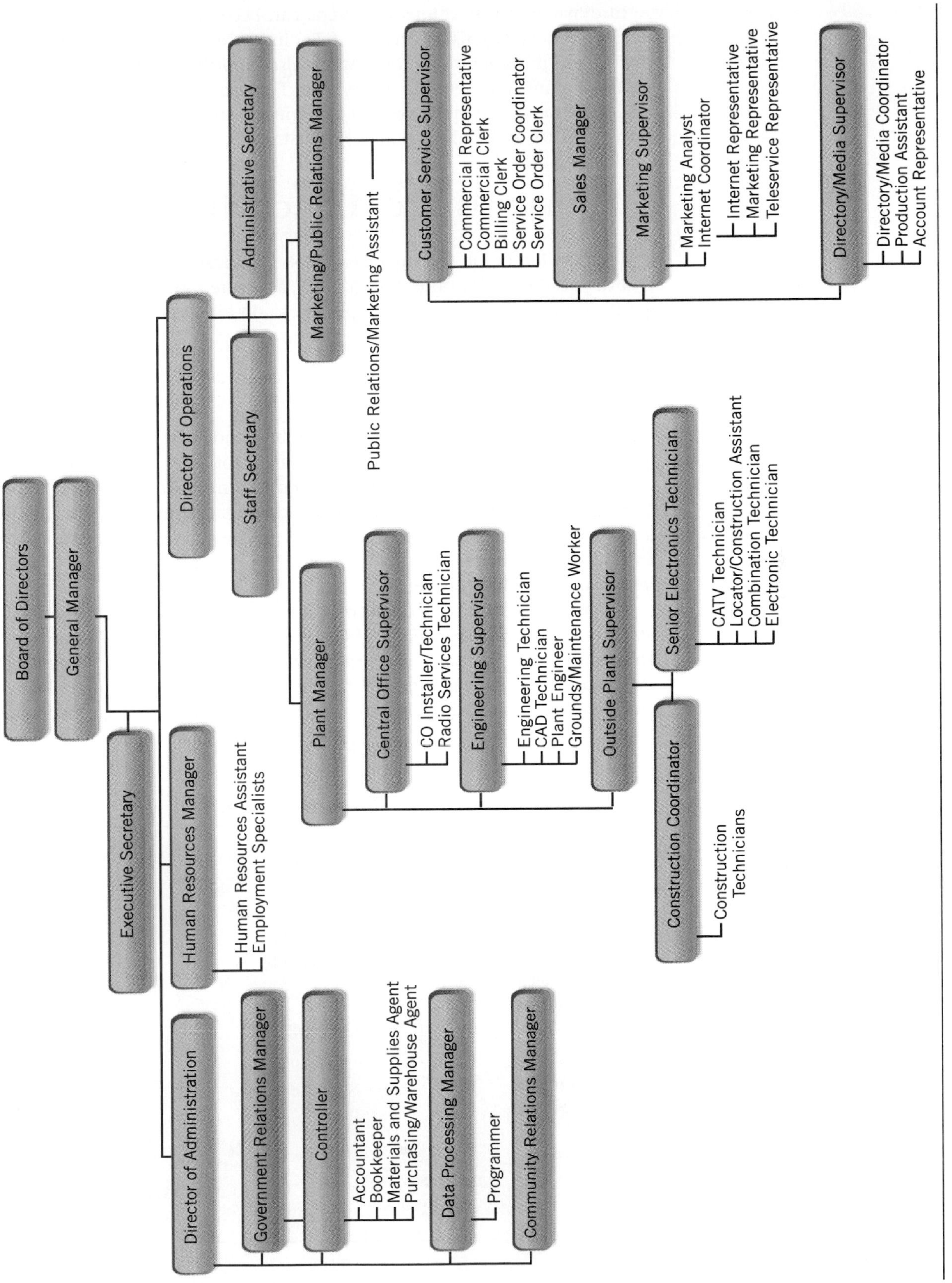

In dynamic organizations the charts can become very complicated because dual reporting relationships may exist. For instance, a design engineer may report to a project manager on a project while also reporting to the chief design engineer for technical review and supervision. This type of organization, often called a *matrix organization,* has grown in usage in recent years, particularly in professional practice and high-technology industries.

# Job Analysis and HR Activities

The completion of job descriptions and job specifications, based on job analysis, is at the heart of many other HR activities, as Figure 7–6 indicates. But even if legal requirements did not force employers to do job analysis, effective HR management would demand it.

## HR Planning

HR planning requires auditing of current jobs, as noted in Chapter 2. Current job descriptions provide the basic details necessary for this internal assessment, including such items as the jobs available, current number of jobs and positions, and reporting relationships of the jobs. By identifying the functions currently being performed and calculating the time being spent to perform them, managers and HR specialists can redesign jobs to eliminate unnecessary tasks and combine responsibilities where desirable.

When reviewing the information provided by both employees and supervisors, a team composed of the HR Manager, the Director of Administration, and an outside consultant noted that several duties associated with maintaining customer service records were divided among three employees. This often led to delays in recording customer payments and scheduling repair services.

**FIGURE 7–6** *Job Analysis and Other HR Activities*

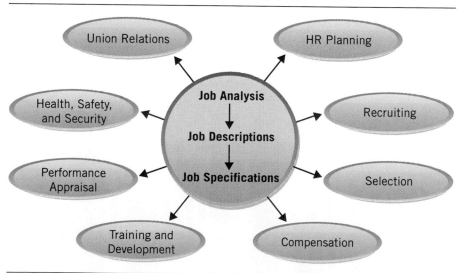

The team regrouped the various customer service duties so that two of the employees performed complete but different functions. Filing activities were concentrated with the third employee, who also served as backup for the other two.

## Recruiting and Selection

Equal employment opportunity guidelines clearly require a sound and comprehensive job analysis to validate recruiting and selection criteria. Without a systematic investigation of a job, an employer may be using requirements that are not specifically job related. For example, if a medical clinic requires a high school diploma for a medical records clerk job, the firm must be able to justify how such an educational requirement matches up to the tasks, duties, and responsibilities of that job. It must be able to show that the knowledge, skills, and abilities needed by the medical records clerk could be obtained only through formal education.

Organizations use job analysis to identify job specifications in order to plan how and where to obtain employees for anticipated job openings, whether recruited internally or externally. For example, a job analysis for a small manufacturer of electric equipment showed that the Accountant II job, which traditionally had required a college-trained person, really could be handled by someone with high school training in bookkeeping and several years of experience. As a result, the company could select from within and promote a current accounting clerk. In addition to saving on recruiting costs, promotion can have a positive impact on employee commitment and career-planning efforts.

## Compensation

Job analysis information is essential when determining compensation. As part of identifying appropriate compensation, job analysis information is used to determine job content for *internal* comparisons of responsibilities and *external* comparisons with the compensation paid by competing employers. Information from job analysis can be used to give more weight, and therefore more pay, to jobs involving more difficult tasks, duties, and responsibilities. Employees' perceptions of fairness and equity are linked not only to how the extrinsic rewards they receive compare with those given to others both inside and outside the organization but also to those rewards they expect for themselves.

Job analysis also can aid in the management of various employee benefits programs. For instance, a job analysis can be used to determine what functions can be performed by workers who have been on workers' compensation disability leave.

## Training and Development

By defining what activities comprise a job, a job analysis helps the supervisor explain that job to a new employee.[12] Information from job descriptions and job specifications can also help in career planning by showing employees what is expected in jobs that they may choose in the future. Job specification information can point out areas in which employees might need to develop in order to further their careers. Employee development efforts by organizations depend on the job descriptions and job specifications generated from job analyses.

## Performance Appraisal

With performance standards to compare what an employee is supposed to be doing with what the person actually has done, a supervisor can determine the employee's performance level. The performance appraisal process should then tie to the job description and performance standards. Developing clear, realistic performance standards can also reduce communication problems in performance appraisal feedback among managers, supervisors, and employees.

## Safety and Health

Job analysis information is useful in identifying possible job hazards and working conditions associated with jobs. From the information gathered, managers and HR specialists can work together to identify the health and safety equipment needed, specify work methods, and train workers.[13]

## Union Relations

Where workers are represented by a labor union, job analysis is used in several ways. First, job analysis information may be needed to determine if the job should be covered by the union agreements. Specifically, management may be able to exclude a supervisory job and its incumbents from the bargaining unit. Second, it is common in unionized environments for job descriptions to be very specific about what tasks are and are not covered in a job. Finally, well-written and specific job descriptions can reduce the number of grievances filed by workers. In one manufacturing plant, a worker refused to sweep up his work area and was disciplined. He filed a grievance and won, because cleaning his work area was not mentioned in the job description.

# Legal Aspects of Job Analysis

Permeating the discussion of equal employment laws, regulations, and court cases in preceding chapters is the concept that legal compliance must focus on the jobs that individuals perform. The 1978 Uniform Selection Guidelines make it clear that HR requirements must be tied to specific job-related factors if employers are to defend their actions as a business necessity.

## Job Analysis and the Americans with Disabilities Act (ADA)

The Americans with Disabilities Act (ADA) has increased the emphasis on job analysis, job descriptions, and job specifications. HR managers and their organizations must identify job activities and then document the steps taken to identify job responsibilities. One result of the ADA is increased emphasis by employers on conducting job analysis, as well as developing and maintaining current and accurate job descriptions.[14] Also, many employers have had to revise their job specifications to reflect the prerequisite KSAs, rather than the "puffed up" ones favored by some managers and employees. It is clear that the ADA has had a major impact on job analysis and the activities derived from it.

**FIGURE 7–7** *Determining Essential and Marginal Functions*

| Considerations | Essential Functions | Marginal Functions |
|---|---|---|
| **Percentage of time spent** | Significant time spent: often 20% of time or more | Generally less than 10% of time |
| **Frequency** | Performed regularly: daily, weekly, monthly | Performed infrequently or when substituting in part of another job |
| **Importance** | Task has consequences to other parts of job and other jobs. | Task is unrelated to job and has little consequence if not performed. |

The ADA requires that organizations identify the *essential functions* of jobs. Specifically, the ADA indicates that **essential job functions** are the fundamental job duties of the employment position that an individual with the disability holds or desires. The term "essential functions" does not include the marginal functions of the positions.[15] **Marginal functions** are those duties that are part of a job but are incidental or ancillary to the purpose and nature of a job.

Figure 7–7 shows three major considerations regarding essential functions and marginal functions. Job analysts, HR staff members, and operating managers must evaluate and make decisions when the information on the three considerations is not clear.

An important part of job analysis is to obtain information about what duties are being performed and what percentage of time is devoted to each duty. As the ADA suggests, it is generally true that the percentage of time spent on a duty indicates its relative importance. How often the duties are performed also becomes important. If duties are performed daily, weekly, and/or monthly, they are more likely to be seen as essential. However, if a task is only performed infrequently or when helping another worker on a totally unrelated job, its essentiality may be more questionable.

Another consideration is the ease or difficulty involved in assigning a duty to be performed by someone else, or in a different job. For instance, assume an assembler of electronic components places the completed parts in a bin next to the work area. At the end of each day, the bin of completed parts must be carried to another room for use in final assembly of a product. Carrying the bin to the other room probably would be defined as a marginal task, because assigning someone else to carry it would not likely create major workflow problems with other jobs and workers.

Another aspect of job analysis is to identify the physical demands and environmental condition of jobs. It is important to identify the skills and capabilities used on a job. For example, it is essential for a customer service representative to be able to hear well enough to take customer orders. However, hearing may be less essential for a heavy equipment operator in a quarry.

## Reasonable Accommodations

Having identified the essential job functions through a job analysis, an employer must be prepared to make reasonable accommodations.[16] Again, the *core* job duties and KSAs must be considered. One manufacturing company with multiple

**Essential job functions**
The fundamental job duties of the employment position that an individual with the disability holds or desires.

**Marginal functions**
Functions that are part of a job but are incidental or ancillary to the purpose and nature of a job.

*BNA*

**Defining Essential Functions 1805.70.40.10**
Review this description of factors to consider when defining the essential functions of jobs and identify those factors for a job you have held.

buildings identified that participation in design planning meetings was an essential job function. To accommodate a physically disabled employee, the firm purchased a motorized cart for the employee and required that all design team meetings be held in first-floor, accessible conference rooms. Generally, the costs of making reasonable accommodation are not great. According to one study, most employers spend $500 or less in making accommodations.[17]

## Job Analysis and Wage/Hour Regulations

Typically, a job analysis identifies the percentage of time spent on each duty in a job. This information helps determine whether someone should be classified as exempt or nonexempt under the wage/hour laws.

As will be noted in Chapter 13, the federal Fair Labor Standards Act (FLSA) and most state wage/hour laws indicate that the percentage of time employees spend on routine, manual, or clerical duties affects whether they must be paid overtime for hours over 40 per week. To be exempt from overtime, the employees must perform their *primary duties* as executive, administrative, or professional employees. *Primary* has been interpreted to mean occupying at least 50% of the time. Additionally, the exemption regulations state that no more than 20% (40% in retail settings) of the time can be spent on manual, routine, or clerical duties.

Other legal-compliance efforts, such as those involving workplace safety and health, can also be aided through the data provided by job analysis. In summary, it is extremely difficult for an employer to have a legal staffing system without performing job analysis. Truly, job analysis is the most basic HR activity.

# Behavioral Aspects of Job Analysis

A detailed examination of jobs, while necessary, can be a demanding and threatening experience for both managers and employees, in part because job analysis can identify the difference between what currently *is* being performed in a job and what *should* be done. Job analysis involves determining what the "core" job is. This determination may require discussion with managers about the design of the job. Often the content of a job may reflect the desires and skills of the incumbent employee. For example, in one firm a woman promoted to office manager continued to spend considerable time opening and sorting the mail because she had done that duty in her old job. Yet she needed to be supervising the work of the eight clerical employees more and should have been delegating the mail duties to one of the clerks. Her manager indicated that opening and sorting mail was not one of the top five tasks of her new job, and the job description was written to reflect this. The manager also met with the employee to discuss what it meant to be a supervisor and what duties should receive more emphasis.

## Job "Inflation"

Employees and managers also have some tendency to inflate the importance and significance of their jobs. Because job analysis information is used for compensation purposes, both managers and employees hope that "puffing up" their jobs will result in higher pay levels.

Titles of jobs often get inflated also, and some HR specialists believe that it is becoming worse. Some firms give fancy titles in place of pay raises, while others do it to keep well-paid employees from leaving for "status" reasons. Some industries, such as banking and entertainment, are known for having more title inflation than others. For instance, banking and financial institutions use officer designations to enhance status. In one small Midwestern bank, an employee who had three years' experience as a teller was "promoted" with no pay increase to Second Vice-President and Senior Customer Service Coordinator. She basically became the lead teller when her supervisor was out of the bank and now could sign a few customer-account forms.

## Managerial Straitjacket

Through the information developed in a job analysis, the job description is supposed to capture the nature of a job. However, if it fails—if some portions of the job are mistakenly left out of the description—some employees may use that to limit managerial flexibility.[18] The resulting attitude, "It's not in my job description," puts a straitjacket on a manager. In some organizations with unionized workforces, very restrictive job descriptions exist.

Because of such difficulties, the final statement in many job descriptions is a *miscellaneous clause,* which consists of a phrase similar to "Performs other duties as needed upon request by immediate supervisor." This statement covers unusual situations that may occur in an employee's job. However, duties covered by this phrase cannot be considered essential functions under the Americans with Disabilities Act (ADA). Also, it may be important to develop flexible work role definitions, particularly in manufacturing operations.[19]

## Current Incumbent Emphasis

As suggested earlier, it is important that a job analysis and the resulting job description and job specifications *should not describe just what the person currently doing the job does and what his or her qualifications are.* The person may have unique capabilities and the ability to expand the scope of the job to assume more responsibilities. The company would have difficulty finding someone exactly like that individual if he or she left. Consequently, it is useful to focus on the *core* jobs and *necessary* KSAs by determining what the jobs would be if the current incumbents quit or were no longer available to do the jobs.

## Employee Anxieties

One fear that employees may have concerns the *purposes* of a detailed investigation of their job. Management should explain why the job analysis is being done, because some employees may be concerned that someone must feel they have done something wrong if such a detailed look is being taken. The attitude behind such a fear might be, "As long as no one knows precisely what I am supposed to be doing, I am safe."

Also, some employees may fear that an analysis of their jobs will put a "straitjacket" on them, limiting their creativity and flexibility by formalizing their duties. However, it does not necessarily follow that analyzing a job will limit job scope or depth. In fact, having a well-written, well-communicated job description can assist employees by clarifying what their roles are and what is expected of them.[20] Perhaps the most effective way to handle anxieties is to involve the employees in the revision process.

**LOGGING ON . . .**

**Job Analysis**

This site is a list server or discussion site for individuals who wish to subscribe. Those in the service receive messages on job analysis, and individuals can post questions and issues.

**http://home.nav.soft.com/ hrmbasics/jobs.htm**

# Job Analysis Methods

Job analysis information can be gathered in a variety of ways. One consideration is who is to conduct the job analysis. Most frequently, a member of the HR staff coordinates this effort. Depending on which of the methods discussed next is used, others who often participate are managers, supervisors, and employees doing the jobs. For more complex analyses, industrial engineers may conduct time and motion studies.

Another consideration is the method to be used. Common methods are observations, interviews, questionnaires, and specialized methods of analysis. Combinations of these approaches frequently are used, depending on the situation and the organization.[21] Each of these methods is discussed in some detail next.

## Observation

When the observation method is used, a manager, job analyst, or industrial engineer observes the individual performing the job and takes notes to describe the tasks and duties performed. Observation may be continuous or based on intermittent sampling.

Use of the observation method is limited because many jobs do not have complete and easily observed job duties or complete job cycles. Thus, observation may be more useful for repetitive jobs and in conjunction with other methods. Managers or job analysts using other methods may watch parts of a job being performed to gain a general familiarity with the job and the conditions under which it is performed. Multiple observations on several occasions also will help them use some of the other job analysis methods more effectively.

**WORK SAMPLING** As a type of observation, work sampling does not require attention to each detailed action throughout an entire work cycle. Instead, a manager can determine the content and pace of a typical workday through statistical sampling of certain actions rather than through continuous observation and timing of all actions. Work sampling is particularly useful for routine and repetitive jobs.

**EMPLOYEE DIARY/LOG** Another method requires that employees "observe" their own performances by keeping a diary/log of their job duties, noting how frequently they are performed and the time required for each duty. Although this approach sometimes generates useful information, it may be burdensome for employees to compile an accurate log. Also, employees sometimes perceive this approach as creating needless documentation that detracts from the performance of their work.

## Interviewing

The interview method of gathering information requires that a manager or HR specialist visit each job site and talk with the employees performing each job. A standardized interview form is used most often to record the information. Frequently, both the employee and the employee's supervisor must be interviewed to obtain a complete understanding of the job. In some situations, such as team-directed jobs, group interviews also can be used, typically involving experienced job incumbents and/or supervisors. It usually requires the presence of a representative from the HR department as a mediator. For certain difficult-to-define jobs, group interviews are probably most appropriate.

The interview method can be quite time consuming, especially if the interviewer talks with two or three employees doing each job. Professional and managerial jobs often are more complicated to analyze and usually require longer interviews. For these reasons, combining the interview with one of the other methods is suggested.

## Questionnaires

The questionnaire is a widely used method of gathering data on jobs. A survey instrument is developed and given to employees and managers to complete. The typical job questionnaire often covers the areas shown in Figure 7–8.

The major advantage of the questionnaire method is that information on a large number of jobs can be collected inexpensively in a relatively short period of time. However, the questionnaire method assumes that employees can accurately analyze and communicate information about their jobs. Employees may vary in their perceptions of the jobs, and even in their literacy. For these reasons, the

**FIGURE 7–8** *Job Analysis Questionnaire*

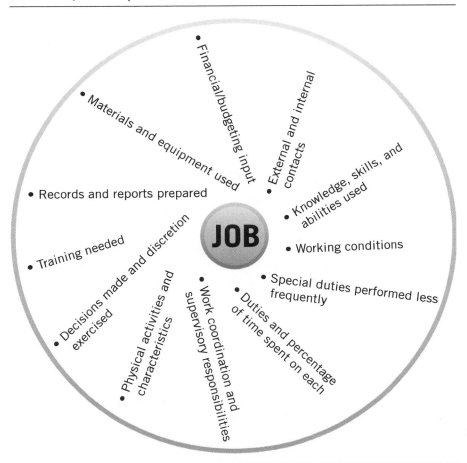

questionnaire method is usually combined with interviews and observations to clarify and verify the questionnaire information.

One type of questionnaire sometimes used is a *checklist*. Differing from the open-ended questionnaire, the checklist offers a simplified way for employees to give information. An obvious difficulty with the checklist is constructing it, which can be a complicated and detailed process.

## Job Analysis and the U.S. Department of Labor

A variety of resources related to job analysis are available from the U.S. Department of Labor (DOL). The resources have been developed and used over many years by various entities with the DOL, primarily the Employment and Training Administration.

**FUNCTIONAL JOB ANALYSIS (FJA)** This method is a comprehensive approach to job analysis. FJA considers: (1) goals of the organization, (2) what workers do to achieve those goals in their jobs, (3) level and orientation of what workers do, (4) performance standards, and (5) training content. A functional definition of what is done in a job can be generated by examining the three components of *data, people,* and *things*.[22] The levels of these components are used to identify and compare important elements of jobs given in the *Dictionary of Occupational Titles (DOT)*, a standardized data source provided by the federal government.

***DICTIONARY OF OCCUPATIONAL TITLES (DOT)*** Functional job analysis, as captured in the *DOT,* is a valuable source of job information, regardless of the job analysis method used. The *DOT* describes a wide range of jobs, samples of which are shown in Figure 7–9. A manager or HR specialist confronted with preparing a large number of job descriptions can use the *DOT* as a starting point. The job description from the *DOT* can then be modified to fit the particular organizational situation.

## Specialized Job Analysis Methods

Several job analysis methods are built on the questionnaire approach. Some of these methods are described next.

**POSITION ANALYSIS QUESTIONNAIRE (PAQ)** The PAQ is a specialized questionnaire method incorporating checklists. Each job is analyzed on 27 dimensions composed of 187 "elements." The PAQ comprises six divisions, with each division containing numerous job elements. The divisions include:[23]

- *Information input:* Where and how does the worker get information to do the job?
- *Mental process:* What levels of reasoning are necessary on the job?
- *Work output:* What physical activities are performed?
- *Relationships with others:* What relationships are required to perform the job?
- *Job context:* What working conditions and social contexts are involved?
- *Other:* What else is relevant to the job?

The PAQ focuses on "worker-oriented" elements that describe behaviors necessary to do the job, rather than on "job-oriented" elements that describe the technical aspects of the work. Although its complexity may deter many potential

**LOGGING ON . . .**
**Using the *DOT***

This web site provides an alphabetical listing of the *DOT* index, classification searches, and the capability of searching the complete *DOT*.

**http://theodora.com/ dot_index.html#MENU**

**FIGURE 7–9** *Sample Job Titles from the Dictionary of Occupational Titles*

# Parts of Occupational Definition

There are seven parts to an occupational definition identified by the U. S. Department of Labor that present data about a job in a systematic fashion. The parts are listed here as they appear in every definition:

1. The Occupational Code Number
2. The Occupational Title
3. The Industry Designation
4. Alternate Titles (if any)

5. The Body of the Definition
   (a) Lead Statement
   (b) Task Element Statements
   (c) "May" Items
6. Undefined Related Titles (if any)
7. Definition Trailer

    1         2        3      4

**166.227-010 TRAINING REPRESENTATIVE (education) alternate titles: training instructor**

5a — Develops and conducts training programs for employees of industrial, commercial, service, or government establishment: Confers with management to gain knowledge of work situation requiring training for employees to better understand changes in policies, procedures, regulations, and technologies. Formulates teaching outline and determines instructional methods, utilizing knowledge of specified training needs and effectiveness of such methods as individual training, group instruction, lectures, demonstrations, conferences, meetings, and workshops. Selects or develops teaching aids, such as training handbooks, demon- 5b — stration models, multimedia visual aids, computer tutorials, and reference works. Conducts training sessions covering specified areas such as those concerned with new employee orientation, on-the-job training, use of computers and software, apprenticeship programs, sales techniques, health and safety practices, public relations, refresher training, promotional development, upgrading, retraining displaced workers, and leadership development. Tests trainees to measure progress and to evaluate effectiveness of training. May 5c — specialize in developing instructional software. — 5 — 5c

**030.162-022 SYSTEMS PROGRAMMER (profess. & kin.)**

Coordinates installation of computer operating system software and tests, maintains, and modifies software, using computer terminal: Reads loading and running instructions for system software, such as task scheduling, memory management, computer file system, or controlling computer input and output, and loads tape into tape drive or transfers software to magnetic disk. Initiates test of system program and observes readout on monitor of computer system to detect errors or work stoppage. Enters code changes into computer system to correct errors. Analyzes performance indicators, such as system's response time, number of transactions per second, and number of programs being processed at once, to ensure that system is operating efficiently. Changes system software so that system performance will meet objectives. Reviews computer system capabilities, workflow, and scheduling limitations to determine if requested changes to operating system are possible. Writes description of steps taken to modify system and procedures required to implement new software. Assists users having problems with use of system software. May train users, — 6 COMPUTER OPERATOR (clerical) 213.362-010, and COMPUTER PROGRAMMER (profess. & kin.) 030.162-010 to use system software. May visit vendors to observe demonstration of systems software. May prepare workflow charts and diagrams to modify system software. May administer and monitor computer program — 7 that controls user access to system. May review productivity reports and problem records to evaluate performance of computer system.

SOURCE: U.S. Department of Labor, Employment and Training Administration, *Dictionary of Occupational Titles*, 4th ed., revised (Washington, D.C.: Government Printing Office, 1991).

users, the PAQ is easily quantified and can be used to conduct validity studies on selection tests. It is also useful in helping to ensure internal pay fairness because it considers the varying demands of different jobs.[24]

**MANAGERIAL JOB ANALYSIS** Because managerial jobs are different in character from jobs with clearly observable routines and procedures, some specialized methods have evolved for their analysis. One of the most well known and widely used methods was developed at Control Data Corporation and is labeled the Management Position Description Questionnaire (MPDQ). Composed of a listing of over 200 statements, the MPDQ examines a variety of managerial dimensions, including decision making and supervising.[25]

## Computerized Job Analysis

As computer technology has expanded, researchers have developed computerized job analysis systems. They all have several common characteristics, including the way they are administered. First, analysts compose task statements that relate to all jobs. They are then distributed as questionnaires that list the task statements. Next, employee responses on computer-scannable documents are fed into computer-based scoring and reporting services capable of recording, analyzing, and reporting thousands of pieces of information about any job.

An important feature of computerized job analysis sources is the specificity of data that can be gathered. All of this specific data is compiled into a job analysis database.

A computerized job analysis system often can reduce the time and effort involved in writing job descriptions. These systems have banks of job duty statements that relate to each of the task and scope statements of the questionnaires.

As is evident, the melding of computer technology with job analysis methodology allows firms to develop more accurate and comprehensive job descriptions, linked to compensation programs, and performance appraisal systems. These processes can also provide better data for legal defensibility than was once available.

## Combination Methods

There are indeed a number of different ways to obtain and analyze information about a job. No specific job analysis method has received the stamp of approval from the various courts in all situations. Therefore, in dealing with issues that may end up in court, care must be taken by HR specialists and those doing the job analysis to document all of the steps taken. Each of the methods has strengths and weaknesses, and a combination of methods generally is preferred over one method alone.

# Stages in the Job Analysis Process

The process of job analysis must be conducted in a logical manner, following appropriate management and professional psychometric practices. Therefore, a multistage process usually is followed, regardless of the job analysis methods

**FIGURE 7-10** *Stages in the Job Analysis Process*

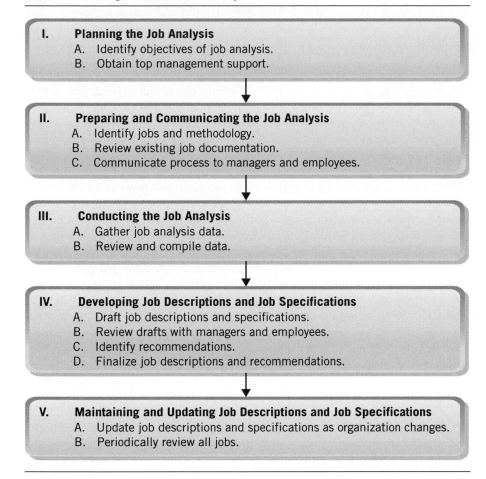

**I.    Planning the Job Analysis**
    A.   Identify objectives of job analysis.
    B.   Obtain top management support.

**II.    Preparing and Communicating the Job Analysis**
    A.   Identify jobs and methodology.
    B.   Review existing job documentation.
    C.   Communicate process to managers and employees.

**III.    Conducting the Job Analysis**
    A.   Gather job analysis data.
    B.   Review and compile data.

**IV.    Developing Job Descriptions and Job Specifications**
    A.   Draft job descriptions and specifications.
    B.   Review drafts with managers and employees.
    C.   Identify recommendations.
    D.   Finalize job descriptions and recommendations.

**V.    Maintaining and Updating Job Descriptions and Job Specifications**
    A.   Update job descriptions and specifications as organization changes.
    B.   Periodically review all jobs.

used. The stages for a typical job analysis are outlined here, but they may vary with the methods used and the number of jobs included. Figure 7–10 illustrates the basic stages of the process.

## Planning the Job Analysis

It is crucial that the job analysis process be planned before beginning the gathering of data from managers and employees. Probably the most important consideration is to identify the objectives of the job analysis. Maybe it is just to update job descriptions. Or, it may include as an outcome revising the compensation programs in the organization. Another objective could be to redesign the jobs in a department or division of the organization. Also, it could be to change the structure in parts of the organization to align it better with business strategies.

Whatever the purpose identified, it is vital to obtain top management support. The backing of senior managers is needed as issues arise regarding changes in jobs or the organizational structure. Support from even the highest levels of management helps when managerial and employee anxieties and resistance arise.

## Preparing and Introducing the Job Analysis

Preparation begins by identifying the jobs under review. For example, are the jobs to be analyzed hourly jobs, clerical jobs, all jobs in one division, or all jobs in the entire organization? In this phase, those who will be involved in conducting the job analysis and the methods to be used are identified. Also specified is how current incumbents and managers will participate in the process and how many employees' jobs will be considered.

Another task in the identification phase is to review existing documentation. Existing job descriptions, organization charts, previous job analysis information, and other industry-related resources all may be useful to review. Having details from this review may save time and effort later in the process.

A crucial step is to communicate and explain the process to managers, affected employees, and other concerned people, such as union stewards. Explanations should address the natural concerns and anxieties people have when someone puts their jobs under close scrutiny. Items to be covered often include the purpose of the job analysis, the steps involved, the time schedule, how managers and employees will participate, who is doing the analysis, and whom to contact as questions arise. When employees are represented by a union, it is essential that union representatives be included in reviewing the job descriptions and specifications to lessen the possibility of future conflicts.

## Conducting the Job Analysis

With the preparation completed, the job analysis can be conducted. The methods selected will determine the time line for the project. Sufficient time should be allotted for obtaining the information from employees and managers. If questionnaires are used, it is often helpful to have employees return them to supervisors or managers for review before giving them back to those conducting the job analysis. The questionnaire should be accompanied by a letter explaining the process and instructions for completing and returning the job analysis questionnaires.

Once data from job analysis has been compiled, it should be sorted by job, the job family, and organizational unit. This step allows for comparison of data from similar jobs throughout the organization. The data also should be reviewed for completeness, and follow-up may be needed in the form of additional interviews or questions to be answered by managers and employees.

## Developing Job Descriptions and Job Specifications

At this stage the job analysts will prepare draft job descriptions and job specifications. Later in this chapter is a section discussing details on how to write job descriptions and job specifications. Our purpose here is to emphasize that the drafts should be relatively complete and identify areas where additional clarifications are needed.

Generally, organizations have found that having managers and employees write job descriptions is not recommended for several reasons. First, there is no consistency in format and details, both of which are important given the legal consequences of job descriptions. Second, managers and employees vary in their writing skills. Also, they may write the job descriptions and job specifications to reflect what they do and what their personal qualifications are, not what the job requires.[26]

Once the drafts are completed, they should be reviewed by managers. Whether employees review the drafts or wait to receive the final job descriptions is often determined by the managerial style of the supervisors/managers and the culture of the organization regarding employee participation and communication.

When finished, job descriptions are distributed by the HR department to managers, supervisors, and employees. It is important that each supervisor or manager review the completed description with individual employees so that there is understanding and agreement on the content that will be linked to performance appraisals, as well as to all other HR activities.

## Maintaining and Updating Job Descriptions and Job Specifications

Once job descriptions and specifications have been completed and reviewed by all appropriate individuals, a system must be developed for keeping them current. Otherwise, the entire process, beginning with job analysis, may have to be repeated in several years. Because organizations are dynamic and evolving entities, rarely do all jobs stay the same for years.

Someone in the HR department usually has responsibility for ensuring that job descriptions and specifications stay current. Employees performing the jobs and their managers play a crucial role because, as those closest to the jobs, they know when changes occur. One effective way to ensure that appropriate reviews occur is to use job descriptions and job specifications in other HR activities. For example, each time a vacancy occurs, the job description and specifications should be reviewed and revised as appropriate *before* recruiting and selection efforts begin. Similarly, in some organizations, managers review the job description during each performance appraisal interview. This review enables the job holder and the supervisor to discuss whether the job description still describes the actual job adequately or whether it needs to be revised. In addition, a comprehensive and systematic review may be done during HR planning efforts. For many organizations, a complete review is made once every three years, or as technology shifts occur, and more frequently when major organizational changes are made.

# Job Descriptions and Job Specifications

The output from analysis of a job is used to develop a job description and job specifications. Together, they summarize job analysis information in a readable format and provide the basis for defensible job-related actions. They also serve the individual employees by providing documentation from management that identifies their jobs.

## Job Description Components

A typical job description, such as the one in Figure 7–11, contains several major parts. Overviews of the most common components are presented next.

**LOGGING ON . . .**
**Rice University Human Resources**
This web site provides guidelines for writing job descriptions, including the essential elements and their importance to organizations.

http://www.ruf.rice.edu/ ~humres/Training/ HowToHire/

**FIGURE 7–11** *Sample Job Description and Specifications*

---

**JOB TITLE:**   Compensation Administrator

**INCUMBENT:**

**SUPERVISOR'S TITLE:**   Vice President of Human Resources

**JOB CODE:** _____

**GRADE:** _____

**FLSA STATUS:** Exempt

**EEOC CLASS:** O/M

**General Summary:**   Responsible for the design and administration of all cash compensation programs, ensures proper consideration of the relationship of compensation to performance of each employee, and provides consultation on compensation administration to managers and supervisors.

**Essential Duties and Responsibilities:**

1. Prepares and maintains all job descriptions for all jobs and periodically reviews and updates all job descriptions. Responds to questions from employees and supervisors regarding job descriptions (25%).

2. Ensures that Company compensation rates are in accordance with the Company philosophy. Maintains current information applicable to pay structure movements taking place in comparable organizations; obtains or conducts pay surveys as necessary and presents recommendations on pay structures on an annual basis. (20%)

3. Develops and administers the performance appraisal program and assists in the development of supervisory training programs. Monitors the use of the performance appraisal instruments to ensure the integrity of the system and its proper use. (20%)

4. Directs the job evaluation process by coordinating committee activities, and reevaluates jobs periodically through the committee process. Resolves disputes over proper evaluation of jobs. Conducts initial evaluation of new jobs prior to hiring and assigns jobs to pay ranges. (15%)

5. Researches and provides recommendations on executive compensation issues. Assists in the development and oversees the administration of all annual bonus payments for senior managers and executives. (15%)

6. Coordinates the development of an integrated Human Resource information system. Assists in identifying needs and interfaces with the Management Information Systems Department to achieve departmental goals for information needs. (5%)

7. Performs related duties as assigned or as the situation dictates.

**Required Knowledge, Skills, and Abilities:**

1. Knowledge of compensation and HR management practices and approaches.

2. Knowledge of effective job analysis methods and of survey development and interpretation practices and principles.

3. Knowledge of performance management program design and administration.

4. Knowledge of federal and state wage and hour regulations.

5. Skill in writing job descriptions, memorandums, letters, and proposals.

6. Skill in making presentations to groups and in explaining compensation policies and practices to employees and supervisors.

7. Ability to plan and prioritize work.

8. Ability to use spreadsheets, presentation graphics, word processing, and database computer software.

*continued*

**FIGURE 7–11** *concluded*

**Education and Experience:**

This position requires the equivalent of a college degree in Business Administration, Psychology, or a related field plus 3–5 years experience in HR management, 2-3 of which should include compensation administration experience. An advanced degree in Industrial Psychology, Business Administration, or HR Management is preferred, but not required.

| Physical Requirements | Rarely (0–12%) | Occasionally (12–33%) | Frequently (34–66%) | Regularly (67–100%) |
|---|---|---|---|---|
| Seeing: Must be able to read reports and use computer. | | | | X |
| Hearing: Must be able to hear well enough to communicate with co-workers. | | | | X |
| Standing/Walking: | X | | | |
| Climbing/Stooping/Kneeling: | X | | | |
| Lifting/Pulling/Pushing: | X | | | |
| Fingering/Grasping/Feeling: Must be able to write, type and use phone system. | | | | X |

**Working Conditions:**   Normal working conditions with the absence of disagreeable elements.

**Note:**   The statements herein are intended to describe the general nature and level of work being performed by employees, and are not to be construed as an exhaustive list of responsibilities, duties, and skills required of personnel so classified. Furthermore, they do not establish a contract for employment and are subject to change at the discretion of the employer.

**IDENTIFICATION** The first part of the job description is the identification section, in which the job title, reporting relationships, department, location, and date of analysis may be given. Usually, it is advisable to note other information that is useful in tracking jobs and employees through human resource information systems (HRIS). Additional items commonly noted in the identification section are:

- Job code
- Pay grade
- Exempt/nonexempt status under Fair Labor Standards Act (FLSA)
- EEOC Classification (from EEO-1 form)

**GENERAL SUMMARY** The second part, the general summary, is a concise statement of the general responsibilities and components that make the job different from others. One HR specialist has characterized the general summary statement as follows: "In thirty words or less, describe the essence of the job."

**ESSENTIAL FUNCTIONS AND DUTIES** The third part of the typical job description lists the essential functions and duties. It contains clear, precise statements on the major tasks, duties, and responsibilities performed. Writing this section is the most time-consuming aspect of preparing job descriptions.

**JOB SPECIFICATIONS** The next portion of the job description gives the qualifications needed to perform the job satisfactorily. The job specifications typically are stated as (1) knowledge, skills, and abilities (KSAs), (2) education and experience, and (3) physical requirements and/or working conditions. The components of the job specifications provide information necessary to determine what accommodations might and might not be possible under Americans with Disabilities Act (ADA) regulations.

**DISCLAIMER AND APPROVALS** The final section on many job descriptions contains approval signatures by appropriate managers and a legal disclaimer. This disclaimer allows employers to change employees' job duties or request employees to perform duties not listed, so that the job description is not viewed as a "contract" between the employer and the employee.

## Preparing Job Descriptions

The ADA focused attention on the importance of well-written job descriptions. Legal compliance requires that they accurately represent the actual jobs. Some guidelines for preparing legally satisfactory job descriptions are noted next.

*BNA*
**Job Descriptions**
**415.40.20**
Review the sample policy on job descriptions to see how the process of developing and maintaining job descriptions can be identified. Also, the sample job description form is useful for generating job descriptions.

**IDENTIFYING TITLES** Job titles should be descriptive of job functions performed. For instance, one firm lumped all clerical jobs into four secretarial categories, even though the actual jobs were for such functions as payroll processor, marketing secretary, and receptionist. When the firm reviewed its descriptions, each job was given a function-related title. However, the jobs were grouped for pay purposes into the same pay grades as before. In summary, job titles should reflect the relative responsibilities in the organization and be linked to the pay grade system.

**WRITING THE GENERAL SUMMARY AND ESSENTIAL FUNCTION STATEMENTS** Most experienced job analysts have found that it is easier to write the general summary *after* the essential function statements have been completed. Otherwise, there is a tendency for the general summary to be too long.

The general format for an essential function statement is as follows: (1) *action verb*, (2) *to what applied*, (3) *what/how/how often*. There is a real art to writing statements that are sufficiently descriptive without being overly detailed. It is important to use precise action verbs that accurately describe the employee's tasks, duties, and responsibilities.[27] For example, it is generally advisable to avoid the use of vague words such as *maintains, handles,* and *processes.* Compare the statement "Processes expense vouchers" to "Reviews employee expense reports, verifies expense documentation, and submits to accounting for payment." The second statement more clearly describes the scope and nature of the duty performed. However, it is just as important to avoid the trap of writing a motion analysis. The statement "Walks to filing cabinet, opens drawer, pulls folder out, and inserts material in correct folder" is an extreme example of a motion statement. The statement "Files correspondence and memoranda to maintain accurate customer policy records" is sufficiently descriptive without being overly detailed.

The language of the ADA has stressed that the essential function statements be organized in the order of importance or "essentiality." If a description has eight statements, it is likely that the last two or three duties described are less essential than the first two or three. Therefore, it is important that job duties be arranged so that the most essential (in criticality and amount of time spent) be listed first and the supportive or marginal ones listed later. Within that framework, specific functional duties should be grouped and arranged in some logical pattern. If a job requires an accounting supervisor to prepare several reports, among other functions, statements relating to the preparation of reports should be grouped together. The *miscellaneous clause* mentioned earlier is typically included to assure some managerial flexibility.

Some job descriptions contain sections about materials or machines used, working conditions, or special tools used. This information is often included in the specific duty statements or in comment sections. Job descriptions of executive and upper-management jobs, because of the wide range of duties and responsibilities, often are written in more general terms than descriptions of jobs at lower levels in the organization.

## Writing Job Specifications

Job specifications can be developed from a variety of information sources. Obviously, the job analysis process provides a primary starting point. But any KSA included must be based on what is needed to perform a job duty. Furthermore, the job specifications listed should reflect what is necessary for satisfactory job performance, not what the ideal candidate would have. For example, it is not appropriate for a manager to list as KSAs five years' experience in the specific industry and an MBA, when satisfactory performance would require only three years' experience and a bachelor's degree in marketing or advertising.

With this perspective in mind, a job analyst can obtain job specification information by talking with the current holders of the jobs and their supervisors and managers about the qualifications needed to perform the jobs satisfactorily. However, caution is needed here, because the characteristics of the current job occupant should not be the sole basis for the job specification statements. The current incumbent's job qualifications often exceed the minimum KSAs required to perform the job satisfactorily. Checking the job requirements of other organizations with similar jobs is another means of obtaining information for job specifications.

## The ADA and Writing KSAs

In writing job specifications, it is important to list specifically those KSAs essential for satisfactory job performance. Only nondiscriminatory, job-related items should be included. For example, a high school diploma should not be required for a job unless the manager can demonstrate that an individual with less education cannot perform the job as well. Because of this concern, some specification

## HR PERSPECTIVE

# Research on Identifying Minimum Qualifications for Jobs

The process of identifying the minimum qualifications for jobs is often somewhat subjective and less clear than it should be. This is especially true given the legal implications of using these minimum qualifications for disqualifying job applications from further consideration.

Levine, Maye, Ulm, and Gordon conducted research on a methodology for developing and validating minimum qualifications for jobs in a state mental health facility. The researchers focused on fourteen different jobs in the state hospital.

First, the researchers gathered information on each job and its specifications. They reviewed the *Dictionary of Occupational Titles (DOT)* and obtained job analysis information on the tasks and KSAs

from those performing each of the jobs.

Next, the researchers identified individuals knowledgeable about each of the jobs, known as subject matter experts (SMEs). Those selected as SMEs included supervisors, managers, incumbent employees, and other knowledgeable persons for each job studied. Each panel of SMEs received the lists of tasks and KSAs, and the members rated each of those items on four scales. The SMEs rated the items independently, and the results were compiled by the researchers.

Following this rating process, the researchers and job analysts reviewed the results and grouped the items into profiles of minimum qualifications in each area identi-

fied. The final product of the process was a listing of the final profile criteria for each job. The completed system was tested by having raters independently evaluate past applicants using the identified minimum qualification profiles.

Using the minimum qualification profiles resulted in four of the nine profiles being validated as most directly applicable to evaluating applicants. Interestingly, using the profiles also led to positive inter-rater reliability, which deals with the consistency of ratings among different raters. In conclusion, the researchers indicated that this methodology appears to be acceptable in identifying minimum qualifications for each of the jobs under consideration.[28]

statements read, "High school diploma or equivalent acceptable experience." As the HR Perspective indicates, it is important to use a process to identify the minimum qualifications associated with jobs.

In light of the ADA, it is crucial that the physical and mental dimensions of each job be clearly identified. If lifting, stooping, standing, walking, climbing, or crawling is required, it should be noted. Also, weights to be lifted should be specified, along with specific visual and hearing requirements of jobs. Refer to Figure 7–11, the sample job description, for examples of KSA statements. Remember, these job specifications are the foundation for evaluating individuals with disabilities for employment.

## Summary

- Job analysis is a systematic investigation of the tasks, duties, and responsibilities necessary to do a job.
- The changing nature of jobs and work has led to additional approaches being used to analyze jobs and work.

- Work analysis examines the workflow, activities, content, and output in an organization.
- Task-based job analysis focuses on the tasks, duties, and responsibilities associated with jobs.

- The competency approach to job analysis identifies competencies, which are the basic characteristics that are linked to performance of individuals or teams.
- Once competencies have been identified, they can be used for HR selection, development, compensation, and performance management.
- The end products of job analysis are (1) job descriptions, which identify the tasks, duties, and responsibilities in jobs, and (2) job specifications, which list the knowledge, skills, and abilities (KSAs) needed to perform a job satisfactorily.
- An organization chart reflects the groupings of job families and reporting relationships among jobs.
- Job analysis information is useful in most HR activities, such as human resource planning, recruiting and selection, compensation, training and development, performance appraisal, safety and health, and union relations.
- Legal compliance in HR must be based on job analysis. The Americans with Disabilities Act (ADA) has increased the importance of job analysis and its components.
- Behavioral factors, including creating a managerial straitjacket and employee anxieties, must be considered when conducting a job analysis.
- Methods of gathering job analysis information include observation, interviews, questionnaires, some specialized methods, and computer job analysis. In practice, a combination of methods is often used.
- The process of conducting a job analysis has the following steps:
  1. Planning the job analysis
  2. Preparing and communicating the job analysis
  3. Conducting the job analysis
  4. Developing job descriptions and job specifications
  5. Maintaining and updating job descriptions and job specifications
- Writing job descriptions and job specifications can be challenging. The essential functions and KSAs should be described clearly.

# Review and Discussion Questions

1. What are the implications for job analysis, considering that some jobs are more varied and require more advanced capabilities compared to other jobs that are more routine and require less knowledge and skills?
2. Why is competency-based job analysis more difficult to conduct than the traditional task-based approach?
3. Obtain an organization chart from an existing organization and evaluate it in light of the suggestions contained in this chapter.
4. Why is job analysis the foundation of many other HR activities?
5. Discuss why the Americans with Disabilities Act (ADA) has heightened the importance of job analysis activities.
6. Describe three methods of analyzing jobs, including some advantages and disadvantages of each method.
7. Explain how you would conduct a job analysis in a company that had never had job descriptions.
8. Discuss how you would train someone to write job descriptions and job specifications for a small bank.

# Terms to Know

competencies   217
duty   216
essential job functions   227
job   214
job analysis   214

job description   221
job family   221
job responsibilities   216
job specifications   221
marginal functions   227

organization chart   221
performance standards   221
position   214
task   216
work analysis   215

# Using the Internet

## Conducting a Job Analysis

Your organization is in need of performing a job analysis on all your current jobs. The top level of management has asked you, the HR manager, to make a presentation on the process. Included in this presentation should be the uses and importance of job analysis, some of the legal consequences of poor job analysis, and just what a job analysis should in-clude according to the EEOC guidelines. Your job is to educate some of the senior managers who are not current on these issues. Prepare a brief summary for your presentation from the web site found at: **http://ijoa.org.**

## CASE

# Job Analysis Guides Reorganization at Bethphage

Bethphage, with approximately 3,000 employees, is a nonprofit organization that provides living and rehabilitative services for individuals with developmental disabilities through operating entities in 15 states and several foreign countries. Dr. David Jacox, CEO, and the Board of Directors identified that due to continuing growth the structure of the organization needed to be reexamined. Previously Bethphage had the parent corporation serving as headquarters and providing corporate functions. Then there were four regional corporations throughout the United States and internationally, each with its own board of directors. Concern about coordination of efforts and the legal issues associated with having so many "governing" bodies led to a need for an organizational restructuring.

Job analysis efforts tied to HR activities provided key information for the parent company board and senior managers throughout all entities. The process of changing Bethphage's organization structure took several years and was done in several phases. Three years ago, Bethphage took a comprehensive look at all jobs. To provide Bethphage's Board, Dr. Jacox, and senior managers with an understanding of the jobs in the organization, a job analysis of all jobs and entities was required.

Raul Saldivar, Senior Vice-President of Human Resources, and a committee of managers and executive directors from throughout Bethphage guided the comprehensive look at all jobs in the firm. Like many organizations, Bethphage had a small HR staff that was busy with many other HR activities. Consequently, Saldivar gave the responsibility for conducting the job analyses and preparing the job descriptions and specifications to Kelli Jorgensen, Bethphage's Compensation and Benefits Manager.

Jorgensen developed an extensive 12-page job analysis questionnaire tailored to the various job functions common throughout Bethphage. Then questionnaires were distributed to all employees in all locations. In spite of grumbling from some employees about the questionnaire length, over 90% of the questionnaires were returned within the allotted period to the appropriate departmental and agency managers for review. They were then sent to Jorgensen and the HR staff. At that point several HR interns from a local university began the arduous task of writing approximately 300 job descriptions and specifications. Once draft descriptions were available, Jorgensen coordinated their review by the appropriate managers and team leaders. Then the drafts were revised, reviewed by the compensation committee, and prepared for use in developing a coordinated compensation system. The entire process of conducting the job analysis and developing final job descriptions and specifications took four months of intensive effort. The process of developing the compensation and performance appraisal systems took another nine months, and the refinement and implementation of all components of the "new and improved" HR activities took over a year.

Once the compensation system had been installed for most of the jobs below the senior management level, the next phase of reorganization proceeded two years later. Bethphage redefined its executive structure, beginning by establishing one Board of Directors for the entire organization and dissolving the separate regional corporations. A revised management structure was created by the addition of a Senior Vice-President of Operations, Linda Timmons, to whom all regional directors report. The structural reorganization affected only about 15–20 jobs at the managerial level; those jobs were analyzed and redesigned before developing new job descriptions, compensation groupings, and ranges.

Now that all phases of the reorganization have been completed, Saldivar and Jorgensen have estab-lished procedures so that all jobs are reviewed each year and the compensation structures are updated. Several beneficial outcomes are based on the comprehensive job analysis developed by Bethphage:

- The HR department has been able to use the job analysis process for developing job descriptions for new jobs.
- Bethphage's new compensation program enables the HR department to ensure a more equitable system of pay increases and to provide a more accurate method for developing pay structures and determining pay levels.
- Over the past few years, Bethphage also has provided managers with a better system for conducting performance evaluations to ensure that they are promptly and accurately completed, and that a pay-for-performance system is developed and used.

As a result of all these activities managers throughout Bethphage are now using the HR department on a consultative basis for organizational decisions of all types. The job analysis activities were the foundation for all of the actions taken by Bethphage.[29]

## Questions

1. Discuss why job analysis was an essential part of the corporate change process at Bethphage.
2. How does the process described in the case illustrate the linkage between job analysis and other HR activities?

# Notes

1. Based on http://www.census.Gov/Press-Release/ff98-04.html; *Human Resources Report*, April 21, 1998, 400; Alan Farnham, "Where Have All the Secretaries Gone?" *Fortune*, May 12, 1997, 152–154.
2. Jody Barnes Nelson, "The Boundary-less Organization: Implications for Job Analysis," *Human Resource Planning* 20, (1997), 39–50.
3. Robert D. Behn, "Job Descriptions vs. Real Performance," *Governing*, January 1997, 60.
4. E. E. Lawler III, "From Job-Based to Competency-Based Organization," *Journal of Organizational Behavior* 15 (1994), 3–15.
5. Michael A. Bennett, "Competencies Under the Microscope," *ACA News*, June 1996, 7–10.
6. For more details on the steps in the interview process, see David D. Dubois, *The Competency Case Book* (Amherst MA: HRD Press, 1998).
7. Patricia K. Zingheim, *et al.* "Competencies and Competency Mod-els: Does One Size Fit All?" *ACA Journal*, Spring 1996, 56–65.
8. Kenneth H. Pritchard, "Introduction to Competencies," White Paper, 1997, Society for Human Resource Management. http://www.shrm.org/docs/whitepapers.
9. Cathy Gedvilas, "Rewarding the 'New Breed' Information Workers," *ACA News* July/August 1998, 30–35.
10. Bennett, "Competencies," 7–10.

11. Robert Adams, "Why Should I Conduct a Job Analysis?" AAIM. http://www.aimmconsult.com/JAreference.html (1998).

12. Marilyn Moats Kennedy, "Can This New Hire Be Saved?" *Across the Board,* May 1997, 53.

13. "Company Finds Job Analysis Key in Relieving Employee 'Discomfort'," *Human Resources Report,* May 11, 1998, 501.

14. Kenneth H. Pritchard, "ADA Compliance: Job Analysis is the Key," SHRM White Paper. http://www.shrm.org/docs/whitepapers/6142.htm (1998).

15. "Equal Employment for Individuals with Disabilities," Federal Register 56 (144), 35735.

16. Barbara Gamble Magill, "ADA Accommodations Don't Have to Break the Bank," *HR Magazine,* July 1997, 85–88.

17. Carolyn Hirschman, "Reasonable Accommodations at a Reasonable Cost," *HR Magazine,* September 1997, 106–114.

18. Sally Ford, "Job Descriptions Should Be Everyday Management Tool," *Kansas City Business Journal,* September 19, 1997, 20.

19. Sharon K. Parlzer, Toby D. Wall, and Paul R. Jackson, "'That's Not My Job': Developing Flexible Employee Work Orientations," *Academy of Management Journal* 40 (1997), 899–929.

20. "The Value of Job Analysis Techniques," http://sol.brunel.ac.uk/~jarvis/bola/job/jobs1/.html (1998).

21. For more details on any of the methods discussed, see Robert D. Gatewood and Hubert S. Feild, *Human Resource Selection,* 4th ed. (New York: The Dryden Press, 1998), 324–369.

22. For more details, see Sidney A. Fine, *Functional Job Analysis Scales: A Disk Aid* (Milwaukee, WI: Sidney A. Fine, 1992).

23. Ernest J. McCormick et al., *PAQ Job Analysis Manual* (Logan, UT: PAQ Services, 1977).

24. James P. Clifford, "Manage Work Better to Better Manage Human Resources: A Comparative Study of Two Approaches to Job Analysis," *Public Personnel Management,* Spring 1996, 89.

25. W.W. Tornow and P. R. Pinto, "The Development of a Managerial Job Taxonomy: A System for Describing, Classifying, and Evaluating Executive Positions," *Journal of Applied Psychology* 61 (1976), 410–418.

26. Phillip C. Grant, "Job Descriptions: What's Missing," *Industrial Management,* November/December 1997, 9–13.

27. "Five Things to Remember When Creating a Job Description," *Manager's Intelligence Report,* March 1997, 13.

28. Edward L. Levine, et al. "A Methodology for Developing and Validating Minimum Qualifications," *Personnel Psychology,* 50 (1997), 1009-1023.

29. Used with permission of Bethphage.

# CHAPTER 8
# Recruiting in Labor Markets

***After you have read this chapter, you should be able to:***

- Specify the strategic decisions that must be made regarding recruiting.

- Compare internal and external sources of candidates.

- Discuss why more employers are using flexible staffing for recruiting.

- Outline a typical recruiting process and identify legal considerations affecting recruiting.

- Identify three internal sources for recruiting.

- List and briefly discuss five external recruiting sources.

- Discuss three factors to consider when evaluating recruiting efforts.

# Innovative Recruiting in Tight Labor Markets

When the unemployment rate is high, recruiting people to work is easy—simply let it be known that jobs are available. But when the unemployment rate is very low and few people are looking for jobs, recruiting becomes much more challenging. In the past few years for many employers, challenging recruiting has become the rule rather than the exception. An examination of some of the recruiting techniques used by employers shows both creativity and desperation facing tight labor markets.

Merit Electric in Largo, Florida, took its pitch for electricians to the *junior high schools.* The owner says, "We are not expecting a decision from an eighth grader, but we want to expose them to the profession." Additionally, in many areas other employers have formed "partnerships" with high schools that include internships, mentoring, and jobs for those graduates who do not wish to go on to college.

In Dubuque, Iowa, when employment hit a low of 3.9%, the city launched a *come-home campaign* during the holidays, hoping parents would convince their adult children visiting from out of state to come back and work in Iowa. Other labor-hungry Iowa communities have added similar programs and have advertised at high school reunions and in college alumni publications. Trying to attract labor rather than businesses is unusual for a state, but it has become common in Iowa, Nebraska, and a number of other states facing low unemployment levels.

Employers in other states also have turned to *"risky" hires* that they would normally not consider. For example, Produce Packaging in Cleveland has hired parolees from Ohio prisons, many of whom had been convicted of violent crimes. For this recruiting source, many of the 1.7 million prisoners in U.S. prisons are released to halfway houses or work-release programs from which they can be hired. Additionally, welfare recipients with little or no job experience are hired, as well as former drug addicts. In fact, one firm—Microboard Processing in Seymour, Connecticut—sets aside 10% of its hires for "high risk" candidates. They do not all work out, because a significant number of them fail to meet production or attendance standards and are terminated. But with a variety of educational and training programs provided by Microboard, others do succeed.

Employers trying to recruit employees in the especially difficult areas of information technology and computer/software engineering go to great lengths to *"steal" employees* from each other. One firm sent a secretary to obtain a competitor's in-house phone book, which could be used to contact employees. In Dallas, National Semiconductor put a billboard right outside the headquarters of its competitor, Texas Instruments. The sign said, "Why did the engineer cross the road? . . . to get a better job." It included National's toll-free phone number.

Other information technology (IT) firms have paid *signing bonuses* to sophomore and junior computer science majors—and promised $60,000 jobs with no college degree. To some 19-year-olds, such offers have proved tempting—but like would-be sports stars, some individuals ultimately have found that they needed to go back and get college degrees for long-term career growth.

In another type of creative recruiting, some firms have opened employment centers in *shopping malls,* and others have stationed remodeled motor homes—all set up for interviews, testing, and hiring—in parking lots at the malls. These centers sport big signs: "Want a job? Apply here!"

Other innovative approaches include advertising over the loudspeaker at San Francisco 49ers games, using a plane towing an advertising banner over beach areas, setting up recruiting tables at minor league baseball games, advertising on the back of grocery receipts, advertising for "moonlighters" (those who want a *second* job), and busing people to work so they do not have to drive.

These are only a few of the ways employers have pursued employees when faced with tight labor markets. But like everything connected to the business cycle, if and when the unemployment rates increase, some employers will be able to return to the traditional approach of advertising in the newspapers to attract candidates for most open jobs.[1]

> *In the past few years for many employers, challenging recruiting has become the rule rather than the exception.*

> 66 *Ability will never catch up with the demand for it.* 99
>
> MALCOLM FORBES

Staffing is the process of matching appropriate people with appropriate jobs. From the viewpoint of organizations, staffing entails using HR planning information to determine the correct numbers and kinds of candidates, locating them, and then selecting those who are most likely to be satisfactory employees. From the standpoint of job applicants, the staffing process affects how they see jobs and organizations, and the likelihood that they will be matched with jobs that are rewarding for them. The organizational perspective is the primary focal point in this chapter and the next.

**Recruiting**

The process of generating a pool of qualified applicants for organizational jobs.

Staffing consists of two parts: recruiting and selection. This chapter examines recruiting, and the next examines selection. **Recruiting** is the process of generating a pool of qualified applicants for organizational jobs. If the number of available candidates only equals the number of people to be hired, there is no real selection—the choice has already been made. The organization must either leave some openings unfilled or take all the candidates.

Many employers currently are facing shortages of workers with the appropriate knowledge, skills, and abilities (KSAs) in tight labor markets, as the chapter opener indicates. However, because business cycles go up *and* down, the demand for labor changes and the number of people looking for work changes. Because the labor market is the environment in which staffing takes place, learning some basics about labor markets aids understanding of recruiting.

# Labor Markets

**Labor markets**

The external sources from which organizations attract employees.

There actually is not one, but several **labor markets** that are the external sources from which employers attract employees. These markets occur because different conditions characterize different geographical areas, industries, occupations, and professions at any given time. For example, the demand for over-the-road truck drivers is very strong at this writing (a tight labor market). Yet with downsizing and mergers in the banking industry, there is a surplus of middle-level banking managers (a loose market).

There are many ways to identify labor markets, including by geographical area, type of skill, and educational level. Some labor market segments might include managerial, clerical, professional and technical, and blue collar. Classified differently, some markets are local, others regional, others national; and there are international labor markets as well. For instance, an interesting labor market segment opened up with the demise of the Soviet Union. A number of excellent Soviet scientists became available due to the absence of job opportunities in their own countries. Several research organizations, including Sun Microsystems, have recruited them for jobs. Many of these recruits have continued to live in their home countries and are linked electronically to their employers in the United States.

Recruiting locally for a job market that is really national likely will result in disappointing applicant rates. For example, attempting to recruit a senior accounting faculty member in a small town is not likely to be successful. Conversely, it may not be necessary to recruit nationally for workers in unskilled positions on the assembly line. The job qualifications needed and the distribution of the labor supply determine which labor markets are relevant.

Changes in a labor market may force changes in recruiting efforts. If a new major employer locates in a regional labor market, then other employers may see a decline in their numbers of applicants. For instance, when three riverboat casinos, employing a total of 3,000 workers, opened in Council Bluffs, Iowa, many employers in the area noticed a dramatic decrease in the number of applicants for job openings outside of the casino industry. Also, some employers, particularly smaller manufacturing firms, had to raise their wages to prevent turnover of existing workers. Similar occurrences have followed the opening of large automobile manufacturing plants in South Carolina, Tennessee, Kentucky, and Alabama.

To understand the components of labor markets in which recruiting takes place, three different concepts must be considered. Those three groups are *labor force population, applicant population,* and *applicant pool.*

The **labor force population** includes all individuals who are available for selection if all possible recruitment strategies are used. This vast array of possible applicants may be reached in very different ways. Different recruiting methods— for example, newspaper ads versus college recruiting—will reach different segments of the labor force population.

The **applicant population** is a subset of the labor force population that is available for selection using a particular recruiting approach. For example, an organization might limit its recruiting for management trainees to MBA graduates from major universities. This recruiting method will result in a very different group of applicants from those who would have applied had the employer chosen to advertise openings for management trainees on a local radio station.

At least four recruiting decisions affect the nature of the applicant population:

- *Recruiting method:* advertising medium chosen and considering use of employment agencies
- *Recruiting message:* what is said about the job and how it is said
- *Applicant qualifications required:* education level and amount of experience necessary
- *Administrative procedures:* time of year recruiting is done, the follow-ups with applicants, and use of previous applicant files

The **applicant pool** consists of all persons who are actually evaluated for selection. Many factors can affect the size of the applicant pool. For example, the organization mentioned previously is likely to interview only a small percentage of the MBA graduates at major universities, because not all graduates will want to be interviewed. The applicant pool at this step will depend on the reputation of the organization and industry as a place to work, the screening efforts of the organization, and the information available to the applicant population. Assuming a suitable candidate can be found, the final selection is made from the applicant pool.

The supply and demand of workers in the labor force population has a substantial impact on the staffing strategies of organizations. Internal labor markets also influence recruiting because many employers choose to promote from within whenever possible, but hire externally for entry-level jobs. A discussion of these and other strategic decisions to be made in recruiting follows.

**Labor force population**
All individuals who are available for selection if all possible recruitment strategies are used.

**Applicant population**
A subset of the labor force population that is available for selection using a particular recruiting approach.

**Applicant pool**
All persons who are actually evaluated for selection.

*BNA: 415.30*
**Recruiting Strategy**
Use the checklist for developing a firm's recruitment strategy and discuss it with an HR manager or other manager at your current employer.

# Planning and Strategic Decisions About Recruiting

The decisions that are made about recruiting help dictate not only the kinds and numbers of applicants, but also how difficult or successful recruiting efforts may be. Figure 8–1 shows an overview of these recruiting decisions.

Recruiting strategy entails identifying where to recruit, who to recruit, and what the job requirements will be. One key consideration is deciding about internal vs. external searches that must be made.

## Internal vs. External Recruiting

Advantages and disadvantages are associated with promoting from within the organization (internal recruitment) and hiring from outside the organization (external recruitment) to fill openings. Promotion from within generally is thought to be a positive force in rewarding good work, and some organizations use it well indeed. However, if followed exclusively, it has the major disadvantage of perpetuating old ways of operating. In addition, there are equal employment concerns with using internal recruiting if protected-class members are not already represented adequately in the organization.

**FIGURE 8–1** *Recruiting Decisions*

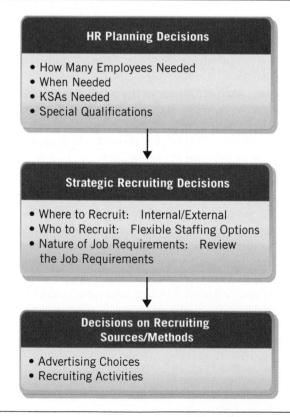

**FIGURE 8–2** *Advantages and Disadvantages of Internal and External Sources*

| Recruiting Source | Advantages | Disadvantages |
|---|---|---|
| Internal | • Morale of promotee<br>• Better assessment of abilities<br>• Lower cost for some jobs<br>• Motivator for good performance<br>• Causes a succession of promotions<br>• Have to hire only at entry level | • Inbreeding<br>• Possible morale problems of those not promoted<br>• "Political" infighting for promotions<br>• Need for management-development program |
| External | • New "blood" brings new perspectives<br>• Cheaper and faster than training professionals<br>• No group of political supporters in organization already<br>• May bring new industry insights | • May not select someone who will "fit" the job or organization<br>• May cause morale problems for internal candidates not selected<br>• Longer "adjustment" or orientation time |

Recruiting externally can infuse the organization with new ideas. Also, it may be cheaper to recruit professionals such as accountants or computer programmers from outside than to develop less-skilled people within the organization. But recruiting from outside the organization for any but entry-level positions presents the problem of adjustment time for the new employees. Another drawback to external recruiting is the negative impact on current employees that often results from selecting an outsider instead of promoting a current employee. Figure 8–2 shows some of the major advantages and disadvantages of internal and external recruiting.

Most organizations combine the use of internal and external methods. Organizations that operate in a rapidly changing environment and competitive conditions may need to place a heavier emphasis on external sources in addition to developing internal sources. However, for those organizations existing in environments that change slowly, promotion from within may be more suitable.

Employers may choose to look globally for some external candidates. However, such external recruiting requires interaction with the federal government to obtain temporary (3-year) H-1B work visas for foreign workers. The employer must attest that the visa will not displace U.S. workers. This approach is most often used for workers in very short supply in the United States.[2]

**LOGGING ON . . .**
**First Place Recruiting**
This website provides additional web links that assist both employers and job candidates with the recruiting process.

**http://www.infogoal.com/fpr/ fprlnk.htm**

## Flexible Staffing as Recruiting

Decisions as to who should be recruited hinge on whether to seek traditional full-time employees or use more "flexible" approaches, which might include temporaries, independent contractors, or professional employer organizations (PEOs) and "leased" employees.

A number of employers feel that the cost of keeping a full-time regular workforce has become excessive and is getting worse because of increasing government-mandated costs. But it is not just the money that is at issue. It is also the number of governmental regulations that define the employment relationship, making many employers reluctant to hire new employees. Using flexible staffing arrangements allows an employer not only to avoid some of the cost of full-time benefits such as vacation pay and pension plans, but also to recruit in a somewhat different market. **Flexible staffing** makes use of recruiting sources and workers who are not traditional employees. These arrangements use temporary workers, independent contractors, and employee leasing.

**Flexible staffing**
Use of recruiting sources and workers who are not employees.

**TEMPORARY WORKERS** Employers who use temporary employees can hire their own temporary staff or use agencies supplying temporary workers. Such firms supply workers on a rate-per-day or per-week basis. Originally developed to provide clerical and office workers to employers, agencies now provide workers in many other areas. Organizations that use temporary workers do not usually provide employee benefits, thus lowering their overall labor costs. But even if they do offer some benefits, employers may see advantages in using temporary workers.

The use of temporary workers may make sense for an organization if its work is subject to seasonal or other fluctuations. Hiring regular employees to meet peak employment needs would require that the employer find some tasks to keep employees busy during less active periods or resort to layoffs.[3]

Some employers hire temporary workers as a way for individuals to move into full-time, regular employment. After 90 days or some other period as a "temp," better-performing workers may move to regular positions when they become available.

Temporary opportunities also are opening up for professional and executive-level jobs, such as chefs, accountants, lawyers, systems analysts, nurses, and managers.[4] Downsizing has taken layers of management out of many firms, and companies may be hesitant to begin adding them back for projects that are temporary. Also, the same downsizing has made available "temporary executives" with experience that would not have been available in years past. Additionally, some of these individuals may have taken early retirement but want to continue working part-time.

Temporary workers can and often do accept regular staff positions after working as temps in firms. This "try before you buy" approach is potentially beneficial both to employers and employees. However, most temporary service firms bill client companies a placement charge if a temporary worker is hired full-time within a certain time period—usually 90 days.

**Independent contractors**
Workers who perform specific services on a contract basis.

**INDEPENDENT CONTRACTORS** Some firms employ **independent contractors** to perform specific services on a contract basis. However, those contractors must be independent as determined by a 20-item test used by the U.S. Internal Revenue Service and the U.S. Department of Labor, which is discussed in greater detail in Chapter 13. Independent contractors are used in a number of areas, including building maintenance, security, and advertising/public relations. Estimates are that employers can save up to 40% by using independent contractors because benefits do not have to be provided.

**PROFESSIONAL EMPLOYER ORGANIZATIONS (PEOS) AND EMPLOYEE LEASING** Employee leasing is a concept that has grown rapidly in recent years. The National Association of Professional Employer Organizations estimates that over 1.6 million individuals are employed by more than 2,200 employee leasing firms.[5] The employee leasing process is simple: An employer signs an agreement with an employee leasing company, after which the existing staff is hired by the leasing firm and leased back to the company. For a fee, a small business owner or operator turns his or her staff over to the leasing company, which then writes the paychecks, pays the taxes, prepares and implements HR policies, and keeps all the required records.

All this service comes at a cost. Leasing companies often charge between 4% and 6% of employees' monthly salaries. Thus, while leasing may save employers money on benefits and HR administration, it can also increase total payroll costs. In addition, employers may encounter some legal problems. For instance, leased workers are employees of the leasing company, but they may sue the client firm for work-related injuries if there has been negligence by the client because these injuries are not covered by workers' compensation.[6] One advantage for employees of leasing companies is that they may receive better benefits than they otherwise would get in many small businesses.

## Reconsider the Job Requirements

In larger organizations, recruiting often begins when a manager notifies someone in the HR unit that an opening needs to be filled. Submitting a *requisition* to the HR unit, much like submitting a supply requisition to the purchasing department, is a common way to trigger recruiting efforts. The HR representative and the manager must review the *job description* and *job specifications* so that both have clear, up-to-date information on the job duties and specific qualifications desired of an applicant. Sometimes the HR rep and the manager may decide that those qualifications need to be altered. For example, deciding whether a job is for a computer programmer or a systems analyst would significantly affect the content of a recruiting advertisement and the screening of applicants.

The job can sometimes be changed specifically in order to alter the recruiting situation. A decision might be made to improve characteristics of vacant positions by raising salaries, increasing benefits, or redesigning the job for a different level of applicant. For example, in high-tech and accounting work, many workers say they prefer working on "projects" to the full-time processing of ongoing work. Perhaps redesigning current jobs would attract more people to the unique advantages of that work. Alternatively, perhaps the job can be changed to take into account the nature or qualifications of available applicants. Ford Motor Company indicated that its recruiters consider 100 applicants to hire 7 employees. Two-thirds of the applicants fail a test in which they are asked to add fractions. Maybe adding fractions would not be necessary if the job were redesigned, or perhaps it could be taught. Similarly, Harley-Davidson screened 9,000 applicants to hire 200 workers in Kansas City.[7] In some cases a better approach may be hiring people with the *aptitude to learn* and teaching them what they need to know rather than hiring those who already have the KSAs needed to perform jobs immediately.[8]

## Retention

Finally, it may be that jobs can be changed to reduce turnover and increase retention of employees, which means less need for recruiting and fewer empty jobs. Nearly two-thirds of HR executives surveyed said they believed their companies needed to change their retention strategies.[9] As the HR Perspective explains, compensation is commonly used to improve retention, along with better opportunities for promotion and transfer, recognition, training, and benefits.

**LOGGING ON . . .**
**TRW—Development and Retention Programs**
An example of retention programs offered by this company can be found at this site, which also emphasizes recruiting and retaining a diverse workforce.

**http://www.trw.com/diversity/ retention.html**

## HR PERSPECTIVE

# The 100 Best Companies to Work for in America

*Fortune* magazine has surveyed over 20,000 employees in 238 companies and devised a list of the 100 best companies to work for in America. More interestingly, the survey also identifies the reasons *why* employees find these companies to be good employers, and in so doing, identifies what it takes to improve retention.

Some companies that downsized only a few years ago have been rehiring as they realize they cut out too much staff, which has damaged their ability to compete for employees. Formal retention programs, which might include cash bonuses for longevity, are better than nothing; but a culture that makes people *want to stay* is more effective.

Why do employees who have many opportunities at other places want to stay? Answers vary: cutting-edge technology, exciting work, a chance to change careers in the same company, possibilities for overseas assignments, promotion from within, flexible work schedules, and terrific benefits. No one mentioned money in the survey—these firms pay well—but people seem to need another reason to go to work. Once people reach a certain level of material comfort, they are most interested in what they do at their jobs all day.

Two themes seem to dominate the employee comments: fun and flexibility. Seventy-four percent said a workplace that "promotes fun and closer work relationships with colleagues" is one where they would like to stay. At the best companies flexibility is given freely, with no need for begging. Flexibility is balanced—for family, work, and life. Retention is easier at companies such as these, and recruiting is not difficult, because the reputations of these organizations are well known.

Among the best companies, according to *Fortune,* are:

- Southwest Airlines (Dallas, TX)
- Kingston Technology (Fountain Valley, CA)
- SAS Institute (Cary, NC)
- MBNA Wilmington, DE)
- W.L. Gore (Newark, DE)
- Microsoft (Redmond, WA)
- Merck (Whitehouse Station, NJ)
- Hewlett-Packard (Palo Alto, CO)[10]

# Decisions on Recruiting Sources/Methods

Before a firm actually proceeds to recruit a pool of applicants, several other decisions should be made. These decisions help determine the exact nature of the recruiting effort (Figure 8–3).

## Recruiting and Legal Considerations

Recruiting as a key employment-related activity is subject to various legal considerations. The wide range of equal employment laws and regulations was discussed in preceding chapters, but it is useful to highlight their impact on recruiting activities here.

**DISPARATE IMPACT AND AFFIRMATIVE ACTION** One facet of legal compliance of the recruiting process is to ensure that external disparate impact is not occurring. Remember that disparate impact occurs when there is underrepresentation of protected-class members in relation to the labor markets utilized by the employer.

To determine if disparate impact is occurring, it is necessary for applicant flow information to be maintained in line with the processes discussed in Chapter 6. If disparate impact exists, then the employer may need to make special efforts to persuade protected-class individuals to apply for jobs. For instance, one major Midwestern insurance company sends announcements of job openings to over

**FIGURE 8–3** *Decisions Affecting Recruiting*

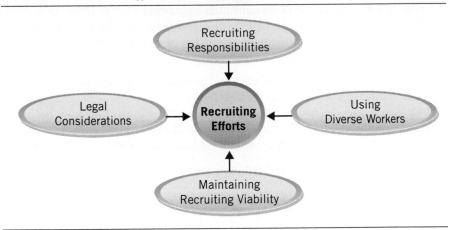

40 different agencies and organizations that specifically service various protected-class members. For employers with affirmative action plans (AAPs), special ways to reduce disparate impact will be identified as goals listed in those plans.

Some employers that emphasize internal recruiting should take actions to obtain protected-class applicants externally if disparate impact exists in the current workforce. Even using current employees as referral sources can create legal concerns. When the organization has an underrepresentation of a particular protected class, word-of-mouth referral has been considered a violation of Title VII of the Civil Rights Act. An organization composed primarily of nonprotected-class individuals presumably would refer more of the same for consideration as employees.

**EMPLOYMENT ADVERTISING** Employers covered by equal employment regulations must take care when preparing the wording for employment advertisements. The Equal Employment Opportunity Commission has issued guidelines stating that no direct or indirect references that have gender or age connotations are permitted. Some examples of likely impermissible terminology include the following: *young and enthusiastic, recent college graduate,* and *journeyman lineman.*

Additionally, employment advertisements should indicate that the employer has a policy of complying with equal employment regulations. Typically, advertisements should contain a general phrase, such as *Equal Opportunity Employer,* or more specific designations, such as *EEO/M-F/AA/ADA.*

## Recruiting Diverse Workers

The growing difficulty that many employers have had in attracting and retaining workers has led them to tap a wide variety of sources. Specifically difficult has been recruiting protected-class individuals under equal employment laws and regulations. If outside agencies are used, equal employment and affirmative action concerns of the actual employers still must be met. What is interesting, though, is that even if the legal stipulations were not present, employers who recruit workers with diverse backgrounds have found these recruits to be valuable employees. Three specific groups that have been attracted into the workforce effectively by some employers are individuals over 55 years of age, persons with disabilities, and persons who are members of racial/ethnic minorities.

**RECRUITING OLDER WORKERS** Demographic data reveals that the percentage of the population over the age of 55 continues to increase each year due to increasing life expectancies. When discussing the recruitment of older workers, the first task is to identify which individuals are included in this group. Senior experienced individuals may include the following:

● *Midlife career changers:* those who are burned out in their jobs and career fields and leave voluntarily to try new fields
● *Displaced workers under age 62:* those who have worked but have been displaced, often involuntarily, through job reductions or plant closings
● *Retirees:* those who took early retirement buyouts or retired at age 62 or later

Here are some concerns expressed by older workers:

● Am I employable if I'm older or lack some education or skills?
● Can I be re-trained, and will employers be patient while I learn new knowledge and skills?
● Are working schedules flexible enough given other life demands?
● How will my Social Security benefits be affected if I earn money working full-time or part-time?

Except for the last question, the reality is that most workers of any age would have similar concerns. Therefore, it is important that older workers not be viewed by their age alone. Rather, they should be viewed as experienced workers who may need some training, much as other workers would. In fact, older individuals often already have good skills and work habits.[11]

**RECRUITING INDIVIDUALS WITH DISABILITIES** Another group of individuals providing a potential pool of recruits for jobs are the over 40 million individuals with disabilities covered by the Americans with Disabilities Act (ADA). Many of them are in the workforce, but others have not been able to find employment, particularly those with severe or multiple disabilities. Yet some 79% of those people surveyed said they want to work despite their disabilities, and 71% of employees in another survey said they would be comfortable working with a person who is disabled.[12]

Two keys to successfully recruiting and utilizing people with disabilities are well-designed jobs and working with associations representing these people. Jobs must be such that accommodation can be made for people with disability. Not every disability lends itself to every job, even with accommodation. However, in many cases changes in job duties, work stations, and equipment might result in a job that a person with a disability can do—and very well. Associations of people with various disabilities can sometimes refer people whose disability will fit with a particular job. Such groups can also often make recommendations for accommodation. Individuals with disabilities have generally been found to be reliable and productive employees when properly placed in the right job.[13]

**RECRUITING MEMBERS OF RACIAL/ETHNIC MINORITIES** Employers that do business with federal and state governments must have affirmative action plans (AAPs), as discussed in Chapter 6. Consequently, those employers face pressures to increase the number of women employees and employees in racial/ethnic minorities. These pressures often are stronger for managerial, professional, and technical jobs than for unskilled, clerical, and blue-collar jobs.

Employers that are successful in diversifying their workforce use recruiting sources that target the appropriate types of applicants. For example, a firm that needs to ensure hiring of minority engineers may use special minority-oriented publications or recruit at colleges with large numbers of minority students. Other means of recruiting have included participating in job fairs sponsored by certain racial/ethnic organizations, establishing a minority internship program, and using current minority employees to recruit others of similar backgrounds.

## Maintaining Recruiting Visibility

Recruiting efforts may be viewed as either continuous or intensive. *Continuous* efforts to recruit have the advantage of keeping the employer in the recruiting market. For example, with college recruiting, it appears to be advantageous for some organizations to have a recruiter on a given campus each year. Those employers that visit a campus only occasionally are less likely to build a following in that school over time.[14]

*Intensive* recruiting may take the form of a vigorous recruiting campaign aimed at hiring a given number of employees, usually within a short period of time. Such efforts may be the result of failure in the HR planning system to identify needs in advance or to recognize drastic changes in workforce needs due to unexpected workloads.

For many people, the only contact they will have with an organization occurs when they apply for a job there. Of course, the probability is that a given individual will not get the job. If 50 people apply for a job and one is hired, 49 were *not* hired and are potentially unhappy. It is at this point that recruiting can do real damage to the perceptions people have of that organization. In addition to the impressions candidates have of the organization, recruiter friendliness and other variables affect decisions of job seekers.

## Organizational Recruiting Responsibilities

In small organizations, the recruiting process is simplified. For many positions, an advertisement in the local paper may be enough to tap into the local labor market. In very small organizations, the owner/manager often places the ad, determines the recruiting criteria, and makes the decision. However, for some specialist jobs, a regional or national search may be undertaken. Figure 8–4 shows a typical distribution of recruiting responsibilities between the HR department and managers in larger organizations.

**FIGURE 8–4** *Typical Recruiting Responsibilities*

| HR Unit | Managers |
|---|---|
| • Forecasts recruiting needs<br>• Prepares copy for recruiting ads and campaigns<br>• Plans and conducts recruiting efforts<br>• Audits and evaluates all recruiting activities | • Anticipate needs for employees to fill vacancies<br>• Determine KSAs needed from applicants<br>• Assist in recruiting effort with information about job requirements<br>• Review recruiting efforts activities |

# Internal Recruiting

Pursuing internal recruiting with the advantages mentioned earlier means focusing on current employees and others with previous contact with an employing organization. Friends of present employees, former employees, and previous applicants may be sources. Promotions, demotions, and transfers also can provide additional people for an organizational unit, if not for the entire organization.

Among the ways in which internal recruiting sources have an advantage over external sources is that they allow management to observe the candidate for promotion (or transfer) over a period of time and to evaluate that person's potential and specific job performance. Further, an organization that promotes its own employees to fill job openings may give those employees added motivation to do a good job. Employees may see little reason to do more than just what the current job requires if management's policy is usually to hire externally. This concern is indeed the main reason why an organization generally considers internal sources of qualified applicants first.

## Job Posting and Bidding

**Job posting and bidding**
A system in which the employer provides notices of job openings within the organization and employees respond by applying for specific openings.

The major means for recruiting employees for other jobs within the organization is a *job posting* system. **Job posting and bidding** is a system in which the employer provides notices of job openings and employees respond by applying for specific openings. The organization can notify employees of all job vacancies by posting notices, circulating publications, or in some other way inviting employees to apply for jobs. In a unionized organization, job posting and bidding can be quite formal; the procedure often is spelled out in the labor agreement. Seniority lists may be used by organizations that make promotions based strictly on seniority, so candidates are considered for promotions in the order of seniority.

Answers to many potential questions must be anticipated: What happens if there are no qualified candidates on the payroll to fill new openings? Is it necessary for employees to inform their supervisors that they are bidding for another job? How much notice should an employee be required to give before transferring to a new department? When should job notices not be posted?

*BNA 1023.10–1023.20*

**Job Postings, Promotions, and Transfers**
Many employers use job postings as a way to identify candidates interested in changing jobs within the organization. Review the issues associated with job postings, promotions, and transfers. See also job posting issues at 415.20.10.50.

A job posting system gives each employee an opportunity to move to a better job within the organization. Without some sort of job posting and bidding, it is difficult to find out what jobs are open elsewhere in the organization. The most common method employers use to notify current employees of openings is to post notices on bulletin boards in locations such as employee lounges, cafeterias, and near elevators. Computer software is now available to handle posting and bidding on PCs and intranets.[15]

Job posting and bidding systems can be ineffective if handled improperly. Jobs generally are posted *before* any external recruiting is done. The organization must allow a reasonable period of time for present employees to check notices of available jobs before it considers external applicants. When employees' bids are turned down, they should have discussions with their supervisors or someone in the HR area regarding the knowledge, skills, and abilities (KSAs) they need in order to improve their opportunities in the future.

## Promotion and Transfer

Many organizations choose to fill vacancies through promotions or transfers from within whenever possible. Although most often successful, promotions from within have some drawbacks as well.[16] The person's performance on one job may not be a good predictor of performance on another, because different skills may be required on the new job. For example, not every good worker makes a good supervisor. In most supervisory jobs, an ability to accomplish the work through others requires skills in influencing and dealing with people that may not have been a factor in nonsupervisory jobs.

It is clear that people in organizations with fewer levels may have less frequent chances for promotion. Also, in most organizations, promotions may not be an effective way to speed the movement of protected-class individuals up through the organization if that is an organizational concern.

## Current Employee Referrals

A reliable source of people to fill vacancies is composed of friends and/or family members of current employees. Employees can acquaint potential applicants with the advantages of a job with the company, furnish letters of introduction, and encourage them to apply. These are external applicants recruited using an internal information source.

Utilizing this source is usually one of the most effective methods of recruiting because many qualified people can be reached at a low cost. In an organization with numerous employees, this approach can develop quite a large pool of potential employees. Some research studies have found that new workers recruited through current employee referral had longer tenure with organizations than those from other recruiting sources.[17]

Some employers pay employees incentives for referring individuals with specialized skills that are difficult to recruit through normal means. One computer firm in the Midwest pays $3,000 to any employee referring a specialized systems analyst after an analyst has worked in the company for six months.[18]

However, as pointed out earlier in the chapter, using only word-of-mouth referrals can violate equal employment regulations if protected-class individuals are underrepresented in the organizational workforce. Therefore, some external recruiting might be necessary to avoid legal problems in this area.

## Recruiting Former Employees and Applicants

Former employees and former applicants are also good internal sources for recruitment. In both cases, there is a time-saving advantage, because something is already known about the potential employee.

**FORMER EMPLOYEES**  Former employees are considered an internal source in the sense that they have ties to the company. Some retired employees may be willing to come back to work on a part-time basis or may recommend someone who would be interested in working for the company. Sometimes people who have left the company to raise a family or complete a college education are willing to come back to work after accomplishing those personal goals. Individuals who left for other jobs might be willing to return for a higher rate of pay. Job sharing and flextime programs may be useful in luring back retirees or others who previously worked for the organization. The main advantage in hiring former employees is that their performance is known.[19]

Some managers are not willing to take back a former employee. However, these managers may change their attitudes toward high-performing former employees as the employment market becomes more competitive. In any case, the decision should depend on the reasons the employee left in the first place. If there were problems with the supervisor or company, it is unlikely that matters have improved in the employee's absence. Concerns that employers have in re-hiring former employees include vindictiveness or fear of morale problems among those who stayed.

**FORMER APPLICANTS AND PREVIOUS "WALK-INS"** Another potential source of applicants can be found in the organizational files. Although not entirely an internal source, those who have previously applied for jobs can be recontacted by mail, a quick and inexpensive way to fill an unexpected opening.

Applicants who have just "walked in" and applied may be considered also. These previous walk-ins are likely to be more suitable for filling unskilled and semiskilled jobs, but some professional openings can be filled by turning to such applications. One firm that needed two cost accountants immediately contacted qualified previous applicants and was able to hire two individuals who were disenchanted with their current jobs at other companies.

## Internal Recruiting Database

Computerized internal talent banks, or applicant tracking systems, are used to furnish a listing of the KSAs available for organizations. Employers that must deal with a large number of applicants and job openings have found it beneficial to use such software as part of a human resource information system (HRIS).

Software of this type allows employers to enter resumes and then sort the resumes by occupational fields, skills, areas of interests, and previous work histories. For instance, if a firm has an opening for someone with an MBA and marketing experience, the key words *MBA* and *marketing* can be entered in a search field, and the program displays a list of all resumes containing these two items.

The advantage of these computerized databases is that they allow recruiters to identify potential candidates more quickly than they could by manually sorting numerous stacks and files of resumes. Employers who have used internal computer databases have found that they reduce recruiting costs associated with advertising expenditures, search-firm fees, and internal processing and record retention expenses.

# External Recruiting

If internal sources do not produce sufficient acceptable candidates for jobs, many external sources are available. These sources include schools, colleges and universities, employment agencies, labor unions, media sources, and trade and competitive sources.

## School Recruiting

High schools or vocational/technical schools may be a good source of new employees for many organizations. A successful recruiting program with these institutions is the result of careful analysis and continuous contact with the individual schools. Major considerations for such a recruiting program include the following:

- School counselors and other faculty members concerned with job opportunities and business careers for their students should be contacted regularly.
- Good relations should be maintained with faculty and officials at all times, even when there is little or no need for new employees.
- Recruiting programs can serve these schools in ways other than the placement of students. For instance, the organization might supply educational films, provide speakers, or arrange for demonstrations and exhibits.

Many schools have a centralized guidance or placement office. Contact can be established and maintained with the supervisors of these offices. Promotional brochures that acquaint students with starting jobs and career opportunities can be distributed to counselors, librarians, or others. Participating in career days and giving tours of the company to school groups are other ways of maintaining good contact with school sources. Cooperative programs in which students work part-time and receive some school credits also may be useful in generating qualified applicants for full-time positions.

Until recently students who were not going on to college received little guidance or training on finding jobs after high school. Yet some 75% of the workforce *does not* receive a bachelor's degree. "Partnerships" with schools, overseen by the federal work-to-school office, have grown to over 1,000 in 45 different states.[20] Companies are entering the classroom not only to recruit, but to tutor students in skills such as reading and math needed for work. Internships during the summer and work/school programs also are being widely used.

Some schools will work with employers in designing programs to fit their needs. This cooperation is occurring at high schools, community colleges and universities. For example, at Vincennes Junior College in Indiana, one firm, Advanced Micro-Electronics (AME), worked with the faculty to create a computer repair program; today, more than a third of AME's employees have been hired from Vincennes Junior College.[21]

## College Recruiting

At the college or university level, the recruitment of graduating students is a large-scale operation for many organizations. Most colleges and universities maintain placement offices in which employers and applicants can meet. However, college recruiting presents some interesting and unique problems.

The major determinants affecting an employer's selection of colleges at which to conduct interviews are:

- Current position requirements
- Experiences with placement offices and previous graduates
- Organizational budget constraints
- Cost of available talent (typical salaries)
- Market competition
- College reputation

College recruiting can be expensive; therefore, an organization should determine if the positions it is trying to fill really require persons with college degrees. A great many positions do not; yet many employers insist on filling them with

# Research on Reactions to Campus Interviews

In a study in the *Academy of Management Journal*, Cynthia Stevens explored whether the job beliefs students held before a campus interview affected how they viewed the recruiter. Two sets of beliefs on the part of students may affect their reaction to a particular company, and therefore the probability that they will accept an offer if made: What they know about a job and company, and how likely they think the company is to give them a job offer.

Stevens studied 106 students who had used placement services at a large university. Average age of the students surveyed was 24 years. Regarding majors, 17% were in Arts and Sciences, 54% in Business, and 30% in Engineering. Stevens collected data by recording the interviews and using a questionnaire to get self-report assessment of job beliefs by the students participating in the study.

The author concluded that the greater the student's perceived likelihood of getting a job with an employer, the greater the student's effort in pursuing that job, and the more positively the recruiter was viewed. Put another way, the view that a candidate has of a company before the interview affects both the perception of the recruiter and the intention to accept a job offer if one is made.

The study suggests that campus recruiting might be made more effective by creating favorable pre-interview impressions through advertising, promotion, and media coverage. The author also noted that campus recruiting is expensive for employers, with most money being spent on travel and on recruiters salaries.[22]

college graduates. The result may be employees who must be paid more and who are likely to leave if the jobs are not sufficiently challenging.

To reduce some of the costs associated with college recruiting, some employers and college or university placement services are developing programs using video interviews. With these systems, students can be interviewed by interviewers hundreds of miles away. There are advantages for both the companies and students. The firms save travel costs and still get the value of seeing and hearing students. For students, the system provides a means of discussing their credentials and job openings without having to miss classes.

There is a great deal of competition for the top students in many college and university programs. However, there is much less competition for those students with less impressive records. Attributes that recruiters seem to value most highly in college graduates—poise, oral and written communication skills, personality, and appearance—all typically are mentioned ahead of grade point average (GPA). However, for many employers, a high GPA is a major criterion when considering candidates for jobs during on-campus interviews. Top graduates in difficult-to-fill specialties are even receiving signing bonuses from employers in some tight labor markets.

Characteristics of recruiters sent to campuses also affect students' attraction to jobs.[23] Further, successful site visits affect the rate of job acceptance. The HR Perspective shows the results of a recent study on recruiting related to campus interviews.

Generally, successful recruiters are those who are enthusiastic and informed, show an interest in the applicant, use interview time well, and avoid overly personal or deliberately stressful questions. Even the gender of recruiters may influence the results.

## Labor Unions

Labor unions are a source of certain types of workers. In some industries, such as construction, unions have traditionally supplied workers to employers. A labor pool is generally available through a union, and workers can be dispatched to particular jobs to meet the needs of the employers.

In some instances, the union can control or influence recruiting and staffing needs. An organization with a strong union may have less flexibility than a nonunion company in deciding who will be hired and where that person will be placed. Unions also can work to an employer's advantage through cooperative staffing programs, as they do in the building and printing industries.

## Media Sources

Media sources such as newspapers, magazines, television, radio, and billboards are widely used. Almost all newspapers carry "Help Wanted" sections, and so do many magazines. For example, *The Wall Street Journal* is a major source used to recruit managerial and professional employees nationally or regionally. Whatever medium is used, it should be tied to the relevant labor market and provide sufficient information on the company and the job.

Newspapers are convenient because there is a short lead time for placing an ad, usually two or three days at most. For positions that must be filled quickly, newspapers may be a good source. However, there can be a great deal of "wasted circulation" with newspaper advertising because most newspapers do not aim to reach any specialized employee markets. Some applicants are only marginally suitable, primarily because employers who compose the ads do not describe the jobs and the necessary qualifications very well. Many employers have found that it is not cost efficient to schedule newspaper ads on days other than Sunday, the only day many job seekers read them.

In addition to newspapers, other media sources include general magazines, television and radio, and billboards. These sources are usually not suitable for frequent use but may be used for one-time campaigns aimed at quickly finding specially skilled workers.

**LOGGING ON . . .**
**Newspaper Employment Ads**
Newspaper employment ads from 19 major cities are available at this website, along with many other recruiting and job-seeking tools.

**http://www.careerpath.com**

**CONSIDERATIONS IN USING MEDIA SOURCES** When using recruitment advertisements in the media, employers should ask five key questions:

- What do we want to accomplish?
- Who are the people we want to reach?
- What should the advertising message convey?
- How should the message be presented?
- In which medium should it run?

Figure 8–5 on the next page shows information a good recruiting advertisement should include. Notice that desired qualifications, details on the job and application process, and an overview of the organization are all important.

**EVALUATING ADS** Economists argue that the value of advertising is to provide good information to make good choices.[24] But to see whether the ads are providing necessary information, HR recruiters should measure the responses they generate.

FIGURE 8–5  *What to Include in an Effective Recruiting Ad*

**INFORMATION ON THE CANDIDATE**

- Years of experience
- Three to five key characteristics of the successful candidate

**INFORMATION ON THE JOB AND PROCESS OF APPLICATION**

- Job title and responsibilities
- Location of job
- Starting pay range
- Closing date for application
- Whether to submit a resume and cover letter
- Whether calls are invited or not
- Where to mail application or resume

**INFORMATION ON THE ORGANIZATION**

- That it is an EEO employer
- Its primary business

To track responses to an ad, an employer first must code the ads used. The easiest way to do this tracking is to use different contact names and addresses (for example, specify a department number). Then the employer can note the source of the advertisement each time an applicant response is received. For coordination purposes, it is best to have one person responsible for opening and coding applicant responses. If one or two people are responsible for screening phone calls, they should ask applicants where they saw the ad. If several people are regularly taking call-in messages, the organization might consider having a special memo pad just for such inquiries, with a "source" section indicated on the form.

Although the total number of responses should be tracked, judging the success of an ad only by this number is a mistake. For example, it is better to have 10 responses with two qualified applicants than 30 responses with only one qualified applicant.

## Trade and Competitive Sources

Other sources for recruiting are *professional and trade associations, trade publications,* and *competitors.* Many professional societies and trade associations publish newsletters or magazines containing job ads. Such publications may be a good source of specialized professionals needed in an industry. Ads in other specialized publications and listings at professional meetings also can be good sources of publicity about professional openings. For example, a newspaper—*The St. Louis Post-Dispatch*—recruits in *Editor and Publisher* for managerial jobs and in *Adver-*

# Cisco Means Successful Recruiting

Effective recruiting is always difficult, but it is an important strategic weapon in the Silicon Valley job market in California. However, Cisco Systems has done recruiting very effectively, often by taking good employees from other companies. Now a firm of over 17,000 employees, Cisco added 4,000 employees in just one year alone to fuel its growth. Cisco's recruiting team identified exactly the kind of people it wanted— the top 10% or 15% of people in the industry. To attract such people, Cisco's HR staff held focus groups with individuals they wanted to hire. Then, rather than listing job openings, they ran an open invitation on the Internet to apply at Cisco. Directing all job seekers to the website provided an inexpensive listing of hundreds of job openings and lots of information about each job. Because

most applicants visited the website from work, Cisco could tell where the prospective applicants currently were working.

With information from the focus groups, Cisco also developed two effective recruiting programs. "Friends" matches Cisco employees with people who have approached the company as prospects. An attempt is made to match individuals with similar backgrounds and skills. Employees call the prospects and tell them in their own words about working for Cisco. Another recruiting program is called "Profiler." Again on the web page, Profiler asks applicants to provide education and background information by choosing selections from an on-screen menu. Thus, the applicants are immediately given a preliminary screening.

Then there is Cisco's acquisition strategy: If it cannot hire the competitor's talent away, just buy the company. Acquisition for the primary purpose of getting research and development talent has worked for the organization. It has acquired 12 companies and seeks to keep virtually all the employees of the companies it buys. Cisco has shown a knack for successfully integrating the employees of the companies it purchases, sometimes by allowing the acquired employees to telecommute rather than relocate to Cisco facilities. In summary, Cisco has shown that being successful in tight recruiting markets requires aggressive tactics, innovation, and regular use of creative HR approaches.[25]

*tising Age* for advertising and marketing jobs. It also uses job banks or computerized applicant listings from the National Association of Business Journalism and the American Association of Industrial Management.[26]

An employer may meet possible applicants who are currently employed by a competitor at professional associations and industry meetings. Some employers directly contact individuals working for competitors. Employees recruited from these sources spend less time in training because they already know the industry. The HR Perspective shows how one firm recruits industry sources successfully.

## Employment Agencies

Every state in the United States has its own state-sponsored employment agency. These agencies operate branch offices in many cities throughout the state and do not charge fees to applicants or employers.

Private employment agencies also are found in most cities. For a fee collected from either the employee or the employer, usually the employer, these agencies do some preliminary screening for an organization and put the organization in touch with applicants. Private employment agencies differ considerably in the level of service, costs, policies, and types of applicants they provide. Employers can reduce the range of possible problems from these sources by giving a precise definition of the position to be filled.

## Executive Search Firms

Some employment agencies focus their efforts on executive, managerial, and professional positions. These executive search firms are split into two groups: (1) contingency firms that charge a fee only after a candidate has been hired by a client company and (2) retainer firms that charge a client a set fee whether or not the contracted search is successful. Most of the larger firms work on a retainer basis.

The fees charged by executive search firms may be 33% or more of the employee's first-year salary. Most employers pay the fees, but there are some circumstances in which employees pay the fees. For placing someone in a high-level executive job, a search firm may receive $300,000 or more, counting travel expenses, the fee, and other compensation. The size of the fees and the aggressiveness with which some firms pursue candidates for openings have led to such firms being called *headhunters*.

Search firms are ethically bound not to approach employees of client companies in their search efforts for another client. As search firms are retained by more corporations, an increasing number of potential candidates become off limits. At some point, the large search firms feel they may lose their effectiveness, because they will have to shun the best candidates for some jobs due to conflict-of-interest concerns.

## Internet Recruiting

Organizations first started using computers as a recruiting tool by advertising jobs on a "bulletin board service" from which prospective applicants would contact the company. Then some companies began to take e-mail applications. Now some employers are not only posting jobs and accepting resumes and cover letters on-line but also are conducting employment interviews on-line. Advantages for such Internet recruiting by employers include:

● Reaching more applicants
● Having lower costs and faster response time frames
● Tapping an applicant pool conversant with the Net

Employers often begin the Internet search process by establishing an organization website and listing jobs on it. Alternatively, companies with a web page that specializes in posting job listings (an Internet job service)—much like the electronic bulletin board of days gone by—can be used by job seekers. Finally, on-line employment agencies can be used to post jobs and find applicants on the Net. Based on the results of one survey, Figure 8–6 shows the percentage of applicants who indicated they planned to use various recruiting resources.

One advantage of Internet recruiting is that it may improve the chances of contacting "passive job seekers"—those people who are not actively seeking work. Listing at popular job-search Internet sites is a good way to attract such browsing high-tech workers.[27] Indeed, recent surveys show that about 37% of companies now use the Net for recruiting, and the rate is increasing rapidly.[28]

# Recruiting Evaluation

Evaluating the success of recruiting efforts is important. That is the primary way to find out whether the efforts are cost effective in terms of time and money spent.

**FIGURE 8–6** *Recruiting Sources Considered by Applicants*

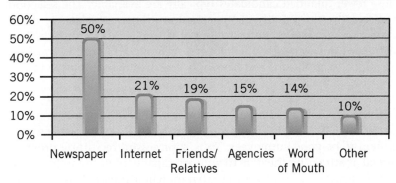

*Respondents may have cited more than one source.

SOURCE: Adapted with permission from *Bulletin to Management (BNA Policy and Practice Series)*, Vol. 49, No. 26, Pp. 205 (July 2, 1998) by The Bureau of National Affairs, Inc. (800-372-1033) <http://www.bna.com>

General areas for evaluating recruiting include the following:

- *Quantity of applicants:* Because the goal of a good recruiting program is to generate a large pool of applicants from which to choose, quantity is a natural place to begin evaluation. Is it sufficient to fill job vacancies?
- *EEO goals met:* The recruiting program is the key activity used to meet goals for hiring protected-class individuals. This is especially relevant when a company is engaged in affirmative action to meet such goals. Is recruiting providing qualified applicants with an appropriate mix of protected-class individuals?
- *Quality of applicants:* In addition to quantity, there is the issue of whether the qualifications of the applicant pool are sufficient to fill the job openings. Do the applicants meet job specifications, and can they perform the jobs?
- *Cost per applicant hired:* Cost varies depending on the position being filled, but knowing how much it costs to fill an empty position puts turnover and salary in perspective. The greatest single expense in recruiting is the cost of having a recruiting staff. Is the cost for recruiting employees from any single source excessive?
- *Time required to fill openings:* The length of time it takes to fill openings is another means of evaluating recruiting efforts. Are openings filled quickly with qualified candidates, so the work and productivity of the organization are not delayed by vacancies?

## Evaluating Recruiting Quantity and Quality

With the broad areas just outlined as a general focus, organizations can see how their recruiting efforts compare with past patterns and with the performance of other organizations. Brief discussions of some measures follow.

**SELECTION RATES** The selection rate is the percentage hired from a given group of applicants. It equals the number hired divided by the number of applicants; for example, a rate of 30% would indicate that 3 out of 10 applicants were hired. The percentage typically goes down as unemployment rates in the job market decrease, because fewer qualified candidates typically are available. The selection rate is also affected by the validity of the selection process. A relatively unsophisticated selection program might pick 8 out of 10 applicants for the job. Four of those might turn out to be good employees. A more valid selection process might pick 5 out of 10 applicants and have only one mediocre employee in this group.

**BASE RATE** In the preceding example, the base rate of good employees in the population is 4 out of 10. That is, if 10 people were hired at random, one would expect 4 of them to be good employees. Thus, a successful recruiting program should be aimed at attracting the 4 in 10 who are capable of doing well on this particular job. Realistically, no recruiting program will attract *only* the 4 in 10 who will succeed. However, efforts to make the recruiting program attract the largest proportion of those in the base rate group can make recruiting efforts more effective.

Certain long-term measures of recruiting effectiveness are quite useful in indicating whether sufficient numbers of the base rate group are being attracted. Information on job performance, absenteeism, cost of training, and turnover by recruiting source helps to adjust future recruiting. For example, some companies find that recruiting at certain colleges or universities furnishes stable, high performers, whereas other schools provide employees who are more prone to turnover.

**Yield ratio**

A comparison of the number of applicants at one stage of the recruiting process to the number at the next stage.

**YIELD RATIOS** Yield ratios can be calculated for each step of the recruiting/selection process. A **yield ratio** is a comparison of the number of applicants at one stage of the recruiting process to the number at the next stage. The result is a tool for approximating the necessary size of the initial applicant pool. Figure 8–7 shows that to end up with 25 hires for the job in question, the company must begin with 300 applicants in the pool, as long as yield ratios remain the same at each step.

A different approach to evaluating recruiting using ratios suggests that over time, organizations can develop ranges for crucial ratios. When a given indicator ratio falls outside that range, there may be problems in the recruiting process. For example, in college recruiting the following ratios might be useful:

$$\frac{\text{College seniors given second interview}}{\text{Total number of seniors interviewed}} = \text{Range of 30–50\%}$$

$$\frac{\text{Number who accept offer}}{\text{Number invited to the company for visit}} = \text{Range of 50–70\%}$$

$$\frac{\text{Number who were hired}}{\text{Number offered a job}} = \text{Range of 70–80\%}$$

$$\frac{\text{Number finally hired}}{\text{Total number interviewed on campus}} = \text{Range of 10–20\%}$$

If an organization needs a Vice President of Marketing *immediately,* having to wait four months to find the right person presents a problem. Generally speaking, it is useful to calculate the average amount of time it takes from contact to hire for each source of applicants, because some sources may be faster than others for a particular employer.

**FIGURE 8–7** *Using Yield Ratios to Determine Needed Applicants*

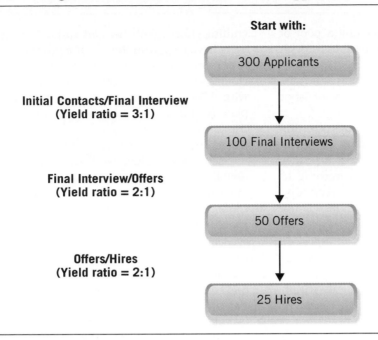

**Start with:**

300 Applicants

**Initial Contacts/Final Interview**
**(Yield ratio = 3:1)**

100 Final Interviews

**Final Interview/Offers**
**(Yield ratio = 2:1)**

50 Offers

**Offers/Hires**
**(Yield ratio = 2:1)**

25 Hires

## Evaluating Recruiting Costs and Benefits

Because recruiting is an important activity, the inability to generate enough qualified applicants can be a serious problem. When recruiting fails to bring in enough applicants, a common response is to raise starting salaries. This action initially may help recruiting, but often at the expense of other employees already in the organization. It also may create resentment on the part of employees who started at much lower salaries than the new hires.

In a cost/benefit analysis to evaluate recruiting efforts, costs may include both *direct costs* (advertising, recruiters' salaries, travel, agency fees, telephone) and the *indirect costs* (involvement of operating managers, public relations, image).[29] Benefits to consider include the following:

- Length of time from contact to hire
- Total size of applicant pool
- Proportion of acceptances to offers
- Percentage of qualified applicants in the pool

Cost/benefit information on each recruiting source can be calculated. Comparing the length of time applicants from each source stay in the organization with the cost of hiring from that source offers a useful perspective. Further, yield ratios from each source can help determine which sources generate the most employees.

In summary, the effectiveness of various recruiting sources will vary depending on the nature of the job being filled and the time available to fill it. But unless calculated, the effectiveness may not be entirely obvious.

# Summary

- Recruiting is the process of generating a pool of qualified applicants for organizational jobs through a series of activities.
- Recruiting must be viewed strategically, and discussions should be held about the relevant labor markets in which to recruit.
- The applicant population is affected by recruiting method, recruiting message, applicant qualifications required, and administrative procedures.
- A growing number of employers are turning to flexible staffing, which makes use of recruiting sources and workers who are not employees. Using temporary employees and employee leasing are two common approaches to flexible staffing.
- Two general groups of recruiting sources exist: internal sources and external sources. An organization must decide whether it will look primarily within the organization or outside for new employees, or use some combination of these sources.
- The decision to use internal or external sources should be based on the advantages and disadvantages associated with each.
- The recruiting process begins with human resource planning and concludes with evaluation of re-

cruiting efforts. Both HR staff and operating managers have responsibilities in the process.
- Recruiting is subject to some legal constraints, including avoidance of disparate impact, compliance with EEO requirements and affirmative action plans (AAPs), and use of nondiscriminatory advertising.
- Efforts should be made to recruit a diverse workforce, including older workers, individuals with disabilities, and individuals who are racial/ethnic minorities.
- Current employees, former employees, and previous applicants are the most common internal sources available.
- External recruiting sources include schools, colleges and universities, labor unions, media sources, trade and competitive sources, employment agencies, and the Internet.
- Recruiting efforts should be evaluated to assess how effectively they are being performed.
- Recruiting evaluation typically includes examining applicant quality and quantity, the time necessary to fill openings, and the costs and benefits of various recruiting sources.

# Review and Discussion Questions

1. Discuss what strategic recruiting considerations should be addressed by HR executives at a mid-sized bank with locations in several cities. Give examples, and be specific.
2. Discuss the advantages and disadvantages of recruiting internally versus externally.
3. What advantages and disadvantages of flexible staffing have you seen in organizations in which you have worked?
4. Design and describe a recruiting process for filling openings for a sales representative's job for a pharmaceutical manufacturer.
5. What internal sources for recruiting have you seen work effectively? What internal sources have you seen work ineffectively? Why?
6. Discuss some ways firms can make college recruiting more effective.
7. What should be considered in evaluating the recruiting efforts of a regional discount retailer with 80–100 stores in a geographic area?

# Terms to Know

| | | |
|---|---|---|
| applicant pool   251 | independent contractors   254 | labor markets   250 |
| applicant population   251 | job posting and bidding   260 | recruiting   250 |
| flexible staffing   254 | labor force population   251 | yield ratio   270 |

# Using the Internet

## Compensation and Recruiting

The president of your organization has asked your HR department to investigate the factors that affect the wages for different supervisory/managerial positions in Human Resources. The information will be used for a new recruiting program being set up on-line to ensure that the compensation program is competitive in the market. Use the website **http://www. abbott-langer.com/prssumm.html** and the free summary data provided to obtain the information that you will present to the president. Address the following issues for the HR supervisory/management jobs:

- Variables affecting compensation
- Regions where these jobs are most highly and least compensated
- Types of employers and compensation levels
- Size of organization and compensation
- Education levels and compensation
- Experience and compensation
- Level of supervisory responsibilities

# CASE

## Spring Break Recruiting

One of the more unusual locations for recruiting is the job fair for college students held on Daytona Beach, Florida, during the last three weeks of March. Begun in the mid 1990s by city promoters trying to enhance the out-of-control image of spring break week, the job fair has become popular with both recruiters and students. Various organizations have been represented, ranging from Walt Disney World Corp. looking for entry-level host jobs to Ernest & Julio Gallo Winery seeking management training prospects. GTE Data Services looked for students to fill internships and training programs, as well as jobs in programming, sales, marketing, and telecommunications. Even the U.S. Secret Service has used the opportunity to interview a large number of college students at one time.

Recruiters can find nearly 200,000 students from a myriad of colleges, with diverse backgrounds, and all in one location at this job fair. With such a large pool of potential applicants, the recruiters work hard to entice students to think about potential jobs and careers rather than vacations.

At the Daytona Beach job fair, recruiting and interviewing practices are different from those at more formal locations. There is definitely a casual atmosphere. Little recruiting occurs in the morning, but afternoons are busier. Application blanks take only five minutes to fill out, so students don't miss much sun time. To encourage students to consider employment, some firms have recruiters give out free sunglasses or passes to nightclubs, offer free breakfast buffets, or sponsor beauty contests. Informal dress by applicants is the norm, so recruiters have to become accustomed to evaluating people on qualities other than grooming and appearance.

Student responses to the idea of job searching while on spring break vary. Some students reject it altogether, but a number of them accept free offers and talk with recruiters. Some students even bring their resumes with them. Over 600 students interviewed with 28 employers during a recent spring break period. Such an approach indicates how a growing number of employers are using innovative means to recruit employees, especially in technical and professional areas.[30]

### Questions

1. From the prospective of a college student, argue the position that this approach is not a good idea for employers to pursue.
2. What difficulties for the employer do you see with this method of recruiting? Evaluate this method by the quality and quantity measures suggested in the chapter.

# Notes

1. Based on Michael M. Phillips, "Iowans Tug at Expatriates' Heart Strings," *The Wall Street Journal,* April 13, 1998, B1; Ellen Neirborne, "Labor Recruiters Get Creative," *USA Today,* July 22, 1997, 1B; Paulette Thomas, "Ex-Cons Find Other Jobs Pay in Labor Pinch," *The Wall Street Journal,* May 12, 1998, B1; Jeffrey Tannebaum, "Making Risky Hires into Valued Workers," *The Wall Street Journal,* June 19, 1997, B1; Del Jones, "Firms Hope to Lure Rivals' Workers," *USA Today,* March 16, 1998, 7B; Stephenie Overman, "A Creative Net Will Snare the Best," *HR Magazine,* May 1998, 88; and "Newest Shop in the Mall: An Employment Center," *Bulletin to Management,* May 14, 1998, 145.

2. Jon Kaufman, "U.S. Recruiter Goes Far Afield to Attract High-Tech Workers," *The Wall Street Journal,* January 8, 1998, A1; and Barry Newman, "Sham System," *The Wall Street Journal,* April 23, 1998, 1A.

3. Rochelle Sharpe, "Off the Dole," *The Wall Street Journal,* July 9, 1997, 1A.

4. Paul Barett, "More Law Firms Turn to Temps with L.L.D.'s," *The Wall Street Journal,* May 19, 1998, B1.

5. Loren J. Julber, "PEO's to the Rescue," *Benefits & Compensation Solutions,* June 1997, 32.

6. John Covaleski, "Working It Out," *Best's Review,* May 1997, 4.

7. Carl Quintanilla, "Work Week," *The Wall Street Journal,* March 3, 1998, 1A.

8. David Freemantle, "Recruit People Who Customers Like—Not Ones Who Just Fit the Description," *Workforce Supplement,* January 1999, 8–12.

9. "Retention," *Bulletin to Management,* October 8, 1998, 1.

10. Adapted from Anne Fisher, "The 100 Best Companies to Work for in America," *Fortune,* January 12, 1998, 69.

11. "How to Recruit Older Workers," *American Association of Retired Persons,* 1998.

12. Patricia Digh, "Finding New Talent in a Tight Market," *Mosaics* (SHRM) March/April 1998; and Albert R. Karr, "Workweek," *The Wall Street Journal,* October 20, 1998, 1A.

13. Carol Patton, "Challenged Workers," *Human Resource Executive,* January 1999, 67–70.

14. Edward Silverman, "On Campus," *Human Resources Executive,* June 9, 1998, 43–45.

15. "Enterprise-Wide Recruiting," *Lotus* (Cambridge, MA: Lotus Development Corp., 1998), 9.

16. Ruth Thaler-Carter, "In-House Recruiters Fill a Specialized Niche," *HR Magazine,* April 1998, 77.

17. Andy Bargerstock and Hank Engel, "Six Ways to Boost Employee Referral Programs," *HR Magazine,* December 1998, 72.

18. "Nepotism," *Human Resources Report,* February 23, 1998, 193.

19. Marilyn M. Kennedy, "Who Says You Can't Go Home Again?", *Across the Board,* November/December 1997, 53.

20. Brandon Cople and Louise Lee, "Formative Years," *The Wall Street Journal,* July 22, 1998, 1A.

21. Christopher Cogglano, "Beyond Campus Recruiting," *INC.,* April 1998, 115.

22. Adapted from Cynthia Kay Stevens, "Effects of Preinterview Beliefs on Applicants Reactions to Campus Interviews," *Academy of Management Journal* 40 (1997), 947.

23. Martin M. Greller, "Dimensions of the Recruiter's Role in the Employment Process," *Perceptual and Motor Skills* 88 (1999), 53–54.

24. "The Money Is the Message," *The Economist,* February 14, 1998, 78.

25. Adapted from Patricia Nakache, "Cisco's Recruiting Edge," *Fortune,* September 29, 1998, 275–276.

26. Ken Liebeskind, "Where to Look for Personnel," *Editor and Publisher,* February 14, 1998, 24.

27. Sherry Kuczynski, "You've Got Job Offers," *HR Magazine,* March 1999, 50–58; and "Employers Step Up to High Stakes Recruiting," *Workforce Strategies,* February 23, 1998, W9.

28. Justin Martin, "Changing Jobs? Try the Net," *Fortune,* March 2, 1998, 205.

29. Ruth Thaler-Carter, "EMA Model Defines Cost-Per-Hire," *HR Magazine,* December 1997, S1.

30. Based on "Job-Hunting College Students May Want to Try the Beach," *Omaha World-Herald,* March 17, 1996, 12A.

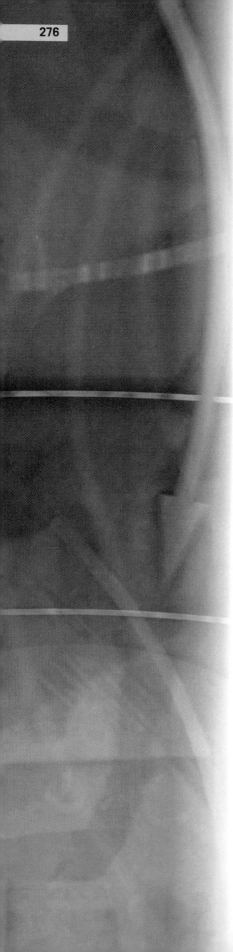

# CHAPTER 9
# Selecting and Placing Human Resources

*After you have read this chapter, you should be able to:*

- Define *selection* and explain the use of selection criteria and predictors.

- Diagram the sequence of a typical selection process.

- Discuss the reception and application phases of the selection process.

- Identify two general and three controversial types of tests.

- Discuss three types of interviews and several key considerations in the selection interview.

- Construct a guide for conducting a selection interview.

- Explain how legal concerns affect background investigations of applicants.

- Discuss why medical examinations, including drug testing, may be useful in the selection process.

## HR TRANSITIONS

# The Search for Useful Selection Tests

One industrial psychologist notes that "it used to be, you would hire someone, and if they didn't work out, fine. That's not the case anymore. This is a competitive work environment and there is much less room for mistakes in hiring. When you make a hire, you need to be right." Testing is being used to increase the chances of being right. If a test that was 100% accurate at identifying good-performing employees and eliminating poor performers could be given to applicants for a job, what would it be worth? Apparently quite a bit, as reflected by the growing frustration employers feel at hiring poor-performing employees. Preemployment testing has boomed to be an industry with revenues over $2 billion yearly. Tests are being used for everything from hiring tow truck drivers to fire chiefs, and they are widely viewed as useful selection tools.

One example of when testing is used is illustrative. When Lori Miller had to hire 40 child-care workers for the new child-care center at Boeing, she had only 4 weeks to do it. Because she did not have time to see all 200 applicants in action with small children, Miller ultimately did as many employers are doing: she used a test to help her pick the "best" 40. The test Miller used was designed for selecting child-care workers, and she used the test score and a follow-up personal interview with those applicants to make her decisions.

The popularity of using tests for selecting employees has grown. There are all kinds of tests: honesty tests, loyalty tests, personality tests, skill tests, leadership tests, genetic tests, drug tests, accident-prone tests, and others. Trends in the use of tests also suggest that more companies are asking more different kinds of potential employees to take tests. More than half of the organizations surveyed in one study require skills tests for hourly workers, 23% ask management candidates to take a skills test, and about 20% ask both management and hourly applicants to take a personality test.

Of course, the perfect test does not exist. There is always room for error; in fact, "accuracy" is really about what is an *acceptable level of error*, not complete accuracy. Tests are only one part of the information-gathering process necessary for effective selection of employees, but they are not the only part of the selection process. For this reason, it is highly recommended that tests be only one element in the decision to hire or not hire.

But while many managers are embracing testing as a tool for putting the right person in the right job, civil libertarians are worrying that probing a job seeker's personality or genetic makeup has the potential for violating individual privacy rights. If an applicant refuses to take a test, it is usually grounds not to hire, and that worries the American Civil Liberties Union (ACLU). Genetic tests that are used to guard against excessive future medical expenses are especially troublesome. As a spokesperson for the ACLU notes, "We all have mutant genes. We will be creating a class of unemployable people if genetic testing becomes the norm."

Testing appeals to employers because it has the potential to reduce the number of employees at work who steal, use drugs, lie, and fail to perform up to standards. But these advantages accrue only if each test used is valid, if it has been interpreted correctly by someone trained to do so, and if it is used as one source of information along with other sources. In summary, testing is a useful but problematic part of selection.[1]

> *Testing appeals to employers because it has the potential to reduce the number of employees who steal, use drugs, lie, and fail to perform up to standards.*

> 66 *Selecting qualified employees is like putting money in the bank.* 99
>
> JOHN BOUDREAU

**Selection**

The process of choosing individuals who have relevant qualifications to fill jobs in an organization.

**Selection** is the process of choosing individuals who have relevant qualifications to fill jobs in an organization. Without qualified employees, an organization is in a poorer position to succeed. A vivid case in point is athletic organizations like the Dallas Cowboys, Atlanta Braves, and Los Angeles Lakers, who fail or succeed on their ability to select the coaches, players, and other employees to win games.

Selection is much more than just choosing the best available person. Selecting the appropriate set of knowledge, skills, and abilities (KSAs)—which come packaged in a human being—is an attempt to get a "fit" between what the applicant can and wants to do, and what the organization needs. The task is made more difficult because it is not always possible to tell exactly what the applicant really can and wants to do. *Fit* between the applicant and the organization affects both the employer's willingness to make a job offer and an applicant's willingness to accept a job. Fitting a person to the right job is called **placement.**

**Placement**

Fitting a person to the right job.

More than anything else, placement of human resources should be seen as a *matching process*. Gaps between an individual's skills and the job requirements are common factors that lead to rejection of an applicant. How well an employee is matched to a job affects the amount and quality of the employee's work. This matching also directly affects training and operating costs. Workers who are unable to produce the expected amount and quality of work can cost an organization a great deal of money and time. Estimates are that hiring an inappropriate employee costs an employer three to five times that employee's salary before it is resolved.[2] Yet hiring mistakes are relatively common.

Good selection and placement decisions are an important part of successful HR management. Some would argue that these decisions are the *most* important part. Productivity improvement for an employer may come from changes in incentive pay plans, improved training, or better job design; but unless the employer has the necessary people with the appropriate KSAs in place, those changes may not have much impact. The very best training will not enable someone with little aptitude for a certain job to do that job well and enjoy it.

To put selection decisions in perspective, consider that organizations on average reject a high percentage of applicants. In some situations about five out of six applicants for jobs are rejected. Figure 9–1 depicts the reasons why employers most often reject applicants. Perhaps the best perspective on selection and placement comes from two traditional HR truisms that clearly identify the importance of effective employment selection.

- *"Good training will not make up for bad selection."* The implication here is that when the right people with the appropriate KSAs are not selected for jobs, it is very difficult for the employer to recover later by somehow trying to train those individuals without the proper aptitude, interests, or other KSA deficiencies.
- *"If you don't hire the right one, your competitor will."* There is an opportunity cost in failure to select the right employee, and that cost is that the "right one" went somewhere else.

**FIGURE 9–1** *Reasons Applicants Are Selected or Rejected*

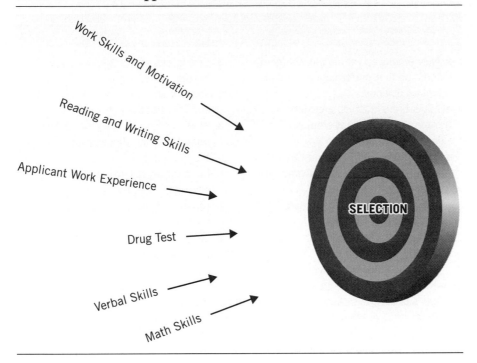

# The Nature of Selection

Already having the needed knowledge, skills, and abilities (KSAs) may be very important for a new employee to do a job well. For example, specific KSAs may be used to hire people for a given job: math skills, ability to weld, or a knowledge of spreadsheets. Job analysis can provide the basis for identifying appropriate KSAs if it is done properly. People already in jobs can help identify the most important KSAs for success as part of job analysis. These KSAs can be used to place an applicant in a suitable job based on how well their KSAs match.

However, specific KSAs may not be *necessary* immediately in some jobs; they can be taught on the job. In fact, for certain jobs it may be good selection strategy to deemphasize the precise matching of applicants' specific KSAs to a job and focus on more general predictors of success.[3] For example, if an employer hires at the entry level and promotes from within for most jobs, specific KSAs might be less important than general ability to learn and conscientiousness. Ability to learn allows a person to grasp new information and make good decisions based on that job knowledge. Conscientiousness might include thoroughness, responsibility, and an organized approach to the job. Figure 9–2 shows some situations when focusing on specific KSAs is a better approach for selection decisions, and when relying on general intelligence and conscientiousness may be better. Whether an employer uses specific KSAs or the more general approach, effective selection of employees involves using *criteria* and *predictors* of job performance.

*BNA*

**465.10.20**
**Picking Selection Tools**
Review this discussion of factors affecting the choice of selection tools and identify the selection tools relevant for a small bank to use in selecting a teller.

**FIGURE 9–2** *Selection Strategy Choices*

| Closely Match Job/Person KSAs for Selection When: | Use General Predictors for Selection When: |
| --- | --- |
| ● New employee will be closely monitored so that performance problems will be obvious.<br>● KSAs brought to job are more important than what employees learn on the job.<br>● Few changes will occur in the jobs —and the changes will be gradual when they occur.<br>● One job candidate clearly has greatly superior KSAs. | ● Employees work independently, having a high degree of autonomy and low structure, which requires conscientiousness to succeed.<br>● KSAs learned on the job are more important than those brought to the job.<br>● Many changes and much problem solving are necessary, and employees must learn very quickly, using creative approaches.<br>● Several job candidates are virtually equal in key KSAs. |

SOURCE: Adapted from Orlando Behling, "Employee Selection: Will Intelligence and Conscientiousness Do the Job?", *Academy of Management Executive*, February 1998, 83.

## Criteria, Predictors, and Job Performance

At the heart of an effective selection system is knowledge of what constitutes appropriate job performance and what characteristics in employees are associated with that performance.[4] Once the definition of employee success (performance) is known, the employee specifications required to achieve that success can be determined. A **selection criterion** is a characteristic that a person must have to do the job successfully. A certain preexisting ability is often a selection criterion. One example is the criterion *appropriate employee permanence*, which considers that a person must stay in a job long enough for the employer at least to break even on the training and hiring expenses incurred to hire the employee. Figure 9–3 shows that ability, motivation, intelligence, conscientiousness, appropriate risk, and permanence might be good selection criteria for many jobs.

To predict whether a selection criterion (such as "motivation" or "ability") is present, employers try to identify **predictors** as measurable indicators of selection criteria. For example, in Figure 9–3 good predictors of the criterion "appropriate permanence" might be individual interests, salary requirements, and tenure on previous jobs.

The information gathered about an applicant should be focused on finding predictors of the likelihood that the applicant will be able to perform the job well. Predictors can take many forms, but they should be job related, valid, and reliable. A test score can be a predictor of success on the job only if it is valid. Previous experience can be a predictor of success if it is related to the necessary performance on the current job. Any selection tool used (for example, application form, test, interview, education requirements, or years of experience

**Selection criterion**
Characteristic that a person must have to do the job successfully.

**Predictors**
Measurable indicators of selection criteria.

**FIGURE 9–3** *Job Performance, Selection Criteria, and Predictors*

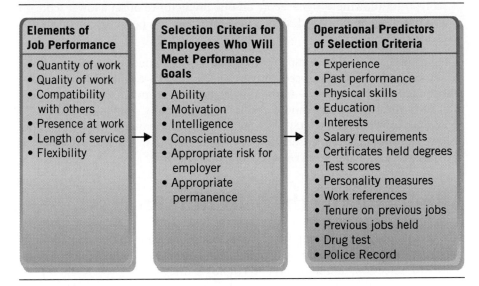

| Elements of Job Performance | Selection Criteria for Employees Who Will Meet Performance Goals | Operational Predictors of Selection Criteria |
|---|---|---|
| • Quantity of work<br>• Quality of work<br>• Compatibility with others<br>• Presence at work<br>• Length of service<br>• Flexibility | • Ability<br>• Motivation<br>• Intelligence<br>• Conscientiousness<br>• Appropriate risk for employer<br>• Appropriate permanence | • Experience<br>• Past performance<br>• Physical skills<br>• Education<br>• Interests<br>• Salary requirements<br>• Certificates held degrees<br>• Test scores<br>• Personality measures<br>• Work references<br>• Tenure on previous jobs<br>• Previous jobs held<br>• Drug test<br>• Police Record |

required) should be used *only* if it is a valid predictor of job performance. Using invalid predictors can result in selecting the "wrong" candidate and rejecting the "right" one.

**VALIDITY**  Validity is the correlation between a predictor and job performance. As mentioned in Chapter 5, validity occurs to the extent that a predictor actually predicts what it is supposed to predict. Validity depends on the situation in which the selection device is being used.[5] For example, a test designed to predict aptitude for child-care jobs might not be valid in predicting sales potential in a candidate for a sales representative.

**RELIABILITY**  Reliability of a predictor is the extent to which it repeatedly produces the same results, over time. For example, if the same person took a test in December and scored 100, but upon taking it in March scored significantly higher, the test would not be highly reliable. Thus, reliability has to do with *consistency,* and predictors that are useful in selection should be consistent.

## Combining Predictors

If an employer chooses to use only one predictor (for example, a test) to select who will be hired, the decision is straightforward. If the test is valid and encompasses a major dimension of a job, and the applicant does well on the test, he or she can be hired. This is the *single predictor* approach. Selection accuracy depends on how valid that single predictor is at predicting performance.

However, if more than one predictor is being used, they must be combined in some way.[6] Two different approaches for combining predictors are:

● *Multiple hurdles:*  A minimum cutoff is set on each predictor, and *each* minimum level must be "passed." For example, in order to be hired a candidate for a sales representative job must achieve a minimum education level, a certain score on a sales aptitude test, and a minimum score on a structured interview.

● *Combined approach:*   In this approach predictors are combined into an overall score, thus allowing a higher score on one predictor to offset a lower score on another. The combined index takes into consideration performance on all predictors.

Figure 9–4 shows how adding more predictors can affect the applicant pool. When several predictors are used, only in the common area shared by the circles will "qualified" candidates be found. But given that no predictor is 100% accurate, each eliminates good candidates. Having too many predictors—especially those with lower accuracy rates—may actually harm the quality of selection decisions.[7] It is important to ensure that only predictors that genuinely distinguish between successful and unsuccessful employees are used.

# Administering the Selection Process

Selecting employees is an important HR activity, but there are certain administrative issues that relate to doing it well: selection and the law, assigning responsibility for selection, and selection and employer image.

## Legal Concerns with Selection

Generally, employers use a variety of preemployment steps and predictors to ensure that applicants will fit available jobs.[8] However, employers may not discrim-

**FIGURE 9–4** *Effect of Adding Predictors to the Selection Process*

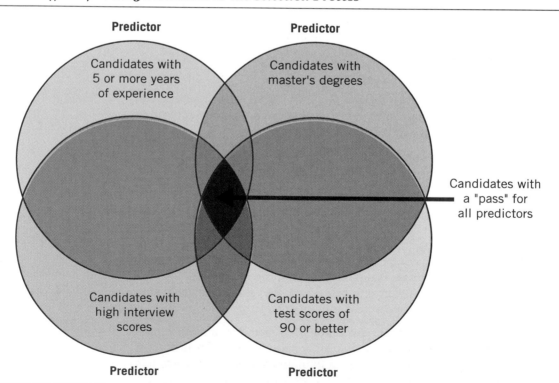

**FIGURE 9–5** *Employment Application Policies*

- Applications are accepted only when there is an opening.
- Only persons filling out application blanks are considered applicants.
- A person's application ceases to be effective after a designated date.
- Only a certain number of applications will be accepted.
- People must apply for specific jobs, not "any job."

inate or otherwise refuse to hire applicants for any reasons that are against the law. Selection is subject to all the equal employment opportunity (EEO) concerns covered in previous chapters. The interview itself is becoming a minefield. One major problem is that there is no standard list of taboo questions, but only general areas about which one cannot ask. Small business owners and managers often are the worst offenders. One of their most common errors is to ask a woman about child-care arrangements, which assumes women are always the ones responsible for child rearing.

It is increasingly important for employers to define carefully exactly who is an *applicant,* given the legal issues involved. If there is no written policy defining conditions that make a person an applicant, any persons who call or send unsolicited resumes might later claim they were not hired because of illegal discrimination. A policy defining *applicant* might include the aspects shown in Figure 9–5.

It is wise for an organization to retain all applications for three years. Applicant flow data should be calculated if the organization has at least 50 employees.

**LOGGING ON . . .**
**LawInfo Forum**
This website provides information on legal issues and their effect on selection. Because this website is a discussion forum, topics will continually change.

**http://www.lawinfo.com/ forum/face-to-face.html**

## Selection Responsibilities

Oganizations vary in how they allocate selection responsibilities between HR specialists and managers. Until the impact of EEO regulations became widespread, selection often was carried out in a rather unplanned manner in many organizations. The need to meet EEO requirements has forced them to plan better in this regard. Still, in some organizations, each department screens and hires its own employees. Many managers insist on selecting their own people because they are sure no one else can choose employees for them as well as they can themselves. This practice is particularly prevalent in smaller firms. But the validity and fairness of such an approach may be questionable.

Other organizations have the HR unit do the initial screening of the candidates, while the appropriate managers or supervisors make the final selection. As a rule, the higher the position within the organization, the greater the likelihood that the ultimate hiring decisions will be made by operating managers rather than HR specialists. Typical selection responsibilities are shown in Figure 9–6 on the next page. These responsibilities are affected by the establishment or existence of a central employment office.

**CENTRALIZED EMPLOYMENT OFFICE** Selection duties may be centralized into a specialized organizational unit that is part of an HR department. In smaller organizations, especially in those with fewer than 100 employees, a full-time employment specialist or unit may be impractical.

The employment function in any organization may be concerned with some or all of the following operations: (1) receiving applications, (2) interviewing

**FIGURE 9–6** *Typical Selection Responsibilities*

| HR Unit | Managers |
|---|---|
| ● Provides initial employment reception<br>● Conducts initial screening interview<br>● Administers appropriate employment tests<br>● Obtains background and reference information<br>● Refers top candidates to managers for final selection<br>● Arranges for the employment physical examination, if used<br>● Evaluates success of selection process | ● Requisition employees with specific qualifications to fill jobs<br>● Participate in selection process as appropriate<br>● Interview final candidates<br>● Make final selection decision, subject to advice of HR specialists<br>● Provide follow-up information on the suitability of selected individuals |

applicants, (3) administering tests to applicants, (4) conducting background investigations, (5) arranging for physical examinations, (6) placing and assigning new employees, (7) coordinating follow-up of these employees, (8) termination interviewing, and (9) maintaining adequate records and reports.

There are several reasons for centralizing employment within one unit:

● It is easier for the applicant to have only one place in which to apply for a job.
● Contact with outside applicant sources is easier because issues can be cleared through one central location.
● Managers can concentrate on their operating responsibilities rather than on interviewing.

With centralization also comes the expectation that better selection may result because it is handled by a staffing specialist. An advantage for applicants is that they may be considered for a greater variety of jobs. Also, selection costs may be cut by avoiding duplication of effort. Additionally, it is important that people well trained in government regulations handle a major part of the process to prevent future lawsuits and costs associated with them.

**USING TEAMS FOR SELECTION** The widespread use of teams presents an interesting selection variation. To be successful, teams have to be allowed to control their destiny as much as possible, which means they should be involved in selecting their teammates. When teams hire new members, they have a vested interest in making sure those persons are successful.

However, a good deal of training is required to make sure that teams understand the selection process, testing, interviewing, and legal constraints. Further, a selection procedure in which the team votes for the top choice is inappropriate; the decision should be made by consensus, which may take longer.

## The Selection Process

Most organizations take certain common steps to process applicants for jobs. Variations on this basic process depend on organizational size, nature of jobs to be filled, number of people to be selected, and pressure of outside forces such as

EEO considerations. This process can take place in a day or over a much longer period of time. If the applicant is processed in one day, the employer usually checks references after selection. Often, one or more phases of the process are omitted or the order changed, depending on the employer.

The selection process shown in Figure 9–7 is typical of a large organization. Assume a woman applicant comes to the organization, is directed to the employment office, and is received by a receptionist. Some firms conduct a job preview/interest screen to determine if an applicant is qualified for open jobs before giving out an application form. Next, the receptionist usually gives the individual an application form to complete. The completed application form serves as the basis for an interview or a test. After the interview or test, the applicant may be told that she does not fit any position the company has available. However, if she does appear to have appropriate qualifications, her background and previous employment history may be checked and/or an additional, more in-depth interview may be conducted. If responses are favorable, the applicant may receive a conditional offer of a job, provided she passes a medical and/or drug test.

**FIGURE 9–7** *Selection Process Flowchart*

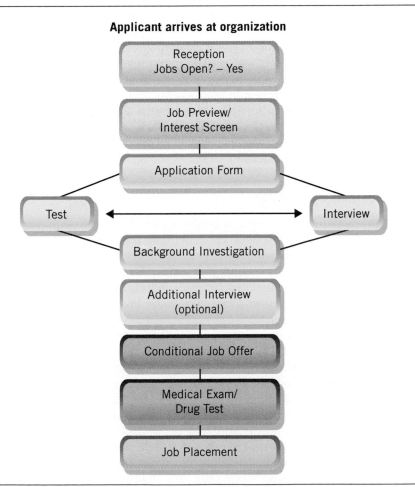

# Reception and Job Preview/Interest Screening

In addition to matching qualified people to jobs, the selection process has an important public-relations dimension. Discriminatory hiring practices, impolite interviewers, unnecessarily long waits, inappropriate testing procedures, and lack of follow-up letters can produce unfavorable impressions of an employer. Providing courteous, professional treatment to all candidates during the selection process is important because for most applicants a job contact of any kind is an extremely personal and significant event. A job applicant's perception of the organization, and even about the products or services it offers, will be influenced by the reception stage of the selection process. Whoever meets the applicant initially should be tactful and able to offer assistance in a courteous, friendly manner. If no jobs are available, applicants can be informed at this point. Any employment possibilities must be presented honestly and clearly.

In some cases, it is appropriate to have a brief interview, called an *initial screening* or a *job preview/interest screen,* to see if the applicant is likely to match any jobs available in the organization before allowing the applicant to fill out an application form. For instance, in most large organizations, this initial screening is done by someone in the employment office or in the HR department. In most situations, the applicant should complete an application form after the screening.

The screening is intended to determine if the applicant is likely to have the ability to perform available jobs. Typical issues might concern job interests, location desired, pay expectations, and availability for work. One firm that hires security guards and armored-car drivers uses the screening interview to verify whether an applicant meets the minimum qualifications for the job, such as having a valid driver's license, being free of any criminal convictions in the past five years, and having been trained to use a pistol. Because these are required minimum standards, it would be a waste of time for any applicant who could not meet them to fill out an application form.

## Computerized Screening

**LOGGING ON . . .**
**Selection Assessment System**
An example of a firm providing computer-based selection assessment systems is found here.

**http://www.selector-pas.com.au/**

The job preview/interest screen can be done effectively by computer as well. Computerized processing of applicants can occur on several different levels. Computers can search resumes or application blanks for key words. Hundreds of large companies use types of "text searching" or artificial-intelligence (AI) software to scan, score, and track resumes of applicants. Some firms using these techniques include Sony Corporation, Coca-Cola, IBM, Paine Webber, Nations Bank, Avis Rent A Car, Microsoft, Pfizer, Shell Oil, and Staples.[9] Companies note that computerized screening saves time and money. It also helps with better placement, thereby reducing turnover. The HR Perspective discusses scannable resumes.

A second means of computerizing screening is conducting initial screening interviews electronically. Coopers & Lybrand, a large accounting and management consulting firm, holds initial screening interviews for college students on an Internet site. Students answer 40 questions, their answers are scored, and they are told at that point whether they qualify for a face-to-face interview. The firm estimates that it eliminates 25% of its 5,000 initial applicants in this way.[10]

Finally, computer-assisted interviewing techniques can use tools such as videotape scenarios to which applicants react. For example, Nike uses computer-

## Scanning Scannable Resumes

Scannable resumes certainly save time and money, and some argue that they "make everyone equal." But of course, some applicants for jobs try to beat the scanning system. The trick, some think, is to list every conceivable skill and to guess which words the computer uses to search. Some applicants use as many buzzwords and as much industry jargon as they can. Of course, it is also possible to pick the wrong words. Some job counselors suggest including in resumes the words that employers use in their help-wanted advertisements.

Employers worry that playing games may cause them to miss a qualified candidate. But some critics point out that selection is not an exact science. Good candidates also are missed when their resumes are submitted "on paper" instead of electronically.[11]

Some scannable key words used to hire for a marketing or sales position follow as an illustration:

Advertising
Budget Preparation
Business Communications
Copywriting
Cost-Benefit Analysis
Customer Service
Data Processing
Database Analysis
Database Management
Direct Marketing Promotion
Direct Sales
Distribution
Entrepreneurial
Financial Markets
Forecast Inventory
Information Distribution
Inventory Control
Market Analysis
Market Research
Market Specialists
Marketing Collateral
Marketing Expense Control
Marketing Plans
Marketing Strategies
Marketing Support Functions
Order Placement
Organizational Skills
Product Sourcing
Productivity Measurement
Promotion
Public Relations
Reporting Systems
Sales
Sales Training Programs
Service-Orientation

assisted interviewing as part of its high-technology selection process. For example, 6,000 applicants responded to ads for 150 positions. After answering eight questions over the phone, 3,500 applicants were screened out. The rest had a computer-assisted interview at the store and finally a personal interview. As part of the computer-assisted interview, applicants watched a video showing three scenarios for helping a retail customer, and they were asked to identify the best scenario. A printer in the next room printed the applicants' responses. Thus, the computer helped screen for people who lost their temper, and it made suggestions to the interviewer on areas to probe in the interview.[12]

## Realistic Job Previews

Most job seekers appear to have little information initially about the organizations to which they apply for jobs. Consequently, the information applicants receive from prospective employers in the recruiting/selection process often is given considerable weight in their decisions whether to accept jobs. Information on pay, nature of the work, geographic location, and opportunity for promotion is important to almost everyone. In addition, information on job security is particularly important to blue-collar applicants.

Some employers oversell their jobs in recruiting advertisements, making them appear better than they really are. The purpose of a **realistic job preview (RJP)** is to inform job candidates of the "organizational realities" of a job, so that

**Realistic job preview (RJP)**
The process through which an interviewer provides a job applicant with an accurate picture of a job.

they can more accurately evaluate their own job expectations. By presenting applicants with a clear picture of the job, the organization hopes to reduce unrealistic expectations and thereby reduce employee disenchantment and ultimately employee dissatisfaction and turnover. A review on research on RJPs found that they do tend to result in applicants having lower job expectations.[13]

A recent court case is of interest here. A federal appeals court heard and upheld an argument that a woman who was fraudulently lured into her job had her career derailed by the employer. The employee (a lawyer) claimed she left the environmental law department of one law firm to head the start-up environmental law department of another firm, but that department never materialized. This and similar rulings should serve as warnings to employers not to exaggerate opportunities.

# Application Forms

Application forms are widely used. Properly prepared, like the one in Figure 9–8, the application form serves four purposes:

- It is a record of the applicant's desire to obtain a position.
- It provides the interviewer with a profile of the applicant that can be used in the interview.
- It is a basic employee record for applicants who are hired.
- It can be used for research on the effectiveness of the selection process.

Many employers use only one application form, but others need several. For example, a hospital might need one form for nurses and medical technicians, another form for clerical and office employees, another for managers and supervisors, and another for support persons in housekeeping and food-service areas.

The information received on application forms may not always be completely accurate. This problem is discussed in greater detail later, but an important point must be made here. In an attempt to prevent inaccuracies, many application forms carry a statement that the applicant is required to sign. In effect, the statement reads: "I realize that falsification of this record is grounds for dismissal if I am hired." The statement has been used by employers to terminate people. In fact, in a recent court case, the court held that when a company can show it would not have hired an applicant if it had known the applicant lied on the application form, the employee's claim of discriminatory discharge will not stand.

Application forms traditionally have asked for references and requested that the applicant give permission to contact them. Rather than asking for personal or general references, though, it may be more useful to request the names of previous supervisors on the application form.

## EEO Considerations and Application Forms

Although application forms may not usually be thought of as "tests," the Uniform Guidelines of the EEOC and court decisions define them as employment tests. Consequently, the data requested on application forms must be job related. Illegal questions typically found on application forms ask for the following:

- Marital status
- Height/weight
- Number and ages of dependents
- Information on spouse
- Date of high school graduation
- Contact in case of emergency

**FIGURE 9–8** *Sample Application Form*

Today's Date _____

## Application for Employment
## An Equal Opportunity Employer*

Personal Information                    Please Print or Type

| Name        (Last)        (First)        (Full Middle Name) | Social Security Number |
|---|---|

| Current Address     City        State      Zip Code | Phone Number<br>(   ) |
|---|---|

| What position are you applying for? | Date available for employment? |
|---|---|

| Are you willing to relocate?<br>☐ Yes   ☐ No | Are you willing to if required?<br>☐ Yes   ☐ No | Any restrictions on hours, weekends, or overtime? If yes, explain. |
|---|---|---|

| Have you ever been employed by this Company or any of its subsidiaries before?<br>☐ Yes          ☐ No | Indicate Locations and Dates |
|---|---|

| Can you, after employment, submit verification of your legal right to work in the United States?<br>☐ Yes   ☐ No | Have you ever been convicted of a felony?<br>☐ Yes   ☐ No | Convictions will not automatically disqualify job candidates. The seriousness of the crime and date of conviction will be considered. |
|---|---|---|

### Performance of Job Functions

| Are you able to perform all the functions of the job for which you are applying, with or without accommodation?<br><br>☐ Yes, without accommodation      ☐ Yes, with accommodation      ☐ No |
|---|
| If you indicated you can perform all the functions with an accommodation, please explain how you would perform the tasks and with what accommodation. |

### Education

| School Level | School Name & Address | No. of Years Attended | Did You Graduate? | Course of Study |
|---|---|---|---|---|
| High School |  |  |  |  |
|  |  |  |  |  |
| Vo-Tech, Business or Trade School |  |  |  |  |
| College |  |  |  |  |
|  |  |  |  |  |
| Graduate School |  |  |  |  |
|  |  |  |  |  |

### Personal Driving Record

| This section is to be completed ONLY if the operation of a motor vehicle will be required in the course of the applicant's employment. |
|---|

| How long have you been a licensed driver? | Driver's license number | Expiration date | Issuing state |
|---|---|---|---|

| List any other state(s) in which you have had a driver's license(s) in the past: |
|---|

| Within the past five years have you had a vehicle accident?<br>☐ Yes  ☐ No | Been convicted of reckless or drunken driving?     If yes, give dates:<br>☐ Yes  ☐ No | Been cited for moving violations? If yes, give dates:<br>☐ Yes  ☐ No |
|---|---|---|

| Has your driver's license ever been revoked or suspended?     If yes, explain:<br>☐ Yes   ☐ No | Is your driver's license restricted?     If yes, explain:<br>☐ Yes   ☐ No |
|---|---|

*We are an Equal Opportunity Employer. We do not discriminate on the basis of race, religion, color, gender, age, national origin or disability.

The reason for concern about such questions is that they can have an adverse impact on some protected groups. For example, the question about dependents can be used to identify women with small children. These women may not be hired because of a manager's perception that they will not be as dependable as those without small children. The high school graduation date gives a close identification of a person's age, which can be used to discriminate against individuals over 40. Or, the question about emergency contact might reveal marital status or other personal information that is inappropriate to ask. See the HR Perspective for examples of how some firms deal unethically with these issues.

One interesting point to remember is that although many employers must collect data on the race and sex of those who apply to fulfill requirements for reporting to the EEOC, the application blank cannot contain these items. As discussed in Chapter 6, the solution used by a growing number of employers is to have applicants provide EEOC reporting data on a separate form. It is important that this form be filed separately and not used in any other HR selection activities, or the employers may be accused of using applicant information inappropriately.

## Weighted Application Forms

One way employers can make the application form more job related is by developing a weighted form. A job analysis is used to determine the knowledge, skills and abilities (KSAs) needed for the job, and an application form is developed to include items related to the selection criteria. Then weights, or numeric values, are placed on possible responses to the items based on their predictive value. The responses of applicants can be scored, totaled, and compared.

One interesting example involves a company that had very high turnover among sewing machine operators. It hired a consultant, who took the applications of 100 successful operators who stayed with the company and 100 operators who left or were fired. He identified 10 variables that differentiated the two groups. Some were unusual; one variable identified was that the better performing sewing machine operators weighed more than 300 pounds and did not own a car, among other factors. Based on this analysis, a weighted application form was developed, but its usefulness could be questioned.

To develop a weighted application blank, it is necessary to develop questions that differentiate between satisfactory and poor performing employees and that can be asked legally. But there are several problems associated with weighted application forms. One difficulty is the time and effort required to develop such a form. For many small employers and for jobs that do not require numerous employees, the cost of developing the weights can be prohibitive. Also, the form must be updated every few years to ensure that the factors previously identified are still valid predictors of job success. However, on the positive side, using weighted forms enables an employer to evaluate and compare applicants' responses numerically to a valid, job-related set of inquiries.

## Resumes

One of the most common methods applicants use to provide background information is the resume. Resumes, also called *vitae* by some, vary in style and length. Technically, a resume used in place of an application form must be treated by an employer as an application form for EEO purposes. Consequently,

# Ethical Issues in Interviewing Women

All HR professionals and most, if not all, managers know the laws and regulations on equal employment. Yet what actually occurs in an interview frequently deviates dramatically from the legally permissible. For years the actual substance of what occurs in many interviews has been a dirty little secret, with no one willing to own up to the sorts of illegal inquiries frequently made of candidates.

Most impermissible areas of inquiry appear to be directed at women. Most typically, the concerns of the interviewer are a young woman's childbearing plans and child-care situations. Managers have great curiosity about such matters because they believe it may affect performance; but how is such information—unlawful if not clearly job related—obtained?

One large manufacturing firm (and a huge federal contractor) uses the simple expedient of having a low-level personnel clerk ask the candidate about her choice of health-insurance plans. An executive from the firm says, "During a lull between interviews, I have a clerk ask whether the applicant wants individual, husband-and-wife, or family coverage, and in choosing an option, the candidate will usually tell the clerk everything we need to know."

Another questionable technique is used by a large financial-services firm, which takes the job candidate to lunch at a nice restaurant. Given the informal atmosphere, the applicant is more easily caught off-guard by a personal inquiry. Typically the prospective supervisor and an assistant eat lunch with the candidate and begin to discuss their children.

One of the firm's supervisors says: "I'll say something like: 'Our car-pool arrangements got messed up this morning and I was almost late for work.' Then I ask the applicant if anything like that ever happens to her. And almost always, the information I want will just come pouring out. The candidate will say something like no, she has no children, isn't even married, or doesn't want children. Or she'll tell me how she's a single mother with two little girls and is always having a problem with car pools and sitters. This tells me what I need to know."

Some employers—often in an informal or cocktail setting—will ask directly about a woman's family situation, putting the candidate in an extremely delicate position. If the female applicant refuses to answer the question, citing its illegality, she runs a very real risk of alienating the interviewer and wrecking her chances of being hired. If she answers the question truthfully, the information may prove fatal to her candidacy.

Many women respond falsely to these illegal inquiries, rationalizing that since the questions are unlawful, they are morally entitled to offer untrue responses. Said one woman, the divorced mother of two children, one of whom is severely handicapped: "Even though I'm a very reliable worker, I knew if I told the truth, I wouldn't get the job, and I needed this job badly. So I said I wasn't married—which was true—and I had no intention of having children—which is sort of true because certainly I don't plan to have any more children . . . I got the job. I figured that my kids were none of their business, so it didn't matter what I told them. Once I was hired, what could they do?"

When disobedience of any law becomes as widespread as it apparently has in these examples, increased enforcement with stiffer penalties probably will not work. Both interviewers and candidates probably would become even more skilled at evading the law—to everyone's detriment.

The best approach is to encourage discussion and education on the subject. If both interviewer and candidate can get beyond the gamesmanship and focus on the optimum fit between the job and the person, everyone will benefit.[14]

even if an applicant furnishes some "illegal information" voluntarily on a resume, the employer should not use that information during the selection process.[15] Because resumes contain only information applicants want to present, some employers require that all who submit resumes complete an application form as well, so similar information will be available on all applicants.[16]

Individuals who mail in resumes may be sent thank-you letters and application forms to be completed and returned. Appendix D contains some suggestions on resume preparation.

## Immigration Requirements

The Immigration Reform and Control Act (IRCA) of 1986, as revised in 1990, requires that within 72 hours of hiring, an employer must determine whether a job applicant is a U.S. citizen, registered alien, or illegal alien. Those not eligible to work in this country must not be hired. The *I-9 form* is used by employers to identify the status of potential employees. Many employers have applicants complete this form during the application process. Others have individuals submit the documents on the first day of employment. Employers do have a responsibility to make sure that documents submitted by new employees, such as U.S. passports, birth certificates, original Social Security cards, and driver's licenses, "reasonably appear on their face to be genuine."[17]

**BNA**
**485.20.10**
**Employee Eligibility**
The basic requirements for employers to confirm employment eligibility under IRCA are discussed here. The I-9 form is available at 485.40.

# Selection Testing

According to the Uniform Selection Guidelines issued by the EEOC, any employment requirement is a "test." The focus in this section is on formal tests. As Figure 9–9 shows, various kinds of tests can be used. Notice that most of them focus on specific job-related aptitudes or skills. Some are paper-and-pencil tests (such as a math test), others are motor-skill tests, and still others use machines (polygraphs, for instance). Some employers purchase prepared tests, while other employers develop their own tests.

Many people feel that formal tests can be of great benefit in the selection process when properly used and administered. Considerable evidence supports this claim. Because of EEO concerns, many employers reduced or eliminated the use of tests a few years ago, fearing that they might be judged discriminatory in some way. However, test usage appears to be increasing again. One recent survey showed that 48% of employers use psychological testing, and 65% said they use some kind of skill testing. The job skills most often tested include typing and data entry and proficiency in accounting or engineering.[18]

Interpreting test results is not always straightforward, even if the test is valid. Individuals trained in testing and test interpretation should be involved in establishing and maintaining a testing system. Furthermore, the role of tests in the overall selection process must be kept in perspective. Tests represent only one possible data source.[19]

## Ability and Aptitude Tests

**Ability tests**
Tests that assess learned skills.

**Aptitude tests**
Tests that measure general ability to learn or acquire a skill.

**Work sample tests**
Tests that require an applicant to perform a simulated job task.

**Ability tests** assess the skills that individuals have already learned. **Aptitude tests** measure general ability to learn or acquire a skill. The typing tests given at many firms to secretarial applicants are commonly used ability tests. Other widely used tests measure mechanical ability and manual dexterity.

A type of ability test used at many organizations simulates job tasks. These **work sample tests,** which require an applicant to perform a simulated job task that is part of the job being applied for, are especially useful. Having an applicant for a financial analyst's job prepare a computer spreadsheet is one such test.

**FIGURE 9–9** *Possible Tests Used for Selection*

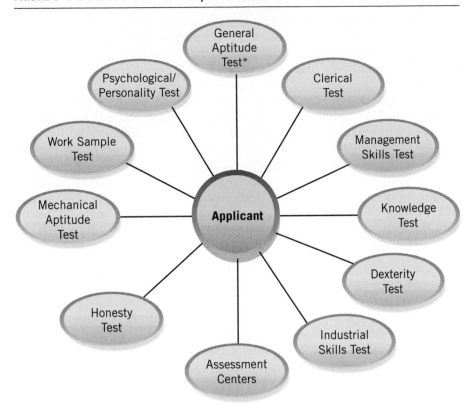

Note: *General aptitude tests are also known as mental ability tests.

Requiring a person applying for a truck driver's job to back a truck to a loading dock is another. An "in basket" test is a work sample test in which a job candidate is asked to respond to memos in a hypothetical in-basket that are typical of the problems faced by people holding that job. The key for any work sample test is the behavioral consistency between the criteria in the job and the requirements of the test.

**Mental ability tests** measure reasoning capabilities. Some of the abilities tested include spatial orientation, comprehension and retention span, and general and conceptual reasoning. The General Aptitude Test Battery (GATB) is a widely used test of this type.

**Mental ability tests**
Tests that measure reasoning capabilities.

## Assessment Centers

An assessment center is not necessarily a place; it is composed of a series of evaluative exercises and tests used for selection and development. The assessment uses multiple exercises and multiple raters. In one assessment center, candidates go through a comprehensive interview, pencil-and-paper test, individual and group simulations, and work exercises. The candidates' performances are then evaluated by a panel of trained raters. It is crucial to any assessment center that the tests and exercises reflect the job content and types of problems faced on the jobs for which individuals are being screened.[20]

## Psychological/Personality Tests

Personality is a unique blend of individual characteristics that affect interaction with the environment and help define a person. Historically, predictive validities have tended to be lower for personality tests used as predictors of performance on the job. However, some studies have shown that carefully chosen personality tests that logically connect to work requirements can help predict the interpersonal aspects of job success.[21] For example, a person's ability to tolerate stress might be a valid concern for a police officer, emotional stability for a nuclear plant operator, and a "people" orientation for a social worker.

There is a never-ending list of characteristics that can be used to differentiate human beings. The multitude of different personality traits has long frustrated psychologists, who have argued that there is a relatively small number of underlying *major* traits. The most widely accepted approach to these underlying personality traits (although not the only one) is often referred to as the "Big Five" personality traits. The Big Five can be considered generally useful predictors of training success and job performance.[22] The Big Five are:

- *Emotional stability:* This is the extent to which a person does *not* suffer from neurosis, depression, anger, worry, and insecurity.
- *Extroversion:* Sociable, gregarious, talkative people are considered extroverted.
- *Agreeableness:* People who are cooperative, good natured, softhearted, tolerant, and trusting score high on the agreeable dimension.
- *Openness/Experience:* This describes people who are flexible in thought and open to new ideas, broad minded, curious, and original.
- *Conscientiousness:* This is the extent to which a person is achievement-oriented, careful, hardworking, organized, and responsible.

As noted earlier in the chapter, conscientiousness has been found to be related to job success across most organizations and occupations. Extroversion predicts success in jobs requiring social interaction, such as many sales jobs. The usefulness of the other three varies depending on the kind of job and organization. When used in selection, psychological or personality testing requires that a solid link be made with job relatedness.[23]

## Polygraph and Honesty Testing

Several types of tests have been devised to assess honesty. These include polygraph tests and paper-and-pencil honesty tests. Both are controversial.

**POLYGRAPHS AND THE EMPLOYEE POLYGRAPH PROTECTION ACT** The polygraph, more generally and incorrectly referred to as the "lie detector," is a mechanical device that measures a person's galvanic skin response, heart rate, and breathing rate. The theory behind the polygraph is that if a person answers incorrectly, the body's physiological responses will "reveal" the falsification through the polygraph's recording mechanisms.

As a result of concerns, Congress passed the Employee Polygraph Protection Act. The act bars polygraph use for preemployment screening purposes by most employers. However, federal, state, and local government agencies are exempt from the act. Also exempted are certain private-sector employers such as security companies and pharmaceutical companies. The act does allow employers to continue to use polygraphs as part of internal investigations of theft or losses. But the polygraph test should be taken voluntarily, and the employee can end the test at any time.

**HONESTY TESTS** Individuals who take honesty tests answer "yes" or "no" to a list of questions. Sample questions include:

- Would you tell your boss if you knew another employee was stealing from the company?
- Is it all right to borrow company equipment to use at home if the property is always returned?
- Have you ever told a lie?
- Have you ever wished you were physically more attractive?

Firms use honesty tests to help reduce losses due to employee theft. With pre-employment polygraph testing no longer allowed, a growing number of firms have turned to such tests. These firms believe that giving honesty tests not only helps them to screen out potentially dishonest individuals, but also sends a message to applicants and employees alike that dishonesty will not be tolerated.

Concerns about the validity of honesty tests continue to be raised. Many firms using them do not do validation studies on their experiences.[24] Instead, they rely on the general validation results given by the test developers, even though that practice is not consistent with the EEOC's Uniform Guidelines.

Honesty tests are valid as broad screening devices for organizations but may not be as good at predicting whether a single individual will steal. Also, the use of these tests can have a negative public-relations impact on applicants. A final concern is that the types of questions asked may constitute invasion of individual privacy.

**QUESTIONABLE TESTS** Some *very* questionable tests are used in employee selection. For instance, graphology, psychics, and blood types all have been used by various employers.

- *Graphology:* Graphology is a type of "test" in which an "analysis" is made of an individual's handwriting. Such characteristics as how people dot an *i* or cross a *t*, whether they write with a left or right slant, and the size and boldness of the letters they form supposedly tell graphologists about the individuals' personalities and their suitability for employment. The cost of a handwriting analysis ranges from $175 to $500 and includes an examination of about 300 personality traits. Formal scientific evaluations of graphology are not easily found. Its value as a personality predictor is very questionable, but it is popular in France, Israel, and several other countries.
- *Psychics:* Similarly, some firms use psychics to help select managerial talent. The psychics are supposedly able to determine if a person is suited for a job both intellectually and emotionally. However, most businesses would not want anyone to know that they used "psychic advisers."
- *Blood type:* If using psychics in selection seems outlandish, how about blood type as a predictor of personality? In Japan, many people think blood type is an excellent predictor. Type O blood supposedly indicates a person who is generous and bold; type A, one who is industrious; type B, one who is impulsive and flexible; and type AB, one who is both rational and creative. A manager at Mitsubishi Electric chose people with type AB blood to dream up the next generation of fax machines. One Japanese nursery school divides children based on their blood types.[25]

There is a lack of formal evidence that handwriting, psychics, or blood type are valid as performance predictors. Some experts have even commented that there may be ethical problems in using these techniques for employee selection.

# Selection Interviewing

**Selection interview**
Interview designed to identify information on a candidate and clarify information from other sources.

A **selection interview** is designed to identify information on a candidate and clarify information from other sources. This in-depth interview is designed to integrate all the information from application forms, tests, and reference checks, so that a decision can be made. Because of the integration required and the desirability of face-to-face contact, the interview is the most important phase of the selection process in many situations. Conflicting information may have emerged from tests, application forms, and references. As a result, the interviewer must obtain as much pertinent information about the applicant as possible during the limited interview time and evaluate this information against job standards. Finally, a selection decision must be made, based on all of the information obtained in the preceding steps.

The interview is not an especially valid predictor of job performance, but it has high "face validity"—that is, it *seems* valid to employers and they like it. Virtually all employers are likely to hire individuals using interviews.[26]

Some interviewers may be better than others at selecting individuals who will perform well. There is very high *intra*rater (the same interviewer) reliability, but only moderate-to-low *inter*rater (different interviewers) reliability. Reliability is the ability to pick the same qualities again and again in applicants. Interrater reliability becomes important if there are several interviewers, each selecting employees from a pool of applicants.

## EEO Considerations and Interviewing

The interview, like a pencil-and-paper test and an application form, is a type of predictor and must meet the standards of job relatedness and nondiscrimination. Some court decisions and EEOC rulings have attacked the interviewing practices of some organizations as discriminatory.

An interviewer making a hiring recommendation must be able to identify the factors that shaped the decision. If that decision is challenged, the organization must be able to show justification. Everything written or said can be probed for evidence in a lawsuit. Lawyers recommend the following to minimize EEO concerns with interviewing:

- Identify objective criteria related to the job to be looked for in the interview.
- Put criteria in writing.
- Provide multiple levels of review for difficult or controversial decisions.
- Use structured interviews, with the same questions asked of all those interviewed for a specific job.

## Types of Interviews

There are six types of selection interviews: structured, situational, behavioral description, nondirective, stress, and panel interviews. Each type is discussed in this section.

**Structured interview**
Interview that uses a set of standardized questions asked of all job applicants.

**STRUCTURED INTERVIEW** The **structured interview** uses a set of standardized questions that are asked of all applicants. Every applicant is asked the same basic questions, so that comparisons among applicants can more easily be made. This type of interview allows an interviewer to prepare job-related questions in advance and then complete a standardized interviewee evaluation form. Completion of such a form provides documentation if anyone, including an EEO enforcement body, should question why one applicant was selected over another. Sample questions that might be asked of all applicants for a production maintenance management opening are as follows:

- Tell me how you trained workers for their jobs.
- How do you decide the amount of work you and the maintenance crew will have to do during a day?
- How does the production schedule of the plant affect what a mechanic ought to repair first?
- How do you know what the needs of the plant are at any given time and what mechanics ought to be doing?
- How did you or would you go about planning a preventive maintenance program in the plant?

As is evident, the structured interview is almost like an oral questionnaire and offers greater consistency and accuracy than some other kinds of interviews. The structured interview is especially useful in the initial screening because of the large number of applicants in this step of the selection process. Obviously, it is less flexible than more traditional interview formats, and therefore it may be less appropriate for second or later interviews.

Even though a series of patterned questions are asked, the structured interview does not have to be rigid. The predetermined questions should be asked in a logical manner, but the interviewer can avoid reading the questions word for word down the list. The applicant should be allowed adequate opportunity to explain answers clearly. The interviewer should probe until he or she fully understands the applicant's responses.

Research on interviews consistently has found the structured interview to be more reliable and valid than other approaches.[27] The format for the interview ensures that a given interviewer has similar information on each candidate, so there is higher intrarater reliability. Also, the fact that several interviewers ask the same questions of applicants has led to better interrater reliability.

Regardless of the type of interview used, interviewers from time to time receive some very "unusual" responses from some job candidates. The HR Perspective describes some of the stranger responses.

**Frank and Ernest**

**Situational interview**
A structured interview composed of questions about how applicants might handle specific job situations.

**SITUATIONAL INTERVIEW** The **situational interview** is a structured interview that is composed of questions about how applicants might handle specific job situations. With experienced applicants, the format is essentially one of a job knowledge or work sample test.

Interview questions are based on job analysis and checked by experts in the job so they will be content valid. There are three types of questions:

- *Hypothetical:* Asking applicant what he or she might do in a certain job situation
- *Related to knowledge:* Might entail explaining a method or demonstrating a procedure
- *Related to requirements:* Explores areas such as willingness to work the hours required and meet travel demands

For some situational interviews job experts also write "good," "average," and "poor" responses to the questions to facilitate rating the answers of the applicant. The interviewer can code the suitability of the answer, assign point values, and add up the total number of points an interviewee received.[28]

**Behavioral description interview**
Interview in which applicants give specific examples of how they have performed or handled problems in the past.

**BEHAVIORAL DESCRIPTION INTERVIEW** When responding to a **behavioral description interview,** applicants are required to give specific examples of how they have performed a certain procedure or handled a problem in the past. For example, applicants might be asked the following:

- How did you handle a situation in which there were no rules or guidelines on employee discipline?
- Why did you choose that approach?
- How did your supervisor react?
- How was the issue finally resolved?

Like other structured methods, behavioral description interviews generally provide better validity than unstructured interviews.[29]

**NONDIRECTIVE INTERVIEW** The **nondirective interview** uses general questions, from which other questions are developed. It should be used mainly in psychological counseling, but it is also used in selection. The interviewer asks general questions designed to prompt the applicant to discuss herself or himself. The interviewer then picks up on an idea in the applicant's response to shape the next question. For example, if the applicant says, "One aspect that I enjoyed in my last job was my supervisor," the interviewer might ask, "What type of supervisor do you most enjoy working with?"

Difficulties with a nondirective interview include keeping it job related and obtaining comparable data on various applicants. Many nondirective interviews are only semiorganized; the result is that a combination of general and specific questions is asked in no set order, and different questions are asked of different applicants for the same job.

**Nondirective interview**
Interview that uses general questions, from which other questions are developed.

**STRESS INTERVIEW** The **stress interview** is a special type of interview designed to create anxiety and put pressure on the applicant to see how the person responds. In a stress interview, the interviewer assumes an extremely aggressive and insulting posture. Those who use this approach often justify its use with individual who will encounter high degrees of stress on the job, such as a consumer-complaint clerk in a department store or an air traffic controller.

The stress interview is a high-risk approach for an employer. The typical applicant is already somewhat anxious in any interview, and the stress interview can easily generate a very poor image of the interviewer and the employer. Consequently, an applicant that the organization wishes to hire might turn down the job offer. Even so, many interviewers deliberately put applicants under stress.

**Stress interview**
Interview designed to create anxiety and put pressure on an applicant to see how the person responds.

**PANEL INTERVIEWS** Usually, applicants are interviewed by one interviewer at a time. But when an interviewee must see several people, many of the interviews are redundant and therefore unnecessarily time consuming. In a **panel interview,** several interviewers interview the candidate at the same time. All the interviewers hear the same respones. On the negative side, applicants are frequently uncomfortable with the group interview format.

**Panel interview**
Interview in which several interviewers interview the candidate at the same time.

## Interviewing Basics

Many people think that the ability to interview is an innate talent, but this contention is difficult to support. Just because someone is personable and likes to talk is no guarantee that the person will be a good interviewer. Interviewing skills are developed through training. Some suggestions for good interviewing follow.

**PLANNING THE INTERVIEW** Effective interviews do not just happen; they are planned. Pre-interview planning is essential to a well-conducted in-depth selection interview. This planning begins with selecting the time and place for the interview. Sufficient time should be allotted so that neither the interviewer nor the interviewee feels rushed. Also, a private location is important, so that both parties can concentrate on the interview content. The interviewer should review the application form for completeness and accuracy before beginning the interview and also should make notes to identify specific areas about which to question the applicant during the interview.

**CONTROLLING THE INTERVIEW** An important aspect of the interview is control. If the interviewer does not control the interview, the applicant usually will. Control includes knowing in advance what information must be collected, systematically collecting it, and stopping when that information has been collected.

Having control of the interview does not mean doing extensive talking. The interviewers should talk no more than about 25% of the time in an in-depth interview. If the interviewer talks more than that, the interviewer is the one being interviewed.

## Questioning Techniques

The questioning techniques that an interviewer uses can and do significantly affect the type and quality of the information obtained. Some specific suggestions follow.

**GOOD QUESTIONS** Many questions an interviewer asks assume that the past is the best predictor of the future, and it usually is. An interviewer is less likely to have difficulty when questioning the applicant's demonstrated past performance than when asking vague questions about the future.

Some types of questions provide more meaningful answers than others. Good interviewing technique depends on the use of open-ended questions directed toward a particular goal. An open-ended questions is one that cannot be answerd yes or no. *Who, what, when, why, tell me, how,* and *which* are all good ways to begin questions that will produce longer and more informative answers. "What was your attendance record on your last job?" is a better question than, "Did you have good attendance on your last job?" because the latter question can be answered with a simple yes, which elicits less information. Figure 9–10 lists questions that are often used for different purposes in selection interviews.

**POOR QUESTIONS** Certain kinds of questions should be avoided:

- *Questions that rarely produce a true answer:* An example is, "How did you get along with your coworkers?" This question is almost inevitably going to be answered, "Just fine."
- *Leading questions:* A leading question is one to which the answer is obvious from the way that the question is asked. For example, "You do like to talk to people, don't you?" Answer: "Of course."
- *Illegal questions:* Questions that involve information such as race, age, gender, national origin, marital status, and number of children are illegal. They are just as inappropriate in the interview as they are on the application form.
- *Obvious questions:* An obvious question is one for which the interviewer already has the answer and the applicant knows it. Questions already answered on the application blank should be probed, not asked again.
- *Questions that are not job related:* All questions asked should be directly related to the job for which the interviewee has applied.

**LISTENING RESPONSES** The good interviewer avoids *listening responses,* such as nodding, pausing, making casual remarks, echoing, and mirroring. A friendly but neutral demeanor is appropriate. Listening responses are an essential part of everyday, normal conversation, but they may unintentionally provide feedback to the applicant. Applicants may try to please the interviewer and look to the

**FIGURE 9–10** *Common Selection Interview Questions by Areas*

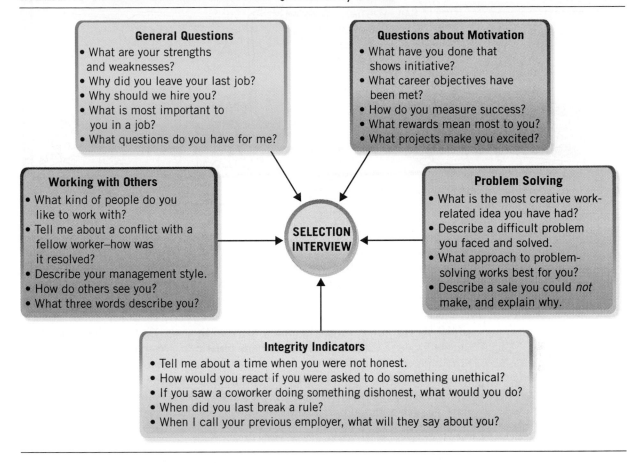

interviewer's listening response for cues. Even though the listening responses may be subtle, they do provide information to applicants.

## Problems in the Interview

Operating managers and supervisors most often use poor interviewing techniques because they do not interview often or have not been trained to interview. Some common problems encountered in the interview are highlighted next.

**SNAP JUDGMENTS** Ideally, the interviewer should collect all the information possible on an applicant before making a judgment. Reserving judgment is much easier to recommend than to do, because it is difficult not to form an early impression. Too often, interviewers form an early impression and spend the balance of the interview looking for evidence to support it. This impression may be based on a review of an individual's application blank or on more subjective factors such as dress or appearance. Consequently, many interviewers make a decision on the job suitability of applicants within the first four or five minutes of the interview.

**NEGATIVE EMPHASIS** As might be expected, unfavorable information about an applicant is the biggest factor considered in interviewers' decisions about overall

suitability. Unfavorable information is given roughly twice the weight of favorable information. Often, a single negative characteristic may bar an individual from being accepted, whereas no amount of positive characteristics will guarantee a candidate's acceptance.

**HALO EFFECT** Interviewers should try to avoid the *halo effect,* which occurs when an interviewer allows a prominent characteristic to overshadow other evidence. The halo effect is present if an interviewer lets a candidate's accomplishments in athletics overshadow other characteristics, which leads the interviewer to hire the applicant because "athletes make good salespeople." *Devil's horns* (a reverse halo effect), such as inappropriate dress or a low grade point average, may affect an interviewer as well.

**BIASES** Interviewers must be able to recognize their personal biases. Interviewers tend to favor or select people whom they perceive to be similar to themselves. This similarity can be in age, race, sex, previous work experiences, personal background, or other factors. As workforce demographics shift, interviewers will have to be even more aware of this "similarity bias."

The selection of an applicant who falls below standards, and the rejection of an applicant who meets standards, indicate that personal bias may have influenced a selection decision. An interviewer should be honest and consider the reasons for selecting a particular applicant. The solution to the problem of bias lies not in claiming that a person has no biases, but in demonstrating that they can be controlled.

**CULTURAL NOISE** The interviewer must learn to recognize and handle *cultural noise*—responses the applicant believes are socially acceptable rather than factual respones. Applicants want jobs; to be hired, they know they must impress the interviewer. They may feel that if they divulge any unacceptable facts about themselves, they will not get the job. Consequently, they may try to give the interviewer responses that are socially acceptable but not very revealing.

An interviewer can handle cultural noise by not encouraging it. If the interviewer supports cultural noise, the applicant will take the cue and continue those kinds of answers. Instead, the applicant can be made aware that the interviewer is not being taken in. An interviewer can say, "The fact that you are the best pitcher on your softball team is interesting, but tell me about your performance on your last job."

## What Interviewers Evaluate

Overall, interviewers look for evidence that an applicant is well rounded, competent, and successful. The factors most often considered are presented in Figure 9–11. These variables do not include all possible criteria that may be taken into account; a wide variety of other variables may be considered, depending on the job and the interviewer.

# Background Investigation

Background investigation may take place either before or after the in-depth interview. It costs the organization some time and money, but it is generally well worth the effort. Unfortunately, applicants frequently misrepresent their qualifications and backgrounds. According to one survey of employers, the most common false information given is length of prior employment, past salary, criminal record, and former job title.[31]

**FIGURE 9–11** *Factors Interviewers Consider in the Interview*

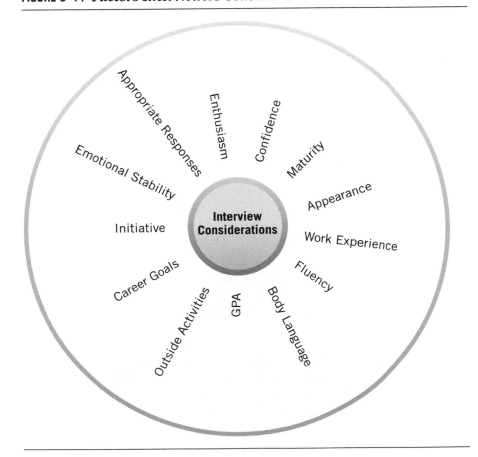

Many universities report that inquiries on graduates and former students often reveal that the individuals never graduated. Some did not even attend the university. Another type of credential fraud uses the mail-order "degree mill." To enhance their chances of employment, individuals purchase unaccredited degrees from organizations that grant them for a fee—as one advertisement puts it, "with no exams, no studying, no classes."[32]

It is estimated that many resumes contain at least one lie or "factual misstatement" (see Figure 9–12). The only way for employers to protect themselves from resume fraud and false credentials is to request verification on proof from applicants either before or after hire. If hired, the employee can be terminated for falsifying employment information. It is unwise for employers to assume that "someone else has already checked." Too often, no one took the trouble.[33]

## Types of References

Background references can be obtained from several sources. Some of the following references may be more useful and relevant than others, depending on the jobs for which applicants are being considered:

- Academic references
- Prior work references
- Financial references
- Law enforcement records
- Personal references

Personal references, such as references from relatives, clergy, or family friends, often are of little value; they probably should not even be required. No applicant will ask somebody to write a recommendation who is going to give a negative response. Instead, greater reliance should be placed on work-related references from previous employers and supervisors.

**FIGURE 9–12** *Common Misrepresentations on Resumes and Applications*

## Legal Constraints on Background Investigations

Various federal and state laws have been passed to protect the rights of individuals whose backgrounds may be investigated during preemployment screening. States vary in what they allow employers to investigate. For example, in some states, employers can request information from law enforcement agencies on any applicant. In some states, they are prohibited from getting certain credit information. Several states have passed laws providing legal immunity for employers who provide information on an employee to another employer. Some legal issues are discussed next.

**THE PRIVACY ACT OF 1974** The most important law passed to protect the privacy of personal information is the Federal Privacy Act of 1974, which applies primarily to government agencies and units. However, bills to extend the provisions of the Privacy Act to private-sector employers have been introduced in Congress at various times. Under the 1974 act, a government entity must have a signed release from a person before it can give information about that person to someone else.

**FAIR CREDIT REPORTING ACT** Many employers check applicants' credit histories. The logic is that if individuals have poor credit histories, then they may be irresponsible. This assumption may be questioned, however, and firms that check applicants' credit records must comply with the federal Fair Credit Reporting Act. This act basically requires disclosing that a credit check is being made, obtaining written consent from the person being checked, and furnishing the applicant a copy of the report.[34]

**RISKS OF GIVING REFERENCES ON FORMER EMPLOYEES** In a number of court cases, individuals have sued their former employers for slander, libel, or defamation of character as a result of what the employers said to other potential employers that prevented the individuals from obtaining jobs. Two examples illustrate why employers should be careful when giving reference information.

*BNA*
**3685.10–3685.40**
**Employment References**
Some of the legal issues associated with references, along with a reference consent and release form, are discussed here. Also state laws on references are available at 3690.

- An executive at one firm remarked that a former employee was a "sociopath." The former employee sued and won $1.9 million in a judgment against the employer and the executive.
- Over $500,000 was paid by both an airline and an insurance company to settle lawsuits on references given on former employees.

Because of such problems, lawyers advise organizations who are asked about former employees to give out only name, employment date, and title; many organizations have adopted policies restricting the release of reference information.[35]

**RISKS OF NEGLIGENT HIRING** The costs of failing to check references may be high. Some organizations have become targets of lawsuits that charge them with negligence in hiring workers who committed violent acts on the job. Lawyers say that an employer's liability hinges on how well it investigates an applicant's fitness. Prior convictions and frequent moves or gaps in employment should be cues for further inquiry. Details provided on the application form by the applicant should be investigated to the greatest extent possible, so the employer can show that due diligence was exercised. Also, applicants should be asked to sign releases authorizing the employer to check references, and those releases should contain a statement releasing the reference givers from any future liability actions.[36]

Clearly, employers are in a difficult position. Because of threats of lawsuit, they must obtain information on potential employees but are unwilling to give out information in return. However, many employers hope that changes may eventually result in a reversal of this situation. One can speculate that we are not too far away from the day when the courts will say that Employer A has the duty to divulge negative information to Employer B on the basis of need to know.

## Reference-Checking Methods

Several methods of obtaining reference information are available to an employer. Telephoning a reference is the most-used method, but many firms prefer written responses.

**TELEPHONE REFERENCE CHECKING** Many experts recommend using a structured telephone reference-check form. Typically, such forms focus on factual verification of information given by the applicant, such as employment dates, salary history, type of job responsibilities, and attendance record. Other questions often include reasons for leaving the previous job, the individual's manner of working with supervisors and other employees, and other less factual information. Naturally, many firms will provide only factual information. But the use of the form can provide evidence that a diligent effort was made.

**LOGGING ON . . .**
**Background Checking Service**
An example of a firm that conducts background checks for employers can be found here.

http://www.emc-corp.com/

**WRITTEN METHODS OF REFERENCE CHECKING** Some organizations send preprinted reference forms to individuals who are giving references for applicants. These forms often contain a release statement signed by the applicant, so that those giving references can see that they have been released from liability on the information they furnish. Specific or general letters of reference also are requested by some employers or provided by applicants.

## Medical Examinations

The Americans with Disabilities Act (ADA) prohibits a company from rejecting an individual because of a disability and from asking job applicants any question relative to current or past medical history until a conditional job offer is made. Figure 9–13 shows proper and improper questions about disabilities. The ADA also prohibits the use of preemployment medical exams, except for drug tests, until a job has been conditionally offered.

**DRUG TESTING** Drug testing may be a part of a medical exam, or it may be done separately. Using drug testing as a part of the selection process has increased in the past few years, though not without controversy. Employers should remember that such tests are not infallible. The accuracy of drug tests varies according to the type of test used, the item tested, and the quality of the laboratory where the test samples are sent. If an individual tests positive for drug use, then a second, more detailed analysis should be administered by an independent medical laboratory. Because of the potential impact of prescription drugs on test results, applicants should complete a detailed questionnaire on this matter before the testing. Whether urine, blood, or hair samples are used, the process of obtaining, labeling, and transferring the samples to the testing lab should be outlined clearly and definite policies and procedures established.

**FIGURE 9–13** *Questioning an Applicant About Disabilities*

**DO NOT ASK:**

- Do you have any physical or other limitations?

- Do you have any disabilities?

- Have you ever filed for or collected workers' compensation?

- How many times were you absent due to illness in the past two years?

- Have you been treated for any of the following medical conditions?

- Do you have any family members with health problems or history of illness or disabilities?

- Why are you using crutches, and how did you become injured?

- Have you ever seen a psychiatrist?

- When did you develop your disabiltiy?

**Interviewer**

**DO ASK:**

- Can you perform the essential functions of the job for which you are applying with or without accommodation? Please describe any accommodations needed.

- How would you perform the essential tasks of the job for which you have applied?

- If hired, how would you perform the tasks outlined in the job description you reviewed?

- Describe your attendance record on your last job.

- Describe any problems you would have reaching the top of a six-foot filing cabinet.

- What did your prior job duties consist of, and which ones were the most challenging?

Drug testing also has legal implications. In a number of cases, courts have ruled that individuals with previous substance-abuse problems who have received rehabilitation are disabled and thus covered by the Americans with Disabilities Act. Also, preemployment drug testing must be administered in a nondiscriminatory manner, not used selectively with certain groups. The results of drug tests also must be used consistently, so that all individuals testing positive are treated uniformly. An applicant for a production-worker position who tests positive should be rejected for employment, just as an applicant to be vice-president of marketing would be.

Challenges to drug testing are less likely to succeed in the private sector than in the government sector. The Fourth Amendment (relating to search and seizure) fails as an argument by employees because the government is not involved.

**GENETIC TESTING** Another controversial area of medical testing is genetic testing. Some large companies currently are using genetic tests and many more are considering their use in the future. However, the general public disapproves strongly of their use.

Employers that use genetic screening tests do so for several reasons. First, the tests may link workplace health hazards and individuals with certain genetic characteristics. Second, genetic testing may be used to make workers aware of genetic problems that could occur in certain work situations. The third use is the most controversial: to exclude individuals from certain jobs if they have genetic conditions that increase their health risks. Because people cannot change their genetic makeup, the potential for discrimination based, for example, on race or sex is very real. For instance, sickle-cell anemia is a condition found primarily in African Americans. If chemicals in a particular work environment can cause health problems for individuals with sickle-cell anemia, African Americans might be screened out on that basis. The question is whether that decision should be made by the individual or the employer.

# Summary

- Selection is a process that matches individuals and their qualifications to jobs in an organization.
- Predictors are used to find criteria of job applicants that make them more likely than others to do well.
- Because of government regulations and the need for better coordination between the HR unit and other managers, many organizations have established a centralized employment office as part of the HR department.
- The selection process—from reception through initial screening, application, testing, interview, and background investigation to physical examination—must be handled by trained, knowledgeable individuals.
- Application forms must meet EEO guidelines and ask only for job-related information.
- All tests used in the selection process must be valid, and employers should use valid predictors to identify candidates who can meet important job criteria.
- Selection tests include ability and aptitude tests, assessment centers, and general psychological/personality tests. Also, selection tests should relate directly to the jobs for which individuals apply.

- Controversial tests used to select employees include polygraph examinations and honesty tests.
- From the standpoints of effectiveness and EEO compliance, the most useful interviews are structured, situational, behavioral description, and panels, although nondirective and stress interviews are also used.
- Sound interviewing requires planning and control. Applicants should be provided a realistic picture of the jobs for which they are applying. Good questioning techniques can reduce interviewing problems.
- Background investigations can be conducted in a variety of areas, but concerns about individual privacy must be addressed.
- Care must be taken when either getting or giving reference information to avoid the potential legal problems of defamation, libel, slander, and negligent hiring.
- Medical examinations may be an appropriate part of the selection process for some employers, but only after a conditional job offer has been made.
- Drug testing has grown in use as a preemployment screening device, in spite of some problems and concerns associated with its accuracy and potential for discrimination on the part of employers.

# Review and Discussion Questions

1. Why do many employers have a specialized employment office?
2. You are starting a new manufacturing company. What phases will you go through to select your employees?
3. Agree or disagree with the following statement: "A good application form is fundamental to an effective selection process." Explain your conclusion.

4. Discuss the following statement: "We stopped giving tests altogether and rely exclusively on interviews for hiring."
5. Make two lists. On one list, indicate what information you would want to obtain from the screening interview; on the other, indicate what information you would want to obtain from the in-depth interview.

6. Develop a structured interview guide for a 20-minute interview with a retail sales clerk applicant.

7. How would you go about investigating a new college graduate's background? Why would this information be useful in making a selection decision?

8. Discuss how the Americans with Disabilities Act (ADA) has modified the use of medical exams in the selection process.

## Terms to Know

ability tests   292
aptitude tests   292
behavioral description interview   298
mental ability tests   293
nondirective interview   299

panel interview   299
placement   278
predictors   280
realistic job preview (RJP)   287
selection   278
selection criterion   280

selection interview   296
situational interview   298
stress interview   299
structured interview   296
work sample tests   292

## Using the Internet

### Defining Hiring Specifications

The president of the company has expressed concerns about the selection process being used for staffing. He has asked you, the HR manager, to define the selection criteria being used for staffing and prepare a memo for him. The senior members have come up with questions regarding the process. Answer the following questions for the senior staff. Use the following website to assist you:

**http://www.appliedhrsolutions.com/**

#### Questions

1. List six job analysis techniques currently used for selection.
2. From the analysis techniques used, what criteria should be developed for the job?
3. List four measurement methods used for each of the criteria.

## CASE

### Selecting Manufacturing Employees

In the United States, Toyota uses a selection assessment test designed to hire individuals to be employed as Toyota auto workers. Called the "Day of Work," this test is the most grueling part of a hiring process that can take months. At Toyota plants in Kentucky and West Virginia, the Day of Work is used regularly. Starting at 6:30 a.m., applicants work on a simulated assembly line for 4 hours and then spend several hours inspecting parts for defects. They also participate in a group problem-solving session and take written tests. This is all necessary just to be *considered* for a job at Toyota.

Another process is used by Carrier Corporation, which makes compressors for air conditioners with its workforce of 150 at its Arkadelphia, Arkansas, plant. If someone wants a job there, he or she must complete a six-week course before even being considered for employment. The selection process weeds out 15 of every 16 applicants and provides Carrier Corporation with a top-quality workforce. High school graduates take a state test for job applicants first. Only one-third advance to the next step. References are closely checked, and then the applicants are interviewed both by managers *and* by the assembly-line workers with whom they will work. Those applicants who have satisfactory interviews take a six-week course that meets five nights a week for three hours, with some extra Saturdays. Attendees learn to read blueprints, do math (including metric calculations and statistical process control), use a computer, and engage in problem solving with others. At the end of the course, the applicants have not been hired (or paid) and have no assurance that they will be.

But this approach does not work everywhere or all the time. During a year, Lincoln Electric considered more than 20,000 job applicants and rejected most of them—yet it has empty positions that it *needs to fill.* Very few of those who applied at Lincoln Electric could do trigonometry (even at the high school level) or read technical drawings. Those skills were needed for even entry-level work.[37]

## Questions

1. Discuss the advantages and disadvantages associated with Toyota's "Day of Work" approach.
2. When using teams to interview applicants, as Carrier Corporation does, what potential problems might exist with the use of invalid predictors and interrater reliability?

# Notes

1. Adapted from Ellen Neuborne, "Employers Score New Hires," *USA Today,* July 9, 1997, 1B; and Maurine Minehan, "The Growing Debate over Genetic Testing," *HR Magazine,* April 1998, 208.
2. Michele Himnelberg, "Firms Alter Hiring Practices to Avoid Mistakes," *The Denver Post,* July 4, 1998, C1.
3. Orlando Behling, "Employee Selection: Will Intelligence and Conscientiousness Do the Job?", *Academy of Management Executive,* February 1998, 77–85.
4. Edward L. Levine, et al., "A Methodology for Developing and Validating Minimum Qualifications (MQs)," *Personnel Psychology* 50 (1997), 1009.
5. Kevin R. Murphy and Ann Harris Sharaella, "Implications of the Multidimensional Nature of Job Performance for the Validity of Selection Tests," *Personnel Psychology* 50 (1997), 823.
6. Calvin Hoffman and G.C. Thornton III, "Examining Selection Utility Where Competing Predictors Differ in Adverse Impact," *Personnel Psychology* 50 (1997), 455.
7. Pierre Mornell, "No Room for Compromise," *INC.,* August 1998, 116.
8. Robert J. Barro, "So You Want to Hire the Beautiful. Well, Why Not?", *Business Week,* March 16, 1998, 18.
9. Ellen Joan Pollock, "Inhuman Resources," *The Wall Street Journal,* July 30, 1998, B1.
10. Diana Kunde, "Computer Screening Helps Both Companies and Job Applicants," *Omaha World-Herald,* November 23, 1997, 17G.
11. Pollock, "Inhuman Resources," *The Wall Street Journal,* B1.
12. Linda Thornburg, "Computer-Assisted Interviewing Shortens the Hiring Cycle," *HR Magazine,* February 1998, 73.
13. Jean M. Phillips, "Effects of Realistic Job Previews on Multiple Organizational Outcomes," *Academy of Management Journal* 41 (1998), 673–690; and Peter W. Horn, et al., "An Exploratory Investigation into Theoretical Mechanisms Underlying Realistic Job Previews," *Personnel Psychology* 51 (1998), 421.
14. Adapted from Paul J. Siegel and Margaret R. Bryant, "A Hiring Checklist," *HR Focus,* April 1997, 22; and A.E. Berkeley, "Job Interviewer's Dirty Little Secrets," *The Wall Street Journal,* March 20, 1989, A13.
15. Jim Jordan, "Truth Often Stretched, Resume Checkers Say," *Omaha World-Herald,* May 24, 1998, 1G.
16. Hal Lancaster, "The Standard Resume Still Has a Role in Job Searches," *The Wall Street Journal,* February 3, 1998, B1.
17. "Cardholder Must Be Dealt With," *Bulletin to Management,* August 27, 1998, 267.
18. "Use of Psychological Testing on the Upswing," *Bulletin to Management,* July 30, 1998, 239.
19. Peter Thompson, "Assessment Tests Are Valuable But Have Limitations," *The Denver Post,* May 31, 1998, G1.
20. Harold W. Goldstein, et al., "The Role of Cognitive Ability in the Subgroup Differences and Incremental Validity of Assessment Center Exercises," *Personnel Psychology* 51 (1998), 357.
21. P.H. Raymark, Mark Schmidt, and Robert Guion, "Identifying Potentially Useful Personality Constructs for Employee Selection," *Personnel Psychology* 50 (1997), 723.
22. John A. Parnell, "Improving the Fit Between Organizations and Employees," *SAM Advanced Management Journal* 63 (1998), 35–42; and Behling, "Employee Selection," 77.
23. Paul Lees-Haley and James McDonald Jr., "The Use (and Misuse) of Psychological Testing in Employment Litigation," *Employee Relations Law Journal,* Summer 1997, 37; and Robert J. Sahl, "The Value of Psychological Assessments," *Benefits & Compensation Solutions,* February 1997, 26.

24. Joyce Hogan and Kimberly Brinkmeyer, "Bridging the Gap Between Overt and Personality-Based Integrity Tests," *Personnel Psychology* 50 (1997), 587.

25. Stephanie Armour, "Fine Print," *USA Today,* July 21, 1998, B1; and Diane E. Lewis, "Prospective Employers Look for the Write Stuff," *The Denver Post,* April 14, 1997, 6E.

26. Pierre Mornell, "Zero Defect Hiring," *INC.,* March 1998, 74.

27. Michael A. Campion, David K. Palmer, and James E. Campion, "A Review of Structure in the Selection Interview," *Personnel Psychology* 50 (1997), 655.

28. Carol Kleiman, "New Interviews Test You on What You Claim You Can Do," *The Denver Post,* November 20, 1997, 1M.

29. H.J. Brackey, "Job Hunters Face New-Styled Interviews," *Omaha World-Herald,* October 18, 1998, G25–26.

30. Adapted from several sources, including "Stupid Resume Tricks," *Fortune,* July 21, 1997, 117; "Job Interviewers Share Horror Stories," *HR Wire,* June 15, 1998; and Larry McShane, "Execs Recall Their Worst Job Interviews," *Laramie Daily Boomerang,* December 13, 1997, 7.

31. Sam Jensen and Mark Schorr, "Lying to Get a Job," *Nebraska Workplace Memo,* February 1999, 1.

32. Andrew McIlvaine, "Internet Helps Job Applicants Get Phony Degrees," *HR Executive,* October 19, 1998, 7.

33. Rob Gardner, "How Well Do You Know Whom You Hire?", *CPA Journal,* March 1998, 62.

34. Gillian Flynn, "Are You Legal Under the Fair Credit Reporting Act?", *Workforce,* March 1998, 79.

35. "Taking Action to Prevent Negligent Hiring," *Bulletin to Management,* July 16, 1998, 24.

36. Jane Easter Bahls, "Available Upon Request?" *HR Magazine Focus,* January 1999, 2-6; and "Firms Giving References for Former Workers Choose to Remain Quiet—Perhaps too Quiet," *Bulletin to Management,* November 19, 1998, 361.

37. Adapted from Micheline Maynard, "Toyota Devises Grueling Workout for Job Seekers," *USA Today,* August 11, 1997, 3B; Raju Narisetti, "Job Paradox," *The Wall Street Journal,* September 8, 1995, A1; and Earle Norton, "Future Factories," *The Wall Street Journal,* January 13, 1993, A1.

# CHAPTER 10
# Training Human Resources

***After you have read this chapter, you should be able to:***

- Define *training* and identify two types of training.

- Discuss at least four learning principles that relate to training.

- Describe four characteristics of an effective orientation system.

- Discuss the three major phases of a training system.

- Identify three ways to determine training needs.

- List and discuss at least four training approaches.

- Give an example for each level of training evaluation.

## HR TRANSITIONS

# Web-Based Training

The explosive growth in use of the Internet is changing how training is being done in organizations. As more and more employees use computers and have access to Internet portals, their employers are seeing the World Wide Web as a means for distributing training to employees who are located in widely diverse locations and jobs. A number of examples illustrate the power of web-based training.

Days Inn, the worldwide lodging chain, has 18,000 employees in almost 2,000 locations. With a staff of only 11 trainers, it would be impossible for sufficient training to be done in classroom settings at company locations. Consequently, Days Inn is making extensive use of interactive web-based training. Customer-service skills are being taught through on-line courses whereby employees at individual hotels can log on and work through an interactive training program. Days Inn is not the only lodging chain to use web-based training either. In conjunction with other firms in the hospitality industry, the American Hotel and Motel Association has established an Education Institute to provide self-paced, web-based training courses to Days Inn and other firms in the industry.

It is no surprise that technology-oriented firms use web-based training. At Sun Microsystems, employees access the web and the company intranet to learn to use standard computer software packages. Bay Networks conducts web-based pre-sales training for its sales representatives nationwide. In this training, audio and graphics presentation slides are used to provide technical information to the firm's sales representatives. A Bay Networks training professional estimates that web-based training saves at least $350 per day per person just in travel and lodging costs. A side benefit is that the company's sales representatives get to stay home for the training, instead of spending time away from their families and offices.

Rather than limiting web-based training to individual, self-paced instruction, Union Pacific, the large nationwide railroad, uses the company's intranet to conduct training for employees in classrooms. Throughout the UP operating areas, employees in ten specially equipped classrooms use computer equipment to take learning retention tests. The results of these tests are used to establish additional training for employees.

The importance of web-based training has been recognized by governmental entities as well. The American Learning Exchange (ALX) has been established by the U.S. Department of Labor, a number of states, and the Public Broadcasting Corporation. Beginning operation in 1998, ALX was started to provide employers and others a web-based source for training resources. Both on-line and other types of training courses and materials are catalogued. There is no fee to those who list training program details or access ALX for information. Once specific information is located, HR professionals can link to other sites for more details on specific training resources (see ALX at www.alx.org).

With all of the web-based resources and options, it is important that managers address some key questions before embarking on extensive use of web-based training. First, top management support is crucial, because the initial costs for equipment and development of training materials may be substantial. Also, employees' computer literacy and access to information technology are critical. Because web-based training requires diffusing training from a central location, managers and HR professionals used to training being controlled must be "retrained" to accept the idea that training is being decentralized and individualized.

It also should be recognized that web-based training may not be appropriate for certain types of training. For instance, leadership skill training or

> *With all of the web-based resources and options, it is important that managers address some key questions before embarking on extensive use of web-based training.*

other behaviorally-focused training and development may be done better face-to-face using increased trainee interactions.

Despite these and other issues that firms are experiencing as web-based training spreads, it is likely that this type of training will grow rapidly in the next few years. Once the initial investment in equipment and content development are made, web-based training becomes a more cost-effective means to training worldwide. Also, training can be simultaneously updated and communicated more easily to employees.

In summary, training using the web is likely to continue replacing classroom instruction in much of the training done by employers. Thus, more training may become distance learning and available on demand.[1]

> *Training is something we hope to integrate into every manager's mind set.*

CHRIS LANDAUER

The strategies that organizations follow have an impact on most HR activities, including training. Increasingly, employers are recognizing that training their human resources is vital. Currently, U.S. employers are spending at least $50 billion annually on training. For many employers, training expenditures average at least 1.5–2% of payroll expenses.

Traditionally, about two-thirds of the training expenses have been devoted to developing professional managers and one-third to first-line workers. But that proportion is changing. Organizations are realizing that they need to develop the capabilities of their first-line workers just as much as the capabilities of their managers. Something else is changing as well. An old axiom in HR management was, "When times get tough, training is the first expenditure cut." Accordingly, often training expenditures are reduced significantly. But a growing number of employers have recognized that training is not just a cost; it is an investment in the human capital of the organization that benefits the entire organization.

Figure 10-1 shows some costs and benefits that may result from training. While some benefits (such as attitude changes) are hard to quantify, comparison of costs and benefits associated with training remains the best way to determine if training is cost effective. For example, one firm evaluated a traditional safety training

**FIGURE 10–1** *Balancing Costs and Benefits of Training*

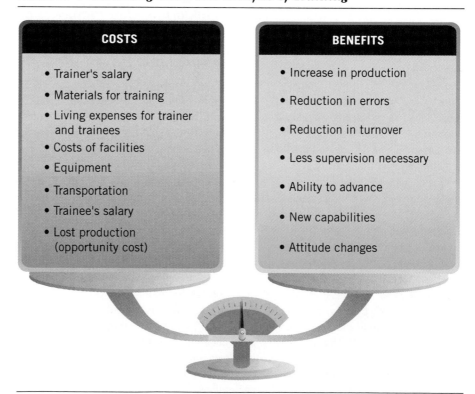

| COSTS | BENEFITS |
|---|---|
| • Trainer's salary | • Increase in production |
| • Materials for training | • Reduction in errors |
| • Living expenses for trainer and trainees | • Reduction in turnover |
| • Costs of facilities | • Less supervision necessary |
| • Equipment | • Ability to advance |
| • Transportation | • New capabilities |
| • Trainee's salary | • Attitude changes |
| • Lost production (opportunity cost) | |

HR PERSPECTIVE

# Research on Identifying the Economic Value of Training

In many organizations, large expenditures are made on training. But whether those expenditures produce value and an economic impact for the organizations that make the expenditures has not been identified clearly. To provide some additional insights on the economic utility of organization-wide training, Morrow, Jarrett, and Rupinski did a study, the results of which were reported in *Personnel Psychology.*

The study was conducted in a large pharmaceutical firm and focused on identifying the economic impact of managerial and sales/technical training efforts. The CEO of the firm had requested that the dollar value of training be identified and its value to the firm be confirmed. The study examined 18 training programs, focusing on the effects of job skills training on employees' behavioral performance on the job. The behavioral performance of those who had received the training was noted by their supervisors, peers, or subordinates, depending upon the skills being evaluated.

Using a variety of statistical analyses, the researchers found that sales/technical training had a greater effect than did managerial training. A return on investment (ROI) on each type of training was determined, with the ROI for the sales/technical training calculated to be 156% and for managerial training to be 84%. Consistent with previous research, the effects of more specific training, such as that in sales/technical skills, apparently have greater immediate payoff. It is possible that the managerial training has a larger payoff over time, but this study focused on first-year returns.

In spite of these issues, the study appears to show that training does produce a return to the organization on its training expenditures. As organizations face strategic changes and more training expenditures are made, it is crucial for the impact of training to be evaluated and documented.[2]

program and found that the program did not lead to a reduction in accidents. Therefore, the training was redesigned so that better safety practices resulted.

What is interesting is that as organizations restructure and implement strategic changes, training becomes more important. Employees who must adapt to the changes need training to update their capabilities. Also, managers must have training and development to enhance their leadership skills and abilities. In a number of situations, effective training often produces productivity gains that more than offset the cost of the training. The HR Perspective describes a study intended to document the economic value of training.

# The Context of Training

**Training** is a process whereby people acquire capabilities to aid in the achievement of organizational goals. Because this process is tied to a variety of organizational purposes, training can be viewed either narrowly or broadly. In a limited sense, training provides employees with specific, identifiable knowledge and skills for use on their present jobs. Sometimes a distinction is drawn between *training* and *development,* with development being broader in scope and focusing on individuals gaining *new* capabilities useful for both present and future jobs.

**Training**
A process whereby people acquire capabilities to aid in the achievement of organizational goals.

## Training Responsibilities

A typical division of training responsibilities is shown in Figure 10–2. The HR unit serves as a source of expert training assistance and coordination. The unit often

**FIGURE 10–2** *Typical Training Responsibilities*

| HR Unit | Managers |
|---|---|
| ● Prepares skill-training materials<br>● Coordinates training efforts<br>● Conducts or arranges for off-the-job training<br>● Coordinates career plans and employee development efforts<br>● Provides input and expertise for organizational development | ● Provide technical information<br>● Monitor training needs<br>● Conduct on-the-job training<br>● Continually discuss employees' growth and future potential<br>● Participate in organizational change efforts |

has a more long-range view of employee careers and the development of the entire organization than do individual operating managers. The difference is especially true at lower levels in the organization.

However, managers are likely to be the best source of technical information used in skills training. They also are in a better position to decide when employees need training or retraining. Because of the close and continual interaction they have with their employees, it is appropriate that managers determine and discuss employee career potentials and plans with individual employees.

It has been increasingly evident that operating managers and HR professionals must work together effectively if training is to be done well. Therefore, a "training partnership" between the HR staff members and operating managers must develop. In this partnership HR serves more as a consultant and training planner with managers, rather than as an entity controlling training.[3]

## Types of Training

Training in organizations is offered in many different areas, and Figure 10–3 shows typical types of training done in organizations. Notice that some of this training is conducted primarily in-house, whereas other types of training make greater use of external training resources.

**INTERNAL TRAINING** Training in on-the-job locations tends to be viewed as being very applicable to the job, it saves the cost of sending employees away for training, and it often avoids the cost of outside trainers. However, trainees who are learning while working can incur costs in the form of lost customers and broken equipment, and they may get frustrated if matters do not go well.

Often, technical training is conducted inside organizations. Technical training is usually skills based, for example, training to run precision computer-controlled machinery. Due to rapid changes in technology, the building and updating of technical skills have become crucial training needs. Basic technical skills training is also being mandated by federal regulations in areas where the Occupational Safety and Health Administration (OSHA), the Environmental Protection Agency (EPA), and other agencies have regulations. As noted in the opening discussion, web-based training and intranets also are growing as internal means of training.

**FIGURE 10–3** *Types of Training*

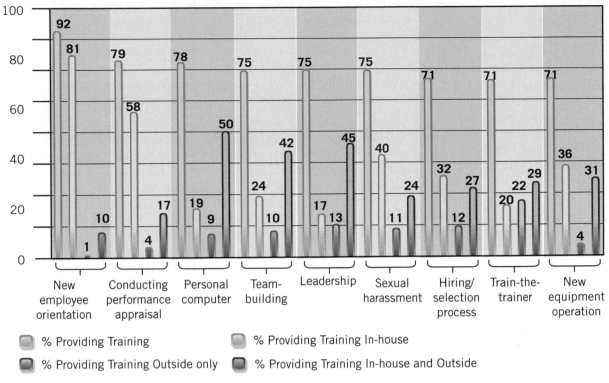

SOURCE: Based on information in *Training*, October 1997 (Lakewood Publications, Minneapolis, MN).

One internal source of training that has grown is **informal training,** which occurs internally through interactions and feedback among employees. One study found that 70% of what employees know about their jobs they learned informally from other employees, not from formal training programs.[4] Several factors account for the amount of informal learning. First, as employees work in teams and on projects with others, they ask questions, receive explanation, and share information with coworkers. Second, rather than relying on the employer to train them and keep their capabilities current, employees request assistance from other employees more knowledgeable or skilled. Third, informal learning occurs among employees striving to meet organizational goals and deadlines. However, problems with informal training include the fact that some training done by fellow employees may not be accurate and may miss certain important details.

At one company in the southeastern United States, managers initially became concerned about the amount of time that employees spent talking with each other in the lunchroom. However, an HR professional who spent time in the lunchroom found that many of the conversations were problem-solving discussions about company projects. Consequently, white boards and flip charts were placed in the lunchroom for employees to use if they wish to do so.[5]

**Informal training**
Training that occurs internally through interactions and feedback among employees.

**LOGGING ON . . .**

**American Society for Training & Development**

This website is a complete guide to training and development. Information on articles, research, educational seminars, and conferences can be found here.

http://www.astd.org/

**EXTERNAL TRAINING** External training occurs for several reasons:

- It may be less expensive for an employer to have an outside trainer conduct training in areas where internal training resources are limited.
- There may not be sufficient time to develop internal training materials.
- The HR staff may not have the level of expertise needed for the subject matter where training is needed.
- There are advantages to having employees interact with managers and peers in other companies in training programs held externally.

One growing trend is the *outsourcing* of training. Vendors are being used to train employees. For example, many software providers have users' conferences where employees from a number of employers receive detailed training on using the software and new features being added. Also, vendors can do training inside the organization if sufficient numbers of employees are to be trained.[6]

Several computer software vendors offer employees technical certifications on their software. For example, being a Master Certified Novell Engineer or Microsoft Certified Product Specialist gives employees credentials that show their level of technical expertise. The certifications also provide employees items to put on their resumes should they decide to change jobs. These certifications also benefit employers, who can use the certifications as job specifications for hiring and promotion purposes. If an employer pays for employees to become certified, employees may view the employer more positively and be less prone to leave.[7]

## Legal Aspects of Training

Training is an area targeted by EEO laws and regulations. One area of concern involves the practices used to select individuals for inclusion in training programs. The criteria used must be job related and must not unfairly restrict the participation of protected-class members. Another concern is differences in pay based on training to which protected-class members have not had equal access. A third is the use of training as a criterion for selecting individuals for promotions. In summary, equal employment laws and regulations definitely apply to training, and employers must be aware of them.

Training is a cost, and some employers have gone to court in an attempt to require individuals who leave their firms after training to repay the cost. For instance, one firm sued a worker in a skilled technical job, who had signed a promissory note to repay the firm $9,000 if he left the firm voluntarily or was fired for cause within 24 months of starting a special training program. The employee contested the suit by saying that he did not learn anything he had not already known and thus had received no benefits from the training. In this case the employer prevailed because of the signed note by the employee.

# Learning Principles: The Psychology of Learning

Working in organizations is a continual learning process, and learning is at the heart of all training activities. Different learning approaches are possible, and learning is a complex psychological process that is not fully understood by practitioners or research psychologists.

Often, trainers or supervisors present information and assume that merely by presenting it they have ensured that it will be learned. But learning takes place only when information is received, understood, and internalized in such a way that some change or conscious effort has been made to use the information. Managers can use the research on learning to make their training efforts more effective. Some major learning principles that guide training efforts are presented next.

## Intention to Learn

People learn at different rates and are able to apply what they learn differently. *Ability* to learn must be accompanied by motivation, or *intention,* to learn. Motivation to learn is determined by answers to questions like these: "How important is my job to me?" "How important is it that I learn that information?" "Will learning this help me in any way?" and "What's in it for me?"

Additionally, people vary in their beliefs about their abilities to learn through training. These perceptions may have nothing to do with their actual ability to learn, but rather reflect the way they see themselves. People with low *self-efficacy* (low level of belief that they can accomplish something) benefit from one-on-one training. People with high self-efficacy seem to do better with conventional training. Because self-efficacy involves a motivational component, it affects a person's intention to learn.[8]

## Whole Learning

It is usually better to give trainees an overall view of what they will be doing than to deal immediately with the specifics. This concept is referred to as *whole learning* or *Gestalt learning.* As applied to job training, this means that instructions should be divided into small elements *after* employees have had the opportunity to see how all the elements fit together.

Another concept is **attentional advice,** which refers to providing trainees information about the processes and strategies that can lead to training success. By focusing the trainees' attention on what they will encounter during training and how it is linked to their jobs, trainers can improve trainees' participation in the training process. For instance, if customer service representatives are being trained to handle varying types of difficult customer calls, the training should give an overview of the types of calls, the verbal cues indicating the different types of calls, and the desired outcomes for each type of call.[9]

**Attentional advice**
Providing trainees information about the processes and strategies that can lead to training success.

## Reinforcement

The concept of **reinforcement** is based on the *law of effect,* which states that people tend to repeat responses that give them some type of positive reward and avoid actions associated with negative consequences. The reinforcers that an individual receives can be either external or internal, and many training situations provide both kinds. A new salesclerk who answers a supervisor's question correctly and is complimented for doing so may receive both an external reward (the compliment) and an internal reward (a feeling of pride). A person who is positively reinforced for learning is more likely to continue to learn.

**Reinforcement**
A concept that people tend to repeat responses that give them some type of positive reward and avoid actions associated with negative consequences.

## Behavior Modification

A comprehensive approach to training has been developed based on the concept of reinforcement. This popular approach, *behavior modification,* uses the theories of psychologist B.F. Skinner, who stated that "learning is not doing; it is changing what we do." Behavior modification makes use of four means of changing behavior, labeled *intervention strategies.* The four strategies are positive reinforcement, negative reinforcement, punishment, and extinction. Each is reviewed next.

**Positive reinforcement**
A person receives a desired reward.

A person who receives a desired reward receives **positive reinforcement.** If an employee is on time every day during the week and, as a result, receives extra pay equivalent to one hour of normal work, the employee has received positive reinforcement of his or her good attendance by receiving a desired award.

**Negative reinforcement**
An individual works to avoid an undesirable consequence.

**Negative reinforcement** occurs when an individual works to avoid an undesirable consequence. An employee who arrives at work on time every day may do so to avoid a supervisor's criticism. Thus, the potential for criticism leads to the employee's taking the desired action.

**Punishment**
Action taken to repel a person from an undesired action.

Action taken to repel a person from undesirable action is **punishment.** A grocery manager may punish a stock clerk for leaving the stockroom dirty by forcing her to stay after work and clean it up.

**Extinction**
The absence of an expected response to a situation.

Behavior can also be modified through a technique known as **extinction,** which is the absence of an expected response to a situation. The hope is that unreinforced behavior will not be repeated.

All four strategies can work to change behavior, and combinations may be called for in certain situations. But research suggests that for most training situations, positive reinforcement of the desired behavior is most effective.

## Immediate Confirmation

**Immediate confirmation**
The concept that people learn best if reinforcement is given as soon as possible after training.

Another learning concept is **immediate confirmation:** people learn best if reinforcement is given as soon as possible after training. Feedback on whether a learner's response was right or wrong should be given as soon as possible after the response. To illustrate, suppose a corporate purchasing department has developed a new system for reporting inventory information. The purchasing manager who trains inventory processors may not have the trainees fill out the entire new inventory form when teaching them the new procedure. Instead the manager may explain the total process and then break it into smaller segments, having each trainee complete the form a section at a time. By checking each individual's form for errors immediately after each section is complete, the purchasing manager can give immediate feedback, or confirmation, before the trainees fill out the next section. This immediate confirmation corrects errors that, if made throughout the whole form, might establish a pattern that would need to be unlearned.

## Learning Practice and Patterns

Learning new skills requires practice and application of what is learned. Both research and experience show that when designing training, behavioral modeling, practice, and learning curves are all important considerations.

**Behavior modeling**
Copying someone else's behavior.

**BEHAVIOR MODELING** The most elementary way in which people learn—and one of the best—is **behavior modeling,** or copying someone else's behavior. A variation of modeling occurs when people avoid making mistakes they see others make. The use of behavior modeling is particularly appropriate for skill training in which the trainees must use both knowledge and practice.

**ACTIVE PRACTICE** **Active practice** occurs when trainees perform job-related tasks and duties during training. It is more effective than simply reading or passively listening. Research has found that active practice was the factor most closely associated with improved performance following training.[10] Once some basic instructions have been given, active practice should be built into every learning situation. It is one of the advantages of good on-the-job training. Assume a person is being trained as a customer service representative. After being given some basic selling instructions and product details, the trainee should be allowed to call a customer to use the knowledge received.

**Active practice**
The performance of job-related tasks and duties by trainees during training.

**SPACED VS. MASSED PRACTICE** Active practice can be structured in two ways. The first, **spaced practice,** occurs when several practice sessions are spaced over a period of hours or days. The other, **massed practice,** occurs when a person does all of the practice at once. Spaced practice works better for some kinds of learning, whereas massed practice is better for others. For example, training cashiers to operate a new machine could be alternated with having the individuals do tasks they already know how to do. Thus, the training is distributed instead of being concentrated into one period.

**Spaced practice**
Several practice sessions spaced over a period of hours or days.

**Massed practice**
The performance of all of the practice at once.

For other kinds of tasks, such as memorizing tasks, massed practice is usually more effective. Can you imagine trying to memorize the list of model options for a dishwasher one model per day for 20 days as an appliance distribution salesperson? By the time you learned the last option, you would have forgotten the first one.

**LEARNING CURVES** People in different training situations learn in different patterns, called *learning curves*. The kind of learning curve typical of a given task has implications for the way the training program is designed. In some situations, the amount of learning and/or the skill level increases rapidly at first, then the rate of improvement slows. For example, when an employee first learns to operate a stamping machine, the rate of production increases rapidly at first and then slows as the normal rate is approached. Learning to perform most routine jobs follows such a curve.

Another common pattern occurs when a person tries to learn an unfamiliar, difficult task that also requires insight into the basics of the job. In this pattern, learning occurs slowly at first, then increases rapidly for a while, and then flattens out. Learning to debug computer systems is one example, especially if the learner has little previous contact with computers.

## Transfer of Training

For effective *transfer of training* from the classroom to the job, two conditions must be met. First, the trainees must be able to take the material learned in training and apply it to the job context in which they work. Second, use of the learned material must be maintained over time on the job.

One way to aid transfer of training to job situations is to ensure that the training is as much like the jobs as possible. In the training situation, trainees should be able to experience the types of situations they can expect on the job. For example, training managers to be better interviewers should include role playing with "applicants" who respond in the same way that real applicants would.

# Orientation: Training for New Employees

**Orientation**
The planned introduction of new employees to their jobs, coworkers, and the organization.

**Orientation** is the planned introduction of new employees to their jobs, coworkers, and the organization. However, orientation should not be a mechanical, one-way process. Because all employees are different, orientation must incorporate a sensitive awareness of the anxieties, uncertainties, and needs of the individual. Orientation in one form or another is offered by most employers.

## Orientation Responsibilities

Orientation requires cooperation between individuals in the HR unit and other managers and supervisors. In a small organization without an HR department, such as a machine shop, the new employee's supervisor or manager has the total responsibility for orientation. In large organizations, managers and supervisors, as well as the HR department, should work as a team in employee orientation.

Figure 10–4 illustrates a common division of orientation responsibilities in which managers work with HR specialists to orient a new employee. Together they must develop an orientation process that will communicate what the employee needs to learn. Supervisors may not know all the details about health insurance or benefit options, for example, but they usually can best present information on safety rules; the HR department then can explain benefits.

## Purposes of Orientation for Employers

The overall goal of orientation is to help new employees learn about the organization as soon as possible, so that they can begin contributing. From the perspective of employers, the orientation process has several specific purposes, which are described next.

**PRODUCTIVITY ENHANCEMENT** Both employers and new employees want individuals starting jobs to become as productive as possible relatively quickly. Texas Instruments found that orientation helps new employees reach full productivity

**FIGURE 10–4** *Typical Orientation Responsibilities*

| HR Unit | Managers |
|---|---|
| ● Places employees on payroll<br>● Designs formal orientation program<br>● Explains benefits and company organization<br>● Develops orientation checklist<br>● Evaluates orientation activities | ● Prepare coworkers for new employee<br>● Introduce new employee to coworkers<br>● Provide overview of job setting and work rules |

levels at least two months sooner than those without effective orientation experiences. Some employers, including a large accounting firm, give new employees computer and intranet access upon acceptance of a job offer. That way new employees can become more familiar with the organization and its operations even before they go through a formal orientation program.[11] This example illustrates that orientation to the organization really begins during the recruiting and selection processes, because the way individuals are treated and what they learn about the organization during the first contacts may shape how they approach new jobs.

Another facet of orientation that affects productivity is training new employees on the proper ways to perform their jobs. One construction company has found that emphasizing safety and instructing new employees in safe work practices has significantly reduced the number of lost-time injuries experienced by new employees.[12]

**TURNOVER REDUCTION**  Some employers have experienced significant turnover of newly hired employees, and it is common for over half of all new hires in hourly jobs to leave within their first year of employment. But employers with effective orientation programs have found that new employees stay longer. Corning Glass identified that 70% of the employees rating orientation highly were likely to stay at least three years. Another firm was able to reduce annual turnover rates by 40%, and much of the decline was attributed to more effective orientation of new employees.[13] As pointed out in Chapter 3, turnover is costly, and if orientation helps reduce turnover, then it contributes to organizational success.[14]

**ORGANIZATIONAL OVERVIEW**  Another purpose of orientation is to inform new employees about the nature of the organization. A general organizational overview might include a brief review of the organization; the history, structure, key executives, purpose, products, and services of the organization; how the employee's job fits into the big picture; and other general information. If the employer prepares an annual report, a copy may be given to a new employee. Also, some organizations give new employees a list of terms that are used in the industry to help them learn regularly used vocabulary. The HR Perspective shows the passport used at ACI Worldwide. It describes an orientation approach that involves executives from throughout the firm, not just HR staff members.

## Purpose of Orientation for New Employees

New employees generally are excited about the "new beginning" and also have anxieties about what they face. Therefore, orientation should help create a favorable impression and enhance interpersonal acceptance of new employees.

**FAVORABLE EMPLOYEE IMPRESSION**  Although the first two purposes of orientation are employer-centered, another goal of orientation is to benefit the new employees. Certainly a good orientation program creates a favorable impression of the organization and its work. This impression begins even before the new employees report to work.[15] Providing sufficient information about when and where to report the first day, handling all relevant paperwork efficiently, and having personable, efficient people assist the new employee all contribute to creating a favorable impression of the organization.

***LOGGING ON . . .***
**Orientation**
At this website, you will find a varied listing of ideas and subjects to incorporate into a new employee orientation program.

**http://www.publiccom.com/ web/change/newemp.html**

## HR PERSPECTIVE
# Passport for New Employee Success

Transaction Systems Architects, Inc., develops, markets, and supports software products for the global electronic funds transfer market. TSA's products are used to process transactions involving credit cards, debit cards, smart cards, home banking services, checks, wire transfers, and automated clearing and settlement. TSA's software solutions are used by more than 2,000 customers in 70 countries on six continents. Of the top 500 banks worldwide (in terms of assets), over 100 use at least one of Transaction Systems' product solutions. More than 2,300 people are employed by TSA in offices in 18 countries. At ACI Worldwide, TSA's support and distribution division, the new employee orientation process picks up the global theme of TSA by using a new employee passport (see photo).

As part of its employee orientation program, ACI in Omaha, Nebraska, gives new employees their own New Employee Passports. The objective of the passport is to provide the employee with an introduction to ACI's senior members—individuals most employees might otherwise never meet. This process also allows senior managers to share their views of the organization and its future prospects.

Modeled after the official U.S. passport, the New Employee Passport is specially prepared for each holder. Inside the passport, in the sections normally reserved for visa stamps, are the names and titles of

the senior managers of the company, including the chief executive officer. In these sections, the management hierarchy specific to the new employee is identified and marked.

Using the passport as an entree, the new employee sets up appointments to meet individually with appropriate senior managers. In these one-on-one meetings, each senior manager describes his/her job and division responsibilities, the strategic directions being pursued, and how the new employee's job fits into the company plans and changes. At the end of these meet-

ings, each senior manager signs the "New Employee Passport," much as a customs official in a foreign country would do. Interestingly, the senior managers uniformly give priority in their schedules for the new employees, thereby emphasizing the importance of the new employee to ACI.

ACI uses its New Employee Passport to communicate the company's informal, open culture. The passport offers a unique introductory process for new employees to learn from senior managers about the strategies and operations of the company.[16]

**ENHANCE INTERPERSONAL ACCEPTANCE** Another purpose of orientation is to ease the employee's entry into the work group. New employees often are concerned about meeting the people in their work units. Further, the expectations of the work group do not always parallel those presented at management's formal orientation. Also, if a well-planned formal orientation is lacking, the new employee may be oriented solely by the group, possibly in ways not beneficial to the organization. For example, at a software company the work group in the section where new employees were assigned delighted in telling the new employees "the way it really works here." Some of their views were not entirely accurate. Therefore, orientation was essential for management to make certain that new employees knew what their supervisors wanted.

## Establishing an Effective Orientation System

A systematic approach to orientation requires attention to attitudes, behaviors, and information that new employees need. Unfortunately, too often orientation is conducted rather haphazardly. The general ideas that follow highlight the major components of an effective orientation system: preparing for new employees, providing them with needed information, presenting orientation information effectively, and conducting evaluation and follow-up on the initial orientation.

**PREPARING FOR NEW EMPLOYEES** New employees must feel that they belong and are important to the organization. Both the supervisor and the HR unit should be prepared to give each new employee this perception. Further, coworkers as well as the supervisor should be prepared for a new employee's arrival. This preparation is especially important if the new employee will be assuming duties that might be interpreted as threatening a current employee's job status or security. The manager or supervisor should discuss the purpose of hiring the new worker with all current employees before the arrival of the new worker.[17]

Some organizations use coworkers or peers to conduct part of the new employees' orientation. It is particularly useful to involve more experienced and higher-performing individuals who can serve as role models for new employees.

*BNA*
**Orientation Pointers**
**495.30**
Review some pointers for supervisors on conducting new employee orientation and compare these pointers to the manner in which you were oriented to a new job.

**PROVIDING NEW EMPLOYEES WITH NEEDED INFORMATION** The guiding question in the establishment of an orientation system is, "What does the new employee need to know *now?*" Often new employees receive a large amount of information they do not immediately need, and they fail to get the information they really need the first day of a new job.

Some organizations systematize this process by developing an orientation checklist. Figure 10–5 on the next page indicates items to be covered by the HR department representative, the new employee's supervisor, or both. A checklist can ensure that all necessary items have been covered at some point, perhaps during the first week. Many employers have employees sign the checklist to verify that they have been told of pertinent rules and procedures.

Often, employees are asked to sign a form indicating that they have received the handbook and have read it. This requirement gives legal protection to employers who may have to enforce policies and rules later. Employees who have signed forms cannot deny later that they were informed about policies and rules.

To help them understand the organization fully, new employees also should be oriented to the culture of the organization. Giving informal information on

**FIGURE 10–5** *Orientation Checklist*

Employee Name_____  Employee Number_____
Starting Date_____  Job Title_____
Department_____  Supervisor_____

**HR DEPARTMENT**

**FIRST DAY**

**OVERVIEW**
____ Company history
____ Organization chart
____ Company business sectors

**WORKING HOURS**
____ Recording work hours
____ Start and stop times
____ Lunch and breaks
____ Overtime policies

**PAY POLICIES**
____ Employee classifications
____ Pay periods
____ Automatic deposits

**DISTRIBUTE EMPLOYEE HANDBOOK**

Employee Signature_____
Date_____

**SECOND DAY**

**PERSONNEL POLICIES**
____ Equal employment
____ Alcohol and drug prohibition
____ Sexual and other harassment
____ Complaints and concerns

**INSURANCE BENEFITS**
____ Group health plan
____ Disability insurance
____ Life insurance
____ Worker compensation

**LEAVE BENEFITS**
____ Sick leave
____ Holiday and vacations
____ Personal leave
____ Family and medical leave
____ Civic duty leave
____ Bereavement leave

**RETIREMENT PLANS**
____ Pension plan
____ 401(k) plan

- - - - - - - - - - - - - - - - - - - - - - - - - - - - - - - - - - - - - - - - - - - - - - - -

Employee Name_____  Employee Number_____
Starting Date_____  Job Title_____
Department_____  Supervisor_____

**SUPERVISOR**

**FIRST DAY**

**OVERVIEW**
____ Introduction to coworkers
____ Tour of department
____ Tour of company

**WORK LOCATION**
____ Parking
____ Dress code
____ Employee lockers
____ Restrooms
____ Telephone (personal usage)

**JOB ORIENTATION**
____ Job overview
____ Job description review
____ Job equipment
____ Safety equipment
____ Safety policies
____ Accident reporting

**EMERGENCIES**
____ Medical
____ Power failure
____ Fire
____ Weather closings

At the end of the employee's first two weeks, the supervisor will ask if the employee has any questions concerning any items. After all questions have been discussed, both the employee and the supervisor will sign and date this form and return it to the HR Department.

Employee Signature_____
Date_____
Orientation Conducted by (supervisor)

_____

such factors as typical dress habits, lunch practices, and what executives are called will help new employees to adjust.

Another important type of initial information to give employees is information on the policies, work rules, and benefits of the company. Policies about sick leave, tardiness, absenteeism, vacations, benefits, hospitalization, parking, and safety rules must be made known to every new employee immediately. Also, the employee's supervisor or manager should describe the routine of a normal workday for the employee the first morning.

**PRESENTING ORIENTATION INFORMATION EFFECTIVELY** Managers and HR representatives should determine the most appropriate ways to present orientation information. One common failing of many orientation programs is *information overload.* New workers presented with too many facts may ignore important details or inaccurately recall much of the information.[18] For example, rather than telling an employee about company sick leave and vacation policies, an employee handbook that includes this information might be presented on the first day. The manager or HR representative then can review this information a few days later to answer any of the employee's questions, and the employee can review it as needed. Some employers have invested considerable time and effort to make their orientation efforts interesting and useful.

Self-paced orientation, whereby employees review orientation information available electronically or on videotape, is growing in usage also. There are several advantages to this approach. Most of the general company information is online for employees to access from home or in offices throughout the world. It also saves several hours of HR staff time, and new employees can return to the information at any time. If they have specific questions, new employees can contact the HR staff either by phone or e-mail.

Indeed, employees will retain more of the orientation information if it is presented in a manner that encourages them to learn. In addition to the videotapes and computers already mentioned, some organizations have successfully used movies, slides, and charts. However, the emphasis should be on presenting information, not on entertaining the new employee. Materials such as handbooks and information leaflets should be reviewed periodically for updates and corrections.

**EVALUATION AND FOLLOW-UP** A systematic orientation program should have an evaluation and/or reorientation phase at some point after the initial orientation. An HR representative or manager can evaluate the effectiveness of the orientation by conducting follow-up interviews with new employees a few weeks or months after the orientation. Employee questionnaires also can be used. Some organizations even give new employees a written test on the company handbook two weeks after orientation. Unfortunately, it appears that most employers do limited or no evaluation of the effectiveness of orientation, according to one survey of employers.[19]

Too often, typical orientation efforts assume that once oriented, employees are familiar with everything they need to know about the organization forever. Instead, orientation should be viewed as a never-ending process of introducing both old and new employees to the current state of the organization. To be assets to their organizations, employees must know current organizational policies and procedures, and these may be altered from time to time.

# Systems Approach to Training

The success of orientation or any other type of training can be gauged by the amount of learning that occurs and is transferred to the job. Too often, unplanned, uncoordinated, and haphazard training efforts significantly reduce the learning that could have occurred. Training and learning will take place, especially through informal work groups, whether an organization has a coordinated effort or not—because employees learn from other employees. But without a well-designed, systematic approach to training, what is learned may not be what is best for the organization. Figure 10–6 shows the relevant components of the three major phases in a training system: (1) the assessment phase, (2) the implementation phase, and (3) the evaluation phase.[20]

## Assessment Phase

In the *assessment* phase, planners determine the need for training and specify the objectives of the training effort. Looking at the performance of clerks in a billing department, a manager might find that their data-entry and keyboard abilities are weak and that they would profit by having instruction in these areas. An objective of increasing the clerks' keyboard entry speed to 60 words per minute without errors might be established. The number of words per minute without errors is the criterion against which training success can be measured, and it represents the way in which the objective is made specific. To make the bridge between assessment and implementation, the clerks would be given a keyboard data-entry test.

**FIGURE 10–6** *Model of a Training System*

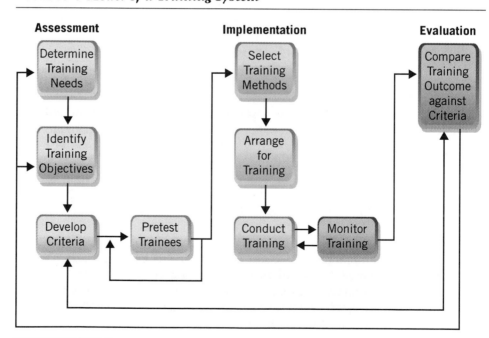

## Implementation Phase

Using the results of the assessment, *implementation* can begin. For instance, a billing supervisor and an HR training specialist could work together to determine how to train the clerks to increase their speeds. Arrangements for instructors, classrooms, materials, and so on would be made at this point. A programmed instruction manual might be used in conjunction with a special data-entry class set up at the company. Implementation occurs when training is actually conducted.

## Evaluation Phase

The *evaluation* phase is crucial. It focuses on measuring how well the training accomplished what its originators expected. Monitoring the training serves as a bridge between the implementation and evaluation phases and provides feedback for setting future training objectives.

# Training Needs Assessment

Training is designed to help the organization accomplish its objectives. Determining organizational training needs is the diagnostic phase of setting training objectives. Just as a patient must be examined before a physician can prescribe medication to deal with an ailment, an organization or an individual employee must be studied before a course of action can be planned to make the "patient" function better. Managers can identify training needs by considering three sources.[21] Figure 10–7 depicts some of the methods used, for each of the three sources.

**FIGURE 10–7** *Levels of Training Needs Assessment*

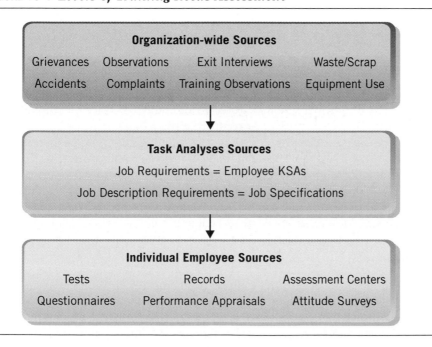

## Organizational Analyses

The first way to diagnose training needs is through organizational analysis, which considers the organization as a system. An important part of the company's strategic human resource planning is the identification of the knowledge, skills, and abilities (KSAs) that will be needed by employers in the future as both jobs and the organization change.

Both internal and external forces that will influence training must be considered when doing organizational analyses. The problems posed by the technical obsolescence of current employees and an insufficiently educated labor pool from which to draw new workers should be confronted before those training needs become critical. To illustrate, consider a medium-sized telecommunications firm that is facing increasing competition and changes in its industry. During its strategic planning, the firm recognized that greater computerization of its operations was needed. The firm identified that establishing an intranet in the company was going to mean that increased internal and external communications were to occur electronically. Many employees needed to be trained to use computer software and given laptops to use both at work and away from the office.

One important source for organizational analyses comes from various operational measures of organizational performance. On a continuing basis, detailed analyses of HR data can show training weaknesses. Departments or areas with high turnover, high absenteeism, low performance, or other deficiencies can be pinpointed. After such problems are analyzed, training objectives can be developed. Specific sources of information and operational measures for an organizational-level needs analysis may include the following:

- Grievances
- Accident records
- Observations
- Exit interviews

- Complaints from customers
- Equipment utilization figures
- Training committee observations
- Waste/scrap/quality control data

## Task Analyses

The second way to diagnose training needs is through analyses of the tasks performed in the organization. To do these analyses, it is necessary to know the job requirements of the organization. Job descriptions and job specifications provide information on the performances expected and skills necessary for employees to accomplish the required work. By comparing the requirements of jobs with the knowledge, skills, and abilities of employees, training needs can be identified.

To continue an example, assume that at a telecommunications firm, analyses were done to identify the tasks to be performed by engineers who were to serve as technical instructors for other employees. By listing the tasks required of a technical instructor, management established a program to teach specific instruction skills needed so the engineers could become successful instructors.

## Individual Analyses

The third means of diagnosing training needs focuses on individuals and how they perform their jobs. Figure 10–8 shows how analyses of the job and the person mesh to identify training needs. The use of performance appraisal data in making these individual analyses is the most common approach. In some

**FIGURE 10-8** *Using Job Performance to Analyze Training Needs*

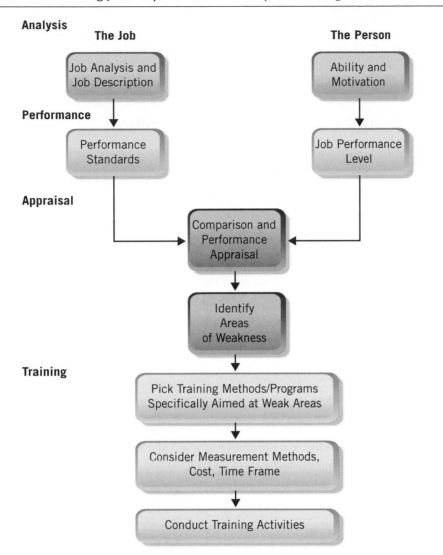

**Analysis**

**The Job**

Job Analysis and Job Description

**The Person**

Ability and Motivation

**Performance**

Performance Standards

Job Performance Level

**Appraisal**

Comparison and Performance Appraisal

Identify Areas of Weakness

**Training**

Pick Training Methods/Programs Specifically Aimed at Weak Areas

Consider Measurement Methods, Cost, Time Frame

Conduct Training Activities

instances, a good HR information system can be used to help identify individuals who require training in specific areas.

To assess training needs through the performance appraisal process, an employee's performance inadequacies first must be determined in a formal review. Then some type of training can be designed to help the employee overcome the weaknesses. Another way of assessing individual training needs is to ask both managerial and nonmanagerial employees about what training they need. The results can inform managers about what employees believe their problems are and what actions they recommend.

A training needs survey can take the form of questionnaires or interviews with supervisors and employees on an individual or group basis. The purpose is to gather information on problems perceived by the individuals involved. The following sources are useful for individual analyses:

- Questionnaires
- Job knowledge tools
- Skill tests
- Attitude surveys

- Records of critical incidents
- Data from assessment centers
- Role-playing results

## Establishing Training Objectives and Priorities

Once training needs have been identified using the various analyses, then training objectives and priorities must be established. All of the gathered data is used to compile a *gap analysis,* which identifies the distance between where an organization is with its employee capabilities and where it needs to be. Training objectives and priorities are set to close the gap.[22]

The success of training should be measured in terms of the objectives set. Useful objectives are measurable. For example, an objective for a new salesclerk might be to "demonstrate the ability to explain the function of each product in the department within two weeks." This objective serves as a check on internalization, or whether the person really learned.

Objectives for training can be set in any area by using one of the following four dimensions:

- *Quantity of work* resulting from training (for example, number of words per minute typed or number of applications processed per day)
- *Quality of work* after training (for example, dollar cost of rework, scrap loss, or errors)
- *Timeliness of work* after training (for example, schedules met or budget reports turned in on time)
- *Cost savings* as a result of training (for example, deviation from budget, sales expense, or cost of downtime)

Because training seldom is an unlimited budget item and there are multiple training needs in an organization, it is necessary to prioritize needs. Ideally, training needs are ranked in importance on the basis of organizational objectives. The training most needed to improve the health of the organization is done first in order to produce visible results more quickly.

# Training Approaches

Once objectives have been determined, the actual training can begin. Regardless of whether the training is job specific or broader in nature, the appropriate training approach must be chosen. The following overview of common training approaches and techniques classifies them into several major groups. Other methods that are used more frequently for management development are discussed in the next chapter, although there can be overlap in the use of some of the methods.

## On-the-Job Training (OJT)

The most common type of training at all levels in an organization is *on-the-job training* (OJT). Whether or not the training is planned, people do learn from their

**LOGGING ON . . .**
**Training Supersite**
This site provides access to *Training* magazine, job openings, products, services, and research articles for training and development professionals.

http://www.trainingsupersite.com/dirset.htm

**FIGURE 10–9** *Job Instruction Training (JIT) Process*

| **Prepare the Learners** | **Present the Information** | **Trainees Practice** | **Do Follow-up** |
|---|---|---|---|
| • Put them at ease<br>• Find out what they know<br>• Get them interested | • Tell, show, question<br>• Present one point at a time<br>• Check, question, repeat<br>• Make sure they know | • Have them do the job<br>• Ask questions<br>• Observe and correct<br>• Make sure they know it | • Put them on their own<br>• Check frequently<br>• Reduce close follow-up as performance improves |

job experiences, particularly if these experiences change over time. On-the-job training usually is done by the manager, other employees, or both. A manager or supervisor who trains an employee must be able to teach, as well as to show, the employee what to do.

**JOB INSTRUCTION TRAINING (JIT)**  A special, guided form of on-the-job training is known as *job instruction training* (JIT). Developed during World War II, JIT was used to prepare civilians with little experience for jobs in the industrial sector producing military equipment. Because of its success, JIT is still used. In fact, its logical progression of steps is an excellent way to teach trainers to train. Figure 10–9 shows the steps in the JIT process.

**PROBLEMS WITH OJT**  On-the-job training is by far the most commonly used form of training because it is flexible and relevant to what the employee is doing. However, OJT has some problems as well. A common problem is that OJT often is haphazardly done. Trainers may have no experience in training, no time to do it, and no desire to participate. Under such conditions, learners essentially are on their own, and training likely will not be effective. Another problem is that OJT can disrupt regular work. Unfortunately, OJT can amount to no training at all in some circumstances, especially if the trainee simply is abandoned by an ineffective trainer to learn the job alone. However, well-planned and well-executed OJT can be very effective.

*BNA: 2030.20.70*
**Training and Compensable Time**
To learn about the requirements for counting time spent in training and work time for overtime determination, review the details in this section.

## Simulation

Simulation is a training approach that uses a training site set up to be identical to the work site. In this setting, trainees can learn under realistic conditions but be away from the pressures of the production schedule. For example, having an employee practice on a PBX console in a simulated setting before taking over as a telephone receptionist allows the person to learn the job more easily and without stress. Consequently, there may be fewer mistakes in handling actual incoming calls.

One type of simulation is called **vestibule training,** which occurs in special facilities that replicate the equipment and work demands of jobs. Examples of vestibule training include airlines that use simulators to train pilots and cabin attendants, astronauts who train in mock-up space capsules, and nuclear power plant operators who use model operations control rooms and consoles.

Behavioral simulations and computer-generated virtual reality have grown as computer technology and use of the Internet for training have grown. Virtual

**Vestibule training**
A type of training which occurs in special facilities that replicate the equipment and work demands of jobs.

reality uses three-dimensional environments to replicate a job. Computers, audio equipment, and video equipment all may be a part of a virtual reality training approach. It is very useful where danger to the learner or to expensive equipment is involved, such as teaching pilots to fly a 757 aircraft or teaching police officers when to use their weapons and when to hold their fire in situations where their lives may be in danger.

## Cooperative Training

Two widely used cooperative training methods are internships and apprenticeships. Both mix classroom training and on-the-job experiences.

**INTERNSHIPS** An internship is a form of on-the-job training that usually combines job training with classroom instruction in trade schools, high schools, colleges, or universities. Internships are advantageous to both employers and interns. Interns get "real-world" exposure, a line on the *vita* (resume), and a chance to examine a possible employer closely. Employers who hire from campuses get a cost-effective selection tool that includes a chance to see an intern at work before a final hiring decision is made.

**APPRENTICESHIPS** Another form of cooperative training that is used by employers, trade unions, and government agencies is apprentice training. An apprenticeship program provides an employee with on-the-job experience under the guidance of a skilled and certified worker. Certain requirements for training, equipment, time length, and proficiency levels may be monitored by a unit of the U.S. Department of Labor. Apprentice training is used most often to train people for jobs in skilled crafts, such as carpentry, plumbing, photoengraving, typesetting, and welding. Apprenticeships usually last two to five years, depending on the occupation. During this time the apprentice receives lower wages than the certified individual.

## Workforce Investment Partnership Act (1998)

The U.S. government and most state governments have programs providing training support to employers who hire new workers, particularly those who are long-term unemployed or have been receiving welfare benefits. Prior to 1998, most federal training was done under the provisions of the Job Training Partnership Act (JTPA). However, in 1998, the JTPA was replaced by the Workforce Investment Partnership Act (WIPA). Through WIPA over 60 federal training support programs were consolidated into three block grant programs. These programs target adult education, disadvantaged youth, and family literacy. Employers hiring and training individuals who meet the WIPA criteria receive tax credits and other assistance for six months or more, depending upon the program regulations.[23]

**Behaviorally experienced training**

Training methods that deal less with physical skills than with attitudes, perceptions, and interpersonal issues.

## Behaviorally Experienced Training

Some training efforts focus on emotional and behavioral learning. **Behaviorally experienced training** focuses less on physical skills than on attitudes, perceptions, and interpersonal issues. As Figure 10–10 shows, there are several different types of behaviorally experienced training. Employees can learn about behavior by *role playing,* in which individuals assume identities in a certain situation and

**FIGURE 10–10** *Common Forms of Behaviorally Experienced Training*

| Type of Training | Nature of Training | Problems with Training |
|---|---|---|
| Role Playing | Participants acting out roles in work-related situations can improve interpersonal skills. | Trainees may see it as a "game," not transferable to the job. |
| Business Games | Computer simulations where the trainee makes management decisions and gets feedback on success. Trains people to make business decisions without actually affecting the business. | Training is expensive and time-consuming. |
| Sensitivity Training | Unstructured attempt to show how others see individual. Can provide insight into interpersonal skills. | Trainees may be personally "threatened"; also may not be seen as job relevant. |
| Diversity Training | Classroom lecture approach to easing racial and gender tensions at work. | Training can create "backlash" or oversensitivity, inhibiting workplace interactions. |
| In-Basket Exercises | A series of memos or letters that must be dealt with, usually in a rapid fashion. Can be made relevant to real job decisions. | Training is time-consuming and must be tailored to jobs under focus. |
| Case Studies/ Incidents | Descriptions of real companies or situations that require dealing with many facts and making decisions. Can provide a great deal of exposure to many different companies and problems. | Care must be taken to ensure that cases are relevant and problems are realistic. |

act them out. *Business games, case studies,* other cases called *incidents,* and short work assignments called *in-baskets* are other behaviorally experienced learning methods. *Sensitivity training,* or *laboratory training,* is an example of a method used for emotional learning. *Diversity training* seeks to shape attitudes about a work environment with differing kinds of employees. Figure 10–10 compares some of the commonly used forms of behaviorally experienced training.

The critical issue is to emphasize the purpose of the exercise. For instance, employees may perceive role playing as fun or annoying, but they should understand clearly that the exercise is attempting to teach something. Also, the trainees must be able to transfer the learning back to their jobs.

## Classroom and Conference Training

Training seminars, courses, and presentations can be used in both skills-related and developmental training. Lectures and discussions are a major part of this training. The numerous management development courses offered by trade associations and educational institutions are examples of conference training.

Company-conducted short courses, lectures, and meetings usually consist of classroom training, whereas company sales meetings are a common type of conference training. Both classroom and conference training frequently make use of training techniques such as case discussions, films, and tapes to enhance the learning experience. Particularly important in classroom training is to recognize that adults in classroom training have different expectations and learning styles than do younger students.[24]

A number of large firms have established their own "universities" to offer classroom and other training as part of curricula for employees. Among the better-known corporate universities are Motorola University, Equifax University, and Northern States Power's Quality Academy.[25]

## Training Media

**LOGGING ON . . .**
**Training Registry**
The Training Registry contains a directory of training courses and vendors, listed by category and topic.

http:/www.tregistry.com/ttr/home.htm

Several aids are available to trainers presenting information. The most common are audiovisual aids and computer-assisted instruction. Another is distance training and learning using interactive two-way television or computer technology. Also, the growth of web-based training and organizational intranets has grown, as mentioned in the chapter opening discussion. Several types of training media are examined next.

**AUDIOVISUAL AIDS**  Technical aids that are audio and visual in nature can include audiotapes and videotapes, films, closed-circuit television, and interactive video teleconferencing. All but interactive video are one-way communications. They may allow the communication of information that cannot be presented in a classroom. Demonstrations of machines, experiments, and examinations of behavior are examples. Interactive video capability adds audio and video capabilities, but it uses touch-screen input instead of a keyboard. Audio and visual aids also can be tied into satellite communications systems to convey the same information, such as new product details, to sales personnel in several states.

**COMPUTER-ASSISTED INSTRUCTION**  *Computer-assisted instruction* (CAI) allows trainees to learn by interacting with a computer. Application of CAI technology is driven by the need to improve the efficiency or effectiveness of a training situation and to enhance the transfer of learning to improve job performance. Computers lend themselves well to instruction, testing, drill and practice, and application through simulation.

Training programs in the United States are becoming increasingly high-tech. Interactive media such as computers can take the place of more expensive instructor-led classroom training. The advancement in computer technology also has led to placing training programs on CD-ROMs, which are distributed to trainees.

Some firms have gone beyond CD-ROMs to distributing updated training materials worldwide. This *streaming of video* allows video clips of training materials to be stored on a firm's network server. Employees then can access the material using the firm's intranet. Changes in training content are loaded directly into the server, rather than having to be distributed on CD-ROMs.[26]

*Virtual reality (VR)* allows trainees to "see" the training situations and react to them using computer interactive technology. For example, VR has been used to "place" police officers, training them how to react, and when to use weapons when chasing suspects in darkened and crowded areas. The U.S. military also has made extensive use of VR in training personnel in several branches of service.

A major advantage of all forms of CAI is that it allows self-directed instruction, which many users prefer. Computers used as a training tool allow self-paced approaches and often can be used at the usual place of business. In contrast, instructor-based teaching in a campus-based setting requires employees to spend considerable time away from their jobs. A survey of 3,700 firms found that training using electronic technologies is growing in use, but that training in instructor-led classrooms is declining in use.[27]

**DISTANCE TRAINING/LEARNING** Many colleges and universities are using interactive two-way television to present classes. The medium allows an instructor in one place to see and respond to a "class" in any number of other locations. If a system is fully configured, employees can take courses from anywhere in the world—while remaining at their jobs or homes. Colleges are designing courses and even degrees for companies who pay for delivering courses to their employees. Both a satellite-based training business and a "World College" based on the Internet are being used. Trainers must avoid becoming dazzled with the technology so that the real emphasis is on performance and training. The effectiveness of the technologies and media needs to be examined when evaluating training.[28]

## Selecting Training Approaches

Once training needs have been assessed and training objectives identified, then the training approaches and methods must be selected. There are many different training methods, and training technology is expanding the number of options available. Figure 10–11 shows that numerous factors must be considered simultaneously when selecting the training approaches to use.

**LOGGING ON . . .**
**Distance Learning**

Information and program details on Distance Learning on the Net can be reviewed at **(www.hoyle.com/distance. htm),** and University Continuing Education Association **(www.educationindex.com)**

**FIGURE 10–11** *Considerations When Selecting Training Approaches*

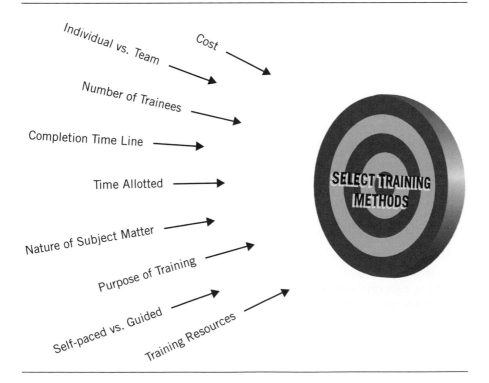

Individual vs. Team

Cost

Number of Trainees

Completion Time Line

Time Allotted

Nature of Subject Matter

Purpose of Training

Self-paced vs. Guided

Training Resources

SELECT TRAINING METHODS

# Evaluation of Training

Evaluation of training compares the post-training results to the objectives expected by managers, trainers, and trainees. Too often, training is done without any thought of measuring and evaluating it later to see how well it worked. Because training is both time-consuming and costly, evaluation should be done. The management axiom that "nothing will improve until it is measured" may apply to training assessment. In fact, at some firms, what employees learn is directly related to what they earn, which puts this principle of measurement into practice.

**Cost/benefit analysis**
Compares costs of training with the benefits received.

One way to evaluate training is to examine the costs associated with the training and the benefits received through **cost/benefit analysis.** As mentioned earlier, comparing costs and benefits is easy until one has to assign an actual dollar value to some of the benefits. The best way is to measure the value of the output before and after training. Any increase represents the benefit resulting from training. However, careful measurement of both the costs and the benefits may be difficult in some situations.[29] Therefore, benchmarking training has grown in usage.

## Benchmarking Training

Rather than doing training evaluation internally, some organizations are using benchmark measures of training that are compared from one organization to others. To do benchmarking, HR professionals in an organization gather data on training and compare it to data on training at other organizations in the industry and of their size. Comparison data is available through the American Society of Training and Development (ASTD) and its Benchmarking Service. This service has training-related data from over 1,000 participating employers who complete detailed questionnaires annually. Training also can be benchmarked against data from the American Productivity and Quality Center and the Saratoga Institute.[30] In both instances, data is available on training expenditures per employee, among other measures.

## Levels of Evaluation

It is best to consider how training is to be evaluated *before* it begins. Donald L. Kirkpatrick identified four levels at which training can be evaluated.[31] As Figure 10–12 shows, the ease of evaluating training becomes increasingly more difficult as training is evaluated using reaction, learning, behavior, and results measures. But the value of the training increases as it can be shown to affect behavior and results instead of reaction and learning-level evaluations. Later research has examined Kirkpatrick's schematic and raised questions about how independent each level is from the others, but the four levels are widely used to focus on the importance of evaluating training.

**REACTION** Organizations evaluate the reaction level of trainees by conducting interviews or by administering questionnaires to the trainees. Assume that 30 managers attended a two-day workshop on effective interviewing skills. A reaction-level measure could be gathered by having the managers complete a survey that asked them to rate the value of the training, the style of the instructors, and the usefulness of the training to them. However, the immediate reaction may

**FIGURE 10–12** *Levels of Training Evaluation*

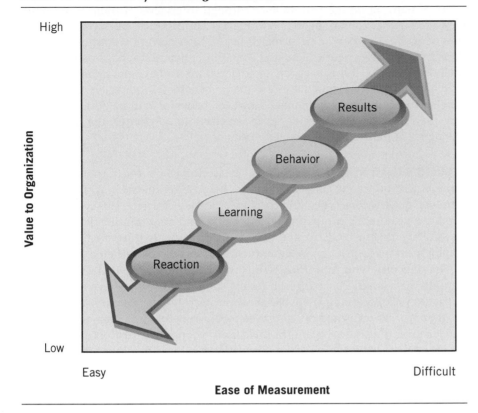

measure only how much the people liked the training rather than how it benefited them.

**LEARNING** Learning levels can be evaluated by measuring how well trainees have learned facts, ideas, concepts, theories, and attitudes. Tests on the training material are commonly used for evaluating learning and can be given both before and after training to compare scores. To evaluate training courses at some firms, test results are used to determine how well the courses have provided employees with the desired content. If test scores indicate learning problems, instructors get feedback, and the courses are redesigned so that the content can be delivered more effectively. To continue the example, giving managers attending the interviewing workshop a test at the end of the session to quiz them on types of interviews, legal and illegal questions, and questioning types could indicate that they learned important material on interviewing. Of course, learning enough to pass a test does not guarantee that the trainee can *do* anything with what was learned or behave differently.

One study of training programs on hazardous waste operations and emergency response for chemical workers found that the multiple-choice test given at the end of the course did not indicate that those trained had actually mastered the relevant material.[32] Also, as students will attest, what is remembered and answered on learning content immediately after the training is different from what may be remembered if the "test" is given several months later.

**BEHAVIOR** Evaluating training at the behavioral level involves (1) measuring the effect of training on job performance through interviews of trainees and their coworkers and (2) observing job performance. For instance, a behavioral evaluation of the managers who participated in the interviewing workshop might be done by observing them conducting actual interviews of applicants for jobs in their departments. If the managers asked questions as they were trained and they used appropriate follow-up questions, then a behavioral indication of the interviewing training could be obtained. However, behavior is more difficult to measure than reaction and learning. Even if behaviors do change, the results that management desires may not be obtained.

**RESULTS** Employers evaluate results by measuring the effect of training on the achievement of organizational objectives. Because results such as productivity, turnover, quality, time, sales, and costs are relatively concrete, this type of evaluation can be done by comparing records before and after training. For the interviewing training, records of the number of individuals hired to the offers of employment made prior to and after the training could be gathered.

The difficulty with measuring results is pinpointing whether it actually was training that caused the changes in results. Other factors may have had a major impact as well. For example, managers who completed the interviewing training program can be measured on employee turnover before and after the training. But turnover is also dependent on the current economic situation, the demand for product, and the quality of employees being hired. Therefore, when evaluating results, managers should be aware of all issues involved in determining the exact effect on the training.

## Evaluation Designs

If evaluation is done internally because benchmarking data are not available, there are many ways to design the evaluation of training programs to measure improvements. The rigor of the three designs discussed next increases with each level.

**POST-MEASURE** The most obvious way to evaluate training effectiveness is to determine after the training whether the individuals can perform the way management wants them to perform. Assume that a manager has 20 typists who need to improve their typing speeds. They are given a one-day training session and then given a typing test to measure their speeds. If the typists can all type the required speed after training, was the training beneficial? It is difficult to say; perhaps they could have done as well before training. It is difficult to know whether the typing speed is a result of the training or could have been achieved without training.

**PRE-/POST-MEASURE** By designing the typing speed evaluation differently, the issue of pretest skill levels could have been considered. If the manager had measured the typing speed before and after training, he could have known whether the training made any difference. However, a question remains. If there was a change in typing speed, was the training responsible for the change, or did these people simply type faster because they knew they were being tested? People often perform better when they know they are being tested on the results.

**FIGURE 10–13** *Pre-/Post-Measure with Control Group*

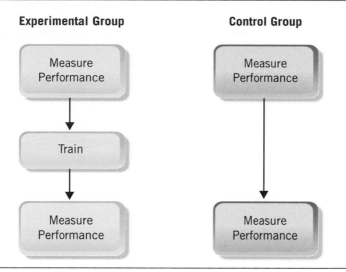

**PRE-/POST-MEASURE WITH CONTROL GROUP** Another evaluation design can address this problem. In addition to the 20 typists who will be trained, a manager can test another group of typists who will not be trained to see if they do as well as those who are to be trained. This second group is called a *control group*. If, after training, the trained typists can type significantly faster than those who were not trained, the manager can be reasonably sure that the training was effective. Figure 10–13 shows the pre-/post-measure design with a control group.

There are some difficulties associated with using this design. First, having enough employees doing similar jobs to be able to create two groups may not be feasible in many situations, even in larger companies. Second, because one group is excluded from training, there may be resentment or increased motivation by those in the control group, which could lead to distorted results, either positive or negative. Additionally, this design also assumes that performance measurement can be done accurately in both groups, so that any performance changes in the experimental group can be attributed to the training.

Other designs also can be used, but these three are the most common ones. When possible, the pre-/post-measure or pre-/post-measure with control group design should be used, because each provides a much stronger measurement than the post-measure design alone.

# Summary

- Training is a learning process whereby people acquire capabilities to aid in the achievement of goals.
- Training can be conducted internally in the organization and can be done formally, informally, or on the job.

- External training is growing in usage, even to the extent that training is being outsourced.
- Training has legal implications, such as who is selected for training, the criteria used for the selection, pay differences based on training, and use of training when making promotion decisions.

- Basic learning principles that guide training efforts include intention to learn, whole learning, reinforcement, immediate confirmation, practice, and transfer of training.
- Orientation is a special kind of training designed to help new employees learn about their jobs, coworkers, and organization.
- Components of an effective orientation system include preparing for new employees; determining what information is needed and when it is needed by the employees; presenting information about the workday, organization, policies, rules, and benefits; and doing evaluation and follow-up.
- A training system includes assessment, implementation, and evaluation.
- Of the many training approaches, on-the-job training (OJT) is the most often used (and abused) method.
- Two widely used cooperative training methods are internships and apprenticeships.
- Training media such as computer-assisted instruction and audio and visual aids each have advantages and disadvantages.
- Evaluation of training success is important. Training can be evaluated at four levels: reaction, learning, behavior, and results.
- A pre-/post-measure with control group design is the most rigorous training evaluation design, but others can be used as well.

# Review and Discussion Questions

1. What are some reasons that external training is growing in usage?
2. Describe how you would use some of the learning concepts discussed in the chapter in training someone to operate a fax machine.
3. Discuss the importance of orientation, and tell how you would orient a new management trainee.
4. What are the three major phases in a training system? Identify the processes within each phase.
5. Assume that you want to identify training needs for a group of sales employees in a luxury-oriented jewelry store. What would you do?
6. You are training someone to use a word-processing computer software program. What training methods would you use?
7. You want to evaluate the training received by some data-input operators:
   (a) Give examples of how to evaluate the training at four different levels.
   (b) What type of training design would you use, and why?

# Terms to Know

active practice   323
attentional advice   321
behaviorally experienced training   336
behavior modeling   322
cost-benefit analysis   340

extinction   322
informal training   319
immediate confirmation   322
massed practice   323
negative reinforcement   322
orientation   324

positive reinforcement   322
punishment   322
reinforcement   321
spaced practice   323
training   317
vestibule training   335

# Using the Internet

## Training and Employee Turnover

You have just been hired as the new training and development manager in a financial institution. This is a new position for the company, and the senior officers have asked you to attend their executive meeting at the end of the week. Your purpose is to explain to them how the training and development of employees will help reduce the increasing turnover they are experiencing. Using the following website list, identify ways that training and development can be used to decrease employee turnover.

**http://www.auxillium.com/humint. htm#training_and_development**

## CASE

## Disney "Magic" Training at Dierberg's

One of the best-known organizations in the world is Walt Disney World. Yes, it is known for the theme parks and resorts it has worldwide, but in HR circles Disney is seen as a model for training employees to deliver outstanding service. At the heart of Disney "magic" is training employees in the Disney culture. Once individuals survive a rigorous selection process and are chosen as *cast members,* training begins with orientation and on-the-job training. Disney has become so well-known for its training that the Disney Institute has been established to share the Disney approach with other employers.

One firm that is a believer in the Disney "magic" is Dierberg's, a supermarket chain based in St. Louis, Missouri. Before Fred Martels, HR director for Dierberg's went to a Disney Institute workshop on customer service and employee orientation, Dierberg's new employees went through a two-hour orientation program. They got an employee handbook, saw a short company history video, and were briefed on safety and company policies. Boring, was how Martels described it. Indications were that upon completing the two-hour orientation, new employees were not excited about their jobs and unclear about customer service expectations and the company.

Then Martels went to a Disney Institute workshop on customer service and Disney's approach to orientation. As a result, Dierberg's totally revamped its orientation program. Following the Disney example, the HR staff had the once-bare walls of the orientation and training rooms decorated with information about company history, pictures of stores, and other company details. That way, new employees can see some of the company history. They are given exercises to get them involved and interacting. They watch new videos that emphasize customer service, company growth, and career opportunities. Throughout the new orientation program, Dierberg's stresses participant involvement and interaction.

Consequently, managers throughout Dierberg's have noticed that new employees are more customer-service oriented and appear more pleasant to customers and coworkers. As a result of this and other changes, Dierberg's has received professional awards for motivating and retaining employees. Evidently, Dierberg's has created its own "magic."[33]

### Questions

1. Discuss why the assessment of training needs at Dierberg's was crucial to the results described in the case.
2. Identify how Dierberg's new orientation program could be evaluated in terms of reaction, learning, behavior, and results.

# Notes

1. Based on Brandon Hall, *The Web-Based Training Cookbook: Everything You Need to Know for Online Training* (New York: Wiley Computer Publishing, 1998); Bill Roberts, "Training Via the Desktop," *HR Magazine,* August 1998, 99–104; Bill Holleran, "Training Resources Are Available on Internet Via ALX," *HR News,* October 1998, 13; and Debra Black, "Live and Online: A WBT Primer," *Training and Development,* September 1998, 34–36.
2. Charles C. Morrow, M. Quintin Jarrett, and Melvin T. Rupinski, "An Investigation of the Effect and Economic Utility of Corporate-Wide Training," *Personnel Psychology* 50 (1997), 91–119.
3. Susan Warner, John Lewison, and Jane Lewis, "Refocusing Competencies Is an Emerging Issue in HR Training," *HR News,* October 1998, 15.
4. Jack Stack, "The Training Myth," *INC.,* August 1998, 41–42.
5. *The Teaching Firm: Where Productive Work and Learning Converge* (Newton, MA: Education Development Center, 1997).
6. Christopher J. Bachler, "Outsourcing Training Helps Companies Keep Up," *Workforce,* June 1997, 100–102.
7. Kathryn Tyler, "Software Certifications Boost Productivity," *HR Magazine,* May 1997, 63–72.
8. J. Kevin Ford, et al, "Relationships of Goal Orientation, Metacognitive Activity, Practice Strategies with Learning Outcomes and Transfer," *Journal of Applied Psychology* 83 (1998), 218–233.
9. Janis A. Cannon-Bowers, et al, "A Framework for Understanding Pre-Practice Conditions and Their Impact on Learning," *Personnel Psychology* 51 (1998), 291–320.
10. Sandra L. Fisher and J. Kevin Ford, "Differentials Effect of Learner Effort and Goal Orientation on Two Learning Outcomes," *Personnel Psychology* 51 (1998), 397–420.
11. Sam Jensen and Mark Schorr, "Employee Retention Begins at Orientation," *Nebraska Workplace Memo,* August 1998, 1.
12. Teri Ellis, "That First Day," *Occupational Health & Safety,* April 1998, 26–29.
13. Rebecca Ganzel, "Putting Out the Welcome Mat," *Training,* March 1998, 54–61.
14. Marilyn Moats Kennedy, "Can This New Hire Be Saved?", *Across the Board,* May 1997, 53.
15. Kathryn Tyler, "Take New Employee Orientation off the Back Burner," *HR Magazine,* May 1998, 49–57.
16. Developed by Geoff Brown, SPHR. Used with permission of ACI.
17. "Helping New Employees Find their Direction," *Bulletin to Management,* October 29, 1998, 343.
18. Eric Raimy, "Lasting Impressions," *Human Resource Executive,* January 1998, 59–61.
19. "Monitor Career Development and Orientation Programs," *HR Magazine,* November 1997, 25.
20. Adapted from I.L. Goldstein, *Training in Organizations* (Monterey, CA: Brooks-Cole, 1993).
21. For more details on conducting training needs analyses, see P. Nick Blanchard and James W. Thacker, *Effective Training: Systems, Strategies, and Practices* (Englewood Cliffs, NJ: Prentice-Hall, 1999), 126–182.
22. Paul Elliott, "Assessment Phase: Building Models and Defining Gaps," in Dana Gaines Robinson and James C. Robinson, *Moving from Training to Performance* (San Francisco: Berrett-Koehler Publishers, Inc., 1998), 63–93.
23. "The Workforce Investment Partnership Act," *HR Magazine,* October 1998, 89.
24. Barb Berquam, "Build a Learning Zone," *Occupational Health & Safety,* August 1998, 62–64.
25. "Corporate Universities Are Catching On," *Workforce,* June 1997, 96.
26. Larry Stevens, "Streamlined Training," *Human Resource Executive,* January 1998, 44–47.
27. Stephanie Armour, "Training Takes Front Seat at Offices," *USA Today,* January 19, 1999, 6B.
28. Kathryn F. Clark, "Virtual Evolution," *Human Resource Executive,* March 18, 1999, 32–34; and Donna J. Abernathy, "The WWW of Distance Learning," *Training & Development,* September 1998, 29–30.
29. Gillian Flynn, "The Nuts & Bolts of Valuing Training," *Workforce,* November 1998, 80–85.
30. "Measuring Training Outcomes," *Workforce Strategies,* June 29, 1998, 31–35.
31. Donald L. Kirkpatrick, "Great Ideas Revisited: Revisiting Kirkpatrick's Four-Level Model," *Training & Development,* January 1996, 54–57.
32. F. Allan Hanson, "Evaluating HAZWOPER Training Programs," *Occupational Health & Safety,* June 1998, 37–66.
33. Based on "The Disney Approach to Human Resource Management," presented to Society for Human Resource Management, Annual Conference, Minneapolis, MN, June 1998; and "Bright Beginnings," *Human Resource Executive,* September 1998, C5.

# CHAPTER 11

# Human Resource Development and Careers

**After you have read this chapter, you should be able to:**

- Define *human resource development,* and explain how it differs from training.

- Describe the development process.

- Discuss specific advantages and problems associated with assessment centers.

- Identify four on-the-job and four off-the-job development methods.

- Differentiate between organization-centered and individual-centered career planning.

- Explain how dual-career ladders for engineers and scientists function.

- Identify how dual-career marriages affect career paths and strategies of individuals and organizations.

# Development in the Professional Sports World

Successful long-term development is something every employer wants from employees. But unlike training, which is relatively well defined and more job specific, development is much less certain and more ill-defined. For instance, can a manager really develop employees so that they use good judgment? How does a supervisor develop an employee to have "appropriate attitude"? Or how does one develop a minimum level of courtesy, table manners, and social skills in relatively uncouth (but talented) technical employees? The classic movie, "My Fair Lady," dealt with a similar set of problems, but professional sports teams may be facing an even greater challenge, given the athletes they often have.

As scandals become common among professional athletes, more teams are offering player development programs to protect their multimillion-dollar investments. For instance, the National Basketball Association has a rookie seminar on potential temptations like groupies, gambling, and drugs. Similarly, major league baseball offers a course to players coming into the big leagues. However, the Texas Rangers baseball club has taken both of those ideas quite a bit further, to help players enjoy their playing days while avoiding trouble. Unfortunately for these young men, trouble is easy to find. Consider: Holly Jenkins, in a recent encounter with one of the

Rangers' young players in his hotel room, laughs and cuddles but suddenly turns angry and storms out of the room. Later, she returns with the police and yells, "That's the one that hit me and offered drugs for sex."

Ms. Jenkins and the police are actors, part of a staged encounter designed to teach the Rangers' youngest ballplayers how to avoid off-the-field trouble that can ruin their major league careers. The Texas Rangers' "Career Development Program" uses role playing, lectures, and guest speakers and covers everything from AIDS to etiquette in six days before spring training. The ball club feels the development is necessary,

unless he throws a game. Another useful development tip for young players is to teach them to drop their beer bottles—and avoid a potentially deadly weapons charge—if accosted in a bar by a drunk who wants to fight a baseball star.

Many young players just a year or two out of high school have little background in the etiquette they will need for banquets and Rotary Club luncheons. As one young prospect notes, "I've never had a meal that required more than one fork." The team stages an actual banquet for the players to test their new development skills, reminding them, "You are not eating, you are dining."

*Development continues throughout everyone's career, but as with these ballplayers, it is not necessarily always easy.*

because as the Rangers' Director of Player Development notes, "These players don't understand what they're getting into."

Some of the development exercises force the young athletes to face very difficult situations—such as conflict between Latino and white players engaged in a name-calling episode. Another role-playing situation forces a player to deal with a mobster who threatens to kill the player's girlfriend

The Rangers' players have evaluated the development program highly —if nothing else, it gets across to *most* players accustomed to scratching and spitting in public that they are judged on how they look, speak, and eat.[1] Development continues throughout everyone's career, but as with these ballplayers, it is not necessarily always easy.

*❝Nothing is more important than growing your "A" players and promptly dealing with your "C" players.❞*

RICHARD BROWN

When organizational strategies seem to involve endless reorganization and downsizing, it is difficult to know what a career is, much less how to develop one. Further, why worry about career "development" for employees when some suggest there will be fewer promotion opportunities in the future? These views are extreme, but three factors do appear to have changed recently regarding employee development:

- The middle-management ladder upward in organizations has been altered—and to some extent replaced—by computers.
- Many firms have sharpened their focus on core competencies, reducing the need for certain types of managers.
- Project-based work is growing, making careers a series of projects, not steps upward in a given organization.

Traditionally, development efforts have targeted managerial personnel. Their development has looked beyond the current job, helping to prepare them for a variety of future jobs in the company. But development for all employees is important for organizations to have the needed human resource capabilities for future growth and change.

Development is different from training, in that it is often the result of experience and the maturity that comes with it. It is possible to train most people to run a postage meter, drive a truck, operate a computer, or assemble a radio. However, development in such areas as judgment, responsibility, decision making, and communications is much more difficult, because such factors may or may not develop over time, either through life experiences or as part of a planned program. While managers may need a variety of experiences to enhance their development, a planned system of development experiences for all employees can help expand the overall level of capabilities in an organization. Figure 11–1 profiles development and contrasts it with training.

# HR Development Today

**Development**

Efforts to improve employees' ability to handle a variety of assignments.

**Development** can be thought of as growing capabilities that go beyond those required by the current job; it represents efforts to improve employees' ability to handle a variety of assignments. Development is beneficial to both the organization and the individuals. Employees and managers with appropriate experiences and abilities enhance the ability of an organization to compete and adapt to a changing competitive environment. In the development process, the individuals' careers also gain focus and evolve.

At the organizational level of analysis, executives responsible for crafting the broader organizational strategies should establish a system for developing the people who will manage and achieve those identified strategies. The successful CEO is likely to have employee and managerial succession plans on several levels and in several different succession pathways as part of that development.[2]

Specific development needs can be identified by HR planning. Currently, more jobs are taking on the characteristics of *knowledge work*. People in such jobs must

**FIGURE 11-1** *Development versus Training*

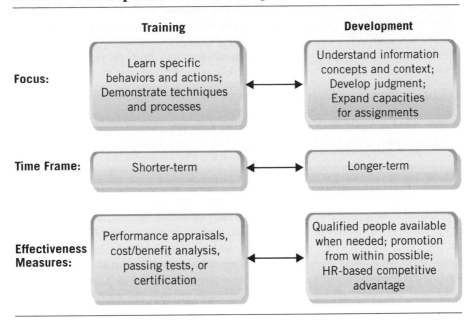

|  | **Training** | | **Development** |
|---|---|---|---|
| **Focus:** | Learn specific behaviors and actions; Demonstrate techniques and processes | ◄──► | Understand information concepts and context; Develop judgment; Expand capacities for assignments |
| **Time Frame:** | Shorter-term | ◄──► | Longer-term |
| **Effectiveness Measures:** | Performance appraisals, cost/benefit analysis, passing tests, or certification | ◄──► | Qualified people available when needed; promotion from within possible; HR-based competitive advantage |

combine mastery of technical expertise with the ability to work in teams with other employees, form relationships with customers, and analyze their own practices. The practice of management increasingly involves guiding and integrating autonomous, highly skilled people.

## Changes in Career Development

As discussed in Chapter 3, merger and acquisition activities, and layoffs for other reasons, have changed the way people and organizations look at careers and development. The "new career" is one in which the individual—not the organization—manages his or her own development.[3] Such self-development consists of the person's educational experiences, training, organizational experiences, projects, and even changes in occupational fields. Under this system, the individual's definition of success is a personal definition, not necessarily the organizational view.

Many organizations have promoted this "self-reliance" as the basis for development, telling employees to focus on creating employability for themselves in the uncertain future.[4] However, employability must be defined in such a way that it has value for the employing organization. To connect employability with organizational strategies, the work to be done must be identified. Then current capabilities of the workforce must be inventoried, paying special attention to the missing necessary capabilities. However, in a dilemma of sorts, employers express concern about giving employees unrestricted access to development opportunities, for fear of not being able to retain talent in some of today's highly competitive labor markets.[5]

Indeed, in fast-paced Silicon Valley, changing companies every year or two is more the norm than the exception. Valued employees are deluged with job offers, and they change jobs at a rate of almost twice the national average.[6] Workers are more loyal to their careers and technologies than to a company. The understandable effect is a hesitancy by Silicon Valley employers to pay for expensive development, only to see the recipients leave and take their newly developed capabilities elsewhere.[7] Not all industries experience these problems of the high-technology industries, but many firms have similar concerns to varying degrees. Developing human resources in an organization can help provide a sustained competitive advantage as long as three basic requirements are met:

- The developed workforce produces more positive economic benefit for the organization than an undeveloped workforce.
- The abilities of the workforce provide an advantage over competitors.
- Those abilities are not easily duplicated by a competitor.

To some extent, employers face a "make or buy" choice: Develop competitive human resources, or "buy" them already developed from somewhere else. Current trends indicate that technical and professional people usually are hired based on the amount of skill development they have already achieved, rather than on their ability to learn or their behavioral traits. Thus, there is an apparent preference to buy rather than "make" scarce employees in today's labor market. However, buying rather than developing human resource capacities does not contribute to the three basic requirements for sustained competitive advantage through human resources.

## Developing Capabilities

Exactly what kind of development a given individual might need to expand his or her capabilities depends on both the person and the capabilities needed. However, the following are some important and common management capabilities to be developed:[8]

- Action orientation
- Quality decisions
- Ethical values
- Technical skills

Equally important but much less commonly developed capabilities for successful managers are team building, developing subordinates, directing others, and dealing with uncertainty.

Developing capabilities requires assessing a person's current capabilities, communicating that assessment to the person, and planning experiences or education to meet the development goals. When organizations take sole responsibility for developing capabilities, research shows that older, longer-service employees, lower-level employees, women, and less-educated employees receive less development than do managers.[9]

As noted earlier, when individuals take responsibility for their own development, they are guided by their development needs as they see and define them. The HR Perspective discusses how a growing number of physicians are taking steps for their own development.

## Lifelong Learning

Learning and development do not occur only once during a person's lifetime; lifelong learning and development are much more likely. To professionals, lifelong learning may mean continuing education requirements to keep certified. For example, lawyers, CPAs, teachers, and dentists have continuing education

# Developing Physicians

When one thinks of professional development for medical doctors, what comes to mind is high-technology diagnostic machinery, or seminars on new treatments, medications, and research discoveries. But the world has changed; some physicians are now pursuing MBA degrees. They travel from as far as Boston, Miami, and Louisiana, flying in late on Thursdays to attend weekend classes at the University of California in Irvine.

Many physicians once sneered at having to know how to use computers and manipulate spreadsheet software, because being a doctor brought all the rewards they needed: big incomes, social status, and a heroic image with patients. But with the advent of managed care, many

physicians are watching helplessly as their incomes lag and their autonomy fades.

These physician students are very bright and motivated but they are not so familiar with team building, innovation, or budgeting. In the typical MBA classroom, content, teaching methods, and other facets are different than they were at med school; memorization and cutthroat competition that were helpful in medical schools are not as appropriate in business. These physician students are learning that they need a different set of competencies to succeed.

However, as the physicians take MBA courses, many doctors begin developing new knowledge, skills, and abilities. Then their biggest challenge is deciding what to do

when they get their MBA degrees. Some physicians continue to practice medicine but use their new business knowledge to manage their investment portfolios; others go to work for one of the large managed care companies. Still others organize smaller physician practices into networks to compete with managed care firms.

Some physicians even become entrepreneurs and start companies in medical related fields. One individual notes: "When I was a doctor, if a managed care company started telling me what to do, my first reaction was: Don't you know who I am? I've published papers, I've done a fellowship! How can you do this to me? Now I realize medicine is like any service."[10]

requirements in most states to keep their licenses to practice. For semi-skilled employees, learning and development may involve training to expand existing skills and prepare for different jobs or promotions.

Employers may help with some of the lifelong development that is necessary, typically done through programs at work or by paying for tuition reimbursement under specified circumstances. However, much of lifelong learning is voluntary, taking place outside the job or work hours. The learning may have no immediate relevance to a person's current job, but might enhance confidence, ideas, or enthusiasm. Of course, much valuable development occurs outside formal coursework as well.

## The HR Development Process

Development should begin with the HR plans of an organization. As discussed in Chapter 2, such plans deal with analyzing, forecasting, and identifying the organizational needs for human resources. Also, HR planning allows anticipating the movement of people through the organization due to retirement, promotion, and transfers. It helps identify the capabilities that will be needed by the organization in the future and the development necessary to have people with those abilities on hand when needed.

Figure 11–2 illustrates the HR development process. As the figure shows, HR plans first identify necessary abilities and capacities. Such capacities can influ-

**FIGURE 11-2** *The HR Development Process in an Organization*

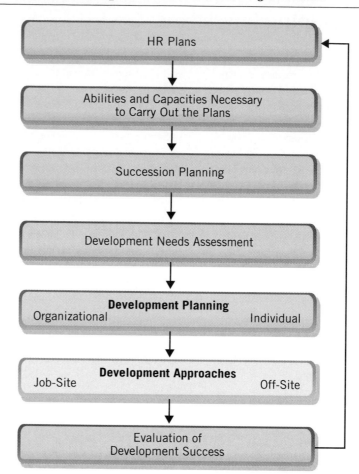

ence planning in return. The specific abilities needed also influence decisions about who will be promoted, and what the succession of leaders will be in the organization. Those decisions influence—and are influenced by—an assessment of the development needs in the organization. Two categories of development planning follow from this needs assessment: organizational and individual. Finally, the success of the developmental process must be evaluated and changes made as necessary over time.

HR planning for needed future abilities was described in Chapter 2. Identifying development needs and succession planning are described next.

# Development Needs Analysis and Succession Planning

Much as with training, employee development must begin with analyses of the needs of both the organization and individuals. There is evidence that this analysis of an individual's development needs is often not given enough attention.

## Development Needs Analysis

Either the company or the individual can analyze what a given person needs by way of development. The goal, of course, is to identify strengths and weaknesses. Methods used by organizations to assess development needs include assessment centers, psychological testing, and performance appraisals.

**ASSESSMENT CENTERS** **Assessment centers** are not places as much as they are collections of instruments and exercises designed to diagnose a person's development needs. They are used both for developing and for selecting managers. Police departments, as well as many other types of large organizations, use assessment centers.

In a typical assessment-center experience, a potential manager spends two or three days away from the job, performing many activities. These activities may include role playing, pencil-and-paper tests, cases, leaderless group discussions, management games, peer evaluations, and in-basket exercises, in which the trainee handles typical problems coming across a manager's desk. For the most part, the exercises are samples of managerial situations that require the use of managerial skills and behaviors. During the exercises, participants are observed by several specially trained judges. Assessment centers are seen as an excellent means for determining management potential. These centers are praised because they are thought to overcome the biases inherent in interview situations, supervisor ratings, and written tests. Experience has shown that such key variables as leadership, initiative, and supervisory skills are almost impossible to measure with paper-and-pencil tests alone. Another advantage of assessment centers is that they help identify employees with potential in large organizations. Supervisors may nominate people for the assessment center, or employees may volunteer. The opportunity to volunteer is especially valuable for talented people whose supervisors may not recognize their abilities

Assessment centers also can raise problems. Some managers may use the assessment center as a way to avoid difficult promotion decisions. Suppose a plant supervisor has personally decided that an employee is not a qualified candidate for promotion. Rather than stick by the decision and tell the employee, the supervisor may send the employee to the assessment center, hoping that the report will show that the employee is not qualified for promotion. Problems between the employee and the supervisor will be worse if the employee earns a positive report. If the report is negative, the supervisor's views are validated. Using the assessment center in this way is not recommended, because it does not aid the development of the employee.[11]

**PSYCHOLOGICAL TESTING** Psychological pencil-and-paper tests have been used for several years to determine employees' developmental potential and needs. Intelligence tests, verbal and mathematical reasoning tests, and personality tests are often used. Such testing can furnish useful information to employers about such factors as motivation, reasoning abilities, leadership styles, interpersonal response traits, and job preferences.

The biggest problem with psychological testing lies in interpretation, because untrained managers, supervisors, and workers usually cannot accurately interpret test results. After a professional reports a test taker's scores to someone in the organization, the interpretation often is left to untrained managers, who may attach their own meanings to the results. It also should be recognized that some

**Assessment center**
A collection of instruments and exercises designed to diagnose a person's development needs.

**LOGGING ON . . .**
**Succession Planning**
This firm specializes in compensation and succession planning for organizations. Check out this website for more information and some statistics regarding succession.

**http://www.mpiweb.com/ index.html**

psychological tests are of limited validity, and test takers can easily fake desirable responses. Thus, psychological testing is appropriate only when the testing and feedback process is closely supervised by a qualified professional throughout.

**PERFORMANCE APPRAISALS** Well-done performance appraisals can be a source of development information. Performance data on productivity, employee relations, job knowledge, and other relevant dimensions can be measured this way. As noted in Chapter 12, appraisals that are designed for development purposes may be more useful than appraisals designed strictly for administrative purposes.

## Succession Planning

Succession planning can be an important part of development. For example, combined with skills training, management development, and promotion from within, it has been linked to "turning around" a plant acquired by another company. The general result for the plant was a large increase in capacity over four years, with virtually no infusion of new managers or employees. Existing talent was developed instead.

**SUCCESSION IN SMALL AND CLOSELY HELD ORGANIZATIONS** Succession planning can be especially important in small- and medium-sized firms, but studies show that these firms have done the least planning. Few small- and medium-sized firms have formal succession plans.[12]

In closely-held family firms (those that are not publicly traded on stock exchanges), many CEOs plan to pass the business on to a family member. Planning in advance for the orderly succession and development needs of the successor is important to avoid a host of potential problems.[13]

**BNA**
**1023.10.30.50**
**Promotion Decisions**
Review the factors affecting promotions of individuals to implement succession plans and develop a checklist for making a promotion decision.

**REPLACEMENT CHARTS** Traditional career paths in a company include a range of possible moves: lateral moves across departments, vertical moves within departments, and others. Each possible path represents actual positions, the experience needed to fill the positions, and the relationships of positions to each other. Replacement charts (similar to depth charts used by football teams to show the backup players at each position) give a simple model of the process. The purpose of replacement charts is to ensure that the right individuals are available at the right time, and that they have had sufficient experience to handle the targeted jobs.

Replacement charts can be part of the development planning process by specifying the nature of development each employee needs to be prepared for the identified promotions. This information can be used to identify development needs and "promotion ladders" for people.

# Planning and Choosing a Development Approach

Possible development approaches are described next, under two major headings: job-site development and off-site development. Both are appropriate in developing managers and other employees. The HR Perspective discusses the variables that facilitate participation in development.

## HR PERSPECTIVE

# Research on Employee Participation in Development

Birdi, Allan, and Warr studied employee participation in development activities, and their findings were reported in the *Journal of Applied Psychology*. The researchers looked at a sample of manufacturing employees in a vehicle manufacturing firm in the United Kingdom. Each employee was asked to describe the level of participation in 13 different development activities over the past year. The major categories were: (1) required development at work, (2) voluntary development at work, and (3) voluntary development off the job.

The researchers found that more educated workers were more active in all three kinds of development activities. This finding may reflect differences in ability and learning confidence. Further, higher-level employees undertook more of all three kinds of development.

An important variable in employee participation in development activities was *management support*. Management and coworkers support can be thought of as part of a "continuous learning culture" that encourages extensive participation in development activities of all kinds. The continuous learning culture involves social pressure, personal responsibility for learning, and assigning difficult job tasks. This support also includes the use of authority by management to ensure that subordinates attend development activities.

The research study also found that job satisfaction was higher in those employees who took part in more development activities. These employees also had higher organizational commitment. However, learning on one's own time was found to be completely *unrelated* to either job satisfaction or commitment, which suggests that individuals' willingness to invest in their own development is not organizationally linked.[14]

When asked, "How does learning occur in your company?", a panel of senior HR executives responded with a mix of methods occurring both on-site and off-premises. Figure 11–3 on the next page shows the specifics, but generally on-the-job methods and off-site methods are used similarly.

Investing in human intellectual capital, whether at work or off the job, seems to be a *requirement* of the "knowledge work" that is becoming more important for almost all employers. Yet identifying exactly the right mix and approaches for development needs remains an art rather than a science.[15]

## Development Approaches: Job-Site Methods

A number of job-site development methods are available. A major difficulty with development that takes place on the job site is that too often, unplanned activities are regarded as development. It is imperative that managers plan and coordinate development efforts so that the desired development actually occurs.

**COACHING** The oldest on-the-job development technique is **coaching,** which is the daily training and feedback given to employees by immediate supervisors. Coaching involves a continual process of learning by doing. For effective coaching, a healthy and open relationship must exist between employees and their supervisors or managers. Many firms conduct formal training courses to improve the coaching skills of their managers.

Unfortunately, like other on-the-job methods, coaching can be temptingly easy to implement without any planning at all. Even if someone has been good at a job or a particular part of a job, there is no guarantee that he or she will be

**Coaching**
Daily training and feedback given to employees by immediate supervisors.

**FIGURE 11–3** *How Development Occurs in Organizations*

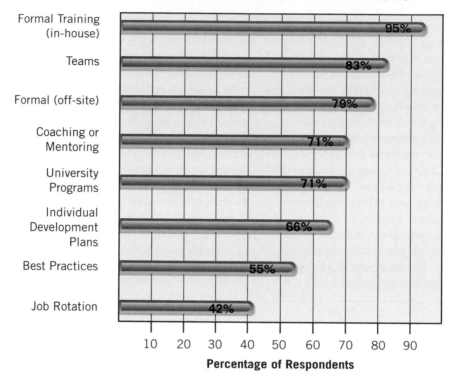

**Results of American Society of Training Directors Executive Survey, asking "How does learning occur in your company?"**

Formal Training (in-house) — 95%
Teams — 83%
Formal (off-site) — 79%
Coaching or Mentoring — 71%
University Programs — 71%
Individual Development Plans — 66%
Best Practices — 55%
Job Rotation — 42%

**Percentage of Respondents**

SOURCE: George Benson, "Battle of the Buzzwords," *Training & Development*, July 1997, 51. ©*Training & Development*, American Society for Training and Development. Reprinted with permission. All rights reserved.

able to coach someone else to do it well—but that assumption is often made. It is easy for the "coach" to fall short in guiding the learner systematically, even if he or she knows which systematic experiences are best. Sometimes, too, doing a full day's work gets priority over learning and coaching. Also, many skills have an intellectual component that might be better learned from a book or lecture before coaching occurs. Sometimes "executive" coaches are hired either by the individual executives or by employers to work with executives who are having problems of one sort or another. Outside coaches are paid well for observing behavior and providing critiques and advice to the individuals.[16]

**COMMITTEE ASSIGNMENTS** Assigning promising employees to important committees can give these employees a broadening experience and can help them to understand the personalities, issues, and processes governing the organization. For instance, assigning employees to a safety committee may give them the safety background they need to become supervisors. Also, they may experience the problems involved in maintaining employee safety awareness. But managers should be aware that it is possible for committee assignments to become time-wasting activities, too.

**JOB ROTATION Job rotation** is the process of shifting an employee from job to job. In some organizations, job rotation is unplanned; other organizations have elaborate charts and schedules, precisely planning the program for each employee.

Job rotation is widely used as a development technique. For example, a promising young manager may spend three months in the plant, three months in corporate planning, and three months in purchasing. When properly handled, such job rotation fosters a greater understanding of the organization. At one large firm, job rotation is used during a 15-month sales training program. Trainees work in at least three areas, such as industrial sales, retail sales, and product training.

Especially when opportunities for promotion are scarce, job rotation through lateral transfers may be beneficial in rekindling enthusiasm and developing new talents. The best lateral moves do one or more of the following:

- Move the person into the core business.
- Provide closer contact with the customer.
- Teach new skills or perspectives.

In spite of its benefits, managers should recognize that job rotation can be expensive. Furthermore, a substantial amount of managerial time is lost when trainees change positions, because they must become acquainted with different people and techniques in each new unit.

**"ASSISTANT-TO" POSITIONS** An "assistant-to" position is a staff position immediately under a manager. Through such jobs, trainees can work with outstanding managers they might not otherwise have met. Some organizations have "junior boards of directors" or "management cabinets" to which trainees may be appointed. Assignments such as these are useful if trainees have the opportunity to deal with challenging or interesting assignments.

## Development Approaches: Off-Site Methods

Off-the-job-site development techniques can be effective because they give the individual an opportunity to get away from the job and concentrate solely on what is to be learned. Moreover, meeting with other people who are concerned with somewhat different problems and come from different organizations may provide an employee with new perspectives on old problems. Various off-site methods are used.

**CLASSROOM COURSES AND DEGREES** Many off-the-job development programs include some classroom instruction. The advantage of classroom training is that it is widely accepted because most people are familar with it. But a disadvantage of classroom instruction is the lecture system, which encourages passive listening and reduced learner participation. Sometimes trainees have little opportunity to question, clarify, and discuss the lecture material. The effectiveness of classroom instruction depends on the group size, ability, instructor, and subject matter.[17]

Organizations often send employees to externally sponsored seminars or professional courses. These programs are offered by many colleges and universities and by professional associations such as the American Management Association. Some larger organizations have established training centers exclusively for their own employees.

**Job rotation**
The process of shifting an employee from job to job.

*LOGGING ON . . .*
**Development Sources**
Information on management development sources is available at this website.

**http://www.tregistry.com/ama.htm**

Many organizations encourage continuing education by paying for employees to take college courses. A very high proportion of organizations reimburses employees for school tuition. Some employers encourage employees to study for advanced degrees such as MBAs in this manner. Employees often earn these degrees at night after their regular workdays end.

**HUMAN RELATIONS TRAINING** Human relations training originated with the well-known Hawthorne studies. Initially, the purpose of the training was to prepare supervisors for "people problems" brought to them by their employees. This type of training focuses on the development of the human relations skills a person needs to work well with others. Many human relations training programs are aimed at new or relatively inexperienced first-line supervisors and middle managers. Human relations programs typically have sessions on motivation, leadership, employee communication, and humanizing the workplace.

The problem with such programs is the difficulty in measuring their effectiveness. The development of human relations skills is a long-range goal; tangible results are hard to identify over the span of several years. Consequently, such programs often are measured only by participants' reactions to them. As mentioned in Chapter 10, reaction-level measurement is the weakest form of evaluating the effectiveness of training.

Figure 11–4 shows some of the reasons managers are most likely to fail after being promoted to management. The most common reason—poor teamwork with subordinates and peers—is a human relations issue.

**CASE STUDIES** The case study is a classroom-oriented development technique that has been widely used. Cases provide a medium through which trainees can study the application of management or behavioral concepts. The emphasis is on application and analysis, not mere memorization of concepts.

One common complaint is that cases sometimes are not sufficiently realistic to be useful. Also, cases may contain information inappropriate to the kinds of decisions that trainees would make in a real situation. This also can be one of the values of case studies, though, if the focus is to test whether students can select appropriate information.

**Role playing**
A development technique requiring the trainee to assume a role in a given situation and act out behaviors associated with that role.

**ROLE PLAYING** **Role playing** is a development technique requiring the trainee to assume a role in a given situation and act out behaviors associated with that role. Participants gain an appreciation of the many behavioral factors influencing on-the-job situations. For instance, a labor relations director may be asked to play the role of a union vice-president in a negotiating situation in order to give the director insight into the constraints and problems facing union bargaining representatives. Role playing is a useful tool in some situations, but a word of caution applies. Trainees are often uncomfortable in role-playing situations, and trainers must introduce the situations well so that learning can occur.

**Simulation**
A development technique that requires participants to analyze a situation and decide the best course of action based on the data given.

**SIMULATIONS (BUSINESS GAMES)** Several business games, or simulations, are available commercially. A **simulation** requires participants to analyze a situation and decide the best course of action based on the data given. Some are computer-interactive games in which individuals or teams draw up a set of marketing plans for an organization to determine such factors as the amount of re-

**FIGURE 11–4** *Reasons New Managers Fail after Being Promoted*

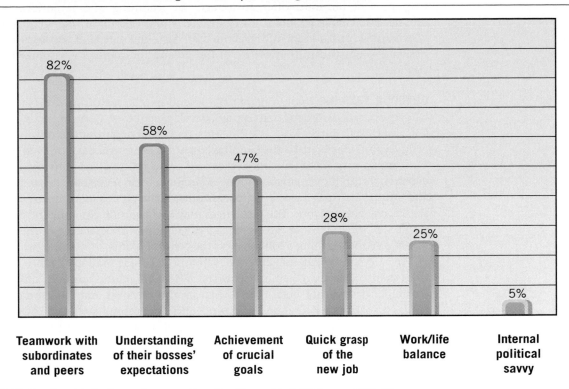

SOURCE: Based on data in *Human Resources Executive*, "Doomed to Fail," January 1998, 82.

sources to allocate for advertising, product design, selling, and sales effort. The participants make a variety of decisions, and then the computer tells them how well they did in relation to competing individuals or teams. Simulations have been used to diagnose organizational problems as well.

When properly done, a simulation can be a useful management development tool. However, simulation receives the same criticism as role playing. Realism is sometimes lacking, so the learning experience is diminished. Learning must be the focus, not just "playing the game."

**SABBATICALS AND LEAVES OF ABSENCE**  A **sabbatical leave** is paid time off the job to develop and rejuvenate oneself. Popular for many years in the academic world, where professors take a leave to sharpen their skills and advance their education or conduct research, sabbaticals have been adopted in the business community as well. More than 10% of U.S. corporations offer sabbaticals.[18] For example, Xerox Corporation gives some of its employees six months or more off with pay to work on "socially desirable" projects. Projects include training people in urban ghettos and providing technical assistance to overseas countries. Sabbaticals are often spent in some form of corporate volunteer program, and they are most commonly given to executives in high-technology businesses with around-the-clock projects. They also are becoming popular in other countries, including the United Kingdom.

**Sabbatical leave**
Paid time off the job to develop and rejuvenate oneself.

Companies offering sabbaticals speak well of the results. They say sabbaticals help prevent burnout, offer advantages in recruiting and retention, boost morale, and enable people to carry heavier workloads upon their return. One disadvantage of paid sabbaticals is the cost. Also, the nature of the learning experience is not within the control of the organization and is left somewhat to chance.[19]

**OUTDOOR TRAINING** Many organizations send executives off to ordeals in the wilderness, called outdoor training, as a development tool. General Foods, Xerox, GE, Honeywell, Burger King, AMEX, Sears, and other organizations have sent executives and managers to the outdoors for stays of several days or even weeks. The rationale for these wilderness excursions is as follows: For individuals, such experiences can increase self-confidence and help them reevaluate personal goals and efforts. For work units, a shared risk outside the office environment can create a sense of teamwork. The challenges may include rock climbing in the California desert, whitewater rafting on the Rogue River, backpacking in the Rocky Mountains, or handling a longboat off the coast of Maine.

The survival-type management development course may have more impact than many other management seminars. There are perils, however, and some participants have not been able to handle the physical and emotional challenges associated with rappeling down a cliff or climbing a 40-foot tower. The decision whether to sponsor such programs should depend on the personalities of the employees who will be involved. Figure 11–5 summarizes the major advantages and disadvantages of the various on-site and off-site approaches to development.

# Management Development

Development is important for all employees, but especially so for managers. Unless managers are appropriately developed, resources (including employees) throughout the organization may not be managed well. Management development should be seen as a way of imparting the knowledge and judgment needed by managers to meet the strategic objectives of the organization. Among these skills are leading, dealing with change, coaching and advising subordinates, controlling operations, and providing feedback.

Some of the discussion earlier in this chapter might lead one to believe that management—especially middle management—is no longer important or even much in evidence today. That is not true; middle management is reduced, but it is *not* gone. There are now 11.17 managers per 100 employees, compared with 11.83 per 100 in 1990. The "massive delayering" portrayed in the popular press is creating some opportunities for managers where they did not exist before.[20] For example, technologies that replace workers need managers to oversee them. More complex white-collar work may actually require *more* managers in some cases. The increasing need for managers to deal with customers rather than just supervise employees makes management both more similar to marketing and more necessary than before. Finally, with responsibility being moved lower in the organization, more people at lower levels are getting management responsibility.

*Experience* is an important part of management development. Indeed, experience often contributes more to the development of senior managers than class-

**FIGURE 11–5** *Advantages and Disadvantages of Major Development Approaches*

| Job-Site Methods | Advantage | Disadvantage |
|---|---|---|
| ● Coaching | Natural and job-related | Difficulty in finding good coaches |
| ● Committee Assignments | Participants are involved in critical processes | Can be time waster |
| ● Job Rotation | Gives excellent overview of the organization | Long start-up time |
| ● "Assistant-to" Positions | Provides exposure to an excellent manager | Possible shortage of good assignments |

| Off-Site Methods | Advantage | Disadvantage |
|---|---|---|
| ● Classroom Courses and Degrees | Familiar, accepted, status | Does not always improve performance |
| ● Human Relations Training | Deals with important management skills | Difficult to measure effectiveness |
| ● Case Studies | Practical; those involved can learn from real management | Information may be inadequate for some decision makers |
| ● Role Playing | May lead to attitude change in difficult interpersonal situations | Trainees may be uncomfortable |
| ● Simulations | Realism and integration | Inappropriate "game playing" |
| ● Sabbaticals | Rejuvenating as well as developmental | Expensive; employees may lose contact with job |
| ● Outdoor Training | Physical challenges can increase self-confidence and teamwork | Not appropriate for all because of physical nature; dangerous |

room training does, because much of that experience occurs in varying circumstances on the job over time. A recent survey by the American Management Association of 4,585 managers and executives concluded that only about one-third of current managers arrived at their current positions by moving up in the same department with the same employer.[21] Experience with varied circumstances and situations contributes to management development, and makes a manager more valuable.

Yet, despite a need for good managers, both middle- and executive-level managers are hard to find. At the middle level, many people are refusing to take management jobs. "You're a backstop, caught in the middle between upper management and the workforce," a cost account manager (who quit management) noted. "I was told 50 hours a week was not enough and that I had to work my people harder. . . . The few dollars more were not worth the pain."[22]

Similarly, few companies seem to take the time to develop their own executive managers anymore. Thirty-five years ago, only 9% of CEOs came from outside a company. Today, nearly a third of the top 1,000 public companies are headed by outsiders, and the number is growing.[23]

Figure 11–6 on the next page shows some lessons and features important in effectively developing both middle- and upper-level managers. Next, the most widely used management development methods are examined individually.

**FIGURE 11–6** *Managerial Lessons and Job Experience*

### INFLUENTIAL EXPERIENCES FOR MANAGERS

| Job Transitions | Task Characteristics | Obstacles |
|---|---|---|
| Being forced to deal with entirely new jobs, problems, people, responsibilities, etc. | Starting or changing some major factor, carrying heavy responsibility, needing to influence others without formal authority | Bad job situation, difficult boss, difficult clients, unsupportive peers, negative economic circumstances, etc. |

**Necessary Lessons To Be Learned**

- **Setting Agendas:** Developing technical/business knowledge, taking responsibility, setting direction

- **Handling Relationships:** Dealing successfully with people

- **Management Values:** Understanding underlying principles that guide successful management behavior

- **Personality Qualities:** Having the temperament necessary to deal with the chaos and ambiguity of executive life

- **Self-Awareness:** Having the ability to understand oneself and how one affects others

## Managerial Modeling

A common adage in management development says that managers tend to manage as they were managed. Another way of saying this is that managers learn by *behavior modeling,* or copying someone else's behavior. This is not surprising, because a great deal of human behavior is learned by modeling. Children learn by modeling the behaviors of parents and older children, which means they are familiar with the process by the time they grow up. Management development efforts can take advantage of natural human behavior by matching young or developing managers with appropriate models and then reinforcing the desirable behaviors exhibited.

It is important to note that modeling is not a straightforward imitation, or copying, process; it is considerably more complex. For example, one can learn what *not* to do by observing a model. Thus, exposure to both positive and negative models can be beneficial to a new manager.

## Management Coaching

Coaching combines observations with suggestions. Like modeling, it is a very natural way for humans to learn. In the context of management development, coaching is best accomplished when it involves a relationship between two

**LOGGING ON . . .**
**Coaching**
This website provides information on a firm specializing in coaching techniques and describes its approach to coaching.

http://www.refocusinc.com/
services.htm#coaching

managers for a period of time as they perform their jobs. Coaching has many applications. It has found some success in solving behavioral problems that threaten to derail managers; abrasive or inflexible managers may benefit from coaching by the right executive. Coaching does not have to be oriented toward aberrant behavior, however; just sharing with another experienced manager how a problem might be approached is coaching, too.

Effective coaching requires patience and good communication skills. A brief outline of good coaching pointers would include:

- Explaining appropriate behavior
- Making clear why actions were taken
- Accurately stating observations
- Providing possible alternatives/suggestions
- Following up/reinforcing

## Mentoring

**Mentoring** is a relationship in which managers at the midpoints in their careers aid individuals in the earlier stages of their careers. Technical, interpersonal, and political skills can be conveyed in such a relationship from the older to the younger person. Not only does the younger one benefit, but the older one may enjoy the challenge of sharing his or her wisdom. The four stages in most successful mentoring relationships are shown in Figure 11–7.

**Mentoring**
A relationship in which managers at midpoints in their careers aid individuals in the earlier stages of their careers.

**FIGURE 11–7** *Stages in Mentoring Relationships*

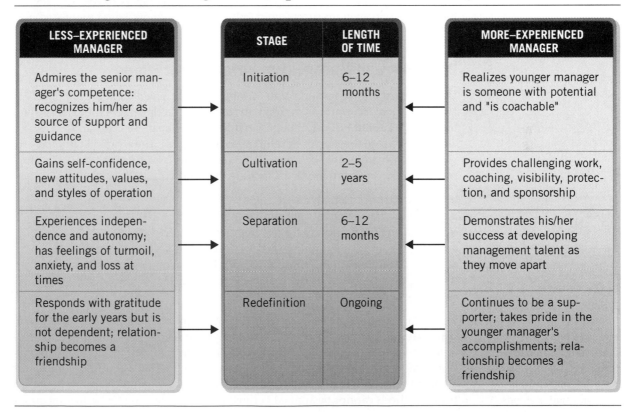

| LESS–EXPERIENCED MANAGER | STAGE | LENGTH OF TIME | MORE–EXPERIENCED MANAGER |
|---|---|---|---|
| Admires the senior manager's competence: recognizes him/her as source of support and guidance | Initiation | 6–12 months | Realizes younger manager is someone with potential and "is coachable" |
| Gains self-confidence, new attitudes, values, and styles of operation | Cultivation | 2–5 years | Provides challenging work, coaching, visibility, protection, and sponsorship |
| Experiences independence and autonomy; has feelings of turmoil, anxiety, and loss at times | Separation | 6–12 months | Demonstrates his/her success at developing management talent as they move apart |
| Responds with gratitude for the early years but is not dependent; relationship becomes a friendship | Redefinition | Ongoing | Continues to be a supporter; takes pride in the younger manager's accomplishments; relationship becomes a friendship |

**WOMEN AND MENTORING** In virtually all countries in the world, the proportion of women holding management jobs is lower than the proportion of men holding such jobs. As mentioned in Chapter 6, the term *glass ceiling* has been used to describe the situation in which women fail to progress into top management positions. One approach to countering the glass ceiling that has been found to be useful is mentoring. For example, in some firms women with mentors have been able to move up more often than those without mentors. But, the extent of mentoring of women and its long-term effects have not been studied extensively; most of the literature on women and mentoring is based on narratives from individuals.

Based on various narratives, successful women executives have suggested that breaking the glass ceiling requires developing political sophistication, building credibility, refining a management style, and shouldering responsibilities. For example, Coopers & Lybrand LLP has a group of employees called C & L 100, made up of women and minority employees with a good chance of making partner some day. The employees are matched with senior partners as mentors who are accountable for their progress. The accounting firm hopes to boost its proportion of protected-class senior partners from 10% to 30% with such programs.[24]

**PROBLEMS WITH MENTORING** Mentoring is not without its problems. Young minority managers report difficulty finding older white mentors. Also, men have been found to be less willing than women to be mentors. Further, mentors who are dissatisfied with their jobs and those who teach a narrow or distorted view of events may not help a young manager's development.[25] However, most managers have a series of advisors or mentors during their careers, and they may find advantages in learning from the different mentors. For example, the experience of having many mentors may help less experienced managers to identify key behaviors in management success and failure. Further, those being mentored may find that their previous mentors are useful sources for networking.[26]

## Problems with Management Development Efforts

Development efforts are subject to certain common mistakes and problems. The HR Perspective illustrates a development problem that Japan is experiencing with managers as a result of the changing nature of the Japanese economy.

Most of the management development problems in the United States have resulted from inadequate HR planning and a lack of coordination of HR development efforts. Common problems include the following:

- Inadequate needs analysis
- Trying out fad programs or training methods
- Abdicating responsibility for development to staff
- Trying to substitute training for selection
- Lack of training among those who lead the development activities
- Using only "courses" as the road to development
- Encapsulated development

**Encapsulated development**

Situation in which an individual learns new methods and ideas in a development course and returns to a work unit that is still bound by old attitudes and methods.

The last item on the list may require some additional explanation. **Encapsulated development** occurs when an individual learns new methods and ideas in a development course and returns to a work unit that is still bound by old attitudes and methods. The reward system and the working conditions have not changed. Although the trainee has learned new ways to handle certain situations, these methods cannot be applied because of resistance from those having an in-

# Management Development Problems in Japan

Japan has been introduced to the hazards of corporate downsizing, which has had an impact on the ranks of Japanese managers. Several habits of Japanese firms have combined to point out the need for changes in management development efforts.

When labor was cheap, it was easy to promise a young "salaryman" a lifetime job. But as the economy matured, those lifetime promises became a liability. Early in their careers, many Japanese managers were rotated through many jobs and locations. Consequently, they did not develop much specialized expertise, but became

generalists with a one-company career. These salarymen invested in the skills they needed for that company (that is, office politics rather than marketing or corporate finance). The result has been called a "battalion of generalists," most of whom are middle managers untrained for anything specific except being a good employee.

But now the promise of a lifelong career with one employer rings hollow in Japan. As in the United States, in Japan young managers must acquire the skills that make them marketable, yet the company that spends money developing those skills may lose the rising young

manager to another firm. A related issue is what to do with all those less mobile and less competent middle-aged managers with only general, company-specific knowledge and skills.

In summary, Japan's system of job rotation and company-specific development provided some advantages in years past. Unfortunately, it seems to be inappropriate in a world where capital is being substituted for labor and uncertainty reigns. Perhaps innovative Japanese firms will find a way to combine the best of both systems and show the world a new model that works better than either of the old models.[27]

vestment in the status quo. The new knowledge remains encapsulated in the classroom setting. Encapsulated development is an obvious waste of time and money. For example, in some organizations, diversity training efforts have been wasted because follow-up and reinforcement were not done and the development was encapsulated as "classroom theory," not reality.

# Careers

A **career** is the sequence of work-related positions a person occupies throughout life. People pursue careers to satisfy deeply individual needs. At one time, identifying with one employer seemed to fulfill many of those needs. Now, the distinction between the individual's career as the organization sees it and the career as the individual sees it is very important.

**Career**
The sequence of work-related positions a person occupies throughout life.

## Organization-Centered vs. Individual-Centered Career Planning

Career planning can be somewhat confusing, because two different perspectives exist. Career planning can be organization centered, individual centered, or both.

**Organization-centered career planning** focuses on jobs and on constructing career paths that provide for the logical progression of people between jobs in an organization. These paths are ones that individuals can follow to advance in certain organizational units. For example, a person might enter the sales department as a sales counselor, then be promoted to account director, to sales manager, and finally to vice-president of sales.

**Organization-centered career planning**
Career planning that focuses on jobs and on constructing career paths that provide for the logical progression of people between jobs in an organization.

**FIGURE 11–8** *Organizationl and Individual Career-Planning Perspectives*

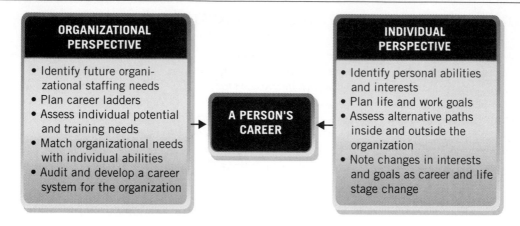

**ORGANIZATIONAL PERSPECTIVE**

- Identify future organizational staffing needs
- Plan career ladders
- Assess individual potential and training needs
- Match organizational needs with individual abilities
- Audit and develop a career system for the organization

**A PERSON'S CAREER**

**INDIVIDUAL PERSPECTIVE**

- Identify personal abilities and interests
- Plan life and work goals
- Assess alternative paths inside and outside the organization
- Note changes in interests and goals as career and life stage change

**Individual-centered career planning**

Career planning that focuses on individuals' careers rather than on organizational needs.

**Individual-centered career planning** focuses on individuals' careers rather than organizational needs. It is done by employees themselves, and individual goals and skills are the focus of the analysis. Such analyses might consider situations both inside and outside the organization that could expand a person's career.[28] Figure 11–8 shows the different perspectives.

Organizational retrenchment and downsizing have changed career plans for many people. They have found themselves in "career transition"—in other words, in need of finding other jobs.[29] Small businesses, some started by early retirees from big companies, have provided many of the new career opportunities.

## How People Choose Careers

Four general individual characteristics affect how people make career choices.

- *Interests:*  People tend to pursue careers that they believe match their interests.
- *Self-image:*  A career is an extension of a person's self-image, as well as a molder of it.
- *Personality:*  This factor includes an employee's personal orientation (for example, whether the employee is realistic, enterprising, and artistic) and personal needs (including affiliation, power, and achievement needs).
- *Social backgrounds:*  Socioeconomic status and the educational and occupation level of a person's parents are a few factors included in this category.

Less is known about how and why people choose specific organizations than about why they choose specific careers. One obvious factor is the availability of a job when the person is looking for work. The amount of information available about alternatives is an important factor as well. Beyond these issues, people seem to pick an organization on the basis of a "fit" between the climate of the organization as they perceive it and their own personal characteristics. Many factors may influence job choice, including the gender of the job informant who passed along job information.[30]

The "dream jobs" of young people ages 13 to 17 change over time, as Figure 11–9 shows. Further, people change jobs more now than ever before. A typical

American holds 8.6 jobs between ages 18 and 32, with most of the job changes occurring earlier rather than later.[31] People clearly make choices about the stops along the way in their careers, basing these stops on many different factors.

## General Career Progression

The typical career today probably will include many different positions, transitions, and organizations—more so than in the past, when employees were less mobile and organizations more stable as long-term employers. In this context, it is useful to think about general patterns in people's careers and in their lives.

Many theorists in adult development describe the first half of life as the young adult's quest for competence and a way to make a mark in the world. According to this view, happiness during this time is sought primarily through achievement and the acquisition of capabilities. The second half of life is different. Once the

**FIGURE 11–9** *"Dream" Jobs for Americans, Ages 13–17*

|  | 1970s | 1990s |
|---|---|---|
| *Boys* | Skilled worker<br>Engineer<br>Lawyer<br>Teacher<br>Athlete | Businessman<br>Computers<br>Lawyer<br>Athlete<br>The Arts |
| *Girls* | Secretary<br>Teacher<br>Nurse<br>Medical Technician<br>Veterinarian | Nurse<br>Teacher<br>Doctor<br>The Arts<br>Businesswoman |

SOURCE: "Dr. Gallup's Finger on America's Pulse," *The Economist*, September 25, 1998, 96.

**FIGURE 11–10** *General Periods in Careers*

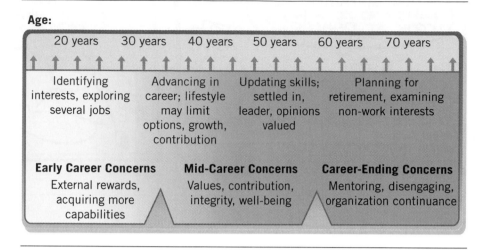

adult starts to measure time from the expected end of his or her life rather than from the beginning. The need for competence and acquisition changes to the need for integrity, values, and well-being. Internal values take precedence over external scorecards for many. In addition, mature adults already have certain skills, so their focus may shift to other interests. Career-ending concerns reflect additional shifts also. Figure 11–10 shows a model identifying general periods in a career and a lifetime.

Contained within this view is the idea that careers and lives are not predictably linear but cyclical. Periods of high stability are followed by transition, by less stability, and by inevitable discoveries, disappointments, and triumphs. Therefore, lives and careers must be viewed as cycles of structure and transition. This view may be a useful perspective for those suffering the negative results of downsizing and early career plateaus in large organizations. Such a perspective argues for the importance of flexibility in an individual's career and may encourage a willingness to acquire diverse skills.[32]

## Retirement

Whether retirement comes at age 50 or 70, it can require a major adjustment for many people. Some common emotional adjustments faced by retirees include:

- *Self-management:*  The person must adjust to being totally self-directed after retirement. There is no longer any supervisor or work agenda dictating what to do and when to do it.
- *Need to belong:*  When a person retires, he or she is no longer a member of the work group that took up so much time and formed an important social structure for so many years. What takes its place?
- *Pride in achievement:*  Achievement reinforces self-esteem and is often centered around work. In retirement, past achievements quickly wear thin as a source of self-esteem.
- *Territoriality:*  Personal "turf," in the form of office, company, and title, is lost in retirement. Other ways to satisfy territorial needs must be found.

- *Goals:* Organizations provide many of a person's goals. Some people may be unprepared to set their own goals when they retire.

Of course, from the standpoint of the organization, retirement is an orderly way to move people out at the ends of their careers. However mindful of the problems that retirement poses for some individuals, some organizations are experimenting with *phased retirement* through gradually reduced workweeks and increased vacation time. These and other preretirement and postretirement programs, aimed at helping employees deal with problems, aid in the transition to a useful retirement.

The phenomenon of "forced" early retirement that began in the 1980s has required thousands of managers and professionals to determine what is important to them while they are still young and healthy and to plan accordingly. Because of economic factors, many organizations have used early retirement to reduce their workforces. Some of these young retirees "go fishing," but many begin second careers.

# Career Planning: Individual Issues

Effective career planning at the individual level first requires self-knowledge. A person must face a number of issues. How hard am I really willing to work? What is most important in life to me? What trade-offs between work and family or leisure am I willing to make? These questions and others must be confronted honestly before personal goals and objectives can be realistically set in a career plan.

As suggested earlier, changing jobs and careers has become an accepted practice in recent years, and it can be financially rewarding. However, "job-hopping" (changing jobs very frequently) can cause problems with retirement, vacation, seniority, and other benefits. Perhaps more important is the perception that job-hopping is a sign of instability, especially among more mature people.

## Career Plateaus

Those who do not job-hop may face another problem: career plateaus. As the baby-boom generation reaches midlife, and as large employers cut back on their workforces, increasing numbers of managers will find themselves at a career plateau. Plateauing may seem a sign of failure to many people, and plateaued employees can cause problems for employers when frustration affects performance.

Perhaps in part because of plateauing, many middle managers' optimism about opportunity for advancement has declined. Even though these managers have more responsibility and less influence in the decision-making process, the result has been leaner, more competitive organizations with few promotion opportunities.

Figure 11–11 shows how a new "portable" career path may be evolving, in keeping with the apparent movement away from an orderly series of cyclic alterations at prescribed chronological ages. This evolution means that careers are less predictable than in previous decades.

## Dual-Career Paths for Technical and Professional Workers

Technical and professional workers, such as engineers and scientists, present a special challenge for organizations. Many of them want to stay in their labs or at their drawing boards rather than move into management; yet advancement

**FIGURE 11–11** *The New "Portable" Career Path*

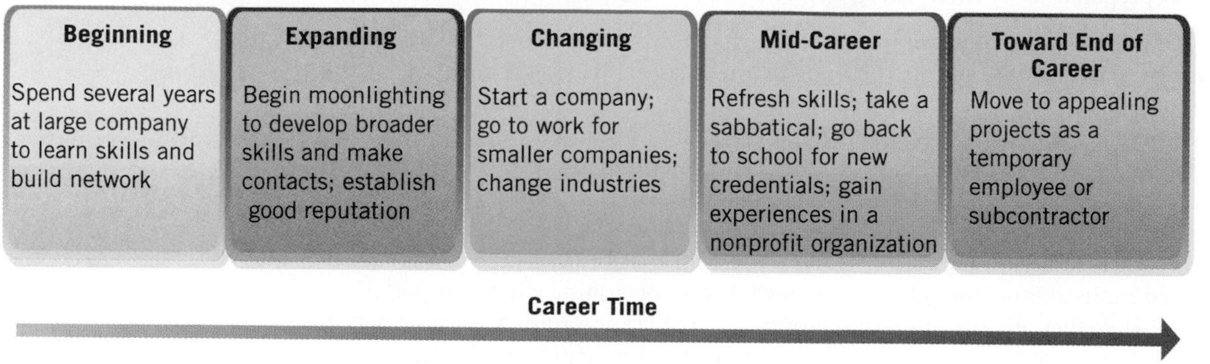

| Beginning | Expanding | Changing | Mid-Career | Toward End of Career |
|---|---|---|---|---|
| Spend several years at large company to learn skills and build network | Begin moonlighting to develop broader skills and make contacts; establish good reputation | Start a company; go to work for smaller companies; change industries | Refresh skills; take a sabbatical; go back to school for new credentials; gain experiences in a nonprofit organization | Move to appealing projects as a temporary employee or subcontractor |

**Career Time** →

frequently *requires* a move into management. Most of these people like the idea of the responsibility and opportunity associated with advancement, but they do not want to leave the technical puzzles and problems at which they excel.

The *dual-career ladder* is an attempt to solve this problem. As shown in Figure 11–12, a person can advance up either the management ladder or a corresponding ladder on the technical/professional side. Dual-career paths have been used at IBM, Union Carbide, and AT&T/Bell Labs for years. They are most common in technology-driven industries such as pharmaceuticals, chemicals, computers, and electronics. Pacific Bell has created a dual-career ladder in its data processing department to reward talented technical people who do not want to move into management. Different tracks, each with attractive job titles and pay opportunities, are provided.[33]

Unfortunately, the technical/professional ladder sometimes is viewed as leading to "second-class citizenship" within the organization. For a second or third career track to be taken seriously, management must apply standards as rigorous as those applied to management promotions.

## Dual-Career Couples

The increasing number of women in the workforce, particularly in professional careers, has greatly increased the number of dual-career couples. The U.S. Bureau of Labor Statistics estimates that 81% of all couples are dual-career couples. Marriages in which both mates are managers, professionals, or technicians have doubled in the past two decades. Leading areas of growth in the number of dual-career couples are the West Coast, Denver, Chicago, New York, and the Washington, DC-Baltimore area. Problem areas involving dual-career couples include retirement, transfer, and family issues.[34]

It is important that the career development problems of dual-career couples be recognized as early as possible, especially if they involve transfer, so that realistic alternatives can be explored. Early planning by employees and their supervisors can prevent crisis. Whenever possible, having both partners involved, even when one is not employed by the company, has been found to enhance the success of such efforts.

For dual-career couples with children, family issues may conflict with career progression. Thus, in job transfer situations, one partner may be more willing to be flexible in this type of job taken for the sake of the family. Part-time work, flextime, and work-at-home arrangements may be options considered, especially for parents with younger children.

**FIGURE 11-12** *Dual-Career Path for Engineers*

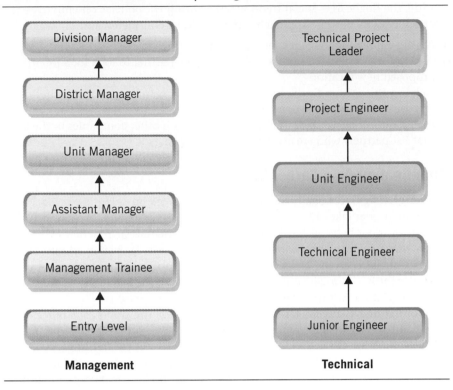

Management                    Technical

**RECRUITMENT PROBLEMS WITH DUAL-CAREER COUPLES** Recruiting a member of a dual-career couple increasingly means having an equally attractive job available for the candidate's partner at the new location. Dual-career couples have more to lose when relocating, and as a result often exhibit higher expectations and request more help and money in such situations.

**RELOCATION OF DUAL-CAREER COUPLES** Traditionally, transfers are part of the path upward in organizations. However, the dual-career couple is much less mobile because one partner's transfer interferes with the other's career.[35] Dual-career couples, besides having invested in two careers, have established support networks of friends and neighbors to cope with their transportation and dependent-care needs. These needs, in a single-career couple, would normally be met by the other partner. Relocating one partner in a dual-career couple means upsetting this carefully constructed network or creating a "commuting" relationship.

If a company has no partner-assistance program, an employee may be hesitant to request such services and may turn down the relocating. The dual-career family has not been the norm for very long, and traditional role expectations remain. A male employee may still fear he will appear "unmanly" should his partner refuse to defer in support of his career, while a female employee may feel guilty about violating the traditional concept of male career dominance.

When relocation is the only way to handle a staffing situation, employers increasingly provide support services to help the couple adapt to the new location. Such companies go so far as to hire the spouse at the new location or find the partner a job with another company. At times, companies have agreed to pay part of the salary or benefits when another company hires the partner and to reciprocate at some future time. When such arrangements cannot be made, professional job search counseling can be obtained for the partner. It makes sense to take into account the dual-career social trend when revising HR policies on employee relocation assistance. Some approaches that could be considered are:

- Paying employment agency fees for the relocating partner
- Paying for a designated number of trips for the partner to look for a job in the proposed new location
- Helping the partner find a job within the same company or in another division or subsidiary of the company
- Developing computerized job banks to share with other companies in the area that list partners who are available for job openings

## Moonlighting As a Career Strategy

**Moonlighting**

Work outside a person's regular employment that takes 12 or more additional hours per week.

**Moonlighting** traditionally has been defined as work outside a person's regular employment that takes 12 or more additional hours per week. More recently, the concept of moonlighting has been expanded to include such activities as self-employment, investments, hobbies, and other interests for which additional remuneration is received. The perception that moonlighting is a fixed outside commitment is no longer sufficiently broad, because the forms that it may take are varied and sometimes difficult to identify.

Moonlighting is no longer just a second job for the underpaid blue-collar worker but also a career development strategy for some professionals. A growing number of managers are dividing their work efforts by moonlighting as consultants or self-employed entrepreneurs. Consulting not only increases their income but also provides new experiences and diversity to their lives. Many individuals also view such activities as providing extra security, especially in these times of layoffs among middle managers.

Most moonlighting managers cannot afford to walk away from their corporate salaries, but they are looking elsewhere for fulfillment. An HR manager at a TV network moonlights by working for a training firm that she and a friend set up. An advertising executive at a cosmetics company accepts freelance assignments from his employer's clients. A computer software expert secretly develops a home computer program to market on his own.

If someone is working for a company and freelancing in the same field, questions about whose ideas and time are involved are bound to arise. Some organizations threaten to fire employees who are caught moonlighting, mainly to keep them from becoming competitors.[36] But that does not seem to stop the activities. Other organizations permit freelance work so long as it is not directly competitive. Many believe that staff members should be free to develop their own special interests.

There is evidence that some people who hold multiple jobs work a second job in preparation for a career change. Whether or not a career change is sought, the concept of "job insurance" plays a role, as mentioned earlier. Moonlighting can be viewed in the same context as auto, car, home, or life insurance. The second job can serve as a backup in the event the primary job is lost.

Moonlighting is not without its problems. The main argument against moonlighting has been that energy is being used on a second job that should be used on the primary job. This division of effort may lead to poor performance, absenteeism, and reduced job commitment. However, these arguments are less valid with a growing number of employees.

Key for employers in dealing with moonlighting employees is to devise and communicate a policy on the subject. Such a policy should focus on defining those areas in which the employer limits employee activities because of business reasons.

# Summary

- Development is different from training because it focuses on less tangible aspects of performance, such as attitudes and values.
- Successful development requires top management support and an understanding of the relationship of development to other HR activities.
- Assessment centers provide valid methods of assessing management talent and development needs.
- Replacement charts are like football depth charts. From them, decisions can be made about whether to develop people internally or go outside for new talent.
- On-the-job development methods include coaching, committee assignments, job rotation, and "assistant-to" positions.
- Off-the-job development methods include classroom courses, human relations training, case studies, role playing, simulations, sabbatical leaves, and outdoor training.
- Mentoring and modeling are two ways for younger managers to acquire the skills and know-how necessary to be successful. Mentoring follows a four-stage progression in most cases.
- Career planning may focus on organizational needs, individual needs, or both.
- A person chooses a career based on interests, self-image, personality, social background, and other factors.
- A person's life is cyclical, as is his or her career. Putting the two together offers a useful perspective.
- Retirement often requires serious emotional adjustments.
- Dual-career ladders are used with scientific and technical employees.
- Dual-career marriages increasingly require relocation assistance for the partners of transferring employees.
- Moonlighting is growing in usage by employees in different fields.

# Review and Discussion Questions

1. What is HR development, and why is top management support so important?
2. Why have many large organizations used assessment centers?
3. You are the head of a government agency. What two methods of on-the-job development would you use with a promising supervisor? What two off-the-job methods would you use? Why?
4. Discuss whether you would prefer organization-centered or individual-centered career planning.
5. List reasons why dual-career paths for professional and technical workers may grow in importance in the future.
6. Assume you must develop a company policy to address concerns about dual-career couples. What would you propose for such a policy?

# Terms to Know

assessment center   355
career   367
coaching   357
development   350
encapsulated development   366

individual-centered career
   planning   368
job rotation   359
mentoring   365
moonlighting   374

organization-centered career
   planning   367
role playing   360
sabbatical leave   361
simulation   360

# Using the Internet

## Coaching Tips

The manager of your telemarketing division has expressed concerns to you, the HR manager, about the coaching skills of his supervisors. He has asked you to provide him with tips the supervisors can use for coaching employees, and with some ideas for improving employee self-confidence. Use the following website with indexed articles to prepare your list. **http://www.CoachCenter.com/masterindex/ learningindex.html**

## CASE

# Development Changes at Chevron

San Francisco–based Chevron Corporation had just revised its career development program when brutal economic realities forced downsizing and layoff of 8,000 employees. Even the name of the previous program, "employee career development," sounded inappropriate after the layoffs. The company knew it could not promise career development, because development implied that upward movement would be possible—and it would *not* be possible. Remaining employees were concerned about job security, and the company was operating in a slow-to-no-growth environment.

To address the problem, the company changed to a "career enrichment" program designed to help employees find meaning in their current work. The process is designed to help employees enhance their effectiveness and satisfaction, develop new skills, and become better prepared to meet future needs of the company. Participation is voluntary, and there is no guarantee of higher salaries or promotions; but the program enables employees to take more responsibility for their own career development.

The key components of the plan are as follows:

- *Preparation:* This phase includes self-assessment, an organizational assessment, and goal-setting sessions.

- *Joint planning:* The employee and the employee's manager review assessment results and agree on an "enrichment plan" for the next year.
- *Plan review:* The plan is presented by the manager to a group of managers, who form a plan review committee. The committee gives the employee feedback on lateral moves, options, and opportunities that might be available.
- *Implementation:* The employee is responsible for implementing the plan, but managers are available for help if needed.
- *End-of-cycle review:* Results are reviewed, and the cycle for the next year is begun.

There was once an understanding that if employees were loyal, they would be assured a job. That is not the case any longer. Employees must understand the business and its needs, as well as their own values and skills, in order to align their personal goals with the goals of the organization.[37]

## Questions

1. What are the advantages and disadvantages of Chevron's development system?
2. What modifications, if any, would you make in the plan? Why?

# Notes

1. Adapted from Scott McCartney, "If the Pitcher Lifts His Pinkie, Odds Are He's a Texas Ranger," *The Wall Street Journal,* March 2, 1998, A1.
2. Hugh P. Gunz, et al., "New Strategy, Wrong Managers? What You Need to Know about Career Streams," *Academy of Management Executive,* May 1998, 21.
3. Douglas T. Hall and Jonathan E. Moss, *Organizational Dynamics,* Winter 1998, 22.
4. William F. Pilder, "Career 'Corporatespeak'," *Human Resource Executive,* May 19, 1998, 73.
5. Nina Monk, "The New Organization Man," *Fortune,* March 16, 1998, 63–82.
6. Julie Schmidt, "Hi-Tech Job Hopping," *USA Today,* August 21, 1998, 1B.
7. JoAnn S. Lublin and J.B. White, "Dilbert's Revenge," *The Wall Street Journal,* September 11, 1997, A1.
8. The following information is based on Michael M. Lombard and Robert W. Eichinger, "HR's Role in Building Competitive Edge Leaders," *Human Resource Management,* Spring 1997, 141.
9. Kamal Birdi, Catrona Allan, and Peter Wahr, "Correlates and Perceived Outcomes of Four Types of Employee Development Activity," *Journal of Applied Psychology,* 82 (1997), 845–857.
10. Adapted from George Anders, "Rx: The MBA," *The Wall Street Journal,* May 13, 1998, 1A.
11. Maria Maciejczyk Claphom and Mark Fulford, "Age Bias in Assessment Center Ratings," *Journal of Managerial Issues,* Fall 1997, 373.
12. "The Secrets of Succession," *The Economist,* October 25, 1997, 73.
13. Ed Silverman, "Gone Awry," *Human Resource Executive,* February 1998, 42.
14. Birdi, et al., "Correlates and Perceived Outcomes," 845–857.
15. Robert F. Pearse, "Maximizing Career Potential: Corporate Investment in Developing Human Capital," *Compensation and Benefits Management,* Winter 1997, 33–39.
16. Patricia Nakache, "Can You Handle the Truth about Your Career?", *Fortune,* July 7, 1997, 208.
17. Anita Bruzzese, "Learning Locomotion," *Human Resource Executive,* July 1998, 28.
18. S. Armour, "Workers View Sabbaticals as a Two-Edged Sword," *USA Today,* August 8, 1997, 3B.
19. Stephanie Mehta, "On Sabbatical Some Go Fishing for Jobs," *The Wall Street Journal,* June 9, 1997, B1.
20. S. Armour, "Once Plagued by Pink Slips, Now They Are in the Driver's Seat," *USA Today,* May 14, 1998, 1B.
21. "Managers are More Mobile, Versatile, AMA Finds," *Bulletin to Management,* August 27, 1998, 265.
22. Tim Schellhardt, "Off the Ladder," *The Wall Street Journal,* April 4, 1997, A1.
23. John Byrne, "Wanted: A Few Good CEO's," *Business Week,* August 11, 1997, 64–70.
24. "To Boost Retention," *The Wall Street Journal,* November 11, 1997, A1.
25. Kathryn Tyler, "Mentoring Programs Link Employees and Experienced Executives," *HR Magazine,* April 1998, 99–103.
26. Roy Furchogott, "You've Come a Short Way, Baby," *Business Week,* November 23, 1998, 82–92.
27. Based on "Japan's Worry About Work," *The Economist,* January 23, 1999, 35–36; and "Sayonara Saraiman," *The Economist,* July 18, 1998, 55–56.
28. Mary Beth Regan, "Your Next Job," *Business Week,* October 13, 1997, 64–72.
29. Hal Lancaster, "Managing Your Career," *The Wall Street Journal,* March 11, 1997, A1.
30. Kevin T. Leight and Jon Marx, "The Consequences of Informal Job Finding for Men and Women," *Academy of Management Journal* 40 (1997), 967.
31. "Work Week: Job Hopping," *The Wall Street Journal,* July 21, 1998, A1.
32. Anne Fisher, "Six Ways to Supercharge Your Career," *Fortune,* January 13, 1997, 46–54.
33. "Lead Report," *Bulletin to Management,* May 18, 1998, 516.
34. "Facts and Figures," *Bulletin to Management,* February 19, 1998, 53–54.
35. Betsy Morris, "It's Her Job Too," *Fortune,* March 17, 1997, 71.
36. Lori Loannov, "Putting Them on Ice," *Fortune,* March 16, 1998, 156; and Gene Koretz, "Those Educated Moonlighters," *Business Week,* August 4, 1997, 22.
37. Adapted from Shari Caudron, "Chevron Changes Focus from Career Development to Career Enrichment," *Personnel Journal* (Special Report), April 1994, 64.

# CHAPTER 12
# Performance Management and Appraisal

*After you have read this chapter, you should be able to:*

- Distinguish between job criteria and performance standards and discuss criterion contamination and deficiency.

- Identify the two major uses of performance appraisal.

- Explain several rater errors by giving examples of them.

- Describe both the advantages and disadvantages of multisource (360°) appraisal.

- Identify the nature of behavioral approaches to performance appraisal and management by objectives (MBO).

- Discuss several concerns about appraisal feedback interviews.

- Identify the characteristics of a legal and effective performance appraisal system.

## HR TRANSITIONS

# 360° Performance Appraisal

The latest attempt to improve performance appraisal—multisource assessment, or 360° performance appraisal (PA)—has found favor with a growing number of organizations. Unlike traditional performance appraisals, which typically come from superiors, 360° appraisal uses feedback from "all around" the appraisee. Superiors, subordinates, peers, customers—and perhaps a self-appraisal as well—provide input for the performance appraisal process. Factors driving the use of 360° PA include the increased use of teams and an emphasis on customer satisfaction that comes from quality enhancement operations. Use of 360° PA with teams presents a problem, however. Should managers even do performance appraisals, should team leaders do them, or should team members evaluate each other?

There also are several other potential problems with 360° assessment:

- The process generates a great deal of paper, with evaluations done by many people.
- Confidentiality is an issue. If people do not believe their comments will be anonymous, they are not as honest as they otherwise would be.
- Determining who will be selected for assessment is important. Friends, enemies, or both?

Intermountain Health Care (IMHC), in Salt Lake City, is a health-care provider that has designed a 360° program around a web-based approach. The company's internally developed system can be customized to the person being rated, eliminates much of the paperwork, and solves data entry problems.

For years, employees at IMHC were evaluated in a traditional way by their supervisors. However, it became clear that due to the nature of the work, supervisors were not able to observe workers in enough situations to evaluate them accurately. Therefore, it was decided that it was more appropriate for employees to be appraised by a team consisting of internal customers, coworkers, and direct reports. Thus,

*Unlike traditional performance appraisals, which typically come from superiors, 360° appraisal uses feedback from "all around" the appraisee.*

the 360° approach to performance appraisal was adopted.

This approach was sound, given the nature of the jobs, but a serious workflow problem was created: how to collect and input into the computer all of the evaluations of each employee who is evaluated by a group of as many as 10 other employees? IMHC tried scanning the paper evaluations into a database,

but that did not eliminate the paper problem.

The new web-based system allows employees to select from a database those questions that apply to them and their jobs. For example, a nurse will select different questions than will someone in marketing. Once the questions are selected, they are approved by the supervisor. The employee and supervisor answer the evaluation questions, as does a "team" of other evaluators agreed to by the employee and supervisor. Then, each team member is e-mailed the list of evaluation questions, and they respond by e-mail. The surveys are kept anonymous, but both employee and supervisor receive copies of the evaluations.

The system is relatively new, but so far IMHC employees and supervisors seem pleased with the way it is working. Feedback occurs quickly with a minimum amount of paper and hassle.[1] Much is left to learn about 360° performance appraisal, but with this new human resource approach, there is great potential to provide *better* feedback where appropriate.

66 *Maximizing performance is a priority for most organizations today.* 99

BOB CARDY

**Performance management system**
Processes used to identify, encourage, measure, evaluate, improve, and reward employee performance.

Employees' job performance is an important issue for all employers. However, satisfactory performance does not happen automatically; therefore, it is more likely with a good performance management system. A **performance management system** consists of the processes used to identify, encourage, measure, evaluate, improve, and reward employee performance at work. In this chapter the focus is on *identifying, measuring,* and *evaluating* performance. The other remaining elements are covered in other chapters. Figure 12–1 shows performance management as part of the link between organizational strategy and results. The figure illustrates common performance management practices and outcomes.

**FIGURE 12–1** *Linkage between Strategy, Outcomes, and Organizational Results*

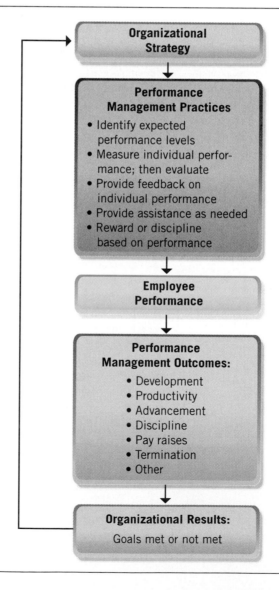

# Identifying and Measuring Employee Performance

Performance is essentially what an employee does or does not do. Performance of employees that affects how much they contribute to the organization could include:

- Quantity of output
- Quality of output
- Timeliness of output
- Presence at work
- Cooperativeness

Obviously other dimensions of performance might be appropriate in certain jobs, but those listed are common to most. However, they are general; each job has specific **job criteria** or job performance dimensions that identify the elements most important in that job. For example, a college professor's job might include the job criteria of teaching, research, and service.[2] Job criteria are the most important factors people do in their jobs; in a sense, job criteria define what the organization is paying an employee to do. Because these criteria are important, individuals' performance on job criteria should be measured, compared against standards, and then the results must be communicated to each employee.

**Job criteria**
Important elements of a job on which performance is measured.

Jobs almost always have more than one job criterion or dimension. For example, a baseball outfielder's job criteria include home runs, batting average, fielding percentage, and on-base performance, to name a few. In sports and many other jobs, multiple job criteria are the rule rather than the exception, and it follows that a given employee might be better at one job criterion than at another.

Some criteria might have more importance than others to the organization. Weights are a way to show the relative importance of several job criteria in one job. In some universities a college professor's teaching might be a bigger part of the job than research or service, so that a weighting of the job criteria at a given university might look like this:

| Job Criterion | Weight |
|---|---|
| Teaching | 60% |
| Research | 30% |
| Service | 10% |
|  | 100% |

## Job Criteria and Information Types

The data or information that managers receive on how well employees are performing their jobs can be of three different types. *Trait-based* information identifies a subjective character trait—such as pleasant personality, initiative, or creativity—and may have little to do with the specific job. Traits tend to be ambiguous, and many court decisions have held that performance evaluations based on traits such as "adaptability" and "general demeanor" are too vague to use as the basis for performance-based HR decisions.[3]

*Behavior-based* information focuses on specific behaviors that lead to job success. For a salesperson, the behavior of "verbal persuasion" can be observed and used as information on performance. Behavioral information is more difficult to identify, but has the advantage of clearly specifying the behaviors management wants to see. A potential problem is that there may be several behaviors, all of which can be successful in a given situation. For example, identifying exactly what "verbal persuasion" is for a salesperson might be difficult.

*Results-based* information considers what the employee has done or accomplished. For jobs in which measurement is easy and appropriate, a results-based approach works very well. However, that which is measured tends to be emphasized, and the equally important but unmeasurable parts of the job may be left out. For example, a car sales representative who gets paid only for sales may be unwilling to do any paperwork or other work not directly related to selling cars. Further, ethical or even legal issues may arise when only results are emphasized and not *how the results were achieved.*

## Relevance of Criteria

When measuring performance, it is important that relevant criteria be used. Generally, criteria are relevant when they focus on the most important aspects of employees' jobs. For example, measuring customer service representatives in an insurance claims center on their "appearance" may be less relevant than measuring the number of calls handled properly. This example stresses that the most important job criteria should be identified and be linked back to the employees' job descriptions.

## Potential Criteria Problems

Because jobs usually include several duties and tasks, if the performance measures leave out some important job duties, the measures are *deficient.* For example, measuring the performance of an employment interviewer only on the number of applicants hired, but not on the quality of those hires, could be deficient. If some irrelevant criteria are included, the criteria are said to be *contaminated.* An example of a contaminated criteria might be appearance for a telemarketing sales representative who is not seen by the customers. Managers use deficient or contaminated criteria for measuring performance much more than they should.

Performance measures also can be thought of as *objective* or *subjective.* Objective measures can be directly counted—for example, the number of cars sold or the number of invoices processed. Subjective measures are more judgmental and more difficult to measure directly. One example of a subjective measure is a supervisor's ratings of an employee's customer service performance. Unlike subjective measures, objective measures tend to be more narrowly focused, which may lead to the objective measures being inadequately defined. However, subjective measures may be prone to contamination or other random errors. Neither is a panacea, and both should be used carefully.

**LOGGING ON . . .**
**Redefining Performance**
This website is for a firm specializing in performance management systems and other tools for HR professionals. The overview explains the firm's approach to increasing employee performance through appraisal systems.

**http://www.btweb.com/**

## Performance Standards

To know that an employee produces 10 "photons" per day does not provide a complete basis for judging employee performance as satisfactory or not. A *standard* against which to compare the information is necessary. Maybe 15 photons is considered a sufficient day's work. **Performance standards** define the expected levels of performance, and are "benchmarks," or "goals," or "targets"— depending on the approach taken. Realistic, measurable, clearly understood

**Performance standards**
Expected levels of performance.

**FIGURE 12–2** *Terms Used to Define Standards at One Company*

**Outstanding.** The person is so successful at this job criterion that special note should be made. Compared with the usual standards and the rest of the department, this performance ranks in the top 10%.

**Very Good.** Performance at this level is one of better-than-average performances in the unit, given the common standards and unit results.

**Satisfactory.** Performance is at or above the minimum standards. This level of performance is what one would expect from most experienced, competent employees.

**Marginal.** Performance is somewhat below the minimum-level standard on this job dimension. However, there appears to be potential to improve the rating within a reasonable time frame.

**Unsatisfactory.** Performance on this item in the job is well below standard, and there is serious question as to whether the person can improve to meet minimum standards.

performance standards benefit both the organization and the employees. In a sense, performance standards define what satisfactory job performance is. It is important to establish standards *before* the work is performed, so that all involved will understand the level of accomplishment expected.

The extent to which standards have been met often is expressed in either numerical or verbal ratings, for example, "outstanding" or "unsatisfactory." It may sometimes be difficult for two or more people to reach agreement on exactly what the level of performance has been relative to the standard. Figure 12–2 shows terms used in evaluating employee performance on standards at one company. Notice that each level is defined in terms of performance standards, rather than numbers, in order to minimize different interpretations of the standards.

Sales quotas and production output standards are familiar numerical performance standards. A nonnumerical standard of performance is that a cashier in a retail store must balance the cash drawer at the end of each day. For example, two nonnumerical performance standards for difficult duties were derived jointly as follows:

---

*Job Criterion.* Keep current on supplier technology.

*Performance Standards.* 1. Every six months, invite suppliers to make presentation of newest technology. 2. Visit supplier plants once per year. 3. Attend trade shows quarterly.

- - - - - - - - - - - - - - - - - - - - - - - - - - - - - - - - - - - - - - - - - - - - -

*Job Criterion.* Do price or cost analysis as appropriate.

*Performance Standard.* Performance is acceptable when employee follows all requirements of the procedure "Price and Cost Analysis."

Standards are often set by someone external to the job, such as a supervisor or a quality control inspector, but they can be written effectively by employees as well. Experienced employees usually know what constitutes satisfactory performance of tasks in their job descriptions, and so do their supervisors.[4] Therefore, these individuals often can collaborate effectively on setting standards.

# Uses of Performance Appraisal

**Performance appraisal (PA)** is the process of evaluating how well employees perform their jobs when compared to a set of standards, and then communicating that information to those employees. Such appraisal also has been called *employee rating, employee evaluation, performance review, performance evaluation,* and *results appraisal.*[5]

Performance appraisal sounds simple enough; and research shows that it is widely used for administering wages and salaries, giving performance feedback, and identifying individual employee strengths and weaknesses. Most U.S. companies have performance appraisal systems for office, professional, technical, supervisory, middle management, and nonunion production workers.

For situations in which an employer deals with a strong union, performance appraisals are usually conducted only on the salaried, nonunion employees. Generally, unions emphasize seniority over merit, which precludes the use of performance appraisal. Because unions officially view all members as equal in ability, the worker with the most experience is considered the most qualified, and a performance appraisal is unnecessary.

Performance appraisal often is many managers' least-favored activity, and there may be good reasons for that feeling. Not all performance appraisals are positive, and discussing ratings with poorly performing employees may not be pleasant. Also, it may be difficult to differentiate among employees if sufficient performance data are not available.[6] Further, some supervisors are uncomfortable "playing God" with employees' raises and careers, which they may feel is a result of conducting performance appraisals.

Performance appraisal has two general uses in organizations, and these roles often are potential conflicts. One role is to measure performance for the purpose of rewarding or otherwise making *administrative* decisions about employees. Promotions or layoffs might hinge on these ratings, often making them difficult for managers to do. Another role is *development* of individual potential. In that role, the manager is featured more as a counselor than as a judge, and the atmosphere is often different. Emphasis is on identifying potential and planning employees' growth opportunities and direction. Figure 12–3 shows the two potentially conflicting roles for performance appraisal.

## Administrative Uses

A performance appraisal system is often the link between the rewards employees hope to receive and their productivity. The linkage can be thought of as follows:

$$\text{productivity} \rightarrow \text{performance appraisal} \rightarrow \text{rewards}$$

Compensation based on performance appraisal is at the heart of the idea that raises should be given for performance accomplishments rather than for seniority. Under performance-oriented systems, employees receive raises based on how well they perform their jobs. The manager's role historically has been as an evaluator of a subordinate's performance, which then leads to managers making

---

**Performance appraisal (PA)**

The process of evaluating how well employees perform their jobs when compared to a set of standards, and then communicating that information.

**FIGURE 12–3** *Conflicting Roles for Performance Appraisal?*

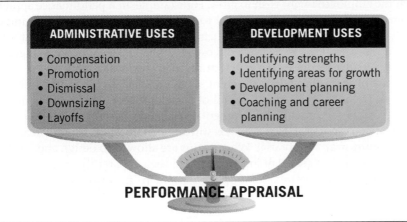

**ADMINISTRATIVE USES**
- Compensation
- Promotion
- Dismissal
- Downsizing
- Layoffs

**DEVELOPMENT USES**
- Identifying strengths
- Identifying areas for growth
- Development planning
- Coaching and career planning

**PERFORMANCE APPRAISAL**

compensation recommendations or decisions for employees. If any part of the process fails, the most productive employees do not receive the larger rewards, resulting in perceived inequity in compensation.

Many U.S. workers see little connection between the levels of their efforts and the sizes of their paychecks. However, the use of performance appraisal to determine pay is very common. Other administrative uses of performance appraisal, such as decisions on promotion, termination, layoff, and transfer assignments, are very important to employees. For example, the order of layoffs can be justified by performance appraisals. For this reason, if an employer claims that the decision was performance-based, the performance appraisals must document clearly the differences in employee performance. Similarly, promotion or demotion based on performance must be documented with performance appraisals.

Performance appraisals are essential when organizations terminate, promote, or pay people differently, because they are a crucial defense if employees sue over such decisions. Thus, necessity likely accounts for the widespread administrative use of performance appraisals. But certain problems, including leniency, are common when ratings are to be used for administrative purposes.

## Development Uses

Performance appraisal can be a primary source of information and feedback for employees, which is key to their future development. When supervisors identify the weaknesses, potentials, and training needs of employees through performance appraisal feedback, they can inform employees about their progress, discuss what skills they need to develop, and work out development plans.

The manager's role in such a situation is like that of a coach. The coach's job is to reward good performance with recognition, explain what improvement is necessary, and show employees *how* to improve. After all, people do not always know where they could improve, and managers really cannot expect improvement if they are unwilling to explain where and how improvement can occur.

The purpose of developmental feedback is to change or reinforce individual behavior, rather than to compare individuals—as in the case of administrative uses of performance appraisal. Positive reinforcement for the behaviors the organization wants is an important part of development.

The development function of performance appraisal also can identify areas in which the employee might wish to grow. For example, in a performance appraisal interview that was targeted exclusively to development, an employee found out that the only factor keeping her from being considered for a management job in her firm was a working knowledge of cost accounting. Her supervisor suggested that she consider taking such a course at night at the local college.

The use of teams provides a different set of circumstances for developmental appraisal. The manager may not see all of the employee's work, but team members do. Teams *can* provide developmental feedback, as we noted earlier in the feature on 360° appraisal. However, it is still an open question whether teams can handle administrative appraisal. When teams are allowed to design appraisal systems, they prefer to "get rid of judgment," and they apparently have a very hard time dealing with differential rewards. Perhaps, then, group appraisal is best used for developmental purposes.

# Informal vs. Systematic Appraisal

*BNA: 1020.10.10–1020.20*

**Performance Appraisal Process**

Compare the steps in the performance appraisal process discussed here with those used at your current employer.

Performance appraisal can occur in two ways, informally or systematically. The *informal appraisal* is conducted whenever the supervisor feels it necessary. The day-to-day working relationship between a manager and an employee offers an opportunity for the employee's performance to be judged. This judgment is communicated through conversation on the job, over coffee, or by on-the-spot examination of a particular piece of work. Informal appraisal is especially appropriate when time is an issue. The longer feedback is delayed, the less likely it is to motivate behavior change. Frequent informal feedback to employees can also prevent surprises when the formal evaluation is communicated. However, informal appraisal can become *too* informal:[7]

> A senior executive at a big auto maker so dreaded face-to-face evaluations that he recently delivered one manager's review while both sat in adjoining stalls in the men's room. The boss told the startled subordinate: "I haven't had a chance to give you a performance appraisal this year. Your bonus is going to be 20%. I am really happy with your performance."

Dilbert reprinted by permission of United Feature Syndicate, Inc.

## HR PERSPECTIVE
# The CEO's Performance Review

Performance reviews are routine at the lower levels in corporations, but they are somewhat less frequent at the top. Some CEOs do not want them, and often when boards of directors do review the chief executive, the focus is on pay rather than leadership or effectiveness.

But that approach can lead to very poor communications. For example, when Gilbert Amelio was fired as Apple Computer CEO, he said his dismissal came as a total surprise. Not a single board member felt comfortable telling him he was in trouble. He indicated that CEOs *really do* want the feedback on how they are doing, so that they can adjust their performance.

More boards of directors are starting to recognize that CEO performance should be appraised, and they are conducting executive performance reviews. For example, Thomas Loarie, Chairman of Kera Vision Inc., a start-up vision care company, was told at one of his last appraisals that he needed to demand more accountability from subordinates and be more realistic about his sales plans. By nature, Mr. Loarie is open and forthright; he was also well liked by the directors. Still, Loarie admitted to feeling some concern before a review, even though negative feedback can be seen as positive because it provides additional information.

When a new Kera Vision product was introduced in Europe, Mr. Loarie had projected a sales increase—but it did not happen. In fact, sales were nonexistent. The board was very critical, suggesting that Loarie had not demanded enough from the European managers. This observation led to the criticism of Loarie about making subordinates accountable.

The Kera Vision board uses specially designed evaluation forms for evaluating the CEO, and the perspective is forward looking rather than only retrospective. The past year's performance is assessed, but —unlike evaluations for lower-level employees—the outlook for the medium- and long-term future also is evaluated. For Kera Vision and other firms, organizational performance is a key factor considered in a CEO's performance appraisal. It is likely that more boards of directors of other firms will adopt a formal process for appraising the performance of CEOs.[8]

---

A *systematic appraisal* is used when the contact between manager and employee is formal, and a system is in place to report managerial impressions and observations on employee performance. Although informal appraisal is useful, it should not take the place of formal appraisal. Even some Chief Executive Officers receive and indeed often *want* formal appraisal. For an example, see the HR Perspective.

## Appraisal Responsibilities

The appraisal process can be quite beneficial to the organization and to the individuals involved if done properly. It also can be the source of a great deal of discontent.

Figure 12–4 shows that the HR unit typically designs a systematic appraisal system. The manager does the actual appraising of the employee, using the procedures developed by the HR unit. As the formal system is being developed, the manager usually offers input on how the final system will work. Only rarely does an HR specialist actually rate a manager's employees.

**TIMING OF APPRAISALS** Appraisals typically are conducted once or twice a year, most often annually, near the employee's anniversary date. For new employees, common timing is to conduct an appraisal 90 days after employment, again at six months, and annually thereafter. "Probationary" or new employees, or those who

**LOGGING ON . . .**
**Performance Appraisal Policies and Procedures**
This website contains an example of the performance appraisal policies and procedures followed by the human resource management of an educational institution.

http://www.hr.rpi.edu/ hartford/policies/ rhpman8.htm

**FIGURE 12–4** *Typical Appraisal Responsibilities*

| HR Unit | Managers |
|---|---|
| ● Designs and maintains formal system<br>● Establishes formal report system<br>● Makes sure reports are on time<br>● Trains raters | ● Typically rate performance of employees<br>● Prepare formal appraisal documents<br>● Review appraisals with employees |

are new and in a trial period, should be evaluated frequently—perhaps weekly for the first month and monthly thereafter until the end of the introductory period for new employees. After that, annual reviews may be sufficient. Indeed, some argue that performance can be appraised too often.[9]

Some companies in high-technology fields are promising accelerated appraisals—six months instead of a year—so that employees receive more frequent raises. The result for some companies has been a reduction in turnover among these very turnover-prone employees.[10]

A regular time interval is a feature of systematic appraisals that distinguishes them from informal appraisals. Both employees and managers are aware that performance will be reviewed on a regular basis, and they can plan for performance discussions. In addition, informal appraisals should be conducted whenever a manager feels they are desirable.

**APPRAISALS AND PAY DISCUSSIONS** Many experts argue that the timing of performance appraisals and pay discussions should be different. The major reason for this view is that employees often focus more on the pay amount than on what they have done well or need to improve. Sometimes managers may manipulate performance appraisal ratings to justify the desired pay treatment for a given individual.

# Who Conducts Appraisals?

Performance appraisal can be done by anyone familiar with the performance of individual employees. Possibilities include the following:

● Supervisors who rate their employees
● Employees who rate their superiors
● Team members who rate each other
● Outside sources
● Employee self-appraisal
● Multisource (360°) appraisal

**BNA**
**1020.20– 1020.50**
**Appraisal Approaches and Methods**
Review additional details on appraisal methods here to expand the considerations discussed in the text.

The first method is the most common. The immediate superior has the sole responsibility for appraisal in most organizations, although it is common practice to have the appraisal reviewed and approved by the supervisor's boss. Any system should include a face-to-face discussion between rater and ratee.

Because of the growing use of teams and a concern with customer input, two fast-growing sources of appraisal information are team members and sources outside the organization. Also, as highlighted in the chapter opening discussion, multisource appraisal (or 360° appraisal) is a combination of all the methods and has grown in usage recently.

## Supervisory Rating of Subordinates

Traditional rating of employees by supervisors is based on the assumption that the immediate supervisor is the person most qualified to evaluate the employee's performance realistically, objectively, and fairly. Toward this end, some supervisors keep performance logs noting what their employees have done. These logs provide specific examples to use when doing ratings. They also serve to jog their memory, because supervisors cannot be expected to remember every detail of performance over a six-month or one-year period. A supervisor's appraisal typically is reviewed by the manager's boss to make sure that a proper job of appraisal has been done. Figure 12–5 shows the traditional review process by which supervisors conduct performance appraisals on employees.

## Employee Rating of Managers

The concept of having supervisors and managers rated by employees or group members is being used in a number of organizations today. A prime example of this type of rating takes place in colleges and universities, where students evaluate the performance of professors in the classroom. Industry also uses employee ratings for management development purposes.

**FIGURE 12–5** *Traditional Performance Appraisal: Logic and Process*

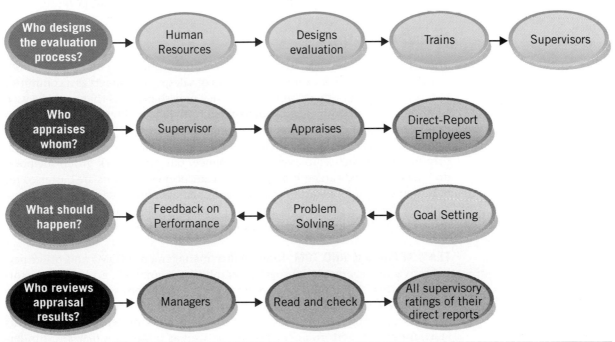

In a very new approach, some corporate boards of directors are being evaluated. Because the fundamental responsibility of the board is to establish goals and direct their accomplishment, that part of their performance should be evaluated. In some instances, evaluation of boards of directors is done by executives if possible, but board self-review or outside evaluation all can be used.[11]

**ADVANTAGES** There are three primary advantages of having employees rate managers. First, in situations where manager-employee relationships are critical, employee ratings can be quite useful in identifying competent managers. The rating of leaders by combat soldiers is an example. Second, this type of rating program can help make the manager more responsive to employees, though this advantage can quickly become a disadvantage if it leads the manager to trying to be "nice" rather than managing. Nice people without other qualifications may not be good managers in many situations. Finally, employee appraisals can be the basis for coaching as part of a career development effort for the managers. The hope is that the feedback will assist their managerial development.

**DISADVANTAGES** A major disadvantage of receiving employee ratings is the negative reaction many superiors have to being evaluated by employees. The "proper" nature of manager-employee relations may be violated by having workers rate managers. Also, the fear of reprisal may be too great for employees to give realistic ratings. In addition, employees may resist rating their bosses because they do not perceive it as part of their jobs. If this situation exists, workers may rate the manager only on the way the manager treats them and not on critical job requirements.

The problems associated with having employees rate managers seem to limit the usefulness of this appraisal approach to certain situations, except for managerial development uses. The traditional nature of most organizations appears to restrict the applicability of employee rating to self-improvement purposes.

## Team/Peer Ratings

The use of peer groups as raters is another type of appraisal with potential both to help and to hurt. For example, if a group of salespersons meets as a committee to talk about one another's ratings, then they may share ideas that could be used to improve the performance of lower-rated individuals. Alternatively, the criticisms could lead to future work relationships being affected negatively.

Peer ratings are especially useful when supervisors do not have the opportunity to observe each employee's performance, but other work group members do.[12] As mentioned earlier, it may be that team/peer evaluations are best used for development purposes rather than for administrative purposes. However, some contend that *any* performance appraisal, including team/peer ratings, can affect teamwork and participative management efforts negatively.

**TEAM APPRAISAL AND TQM** Total quality management (TQM) and other participative management approaches emphasize teamwork and team performance rather than individual performance. Effectiveness is viewed as the result of systematic factors rather than the product of individual efforts.[13] Individual accomplishment occurs only through working with others. In this view, individual performance appraisal is seen as producing fear and hindering the development of teamwork. If management does not appraise team members in high-involvement/high-commitment groups, some contend that it is more likely that other team members will focus informally on helping those whose performance is deficient. But even if formal appraisals seem inappropriate, informal appraisals by peers or team leaders still may be necessary at times.

**TEAM RATING DIFFICULTIES** Although team members have good information on one another's performance, they may not choose to share it. They may unfairly attack or "go easy" to spare feelings. Some organizations attempt to overcome such problems by using anonymous appraisals and/or having a consultant or manager interpret peer ratings. However, there is some evidence that using outsiders to facilitate the rating process does not necessarily result in the system being seen as more fair by those being rated. Whatever the solution, team/peer performance ratings are important and probably inevitable, especially where work teams are used extensively.[14]

## Self-Ratings

Self-appraisal works in certain situations. Essentially, it is a self-development tool that forces employees to think about their strengths and weaknesses and set goals for improvement. If an employee is working in isolation or possesses a unique skill, the employee may be the only one qualified to rate his or her own behavior. However, employees may not rate themselves as supervisors would rate them; they may use quite different standards.[15] Some research shows that people tend to be more lenient when rating themselves, whereas other research does not. Despite the difficulty in evaluating self-ratings, employee self-ratings can be a valuable and credible source of performance information.[16]

## Outside Raters

Rating also may be done by outsiders. Outside experts may be called in to review the work of a college president, for example; or a panel of division managers might evaluate a person's potential for advancement in an organization. Outsiders may furnish managers with professional assistance in making appraisals, but there are obvious disadvantages. The outsider may not know all the important contingencies within the organization. In addition, outsider appraisals are time consuming and expensive.

The customers or clients of an organization are obvious sources for outside appraisals. For salespeople and other service jobs, customers may provide the only really clear view of certain behaviors. One corporation uses measures of customer satisfaction with service as a way of helping to determine bonuses for top marketing executives.

## Multisource Rating

As noted in the chapter opening discussion, multisource—or 360°—rating is growing in popularity. Figure 12–6 shows graphically some of the parties who may be involved in 360° rating. Multisource feedback recognizes that the manager is no longer the sole source of performance appraisal information. Instead, feedback from various colleagues and constituencies is obtained and given to the manager, thus allowing the manager to help shape the feedback from all sources. The manager remains a focal point both to receive the feedback initially and to engage in appropriate follow-up, even in a 360° system. Thus, the manager's perception of an employee's performance is still an important part of the process.

The research on 360° feedback is relatively new and not large in volume. A review of the research suggests there is typically limited agreement among rating sources.[17] However, it should be remembered that the purpose of 360° feedback is *not* to increase reliability by soliciting like-minded views. Rather, the intent is to capture all of the differing evaluations that bear on the individual employee's different roles.

Multisource feedback has been seen by participants as useful, but follow-up on the development activities identified as a result of the feedback has been found to be the most critical factor in the future development of a manager's skills. Appraisees are generally supportive of subordinate appraisal when they receive feedback from *both* their managers and their subordinates. However, supervisors' enthusiasm for subordinates' ratings dims considerably when such ratings are used to help determine pay.

Some potential problems clearly are present when 360° feedback is used for administrative purposes. Differences among raters can present a challenge, especially in the use of 360° ratings for discipline or pay decisions.[18] Bias can just as easily be rooted in customers, subordinates, and peers as in a boss, and their lack of accountability can affect the ratings. Multisource approaches to performance appraisal are possible solutions to the well-documented dissatisfaction with today's legally necessary administrative performance appraisal. But a number of questions arise as multisource appraisals become more common. One concern is whether 360° appraisals improve the process or simply multiply the number of problems by the total number of raters. Also, some wonder if multisource appraisals really will create better decisions than conventional methods, given the additional time investment.[19]

**FIGURE 12–6** *Multisource Appraisal*

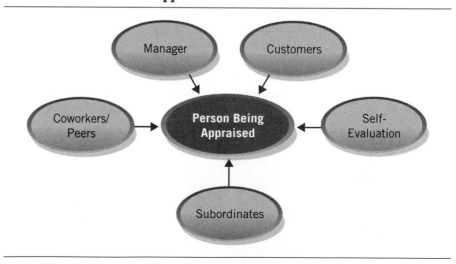

**FIGURE 12–7** *Performance Appraisal Methods*

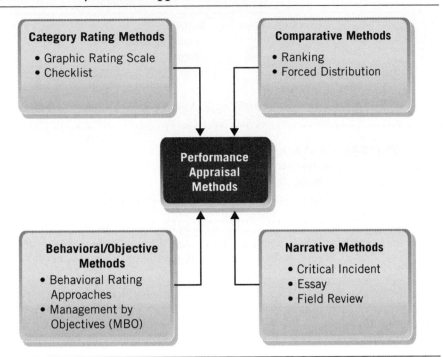

It seems reasonable to assume that these issues are of less concern when the 360° feedback is used *only for development,* because the process is usually less threatening. But those concerns may negate multisource appraisals as an administrative tool in many situations.[20]

# Methods for Appraising Performance

Performance can be appraised by a number of methods. In Figure 12–7, various methods are categorized into four major groups. In this section, after describing each method, the discussion considers combinations of methods. Combinations occur across different jobs in the same organization and even within the same jobs when appropriate.

## Category Rating Methods

The simplest methods for appraising performance are category rating methods, which require a manager to mark an employee's level of performance on a specific form divided into categories of performance. The graphic rating scale and checklist are common category rating methods.

**GRAPHIC RATING SCALE** The **graphic rating scale** allows the rater to mark an employee's performance on a continuum. Because of its simplicity, this method is the one most frequently used. Figure 12–8 shows a graphic rating scale form

**Graphic rating scale**
A scale that allows the rater to mark an employee's performance on a continuum.

FIGURE 12–8 *Sample Performance Appraisal Form (simplified)*

Date Sent     **4/19/00**                              Return by          **5/01/00**
Name          **Jane Doe**                             Job Title          **Receiving Clerk**
Department        **Receiving**                         Supervisor         **Fred Smith**
Full-time    **x**                    Part-time_____    Date of Hire     **5/12/98**
Rating Period:    From    **5/12/99**          To:    **5/12/00**
Reason for appraisal (check one): Regular Interval    **x**      Introductory___    Counseling only___    Discharge___

**Utilizing the following definitions, rate the performance on as I, M, or E.**
 I - Performance is below job requirements and **improvement is needed.**
 M - Performance meets job requirements and is **meeting standards.**
 E - Performance **exceeds** job requirements a **majority** of the time and is **exceeding standards.**

**SPECIFIC JOB RESPONSIBILITIES:** List the principal activities from the job summary, rate the performance on each job duty by placing an "X" on the rating scale at the appropriate location, and make appropriate comments to explain the rating.

| I | M | E |
|---|---|---|

**Job Duty #1:**      **Inventory receiving and checking**
Explanation:_____
_____

| I | M | E |
|---|---|---|

**Job Duty #2:**      **Accuracy of records kept**
Explanation:_____
_____

| I | M | E |
|---|---|---|

**Attendance** (including absences and tardies):    Number of absences_____    Number of tardies_____
Explanation:_____

**Overall Rating:** Based on the total performance, place the letter **I, M, or E** in the box provided that best describes the employee's overall performance.
Explanation:_____
_____

used by managers to rate employees. The rater checks the appropriate rating on the scale for each duty listed. More detail can be added in the space for comments following each factor rated.

There are actually two types of graphic rating scales in use today. They are sometimes *both* used in rating the same person. The first and most common type lists job criteria (quantity of work, quality of work, etc.). The second is more behavioral, with specific behaviors listed and the effectiveness of each rated.

There are some obvious drawbacks to the graphic rating scale as well. Often, separate traits or factors are grouped together, and the rater is given only one box to check. Another drawback is that the descriptive words sometimes used in such scales may have different meanings to different raters. Terms such as *initiative* and *cooperation* are subject to many interpretations, especially if used in conjunction with words such as *outstanding, average,* and *poor.*

Graphic rating scales in many forms are used widely because they are easy to develop; but they encourage errors on the part of the raters, who may depend too heavily on the form itself to define performance. Both graphic rating scales and the checklist (which follows) tend to focus much emphasis on the rating instrument itself and its limitations. In so far as they fit the person and job being rated, the scales work well. However, if the instrument is a poor fit, managers who must use them frequently complain about "the rating form."

**CHECKLIST** The **checklist** is composed of a list of statements or words. Raters check statements most representative of the characteristics and performance of employees. The following are typical checklist statements:

**Checklist**
Performance appraisal tool that uses a list of statements or words that are checked by raters.

_____ can be expected to finish work on time
_____ seldom agrees to work overtime
_____ is cooperative and helpful
_____ accepts criticism
_____ strives for self-improvement

The checklist can be modified so that varying weights are assigned to the statements or words. The results can then be quantified. Usually, the weights are not known by the rating supervisor because they are tabulated by someone else, such as a member of the HR unit.

There are several difficulties with the checklist: (1) as with the graphic rating scale, the words or statements may have different meanings to different raters; (2) raters cannot readily discern the rating results if a weighted checklist is used; and (3) raters do not assign the weights to the factors. These difficulties limit the use of the information when a rater discusses the checklist with the employee, creating a barrier to effective developmental counseling.

## Comparative Methods

Comparative methods require that managers directly compare the performance of their employees against one another. For example, a data-entry operator's performance would be compared with that of other data-entry operators by the computing supervisor. Comparative techniques include ranking, paired comparison, and forced distribution.

**RANKING** The **ranking** method consists of listing all employees from highest to lowest in performance. The primary drawback of the ranking method is that the size of the differences among individuals is not well defined. For example, there may be little difference in performance between individuals ranked second and third, but a big difference in performance between those ranked third and fourth. This drawback can be overcome to some extent by assigning points to indicate

**Ranking**
Listing of all employees from highest to lowest in performance.

the size of the gaps. Ranking also means that someone must be last. It is possible that the last-ranked individual in one group would be the top employee in a different group. Further, ranking becomes very unwieldy if the group to be ranked is very large.

**FORCED DISTRIBUTION** Forced distribution is a technique for distributing ratings that can be generated with any of the other methods. However, it does require a comparison among people in the work group under consideration.

**Forced distribution**

Performance appraisal method in which ratings of employees' performance are distributed along a bell-shaped curve.

With the **forced distribution** method, the ratings of employees' performance are distributed along a bell-shaped curve. Using the forced distribution method, for example, a head nurse would rank nursing personnel along a scale, placing a certain percentage of employees at each performance level. Figure 12–9 shows a scale used with a forced distribution.

This method assumes that the widely known bell-shaped curve of performance exists in a given group. In fact, generally, the distribution of performance appraisal ratings does not approximate the normal distribution of the bell-shaped curve. It is common for 60% to 70% of the workforce of an organization to be rated in the top two performance levels. This pattern could reflect outstanding performance by many employees, or it could reflect *leniency bias,* discussed later in this chapter.

There are several drawbacks to the forced distribution method. One problem is that a supervisor may resist placing any individual in the lowest (or the highest) group. Difficulties may arise when the rater must explain to the employee why he or she was placed in one grouping and others were placed in higher groupings. Further, with small groups, there may be no reason to assume that a bell-shaped distribution of performance really exists. Finally, in some cases the manager may feel forced to make distinctions among employees that may not exist.

**FIGURE 12–9** *Forced Distribution on a Bell-Shaped Curve*

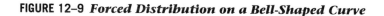
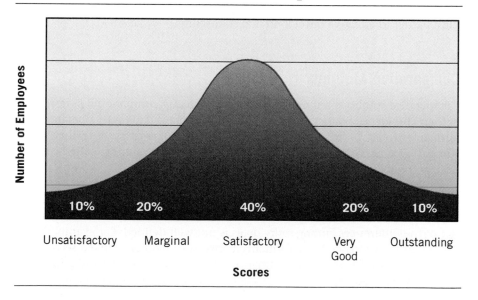

## Narrative Methods

Managers and HR specialists frequently are required to provide written appraisal information. Documentation and description are the essence of the critical incident, the essay, and the field review methods. These records describe an employee's actions rather than indicating an actual rating.

**CRITICAL INCIDENT**  In the critical incident method, the manager keeps a written record of both highly favorable and unfavorable actions in an employee's performance. When a "critical incident" involving an employee occurs, the manager writes it down. A list of critical incidents is kept during the entire rating period for each employee. The critical incident method can be used with other methods to document the reasons why an employee was rated in a certain way.

The critical incident method also has its unfavorable aspects. First, what constitutes a critical incident is not defined in the same way by all supervisors. Next, producing daily or weekly written remarks about each employee's performance can take considerable time. Further, employees may become overly concerned about what the superior writes and begin to fear the manager's "black book."

**ESSAY**  The essay, or "free-form," appraisal method requires the manager to write a short essay describing each employee's performance during the rating period. The rater usually is given a few general headings under which to categorize comments. The intent is to allow the rater more flexibility than other methods do. As a result, the essay is often combined with other methods.

**FIELD REVIEW**  The field review has as much to do with *who* does the evaluation as the method used. This approach can include the HR department as a reviewer, or a completely independent reviewer outside the organization. In the field review, the outside reviewer becomes an active partner in the rating process. The outsider interviews the manager about each employee's performance, then compiles the notes from each interview into a rating for each employee. Then the rating is reviewed by the supervisor for needed changes. This method assumes that the outsider knows enough about the job setting to help supervisors give more accurate and thorough appraisals.

The major limitation of the field review is that the outsider has a great deal of control over the rating. Although this control may be desirable from one viewpoint, managers may see it as a challenge to their authority. In addition, the field review can be time consuming, particularly if a large number of employees are to be rated.

## Behavioral/Objectives Methods

In an attempt to overcome some of the difficulties of the methods just described, several different behavioral approaches have been used. Behavioral approaches hold promise for some situations in overcoming some of the problems with other methods.

**BEHAVIORAL RATING APPROACHES**  **Behavioral rating approaches** attempt to assess an employee's *behaviors* instead of other characteristics. Some of the different behavioral approaches are *behaviorally anchored rating scales* (BARS), *behavioral observation scales* (BOS), and *behavioral expectation scales* (BES). BARS match

**Behavioral rating approach**
Assesses an employee's behaviors instead of other characteristics.

descriptions of possible behaviors with what the employee most commonly exhibits. BOS are used to count the number of times certain behaviors are exhibited. BES order behaviors on a continuum to define outstanding, average, and unacceptable performance. BARS were developed first and are used here as an example of behavioral rating approaches.

Behavioral rating approaches describe examples of employee job behaviors. These examples are "anchored," or measured, against a scale of performance levels. Figure 12–10 shows a behavioral observation rating scale that rates customer service skills. What constitutes various levels of performance is clearly defined in the figure. Spelling out the behavior associated with each level of performance helps minimize some of the problems noted earlier for other approaches.

**CONSTRUCTING BEHAVIORAL SCALES** Construction of a behavioral scale begins with identifying important *job dimensions*. These dimensions are the most important performance factors in an employee's job description. For example, for a college professor, the major job dimensions associated with teaching might be (a) course organization, (b) attitude toward students, (c) fair treatment, and (d) competence in subject area.

Short statements, similar to critical incidents, are developed that describe both desirable and undesirable behaviors (anchors). Then they are "retranslated," or assigned to one of the job dimensions.[21] This task is usually a group project, and assignment to a dimension usually requires the agreement of 60% to 70% of the group. The group, consisting of people familiar with the job, then assigns each "anchor" a number, which represents how good or bad the behavior is. When numbered, these anchors are fitted to a scale. Figure 12–11 shows a flow diagram for developing behavioral anchors.

**FIGURE 12–10** *Customer Service Skills*

Example behaviors of a telephone customer service representative taking orders for a national catalog retailer.

**The customer service representative:**

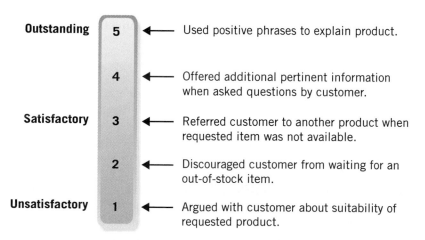

| | | |
|---|---|---|
| Outstanding | 5 | ← Used positive phrases to explain product. |
| | 4 | ← Offered additional pertinent information when asked questions by customer. |
| Satisfactory | 3 | ← Referred customer to another product when requested item was not available. |
| | 2 | ← Discouraged customer from waiting for an out-of-stock item. |
| Unsatisfactory | 1 | ← Argued with customer about suitability of requested product. |

**FIGURE 12–11** *Development Process for Behavioral Anchors*

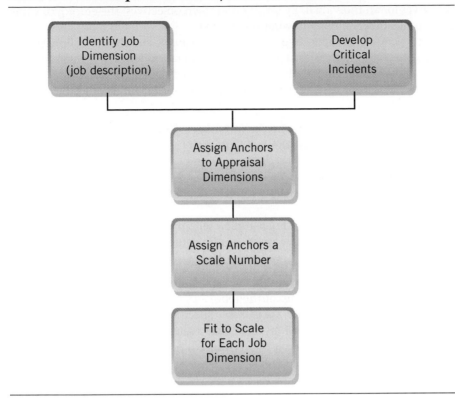

There are several problems associated with the behavioral approaches that must be considered. First, developing and maintaining behaviorally anchored rating scales require extensive time and effort. In addition, several appraisal forms are needed to accommodate different types of jobs in an organization. In a hospital, nurses, dietitians, and admission clerks all have different jobs; separate BARS forms would need to be developed for each distinct job.

## Management by Objectives (MBO)

**Management by objectives (MBO)** specifies the performance goals that an individual hopes to attain within an appropriate length of time. The objectives that each manager sets are derived from the overall goals and objectives of the organization, although MBO should not be a disguised means for a superior to dictate the objectives of individual managers or employees. Although not limited to the appraisal of managers, MBO is most often used for this purpose. Other names for MBO include *appraisal by results, target-coaching, work planning and review, performance objectives,* and *mutual goal setting.*

**KEY MBO IDEAS** Three key assumptions underlie an MBO appraisal system. First, if an employee is involved in planning and setting the objectives and determining the measure, a higher level of commitment and performance may result.

Second, if the objectives are identified clearly and precisely, the employee will do a better job of achieving the desired results. Ambiguity and confusion—and

**Management by objectives (MBO)**
Specifies the performance goals that an individual hopes to attain within an appropriate length of time.

therefore less effective performance—may result when a superior determines the objectives for an individual. By setting their own objectives, the employee gains an accurate understanding of what is expected.

Third, performance objectives should be measurable and should define results. Vague generalities such as "initiative" and "cooperation," which are common in many superior-based appraisals, should be avoided. Objectives are composed of specific actions to be taken or work to be accomplished. Sample objectives might include:

- Submit regional sales report by the fifth of every month.
- Obtain orders from at least five new customers per month.
- Maintain payroll costs at 10% of sales volume.
- Have scrap loss of less than 5%.
- Fill all organizational vacancies within 30 days after openings occur.

**THE MBO PROCESS** Implementing a guided self-appraisal system using MBO is a four-stage process. These phases are shown in Figure 12–12 and discussed next.

1. *Job review and agreement:* The employee and the superior review the job description and the key activities that comprise the employee's job. The idea is to agree on the exact makeup of the job.
2. *Development of performance standards:* Specific standards of performance must be mutually developed. In this phase a satisfactory level of performance that is specific and measurable is determined. For example, a quota of selling

**FIGURE 12–12** *MBO Process*

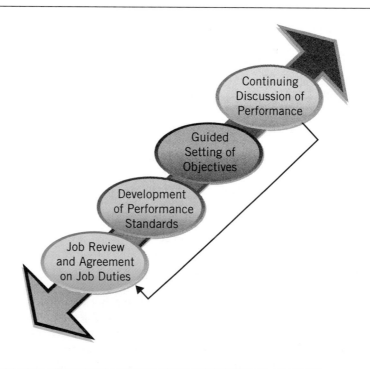

five cars per month may be an appropriate performance standard for a sales-person.

3. *Guided objective setting:* Objectives are established by the employee in conjunction with, and guided by, the superior. For the automobile salesperson, an objective might be to improve performance; the salesperson might set a new objective of selling six cars per month. Notice that the objective set may be different from the performance standard. Objectives should be realistically attainable.

4. *Continuing performance discussions:* The employee and the superior use the objectives as bases for continuing discussions about the employee's performance. Although a formal review session may be scheduled, the employee and the manager do not necessarily wait until the appointed time to discuss performance. Objectives are modified mutually, and progress is discussed during the period.

**MBO CRITIQUE** No management tool is perfect, and certainly MBO is not appropriate for all employees or all organizations. Jobs with little or no flexibility are not compatible with MBO. For example, an assembly-line worker usually has so little job flexibility that performance standards and objectives are already determined. The MBO process seems to be most useful with managerial personnel and employees who have a fairly wide range of flexibility and control over their jobs. When imposed on a rigid and autocratic management system, MBO may fail. Extreme emphasis on penalties for not meeting objectives defeats the development and participative nature of MBO.

## Combinations of Methods

There is no one best appraisal method. Indeed, research has suggested that the method used does not change the accuracy or solve rater errors. A performance measurement system that uses a combination of the preceding methods is possible and may be sensible in certain circumstances. Consider combinations to offset the following advantages and disadvantages: Category rating methods are easy to develop, but they usually do little to measure strategic accomplishments. Further, they may make inter-rater reliability problems worse. Comparative approaches help reduce leniency, central tendency, and strictness errors, which makes them useful for administrative decisions such as pay raises. *But* the comparative approaches do a poor job of linking performance to organizational goals, and they do not provide feedback for improvement as well as other methods.

Narrative methods work best for development because they potentially generate more feedback information. However, without good definitions of criteria or standards, they can be so unstructured as to be of little value. Also, these methods are poor for administrative uses. The behavioral/objective approaches work well to link performance to organizational goals, but both can require much more effort and time to define expectations and explain the process to employees. These approaches may not work well for lower-level jobs.

When managers can articulate what they want a performance appraisal system to accomplish, they can choose and/or mix the methods just mentioned to get the combinations of advantages they want.[22] For example, one combination might include a graphic rating scale of performance on major job criteria, a narrative of developmental needs, and an overall ranking of employees in a department.[23] Different categories of employees (e.g., salaried exempt, nonexempt salaried, maintenance) might require different combinations.

# Rater Errors

There are many possible sources of error in the performance appraisal process. One of the major sources is mistakes made by the rater. There is no simple way to completely eliminate these errors, but making raters aware of them through training is helpful. Various types of rater errors are discussed next.

## Problems of Varying Standards

When appraising employees, a manager should avoid using different standards and expectations for employees performing similar jobs, which is certain to incur the anger of employees. Such problems are likely to exist when ambiguous criteria and subjective weightings by supervisors are used.

Even if an employee actually has been appraised on the same basis as others, his or her perception is crucial. If a student felt a professor had graded his exam harder than another student's exam, he might ask the professor for an explanation. The student's opinion might not be changed by the professor's claim that she had "graded fairly." So it is with performance appraisals in a work situation. If performance appraisal information is to be helpful, the rater must use the same standards and weights for every employee and be able to defend the appraisal.

## Recency Effect

**Recency effect**
Error in which the rater gives greater weight to recent events when appraising an individual's performance.

The **recency effect** occurs when a rater gives greater weight to recent events when appraising an individual's performance. Giving a student a course grade based only on his performance in the last week of class, or giving a drill press operator a high rating even though she made the quota only in the last two weeks of the rating period are examples.

The recency effect is an understandable rater error. It may be difficult for a rater to remember performance that took place seven or eight months ago. Employees also become more concerned about performance as formal appraisal time approaches. Some employees may attempt to take advantage of the recency effect by currying favor with their supervisors shortly before their appraisals are conducted. The problem can be minimized by using some method of documenting both positive and negative performance.

## Central Tendency, Leniency, and Strictness Errors

**Central tendency error**
Rating all employees in a narrow band in the middle of the rating scale.

Students are well aware that some professors tend to grade easier or harder than others. A manager may develop a similar *rating pattern*. Appraisers who rate all employees within a narrow range (usually the middle or average) commit a **central tendency error.** For example, Dolores Bressler, office manager, tends to rate all her employees as average. Even the poor performers receive an average rating from Dolores. However, Jane Carr, the billing supervisor, believes that if employees are poor performers, they should be rated below average. An employee of Jane's who is rated average may well be a better performer than one rated average by Dolores.

# Research on Influence Tactics

Performance ratings can be subject to leniency and other errors, but what can subordinates do to influence the ratings their way? Research reported in *Personnel Psychology* by Wayne, Linden, Graf, and Ferris helps answer that question.

Previous research has suggested that employees are not passive, but actively engage in efforts to improve their work environments. The employees use "upward influence," which is behavior directed at persons higher in the hierarchy in an attempt to favorably influence performance ratings as well as other outcomes. Three such influence attempts and their effect on performance appraisal were considered in this research study.

One influence attempt focuses on a manager's perceptions of a subordinate's *skills with other people* that could affect performance ratings. If the subordinate uses interpersonal skill and reasoning in

dealing with the manager, the manager may then assume the subordinate treats all people that way and rate him or her well.

Another possible area for influence occurs when a manager likes the individual because he or she *does favors* for the manager. In turn this means the manager appreciates the employee and perhaps feels that employee is "owed" something.

A pervasive effect in social psychology is that people tend to perceive themselves as *being similar* to a person who engages in desirable behavior. The third area for influence could occur if managers view some subordinates as similar to themselves, and these perceptions could affect the performance ratings given by managers.

In a large corporation that produces chemicals and machinery, the researchers studied 247 pairs of managers and subordinates. The average age of subordinates was 48,

they had been with the company on average a bit over 16 years, and their average education was a bachelor's degree. A questionnaire designed to cover "career-related issues" was mailed to the employees' and managers' homes. Interpersonal skills, liking, similarity, and performance ratings were measured on the questionnaire.

The research study found that the manager's perceptions of a subordinate's interpersonal skills and similarity to the manager showed significant positive links with performance ratings. But "liking" showed no significant linkage. Apparently, influence attempts *do* affect manager's perceptions of an employee. The study also found that perceptions of an employee and perceptions of interpersonal skills and similarity do affect performance ratings, although simply liking the subordinate does not.[25]

Rating patterns also may exhibit leniency or strictness. The *leniency error* occurs when ratings of all employees are at the high end of the scale. The *strictness error* occurs when a manager uses only the lower part of the scale to rate employees. Recent research on leniency strongly suggests that when performance evaluation is done for administrative purposes (e.g., pay or promotion), the ratings are on average one-third standard deviation higher than when they are done for development purposes.[24] This finding illustrates that to avoid conflict, managers often rate employees higher than they should be. This "ratings boost" is especially likely when no manager or HR representative reviews the completed appraisals. For related research, see the HR Perspective.

## Rater Bias

**Rater bias** occurs when a rater's values or prejudices distort the rating. Rater bias may be unconscious or quite intentional. If a manager has a strong dislike of certain ethnic groups, this bias is likely to result in distorted appraisal information

**Rater bias**
Error that occurs when a rater's values or prejudices distort the rating.

for some people. Age, religion, seniority, sex, appearance, or other arbitrary classifications may be reflected in appraisals if the appraisal process is not properly designed. Examination of ratings by higher-level managers may help correct this problem.

One reason that positive rater bias or leniency may exist is that supervisors are concerned about damaging a good working relationship by giving an unfavorable rating. Or they may wish to avoid giving negative feedback, which is often unpleasant, so they inflate the ratings. Reasons for a rating biased on the low side might include sending the employee a "message" or documenting a case leading to dismissal. Rater bias is difficult to overcome, especially if a manager is not aware of the bias or will not admit to it.

## Halo Effect

**Halo effect**
Rating a person high or low on all items because of one characteristic.

The **halo effect** occurs when a manager rates an employee high or low on all items because of one characteristic. For example, if a worker has few absences, her supervisor might give her a high rating in all other areas of work, including quantity and quality of output, because of her dependability. The manager may not really think about the employee's other characteristics separately.

An appraisal that shows the same rating on all characteristics may be evidence of the halo effect. Clearly specifying the categories to be rated, rating all employees on one characteristic at a time, and training raters to recognize the problem are some ways of reducing the halo effect.

## Contrast Error

**Contrast error**
Tendency to rate people relative to other people rather than to performance standards.

Rating should be done using established standards. The **contrast error** is the tendency to rate people relative to other people rather than to performance standards. For example, if everyone else in a group is doing a mediocre job, a person performing somewhat better may be rated as excellent because of the contrast effect. But in a group performing well, the same person might have received a poor rating. Although it may be appropriate to compare people at times, the rating should reflect performance against job requirements, not against other people.

# Appraisal Feedback

Once appraisals have been completed, it is important to communicate them so that employees have a clear understanding of how they stand in the eyes of their immediate superiors and the organization. It is fairly common for organizations to *require* that managers discuss appraisals with employees. The appraisal feedback interview can be used to clear up misunderstandings on both sides. In this interview, the manager should emphasize counseling and development, not just tell the employee, "Here is how you rate and why." Focusing on development gives both parties an opportunity to consider the employee's performance—what has been done well and what has potential for improvement. Because feedback is an important part of appraisal, a brief look at feedback and how it works is a useful aid to understanding of the appraisal interview.

# Feedback as a System

There are three commonly recognized components of a feedback system. They are *data, evaluation of that data,* and some *action* based on the evaluation.

*Data* are factual information regarding observed actions or consequences. Feedback systems may be judged in terms of the accuracy, completeness, and appropriateness of the data they capture. Most often data are facts that report what happened, such as "Charlie broke a photon," or "Mary spoke harshly to an engineer." For instance, when Mary spoke harshly to the engineer, it may have been an instance of poor human relations reflecting a lack of sensitivity. However, it also may have been a proper and necessary action. Someone will have to judge the meaning or value of the data, which is evaluation.

*Evaluation* is the way the feedback system reacts to the facts, and it requires performance standards. Evaluators, of course, might come to very different conclusions on the same performance given different standards. Management might evaluate the same factual information differently than would customers (for example, regarding merchandise exchange or credit decisions) or coworkers. Evaluation can be done by the person supplying the data, by a supervisor, or by a group.

For feedback to cause change some decision must be made regarding subsequent *action.* A system in which data and evaluation did *not* influence action would not be a feedback system. In traditional appraisal systems, the manager makes specific suggestions regarding future actions the employee might take. In 360° feedback, those people from whom information was solicited might also suggest actions that the individual may consider in some decisions (for example, job assignments) but not in others (salary increases) depending on circumstances.[26]

It may be necessary to involve information providers if the subsequent actions are highly interdependent and require coordination with the people providing the information. All three components (data, evaluation, and action) are necessary parts of a successful feedback system.

# The Appraisal Interview

The appraisal interview presents both an opportunity and a danger. It is an emotional experience for the manager and the employee, because the manager must communicate both praise and constructive criticism. A major concern for managers is how to emphasize the positive aspects of the employee's performance while still discussing ways to make needed improvements. If the interview is handled poorly, the employee may feel resentment, and conflict may result, which could be reflected in future work.

Employees usually approach an appraisal interview with some concern. They often feel that discussions about performance are very personal and important to their continued job success. At the same time, they want to know how the manager feels they have been doing.[27] Figure 12–13 on the next page summarizes hints for an effective appraisal interview for supervisors and managers.

# Reactions of Managers

Managers and supervisors who must complete appraisals of their employees often resist the appraisal process. Managers may feel they are put in the position of

**FIGURE 12–13** *Hints for Managers in the Appraisal Interview*

| DO | DO NOT |
|---|---|
| • Prepare in advance<br>• Focus on performance and development<br>• Be specific about reasons for ratings<br>• Decide on specific steps to be taken for improvement<br>• Consider the supervisor's role in the subordinate's performance<br>• Reinforce desired behaviors<br>• Focus on future performance | • Lecture the employee<br>• Mix performance appraisal and salary or promotion issues<br>• Concentrate only on the negative<br>• Do all the talking<br>• Be overly critical or "harp on" a failing<br>• Feel it is necessary that both parties agree in all areas<br>• Compare the employee with others |

"playing God." A major part of the manager's role is to assist, encourage, coach, and counsel employees to improve their performance. However, being a judge on the one hand and a coach and counselor on the other may cause internal conflict and confusion for the manager.

The fact that appraisals may affect an employee's future career may cause raters to alter or bias their ratings. This bias is even more likely when managers know that they will have to communicate and defend their ratings to the employees, their bosses, or HR specialists. From the manager's viewpoint, providing negative feedback to an employee in an appraisal interview can be easily avoided by making the employee's ratings positive. Reactions such as these are attempts to avoid unpleasantness in an interpersonal situation. But avoidance helps no one. A manager *owes* an employee a well-considered appraisal.

## Reactions of Appraised Employees

Many employees view appraising as a zero-sum game—that is, one in which there must be a winner and a loser. Employees may well see the appraisal process as a threat and feel that the only way to get a higher rating is for someone else to receive a low rating. This win/lose perception is encouraged by comparative methods of rating. However, appraisals can also be non-zero-sum in nature—that is, both parties can win and no one must lose. Emphasis on the self-improvement and developmental aspects of appraisal appears to be the most effective means to reduce zero-sum reactions from those participating in the appraisal process.

Another common employee reaction is similar to students' reactions to tests. A professor may prepare a test he or she feels is fair, but it does not necessarily follow that students will feel the test is fair. They simply may see it differently. Likewise, employees being appraised may not necessarily agree with the manager doing the appraising.[28] In most cases, however, employees will view appraisals done well as what they are meant to be—constructive feedback.

# Legal and Effective Performance Appraisals

A growing number of court decisions have focused on performance appraisals, particularly in relation to equal employment opportunity (EEO) concerns. The Uniform Guidelines issued by the Equal Employment Opportunity Commission (EEOC) and other federal enforcement agencies make it clear that performance appraisal must be job related and nondiscriminatory.

## Performance Appraisals and the Law

It may seem unnecessary to emphasize that performance appraisals must be job related, because appraisals are supposed to measure how well employees are doing their jobs. Yet in numerous cases, courts have ruled that performance appraisals were discriminatory and not job related.[29]

The elements of a performance appraisal system that can survive court tests can be determined from existing case law. Various cases have provided guidance. The elements of a legally defensible performance appraisal are as follows:

- Performance appraisal criteria based on job analysis
- Absence of disparate impact and evidence of validity
- Formal evaluation criteria that limit managerial discretion
- Formal rating instrument
- Personal knowledge of and contact with appraised individual
- Training of supervisors in conducting appraisals
- Review process that prevents one manager acting alone from controlling an employee's career
- Counseling to help poor performers improve

It is clear that the courts are interested in fair and nondiscriminatory performance appraisals. Employers must decide how to design their appraisal systems to satisfy the courts, enforcement agencies, and their employees.[30]

## Effective Performance Management

Regardless of which approach is used, an understanding of what performance management is supposed to do is critical. When performance appraisal is used to develop employees as resources, it usually works. When management uses performance appraisal as a punishment or when raters fail to understand its limitations, it fails. The key is not which form or which method is used, but whether managers and employees understand its purposes. In its simplest form, a performance appraisal is a manager's observation: "Here are your strengths and weaknesses, and here is a way to shore up the weak areas." It can lead to higher employee motivation and satisfaction if done right.

But in an era of continuous improvement, an ineffective performance management system can be a huge liability.[31] Figure 12–14 shows the areas where respondents to one survey felt performance management had "opportunities for improvement." An effective performance management system will be:

- Consistent with the strategic mission of the organization
- Beneficial as a development tool
- Useful as an administrative tool
- Legal and job-related
- Viewed as generally fair by employees
- Useful in documenting employee performance

Most systems can be improved by training supervisors, because conducting performance appraisal is a big part of a performance management system. Training should focus on minimizing rater errors and providing a common frame of reference on how raters observe and recall information.

Organizationally, there is a tendency to distill performance into a single number that can be used to support pay raises. Systems based on this concept reduce the complexity of each person's contribution in order to satisfy compensation-system requirements.[32] Such systems are too simplistic to give employees useful feedback or help managers pinpoint training and development needs. In fact, use of a single numerical rating often is a barrier to performance discussions, because

**FIGURE 12–14** *Performance Management Improvements Needed*

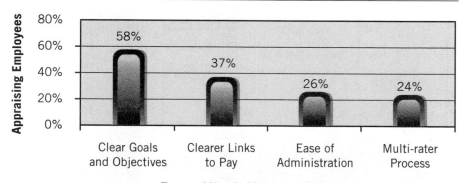

SOURCE: Adapted from "Survey of Human Resource Trends," *HR Magazine Supplement*, August 1997, 4.

what is emphasized is attaching a label to a person's performance and defending or attacking that label. Effective performance management systems evolve from the recognition that human behaviors and capabilities collapsed into a single score have limited use in shaping the necessary range of performance.

# Summary

- Performance management systems attempt to identify, encourage, measure, evaluate, improve, and reward employee performance.
- Performance is the critical link between organizational strategies and results.
- Job criteria are important job dimensions, such as teaching for a college professor, runs batted in for a major-league outfielder, or orders completed by a warehouse shipping worker.
- Relevance, contamination, and deficiency of criteria affect performance measurement.
- Appraising employee performance is useful for development and administrative purposes.
- Performance appraisal can be done either informally or systematically. Systematic appraisals usually are done annually.
- Appraisals can be done by superiors, employees, teams, outsiders, or a combination of raters. Employees also can conduct self-appraisals.
- Superiors' ratings of employees are most frequently used.
- Four types of appraisal methods are available: category rating methods, comparative methods, narrative methods, and behavioral objective methods.
- Category rating methods, especially graphic rating scales and checklists, are widely used.
- Ranking and forced distribution are comparative methods.

- Narrative methods include the critical incident technique, the essay approach, and the field review.
- Two behavioral/objectives methods of appraisal include behavioral rating approaches and management by objectives (MBO).
- Construction of a behaviorally-oriented rating scale requires a detailed job analysis so that the rating criteria and anchors are job specific.
- Management by objectives (MBO) is an approach that requires joint goal setting by a superior and an employee.
- A major source of performance appraisal problems is rater error. Rater errors include varying standards, recency effect, rater bias (such as leniency bias), rating patterns (such as central tendency error), halo effect, and contrast error.
- The appraisal feedback interview is a vital part of any appraisal system.
- Both managers and employees may resist performance appraisals, and perfect systems do not exist.
- Federal employment guidelines and numerous court decisions have scrutinized performance appraisals. The absence of specific job relatedness can create legal problems, as can subjectivity.
- Training appraisers and guarding against the tendency to reduce performance to a single number are important for an effective performance management system.

# Review and Discussion Questions

1. What is the difference between performance standards and job criteria, and why do the criteria problems of contamination and deficiency exist?
2. How can the developmental and administrative uses of performance appraisals conflict?
3. Suppose you are a supervisor. What errors might you make when preparing a performance appraisal on a clerical employee?
4. What sources are typically included in many 360° performance appraisals?

5. Explain the similarities and differences between the behavioral approaches to performance appraisal and management by objectives (MBO).
6. Construct a plan for a post-appraisal interview with an employee who has performed poorly.
7. Discuss the following statement: "Most performance appraisal systems in use today would not pass legal scrutiny."

## Terms to Know

behavioral rating approach   397
central tendency error   402
checklist   395
contrast error   404
forced distribution   396
graphic rating scale   393
halo effect   404

job criteria   381
management by objectives (MBO)   399
performance appraisal (PA)   384
performance management system   380
performance standards   382

ranking   395
rater bias   403
recency effect   402

# Using the Internet

## Conducting Team-Based Performance Appraisals

Your company has recently changed from an individual-based performance appraisal system for sales associates into one stressing team performance. As the HR manager, it is your job to change your current performance appraisal system to a team-based performance appraisal system. You are meeting with the sales managers at the end of the week to review the steps in your plan. Use the following website to assist you:

**http://www.zigonperf.com/**
**Team_Friendly.htm**

# CASE

## Revising the Performance Appraisal System at St. Luke's Hospital

Recently St. Luke's Hospital, a thoroughly modern hospital in Jacksonville, Florida, had a thoroughly modern problem. Its performance appraisal system was rapidly becoming an insurmountable pile of papers; and with 1,325 employees, the HR staff recognized that changes were needed.

Performance appraisal forms can range from a simple sheet of paper to very lengthy and complex packets. St. Luke's performance appraisal system had evolved over the years into a form with about 20 pages per employee. Although some of the length was due to concerns about meeting numerous federal, state, and health-care industry requirements, other facets of the system had been developed for administrative reasons.

The existing performance appraisal system was based on a combination of job descriptions and a performance appraisal. In addition, health-care accreditation requirements necessitated using a competency management program focusing on employee development and education. As a result, St. Luke's had combined the competency profiles with the job descriptions and performance appraisal forms. To complete an appraisal on employees, supervisors and managers scored employee performance on formal weighted criteria and then summarized the information by compensation and benefits class. Those summaries were reviewed by upper management for consistency, as one would expect. The overall performance appraisal process was paper-intensive, slow, and frustrating because it required a total of 36 different steps.

A steering committee was formed to oversee the process of changing to a better performance appraisal system. The committee established that it was crucial for the new system to better fit the needs of those using it. Also, the committee wanted the system to use more technology and less paper. Based on these general objectives, brainstorming was conducted to find bottlenecks and identify what the ideal automated process would look like. At this point, the committee understood the current systems and what key users wanted. After reviewing literature on performance appraisal systems, surveying other hospitals, and looking at software packages, the committee decided it would have to design its own system.

The option chosen consisted of moving the numerical criteria scores from the individual pages of the job description to a summary sheet that provided for scoring up to six employees on one form. Then total scores were calculated by the computer. Also, written comments were moved to a summary sheet dealing only with exceptions to standards.

The most difficult part proved to be the design of the database. It had to be designed from scratch and had to interface with existing HR systems. A software program was written to do the calculations using data already in place, and another program was written to do the calculations. The new process reduced the paperwork from 20 to 7 pages per employee. Supervisors and managers were given the option of using computerized comment sheets. Another time-saver was the ability to use the system to record and document noteworthy employee performance incidents, both positive and negative in nature, as they occurred throughout the year. This documentation feature eliminated the need for a separate note-keeping system that many managers had been using.

To implement the new performance appraisal system, training for supervisors and managers was crucial. When the training program was developed for the new system, all 97 supervisors and managers were required to attend. During the training, attendees were given a sample package with appraisal forms, a checkoff time line, a resource text, and directions for using the on-line performance appraisal forms.

To determine if the original goals had been met, the committee developed an evaluation form. After the new appraisal system had been in use, an evaluation revealed that 90% of the supervisors and managers felt that the process had indeed been streamlined. The new process was viewed as easier to understand, a significant reduction in paper had occurred, arithmetic errors were prevented, and the appraisal information was clearer and more concise.

The next year the committee reconvened to examine the first year of operation and identify areas for improvement. Since then minor revisions have been made in the performance appraisal system, updates on computer hardware and software were undertaken, and data screens have been simplified for management users. Also, efforts have begun to fully automate the performance appraisal system. In summary, the revision of St. Luke's performance appraisal system met its objectives.[33]

## Questions

1. Explain why the new performance appraisal system at St. Luke's Hospital is more likely to result in more accurate performance appraisals.
2. Describe some of the advantages and disadvantages of combining job descriptions, performance appraisals, and competency profiles for development as St. Luke's did.

# Notes

1. Adapted from Larry Stevens, "Rave Reviews," *Human Resource Executive,* January 1998, 41–43.
2. David Westman, "Seven Steps to Successful Performance Appraisal," *ACA News,* July/August 1998, 13–16.
3. R. J. Mirabile, "Everything You Wanted to Know about Competency Modeling," *Training & Development,* August 1997, 73–75.
4. Fred Kniggendorf, "Helping Supervisors Define Standards of Performance," *HR Focus,* February 1998, 13.
5. Allen D. Heuerman, "Using Performance Management to Energize the Results Act," *The Public Manager,* Fall 1997, 17–21.
6. "Manipulations of Evaluations Suggested," *EEO Diversity,* July 6, 1998, 716.
7. Joann S. Lublin, "It's Shape-up Time for Performance Reviews," *The Wall Street Journal,* October 3, 1994, B1.
8. Based on Tim Schellhardt, "Behind the Scenes at One CEO's Performance Review," *The Wall Street Journal,* April 27, 1998, B1.
9. Devaun M. Kite, et al., "Can Managers Appraise Performance Too Often?", *Journal of Applied Business Research* 13 (n.d.), 41–51.
10. Joann S. Lublin, "New Hires Win Fast Raises in Accelerated Job Reviews," *The Wall Street Journal,* October 6, 1998, B1.
11. Mary Jane Kolar, "Evaluating Board Performance," *Association Management,* January 1998, 82.
12. Carol Patton, "Panel of Peers," *Human Resource Executive,* June 5, 1998, 84–86.

13. Charles S. Osborn, "Systems for Sustainable Organizations," *Journal of Management Studies* 35 (July 1998), 481–510.

14. Margaret A. Jacobs, "Red Lobster Tale: Peers Decide Fired Waitress's Fate," *The Wall Street Journal,* January 20, 1998, B1.

15. Hilary Stout, "Self-Evaluation Brings Change to a Family's Ad Agency," *The Wall Street Journal,* January 6, 1998, B1.

16. Christine Bunish, "Reviewing the Review Process," *Business Marketing,* December 1997, 41.

17. David Waldman and David Bowen, "The Acceptability of 360° Appraisals," *Human Resource Management,* Summer 1998, 117–129.

18. R. Lepsinger and A.D. Lucia, "360 Degree Feedback and Performance Appraisal," *Training,* September 1997, 62.

19. Dianne M. LaMountain, "Assessing the Value of Multisource Feedback," *Employment Relations Today,* Autumn 1997, 75–90.

20. John H. Jackson and Martin M. Greller, "Decision Elements for Using 360° Feedback," *Human Resource Planning,* 20 (1998), 18–28.

21. Joseph Maiorca, "How to Construct BARS," *Supervision,* August 1997, 15–19.

22. John G. Simonds Jr. and Robert G. Bell, "Creating Individual and Team Performance Measures," *Employment Relations Today,* Winter 1997, 27–36.

23. Michael Kramer, "Designing an Individualized Performance Evaluation System," *FBI Law Enforcement Bulletin,* March 1998, 20–27.

24. I. M. Jawahar and Charles R. Williams, "Where All the Children Are Above Average," *Personnel Psychology* 50 (1997), 905–926.

25. Sandy Wayne, et al., "The Role of Upward Influence Tactics in Human Resource Decisions," *Personnel Psychology* 50 (1997), 979–1005.

26. David A. Waldman, Leanne E. Atwaker, and David Antonioni, "Has 360° Feedback Gone Amok?", *Academy of Management Executive,* May 1998, 86–94.

27. Dick Gnote, "Painless Performance Appraisals Focus on Results, Behaviors," *HR Magazine,* October 1998, 52–58.

28. Theresa M. Wellbourne, Diane E. Johnson, and Emir Erez, "The Role-Based Performance Scale," *Academy of Management Journal* 41 (1998), 540–555.

29. John M. Werner and Mark C. Bolino, "Explaining U.S. Court of Appeals Decisions Involving Performance Appraisal," *Personnel Psychology* 50 (1997), 1–24.

30. "Minimize Performance Evaluation Legal Risks," *Journal of Accountancy,* February 1998, 10.

31. Clinton O. Longnecker and Laurence S. Fink, "Keys to Designing and Running an Effective Performance Appraisal System," *Journal of Compensation and Benefits,* November/December 1997, 28.

32. Jean-Francois Manzoni and Jean-Louis Barsoux, "The Set-up-to-Fail Syndrome," *Harvard Business Review,* March-April 1998, 101–114.

33. Based on LaJuan Aderhold, Nancy L. O'Keefe, and Darrell E. Burke, "Critical Care for Review Process," *Personnel Journal,* April 1996, 115–120.

# CHAPTER 13

# Compensation Strategies and Practices

*After you have read this chapter, you should be able to:*

- Identify the two general types of compensation and the components of each.

- Give examples of two different compensation philosophies in organizations.

- Discuss four strategic compensation design issues currently being used.

- Describe three behavioral considerations affecting compensation activities.

- Identify the basic provisions of the Fair Labor Standards Act (FLSA).

- Define *job evaluation* and discuss four methods of performing it.

- Outline the process of building a wage and salary administration system.

- Discuss how a pay-for-performance system is established.

# Strategic Redesign of Compensation at Bayer

The important link between a firm's strategic objectives and its compensation system is illustrated by what has occurred at Bayer Corporation. The process used and experiences at Bayer also illustrate how compensation systems must be compatible with the culture of an organization.

Bayer Corporation is a subsidiary of Bayer Group AG, a Germany-based global chemical company. Several years ago, Bayer Corporation was created by combining three different operating companies, each with its own markets, products, and cultures—Mobay Chemicals, Miles, Inc., and Agfa. Bayer executives recognized that compensation systems were a critical component of creating a corporate culture that embodies the values and visions developed during the strategic planning for the new firm. Once the merger of the three entities had occurred, a new organizational structure was implemented. This structure had fewer layers and levels, and was developed to give Bayer employees the flexibility to move across organizational units and internationally.

Bayer, like many organizations today, compensated people for doing specific jobs. But they wanted to reward people for their flexibility in playing different roles in the organization and moving between jobs. At the same time, Bayer executives wanted a simple compensation system that was tied to the core values and culture that Bayer hoped would evolve.

Bayer began its transition to a different compensation system by establishing a task force of 14 executives chaired by Bayer's Vice-President of Benefits. This Job Advisory Committee, as it was labeled, was to recommend the processes needed to move to a job evaluation system more aligned with the new organization. Job evaluation, the systematic process of determining the internal value of jobs in relation to other jobs, had previously been done in two of the companies using a traditional point factor system; however the third entity had not used a formal job evaluation system.

The committee began by identifying the advantages and disadvantages of the existing point system. The committee identified many features of the old system that were working well, particularly the involvement of managers and employees in the job evaluation "pointing" process. But the committee felt that the existing point factors and dimensions were too task-based, and they did not reflect the flexibility desired as part of the organizational culture. Also, greater recognition of employees' capabilities, not just their jobs and budgetary responsibilities, needed to be considered.

Assisted by a major consulting firm over a period of time and a number of meetings, the committee decided to redesign the job evaluation system and focus on work-value competencies.

The new work-value clusters defined were:

- Improvement opportunity
- Contribution
- Capability
- Expertise and complexity
- Leadership and integration
- Relationship-building skills

For these six clusters, the committee identified scales and point values. The process of developing the new factors and points took about a year.

Once the new system had been tested by pointing jobs on both the old and new systems, fine-tuning was needed. Ultimately, a cross-section of benchmark jobs was pointed using the new system and the results calibrated statistically to the old system, rather than having all jobs in the organization repointed again.

The ultimate test of the new job evaluation system has been its acceptance and use throughout Bayer. Based on feedback from managers and employees alike, the new system is working well. Bayer's job evaluation system has become the means of aligning its compensation system with the business values of the new corporate culture being created. The compensation plan also supports business strategies and rewards employees as Bayer grows and meets its strategic objectives.[1]

*Greater recognition of employees' capabilities, not just their jobs and budgetary responsibilities, needed to be considered.*

> ❝*Organizations need to be fluid to move as markets move. That necessitates a more flexible approach to compensation.*❞
>
> KATHRYN MCKEE, SPHR, CCP

Compensation systems in organizations must be linked to organizational objectives and strategies, as the opening discussion of Bayer Corporation indicates. But compensation also requires balancing the interests and costs of the employer with the expectations of employees.[2] A compensation program in an organization should have four objectives:

- Legal compliance with all appropriate laws and regulations
- Cost effectiveness for the organization
- Internal, external, and individual equity for employees
- Performance enhancement for the organization

For employers, compensation costs must be at a level that both ensures organizational competitiveness and provides sufficient rewards to employees for their knowledge, skills, abilities, and performance accomplishments. Balancing these facets so that the employer can attract, retain, and reward the performance of employees requires considering several types of compensation.

# Nature of Compensation

Compensation is an important factor affecting how and why people choose to work at one organization over others. Employers must be reasonably competitive with several types of compensation in order to hire, keep, and reward performance of individuals in the organization.

## Types of Compensation

Rewards can be both *intrinsic* and *extrinsic*. *Intrinsic* rewards often include praise for completing a project or meeting some performance objectives. Other psychological and social effects of compensation reflect the intrinsic type of rewards. *Extrinsic* rewards are tangible, having the form of both monetary and nonmonetary rewards. Tangible components of a compensation program are of two general types (Figure 13–1). With the direct type of compensation, monetary rewards are provided by the employer. *Base pay* and *variable pay* are the most common forms of direct compensation. Indirect compensation commonly consists of employee *benefits*.

**BASE PAY**  The basic compensation that an employee receives, usually as a wage or salary, is called **base pay.** Many organizations use two base pay categories, *hourly* and *salaried,* which are identified according to the way pay is distributed and the nature of the jobs. Hourly pay is the most common means of payment based on time; employees who are paid hourly are said to receive **wages**, which are payments directly calculated on the amount of time worked. In contrast, people who are paid **salaries** receive payments that are consistent from period to period despite the number of hours worked. Being salaried typically has carried higher status for employees than being paid wages. Some organizations have

*LOGGING ON . . .*
**Compensation Systems**
Benchmark compensation systems are outlined on this site, including information on both traditional and variable pay systems.

**http://www.banschke.com/ Bau_BCSi.htm**

**Base pay**
The basic compensation an employee receives, usually as a wage or salary.

**Wages**
Payments directly calculated on the amount of time worked.

**Salaries**
Payments that are consistent from period to period despite the number of hours worked.

**FIGURE 13–1** *Components of a Compensation Program*

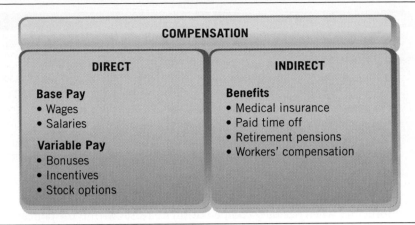

switched to an all-salaried approach with their manufacturing and clerical employees in order to create a greater sense of loyalty and organizational commitment. But they still must pay overtime to certain employees in jobs covered by federal and state pay laws.

**VARIABLE PAY** Another type of direct pay is **variable pay**, which is compensation linked directly to performance accomplishments. The most common types of variable pay for most employees are bonuses and incentive program payments. For executives, it is common to have longer-term rewards such as stock options. Variable pay, including executive compensation, is discussed in Chapter 14.

**BENEFITS** Many organizations provide numerous extrinsic rewards in an indirect manner. With indirect compensation, employees receive the tangible value of the rewards without receiving the actual cash. A **benefit** is an indirect reward, such as health insurance, vacation pay, or retirement pensions, given to an employee or group of employees as a part of organizational membership.

**Variable pay**
Compensation linked to individual, team, and/or organizational performance.

**Benefit**
An indirect reward given to an employee or group of employees as a part of organizational membership.

## Compensation Responsibilities

Compensation costs are significant expenditures in most organizations. For instance, at one large hotel, employee payroll and benefits expenditures comprise about 50% of all costs. Although compensation costs are relatively easy to calculate, the value derived by employers and employees is more difficult to identify. To administer these expenditures wisely, HR specialists and other managers must work together.

A typical division of compensation responsibilities is illustrated in Figure 13–2. HR specialists usually guide the overall development and administration of an organizational compensation system by conducting job evaluations and wage surveys. Also, because of the technical complexity involved, HR specialists typically are the ones who develop base pay programs and salary structures and policies. Operating managers evaluate the performance of employees and consider

**FIGURE 13–2** *Typical Compensation Responsibilities*

| HR Unit | Managers |
|---|---|
| • Develops and administers compensation system <br> • Conducts job evaluation and wage surveys <br> • Develops wage/salary structures and policies | • Attempt to match performance and rewards <br> • Recommend pay rates and increases based on guidelines from HR unit <br> • Evaluate employee performance for compensation purposes |

that performance when deciding compensation increases within the policies and guidelines established by the HR unit.

# Strategic Compensation

Compensation decisions must be viewed strategically. Because so many organizational funds are spent on compensation-related activities, it is critical for top management and HR executives to view the "strategic" fit of compensation with the strategies and objectives of the organization. The changes in the global marketplace for products and services have led to organizational changes in business philosophies, strategies, and objectives. Increasingly, organizations are recognizing that compensation philosophies must change also. The example of Bayer Corporation illustrates this alignment. The compensation practices that typically exist in a new organization may be different from those in a mature, bureaucratic organization. For example, if a firm wishes to create an innovative, entrepreneurial culture, it may offer bonuses and stock equity programs so that employees can participate in the growth and success of the company, but set its base pay and benefits at relatively modest levels. However, for a large, stable organization, highly structured pay and benefit programs may be more common.

## Compensation Philosophies

There are two basic compensation philosophies, which should be seen as opposite ends of a continuum. At one end of the continuum in Figure 13–3 is the *entitlement* philosophy; at the other end, the *performance-oriented* philosophy.

**ENTITLEMENT ORIENTATION** The entitlement philosophy can be seen in many organizations that traditionally have given automatic increases to their employees every year. Further, most of those employees receive the same or nearly the same percentage increase each year. Employees and managers who subscribe to the entitlement philosophy believe that individuals who have worked another year are *entitled* to a raise in base pay, and that all incentives and benefit programs should continue and be increased, regardless of changing industry or economic conditions. Commonly, in organizations following an entitlement philosophy, pay increases are referred to as *cost-of-living* raises, whether or not they are tied specifically to economic indicators. Following an entitlement

**FIGURE 13–3** *Continuum of Compensation Philosophies*

| ◀ • • • • •   Entitlement  • • • • • • • • • • • • • • • • • • • • • • • • • • • • • • • Performance • • • • • • • • • • ▶ |
| --- |
| • Seniority-based | • No raises for length of service |
| • Across-the-board raises | • No raises for longer-service poor performers |
| • "Guaranteed" movement of scales | • Market adjusted pay structures |
| • Industry comparisons only | • Broader industry comparison |
| • "Santa Claus" bonuses | • Bonuses tied to performance results |

philosophy ultimately means that as employees continue their employment lives, employer costs increase, regardless of employee performance or other organizational competitive pressures. Market comparisons tend to be made within an industry, rather than more broadly considering compensation in firms of all types. Bonuses in many entitlement-oriented organizations are determined very paternalistically and often do not reflect operating results. Instead, the CEO or owner acts as Santa Claus at the end of the year, passing out bonus checks that generally do not vary from year to year. Therefore employees "expect" to receive the bonuses as another form of entitlement.

**PERFORMANCE ORIENTATION** Where a *performance-oriented* philosophy is followed, no one is guaranteed compensation just for adding another year to organizational service. Instead, pay and incentives are based on performance differences among employees. Employees who perform well get larger compensation increases; those who do not perform satisfactorily receive little or no increase in compensation. Thus, employees who perform satisfactorily should keep up or advance in relation to a broad view of the labor market for their jobs, whereas poor or marginal performers should fall behind.

Bonuses are paid based on individual, group, and/or organizational performance results. Few organizations are totally performance-oriented in all facets of their compensation practices. However, breaking the entitlement mode is increasingly occurring in the organizational restructuring common throughout many industries. A study of public-sector HR managers found that there is a desire and need to shift toward more performance-oriented compensation practices in many public-sector organizations.[3] How fast that occurs, given the historical traditions and the strength of public-sector unions, remains to be seen.

## Strategic Compensation Design

Designing a compensation system for an organization requires knowledge of the strategic issues facing the organization and the culture of the organization. Organizations today are facing more pressures and greater demands for flexibility from their managers and employees. As Figure 13–4 on the next page notes, compensation strategies used in organizations have shifted. Organizations that are more static have fixed salaries, limited participation in bonuses, and other features clearly focused internally. However, dynamic, rapidly changing organizations have more varied compensation systems that reward current performance and growth.

**FIGURE 13–4** *Changing Compensation Strategies*

| Yesterday | Today | Tomorrow |
|-----------|-------|----------|
| • Fixed salary | • Variable pay as add-on to salary | • Low fixed salary, more variable pay |
| • Bonuses/perks for executives only | • Variable pay emerging throughout organization | • Variable pay common throughout the organization |
| • Fixed benefits, reward long tenure | • Flexible benefits | • Portable benefits |
| • Company-based career, "moving up" | • Industry-based career, "moving around" | • Skill-based career, interim employment |
| • Hierarchical organizations | • Flatter, team-based organizations | • Networked "virtual" organizations |
| • "Cookie cutter" pay plans | • Total compensation (Look at benefits, too) | • Customized, integrated pay systems; pay, benefits, intangibles |

SOURCE: Reprinted from September 1996 *ACA News,* with permission from the American Compensation Association (ACA), 14040 N. Northsight Blvd., Scottsdale, Arizona 85260; telephone 602/951-9191; fax 602/483-8352. © ACA. http://www.acaonline.org

**COMPENSATION AND ORGANIZATIONAL CULTURE** It is critical that organizations align their compensation practices with their organizational cultures, especially if efforts are made to change the cultures because of competitive pressures. For instance, a telecommunications firm faced major changes in the industry after government restrictions on pricing were removed and cable television firms were allowed to provide telephone service. The firm could not continue to offer the wages it had paid when government agencies allowed the pricing of services to obtain full cost recovery and a set level of profits. When changing organizational culture, organizations must change their compensation systems if they are to avoid sending mixed signals to employees. The opening discussion about Bayer Corporation illustrates the importance of matching compensation practices to the organizational culture.

**COST-EFFECTIVENESS AND LABOR MARKET POSITIONING** Another strategic design consideration for compensation systems is to balance the costs of attracting and retaining employees with the competitive pressures in its industry. Considering these pressures is particularly important when the organization faces a very tight labor market for workers with specific skills. The cost pressures of industry competition with organizations in lower-wage countries such as China or Mexico must also be addressed, while maintaining competitive pricing for the firm's products and services.

Some organizations have specifically stated policies about where they wish to be positioned in the labor market. These policies use a *quartile strategy,* and Figure 13–5 illustrates the three different quartiles. Data in pay surveys reveals that the actual dollar difference between quartiles is generally 15–20%.

Most employers position themselves in the *second quartile,* in the middle of the market, based on pay survey data of other employers' compensation plans.

Choosing this level attempts to balance employer cost pressures and the need to attract and retain employees by mid-level compensation plans.

An employer using a *first-quartile* approach is choosing to pay below market compensation. This may be done for several reasons. One is because of a shortage of funds and the inability to pay more and still meet strategic objectives. Also, if there is an abundance of workers, particularly those with lower skills, then a below-market approach can be used to attract sufficient workers at a lesser cost. The downside of this strategy is that higher turnover of workers is more likely. If the labor market supply tightens, then difficulty in attracting and retaining workers will probably result.

A *third-quartile* approach is an aggressive, above-market emphasis. This strategy may be chosen to ensure that sufficient workers with the required capabilities are attracted and retained. It also may allow the organization to be more selective when hiring workers. However, because it is a higher-cost approach, it is crucial that those paid above-market wages be more productive.

Most compensation programs are designed to reward employees for the tasks, duties, and responsibilities performed. It is the jobs done that determine, to a large extent, which employees have higher base rates than others. Employees are paid more for doing jobs that require more variety of tasks, more knowledge and skills, greater physical effort, or more demanding working conditions.

**COMPETENCY-BASED PAY** However, as discussed in Chapter 7 on job analysis, some organizations are emphasizing competencies more than tasks. A growing number of organizations, including Bayer Corporation, are paying employees for the competencies they have rather than just for the specific tasks being performed. Paying for competencies rewards employees who are more versatile and have continued to develop their competencies. In *knowledge-based pay* (KBP) or

**FIGURE 13–5** *Compensation Quartile Strategies*

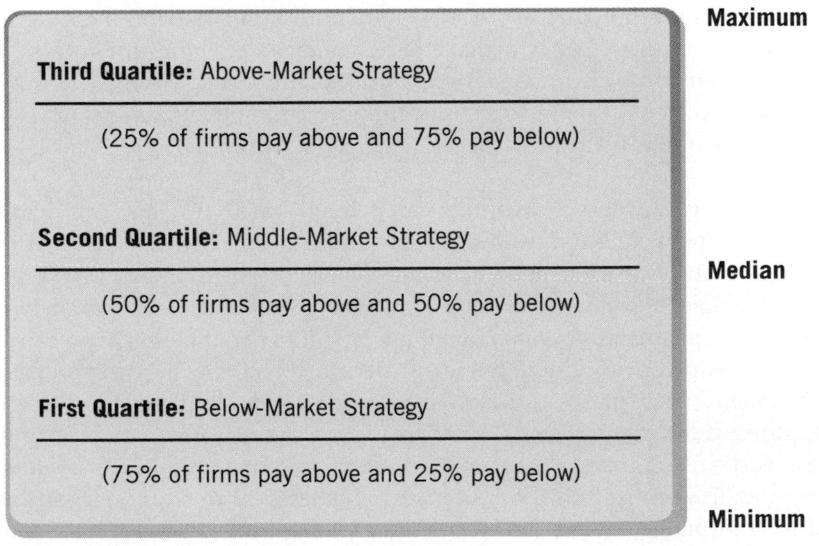

Maximum

**Third Quartile:** Above-Market Strategy

(25% of firms pay above and 75% pay below)

**Second Quartile:** Middle-Market Strategy

Median

(50% of firms pay above and 50% pay below)

**First Quartile:** Below-Market Strategy

(75% of firms pay above and 25% pay below)

Minimum

# Research on Skill-Based Pay and Organization Performance

A growing number of organizations have adopted competency-based pay programs that focus on employee skills. But whether these skill-based pay programs result in organizational performance and productivity increases has not been documented. Murray and Gebhart conducted a study, published in the *Academy of Management Journal*, that focused on providing data on this issue.

The researchers gathered data from an organization that had adopted a skill-based pay (SBP) plan and a comparable organization that was using a traditional task-based plan. Both organizations were component assembly plants of the same large manufacturing corporation.

First, the researchers interviewed managers at the plant using the SBP plan and obtained details on the plan. In the SBP plan five skill blocks had been identified, and employees progressed through them as they acquired more capabilities. Employees were offered training on the skills, and they had to demonstrate skill mastery both initially and ongoing.

Next, data was gathered from both plants to track labor costs per part, productivity, and quality. Using statistical analyses, the researchers found that the plant using SBP had 58% greater productivity, 82% better scrap reduction, and 16% lower cost per part produced than in the comparable facility not using SBP. Based on these results, the researchers suggested that the positive effects found in the plant using an SBP plan are due to the comprehensive HR efforts needed to make the SBP plan work.[4]

***LOGGING ON . . .***
**American Compensation Association**
This web site has a listing of products, services, and the latest research on compensation and benefit issues.

**http://www.acaonline.org**

*skill-based pay* (SBP) systems, employees start at a base level of pay and receive increases as they learn to do other jobs or gain other skills and therefore become more valuable to the employer. For example, a printing firm has two-color, four-color, and six-color presses. The more colors, the more skill required of the press operators. Under a KBP or SBP system, press operators increase their pay as they learn how to operate the more complex presses, even though sometimes they may be running only two-color jobs. The HR Perspective describes research on such a plan.

A survey sponsored by the American Compensation Association (ACA) found that the success of competency plans requires managerial commitment to a philosophy different from the one that has existed traditionally in organizations.[5] This approach places far more emphasis on training employees and supervisors. Also, workflow must be adapted to allow workers to move from job to job as needed.

When an organization moves to a competency-based system, considerable time must be spent identifying what the required competencies are for various jobs.[6] Then each *block* of competencies must be priced using market data. Progression of employees must be possible, and they must be paid appropriately for all of their competencies. Any *limitations* on the numbers of people who can acquire more competencies should be clearly identified. *Training* in the appropriate competencies is particularly critical. Also important to a competency-based system is a means for *certification* of employees who have acquired certain competencies. Further, a process must exist for verifying that employees *maintain competencies*. In summary, use of a competency-based system requires significant investment of management time and needs a continuous commitment by top management.

Both the organization and employees can benefit from a competency-based system that is properly designed and implemented. Some outcomes are:

**Organization-Related Outcomes**

- Greater workforce flexibility
- Increased effectiveness of work teams
- Fewer bottlenecks in workflow
- Increased worker output per hour

**Employee-Related Outcomes**

- Enhanced employee understanding of organizational "big picture"
- Greater employee self-management capabilities
- Improved employee satisfaction
- Greater employee commitment

Because competency plans focus on growth and development of employee competencies, those employees who continue to develop their competencies to receive pay raises are the real winners. As more organizations recognize the value of human resources, it is likely that competency-based systems may spread.

**BROADBANDING AND CAREER DEVELOPMENT** Using an approach closely related to competency-based compensation, many organizations have revised their hierarchical pay structures. **Broadbanding**, which uses fewer pay grades having broader ranges than traditional compensation systems, is increasingly being used. Figure 13–6 depicts the difference between traditional pay structures and broadbanding. Interest in broadbanding also has spread globally. One survey of global companies found increased usage of broadbanding and career bands in 15 different countries.[7]

There are several reasons why it is beneficial to reduce the number of pay grades and broaden pay ranges. First and foremost, broadbanding is more consistent with the flattening of organizational levels and the growing use of jobs that are multidimensional. With fewer bands and broader ranges, employees can

**Broadbanding**
Practice of using fewer pay grades having broader ranges than traditional compensation systems.

**FIGURE 13–6** *Traditional Pay Structure vs. Broadbanding*

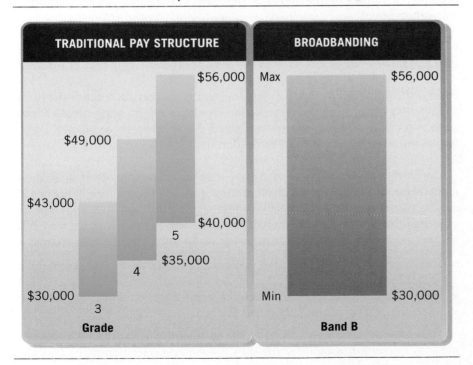

shift responsibilities as market conditions and organizational needs change. Traditional questions from employees about when a promotion to a new grade occurs, and what pay adjustments will be made for temporarily performing some new job responsibilities, are unnecessary.[8]

Another advantage of broadbanding is that employee career development can be enhanced when the artificial barriers of numerous pay grades are removed. With broadbanding, many of the control mechanisms traditionally enforced by HR departments also are removed, and authority for more compensation decisions is decentralized to the operating managers. By allowing employees to move into other job areas and broaden their knowledge, skills, and abilities without having to deal with a large number of constraints imposed by a compensation program, the organization encourages employees to move between departments, divisions, and locations. In firms that have adopted broadbanding, employees are encouraged to move across business units and apply for openings in areas of the company other than where they have been working. This cross-functional development is beneficial because it creates more employees who have greater flexibility and broader sets of capabilities. One study of companies using broadbanding found that the primary reasons for its use were (1) creating more flexible organizations, (2) encouraging competency development, and (3) emphasizing career development.[9]

However, broadbanding is not appropriate for every organization. Many organizations still operate in a relatively structured manner, and the flexibility associated with broadbanding is not consistent with the traditional hierarchial culture in which executives and managers have been operating.

Another problem with broadbanding is that many employees have become "conditioned" to the idea that a promotion is accompanied by a pay raise and movement to a new pay grade. As a result of removing this grade progression, the organization may be seen as having fewer upward promotion opportunities. Furthermore, a number of individuals do not want to move across the organization into other areas.

Despite these and other problems, it is likely that broadbanding will continue to grow in usage. As more and more organizations face changes due to competition and other strategic factors, the flexibility of broadbanding may be needed.[10]

**BASE AND VARIABLE PAY** Another growing compensation approach is the use of variable pay throughout the organization. Traditionally in many organizations, most employees receive compensation based either on wages or salaries. Except for executives, few individuals receive additional pay tied to performance except for annual raises in their base pay amounts.

Currently, variable pay programs have been extensively adopted throughout many organizations and for all levels of employees. Widespread use of various incentive plans, team bonuses, organizational gainsharing programs, and other designs have been implemented in order to link growth in compensation to results. Management must address two main issues when using variable pay systems:

- Should performance be measured and rewarded based on individual, group, or organizational performance?
- Should the length of time for measuring performance be short-term (less than one year) or longer-term (more than one year)?

The various types and facets of variable pay are discussed in the next chapter. But it is important to monitor the shift toward compensation being allocated

## HR PERSPECTIVE
# Team-Based Rewards

As more organizations have established work teams, they have developed team-based reward systems. Several company examples illustrate some of the factors associated with having a successful team-based compensation program.

At Libby, Inc., workers at its Toledo, Ohio, manufacturing plants set plant goals. These goals then are used to peg 60% of performance targets, while the other 40% are based on corporate operations and improvements in income. The plants use cross-functional teams for the production work, and a gainsharing program has been established that provides variable pay based on performance against those goals. The program illustrates the importance of using business unit goals, not just corporate or team goals.

Base pay for teams is generally recommended to be built on a skill-based system of competencies. Teams at Eastman Chemical Company in Tennessee have a pay program for applied knowledge and skills set up in six levels.

But team-based pay does not always succeed easily. At a Frito-Lay facility in Missouri, the team-based compensation program was installed by management in the plant. Training in "team behavior" was necessary to change the organizational culture. All went satisfactorily until an announcement was made that the pay program was being changed from pay raises being given across-the-board to a pay-for-performance system using team member input. Many workers objected to their team members influencing pay decisions, and the plant management had to defer implementing team-based rewards. This experience illustrates that team-based compensation should be used only when the organizational culture is compatible with it, and there has been extensive employee involvement and acceptance.[11]

through such plans, rather than the organization relying solely on base pay to reward employees at all levels for attaining strategic organizational objectives.

**TEAM-BASED COMPENSATION** Another compensation design issue that has grown in importance is team-based compensation. As organizations have shifted to using work teams, a logical concern is how to develop compensation programs that build on the team concept. It becomes even trickier because organizations are compensating *individuals* who work in teams. Paying everyone on teams the same amount even though there are differing competencies and levels of performance obviously may create equity concerns for individual employees.

Many organizations use team rewards as variable pay above base pay. For base pay, individuals are compensated using competency- or skill-based approaches. A study of organizations using team-based rewards, and of individuals serving on the teams, identified that team rewards are most frequently distributed annually (58%) as a specified dollar amount (56%), not as a percentage of base pay (44%).[12]

Based on experiences in the team-based environment, as the HR Perspective illustrates, several factors should be considered when using team-based reward systems:[13]

- Use skill-based pay for the base.
- Make the system simple and understandable.
- Use variable pay based on business entity performance.
- Distribute rewards at the team level.
- Have a high degree of employee involvement.

In summary, the most successful uses of team-based compensation have been as variable pay on top of base pay. Rather than substituting for base pay programs, team-based rewards appear to be useful in rewarding performance of a team beyond the satisfactory level. More discussion on team-based incentives is contained in the next chapter.

# Behavioral Aspects of Compensation

Behavioral factors affect all types of compensation. Most people in work organizations are working in order to gain rewards for their efforts. Except in volunteer organizations, people expect to receive fair value in the form of compensation for their efforts. Whether regarding base pay, variable pay, or benefits, the extent to which employees perceive they are receiving fair value often affects their performance and how they view their jobs and employers.

## Equity

**Equity**

The perceived fairness of the relation between what a person does (inputs) and what the person receives (outcomes).

People want to be treated fairly in all facets of compensation, including base pay, incentives, and benefits. This is the concept of **equity,** which is the perceived fairness of the relation between what a person does (inputs) and what the person receives (outcomes). *Inputs* are what a person brings to the organization and includes educational level, age, experience, productivity, and other skills or efforts. What a person receives from the organization, or *outcomes,* are the rewards obtained in exchange for inputs. Outcomes include pay, benefits, recognition, achievement, prestige, and any tangible or intangible reward received. Individuals judge equity in compensation by comparing the effort and performance they give with the effort and performance of others and the rewards those others receive. But it must be stressed that these comparisons are personal and based on individual perceptions, not just facts.

A sense of inequity occurs when the comparison process results in an imbalance between input and outcomes. As Figure 13–7 indicates, there are individual, organizational, and external dimensions to equity.

**PROCEDURAL AND DISTRIBUTIVE JUSTICE IN COMPENSATION** Internally, equity means that employees receive compensation in relation to the knowledge, skills, and abilities (KSAs) they use in their jobs as well as their responsibilities and accomplishments. Two key issues that relate to internal equity are *procedural justice* and *distributive justice.*

**Procedural justice**

The perceived fairness of the process and procedures used to make decisions about employees.

**Procedural justice** is the perceived fairness of the process and procedures used to make decisions about employees, including their pay. Procedural fairness is viewed both in terms of the policies and procedures and the actions of supervisors and managers who implement the policies and procedures.[14] As it applies to compensation, the process of determining the base pay for jobs, the allocation of pay increases, and the measurement of performance must be perceived as fair. Two critical issues are (1) how appropriate and fair is the process used to assign jobs to pay grades? and (2) how are the pay ranges for those jobs established?

**Distributive justice**

The perceived fairness in the distribution of outcomes.

Another related issue that must be considered is **distributive justice,** which refers to the perceived fairness of the amounts given for performance. This facet of equity refers to how pay relates to performance. For instance, if a hard-working employee whose performance is outstanding receives the same across-the-board raise as an employee with attendance problems and mediocre perfor-

**FIGURE 13–7** *Equity Considerations in Compensation*

mance, then greater inequity may be perceived. Likewise, if two employees have similar performance records but one receives a significantly greater pay raise, the other one may perceive that the inequity is due to supervisory favoritism or other factors not related to the job.

To address concerns about justice, some organizations establish *appeals procedures*. In public-sector organizations, appeals procedures usually are identified formally, whereas in private-sector firms they are usually more informal. Typically, employees can contact the HR department after they have discussed their concerns with their immediate supervisors and managers.

**PAY OPENNESS** Another equity issue concerns the degree of openness or secrecy that organizations allow regarding their pay systems. Pay information kept secret in "closed" systems includes how much others make, what raises others have received, and even what pay grades and ranges exist in the organization.

A growing number of organizations are opening up their pay systems to some degree by informing employees of compensation policies, providing a general description of the basis for the compensation system, and indicating where an individual's pay is within a pay grade. Such information allows employees to make more accurate equity comparisons. It is crucial in an open pay system that managers be able to explain satisfactorily any pay differences that exist.

**EXTERNAL EQUITY** Externally, the organization must provide compensation that is seen as equitable in relation to the compensation provided employees performing similar jobs in other organizations. If an employer does not provide compensation that is viewed as fair by its employees, that organization may have higher turnover of employees, may have more difficulty recruiting qualified and scarce-skill employees, and may attract and retain individuals with less knowledge, skills, and abilities, resulting in lower overall organizational productivity. Organizations track external equity by using pay surveys, which are discussed later in the chapter.

## Importance of Equity and Compensation Activities

It is important for HR professionals and managers to develop, administer, and maintain compensation programs that are perceived equitably by employees. The consequence of an equitable compensation program is that individuals are more likely to be attracted to and take jobs in organizations where employees do not voice widespread concerns about equity. Greater loyalty, less turnover, and higher commitment to achieve organizational performance objectives are more likely if employees believe they are compensated fairly and will share in the growth of the organization. Also, the organization must have policies, procedures, and administrative support systems that are viewed as job-related and are not manipulated by favoritism or personality preferences of managers and supervisors.

Finally, external equity is crucial if the organization is going to compete effectively in the labor market. Increasingly in many labor markets, some employers are finding it difficult to attract and retain a workforce with the necessary capabilities to compete in a global marketplace. Regularly tracking external pay data and updating pay structures are integral to ensuring external equity in any organization.

# Legal Constraints on Pay Systems

Compensation systems must comply with a myriad of government constraints. Minimum wage standards and hours of work are two important areas addressed by the laws. The following discussion examines the laws and regulations affecting base compensation; laws and regulations affecting incentives and benefits are examined in later chapters.

**LOGGING ON . . .**
**Information on Fair Labor Standards Act**
This web site includes background information on Fair Labor Standards Act provisions affecting compensation policies and practices.

**http://humanresources.ucr. edu/hrunits/compensation/ FLSA.htm**

## Fair Labor Standards Act (FLSA)

The major law affecting compensation is the Fair Labor Standards Act (FLSA). Passed in 1938, the FLSA has been amended several times to raise minimum wage rates and expand employers covered. Unless otherwise noted in the discussion that follows, both private- and public-sector employers are affected by the act. Generally, private-sector employers engaged in interstate commerce and retail service firms with two or more employees and gross sales of at least $500,000 per year are covered by the act. Very small, family-owned and -operated entities and family farms generally are excluded from coverage. Most federal, state, and local government employers are also subject to the provisions of the act, except for military personnel, volunteer workers, and a few other limited groups.[15]

Compliance with FLSA provisions is enforced by the Wage and Hour Division of the U.S. Department of Labor. To meet FLSA requirements employers must keep accurate time records and maintain these records for three years. Inspectors from the Wage and Hour Division investigate complaints filed by individuals who believe they have not received the overtime payments due them. Also, certain industries that historically have had a large number of wage and hour violations can be targeted, and firms in those industries can be investigated. Penalties for wage and hour violations often include awards of back pay for affected current and former employees for up to *two years*.

The act has three major objectives:

● Establish a minimum wage floor.
● Discourage oppressive use of child labor.
● Encourage limits on the number of weekly hours employees work through overtime provisions (exempt and nonexempt status).

## Ethical Debate on a Minimum Wage vs. a "Living" Wage

Since 1938 when the Fair Labor Standards Act was passed, a minimum wage has been in existence in the United States. First established at 25¢/hour, the minimum wage has increased significantly. But the concept of a minimum wage and an appropriate level for it have been subjects of considerable debate by economists, politicians, employers, unions, and others. One view of the minimum wage is that it should be set at a relatively low level, so that smaller employers can afford to hire workers. Also, having a lower minimum wage encourages employers to hire workers with minimal work histories and those with limited knowledge, skills and abilities (KSAs).

Considerable research has been done regarding the effects of raising the minimum wage on the creation of new jobs and job opportunities for lower-skilled workers. The research results generally have been mixed: Some studies show that a minimum-wage increase reduces job opportunities for some workers; other studies show little impact. Obviously, the overall state of the U.S. economy is a major mediating factor.

A new dimension to the debate on minimum wage has emerged in the past few years: the concept of a "living wage." Some politicians in the United States and other countries with minimum-wage laws have argued that the minimum wage should be set at a level that provides a living wage for workers. In the United States the living-wage level typically has been identified as the amount needed for a family of four to be supported by one worker so that family income is above the officially identified "poverty" level. Currently in the United States, that is about $7.50/hour, which is significantly higher than the current minimum wage.

A number of cities have not waited for U.S. federal laws to change and they have passed living-wage laws. Here are some examples:

Baltimore, MD: $7.50/hour
Duluth, MN: $7.25 or $6.50 plus
    health insurance
Los Angeles, CA: $7.25 with benefits or $8.50 without benefits

Other cities—such as Boston, MA; Minneapolis, MN; and New Haven, CT—require a living-wage minimum at 100% or more of the poverty level established by U.S. government statistics.

Those favoring living-wage laws stress that they are needed so that even the lowest-skilled workers can earn wages above the poverty level. Those opposed to living-wage laws point out that because many of the lowest-paid workers are single, using the "family of four" test is inappropriate. Obviously there are ethical, economic, and employment implications on both sides of this issue. What do you think?[16]

**MINIMUM WAGE** The FLSA sets a minimum wage to be paid to the broad spectrum of covered employees. The actual minimum wage can be changed only by congressional action. A lower minimum-wage level is set for "tipped" employees who work in such firms as restaurants, but their payment must at least equal the minimum wage when *average* tips are included. The level at which the minimum wage should be set has led to significant political discussions and legislative maneuvering. But, as the HR Perspective indicates, some ethical issues are being debated regarding the purpose of the minimum wage and how it should be changed.

**CHILD-LABOR PROVISIONS** The child-labor provisions of the FLSA set the minimum age for employment with unlimited hours at 16 years. For hazardous occupations (see Chapter 16), the minimum is 18 years of age. Those aged 14 to 15 years old may work outside school hours with certain limitations.

Many employers require age certificates for employees because the FLSA places the responsibility on the employer to determine an individual's age.[17] The certificates may be issued by a representative of a state labor department, a state education department, or a local school district.

**Exempt employees**
Employees to whom
employers are not required
to pay overtime under the
Fair Labor Standards Act.

**Nonexempt employees**
Employees who must be
paid overtime under the
Fair Labor Standards Act.

**EXEMPT AND NONEXEMPT STATUS** Under the FLSA, employees are classified as exempt or nonexempt. **Exempt** employees are those who hold positions classified as *executive, administrative, professional,* or *outside sales,* to whom employers are not required to pay overtime. **Nonexempt** employees are those who must be paid overtime under the Fair Labor Standards Act.

In base pay programs, employers often categorize jobs into three different groupings that tie the FLSA status and the method of payment together:

● Hourly
● Salaried-nonexempt
● Salaried-exempt

*Hourly* jobs require employers to pay overtime and comply with the FLSA. Each salaried position must be identified as *salaried-exempt* or *salaried-nonexempt.* Employees in positions classified as salaried-nonexempt are covered by the overtime provisions of the FLSA and therefore must be paid overtime. Salaried-nonexempt positions sometimes include secretarial, clerical, and salaried blue-collar positions.

Salaried-exempt employees are not required by the FLSA to be paid overtime, although some organizations have implemented policies to pay a straight rate for extensive hours of overtime. For instance, some electric utilities pay first-line supervisors extra using a special rate for hours worked over 50 per week during storm emergencies. A growing number of salaried-exempt information professionals also receive additional compensation for working extensive hours.

Three major factors are considered in determining whether an individual holds an exempt position:

● Discretionary authority for independent action
● Percentage of time spent performing routine, manual, or clerical work
● Earnings level

Figure 13–8 shows the impact of these factors on each type of exemption. It is useful to note that the earnings levels are basically meaningless, because they have not changed in years despite increases in the minimum wage. These inconsistencies are due to political disagreements among employers, unions, legislators, and federal regulations.

**COMPUTER-RELATED OCCUPATIONS** Due to the growth of information systems and computer jobs, a special category of professionals was added in 1990. For those working in computer-related occupations who are paid at least the equivalent of $27.63 per hour on a salaried basis, the FLSA does not require overtime pay. Because the wage level in this case is set at approximately $58,000 per year, a limited number of jobs and individuals are affected. For all other occupations, the FLSA has no set dollar level above which overtime is not required.

*BNA:*
**Regular Pay and Overtime**
To review FLSA regulations
on determining regular
base pay rates and over-
time rate determination
considering several factors,
see 2035.10–2035.70.

**OVERTIME PROVISIONS** The FLSA establishes overtime pay requirements. Its provisions set overtime pay at one and one-half times the regular pay rate for all hours in excess of 40 per week, except for employees who are not covered by the FLSA. Overtime provisions do not apply to farm workers, who also have a lower minimum-wage schedule.

The work week is defined as a consecutive period of 168 hours (24 hours × 7 days) and does not have to be a calendar week. Hospitals are allowed to use a 14-day period instead of a 7-day week as long as overtime is paid for hours worked

## FIGURE 13–8 *Wage/Hour Status Under Fair Labor Standards Act*

| Exemption Category | A Discretionary Authority | B Percent of Time | C Earnings Levels |
|---|---|---|---|
| **Executive** | 1. Primary duty is managing<br>2. Regularly directs work of at least two others<br>3. Authority to hire/fire or recommend these | 1. Must spend 20% or less time doing clerical, manual, routine work (less than 40% in retail or service establishments) | 1. Paid salary at $155/wk or $250/wk if meets A1–A2 |
| **Administrative** | 1. Primarily responsible for nonmanual or office work related to management policies<br>2. Regularly exercises discretion and independent judgment and makes important decisions<br>3. Regularly assists executives and works under general supervision | 1. Must spend 20% or less time doing clerical, manual, routine work (less than 40% in retail or service establishments) | 1. Paid salary at $155/wk or $250/wk if meets A1–A2 |
| **Professional** | 1. Performs work requiring knowledge of an advanced field *or* creative and original artistic work *or* works as teacher in educational system<br>2. Must do work that is predominantly intellectual and varied | 1. Must spend 20% or less time doing nonprofessional work | 1. Paid salary at least $170/wk or $250/wk if meets A1 |
| **Outside Sales** | 1. Customarily works away from employer site *and*<br>2. Sells tangible or intangible items *or*<br>3. Obtains orders or contracts for services | 1. Must spend 20% or less time doing work other than outside selling | 1. No salary test |

NOTE: For more details, see *Executive, Administrative, Professional, and Outside Sales Exemptions under the Fair Labor Standards Act*, WH Publication no. 1363 (Washington, DC: U.S. Department of Labor, Employment Standards Administration, Wage and Hour Division).

beyond 8 in a day or 80 in a 14-day period. No daily number of hours requiring overtime is set, except for special provisions relating to hospitals and other specially designated organizations. Thus, if a manufacturing firm has a 4-day/10-hour schedule, no overtime pay is required by the act.

**COMPENSATORY TIME OFF** Often called *comp-time,* **compensatory time off** is given in lieu of payment for extra time worked. However, unless it is given at the rate of one and one-half times the hours worked over a 40-hour week, comp-time is illegal in the private sector. Also, comp-time cannot be carried over from one pay period to another.

The only major exception to those provisions is for public-sector employees, such as fire and police employees, and a limited number of other workers. Because they often are on 24-hour duty, these individuals may receive compen-

**Compensatory time off**
That given in lieu of payment for extra time worked.

satory time off. Police and fire officers can accumulate up to 480 hours; all other covered public-sector employees can accumulate up to 240 hours. When those hours are used, the employees must be paid their normal rates of pay, and the comp-time hours used *do not* count as hours worked in the paid week.

## Independent Contractor Regulations

The growing use of contingent workers by many organizations has called attention to another group of legal regulations—those identifying the criteria that independent contractors must meet. Classifying someone as an independent contractor rather than an employee offers two primary advantages.[18] First, the employer does not have to pay Social Security, unemployment, or workers' compensation costs. These additional payroll levies could add 10% or more to the costs of hiring the individual as an employee. Second, if the person is classified as an employee and is doing a job considered nonexempt under the federal Fair Labor Standards Act, then the employer may be responsible for overtime pay at the rate of time-and-a-half for any week in which the person works more than 40 hours.

The criteria for deciding independent contractor status have been identified by the Internal Revenue Service (IRS), and most other federal and state entities rely on those criteria. The IRS has identified 20 factors that must be considered in making such a determination. Figure 13–9 illustrates some of the key differences between an employee and an independent contractor.

## Acts Affecting Government Contractors

Several compensation-related acts apply to firms having contracts with the U.S. government. The first one passed was the *Davis-Bacon Act of 1931,* which affects compensation paid by firms engaged in federal construction projects valued in excess of $2,000. It deals only with federal construction projects and requires that the "prevailing" wage rate be paid on all federal construction projects. The

**FIGURE 13–9** *Employees or Independent Contractors?—The IRS Test*

| An Employee | An Independent Contractor |
|---|---|
| • Must comply with instructions about when, where, and how to work<br>• Renders services personally<br>• Has a continuing relationship with an employer<br>• Usually works on the premises of the employer<br>• Normally is furnished significant tools, materials, and other equipment by the employer<br>• Can be fired by an employer<br>• Can quit at any time without incurring liability | • Can hire, supervise, and pay assistants<br>• Generally can set his or her own hours<br>• Usually is paid by the job or on straight commission<br>• Has made a significant investment in facilities<br>• Can make a profit or suffer a loss<br>• Generally is free to provide services to two or more unrelated persons or firms at the same time<br>• Makes his or her services available to the public |

SOURCE: Internal Revenue Service

*prevailing wage* is determined by a formula that considers the rate paid for a job by a majority of the employers in the appropriate geographic area.

Two other acts require firms with *federal supply or service contracts* exceeding $10,000 to pay a prevailing wage. Both the *Walsh-Healy Public Contracts Act* and the *Service Contracts Act* apply only to those who are working directly on a federal government contract or who substantially affect its performance.

## Equal Pay and Pay Equity

Various legislative efforts have addressed the issue of wage discrimination on the basis of gender. The Equal Pay Act was passed as a major amendment to the FLSA in 1963. The original act and subsequent amendments focus on wage discrimination on the basis of sex. The act applies to both men and women and prohibits paying different wage scales to men and women performing substantially the same jobs. Pay differences are justifiable on the basis of merit (better performance), seniority (longer service), quantity or quality of work, or any factor other than sex. Similar pay must be given for jobs requiring equal skills, equal effort, or equal responsibility or jobs done under similar working conditions.

Most of the equal-pay cases decided in court have involved situations in which women were paid less than men for doing similar work, though under different job titles. For example, equal-pay violations have been found in health-care institutions in which male "physician assistants" were paid significantly more than females with equal experience and qualifications who were called "nurse practitioners" but performed the same job duties.

There has been growing pressure to pay jobs requiring comparable capabilities similarly even if actual duties and market rates vary. Growing concerns about *comparable worth* have been translated into laws designed to address disparities between the pay levels of men and women. These laws focus on public-sector jobs, especially those in state governments. States with comparable-worth laws include Hawaii, Iowa, Maine, Michigan, Minnesota, Montana, Ohio, Oregon, Washington, and Wisconsin.

Pay equity is a different issue from that of equal pay for equal work. **Pay equity** is the concept that the pay for all jobs requiring comparable knowledge, skills, and abilities should be similar even if actual duties and market rates differ significantly. Except where state (in the United States) or provincial (in Canada) laws have required pay equity, simply showing that there are pay differences for jobs that are different has not been sufficient to prove discrimination in court.

Because the U.S. Supreme Court and other lower-court decisions generally have not supported the concept of pay equity, some advocacy groups have urged passage of a federal act mandating pay equity.[19] For instance, in 1997 a bill called the Fair Pay Act was introduced in the U.S. Senate, but it has not been passed into law.

**Pay equity**
Similarity in pay for all jobs requiring comparable levels of knowledge, skills, and abilities, even if actual duties and market rates differ significantly.

## State Laws

Modified versions of federal compensation laws have been enacted by many state and municipal government bodies. These laws tend to cover workers included in intrastate commerce not covered by federal law. If a state has a higher minimum wage than that set under the Fair Labor Standards Act, the higher figure becomes the required minimum wage.

Many states once had laws that limited the number of hours women could work. However, these laws generally have been held to be discriminatory in a variety of court cases. Consequently, most states have dropped such laws.

## Garnishment Laws

**Garnishment**
A court action in which a portion of an employee's wages is set aside to pay a debt owed a creditor.

**Garnishment** of an employee's wage occurs when a creditor obtains a court order that directs an employer to submit a part of the employee's pay to the creditor for debts owed by the employee. Regulations passed as a part of the Consumer Credit Protection Act established limitations on the amount of wages that can be garnished and restricted the right of employers to discharge employees whose pay is subject to a single garnishment order. All 50 states have laws applying to wage garnishments.

# Wage and Salary Administration

**Wage and salary administration**
Activities involved in the development, implementation, and maintenance of a base pay system.

The development, implementation, and ongoing maintenance of a base pay system usually is described as **wage and salary administration.** The purpose of wage and salary administration is to provide pay that is both competitive and equitable. Underlying the administered activities are pay policies that set the overall direction of pay within the organization.

## Pay Policies

Organizations must develop policies as general guidelines to provide for coordination, consistency, and fairness in compensating employees. The pay policies are an outgrowth of the answers to the compensation philosophy issues discussed earlier. For example, following a pay-for-performance philosophy requires incorporating performance appraisal results into the pay adjustment process. However, a more entitlement-oriented philosophy will require developing policies in automatic step increases based on length of service for hourly employees. Figure 13–10 identifies some questions about pay policy organizations must address. Many of these items are mentioned in the discussion that follows.

**MARKET POSITIONING** A major policy decision must be made about the comparative level of pay the organization wants to maintain. Specifically, an employer must identify how competitive it wishes to be in the market for employees. Organizations usually want to "pay market"—that is, to *match* the "going rates" paid to employees by competitive organizations in order to ensure external equity.

Some organizations choose to *lead* the market by paying above-market rates. This policy aids in attracting and retaining employees. One transportation firm that pays about 10% to 15% above local-market medians for clerical employees consistently has a waiting list for qualified word processing workers and other specialized office workers. By paying above market, the firm feels that it also deters efforts of its office workers to unionize.

In contrast, some employers may deliberately choose to *lag* the market by paying below market. If there is an excess of qualified workers in an area, an adequate number of people are willing to work for lower pay. Also, organizations in declining industries and some small businesses may not be able to afford to pay

**FIGURE 13–10** *Pay Policies Considerations*

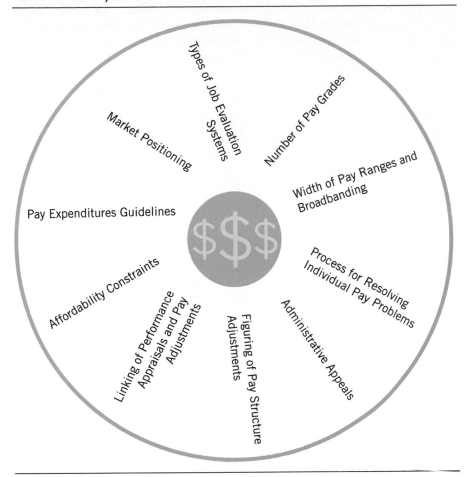

going rates because of financial pressures. However, paying rates below market can result in higher turnover or in having to hire less-qualified employees.

**MARKET PRICING** Some employers do not establish a formal wage and salary system. Smaller employers particularly may assume that the pay set by other employers is an accurate reflection of a job's worth, so they set their pay rates at **market price,** the typical wage paid for a job in the immediate labor market.

One difficulty with this approach is the assumption that jobs are the same from organization to organization, which is not necessarily the case. Also, obtaining market information often means calling one or two other firms, which may not give an accurate picture of the market. Further, direct market pricing does not adequately consider the impact of economic conditions, employer size, and other variables. Consequently, more complex methods have been developed.

**Market price**

Typical wage paid for a job in the immediate labor market.

## Unions and Compensation

A major variable affecting an employer's pay policies is whether any employees are represented by a labor union. In nonunion organizations, employers have significantly more flexibility in determining pay levels and policies. Unionized employees usually have their pay set according to the terms of a collective bargaining contract between their employer and the union that represents them. Because pay is a visible issue, it is natural for unions to emphasize pay levels.

According to U.S. Bureau of Labor Statistics data, employers having unionized employees generally provide higher wage levels than nonunion employers. The strength and extent of unionization in an industry and in an organization affect wage levels. The levels generally are higher in firms in heavily unionized industries with highly unionized workforces. As union strength in heavily unionized industries has declined, pay increases on a percentage basis for union employees have diminished somewhat in recent years; in many areas, they have lagged those of nonunion employees.

# Development of a Base Pay System

Once pay policies have been determined, the actual development of a base pay system begins. Because most organizations use task-based systems focusing on work done in specific jobs, that is the emphasis of this discussion. If skill-based or team pay systems are used, then many of the activities discussed here must be modified.

As Figure 13–11 shows, the development of a wage and salary system assumes that accurate job descriptions and job specifications are available. The job

**FIGURE 13–11** *Compensation Administration Process*

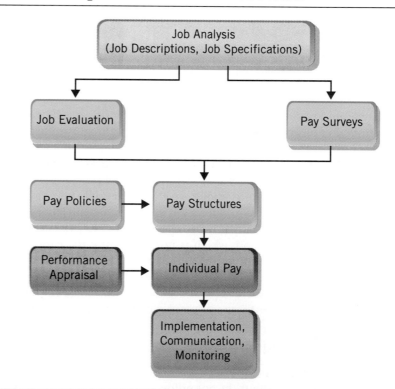

descriptions then are used in two activities: *job evaluation* and *pay surveys*. These activities are designed to ensure that the pay system is both internally equitable and externally competitive. The data compiled in these two activities are used to design *pay structures,* including *pay grades* and minimum-to-maximum *pay ranges*. After the pay structures have been developed, individual jobs must be placed in the appropriate pay grades and employees' pay adjusted based on length of service and performance. Finally, the pay system must be monitored and updated.

## Job Evaluation

**Job evaluation** provides a systematic basis for determining the relative worth of jobs within an organization. It flows from the job analysis process and is based on job descriptions and job specifications. In a job evaluation, every job in an organization is examined and ultimately priced according to the following features:

- Relative importance of the job
- Knowledge, skills, and abilities (KSAs) needed to perform the job
- Difficulty of the job

**Job evaluation**
The systematic determination of the relative worth of jobs within an organization.

It is important that employees perceive their pay as appropriate in relation to pay for jobs performed by others. Because jobs may vary widely in an organization, it is particularly important to identify **benchmark jobs**—jobs that are found in many other organizations and are performed by several individuals who have similar duties that are relatively stable and that require similar KSAs. For example, benchmark jobs commonly used in clerical/office situations are accounts payable processor, word processing operator, and receptionist. Benchmark jobs are used with all of the job evaluation methods discussed here because they provide "anchors" against which unique jobs can be evaluated.

**Benchmark job**
Job found in many organizations and performed by several individuals who have similar duties that are relatively stable and require similar KSAs.

Several methods are used to determine internal job worth through job evaluation. All methods have the same general objective, but they differ in complexity and means of measurement. Regardless of the method used, the intent is to develop a usable, measurable, and realistic system to determine compensation in an organization.

**RANKING METHOD** The ranking method is one of the simplest methods of job evaluation. It places jobs in order, ranging from highest to lowest in value to the organization. The entire job is considered rather than the individual components.[20] Several different methods of ranking are available, but all present problems.

Ranking methods are extremely subjective, and managers may have difficulty explaining why one job is ranked higher than another to employees whose pay is affected by these rankings. When there are a large number of jobs, the ranking method also can be awkward and unwieldy. Therefore, the ranking method is more appropriate in a small organization having relatively few jobs.

**CLASSIFICATION METHOD** In the classification method of job evaluation, descriptions of each class of jobs are written, and then each job in the organization is put into a grade according to the class description it matches the best.

The major difficulty with the classification method is that subjective judgments are needed to develop the class descriptions and to place jobs accurately in them. With a wide variety of jobs and generally written class descriptions, some jobs may appear to fall into two or three different grades.

Another problem with the classification method is that it relies heavily on job titles and duties and assumes that they are similar from one organization to another. For these reasons, many federal, state, and local government entities, which traditionally used the classification method, have shifted to point systems.

**POINT METHOD**  The point method, the most widely used job evaluation method, is more sophisticated than the ranking and classification methods. It breaks down jobs into various compensable factors and places weights, or *points,* on them. A **compensable factor** is one used to identify a job value that is commonly present throughout a group of jobs. The factors are determined from the job analysis. For example, for jobs in warehouse and manufacturing settings, *physical demands, hazards encountered,* and *working environment* may be identified as factors and weighted heavily. However, in most office and clerical jobs, those factors are of little importance. Consequently, the compensable factors used and the weights assigned must reflect the nature of the job under study and the changes in it.[21]

Figure 13–12 helps to illustrate how the system is used. The individual using the point chart in the figure looks at a job description and identifies the degree to which each element is necessary to perform the job satisfactorily. For example, the points assigned for a payroll clerk for education might be 42 points, third degree. To reduce subjectivity, such determinations often are made by a group of people familiar with the jobs. Once points have been identified for all factors, the total points for the payroll clerk job are computed. After point totals have been determined for all jobs, the jobs are grouped together into pay grades.

A special type of point method used by a consulting firm, the Hay Group, has received widespread application, although it is most often used with exempt employees. The *Hay system* uses three factors and numerically measures the degree to which each of these factors is required in each job. The three factors and their sub-factors are as follows:[22]

**Compensable factor**

That used to identify a job value that is commonly present throughout a group of jobs.

*LOGGING ON . . .*

**Job Evaluation Factors**

This web site includes a chart of job evaluation factors.

**http://www.qp.gov.bc.ca/ PSERC/CHIPS/Manual/ Lrjfact2.htm**

| Know-How | Problem Solving | Accountability |
|---|---|---|
| • Functional expertise | • Environment | • Freedom to act |
| • Managerial skills | • Challenge | • Impact of end results |
| • Human relations | | • Magnitude |

The point method has grown in popularity for several reasons. It is a relatively simple system to use. It considers the components of a job rather than the total job and is much more comprehensive than either the ranking or classification method. Once points have been determined and a job evaluation point manual has been developed, the method can be used easily by people who are not specialists. The system can be understood by managers and employees, which gives it a definite advantage.

Another reason for the widespread use of the point method is that it evaluates the components of a job and determines total points before the current pay structure is considered. In this way, an employer can assess relative worth instead of relying on past patterns of worth.

One major drawback to the point method is the time needed to develop a system. For this reason, employers often use manuals and systems developed by management consultants or other organizations. Point systems have also been criticized for reinforcing traditional organizational structures and job rigidity.

**FIGURE 13–12** *Job Evaluation Point Chart*

| Factor | 1st Degree Points | 2nd Degree Points | 3rd Degree Points | 4th Degree Points |
|---|---|---|---|---|
| **CLERICAL GROUP** | | | | |
| 1. Education | 14 | 28 | 42 | 56 |
| 2. Experience | 22 | 44 | 66 | 88 |
| 3. Initiative and ingenuity | 14 | 28 | 42 | 56 |
| 4. Contacts with others | 14 | 28 | 42 | 56 |
| Responsibility | | | | |
| 5. Supervision received | 10 | 20 | 35 | 50 |
| 6. Latitude and depth | 20 | 40 | 70 | 100 |
| 7. Work of others | 5 | 10 | 15 | 20 |
| 8. Trust imposed | 10 | 20 | 35 | 50 |
| 9. Performance | 7 | 14 | 21 | 28 |
| Other | | | | |
| 10. Work environment | 10 | 25 | 45 | |
| 11. Mental or visual demand | 10 | 20 | 35 | |
| 12. Physical effort | 28 | | | |

*The specific degrees and points for education are as follows:

*Education* is the basic prerequisite knowledge essential to satisfactorily perform the job. This knowledge may have been acquired through formal schooling, as well as correspondence courses, company education programs, or through equivalent experience in allied fields. Analyze the minimum requirements of the job and not the formal education of individuals performing it.

*1st Degree*—Requires knowledge usually equivalent to a two-year high school education. Requires ability to read, write, and follow simple written or oral instructions and to use simple arithmetic processes involving counting, adding, subtracting, dividing, and multiplying whole numbers. May require basic typing ability.

*2nd Degree*—Requires knowledge equivalent to a four-year high school education. Requires ability to perform advanced arithmetic process involving adding, subtracting, dividing, and multiplying or decimals and fractions and ability to maintain or prepare routine correspondence, records, and reports. May require knowledge of advanced typing and/or basic knowledge of bookkeeping, drafting, etc.

*3rdDegree*—Requires knowledge equivalent to a four-year high school education plus some specialized knowledge/training in a particular field, such as elementary accounting; or general blueprint reading or engineering practices.

*4th Degree*—Requires knowledge equivalent to two years of college education. Requires ability to understand and perform work involving general engineering or accounting theory. Requires ability to originate and compile statistics and interpretive reports and prepare correspondence of a difficult or technical nature.

Although not perfect, the point method of job evaluation generally is better than the classification and ranking methods because it quantifies job elements.

**FACTOR COMPARISON** The factor-comparison method is a quantitative and complex combination of the ranking and point methods. It involves first determining the benchmark jobs in an organization, selecting compensable factors, and ranking all benchmark jobs factor by factor. Next, the jobs are compared with market rates for benchmark jobs, and monetary values are assigned to each factor. The final step is to evaluate all other jobs in the organization by comparing them with the benchmark jobs.

A major advantage of the factor-comparison method is that it is tailored specifically to one organization. Each organization must develop its own key jobs and its own factors. For this reason, buying a packaged system may not be appropriate. Further, factor comparison not only tells which jobs are worth more but also indicates how much more, so that factor values can be more easily converted to monetary wages.

The major disadvantages of the factor-comparison method are its difficulty and complexity. It is not an easy system to explain to employees, and it is time consuming to establish and develop. Also, a factor-comparison system may not be appropriate for an organization with many similar types of jobs. Managers attempting to use the method should consult a specialist or one of the more detailed compensation books or manuals that discuss the method.

**INTEGRATED AND COMPUTERIZED JOB EVALUATION** Increasingly, organizations are linking the components of wage and salary programs through computerized and statistical techniques. Using a bank of compensable factors, employers can select those factors that are most relevant for the different job families in the organization. Then these integrated systems can perform the following tasks:

- Create job descriptions that identify the compensable functions for each job.
- Link to pay survey data available on the Internet.
- Use multiple regression and other statistical methods to analyze job evaluation and pay survey relationships.
- Compare current employee pay levels in a database to the job evaluation and pay survey data.
- Develop costing models and budgetary implications of various implementation approaches.

Because of the advanced expertise needed to develop and computerize the integrated systems, management consultants are the primary source for them. These systems really are less a separate method and more an application of information technology and advanced statistics to the process of developing a wage and salary program. Integrated systems, including the consulting expertise necessary to work through and implement them, are relatively expensive to purchase. Therefore they generally are used only by medium- to large-sized employers.

## Legal Issues and Job Evaluation

Employers usually view evaluating jobs to determine rates of pay as a separate issue from selecting individuals for those jobs or taking disciplinary action against individuals. But because job evaluation affects the employment relationship, specifically the pay of individuals, it involves legal issues that must be addressed.

**JOB EVALUATION AND THE AMERICANS WITH DISABILITIES ACT (ADA)** As emphasized in Chapter 7, the Americans with Disabilities Act requires employers to identify the essential functions of a job. However, all facets of jobs are examined during a job evaluation. For instance, assume a production job requires a punch press operator to drill holes in parts and place them in a bin of finished products. Every three hours the operator must push that bin, which may weigh two hundred pounds or more, to the packaging area. The movement of the bin probably is not an essential function. But if job evaluation considers the physical demands associated with pushing the bin, then the points assigned may be different from the points that would be assigned if only the essential functions were considered.

**GENDER ISSUES AND JOB EVALUATION** Critics have charged that traditional job evaluation programs place less weight on knowledge, skills, and working conditions for many female-dominated jobs in office and clerical areas than on the same factors for male-dominated jobs in craft and manufacturing areas. Also, jobs typically are compared only with others in the same job "family." As discussed earlier, advocates of pay equity view the disparity between men's jobs and women's jobs as evidence of gender discrimination. These advocates also have attacked typical job evaluations as being gender biased.

Employers counter that because they base their pay rates heavily on external equity comparisons in the labor market, they are not the ones who are discriminating; they are just reflecting rates the "market economy" sets for jobs and workers. A number of different methodologies can be used to evaluate the differences in pay based on gender.[24] Undoubtedly, with further developments in court decisions, government actions, and research, job evaluation activities will face more pressures to address gender differences.

## Pay Surveys

Another part of building a pay system is surveying the pay that other organizations provide for similar jobs. A **pay survey** is a collection of data on compensation rates for workers performing similar jobs in other organizations. An employer may use surveys conducted by other organizations, or it may decide to conduct its own survey.

**USING PREPARED PAY SURVEYS**  Many different surveys are available from a variety of sources. As the HR Perspective indicates, the growth of the Internet has resulted in a large amount of pay survey sources and data being available on-line. Whether available electronically or in printed form, national surveys on many jobs and industries come from the U.S. Department of Labor, Bureau of Labor Statistics, and through national trade associations. In many communities, employers participate in a wage survey sponsored by the local Chamber of Commerce to provide information to new employers interested in locating in the community.

When using surveys from other sources, it is important to use them properly. Some questions to be addressed before using a survey are:

- *Participants:*  Is the survey a realistic sample of those employers with whom the organization competes for employees?
- *Broad-based:*  Is the survey balanced so that organizations of varying sizes, industries, and locales are included?
- *Timeliness:*  How current is the data (determined by the date when the survey was conducted)?
- *Methodology:*  How established is the survey, and how qualified are those who conducted it?
- *Job matches:*  Does it contain job summaries so that appropriate matches to organization job descriptions can be made?

**DEVELOPING A PAY SURVEY**  If needed pay information is not already available, the employer can undertake its own pay survey. Employers with comparable positions should be selected. Employers considered to be "representative" should also be surveyed. Even if the employer conducting the survey is not unionized, the pay survey probably should examine union as well as nonunion organizations. Developing pay competitive with union wages may deter employees from joining a union.

**Pay survey**
A collection of data on existing compensation rates for workers performing similar jobs in other organizations.

***LOGGING ON . . .***
**Pay Survey Sources**
Sources are identified and reviewed by the Institute of Management & Administration, Inc. at:

**http://www.ioma.com**

# HR PERSPECTIVE

## The Internet and Pay Survey Data

The growth of the Internet has provided HR professionals expanded access to pay survey data. There are numerous ways to access electronic pay surveys done by governmental entities, associations, and consulting firms. Following are some useful World Wide Web sites, with the specific web addresses in parentheses.

Many surveys that are conducted by governmental agencies can be tapped using web sources. Here are some useful federal and state government sources for pay survey data:

- *U.S. Department of Labor, Bureau of Labor Statistics (BLS):* By starting at the BLS home page (www.bls.gov), users can then move to a search by states, occupational titles, covered employment, and wages.
- *U.S. Securities and Exchange Commission:* This web site gives pay data for some executive salaries (www.sec.gov).
- *State Governments:* Many states compile pay survey data that can be accessed on the web.

For example, see New York (www.labor.state.ny/wages/man.htm) and South Dakota (www.state.sd.us/dol).

Many private-sector survey sources also provide pay survey data on the web. Many of them require users to pay subscription fees to access the actual data banks. One useful general source is the American Compensation Association (www.acaonline.org). Another web site that reviews the executive pay and incentives of 300 CEOs is compiled by the AFL-CIO union organization (www.aflcio.paywatch.org).

Consulting firms are a major source of pay survey data on the web. Many firms, both large and small, conduct annual surveys on various industries, job fields, and geographic regions. Some of the more prominent ones are William M. Mercer, Inc. (www.mercer.com); Watson, Wyatt Worldwide (www.watsonwyatt.com); Hewitt Associates (www.hewitt.com); and Hay Group (www.haygroup.com). Various

professional and trade associations also have pay survey data available. A few examples are

- *Computer professionals:* Pencom (www.pencomsi.com)
- *Accounting:* ACSYS Resources, Inc. (www.ascysresources.com/acct.htm)
- *Advertising:* Ad Age Data Place (www.adage.com/egibin/)

Even international pay survey data can be obtained electronically. For instance, if data on pay in the United Kingdom is needed, an international HR professional can access the Eclipse Group, a private source for pay survey data at (www.ireclipse.co.uk). Or, for data in Venezuela, try a government site at (www.ocei.gov.ve).

This brief discussion illustrates that pay survey data that was formerly available only in printed form now can be downloaded from electronic sources. These electronic sources definitely provide greater access to data.[23]

Jobs to be surveyed also must be determined. Because not all of the jobs in all organizations can be surveyed, those designing the pay survey should select jobs that can be easily compared, have common job elements, and represent a broad range of jobs. Key or benchmark jobs are especially important ones to include. It is also advisable to provide brief job descriptions for jobs surveyed in order to ensure more accurate matches. For executive-level jobs, data on total compensation (base pay and bonuses) is often gathered as well.

In the next phase of designing the pay survey, managers decide what information is needed for various jobs. Information such as starting pay, base pay, overtime rate, vacation and holiday pay policies, and bonuses all can be included in a survey. However, requesting too much information may discourage survey returns.

The results of the pay survey usually are made available to those participating in the survey in order to gain their cooperation. Most surveys specify confidentiality, and data is summarized to assure anonymity. Different job levels often are included, and the pay rates are presented both in overall terms and on a city-by-city basis to reflect regional differences in pay.

There has been some debate about how essential pay survey data will continue to be, as jobs continue to change and more "hybrid" jobs that are combinations of traditional jobs emerge.[25] Also, as more disparate jobs are placed into broader pay bands, the difficulty of comparing diverse jobs increases.[26]

**LEGAL ISSUES AND PAY SURVEYS** One reason for employers to use outside consultants to conduct pay surveys is to avoid charges that the employers are attempting "price-fixing" on wages. The federal government has filed suit in the past alleging that by sharing wage data, employers may be attempting to hold wages down artificially in violation of the Sherman Anti-Trust Act.

A key case involved the Utah Society for Healthcare Human Resource Administration and nine hospitals in the Salt Lake City area. The consent decree that resulted prohibits all health-care facilities in Utah from designing, developing, or conducting a wage survey. The hospitals can participate in surveys conducted by independent third-party firms only if privacy safeguards are met. Specifically, only aggregate data that is summarized may be provided, and no data from an individual firm may be identified.[27] As a result, it is likely that fewer firms will conduct their own surveys, and the use of outside consultants to do pay surveys will continue to grow.

## Pay Structures

Once survey data has been gathered, pay structures can be developed by the process depicted in Figure 13–13 on the next page. As indicated in that figure, one means of tying pay survey information to job evaluation data is to plot a *wage curve,* or *scattergram.* This plotting involves first making a graph that charts job evaluation points and pay survey rates for all surveyed jobs. In this way, the distribution of pay for surveyed jobs can be shown, and a linear trend line can be developed by use of the *least-squares regression method.* Also, a curvilinear line can be developed by use of multiple regression and other statistical techniques. The end result is the development of a **market line.** This line shows the relationship between job value, as determined by job evaluation points, and pay survey rates. (Details on these methods can be found in any basic statistics text.)

**Market line**
The line on a graph showing the relationship between job value, as determined by job evaluation points, and pay survey rates.

**DIFFERENT PAY STRUCTURES** In organizations there are a number of different job families. The pay survey data may reveal that there are different levels of pay due to market factors, which may lead to firms establishing several different pay structures, rather than just one structure. Examples of some common pay structures are (1) hourly and salaried; (2) office, plant, technical, professional, and managerial; and (3) clerical, information technology, professional, supervisory, management, and executive.

One basis for determining how many and which pay structures to have is the nature and culture of the organization. Another basis is the results of the statistical analysis done when determining market lines, particularly the $r^2$ levels when the data is analyzed by different job families and groups. Generally, an $r^2$ of $+.85$ or higher is desired.

**ESTABLISHING PAY GRADES** In the process of establishing a pay structure, organizations use **pay grades** to group individual jobs having approximately the

**Pay grade**
A grouping of individual jobs having approximately the same job worth.

**FIGURE 13–13** *Establishing Pay Structures*

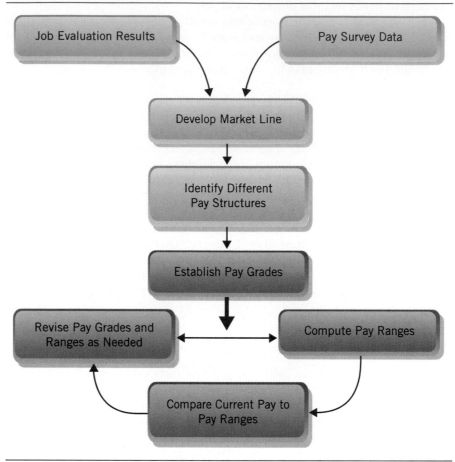

same job worth. While there are no set rules to be used in establishing pay grades, some overall suggestions have been made. Generally, from 11 to 17 grades are used in small companies. However, as discussed earlier, a growing number of employers are reducing the number of grades by *broadbanding.*

By using pay grades, management can develop a coordinated pay system without having to determine a separate pay rate for each job in the organization. All the jobs within a grade have the same range of pay regardless of points. As discussed previously, the factor-comparison method of job evaluation uses monetary values, so an employer using that method can easily establish and price pay grades. A vital part of the classification method is developing grades. Organizations that use the ranking method can group several ranks to create pay grades.

**PAY RANGES** The pay range for each pay grade also must be established. Using the market line as a starting point, the employer can determine maximum and minimum pay levels for each pay grade by making the market line the midpoint line of the new pay structure. (See Figure 13–14.) For example, in a particular pay grade, the maximum value may be 20% above the midpoint and the minimum value 20% below it.

**FIGURE 13–14** *Pay Scattergram*

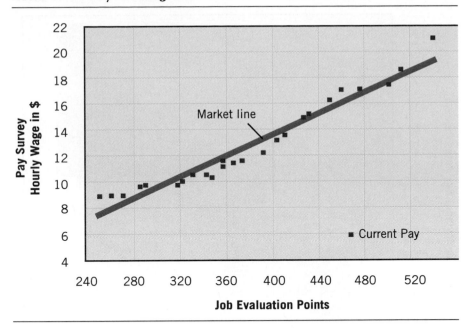

As Figure 13–15 shows, a smaller minimum-to-maximum range should be used for lower-level jobs than for higher-level jobs, primarily because employees in lower-level jobs tend to stay in them for shorter periods of time and have greater promotion possibilities. For example, a clerk-typist might advance to the position of secretary or word processing operator. In contrast, a design engineer likely would have fewer possibilities for upward movement in an organization. This "expanding" approach also recognizes that individual performance can vary more greatly among people in upper-level jobs than in lower-level jobs. However, using the same percentage range at all levels can make administration of a pay system easier in small firms. If broadbanding is used, then much wider ranges, often exceeding 100%, may be used.

Experts recommend having overlap between grades, as in Figure 13–16 on the next page. This structure means that an experienced employee in a lower grade can be paid more than a less-experienced employee in a job in the next pay grade.

Once pay grades and ranges have been computed, then the current pay of employees must be compared to the draft ranges. If a significant number of employees are out of range, then a revision of the pay grades and ranges may need to be computed. Also, once costing and budgeting scenarios are run in order

**FIGURE 13–15** *Typical Pay Range Widths*

| Types of Jobs | Range Above Minimum | % Around Midpoint |
| --- | --- | --- |
| Executives | 50%–70% | ± 20–25% |
| Mid Management/Professionals | 40%–50% | ± 16–20% |
| Technicians/Skilled Craft & Clerical | 30%–40% | ± 13–16% |
| General Clerical/Others | 25%–35% | ± 11–15% |

FIGURE 13–16 *Example of Pay Grades and Pay Ranges*

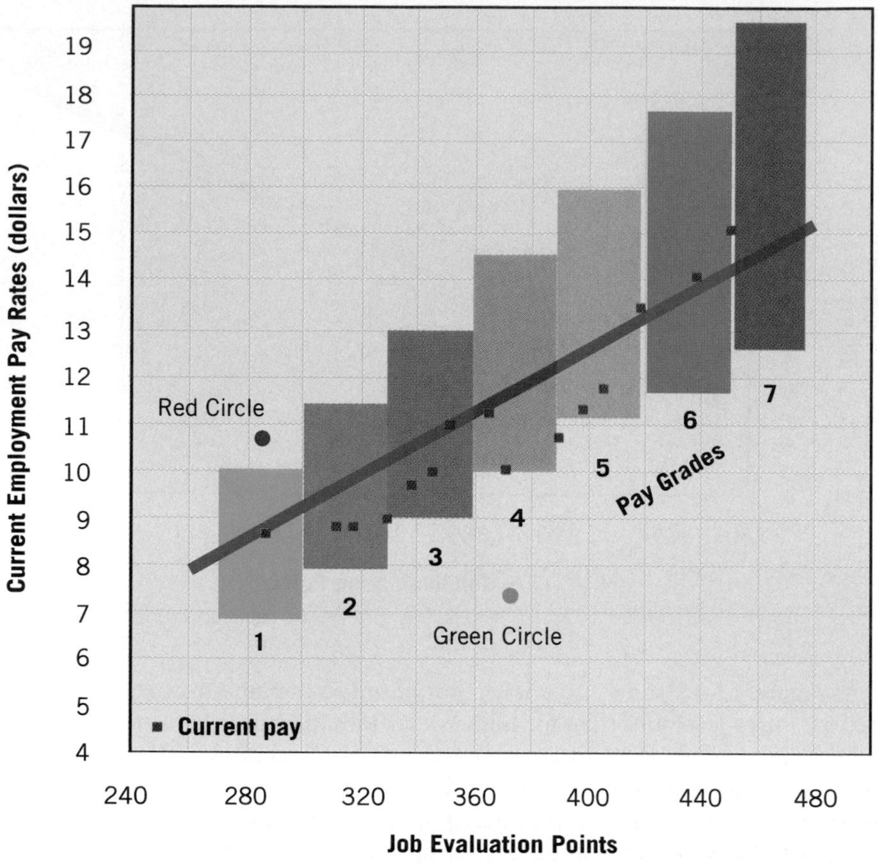

| Grade | Point Range | Minimum Pay | Midpoint Pay | Maximum Pay |
|---|---|---|---|---|
| 1 | Below 300 | 6.94 | 8.50 | 10.06 |
| 2 | 300–329 | 7.96 | 9.75 | 11.54 |
| 3 | 330–359 | 8.98 | 11.00 | 13.02 |
| 4 | 360–389 | 10.00 | 12.25 | 14.50 |
| 5 | 390–419 | 11.01 | 13.49 | 15.97 |
| 6 | 420–449 | 11.79 | 14.74 | 17.69 |
| 7 | Over 450 | 12.79 | 15.99 | 19.18 |

to see the financial input of the new pay structures, then pay policy decisions about market positioning may have to be revised. As a result, changes to the pay ranges may lead to lowering or raising the ranges.

## Individual Pay

Once managers have determined pay ranges, they can set the specific pay for individuals. Each dot on the graph in Figure 13–16 represents an individual employee's current pay in relation to the pay ranges that have been developed. Setting a range for each pay grade gives flexibility by allowing individuals to progress within a grade instead of having to be moved to a new grade each time they receive a raise. A pay range also allows managers to reward the better-performing employees while maintaining the integrity of the pay system.

## Rates Out of Range

Regardless of how well constructed a pay structure is, there usually are a few individuals whose pay is lower than the minimum or higher than the maximum. These situations occur most frequently when firms that have had an informal pay system develop a new, more formalized one.

**RED-CIRCLED EMPLOYEES** A red-circled job is shown on the graph in Figure 13–16. A **red-circled employee** is an incumbent who is paid above the range set for the job. For example, assume that an employee's current pay is $10.92 per hour but the pay range for that grade is between $6.94 and $10.06. The person would be red circled, and attempts would be made over a period of time to bring the employee's rate into grade. Typically, the red-circled job is filled by a longer-service employee who has declined promotions or has been viewed as unpromotable due to insufficient education or other capabilities. Yet the individual may have continued to receive large pay increases.

Several approaches can be used to bring a red-circled person's pay into line. Although the fastest way would be to cut the employee's pay, that approach is not recommended and is seldom used. Instead, the employee's pay may be frozen until the pay range can be adjusted upward to get the employee's pay rate back into the grade. The employee can also be transferred to a job with a higher grade or given more responsibilities. This method will result in greater job evaluation worth, thus justifying the job's being upgraded. Another approach is to give the employee a small lump-sum payment but not adjust the pay rate when others are given raises.

**GREEN-CIRCLED EMPLOYEES** An individual whose pay is below the range is a **green-circled employee.** Promotion is a major cause of this situation. Assume someone receives a promotion that significantly increases his or her responsibilities and pay grade. Typical promotion adjustments are 8% to 15%, but such an adjustment may still leave the individual below the minimum of the new pay range. Because the promotion represents such a significant increase in responsibilities, the employer may not work to increase the person's pay to the minimum until all facets of the new job are being fully performed. Generally, it is recommended that the green-circled individual receive pay increases to get to the pay grade minimum fairly rapidly. More frequent increases can be given if the increase to minimum would be large.

## Pay Compression

One major problem many employers face is **pay compression,** which occurs when the range of pay differences among individuals with different levels of experience and performance becomes small. Pay compression occurs for a number of reasons, but the major one involves the situation in which labor market pay levels increase more rapidly than an employee's pay adjustments. Such situations

**Red-circled employee**
An incumbent who is paid above the range set for the job.

**Green-circled employee**
An incumbent who is paid below the range set for the job.

**Pay compression**
Situation in which pay differences among individuals with different levels of experience and performance in the organization becomes small.

have become prevalent in many occupational areas, particularly those in the information technology field.[28]

Occasionally, in response to competitive market shortages of particular job skills, managers may have to deviate from the priced grades to hire people with scarce skills. For example, suppose the worth of a specialized information systems analyst's job is evaluated at $38,000 to $48,000 annual salary in a company, but qualified individuals are in short supply and other employers are paying $60,000. The firm must pay the higher rate. But suppose several analysts who have been with the firm for several years started at $38,000 and have received 6% increases each year. These current employees may still be making less than salaries paid to attract and retain new analysts from outside with lesser experience. One solution to pay compression is to have employees follow a step progression based on length of service, assuming performance is satisfactory or better.

## Pay Increases

Once pay ranges have been developed and individuals' placements within the ranges identified, managers must look at adjustment to individual pay. Decisions about pay increases often are critical ones in the relationships among employees, their managers, and the organization. Individuals have expectations about their pay and about how much increase is "fair," especially in comparison with the increases received by other employees. There are several ways to determine pay increases.

**PAY-FOR-PERFORMANCE SYSTEMS** Many employers profess to have a pay system based on performance. But relying on performance-appraisal information for making pay adjustments assumes that the appraisals are done well, and this is not always the case, especially for employees whose work cannot be measured easily. Consequently, some system for integrating appraisals and pay changes must be developed and applied equally. Often, this integration is done through the use of a *pay adjustment matrix,* or *salary guide chart* (see Figure 13–17). Pay adjustment matrices base adjustments in part on a person's **compa-ratio,** which is the pay level divided by the midpoint of the pay range. To illustrate from Figure 13–17, the compa-ratio for two employees would be:

**Compa-ratio**

Pay level divided by the midpoint of the pay range.

$$\text{Employee R} = \frac{\$16.50 \text{ (current pay)}}{15.00 \text{ (midpoint)}} \times 100 \rightarrow \text{Compa-ratio} = 110$$

$$\text{Employee J} = \frac{\$13.05 \text{ (current pay)}}{15.00 \text{ (midpoint)}} \times 100 \rightarrow \text{Compa-ratio} = 87$$

Such charts reflect a person's upward movement in an organization. Upward movement depends on the person's performance, as rated in an appraisal, and on the person's position in the pay range, which has some relation to experience as well. A person's placement on the chart determines what pay raise the person should receive. For example, if employee J is rated as exceeding expectations (3) with a compa-ratio of 89, that person is eligible for a raise of 7% to 9% according to the chart in Figure 13–17.

The sample matrix has several interesting facets that illustrate the emphasis on paying for performance. First, those individuals whose performance is below expectations receive no raises, not even a so-called cost-of-living raise. This approach sends a very strong signal that poor performers will not continue to receive increases just by completing another year of service.

Second, notice that as employees move up the pay range, they must exhibit higher performance to obtain the same percentage raise as those lower in the range performing at the "meets performance expectations" (2) level. This approach is taken because the firm is paying above the market midpoint but receiving only satisfactory performance rather than above-market performance. Charts can be constructed to reflect the specific pay-for-performance policy and philosophy in an organization.

In many organizations, pay-for-performance systems are becoming a popular way to change the way pay increases are distributed. In a truly performance-oriented system, no pay raises are given except for increases in performance. Giving pay increases to people because they have 10 to 15 years' experience, even though they are mediocre employees, defeats the approach. Further, unless the performance-based portion of a pay increase is fairly significant, employees may feel it is not worth the extra effort.[29] Giving an outstanding industrial designer making $40,000 a year the "standard raise" of 4% plus 1% for merit means only $400 for merit versus $1,600 for "hanging around another year."

**FIGURE 13–17** *Pay Adjustment Matrix*

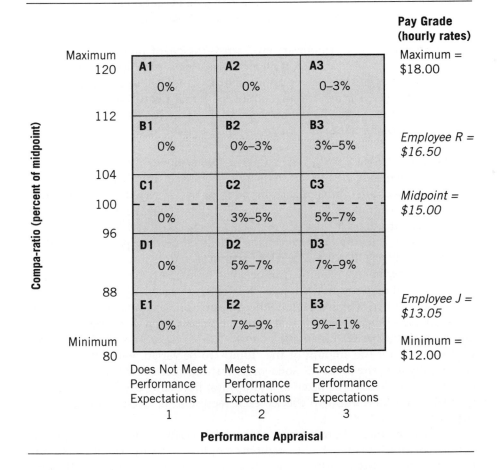

**SENIORITY** Seniority, or time spent in the organization or on a particular job, can be used as the basis for pay increases. Many employers have policies requiring that persons be employed for a certain length of time before they are eligible for pay increases. Pay adjustments based on seniority often are set as automatic steps once a person has been employed the required length of time, although performance must be at least satisfactory in many nonunion systems.

**Maturity curve**
Curve that depicts the relationship between experience and pay rates.

A closely related approach uses a **maturity curve,** which depicts the relationship between experience and pay rates. Pay rises as an employee's experience increases, which is especially useful for professionals and skilled craft employees. Unlike a true seniority system, in which a pay raise occurs automatically once someone has put in the required time, a system using maturity curves is built on the assumption that as experience increases, proficiency and performance also increase, so pay raises are appropriate. If proficiency does not increase, theoretically pay adjustments are reduced, although that seldom happens in practice. Once a person plateaus in proficiency, then the pay progression is limited to following the overall movement of the pay structure.

*BNA:*
**General Increases**
Different methods of determining general pay increases, including the cost-of-living approach and others, are discussed at 2225.10.

**COST-OF-LIVING ADJUSTMENTS (COLA)** A common pay-raise practice is the use of a *standard raise* or *cost-of-living adjustment* (COLA). Giving all employees a standard percentage increase enables them to maintain the same real wages in a period of economic inflation. Often, these adjustments are tied to changes in the Consumer Price Index (CPI) or some other general economic measure. However, numerous studies have revealed that the CPI overstates the actual cost of living.

Unfortunately, some employers give across-the-board raises and call them *merit raises,* which they are not. If all employees get a pay increase, it is legitimately viewed as a cost-of-living adjustment having little to do with merit or good performance. For this reason, employers should reserve the term *merit* for any amount above the standard raise, and they should state clearly which amount is for performance and which is the "automatic" COLA adjustment.

**LUMP-SUM INCREASES (LSI)** Most employees who receive pay increases, either for merit or seniority, first have their base pay adjusted and then receive an increase in the amount of their regular monthly or weekly paycheck. For example, an employee who makes $12.00 per hour and then receives a 3% increase will move to $12.36 per hour.

**Lump-sum increase (LSI)**
A one-time payment of all or part of a yearly pay increase.

In contrast, a **lump-sum increase (LSI)** is a one-time payment of all or part of a yearly pay increase. The pure LSI approach does not increase the base pay. Therefore, in this example the person's base pay remains at $12.00 per hour. If an LSI of 3% is granted, then the person received $748.80 (computed as 36¢ per hour × 2080 working hours in the year.) However, the base rate remains at $12.00 per hour. It is that base rate upon which overtime is figured, and keeping the base rate static slows down the progression of the base wages. It also allows for the amount of the "lump" to be varied, without having to continually raise the base rate. Some organizations place a limit on how much of a merit increase can be taken as a lump-sum payment. Other organizations split the lump sum into two checks, each representing one-half of the year's pay raise.

As with any plan, there are advantages and disadvantages. The major advantage of an LSI plan is that it heightens employees' awareness of what their performance "merited." A lump-sum check also gives employees some flexibility in their spending patterns so that they can buy big-ticket items without having to take out a loan. In addition, the firm can slow down the increase of base pay, so that the compounding effect of succeeding raises is reduced. Unionized employers, such as Boeing and Ford, have negotiated LSI plans as a way to hold down base wages, which also holds down the rates paid for overtime work. Pension costs and some other benefits, often tied to base wages, can be reduced as well.

One disadvantage of LSI plans is administrative tracking, including a system to handle income tax and Social Security deductions from the lump-sum check. Also, workers who take a lump-sum payment may become discouraged because their base pay has not changed. Unions generally resist LSI programs because of this and because of the impact on pensions and benefits. To some extent, this problem can be reduced if the pay increase is split to include some in the base pay and the rest in the lump-sum payment.

# Summary

- Compensation provided by an organization can come both directly through base pay and variable pay, and indirectly through benefits.
- Compensation responsibilities of both HR specialists and managers must be performed well. Compensation practices are closely related to organizational culture, philosophies, strategies, and objectives.
- A continuum of compensation philosophies exists, ranging from an entitlement-oriented philosophy to a performance-oriented philosophy.
- Compensation strategies are shifting, and organizations must balance cost-effectiveness with labor market realities.
- Competency-based pay that focuses on what capabilities people have is growing in usage.
- Broadbanding, which uses fewer pay grades with wider ranges, provides greater career movement possibilities for employees.
- Variable-pay programs, including those that are team based, are being used to enhance organizational performance and reward greater employee participation in work teams.
- When designing and administering compensation programs, behavioral aspects must be considered. Equity, organizational justice, pay openness, and external equity are all important.
- The Fair Labor Standards Act (FLSA), as amended, is the major federal law that affects pay systems. It requires most organizations to pay a minimum wage and to comply with overtime provisions,

- including appropriately classifying employees as exempt or nonexempt and as independent contractors or employees.
- Other laws place restrictions on employers who have federal supply contracts or federal construction contracts, or on those employers who garnish employees' pay.
- Administration of a wage and salary system requires the development of pay policies that incorporate internal and external equity considerations.
- Job evaluation determines the relative worth of jobs. Several different evaluation methods exist, with the point method being the most widely used.
- Once the job evaluation process has been completed, pay survey data must be collected and a pay structure developed. An effective pay system requires that changes continue to be made as needed.
- Developing a pay structure includes grouping jobs into pay grades and establishing a pay range for each grade. Broadbanding, which uses fewer pay grades with broader ranges, is growing in popularity.
- Individual pay must take into account employees' placement within pay grades. Problems involving rates above or below range and pay compression must be addressed.
- Individual pay increases can be based on performance, cost-of-living adjustments, seniority, or a combination of approaches.

# Review and Discussion Questions

1. Give examples of direct and indirect compensation at a recent job that you have had.
2. Discuss what compensation philosophies seemed to be used at organizations where you have worked. What were the consequences of those philosophies?
3. Why are competency-based compensation, broadbanding, and variable pay all related to changing strategies for compensating employees?
4. Discuss the following statement: "If employees believe that subjectivity and favoritism shape the pay system in an organization, then it does not matter that the system was properly designed and implemented."
5. What factors should be considered to determine if an employee who works over 40 hours in a week is due overtime under the FLSA?
6. Considering all methods, why is the point method the most widely used for job evaluation?
7. You have been named compensation manager for a hospital. How would you establish a pay system?
8. Why are pay-for-performance systems growing in importance?

# Terms to Know

base pay   416
benchmark job   437
benefit   417
broadbanding   423
compa-ratio   448
compensable factor   438
compensatory time off   431
distributive justice   426
equity   426
exempt employees   430

garnishment   434
green-circled employee   447
job evaluation   437
lump-sum increase (LSI)   450
market line   443
market price   435
maturity curve   450
nonexempt employees   430
pay compression   447
pay equity   433

pay grade   443
pay survey   441
procedural justice   426
red-circled employee   447
salaries   416
variable pay   417
wage and salary administration   434
wages   416

# Using the Internet

## Using Pay Survey Data

As an HR manager, you are responsible for recruiting top job applicants. Your firm has just lost several administrative and marketing employees to other organizations. To prepare for the hiring process, you need to research market pay data to ensure that your firm is offering a competitive salary to top applicants.

Using the web site at **http://www.ioma.com**, access IOMA's Salary of the month and identify the base pay and average bonus information for administrative and marketing jobs.

The information in the survey is according to Gross Annual Fee Range. Assume the fee range for your firm is "More than $6 Million." The jobs are:

**Administrative**
● Secretary/Administrative Assistant
● Word Processor
● Receptionist

**Marketing**
● Marketing Director
● Network Administrator
● Computer Operator

# CASE

# Implementing a New Compensation Program

The changing nature of jobs in organizations has led to companies redesigning their compensation programs to reflect the changes. As mentioned in the chapter, one approach being used by some employers is competency-based pay. One firm has had success with using a knowledge-based program to measure and reward employees.

This medium-sized manufacturing firm has about 5,000 employees in one location, and none are represented by unions. As a result of continuing efforts by the firm's management to examine and apply innovative organization and management practices, the senior managers at the company decided to redesign work processes and compensation in three production departments. A task force of employees analyzed the work in each of the production departments and recommended some changes.

First, individual jobs and job descriptions were changed to using a team-work approach. In the new system, workers were expected to become skilled in several tasks and rotate throughout the different tasks, depending upon the production schedule and workflow. Workers also were expected to perform their own quality control. Finally a pay-for-performance program was developed to encourage workers to broaden their capabilities and to reward them as they did so.

A series of "skill blocks" was identified by HR specialists and others familiar with the jobs, with each skill block containing what a worker was required to know and do. Skill blocks were developed for all processes in the production departments. As employees mastered a skill block, they received pay increases of 20 cents per hour, except for the basic skill block mastery, which provided a 30-cent-per-hour increase. Because pay is based on the number of skill blocks mastered, no maximum pay levels were set. These increases were granted on top of the entry-level pay rate of $9.81 per hour.

Following the communication of the new program, employees could choose to convert to the new program or transfer to other departments still using the traditional job-based pay plan. Only one production worker opted to transfer out of the new production compensation program and the department. HR specialists and production mnagers spent considerable time meeting with workers on the processes to be used to assess their competencies. Also, extensive training support had to be implemented so that employees could develop additional mastery of other skill blocks. Other coordination and program administration issues had to be addressed as well.

As a result of the changes to the new program, production technicians are rewarded continually for learning more and enhancing their capabilities. Also, greater workforce flexibility has resulted, so that workers can move between jobs and tasks as production needs dictate. Productivity has increased and production employees have become more knowledgeable about the linkage between compensation, their capabilities, and productivity.[30]

## Questions

1. Discuss how changing the compensation program was consistent with the strategic shifts occurring in the organization.
2. What difficulties can you identify with shifting to the new compensation program from the traditional ones used in many production settings?

# Notes

1. Adapted from Jennifer J. Laabs, "Rating Jobs Against New Values," *Workforce*, May 1997, 38–49.
2. Eamon Cassidy and Carol Ackah, "A Role for Reward in Organizational Change?" *IBAR* 18 (1997), 52–62.
3. Howard Risher, "The Search for a New Model for Salary Management: Is There Support for Private Sector Practices?" *Public Personnel Management*, Winter 1997, 431–439.
4. Adapted from Brian Murphy and Barry Gebhart, "An Empirical Analysis of a Skill-Based Pay Program and Plant Performance Outcomes," *Academy of Management Journal* 41 (1998) 68–78.
5. "The State of Competencies: ACA's Research One Year Later," *ACA Journal*, Autumn 1997, 54–61.

6. Duncan Brown and Michael Armstrong, "Terms of Enrichment," *People Management,* September 11, 1997, 36–38.

7. Kenan S. Abosch and Beverly L. Hmurovic, "A Traveler's Guide to Broadbanding," *ACA Journal,* Summer 1998, 38–47.

8. Kathryn Tyler, "Compensation Strategies Can Foster Lateral Moves and Growing in Place," *HR Magazine,* April 1998, 64–71.

9. Barbara Parus, "Broadbanding Highly Effective, Survey Shows," *ACA News,* July/August 1998, 40–42.

10. Christian M. Ellis and Jeff McCutheon, "Critical Success Factors for Implementing Banding in Complex Organizations," *ACA News,* February 1999, 30–32; and Neil Merrick, "Broadbanding Not a 'Quick Fix'," *People Management,* February 20, 1997, 16.

11. Adapted from C. James Novak, "Proceed with Caution when Paying Teams," *HR Magazine,* April 1997, 73–78.

12. Jacquelyn S. DeMatteo, et al., "Factors Related to the Successful Implementation of Team-Based Rewards," *ACA Journal,* Winter 1997, 16–27.

13. Patricia K. Zingheim and Jay R. Schuster, "Best Practices for Small-Team Pay," *ACA Journal,* Spring 1997, 40–49.

14. Anthony T. Cobb, Mike Vest, and Fred Hills, "Who Delivers Justice?: Source Perceptions of Procedural Fairness," *Journal of Applied Social Psychology* 27 (1997), 1021–1040.

15. For more specifics, see *Handy Reference Guide to the Fair Labor Standard Act,* WH Publication no. 1282 (Washington, DC: U.S. Department of Labor, Employment Standards Administration, Wage and Hour Division).

16. "New Demands for a Higher Minimum Wage," *Compensation & Benefits Review,* March/April 1998, 22–23; "City by City, Employers Forced to Pay 'Living Wage'," *Bulletin to Management,* October 30, 1997, 345; Tim Harcourt, "The Economics of the Living Wage," *Australian Economic Review,* June 1997, 194–203; and William Van Lear, "Reflections on the Minimum Wage," *Journal of Economic Issues,* 31 (1997), 263–265.

17. For more details see J. E. Kalet, *Primer on FLSA and Other Wage and Hour Laws,* 3rd ed. (Washington, DC: Bureau of National Affairs, 1994).

18. Michael N. Wolfe, "Classification of Workers: Independent Contractor vs. Employee," *ACA Journal,* Summer 1998, 6–15.

19. Deborah Shalowitz Cowans, "Equal Pay Ranks First for Women," *Business Insurance,* September 15, 1997, 71.

20. "Job Evaluation Products," Organisatieadvies Worst, http://www1.tip.nl/~t169028/homepag3.htm.

21. Anne Woodsworth, "Putting Our Salaries Where Our Jobs Are," *Library Journal,* January 1997, 61.

22. For a detailed discussion of the Hay system, see Richard I. Henderson, *Compensation Management in a Knowledge-Based World,* 7th ed. (Englewood Cliffs, NJ: Prentice-Hall, 1997), 277–294.

23. Adapted from Fay Hansen, "Guide to Salary Survey Data on the Web," *Compensation & Benefits Review,* March/April 1998, 16–20.

24. Michael O'Malley, "Testing for Gender Differences on Pay," *ACA Journal,* Summer 1998, 6–15.

25. Joyce A. Cain, et al., "The Future of Salary Surveys," *ACA News,* October 1997, 32–36.

26. John Yurkat, "Is 'The End of Jobs' the End of Pay Surveys Too?" *Compensation & Benefits Review,* July/August 1997, 24+.

27. *District of Utah, U.S. District Court v. Utah Society for Healthcare Human Resources Administration, et al. Federal Register,* March 1994, 14203.

28. Marilyn Moats Kennedy, "Are you A Victim of 'Salary Compression'?" *Manager's Intelligence Report,* 1998, www.ragan.com.

29. Atul Mitra, Nina Gupta, and G. Douglas Jenkins, "A Drop in the Bucket: When Is a Pay Raise a Pay Raise?" *Journal of Organizational Behavior* 18 (1997), 117–137.

30. Adapted from Gerald D. Klein, "Case Study: A Pay-for-Knowledge Compensation Program That Works," *Compensation & Benefits Review,* March 1998, 69–75.

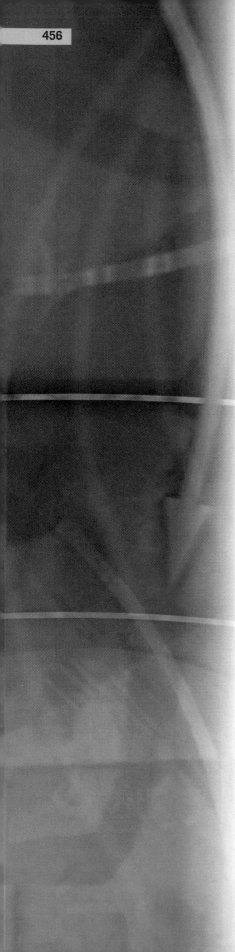

# CHAPTER 14

# Variable Pay and Executive Compensation

***After you have read this chapter, you should be able to:***

- Define *variable pay* and give examples of three types of variable pay.

- Identify four guidelines for successful incentive programs.

- Discuss three types of individual incentives.

- Explain the three different ways that sales employees typically are compensated.

- Identify key factors that must be addressed when using team variable pay plans.

- Discuss why gainsharing, profit-sharing, and employee stock ownership plans (ESOPs) have grown as organizational incentive plans.

- Identify the components of executive compensation and discuss criticisms of the reasonableness of executive compensation.

## HR TRANSITIONS

# Employees Stock Up

Variable pay in the form of incentives for employees can take many forms, ranging from commissions for sales representatives to annual bonuses for managers. But a growing number of companies are moving beyond the typical incentives given to lower-level workers and using stock options throughout the organization. Traditionally, stock options have been provided only to a limited number of top-level executives and senior managers. Now employee stock incentives at all levels are creating strong results for employers and employees alike.

One well-known firm using stock options effectively is Home Depot. Founded in 1978, Home Depot has numerous home improvement and building supply stores throughout the United States. Since its early years, Home Depot has provided stock option incentives for management and administrative employees. Additionally, the firm has a plan that permits virtually all other employees to buy Home Depot stock at a discounted price. Home Depot's CEO, Arthur Blank, has stated that the employee stock plans are at the heart of the firm's success. Black believes that the stock plan has contributed to the feeling among all employees that they "own" their stores, which leads to higher internal morale and greater attention to customer service. Another benefit of the stock program is that Home Depot employees are more likely to resist recruiting efforts by other employers because of their stock ownership in the company.

The Home Depot stock ownership program has paid off for employees, as well. One share of Home Depot stock bought in 1981 would be worth over 100 shares today. As a result, over 1,000 Home Depot employees have company stock valued at $1 million or

more. Many of these "millionaires" are not executives, but administrative and sales employees throughout the company and its stores. In early 1998 Home Depot stock split 2 for 1, and some managers reported that employees were cheering and yelling like they were at a sports pep rally.

Home Depot's biggest competitor also has established employee stock programs. Lowe's, based in North Carolina, provides stock equivalents up to 13% of base pay to employees with one year of service or more. Lowe's has found that its stock program provides a significant recruiting leverage when Lowe Stores are opened in tight labor markets.

Employee stock programs are spreading to other industries as well. One of the most interesting employee stock programs established recently is at the Edison Project. This firm contracts with public schools to operate public schools for fees equivalent to the costs currently incurred by local school districts. Despite significant resistance by traditional educational administrators and teachers' unions, the Edison Project has had significant success in raising student test scores and improving the educational performance of students, many of whom are in lower socioeconomic neighborhoods. Several years after starting the Edison Project, Chris Whittle—its founder—developed a plan to begin providing stock options. In the year 2000, teachers and administrators in over 50 schools that Edison operates in Florida, Colorado, Kansas, and other states will receive shares of

Edison Project stock. When the stock goes public, all full-time staff members can purchase stock at a price set lower than the market price. Employees must stay with Edison for at least five years to fully vest all of their shares, and then the employees can keep any appreciated value of the stock. A sliding scale based on job responsibilities identifies the number of Edison shares that can be purchased. In addition to the stock purchase plan, Edison teachers and administrative staff can earn annual cash bonuses upon the performances of their students against yearly objectives set by local school districts.

Many other firms have employee

> *Now, employee stock incentives at all levels are creating strong results for employers and employees alike.*

stock plans as well, and these plans have significantly rewarded employees for organizational peformance. The major concern with such programs is if the value of the stock declines significantly over time. The incentive value of the stock is reduced when employees' stock value declines, as happened in 1998 when the stock market temporarily dropped. However, these stock plans are designed to reward longer-term performance and employee loyalty, and many of the stock prices rebounded. Obviously, stock prices do not always go up; and when stock values decline, employee anxiety increases. Nevertheless, using stock plans as a means of providing additional compensation to employees appears to help focus employee efforts on increasing organizational performance. Certainly, the "millionaires" at Home Depot, Lowe's, and other firms would agree.[1]

> 66 *The new world of work demands employee performance instead of loyalty, creativity instead of compliance, and earned rewards instead of entitlements.* 99
>
> THE ECONOMIST

A growing number of employers have established compensation programs for employees that provide additional compensation linked to individual, group or team, and organizational performance. For example, individual employees at a telecommunications company receive extra pay if they describe special calling features, such as call-waiting and caller identification, and customers mention their names when signing up for the services. For many sales representatives, commissions tied to sales performance are a significant portion of total compensation. At the executive level, many individuals receive stock options tied to the longer-term performance of firms and their stock prices. All of these examples are illustrations of variable pay plans.

# Variable Pay: Incentives for Performance

**Variable pay**

Compensation linked to individual, team, and/or organization performance.

**Variable pay** is compensation linked to individual, team, and/or organization performance. Traditionally also known as *incentives,* variable pay plans are attempts to tie additional tangible rewards given to employees for performance beyond normal expectations. The philosophical foundation of variable pay rests on several basic assumptions:

● Some jobs contribute more to organizational success than others.
● Some people perform better than others.
● Employees who perform better should receive more compensation.
● A portion of some employees' total compensation should be given to reward above-satisfactory performance.

Contrast the assumptions above with a pay system based on seniority or length of service:

● Time spent each day is the primary measure of short-term contribution.
● In the long term, length of service with the organization is the primary differentiating factor among people.
● Differences in individual contributions to the organiation are recognized through different base pay levels.
● Giving additional performance rewards to some people but not others is divisive and hampers employees working together.

The prevalence of variable pay programs can be seen in a study of over 400 large companies. As Figure 14–1 shows, almost half of all surveyed firms offer variable pay programs to hourly employees, while most offer such plans to executives. Generally, sales employees and executives have higher amounts of variable pay, which usually is linked to sales performance.[2] It is evident that variable pay plans have become significant to both employers and employees.

## Types of Variable Pay

Variable pay plans can be established that focus on individual performance, team or group performance, and on organization-wide performance. An important fea-

**FIGURE 14–1** *Variable Pay Plan Participation by Employee Groups*

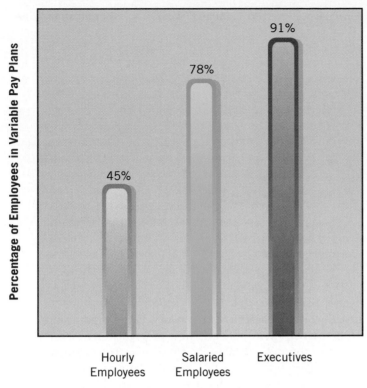

SOURCE: Based on data in *1998/1999 Compensation Budget Survey of Fortune 1000 Companies* (Secaucus, NJ: Buck Consultants, 1998).

ture of variable pay plans is that incentives increase the degree of cooperation in teams, whereas individual incentives do not.

*Individual incentives* are given to reward the effort and performance of individuals. Some of the most common means of providing individuals variable pay are piece-rate systems, sales commissions, and bonuses. Other means include special recognition rewards such as trips or merchandise. Two widely used individual incentives focus on employee safety and attendance. One of the difficulties with individual incentives is that an employee may focus on what is best individually and may block or inhibit performance of other individuals with whom the employee is competing. That competition particularly occurs if only the top performer or winner receives incentives. This is one reason why team or group incentives have been developed.

When an entire work group or *team* is rewarded for its performance, more cooperation among the members is required and usually forthcoming. However, competition among different teams for rewards can lead to decline in overall performance under certain circumstances. The most common types of *team* or *group incentives* are gainsharing plans where employee teams that meet certain goals share in the gains measured against performance targets. Often, gainsharing programs focus on quality improvement, labor-cost reduction, and other measurable results.

*Organization incentives* reward people for the performance of the entire organization. This approach reduces individual and team competition and assumes that

**FIGURE 14–2** *Types of Variable Pay Plans*

| Individual | Group (Team) | Organization-Wide |
|---|---|---|
| • Piece rate<br>• Sales commissions<br>• Bonuses<br>• Special recognitions<br>  (trips, merchandise)<br>• Safety awards<br>• Attendance bonuses | • Gain sharing<br><br>• Quality<br>  improvement<br><br>• Labor-cost<br>  reduction | • Profit sharing<br><br>• Employee stock<br>  options<br><br>• Executive stock<br>  options<br><br>• Deferred<br>  compensation |

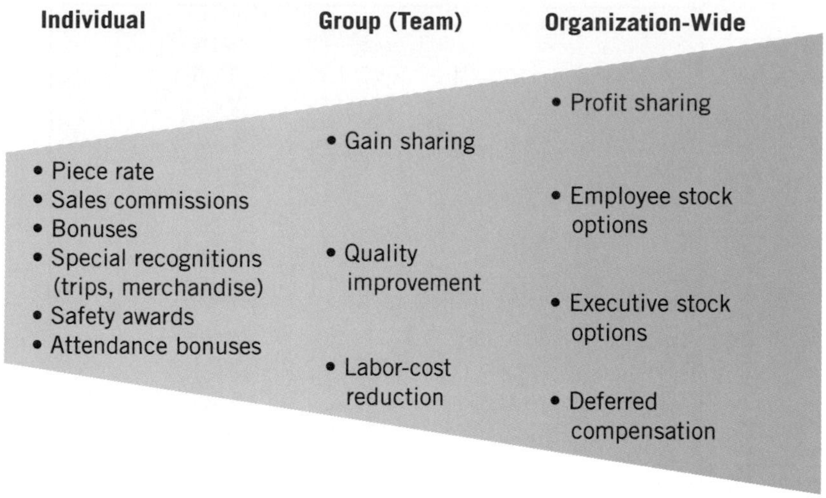

all employees working together can generate better organizational results that lead to better financial performance. These programs share some of the financial gains to the firm through payments to employees. The payments often are paid as an additional percentage of each employee's base pay. Also, organizational incentives may be given as a lump-sum amount to all employees, or different amounts may be given to different levels of employees throughout the organization. The most prevalent forms of organization-wide incentives are profit-sharing plans and employee stock plans. For senior managers and executives, variable pay plans often are established to provide stock options and other forms of deferred compensation that minimize the tax liabilities of the recipients. Figure 14–2 shows some of the programs under each type.

## Successes and Failures of Variable Pay Plans

As variable pay has grown in popularity, it is becoming evident that these plans have both succeeded and failed. One study of employers found that despite the fact that 61% of the companies have variable pay plans, almost half of them did not achieve their performance targets for the year. But to avoid negative employee reactions, many of those companies paid out 85% of the incentives anyway. The good news from the study is that over half of the variable pay plans achieved their performance objectives.[3] Executive-focused variable pay plans tend to be viewed as more successful than those used with lower-level, nonmanagement employees.[4]

The reactions of employees are crucial to how variable pay plans are accepted. It is interesting that in a study of over 2,000 workers from a variety of companies, most respondents said they want performance rewards included in their base pay, rather than as one-time payments. Also, the employees strongly preferred individual rewards over team or organization incentives.[5]

These studies and others highlight the fact that neither of the polar extremes —the view that incentives do not work versus the view that incentives are a panacea—appears to be the case. Also, the enthusiasm that many employers and managers have for variable pay plans is not matched by many workers. The key to success seems to be to combine incentives with employee participation in the process.

In summary, it appears that variable pay plans are successful under certain circumstances. As Figure 14–3 indicates, a number of factors affect the success of variable pay plans. The next section discusses the guidelines for establishing successful variable pay plans.

## Guidelines for Variable Pay Plans

Providing variable pay through incentive systems can be complex and can take many forms. However, certain general guidelines are useful in establishing and maintaining successful variable pay systems.

**RECOGNIZE ORGANIZATIONAL CULTURE AND RESOURCES** An important factor in the success of any variable pay program is that it be consistent with both the culture and the financial resources of the organization. For example, if an organization is autocratic and adheres to traditional rules and procedures, an incentive

**FIGURE 14–3** *Conditions for Successful Variable Pay Plans*

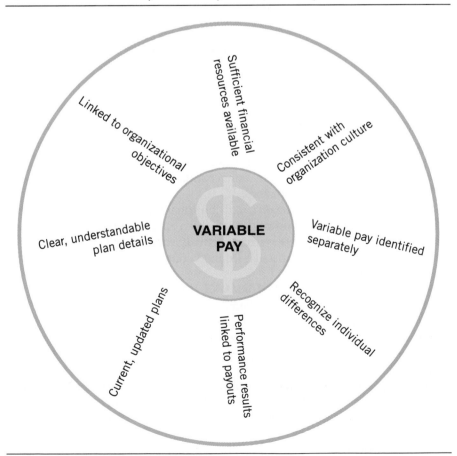

system that rewards flexibility and teamwork is likely to fail. The incentive plan is being "planted" in the wrong growing environment.[6]

Any variable pay system requires an organizational climate of trust and cooperation between employees and managers.[7] As the amount of trust between employees and managers increases, and the objectivity of the criteria used for determining rewards becomes greater, the likelihood of a successful incentive program increases. If workers have a high level of trust and good working relationships with their superiors, they may accept more subjective performance measures. But low trust of management leads to a low probability of success for a variable pay system.

**MAKE VARIABLE PAY PLANS UNDERSTANDABLE** Another key factor for establishing effective variable pay plans is to make them easy for employees to understand. If these plans are clear, employees can track performance against the objectives of the plan and see what variable pay they are earning. However, if plans are developed that are too complicated and employees need calculators, worksheets, and assistance from analysts to determine where they are against incentive target levels, then the plans have lost some of their motivational value. The more complicated a plan is, the more difficult it will be to communicate it meaningfully to employees.[8]

Many plans include several performance criteria, which generally are recommended by experts in variable pay designs. But having two or three areas to focus on should not result in a significant number of steps being required for employees to compute their incentive amounts and for managers to be able to explain what further performance targets need to be met. In summary, effective variable pay plans give employees clear information on why the employer is establishing the plan, how the employees' performance will be evaluated, what their contributions will produce for the organization, and what rewards they will receive.[9]

**LOGGING ON . . .**
**Strategies for Incentives**
This website is from a company specializing in incentive programs. An overview of the strategies and philosophies used when developing an incentive program is available.

**http://www.hinda.com/ index.htm**

**KEEP INCENTIVE PLANS CURRENT** An incentive system should consistently reflect current technological and organizational conditions. Offering an incentive for sales representatives to sell older-generation equipment in order to clear it out of stock might be appropriate until that merchandise is gone, but no incentive may be needed to sell high-demand items.

Incentive systems should be reviewed continually to determine whether they are operating as designed. Follow-up, through an attitude survey or other means, will determine if the incentive system is actually encouraging employees to perform better. If it is not, then managers should consider changing the system.

**TIE VARIABLE PAY TO DESIRED PERFORMANCE** Variable pay sytems should be tied as much as possible to desired performance. Employees must see a direct relationship between their efforts and their financial rewards.[10] Further, both employees and managers must recognize that incentives are most effective when employees can see clearly that their extra efforts lead to increased performance and desirable rewards.[11]

Because people tend to produce what is measured and rewarded, it is important to make sure that what is being rewarded ties to organizational objectives. Also, often multiple measures are used to assure that various performance dimensions are not omitted. For example, assume a hotel reservation center sets incentives for its employees to increase productivity by lowering their time spent per call. That reduction may occur, but customer service and the number of reservations made might drop as employees rush callers to reduce talk time.

Indeed, linking pay to performance may not always be appropriate. For example, if the output cannot be objectively measured, management may not be able to reward the higher performers with more pay. Managers may not even be able to accurately identify the higher performers.

**RECOGNIZE INDIVIDUAL DIFFERENCES** Incentive plans should provide for individual differences. People are complex, and a variety of incentive systems may have to be developed to appeal to various organizational groups and individuals. Therefore, variable pay plans must be designed carefully. As illogical as it may seem, informal group pressure and sanctions commonly are used to restrict the amount that individuals produce, even if individual pay is reduced as a result. Those who seek to maximize their earnings by exceeding group-imposed limits are labeled "rate busters" or something even more graphic. Rate restrictors often feel they are being made to suffer by comparison with the higher producers. Therefore, designers of incentive plans first must look at individual issues.

**IDENTIFY VARIABLE PAY SEPARATE FROM BASE PAY** Successful variable pay plans clearly identify how much the variable pay plan provides to employees separate from their base pay amounts. That separation makes a clear connection between performance and pay. It also reinforces the notion that one part of the employees' pay must be "re-earned" in the next performance period.

*BNA: 2249.20*
**Incentive Plan Design**
Read this section containing incentive plan design issues and list them, so that they can be reviewed as you read the information on individual and group incentives.

# Individual Incentives

Individual incentive systems attempt to relate individual effort to pay. Conditions necessary for the use of individual incentive plans are as follows:

- *Identification of individual performance:* The performance of each individual can be measured and identified because each employee has job responsibilities and tasks that can be categorized from those of other employees.
- *Independent work:* Individual contributions result from independent work and effort given by individual employers.
- *Individual competitiveness desired:* Because individuals generally will pursue the individual incentives for themselves, competition among employees will occur. Therefore, independent competition whereby some individuals "win" and others do not must be desired.
- *Individualism stressed in organizational culture:* The culture of the organization must be one that emphasizes individual growth, achievements, and rewards. If an organization emphasizes teamwork and cooperation, then individual incentives will be counterproductive.

## Piece-Rate Systems

The most basic individual incentive system is the piece-rate system, whether of the straight or differential type. Under the **straight piece-rate system,** wages are determined by multiplying the number of units produced (such as garments sewn or customers contacted) by the piece rate for one unit. The rate per piece does not change regardless of the number of pieces produced. Because the cost is

**Straight piece-rate system**
A pay system in which wages are determined by multiplying the number of units produced by the piece rate for one unit.

## HR PERSPECTIVE

# Piece-Rate Plan Clear Winner at Safelite Glass

Many organizations attempt to link employee performance to compensation. One of the oldest programs of this type is a piece-rate plan, whereby employees are paid only for what they produce. At Safelite Glass Corporation, this traditional plan appears to have produced payoffs in higher productivity for the company and more pay for employees.

Safelite operates nationally, providing auto glass installation services. Several years ago, Safelite management decided to change from hourly pay for installation employees to a piece-rate plan. To avoid creating employee anxiety, Safelite guaranteed a base wage of $11 per hour to installers. But Safelite also offered the installers an alternative plan, under which they could receive $20 per installed unit. To ensure that quality standards were met, windshields installed improperly or broken were replaced at no additional pay. Using a workflow and tracking system, the firm could identify each installer's work.

The success of the program exceeded most expectations. Individual productivity increased on average 20%, resulting in installer's average pay increasing by 10%. The company output also increased. Closely related, employee turnover and absenteeism declined, especially among the most productive workers. Thus, Safelite could see clearly the link between managers and employees, organizational and individual performance, and the rewards generated by that performance.[12]

**Differential piece-rate system**
Pays employees one piece-rate wage for units produced up to a standard output and a higher piece-rate wage for units produced over the standard.

### BNA 2035.20.70
**Piece-Rate Determination**
To review the wage and hour regulations regarding determining the overtime rates for employees paid on piece rate plans, see this section.

**Bonus**
A one-time payment that does not become part of the employee's base pay.

the same for each unit, the wage for each employee is easy to figure, and labor costs can be accurately predicted.

A **differential piece-rate system** pays employees one piece-rate wage for units produced up to a standard output and a higher piece-rate wage for units produced over the standard. Developed by Frederick W. Taylor in the late 1800s, this system is designed to stimulate employees to achieve or exceed established standards of production.

Managers often determine the standards, or quotas, by using time and motion studies. For example, assume that the standard quota for a worker is set at 300 units per day and the standard rate is 14 cents per unit. For all units over the standard, however, the employee receives 20 cents per unit. Under this system, the worker who produces 400 units in one day will get $62 in wages (300 × 14 cents) + (100 × 20 cents). There are many possible combinations of straight and differential piece-rate systems. The specific system used by a firm depends on many situational factors. The effects of a piece-rate system can be seen in the HR Perspective on Safelite Glass Corporation in Columbus, Ohio.

Despite their incentive value, piece-rate systems are difficult to use because standards for many types of jobs are difficult and costly to determine. In some instances, the cost of determining and maintaining the standards may be greater than the benefits derived. Jobs in which individuals have limited control over output or in which high standards of quality are necessary also may be unsuited to piecework.

## Bonuses

Individual employees may receive additional compensation payments in the form of a **bonus,** which is a one-time payment that does not become part of the employee's base pay. Generally, bonuses are less costly to the employer than other pay increases because they do not become part of employees' base wages, upon which future percentage increases are figured. Growing in popularity, individual incentive compensation in the form of bonuses often is used at the executive levels of an organization, but bonus usage also is spreading to lower-level jobs, as Figure 14–4 indicates.

Bonuses also can be used to reward employees for contributing new ideas, developing skills, or obtaining professional certifications. When the skills or certification requirements are acquired by an employee, a pay increase or a one-time bonus may follow. For example, a financial services firm provides the equivalent of two week's pay to employees who master job-relevant computer skills. Another firm gives one week's pay to members of the HR staff who obtain their professional certifications such as PHR, SPHR, CCP, and others discussed in Chapter 1. Firms in the information technology industry pay bonuses for obtaining special technical skills in order to keep employees from looking for new jobs elsewhere using their newly acquired skills and certification.[13]

A bonus recognizes performance by both the employee and the company. When both types of performance are good, bonuses go up. When both are bad, bonuses go down. When an employee has done poorly in a year that was good for the company, most employers base the employee's bonus on individual performance. It is not always as clear what to do when an employee does well but the company does not. However, a growing number of companies are asking employees to put a portion of their pay "on the line." While offering big incentive bonuses for high performance, they are withholding them when performance is poor and insisting that employees share *both* the risks and rewards of business.

**FIGURE 14–4** *Bonuses as Percentage of Salary (averages for non-sales employees)*

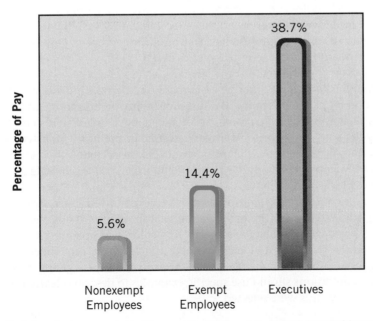

SOURCE: Buck Consultants, as reported in "Compensation Trends and Strategies," *Journal of Accountancy,* January 1998, 87.

One method of determining an employee's annual bonus is to compute it as a percentage of the individual's base salary. Often, such programs pay bonuses only if specific individual and organizational objectives have been achieved. Though technically this type of bonus is individual, it comes close to being a group or organizational incentive system. Because it is based on the profits of the division, management must consider the total performance of the division and its employees.

Whatever method of determining bonuses is used, legal experts recommend that bonus plans be described in writing, especially for key managers. A growing number of lawsuits are being filed by employees who leave organizations either voluntarily or involuntarily, demanding payment of bonuses promised to them.[14]

## Special Incentive Programs

There are numerous special incentive programs that provide awards to individuals. These programs can take various forms, ranging from one-time contests for meeting performance targets to rewards for performance over time. For instance, safe-driving awards are given for truck drivers who have no accidents or violations during a year. Although special programs also can be developed for groups and for entire organizations, these programs often focus on rewarding only high-performing individuals.

**INCENTIVE PROGRAM AWARDS** Cash merchandise, gift certificates, and travel are the most frequently used rewards, as Figure 14–5 shows. Cash is still highly valued by many employees because they have discretion on how to spend it; however, travel awards, particularly those to popular destinations such as Disney World, Las Vegas, Hawaii, and international locations, appeal to many employees. In one study, Goodyear Tire & Rubber Company conducted an experiment in which some employees received cash and another set of employees received merchandise and other non-cash rewards. The employees receiving the non-cash incentives outperformed those receiving only cash by 46%. The study concluded that many employees like the continuing "trophy" value of merchandise rather than the short-term usage of cash.[15]

**RECOGNITION AWARDS** Another type of program recognizes individual employees for their performance or service. For instance, many organizations in service industries such as hotels, restaurants, and retailers have established "employee of the month" and "employee of the year" awards. In the hotel industry over half of the hotels surveyed have recognition awards for desk clerks, housekeepers, and other hourly employees, with the awards being triggered by favorable guest comment cards.[16]

It is important that recognition awards be given to recognize specific efforts and activities targeted by the organization as important.[17] While the criteria for selecting award winners may be subjectively determined in some situations, formally identified criteria provide greater objectivity and are more likely to reward performance, rather than being seen as favoritism. When giving recognition awards, organizations should use specific examples to describe clearly how those receiving the awards were selected.

**SERVICE AWARDS** Another common type of reward given to individual employees is the *service award*. Although these awards often may be portrayed as

**FIGURE 14–5** *Special Incentive Award Types*

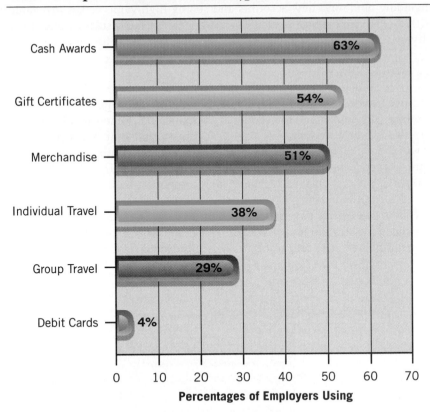

SOURCE: *A Study of the Incentive Merchandise and Travel Marketplace* (Westfield, NJ: The Incentive Federation, Inc., 1997). Used with permission.

rewarding performance over a number of years, the reality is that they are determined by length of service, and performance plays little or no role.

# Sales Compensation and Incentives

The compensation paid to employees involved with sales and marketing is partly or entirely tied to sales performance. Better-performing salespeople receive more total compensation than those selling less.

## Sales Performance Measurement

Successfully using variable sales compensation requires establishing clear performance criteria and measures. Generally, no more than three sales performance measures should be used in a sales compensation plan.[18] Consultants criticize many sales commission plans as being too complex to motivate sales representatives. Other plans may be too simple, focusing only on the salesperson's pay, not on organizational objectives. Although many companies use an individual's sales revenue compared to established quotas as the primary performance measure, performance would be much better if these organizations used a variety of criteria, including obtaining new accounts and selling high-value versus low-value items that reflect marketing plans. Figure 14–6 shows the results of one study identifying the criteria used to determine incentive payments for salespeople.

## Sales Compensation Plans

Sales compensation plans are generally of several different types. The types are based on the degree to which total compensation includes some variable pay tied to sales performance. A survey of over 260 firms found that plans providing salary with bonus (37%) and salary with commission and bonus (35%) were the most used types. Less used were plans providing commission only (24%) and salary only (5%).[19] A look at each type of sales compensation follows next.

**SALARY ONLY** Some firms pay salespeople only a salary. The salary-only approach is useful when serving and retaining existing accounts is being emphasized more than generating new sales and accounts. This approach is frequently used to pro-

**FIGURE 14–6** *Sales Performance Criteria*

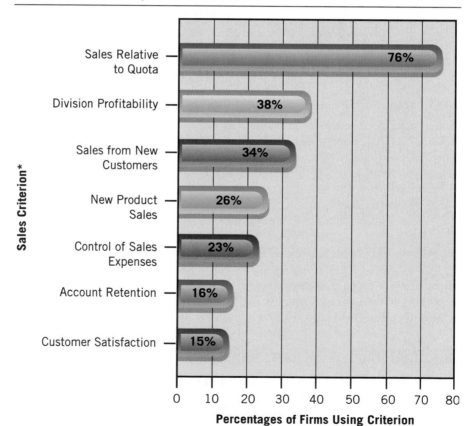

*NOTE: Because multiple criteria may be used, the totals exceed 100%.
SOURCE: Based on data in Kisson Joseph and Manohar U. Kalwani, "The Role of Bonus Pay in Salesforce Compensation Plans," *Industrial Marketing Management* 27 (1998), 147–159.

# Balancing Sales Compensation and Ethical Concerns

Sales commission programs are widely used to compensate sales representatives. These programs are very effective at driving the behavior of sales representatives, especially if the sales performance measures are based wholly or mostly on sales volume and revenues. However, in a number of instances, performance-based sales employees have acted unethically. For instance, a major retailer paid commissions to employees for generating sales volume and revenue for auto parts in its auto repair centers. Upon closer scrutiny, the retailer discovered that in several cases representatives were convincing customers to buy unnecessary part replacements and have unnecessary repairs done. By doing so, the sales reps received higher commissions and met corporate performance targets. As a result of the investigation, which received widespread, negative press coverage, the retailer had to revamp its incentive plans.

Other industries have seen similarly shady behavior as well. Several brokerage and insurance firms have been investigated because sales representatives have misrepresented financial products and services that were marketed to a wide range of customers. In some cases large fines and criminal indictments have been handed down.

Some legal experts and academics have voiced concerns that performance-driven sales incentives encourage unethical behavior, particularly if commissions are the sole basis for determining the compensation of sales representatives. These critics charge that sales commission programs align the interest of sales reps with the firm, rather than with those of customers and clients. This concern is especially true if the customer purchases are likely to be "one-time" purchases, such as a used car or a life insurance policy, where the likelihood of repeat pur-

chases and a continuing customer relationship is lower.

Some solutions to address these ethical issues have included discontinuing commission-only plans, so that the basic income of sales reps does not solely depend on what they "hunt and kill." Instead, proponents urge using a mixture of guaranteed base salary and lowered commission rates. Critics of sales compensation also suggest that other sales-related dimensions be used, such as customer service, repeat business, or customer satisfaction. For instance, sales commissions for investment brokers might be linked to increasing a client's net portfolio value, rather than only to the trading commissions generated. How realistic such changes are in a variety of sales situations may be debated. But it is clear that ethical issues must be considered when developing and managing sales incentive plans.[20]

---

tect the income of new sales representatives for a period of time while they are building up their sales clientele. It is also used when both new and existing sales reps have to spend considerable time learning about and selling customers new products and service lines. Generally, the salary-only approach may extend no more than six months, at which point sales plus commission or bonuses are implemented. However, one study found that salespeople who wanted extrinsic rewards were less effective in salary-only plans. They were less motivated to sell without additional performance-related compensation.[21]

**STRAIGHT COMMISSION** An individual incentive system widely used in sales jobs is the **commission,** which is compensation computed as a percentage of sales in units or dollars. Commissions are integrated into the pay given to sales workers in three common ways: straight commission, salary plus commission, and bonuses.

In the straight commission system, a sales representative receives a percentage of the value of the sales made. Consider a sales representative working for a

**Commission**
Compensation computed as a percentage of sales in units or dollars.

consumer products company. She receives no compensation if no sales are made, but for all sales made in her territory, she receives a percentage of the total amount. The advantage of this system is that the sales representative must sell to earn. The disadvantage is that it offers no security for the sales staff. This disadvantage can be especially pronounced when the product or service sold is one that requires a long lead time before purchasing decisions are made. Also, as the HR Perspective on the previous page indicates, commission-only plans may lead to unethical behavior of sales employees.

**Draw**

An amount advanced from and repaid to future commissions earned by the employee.

For these reasons just mentioned, some employers use a **draw** system, in which the sales representative can draw advance payments against future commissions. The amount drawn then is deducted from future commission checks. From the employer's side, one of the risks in a draw system is that future commissions may not be large enough to repay the draw, especially for a new or marginally successful salesperson. In addition, arrangements must be made for repayment of drawn amounts if an individual leaves the organization before earning the draw in commission.

**SALARY PLUS COMMISSION OR BONUSES** The most frequently used form of sales compensation is the *salary plus commission,* which combines the stability of a salary with the performance aspect of a commission. Many organizations also pay salespeople salaries and then offer bonuses as a percentage of base pay tied to meeting various levels of sales targets or other criteria. A common split is 70% salary to 30% commission, although the split varies by industry and with other factors.

Some sales organizations combine both individual and group sales bonus programs. In these programs, a portion of the sales incentive is linked to the attainment of group sales goals. This approach encourages cooperation and teamwork for the salespersons to work together. Team incentives in situations other than sales jobs are discussed next.

# Team-Based Variable Pay

The growing use of work teams in organizations has implications for compensation of the teams and their members. Interestingly, while the use of teams has increased significantly in the past few years, the question of how to equitably compensate the individuals who compose the team remains one of the biggest challenges. As Figure 14–7 notes, there are several reasons why organizations have established group or team variable pay plans, and evidently these goals are being met in a number of organizations.

As seen in the results of a survey of the *Fortune* 1000 large companies, almost 70% of these large firms are using work teams in some manner. About 87% of the executives and HR professionals surveyed were positive about the use of teams. However, only 45% of those surveyed were positive about the ways those teams were being paid. Also, the satisfaction with team-based pay plans was lower than two years before, despite a significant increase in the use of teams.[22]

## Types of Team Incentives

Team-based reward systems use various ways of compensating individuals. The components often include individual wages and salaries in addition to team-

**FIGURE 14–7** *Why Organizations Establish Team Variable Pay Plans*

TEAM VARIABLE PAY

- Enhances Productivity
- Ties Earnings to Team Performance
- Improves Quality
- Aids Recruiting and Retention of Employees
- Improves Employee Morale

based rewards. Most team-based organizations continue to pay individuals based either on the jobs performed or the individuals' competencies and capabilities. Several decisions about methods of distributing and allocating team rewards must be made.

## Distributing Team Incentives

The two primary approaches for distributing team rewards are as follows:

- *Same size reward for each team member:* In this approach, all team members receive the same payout, regardless of job levels, current pay, or seniority.
- *Different size rewards for each team member:* Using this approach, individual rewards vary based upon such factors as contribution to team results, current pay, years of experience, and skill levels of jobs performed.

Generally more organizations use the same-size team reward approach as an addition to different levels of individual pay. This approach is used to reward team performance by making the team incentive equal, while still recognizing that individual pay differences exist and are important to many persons. The size of the team incentive can be determined either by using a percentage of base pay for the individuals or the team as a whole, or by offering a specific dollar amount. For example, one firm pays team members individual base rates that reflect years of experience and any additional training that team members have. The team reward is distributed to all as a flat dollar amount.

**TIMING OF TEAM INCENTIVES** How often team incentives are paid out is another important consideration. Some of the choices seen in firms with team-based incentives include payment monthly, quarterly, biannually, or annually. As Figure 14–8 on the next page shows, yearly is the most common period used. The shorter the time period, the more likely it is that employees will see a closer link to their efforts and the performance results that trigger the award payouts. A study of team rewards for quality management found that companies generally limited the team rewards to $500 or less, so that the rewards could be paid out more frequently.[23] Naturally, the nature of the teamwork, measurement criteria, and organizational results must all be considered when determining the appropriate time period.

**DECISION MAKING ABOUT TEAM-INCENTIVE AMOUNTS** To reinforce the team concept, some team incentive programs allow group members to make decisions

**FIGURE 14–8** *Characteristics of Team-Based Rewards*

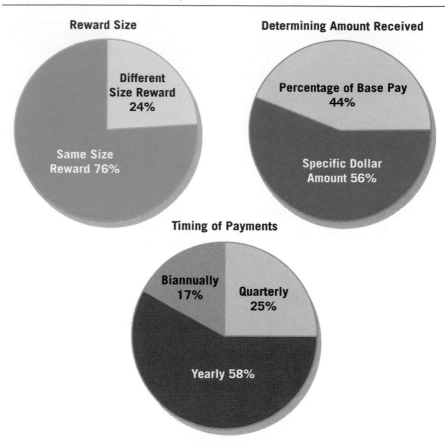

SOURCE: Jacquelyn S. DeMatteo, et al., "Factors Related to the Successful Implementation of Team-Based Rewards," *ACA Journal*, Winter 1997, 20. Used with permission.

about how to allocate the team rewards to individuals. For example, in one division of Motorola, teams are given a lump sum amount and they decide how to divide up the money. Some teams vote, while others have a team leader decide.[24] In other companies teams divide the team "pot" equally, thus avoiding conflict and recognizing that all members contributed to the team results.

Although some teams actually make decisions on bonuses for their members, this practice seems to be the exception rather than the rule. Many companies find teams unwilling to handle pay decisions for coworkers. Team-based bonus plans present other problems as well. Should a member be rewarded for trying hard but not quite succeeding? What happens when extra money for a "superstar" has to come from other group members' forgoing their own bonuses to some extent? Team-based incentives present both opportunities and challenges when they are developed and implemented.

## Problems with Team-Based Incentives

The difference between rewarding team members *equally* or *equitably* triggers many of the problems associated with team-based incentives. Rewards that are distributed equally in amount to all team members may be perceived as "unfair" by employees who may work harder, have more capabilities, and perform more difficult jobs. This problem is compounded when a poorly performing individual negatively influences the team results. For instance, suppose that holding data-entry errors to below 2% is an objective that triggers payment of a group incentive. The presence of one or two poor performers who make numerous errors can result in the group being denied an incentive payment for a month. Unfortunately, even if management retrains or removes the poor performers, some incentive amounts already have been lost.

Equitable pay in the minds of many people means distributing the team rewards individually to recognize individual efforts and capabilities. One survey of employees working in teams found a relatively low level of employee satisfaction with rewards that are the same for all, rather than different amounts based on performance, which may be viewed more equitably.[25]

In summary, it seems that the concept of people working in teams is seen as beneficial by managers and organization leaders. But employees still expect to be paid based on individual performance, to a large extent. Until this individualism is recognized and compensation programs developed that are viewed as more equitable by more "team members," caution should be used in developing and implementing team-based incentives.

## Successful Team-Based Incentives

The unique nature of the team and its members is important when establishing successful team-based rewards. One consideration is the history of the group and its past performance.[26] Use of incentives is more successful where groups have been used in the past and where those groups have performed well. However, simultaneously introducing the teamwork concept and changing to team-based incentives has not been as successful.

Another consideration for the success of team-based incentives is the size of the team. If a team becomes too large, employees may feel their individual efforts will have little or no effect on the total performance of the group and the resulting rewards. Incentive plans for small groups are a direct result of the growing number of complex jobs requiring interdependent effort. Team-based incentive plans may encourage teamwork in small groups where interdependence is high. Therefore, it is recommended that team-based performance measures be used.[27] Such plans have been used in many service-oriented industries, where a high degree of contact with customers requires teamwork.

Team incentives seem to work best when the following criteria are present:

- Significant interdependence exists among the work of several individuals, and teamwork and cooperation are essential.
- Difficulties exist in identifying exactly who is responsible for differing levels of performance.
- Management wants to create or reinforce teamwork and cooperation among employees.
- Rewards are seen as being allocated in a fair and equitable manner.
- Employee input is obtained in the design of the team-incentive plan.

If these conditions cannot be met, then either individual or organizational incentives may be more appropriate.

# Organizational Incentives

An organizational incentive system compensates all employees in the organization based on how well the organization as a whole performs during the year. The basic concept behind organizational incentive plans is that overall efficiency depends on organizational or plant-wide cooperation. The purpose of these plans is to produce teamwork. For example, conflict between marketing and production can be overcome if management uses an incentive system that emphasizes organizational profit and productivity. To be effective, an organizational incentive program should include everyone from nonexempt employees to managers and executives. Common organizational incentive systems include gainsharing, profit sharing, and employee stock ownership plans (ESOPs).

## Gainsharing

**Gainsharing**

The sharing with employees of greater-than-expected gains in profits and/or productivity.

**Gainsharing** is the sharing with employers of greater-than-expected gains in profits and/or productivity. Gainsharing attempts to increase "discretionary efforts"—that is, the difference between the maximum amount of effort a person can exert and the minimum amount of effort necessary to keep from being fired. It can be argued that workers currently are not paid for discretionary effort in most organizations. They are paid to meet the minimum acceptable level of effort required. However, when workers do exercise discretionary efforts, the organization can afford to pay them more than the going rate, because the extra efforts produce financial gains over and above the returns of minimal efforts.

**DETERMINING PAYMENT AND PERFORMANCE MEASURES** To begin a gainsharing program, management must identify the ways in which increased productivity, quality, and financial performance can occur and decide that some of the gains should be shared with employees. The most critical step is to involve employees at all levels in the gainsharing process, often by establishing a gainsharing task force or design team composed of managers and nonmanagers alike. Once the task force meets, there are two crucial decisions to be made: (1) How much gain is to be shared with employees? (2) What are the performance measures to be used?[28]

Payouts of the gains can be made monthly, quarterly, semiannually, or annually, depending on management philosophy and the performance measures used. The more frequent the payouts, the greater the visibility of the rewards to employees. Therefore, given a choice, most firms with gainsharing plans have chosen to make the payouts more frequently than annually.

The rewards can be distributed in four ways:

- A flat amount for all employees
- Same percentage of base salary for all employees
- Percentage of the gains by category of employees
- Amount of percentage based on individual performance against measures

The first two methods generally are preferred because they promote and reward teamwork and cooperation more than the other two methods. Where performance measures are used, only those measures that employees actually can affect should be considered. Often, measures such as labor costs, overtime hours, and quality benchmarks are used. Both organizational measures and departmental measures may be used, with the gainsharing weighting being split between the two categories. Naturally, an individual's performance must be satisfactory in order for that individual to receive the gainsharing payments.

**SUCCESS IN GAINSHARING** The success or failure of incentive programs begins with the culture of the organization. Putting a gainsharing program in autocratically or in desperation to save a badly managed firm virtually guarantees failure. Inadequate financial systems, severe external competitive conditions, and government constraints also inhibit the success of gainsharing programs. Simply offering gainsharing payouts may not be enough to generate much participation in the plan. Negative attitudes toward the gainsharing plan and management can lead to nonparticipation by the employees. However, gainsharing certainly *can* work to improve performance, as the closing case in this chapter on Baltimore County indicates.

**IMPROSHARE** A number of gainsharing-type plans have been devised. One is Improshare, which stands for Improved Productivity through Sharing. Improshare was created by Mitchell Fein, an industrial engineer. It is similar to a piece-rate plan except that it rewards all workers in the organization. Input is measured in hours and output in physical units. A standard is calculated and weekly bonuses are paid based on the extent to which the standard is exceeded. Generally, the Improshare programs have resulted in productivity gains.

**SCANLON PLAN** Since its development in 1927, the Scanlon plan has been implemented in many organizations, especially in smaller unionized industrial firms. The basic concept underlying the Scanlon plan is that efficiency depends on teamwork and plant-wide cooperation.

The system is activated through departmental employee committees that receive and review cost-saving ideas submitted by employees. Suggestions beyond the scope of the departmental committees are passed to the plant screening committee for review. Savings that result from suggestions are passed on to all members of the organization.

Incentive rewards are paid to employees on the basis of improvements in preestablished ratios. Ratios of labor costs to total sales value or total production or total hours to total production are the most commonly used. Savings due to differences between actual and expected ratios are placed in a bonus fund. A predetermined percentage of this fund is then split between employees and the organization.

The Scanlon plan is not a true profit-sharing plan, because employees receive incentive compensation for reducing labor costs, regardless of whether the organization ultimately makes a profit. Organizations that have implemented the Scanlon plan have experienced an increase in productivity and a decrease in labor costs. Also, employee attitudes have become more favorable, and cooperation between management and workers has increased.

**RUCKER PLAN** The Rucker plan, almost as old as the Scanlon plan, was developed in the 1930s by the economist Allan W. Rucker. The Scanlon formula measures performance against a standard of labor costs in relation to the dollar value of production, whereas the Rucker formula introduces a third variable: the dollar value of all materials, supplies, and services that the organization uses.

The Rucker formula is calculated as follows:

$$\frac{\$ \text{ Value of Labor Costs}}{\$ \text{ Value of Production } - \$ \text{ Value of Materials, Supplies, Services}}$$

The result is what economists call the "value added" to a product by the organization. The use of value added rather than the dollar value of production builds in an incentive to save on other inputs.

## Profit Sharing

**Profit sharing**

A system to distribute a portion of the profits of the organization to employees.

As the name implies, **profit sharing** distributes a portion of organizational profits to employees. Typically, the percentage of the profits distributed to employees is agreed on by the end of the year before distribution. In some profit-sharing plans, employees receive portions of the profits at the end of the year; in others, the profits are deferred, placed in a fund, and made available to employees on retirement or on their leaving the organization. Figure 14–9 shows how profit-sharing plans can be set up.

Unions sometimes are skeptical of profit-sharing plans, because such plans only work when there are profits to be shared. Often, the level of profits is influenced by factors not under the employees' control, such as marketing efforts, competition, and elements of executive compensation. However, in recent years, organized labor has supported profit-sharing plans in which employees' pay increases are tied to improved company performance.

**OBJECTIVES OF PROFIT-SHARING PLANS** The primary objectives of profit-sharing plans are to:

● Improve productivity
● Recruit or retain employees
● Improve product/service quality
● Improve employee morale

**DRAWBACKS OF PROFIT-SHARING PLANS** When used throughout an organization, including lower-echelon workers, profit-sharing plans can have some drawbacks. First, management must be willing to disclose financial and profit information to

**FIGURE 14–9** *Profit-Sharing Plan Framework*

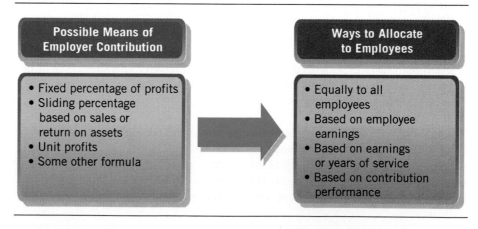

employees. As many people know, both the definition and level of profit can depend on the accounting system used and decisions made. Therefore, to be credible, management must be willing to disclose sufficient financial and profit information to alleviate the skepticism of employees, particularly if profit-sharing levels are reduced from previous years. Second, profits may vary a great deal from year to year—resulting in windfalls and losses beyond the employees' control. Third, the payoff may be seen as too far removed from employees' efforts to serve as a strong link between better performance and higher rewards.

## Employee Stock Ownership Plans (ESOPs)

A common type of profit sharing is the **employee stock ownership plan (ESOP).** An ESOP is designed to give employees stock ownership of the organization for which they work, thereby increasing their commitment, loyalty, and effort. According to the National Center for Employee Ownership, an estimated 15,000 firms in the United States have established broad employee-ownership programs. Of these firms, about 10,000 have formed ESOPs, covering about 9 million workers.[29]

**Employee stock ownership plan (ESOP)**
A plan whereby employees gain stock ownership in the organization for which they work.

**ESTABLISHING AN ESOP** An organization establishes an ESOP by using its stock as collateral to borrow capital from a financial institution. Once the loan repayment begins through the use of company profits, a certain amount of stock is released and allocated to an employee stock ownership trust (ESOT). Employees are assigned shares of company stock kept in the trust, based on length of service and pay level. On retirement, death, or separation from the organization, employees or their beneficiaries can sell the stock back to the trust or on the open market, if the stock is publicly traded.

Employee stock ownership plans are subject to certain tax laws. Generally, the employers who have treated all employees alike are most advantaged. Those that provide different levels of benefits for different groups of employees are penalized in the tax laws.

**ADVANTAGES AND DISADVANTAGES OF ESOPS** Establishing an ESOP creates several advantages. The major one is that the firm can receive favorable tax treatment of the earnings earmarked for use in the ESOP. Second, an ESOP gives employees a "piece of the action" so that they can share in the growth and profitability of their firm. As a result, employee ownership may be effective in motivating employees to be more productive and focused on organizational performance. In one survey of over 1,100 ESOP companies, about 60% said productivity had increased, and 68% said financial performance was higher since converting to an ESOP.[30]

Almost everyone loves the concept of employee ownership as a kind of "people's capitalism." However, the sharing also can be a disadvantage because employees may feel "forced" to join, thus placing their financial future at greater risk. Both their wages or salaries and their retirement benefits depend on the performance of the organization. This concentration is even riskier for retirees because the value of pension fund assets also depends on how well the company does.

Another drawback is that ESOPs have been used as a management tool to fend off unfriendly takeover attempts. Holders of employee-owned stock often align with management to turn down bids that would benefit outside stockholders but would replace management and restructure operations. Surely, ESOPs were not created to entrench inefficient management. Despite these disadvantages, ESOPs have grown in popularity.

**FASB RULES ON ESOPS** Perhaps in part because of the increase in popularity of ESOPs, companies have been required to disclose how much they would have earned if the stock options they gave employees had been charged against company income. The Financial Accounting Standards Board (FASB) now requires companies to report the value of the stock options they give employees—but there is some real controversy over how to value the options.

# Executive Compensation

Many organizations, especially large ones, administer executive compensation somewhat differently than compensation for lower-level employees. An executive typically is someone in the top two levels of an organization, such as Chief Executive Officer (CEO), President, or Senior Vice-President. As Figure 14–10 shows, the common components of executive compensation are *salaries,* annual *bonuses, long-term incentives, supplemental benefits,* and *perquisites.*

Two objectives influence executive compensation: (1) ensuring that the total compensation packages for executives are competitive with the compensation packages in other firms that might employ them, and (2) tying the overall performance of the organization over a period of time to the compensation that is paid to executives. It is the second objective that critics of executive compensation believe is not being met. In many organizations, it appears that the levels of executive compensation may be unreasonable and not linked closely to organizational performance.

## Elements of Executive Compensation

At the heart of most executive compensation plans is the idea that executives should be rewarded if the organization grows in profitability and value over a

**FIGURE 14–10** *Executive Compensation Components*

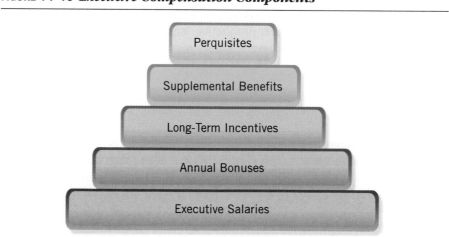

period of years. Because many executives are in high tax brackets, their compensation often is provided in ways that offer significant tax savings. Therefore, their total compensation packages are more significant than their base pay. Especially when the base salary is $1 million or more, the executive often is interested in the mix of items in the total package, including current and deferred compensation.

**EXECUTIVE SALARIES** Salaries of executives vary by type of job, size of organization, region of the country, and industry. On average, salaries make up about 40–60% of the typical top executive's annual compensation total. A provision of a 1993 tax act prohibits a publicly traded company from deducting pay of more than $1 million for each of its top five officers unless that pay is based on performance criteria approved by outside directors and shareholders.

**EXECUTIVE BONUS PLANS** Because executive performance may be difficult to determine, bonus compensation must reflect some kind of performance measure if it is to be meaningful. As an example, a retail chain with over 250 stores ties annual bonuses for managers to store profitability. The bonuses have amounted to as much as 35% of a store manager's base salary.

Bonuses for executives can be determined in several ways. A discretionary system whereby bonuses are awarded based on the judgments of the chief executive officer and the board of directors is one way. However, the absence of formal, measurable targets is a major drawback of this approach. Also, as noted, bonuses can be tied to specific measures, such as return on investment, earnings per share, or net profits before taxes. More complex systems create bonus pools and thresholds above which bonuses are computed. Whatever method is used, it is important to describe it so that executives trying to earn bonuses understand the plan; otherwise, the incentive effect will be diminished.

**PERFORMANCE INCENTIVES—LONG TERM VS. SHORT TERM** Performance-based incentives attempt to tie executive compensation to the long-term growth and success of the organization. However, whether the emphasis is really on the long term or merely represents a series of short-term rewards is controversial. Short-term rewards based on quarterly or annual performance may not result in the kind of long-run-oriented decisions necessary for the company to continue to do well.

A **stock option** gives an individual the right to buy stock in a company, usually at an advantageous price. Different types of stock options have been used depending on the tax laws in effect. Stock options have increased in use as a component of executive compensation during the past 10 years, and employers may use a variety of very specialized and technical approaches to them, which are beyond the scope of this discussion. However, the overall trend is toward using stock options as performance-based long-term incentives.

Where stock is closely held, firms may grant "stock equivalencies" in the form of *phantom stock* or *share appreciation rights*. These plans pay recipients the increased value of the stock in the future, determined by a base valuation made at the time the phantom stock or share appreciation rights are given. Depending on how these plans are established, the executives may be able to defer taxes or be taxed at lower capital-gains tax rates.

**BENEFITS FOR EXECUTIVES** As with benefits for non-executive employees, executive benefits may take several forms, including traditional retirement, health

**LOGGING ON . . .**
**Crystal Report**
The Crystal Report evaluates executive compensation levels and issues. Details on the report can be found at

**www.crystalreport.com.**

**Stock option**
A plan that gives an individual the right to buy stock in a company, usually at a fixed price for a period of time.

insurance, vacations, and others. However, executive benefits may include some items that other employees do not receive. For example, executive health plans with no co-payments and with no limitations on deductibles or physician choice are popular among small and middle-sized businesses. Corporate-owned life insurance on the life of the executive is popular and pays *both* the executive's estate *and* the company in the event of death. Trusts of various kinds may be designed by the company to help the executive deal with estate issues. Deferred compensation is another possible means used to help executives with tax liabilities caused by incentive compensation plans.

**Perquisites (perks)**
Special benefits—usually noncash items—for executives.

**EXECUTIVE PERQUISITES** In addition to the regular benefits received by all employees, executives often receive benefits called perquisites. **Perquisites (perks)** are special executive benefits—usually noncash items. Perks are useful in tying executives to organizations and in demonstrating their importance to the companies. It is the status enhancement value of perks that is important to many executives. Visible symbols of status allow executives to be seen as "very important people (VIPs)" both inside and outside their organizations. In addition, perks can offer substantial tax savings because many perks are not taxed as income. Figure 14–11 on the next page lists some perks that are commonly available.

## Board of Directors' Role with Executive Compensation

In most organizations the board of directors is the major policy-setting entity. For publicly traded companies covered by federal regulatory agencies, such as the Securities and Exchange Commission (SEC), the board of directors must approve executive compensation packages. Even many nonprofit organizations are covered by Internal Revenue Service requirements to have boards of directors review and approve the compensation for top-level executives. In family-owned or privately owned firms, boards of directors may have less involvement in establishing and reviewing the compensation packages for key executives.

**Compensation committee**
Usually a subgroup of the board of directors composed of directors who are not officers of the firm.

**BOARD COMPENSATION COMMITTEE** The **compensation committee** usually is a subgroup of the board of directors composed of directors who are not officers of the firm. Compensation committees generally make recommendations to the board of directors on overall pay policies, salaries for top officers, supplemental compensation such as stock options and bonuses, and additional perquisites ("perks") for executives. But the "independence" of board compensation committees increasingly has been criticized.[31]

One major concern voiced by many critics is that the base pay and bonuses of CEOs often are set by board compensation members, many of whom are CEOs of other companies with similar compensation packages. However, one study found little relationship between the composition of compensation committees of boards and the level of CEO compensation.[32] Also, the compensation advisors and consultants to the CEOs often collect large fees, and critics charge that those fees distort the objectivity of the advice given.

To counter criticism, some corporations are changing the composition of the compensation committee and giving it more independence. Some of the changes include prohibiting "insider" company officers and board members from serving on compensation committees. Also, some firms empower the compensation committee to hire and pay compensation consultants without involving executive management.

**FIGURE 14–11** *Executive Perquisites*

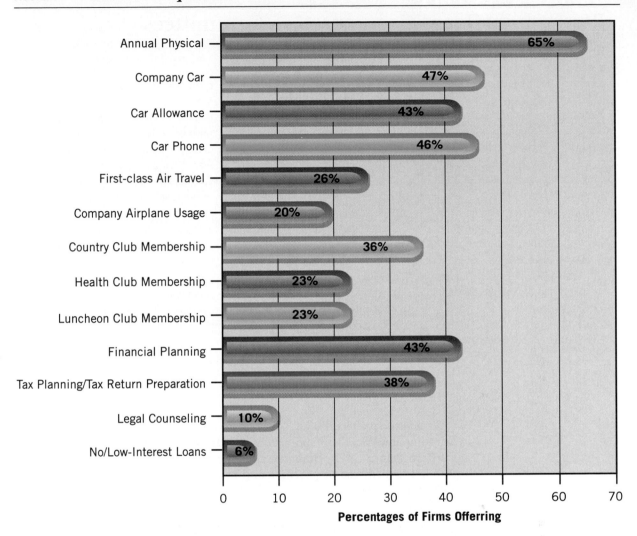

*Percentages based on 767 total responses.
SOURCE: Based on data in *1998 Executive Compensation Survey* (Louisville, KY: William M. Mercer, Inc., 1998), 11.

More importantly, the link between the independence of board compensation committees and organization performances is crucial. If the compensation committee's decisions about executive variable pay lead to higher organizational performance, then the composition of the compensation committee is less of an issue. Research on compensation committees and organizational performance indicates that having more "outside" directors is linked to better organizational performance results, as the HR Perspective on the next page indicates.

**BOARD MEMBERS' COMPENSATION** Although they are not executives of the firm, outside members of boards of directors receive compensation as well. Generally, they receive directors' fees, either as a set amount per year or a per-meeting fee. To counter some criticisms of the independence of board members,

## Research on Board Compensation Committees and Organizational Performance

There has been a growing debate about how the composition of the compensation committees of corporate boards of directors affects executive compensation. One study that gathered research on this area was published in the *Academy of Management Journal*.

The study by Conyon and Peck examined performance data on publicly traded firms in the United Kingdom (U.K.) and compared those results to the composition of board compensation committees. Data were collected from the top 100 companies in market value in the U.K. Details on composite performance, organization size, and corporate governance were gathered by the researchers. Data on a total of 94 companies were used in the study. The researchers examined the proportion of "outside" directors and the existence of board compensation committees. Another factor examined was whether the corporate CEOs also served as the Chairman of the board of directors.

The researchers concluded that top management pay was more aligned with corporate performance in companies with a greater number of "outsiders" and use of a compensation committee to make executive compensation decisions. The results of this study suggest that outsiders do play a role in ensuring that executive incentives are linked more closely to organizational results. Also, having a higher proportion of outsiders on board compensation committees seemed to be related to even higher performance. The authors conclude by stating, "The evidence appears to clearly indicate that the composition of both a company's main board and its compensation committee are important in the closer alignment of management pay and corporate performance."[33]

some experts have recommended that board members be paid totally or in part with company stock. This approach is seen as linking board members' pay more closely to that of the stockholders they represent. Also, some corporations require board members to purchase and own a minimum number of shares of stock in the company.

## Reasonableness of Executive Compensation

The expansion of executive compensation to include significant stock options and other components may be necessary for firms to be competitive for top executive talent, especially in larger, publicly traded corporations.[34] The purpose of including the stock and other components is to link organizational performance to executive compensation.

**ORGANIZATIONAL PERFORMANCE AND EXECUTIVE COMPENSATION** Whether executive compensation levels are linked to organizational performance has been the subject of numerous studies. One key in evaluating all of the studies is to examine the performance measures used. In many settings, financial measures such as return on equity, return to shareholders, earnings per share, net income before taxes, and other criteria are used. However, a number of firms also incorporate nonfinancial organizational measures of performance when determining executive bonuses and incentives. Customer satisfaction, employee satisfaction, market share, productivity, quality, and other areas are measured and considered when executive performance rewards are given.[35]

There are some indications that executive compensation, particularly when stock and stock options are included, has a positive effect on the total returns to shareholders. One study by Wyatt-Watson, a large consulting firm, found that high levels of CEO stock ownership has led to total returns to shareholders of 21% annually, compared to firms with lower levels of CEO stock ownership having total shareholder returns of 15% annually.[36] However, reviews of numerous studies have found that the overall linkage between executive compensation and organizational performance is somewhat weak and statistically insignificant.[37] Consequently, criticisms of executive compensation regularly are voiced.

**CRITICISM OF EXECUTIVE COMPENSATION** Critics point out that many U.S. corporate CEOs make almost 200 times more than average workers in their firms make, up from 35 to 1 in the 1970s.[38] Moreover, in Japan the ratio is 15 to 1 and in Europe 20 to 1. Also, Japanese CEOs are paid about one-third of what U.S. CEOs in comparable-sized firms are paid. Stock options are seldom used in Japan and many other countries, and base salaries and bonuses often are significantly lower as well.

The biggest criticism of executive compensation levels is that even though the various elements of executive compensation are supposed to be linked to organizational performance, in far too many companies the reality is that many executives get large compensation packages and produce mediocre to poor organizational results. Critics point to numerous examples of CEOs and other senior managers getting large rewards even when organizational performance declines.[39] A noted critic of excessive levels of executive compensation, Graef Crystal, even publishes a newsletter annually identifying the most overpaid CEOs.

**LOGGING ON . . .**
**Executive PayWatch**
This site developed by labor unions provides a CEO compensation database index by company, including data on both base pay and stock options. Over 400 companies are tracked in this database.

**http://www.aflcio.org/ paywatch/ceoyou/aflcio.pl**

© Mike Keefe, The Denver Post 1998

## HR PERSPECTIVE

# Ethics of Huge Golden Parachutes

"Out of control," "obscene," "sickening," "outrageous and irresponsible." No, these comments are not being made about toxic waste or organized crime. Instead, they are comments made about golden parachutes received by individuals who had been Chief Executive Officers (CEOs) of corporations during the past few years. Some examples include the following:

- Michael Ovitz served as the second highest executive at Walt Disney for about a year. When he quit, he received a golden parachute estimated to be as high as $90 million! The reason for his departure was incompatibility with Michael Eisner, CEO of Disney.
- When Tandem Computers was acquired by Compaq, Roel Pieper got a parachute paying him $6 million plus options on company shares worth over $10 million.

These rewards were given, despite Tandem's corporate performance being mediocre for several years before the acquisition.

- When Union Pacific Corp (UP) acquired Southern Pacific Railroad, the CEO of UP, Drew Lewis, got a $4 million bonus and a five-year consulting contract paying $3.75 million. Unfortunately, the merger was handled badly for a few years, resulting in rail traffic delays, safety problems, and a significant decline in the financial results of the combined companies.

Critics of these and other large golden parachutes for a few top executives point out that these parachutes were suggested and pushed by the executives who were to receive them. Despite these parachutes being approved by boards of directors, critics also question how independent the board decisions

really are, given the fact that the CEOs and other senior executives serve on those same boards.

Just as troubling, these golden parachutes go to only a few people, whereas the numerous employees who lose their jobs after mergers and acquisitions receive limited or no parachute protection. Finally, golden parachutes are often given to top executives who have presided over firms whose performance has been mediocre to poor. Thus, a few executives get rewarded, even though corporate performance has not produced returns to stockholders. Despite the criticisms of golden parachutes, financial experts are projecting that the increasing number of mergers and consolidations in many industries will lead to even more outlandish golden parachutes being given to a limited number of executives.[41]

**Golden parachute**

A severance benefit that provides protection and security to executives in the event that they lose their jobs or that their firms are acquired by other firms.

**"GOLDEN PARACHUTES" FOR EXECUTIVES** A special perk available to some executives, a **golden parachute,** provides protection and security to executives in the event that they lose their jobs or their firms are acquired by other firms. Typically, employment contracts are written to give special compensation to executives if they are negatively affected in an acquisition or merger.

Estimates are that over half of all CEOs and other senior executives in the largest major corporations have golden parachutes. A typical golden parachute gives a CEO a lump sum amount equal to 2–4 times their annual salary and bonus, extra pension credits, immediate vesting of stock options, outplacement assistance, and other sweeteners. Additionally, some golden parachutes provide consulting contracts of up to 10 years at the final annual salary and bonus.[40] But the huge size of some parachute packages raises some ethical concerns, as the HR Perspective discusses.

There are a number of criticisms of golden parachutes. First, golden parachutes often are criticized for giving executives protection, while lower- and middle-level managers and other employees are left vulnerable when mergers or acquisitions occur. As a result, some firms have established **silver parachutes**, severence and benefit plans to protect nonexecutives if their firms are acquired

**Silver parachute**

A severance and benefits plan to protect nonexecutives if their firms are acquired by other firms.

by other firms. For example, one manufacturer has a generous severance pay and benefits plan that goes into effect if a hostile takeover threatens any of the 3,500 employees' jobs. Whether golden or silver, the parachute phenomenon is a clear response to the takeover strategy that many organizations have faced.

Another problem with golden parachutes is that many parachute provisions are not tied to organizational performance. One study of the banking industry found that adoption of golden parachutes for top executives was correlated with poor bank operating performance, both before and after the adoption of the parachutes.[42]

Additionally, there are indications that executives push boards to adopt golden parachutes in order to deter takeover attempts.[43] In this way the executives, particularly those in underperforming organizations, can continue in their jobs—for which they receive extensive compensation.

Another criticism of executive compensation is that a short-term focus of one year is used in some executive compensation packages. Instead, performance in a given year may lead to large rewards even though corporate performance over a multi-year period may be mediocre. This difference is especially apparent if the yearly measures are carefully chosen. Executives can even manipulate earnings per share by selling assets, liquidating inventories, or reducing research and development expenditures. All these actions may make organizational performance look better, but they may impair the long-term growth of the organization.

Overall, the reasonableness of executive compensation is often justified by comparison to compensation market surveys, but these surveys usually provide a range of compensation data that requires interpretation. A tax court case suggested some interesting criteria to determine if executive pay was "reasonable" in a specific instance.[44]

- Would another company hire this person as CEO?
- Is the company so tenuous that a premium must be paid?
- How does this compensation compare with that in similar companies?
- Is the CEO's pay consistent with pay for the other employees?
- What would an investor pay for this CEO's level of performance?

Undoubtedly, the criticisms of executive compensation will continue as huge payouts occur, particularly if organizational performance has been weak. Hopefully, boards of directors of more corporations will address the need to better link organizational performance with variable pay rewards for executives and other employees.

# Summary

- Variable pay is additional compensation linked to individual, team (group), and/or organizational performance. Variable pay traditionally has been referred to as incentives.
- Effective variable pay plans should recognize organizational culture and resources, be clear and understandable, be kept current, tie incentives to performance, recognize individual differences, and identify plan payments separate from base pay.

- Sales employees may have their compensation tied to their performance on a number of sales-related criteria. Sales compensation can be provided as salary only, commission only, and salary plus commissions or bonuses.
- Design of team (group) variable pay plans must consider how team incentives are to be distributed, the timing of the incentive payments, and how decisions are made about who receives how much of the variable payout.

- To overcome some problems associated with individual incentives, team (group) variable pay plans encourage and reward teamwork and group effort.
- One prominent organization-wide variable pay plan is gainsharing, which provides rewards based on greater-than-expected gains in profits and/or productivity.
- Other organization-wide incentive plans include Improshare, Scanlon, and Rucker plans.
- Profit-sharing plans set aside a portion of the profits earned by organizations for distribution to employees.
- An employee stock ownership plan (ESOP) enables employees to gain ownership in the firm for which they work.
- Executive compensation must be viewed as a total package composed of salaries, bonuses, long-term performance-based incentives, benefits, and perquisites (perks).
- A compensation committee, which is a subgroup of the board of directors, has authority over executive compensation plans.
- Performance-based incentives often represent a significant portion of an executive's compensation package. Stock options, phantom stock, and stock appreciation rights are widely used.
- Perks provide additional noncash compensation to executives.

## Review and Discussion Questions

1. Identify what variable pay is and discuss why its usage has increased.
2. Describe why incentive plans you have received at work have been successful and/or unsuccessful.
3. Give several examples of individual incentives that have been used by an organization in which you were employed.
4. What are the positives and negatives associated with using salary-only and commission-only sales compensation plans?
5. Describe situations in which team incentive plans are likely to be successful.
6. Why would an employee stock ownership plan (ESOP) be seen by employees both as an attraction and as a risk?
7. Locate a corporate annual report and review it to identify the components of executive compensation discussed in it. How reasonable is the compensation of the CEO compared with the corporate results described in the report?

## Terms to Know

bonus   464
commission   469
compensation committee   480
differential piece-rate system   464
draw   470

employee stock ownership plan
   (ESOP)   477
gainsharing   474
golden parachute   484
perquisites (perks)   480

profit sharing   476
silver parachute   484
stock option   479
straight piece-rate system   463
variable pay   458

## Using the Internet

## Executive Compensation Issues

The board of directors has asked you, as HR Director, to research some issues on CEO compensation. The board and some of the stockholders have expressed some concerns about the compensation plan for the CEO. They are not sure if it is justified, or if it is the market rate for a CEO. Using the following website, research six reasons why a large compensation plan for the CEO may not be justified.
**http://aflcio.org/paywatch/problem/
index.htm**

# CASE

# County Governments and Incentive Programs

The spread of incentive programs is not limited to private-sector employers. A number of local and state governmental entities have established incentive programs, including public school districts, state-operated institutions, and county governments. Two county government programs illustrate both the advantages and the reactions to the use of incentives in the public sector.

In Maryland several years ago, Baltimore County employee morale was very low, and for good reason. Over the previous five years, employees had received raises in only one of the years, the number of employees had declined, and some layoffs had occurred. During the same period of time the population in Baltimore County had increased significantly, which meant more work for fewer workers who had received limited pay increases. Also, the quality of the services delivered by the county employees had declined somewhat.

Then changes began to be made when a new county executive, Dutch Ruppensberger, took office. Ruppensberger, who previously had served on the council, recruited outside consultants to help design an employee gainsharing program. Ruppensberger saw this program as a way to improve quality and productivity in delivering county services while also rewarding employees for their efforts. The program began by gathering employee ideas and obtaining employee input through some employee teams. Then a pilot program was begun in two very different divisions, Dietary Services and Recreational and Parks Maintenance. Employees in the two divisions participated in training on teamwork and resolving conflicts. Then the teams met to draft program objectives and action plans. The Dietary Services Division, which provided meals to prisoners in the county jails, identified potential savings of $88,000 that could be made. The Recreation and Parks Maintenance employees estimated that savings of $126,000 could be reached. Both divisions submitted their plans to county management and then the County Council. With approvals granted, the gainsharing program was implemented. Under the plan half of the estimated savings in each division go to the county, while the other half of the savings are divided equally among participating division employees up to an identified maximum amount. Based upon the first year of the plan in these two divisions, significant savings have been obtained, and participating employees received their appropriate payments. The success of programs at Baltimore County appears to be due to its focus on rewarding employees directly involved in delivering county services.

However, a bonus incentive plan for executive-level managers in San Diego County in California created a firestorm of controversy. Under the San Diego County plan, executive-level, across-the-board pay increases were eliminated. Performance bonuses were paid only to executives who attained established performance objectives. A total of 180 executives and administrators received bonus payments totaling $1.34 million; but one-third of all executives received no bonus, and several had their base pay cut because of missing performance objectives.

When the amounts of the bonuses were made public, a furor resulted. The local union representing lower-paid county employees protested that executives—including the top county executive, who got a $45,000 bonus—were getting huge sums, while lower-level employees got only a 3% raise. Further, the union noted that some of the bonus amounts were more than the annual income of many lower-level county employees. Also, the bonus program for executives cost $500,000 more than if 3% across-the-board raises had been given to those executives. As a result of the controversy, the county board directed that the program be revised.[45]

## Questions

1. What factors determined the success and failure of the two programs described in the case?
2. Given the strength of public-sector unions, some experts believe that incentive programs in public-sector organizations will never become widespread. Comment on this view and discuss why it may or may not prevail.

# Notes

1. Based on Tamara Henry, "Edison Project to Offer Stock Options to Teachers," *USA Today,* October 22, 1998, D1–2; and "Home Depot Employees Build Fortunes with Firm's Stock," *Omaha World-Herald,* August 3, 1998, p. 15.
2. "Alternative Reward Strategies Gaining Mainstream Appeal," *Bulletin to Management,* November 5, 1998, 348.
3. Valerie Frazee, "Variable Compensation Plans Yield Low Returns," *Workforce,* April 1997, 21–24.
4. "New Study Tracks What's Working and What's Not in Incentive Plan Design," *IOMA's Report on Salary Surveys,* January 1998, http://www.ioma.com.
5. Peter V. LeBlanc and Paul W. Mulvey, "How American Workers See the Rewards of Work," *Compensation & Benefits Review,* January/February 1998, 24–29.
6. Robert J. Greene, "Effective Variable Compensation Plans," *ACA Journal,* Spring 1997, 32–39.
7. "Alternative Pay Breaks New Ground," *Bulletin to Management,* March 12, 1998, 80.
8. Don Barksdale, "Leading Employees through the Variable Pay Jungle," *HR Magazine,* July 1998, 111–118.
9. Kenan S. Abosch, "Variable Pay: Do We Have the Basics in Place?" *Compensation & Benefits Review,* July/August 1998, 12–21.
10. Nina Gupta and Atul Mitra, "The Value of Financial Incentives," *ACA Journal,* Autumn 1998, 58–65.
11. James Shah, E. Tory Higgins, and Ronald S. Friedman, "Performance Incentives and Means: How Regulatory Focus Influences Goal Attainment," *Journal of Personality and Social Psychology* 74 (1998), 285–293.
12. Adapted from Gene Koretz, "Truly Tying Pay to Performance," *Business Week,* February 17, 1997, 25.
13. Renee Gotcher, "Keeping Employees On Board: Combine Bonuses with Rewards," *Infoworld,* October 20, 1997, 119.
14. Edward S. Silverman, "Bonus Onus," *Human Resource Executive,* February 1999, 40–42; and Richard

H. Block and David R. Lagasse, "Making a Bonus Plan Work for You," *HR Magazine,* November 1997, 126–129.
15. "The Power of Merchandise," *Incentives Solve Business Problems* 1 (1997), 1–2.
16. "Money Talks," *The Wall Street Journal,* January 6, 1998, A1.
17. Kevin Wallsten, "Targeted Rewards Have Greater Value—and Bigger Impact," *Workforce,* November 1998, 67–71.
18. David J. Cichell, "Solving the Seven Riddles of Sales Compensation Design," *ACA News,* September 1998, 33–35.
19. Kisson Joseph and Manohar U. Kalwani, "The Role of Bonus Pay in Salesforce Compensation Plans," *Industrial Marketing Management* 27 (1998), 147–159.
20. Based on ideas in Jim Settel and Nancy B. Kurland, "Can We Create a Conflict-Free Commission Payment System?", *Business and Society Review* 100/101 (1998), 33–44.
21. Dong Hwan Lee, "Moderating Effect of Salesperson Reward Orientation on the Relative Effectiveness of Alternative Compensation Plans," *Journal of Business Research* 43 (1998), 65–77.
22. C. James Novak, "Proceed with Caution When Paying Teams," *HR Magazine,* April 1997, 73–78.
23. David B. Balkin, Shimon Dolan, and Kim Forgues, "Rewards for Team Contributions to Quality," *Journal of Compensation and Benefits,* July/August 1997, 41–46.
24. "Team Structures Can Complicate Reward Programs," *InfoWorld,* May 25, 1998, 132.
25. Jacquelyn S. De Matteo, et al., "Factors Related to the Successful Implementation of Team-Based Rewards," *ACA Journal,* Winter 1997, 16–28.
26. Haig R. Nalbantian and Andrew Schotter, "Productivity Under Group Incentives: An Experimental Study," *The American Economic Review,* 87 (1997), 314–341.
27. Patricia K. Zingheim and Jay R. Schuster, "Best Practices for Small-Team Pay," *ACA Journal,* Spring 1997, 40–49.

28. Robert Masternak, "How to Make Gainsharing Successful," *Compensation & Benefits Review,* September/October 1997, 43–52.
29. Jeff Gates, *The Ownership Solution* (Reading, MA: Addison-Wesley, 1998).
30. "More Companies See Value in Employee Stock Plans," *Omaha World-Herald,* January 26, 1997, 46R.
31. Charles M. Elson, "Executive Overcompensation and Board Independence," *ACA News,* October 1998, 6–7.
32. Catherine M. Daily, et al., "Compensation Committee Composition as a Determinant of CEO Compensation," *Academy of Management Journal* 41 (1998), 209–220.
33. Based on Martin J. Conyon and Simon I. Peck, "Board Control, Remuneration Committees, and Top Management Compensation," *Academy of Management Journal* 41 (1998), 146–157.
34. Gary Strauss, "Firms Supersize Executive Perks," *USA Today,* March 17, 1999, 1B; Brenda Paik Sunoo, "Shareholder Revolt: Is Your CEO Worth $39 Million?" *Workforce,* January 1999, 38–45; and "Attracting and Hiring Top Talent," *ACA News,* June 1998, 23–27.
35. Christopher D. Ittner, David Larcker, and Madhav V. Rajan, "The Choice of Performance Measures in Annual Bonus Contracts," *The Accounting Review* 72 (1997), 231–255.
36. Ira T. Kay, "How Stock Drives CEO and Company Performance," *Across the Board,* quoted in *ACA News,* October 1997, 19–22.
37. Harry G. Bartema and Luis R. Gomez-Mejia, "Managerial Compensation and Firm Performance: A General Research Framework," *Academy of Management Journal* 41 (1998), 135–145.
38. Robert H. Frank, "Executive Pay Excesses: Whose Ethical Responsibility?" in *CEO Pay: A Comprehensive Look* (Scottsdale, AZ: American Compensation Association, 1997), 77–79.

39. Ronald Bottano, "Equity Incentives," *ACA News,* January 1999, 6–7; and "Executive Pay," *Business Week,* April 19, 1999, 73–90.

40. Jennifer Reingold, "When Bosses Get Rich from Selling the Company," *Business Week,* March 30, 1998, 33–34.

41. Based on "Golden Parachutes Soften Blow to Executives," *Omaha World-Herald,* February 2, 1997, 1G; and "The Sweet Hereafter," *Business Week,* March 30 ,1998, 33.

42. Jacelyn Evans, Thomas H. Noe, and John H. Thornton, Jr., "Regulatory Distortion of Management Compensation: The Case of Golden Parachutes for Bank Managers," *Journal of Banking & Finance* 21 (1997), 825–848.

43. Gary Strauss, "Sweet Exit Deals Get Sweeter," *USA Today,* April 1, 1999, 1B; and Pamela L. Hall and Dwight C. Anderson, "The Effect of Golden Parachutes on Shareholder Wealth and Takeover Probabilities," *Journal of Business Finance & Accounting* 24 (1997), 445–463.

44. Ira Weinberg and John Heller, "How to Determine the Reasonableness of Executive Pay," *Journal of Compensation and Benefits* (May-June 1994), 39–44.

45. Based on James Fox and Bruce Lawson, "Gainsharing Lifts Baltimore Employees' Morale," *American City & County,* September 1997, 93; and Ellen Perlman, "Bonus Bucks Cause a Ruckus," *Governing,* December 1997, 82.

**CHAPTER 15**

# Managing Employee Benefits

*After you have read this chapter, you should be able to:*

- Define what a benefit is and identify two strategic reasons why employers provide benefits.

- Distinguish between mandated and voluntary benefits and list three examples of each.

- Describe two security benefits.

- List and define at least six pension-related terms.

- Explain why health-care cost management has become important and identify some methods of achieving it.

- Discuss why family-oriented and time-off benefits have grown in importance to many employees.

- Discuss benefits communication and flexible benefits as considerations in benefits administration.

# Competing with Employee Benefits

In competing for workers, many employers are offering their employees a wide range of benefits other than those considered standard. Food services, counseling services, paid professional memberships, uniforms, and employee discounts are common. But some other employers offer more unusual benefits, as the following examples illustrate:

- At Autodesk, employees can have dry cleaning picked up and delivered to their desks.
- At some locations of Barnett Banks in Florida, employees can arrange for car washes.
- At Netscape Communications a dental van comes to the office complex twice a week and dentists perform root canals, teeth cleaning, and other general dental services.
- On his or her birthday, each employee at Mary Kay Cosmetics in Dallas, Texas, receives a birthday card and a coupon for a free lunch or movie tickets for two. After five years with the company, employees receive a $100 U.S. Savings Bond.
- At Con Agra's frozen food division in Omaha, Nebraska, an employee who has a sick child can request that a trained babysitter go to the employee's house so that the employee can go to work. Con Agra pays 75% of the cost for the "sick kid" sitter.

Organizations are offering such benefits in order to retain employees using means not readily available elsewhere. These organizations hope to create greater employee loyalty, which will enhance employee retention. They also hope that offering unusual benefits will help differentiate them when

recruiting workers, particularly professionals and managers who have scarce skills. An employer with a more attractive benefits package may have an advantage over other employers in hiring qualified employees if the base pay is similar to that of competing firms. In fact, such benefits may create "golden handcuffs," whereby employees may be more reticent to move to another employer.

In traditional organizational environments, most workers are full-time employees who have a high degree of job security and comprehensive benefits plans. However, in many organizations today, a large percentage of workers are part-time or con-

*An employer with a more attractive benefits package may have an advantage over other employers in hiring qualified employees if the base pay is similar to that of competing firms.*

tingent workers. Many workers, especially those with capabilities that are in high demand, leave jobs after one or two years. Organizations are "rightsizing" some people out of jobs, while they continue to hire others. Consequently, employees are looking for benefits that they can move from employer to employer and manage themselves. The rapid growth of 401(k) plans, in which employees and employers both contribute to funding of retirement benefits, illustrates this change to greater individual employee responsibility. Even part-time workers are sometimes participating in benefits programs, doing so in proportion to the

percentage of full-time equivalent hours worked.

The benefits offered also are expanding to reflect changes in employee lifestyles and demographics. Due to the aging of the population, long-term care insurance is being added by some employers. According to a study by Hewitt Associates, a growing number of employers will be offering the opportunity for employees to purchase long-term care insurance. Providing employees benefits more often purchased individually also is seen as the way to save employees time and money, while costing the employers little.

Employees with family responsibili-

ties see both child-care and elder-care benefits as valuable. On-site child-care centers, elder-care referral networks, alternative work schedules, and telecommuting are just some of the benefits options available to assist employees attempting to balance work and family demands.

From the employers' perspective, employee benefits are a double-edged sword. On one side, employers are trying to cut costs, or at least restrain the growth of benefit costs. On the other side, employers are learning that in order to attract and retain employees with the necessary capabilities means that employers will have to offer more and varied benefits.

> 66 *In this era of greater personal responsibility and demographic changes, government, employers and individuals are changing their approaches to financial security and how it can be maintained through employee benefits.* 99

ANNA M. RAPPAPORT

**Benefit**

An indirect reward given to an employee or group of employees as a part of organizational membership.

Employee benefits are available in a smorgasbord of indirect compensation, such as pensions, health insurance, time off with pay, and many others. A **benefit** is a form of indirect compensation. Unlike employers in many other countries, employers in the United States have become a major provider of benefits for citizens. In many other nations, citizens and employers are taxed to pay for government-provided benefits such as health care and retirement. Although U.S. employers are required to provide some benefits, they voluntarily provide many others.

Benefits must be viewed as part of the total compensation package offered to employees. Total compensation includes money paid directly (such as wages and salaries) and money paid indirectly (such as benefits). Too often, both managers and employees think of only wages and salaries as compensation and fail to consider the additional costs associated with benefits expenditures.

Total labor compensation amounts to over half of all total costs at many employers' operations and even more in some service operations. For example, around 80% of the U.S. Post Office budget is labor compensation. Because all of the compensation components of base pay, variable pay, and benefits are such a significant part of organizational cost, it is important that these costs be viewed realistically.

The scope of benefits costs is seen in Figure 15–1. According to a study by the U.S. Chamber of Commerce, employer spending on benefits equals 41.39% of overall payroll costs.[2] Using data from the Chamber of Commerce survey, average employee's annual base pay is $29,371, and that "average" employee has benefits totaling $14,086 added to the base pay. This results in a total average annual cost of $43,457 for that typical employee. In manufacturing industries, the total annual individual benefits expenditure averages over $19,000; in non-manufacturing industries, the average is about $13,000. Figure 15–1 shows how the average benefit costs are divided. Notice that payments for time not worked, insurance payments, and legally required payments compose about 70% of the total benefits expenditures.

# Strategic Perspectives on Benefits

Increasingly, employers consider benefits and the expenditures associated with them as linked to organizational strategic goals.[3] This linkage is especially true as one considers some of the changing demographics affecting organizations and their implications in employee benefit plans. First, employers must offer competitive compensation packages if they are to compete in the tight labor markets present in many geographic locales and occupational fields. Second, the aging of the workforce places greater demands on employers to monitor the costs associated with health-care and retirement-related benefits plans. Additionally, with more dual-career couples and single-parent families, the benefits associated with

**FIGURE 15–1** *How the Benefit Dollar Is Spent*

Insurance payments
(medical premiums,
vision care, dental
care, life insurance, etc.)
24.1%

Payment for time
not worked (leaves,
vacations, and
holidays)
24.7%

Legally required
(Social Security,
Unemployment, and
Workers' Compensation)
21.4%

Paid rest periods
(coffee breaks,
lunch period, travel
time)
9.0%

Miscellaneous
(educational
assistance,
severance pay,
child care, etc.)
5.6%

Retirement plans
15.2%

SOURCE: Based on information in *Employee Benefits*, 1997 edition (Washington, DC: U.S. Chamber of Commerce, 1997).

work and family issues—such as family leaves, working schedules, and dependent care—are having to be addressed daily by HR professionals.

## Nature of Benefits

Benefits attempt to protect employees and their dependents from financial risks associated with illness, disability, and unemployment. Also, as discussed at the beginning of the chapter, from management's perspective benefits are thought to contribute to attracting, retaining, and maintaining human resources. Two factors that have influenced the growth of benefits are federal tax laws and other legislation affecting benefits.

**TAX ADVANTAGES OF BENEFITS** Benefits generally are not taxed as income to employees. For this reason, they represent a somewhat more valuable reward to employees than an equivalent cash payment. For example, assume that employee Henry Schmidt is in a 25% tax bracket. If Henry earns an extra $400, he must pay $100 in taxes on this amount (disregarding exemptions). But if his employer provides prescription drug coverage in a benefit plan, and he receives the $400 as payments for prescription drugs, he is not taxed on the amount; he receives the value of the entire $400. This feature makes benefits a desirable form of compensation to employees, and more benefits are more desirable.

*LOGGING ON . . .*
**The Benefits Link**
This website is an Internet link to information and services for employers and employees regarding benefit plans, products, services, and job opportunities in benefits. It also offers a benefits search engine for specific inquiries.

**http://www.benefitlink.com/ index.shtml**

**FEDERAL SOCIAL LEGISLATION AND BENEFITS** A variety of laws, from the Social Security Act to the Family and Medical Leave Act (FMLA), have required that certain employers provide benefits to certain employees. These laws are covered later in this chapter. The number and total cost of mandated benefits have increased over the years, causing the total cost of keeping employees on the job to increase as well, even for employers who offer no voluntary benefits. As a result, a growing number of employers show a preference for having existing employees work overtime, rather than hiring new employees, in an attempt to save on such benefit costs.

## Evaluating Benefits Strategically

As with any expenditure, it is important that a strategic evaluation of benefits expenditures be done. Given the significant dollars spent on benefits by many employers, HR professionals are the ones who must provide "cost-benefit" analyses on benefits. As part of their evaluative efforts, HR professionals should address a number of strategic concerns about benefits:

- What is expected from benefits?
- What is an appropriate mix of benefits?
- How much total compensation, including benefits, should be provided?
- What part should benefits comprise of the total compensation of individuals?
- What expense levels are acceptable for each benefit offered?
- Why is each type of benefit offered?
- Which employees should be given or offered which benefits?
- What is being received in return for each benefit?
- How does having a comprehensive benefits package aid in minimizing turnover or maximizing recruiting and retention of employees?
- How flexible should the package of benefits be?

## Types of Benefits

Many different types of benefits are offered by employers. As Figure 15–2 indicates, some of the benefits are legally mandated by federal, state, and local laws. Employers have little choice but to pay for these benefits.

**Mandated benefits**
Those benefits which employers in the United States must provide to employees by law.

**MANDATED BENEFITS** **Mandated benefits** are those benefits which employers in the United States must provide to employees by law. Social Security and unemployment insurance are funded through a tax paid by the employer based on the employee's compensation. Workers' compensation laws exist in all states. In addition, under the Family and Medical Leave Act (FMLA), employers must offer unpaid leaves to employees with certain medical or family difficulties. Other mandated benefits are available through Medicare, which provides health care for those age 65 and over. It is funded in part by an employer tax through Social Security. The Consolidated Omnibus Budget Reconciliation Act (COBRA) and the Health Insurance Portability and Accountability Act (HIPAA) mandate that an employer extend health-care coverage to employees after they leave the organization, and that most employees be able to obtain coverage if they were previously covered in a health plan.

**FIGURE 15–2** *Benefits Classified by Type*

| Government Mandated | Employer Voluntary | |
|---|---|---|
| **Security** | **Health Care** | **Family-Oriented** |
| Workers' compensation | COBRA and HIPAA provisions | Family and Medical Leave Act |
| Unemployment compensation | Medical | Dependent care |
| Supplemental unemployment benefits (SUB) | Dental | Alternative work arrangements |
| Severance pay | Vision care | **Time Off** |
| **Retirement Security** | Prescription drugs | Military reserve time off |
| Social Security | Psychiatric counseling | Election and jury leaves |
| Early retirement options | Wellness programs | Lunch and rest breaks |
| Pre-retirement counseling | HMO or PPO health-care plans | Holidays and vacations |
| Disability retirement benefits | **Financial, Insurance and Related** | Funeral and bereavement leaves |
| Health care for retirees | Life insurance | **Social and Recreational** |
| Pension plans | Legal insurance | Tennis courts |
| Individual retirement accounts (IRAs) | Disability insurance | Bowling leagues |
| 401(k) and 403(b) plans | Financial counseling | Service awards |
| | Credit unions | Sponsored events (athletic and social) |
| | Company-provided car and expense account | Cafeteria and food services |
| | Educational assistance | Recreation programs |

Mandated benefits have been *proposed* for many other areas, but as yet none of the proposals have been adopted. Areas in which coverage has been proposed are as follows:

- Universal health-care benefits for all workers
- Child-care assistance
- Pension plan coverage that can be transferred by workers who change jobs
- Core benefits for part-time employees working at least 500 hours per year

A major reason for these proposals is that federal and state governments want to shift many of the social costs for health care and other expenditures to employers. This shift would relieve some of the budgetary pressures facing governments to raise taxes and cut spending.

**VOLUNTARY BENEFITS** Most of the other types of benefits are provided by employers voluntarily in order to compete for and retain employees. By offering additional benefits, organizations are recognizing the need to provide greater security and benefit support to workers with widely varied personal circumstances. By offering more benefits, employers hope to strengthen the ties between the organizations and employees as valuable human resources. Also, as the workforce ages and more individuals retire, financial security in retirement is an issue that employees and employers are addressing. In addition, with the changes in work and jobs emphasizing flexibility and choice, both workers and employers are seeing benefits choices as necessary. As a result, flexible benefits and cafeteria benefit plans have expanded. The following sections describe the different types of benefits that were shown in Figure 15–2.

# Security Benefits

A number of benefits provide employees security. Some of these benefits are mandated by laws, while others are offered by employers voluntarily. Workers' compensation, unemployment compensation, and severance pay are primary benefits existing in most organizations.

## Workers' Compensation

**Workers' compensation**
Benefits provided to persons injured on the job.

**Workers' compensation** provides benefits to persons injured on the job. State laws require most employers to provide workers' compensation coverage by purchasing insurance from a private carrier or state insurance fund or by providing self-insurance. Employers that self-insure are required to post a bond or deposit securities with the state industrial commission. State laws usually require that employers have a minimum number of employees before they are permitted to self-insure. Group self-insurance is permitted in some states and is useful for groups of small businesses. U.S. government employees are covered under the Federal Employees' Liability Act, administered by the U.S. Department of Labor.

**WORKERS' COMPENSATION REQUIREMENTS** The workers' compensation system requires employers to give cash benefits, medical care, and rehabilitation services to employees for injuries or illnesses occurring within the scope of their employment. Employees are entitled to quick and certain payment from the workers' compensation system without proving that the employer is at fault. In exchange, employees give up the right of legal actions and awards; so employers enjoy limited liability for occupational illnesses and injury.

**CONTROLLING WORKERS' COMPENSATION COSTS** Workers' compensation costs have increased dramatically in the past and have become a major issue in many states. These costs comprise from 2% to 10% of payroll costs for most employers. Major contributors to the increases have been higher litigation expenses and medical costs.

Employers continually must monitor their workers' compensation expenditures.[4] To reduce accidents and workers' compensation costs, an employer should have a well-managed safety program, which typically results in: (1) reduction in insurance premiums, (2) savings of litigation costs, (3) fewer wages paid for lost time, (4) less expense in training new workers, (5) less overtime, and (6) greater productivity. Efforts to reduce workplace injuries and illnesses can reduce workers' compensation premiums and claims costs. Many of the safety and health management suggestions discussed in Chapter 16 can be used to reduce workers' compensation costs.

## Unemployment Compensation

Another benefit required by law is unemployment compensation, established as part of the Social Security Act of 1935. Each state operates its own unemployment compensation system, and provisions differ significantly from state to state.

Employers finance this benefit by paying a tax on the first $7,000 (or more, in 37 states) of annual earnings for each employee. The tax is paid to state and federal unemployment compensation funds. The percentage paid by individual employers is based on "experience rates," which reflect the number of claims filed by workers who leave. An employee who is out of work and is actively looking for employment normally receives up to 26 weeks of pay, at the rate of 50% to 80% of normal pay. Most employees are eligible. However, workers fired for misconduct or those not actively seeking employment generally are ineligible.

**CRITICISM OF UNEMPLOYMENT INSURANCE** Changes in unemployment insurance laws have been proposed at both state and federal levels, for two reasons: (1) Abuses are estimated to cost billions each year, and (2) many state unemployment funds are exhausted during economic slowdowns. Some states allow union workers who are on strike to collect unemployment benefits, a provision bitterly opposed by many employers.

**SUPPLEMENTAL UNEMPLOYMENT BENEFITS (SUB)** Supplemental unemployment benefits (SUB) are closely related to unemployment compensation, but they are *not required by law.* First obtained by the United Steelworkers in 1955, a SUB program is a benefit provision negotiated by a union with an employer as part of a collective bargaining agreement. The provision requires organizations to contribute to a fund that supplements the unemployment compensation available to employees from federal and/or state sources.

## Severance Pay

**Severance pay** is a security benefit voluntarily offered by employers to employees who lose their jobs. Severed employees may receive lump-sum severance payments if their employment is terminated by the employer. For example, if a facility closes because it is outmoded and no longer economically profitable to operate, the employees who lose their jobs may receive lump-sum payments based on their years of service. Severance pay provisions often appear in union/management agreements and usually provide larger payments for employees with longer service. Figure 15–3 on the next page depicts a study of severance practices in the health-care industry. Notice that senior-level executives typically receive more severance per year of service than do lower-level managers and employees.

Many employers have begun reducing the amount of cash severance given, but replacing some of the severance value by offering continued health insurance and outplacement assistance.[5] With *outplacement* assistance ex-employees receive resume-writing instruction, interviewing skills workshops, and career counseling.

**Severance pay**
A security benefit voluntarily offered by employers to employees who lose their jobs.

**FIGURE 15–3** *Severance Pay in the Health-Care Industry*

| Calculation of Severance | Percent of companies giving each amount of severance pay | | | | | | |
|---|---|---|---|---|---|---|---|
| Based on Years of Service | President, CEO, COO | Senior Execs: CFO Vps, etc. | Dept Heads & Mgrs | Physicians | Supervisory/ Technical | Other Primary Care Personnel | Maintenance/ Housekeeping |
| Less than 1 week/ year of service | 8 | 7 | 6 | 13 | 10 | 11 | 12 |
| 1 week/year of service | 33 | 31 | 48 | 50 | 65 | 70 | 70 |
| 2 weeks/year of service | 13 | 16 | 28 | 20 | 16 | 15 | 14 |
| 3 weeks/year of service | 4 | 4 | 3 | 0 | 1 | 1 | 1 |
| 1 month/year of service | 26 | 29 | 12 | 13 | 5 | 2 | 2 |
| Over 1 month/ year of service | 17 | 13 | 3 | 4 | 3 | 1 | 1 |

*Column percentages do not total 100% due to multiple answers by respondents.

SOURCE: *Severance Practices in the Health-care Industry* (Philadelphia: Right Management Consultants, 1997), 25. Used with permission.

The Worker Adjustment and Retraining Notification Act (WARN) of 1988 requires that many employers give 60 days' notice if a mass layoff or facility closing is to occur. The act does not require employers to give severance pay.

# Retirement Security Benefits

Few people have financial reserves to use when they retire, so retirement benefits attempt to provide income for employees who have retired. Except for smaller employers with fewer than 100 employees, most employers offer some kind of retirement plan. Generally, private pensions are a critical part of providing income for people after retirement. With the baby boomer generation closing in on retirement, pressures on such funds are likely to grow.

## Retirement Benefits and Age Discrimination

As a result of a 1986 amendment to the Age Discrimination in Employment Act (ADEA), most employees cannot be forced to retire at any age. As a result, employers have had to develop different policies to comply with these regulations. In many employer pension plans "normal retirement" is the age at which employees can retire and collect full pension benefits. Employers must decide whether individuals who continue to work past age 65 should receive the full benefits package, especially pension credits. As possible changes in Social Security increase the age for full benefits past 65, these policies likely will be modified. Despite the removal of mandatory retirement provisions, the age at which individuals retire has continued to decline in the United States. About 75% of all workers retire before the age of 65 years.[6]

**EARLY RETIREMENT** Provisions for early retirement currently are included in many pension plans. Early retirement gives people an opportunity to get away from a long-term job; individuals who have spent 25 to 30 years working for the same employer may wish to use their talents in other areas. Phased-in and part-time retirements also are used by some individuals and firms.

Some employers use early reitrement buyout programs to cut back their work-forces and reduce costs. Care must be taken to make these early retirement programs truly voluntary. Forcing workers to take advantage of an early retirement buyout program led to the passage of a federal law entitled the Older Workers Benefit Protection Act (OWBPA).

**OLDER WORKERS BENEFIT PROTECTION ACT (OWBPA)** Passed in 1990, the Older Workers Benefit Protection Act (OWBPA) amended the ADEA and overturned a 1989 decision by the U.S. Supreme Court in *Public Employees Retirement System of Ohio v. Betts*.[7] This act requires equal treatment for older workers in early retirement or severance situations. It sets forth some very specific criteria that must be met when older workers sign waivers promising not to sue for age discrimination.

**RETIREE BENEFITS** Some employers choose to offer their retirees benefits, which are paid by the retirees, the company, or both. These benefits are usually available until the retiree is eligible for Medicare. Figure 15–4 shows the retiree health-benefit coverage by employer size. The costs of such coverage have risen dramatically, and to ensure that firms adequately reflect the liabilities for retiree health

**FIGURE 15–4** *Retiree Health Benefits by Employer Size*

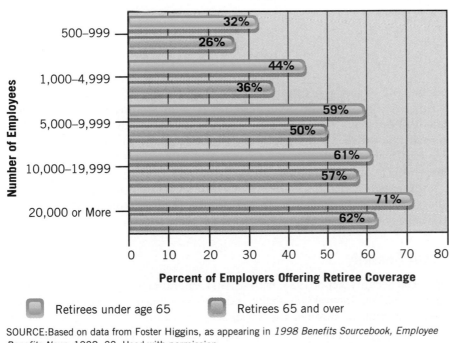

**Percent of Employers Offering Retiree Coverage**

☐ Retirees under age 65        ☐ Retirees 65 and over

SOURCE: Based on data from Foster Higgins, as appearing in *1998 Benefits Sourcebook, Employee Benefits News*, 1998, 22. Used with permission.

## HR PERSPECTIVE

# Ethics of Cutting Retiree Benefits

For many retirees the pension and health-care benefits provided by their former employers are the core of their retirement security, both financial and emotional. At the same time, pension benefits and retiree health-care costs represent major expenses and/or a source of additional savings for employers. The two perspectives raise a serious question: *How ethical is it for a firm to cap or cut the pensions and health-care benefits provided to retired former employees?*

Many of the retirees worked for their employers for twenty, thirty, forty, or more years. Yet for retirees from some employers, the reward for long and loyal service increasingly is a reduction in benefits. Employers have tried to combat rising costs by trying such strategies as the following:

- Canceling retiree health-care benefits, especially if the retiree takes another job offering some benefit coverage, even if the job is part-time.
- Restricting retirement benefits for current retirees by raising deductibles, cutting coverage, or reducing employer contributions.
- Changing retiree health benefits to require retirees to switch to managed health-care programs such as HMOs.
- Lobbying for tax law changes to allow employers to tap excess pension benefits to fund retiree health-care costs, resulting in lower pension payments to retirees. One survey of 1,500 employers found that 12% of the firms increased retiree premiums, and about 6% required retirees to contribute more for their health-care benefits.

Employers have received support from the U.S. Supreme Court. In a 1998 decision, the Supreme Court rejected an appeal to a lower court decision affecting 84,000 General Motors (GM) workers. The GM workers claimed that GM had promised free lifetime health-care coverage. However, in supporting the appeals court decision, the Supreme Court ruled that GM had reserved the right to change its benefits plan in some of its plan documents, despite some oral and written promises that retirees would be provided lifetime benefits.

Despite the legal ruling, there is still a troubling ethical issue that a growing number of employers will be facing. That issue is whether to cut benefits to individuals who loyally worked for many years and live for a number of years in the future.[8]

benefits, the Financial Accounting Standards Board (FASB) issued Rule 106 requiring that firms establish accounting reserves for funding retiree health-care benefits. FASB Rule 106 affected many firms, which now must reflect the liability on financial statements and reduce their current earnings each year to fund retiree health-care benefits. Huge write-offs against earnings have been taken by many firms in order to comply with FASB 106.

Another way employers have responded to FASB 106 is to change or discontinue some retiree benefits.[9] The HR Perspective discusses ethical and legal issues associated with this practice.

## Social Security

The Social Security Act of 1935, with its later amendments, established a system providing *old age, survivor's, disability,* and *retirement benefits.* Administered by the federal government through the Social Security Administration, this program provides benefits to previously employed individuals. Employees and employers share in the cost of Social Security through a tax on employees' wages or salaries.

**SOCIAL SECURITY CHANGES** Since the system's inception, Social Security payroll taxes have risen to 15.3% currently, with employees and employers each paying 7.65% up to an established maximum.[10] In addition, Medicare taxes have more than doubled, to 2.9%. But benefits also became increasingly generous during the 1960s and 1970s. When generous benefits collided with a steep drop in labor-force growth, which slowed the growth of the amount being paid in to the system, problems emerged. Several other factors have created additional pressures: Social Security payments were tied to the cost of living (through the Consumer Price Index), which brought about automatic increases in payments. Increasing numbers of persons are covered by the Social Security system. Further, the aging of the U.S. population—and more people living longer—places increasingly severe strains on the system for the future as more and more people become eligible for payments. All of these problems have raised concerns about the availability of future funds from which to pay benefits.[11] The political cartoon captures these concerns.

Because the Social Security system affects a large number of individuals and is government operated, it is a politically sensitive program. Congress has in part been responding to popular pressure when it has raised payments *and* introduced cost-of-living adjustments. At the same time, Congress must respond to criticism that the system is in trouble. Yet critics believe that further changes will be needed to ensure the future viability of the Social Security system.

## Pension Plans

**Pension plans** are retirement benefits established and funded by employers and employees. Organizations are not required to offer pension plans to employees, and only 40% to 50% of U.S. workers are covered by them. Smaller firms offer them less often than large ones. Many employers do not offer pension plans

**Pension plans**
Retirement benefits established and funded by employers and employees.

© Mike Keefe, The Denver Post 1998

**BNA: 2640.10–2640.20**

**ERISA Benefit Plan Requirements**

This section contains an overview of the primary provisions of ERISA as they affect employee benefit plans, specifically pension and welfare plans.

**Contributory plan**

Pension plan in which the money for pension benefits is paid in by both employees and employers.

**Noncontributory plan**

Pension plan in which all the funds for pension benefits are provided by the employer.

**Defined-contribution plan**

Pension plan in which the employer makes an annual payment to an employee's pension account.

**Defined-benefit plan**

Pension plan in which an employee is promised a pension amount based on age and service.

**Vesting**

The right of employees to receive benefits from their pension plans.

primarily because of the costs and administrative burdens imposed by government legislation, such as the law discussed next.

**EMPLOYEE RETIREMENT INCOME SECURITY ACT (ERISA)** It was widespread criticism of many pension plans that led to the passage of the Employee Retirement Income Security Act (ERISA) in 1974. The purpose of this law is to regulate private pension plans in order to assure that employees who put money into them or depend on a pension for retirement funds actually will receive the money when they retire.

ERISA essentially requires many companies to offer retirement plans to all employees if they are offered to any employees. Accrued benefits must be given to employees when they retire or leave. The act also sets minimum funding requirements. Plans that do not meet these requirements are subject to IRS financial penalties. Employers are required to pay plan termination insurance to ensure that employee pensions will be there even if the company goes out of business.

**PENSION CONTRIBUTIONS** Pension plans can be either contributory or noncontributory. In a **contributory plan,** money for pension benefits is paid in by both the employee and the employer. In a **noncontributory plan,** the employer provides all the funds. As would be expected, the noncontributory plan is preferred by employees and labor unions.

**PENSION BENEFITS** Payment of benefits can follow one of two plans. In a **defined-contribution plan,** the employer makes an annual payment to an employee's pension account. The key to this plan is the *contribution rate;* employee retirement benefits depend on fixed contributions and employee earnings levels. Profit-sharing plans, employee stock ownership plans (ESOPs), and thrift plans often are defined-contribution plans. Because these plans hinge on the investment returns on the previous contributions, which can vary according to profitability or other factors, employees' retirement benefits are somewhat less secure and predictable. But because of their structure, these plans are preferred by younger, shorter-service employees, as shown in Figure 15–5.

In a **defined-benefit plan,** an employee is promised a pension amount based on age and service. The employers' contributions are based on actuarial calculations that focus on the *benefits* to be received by employees after retirement and the *methods* used to determine such benefits. The amount of an individual employee's benefits is determined by the person's length of service with the organization and the person's average earnings over a five-year or longer period. A defined-benefit plan gives the employee greater assurance of benefits and greater predictability in the amount of benefits that will be available for retirement. As Figure 15–5 shows, defined-benefit plans are often more preferred by older workers.[12]

If the funding in a defined-benefit plan is insufficient, the employers may have to make up the shortfall. Therefore, a growing number of employers are dropping defined-benefit plans in favor of defined-contribution plans so that their contribution liabilities are known.[13]

**VESTING RIGHTS** Certain rights are attached to employee pension plans. The right of employees to receive benefits from their pension plans is called **vesting.** Typically, vesting assures employees of a certain pension, provided they have worked a minimum number of years. If employees resign or are terminated before

**FIGURE 15–5** *Employee Preference for Retirement Plan Type*

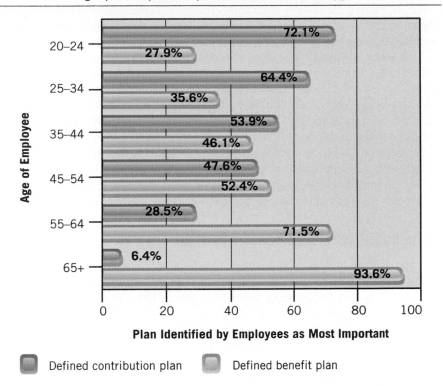

Defined contribution plan      Defined benefit plan

SOURCE: R. Evan Ingle, "Defined Benefit Plans Still Measure Up," *HR Magazine*, June 1997, 127. Reprinted with permission of *HR Magazine* published by the Society for Human Resource Management, Alexandria, VA.

they are vested (that is, before they have been employed for the required time), no pension rights accrue to them except the funds that they have contributed. If employees stay the allotted time, they retain their pension rights and receive benefits from the funds contributed by both the employer and themselves.

**PORTABILITY** Another feature of some employee pensions is **portability.** In a portable plan, employees can move their pension benefits from one employer to another. A commonly used portable pension system in colleges and universities is the Teacher Insurance Annuity Association (TIAA) system. Under this system, any faculty or staff member who accumulates pension benefits at one university can transfer these benefits to another university within the TIAA system. If they leave before retirement, individuals who are not in a portable system must take a *lump-sum settlement* made up of the money that they contributed to the plan plus accumulated interest on their contributions.

A growing number of firms are switching to portable pension plans. Instead of a traditional pension plan in which workers must wait until they retire to receive their pension benefits, the portable plan takes a different approach. Once workers have vested in a plan for a period of time, such as five years, they can transfer their fund balances to other retirement plans if they change jobs. Over 400 firms, including Bell Atlantic, Xerox, and Cigna, have switched to portable plans in the past few years.[14]

**Portability**
A pension plan feature that allows employees to move their pension benefits from one employer to another.

**GENDER DISCRIMINATION IN PENSION PLANS** The pension area is like many others in HR management—it is constantly changing. Some relatively recent changes are concerned with making pension plans nondiscriminatory. Here, the term *nondiscriminatory* refers to discrimination against women.

Statistics have shown that women generally live longer than men. As a result, before 1983, women received lower benefits than men for the same contributions. However, this kind of discrimination was declared illegal by a U.S. Supreme Court decision. The *Arizona Governing Committee v. Norris* ruling forced pension plan administrators to use "unisex" mortality tables that do not reflect the gender differential in mortality.[15] To bring legislation in line with this decision, the Retirement Equity Act was passed in 1984 as an amendment to ERISA and the Internal Revenue Code. It liberalized pension regulations that affect women, guaranteed access to benefits, prohibited pension-related penalties owing to absences from work such as maternity leave, and lowered the vesting age.

## Individual Retirement Benefit Options

The availability of several retirement benefit options makes the pension area more complex. The most prominent options are individual retirement accounts (IRAs), 401(k) and 403(b) plans, and Keogh plans. These may be available *in addition* to pension plans.

**Individual retirement account (IRA)**

A special account in which an employee can set aside funds that will not be taxed until the employee retires.

**INDIVIDUAL RETIREMENT ACCOUNTS (IRAs)** An **individual retirement account (IRA)** is a special account in which an employee can set aside funds that will not be taxed until the employee retires. The major advantages of an IRA are the ability to accumulate extra retirement funds and the shifting of taxable income to later years, when total income—and therefore taxable income—is likely to be lower. Until 1987, many workers took advantage of IRAs offered by financial institutions, insurance companies, and brokerage firms. However, with the passage of the Tax Reform Act of 1986, IRA use became more limited. Due to federal law changes in 1997, a special type of IRA, called the Roth IRA, was authorized, which likely will make the usage of IRAs grow.

**401(K) AND 403(B) PLANS** Both the 401(k) and 403(b) plans allow employees to elect to have their current pay reduced by a certain percentage and have that amount paid into a retirement plan. The 403(b) plan is available to nonprofit employers, while 401(k) plans are available to the greatest number of employers, particularly those in the private sector. Therefore, for discussion purposes, the focus will be on 401(k) plans due to their greater prominence.

**401(k) plan**

An agreement in which a percentage of an employee's pay is withheld and invested in a tax-deferred account.

The **401(k) plan** gets its name from Section 401(k) of the federal tax code and is an agreement in which a percentage of an employee's pay is withheld and invested in a tax-deferred account. It allows employees to choose whether to receive cash or have employer contributions from profit-sharing and stock-bonus plans placed into tax-deferred accounts.

The use of 401(k) plans and the assets in them have grown significantly in the past few years.[16] The advantage to employees is that they can save approximately $10,000 per year (as a ceiling) of pretax income toward their retirement. Typically, employers match employee contributions at a 50% rate up to a certain percentage of employee pay, and often employees can contribute additional funds of their own up to the ceiling set by the Internal Revenue Service.

**FIGURE 15-6** *Pension & Retirement Functions on the Internet*

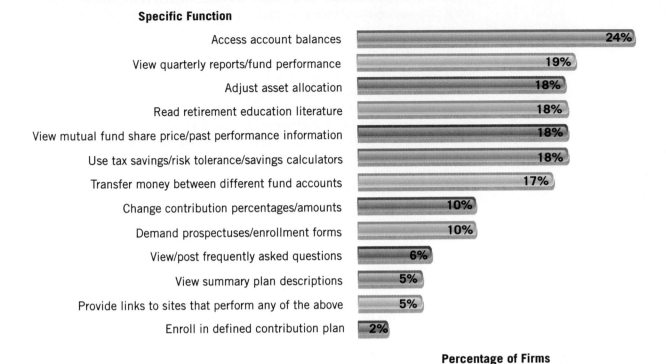

**Specific Function**

| Function | Percentage |
|---|---|
| Access account balances | 24% |
| View quarterly reports/fund performance | 19% |
| Adjust asset allocation | 18% |
| Read retirement education literature | 18% |
| View mutual fund share price/past performance information | 18% |
| Use tax savings/risk tolerance/savings calculators | 18% |
| Transfer money between different fund accounts | 17% |
| Change contribution percentages/amounts | 10% |
| Demand prospectuses/enrollment forms | 10% |
| View/post frequently asked questions | 6% |
| View summary plan descriptions | 5% |
| Provide links to sites that perform any of the above | 5% |
| Enroll in defined contribution plan | 2% |

**Percentage of Firms
Using Internet**

*Percentage of companies with web technology for 401(k) information.

SOURCE: Adapted from *Managing HR Information System*, October 1998, 9. Based on data from the International Foundation of Employee Benefit Plans.

The growing use of the Internet allows employees in a growing number of organizations to check their 401(k) balances and move funds among various financial options. The use of the web-based services is likely to grow in the next few years. The range of options is shown in Figure 15–6.

**KEOGH PLANS** A **Keogh plan** is a special type of individualized pension plan for self-employed persons. These individuals can set aside a percentage of their incomes in pension accounts. Keogh plans can be either defined-contribution or defined-benefit plans. Because of the complexity of Keogh plans and the special regulations covering them, many self-employed individuals seek advice from tax specialists before establishing one.

**Keogh plan**
A type of individualized pension plan for self-employed individuals.

# Health-Care Benefits

Employers provide a variety of health-care and medical benefits, usually through insurance coverage. The most common plans cover medical, dental, prescription-drug, and vision-care expenses for employees and their dependents. Basic health-care insurance to cover both normal and major medical expenses is highly desired by employees. Dental insurance is also important to many employees. Many dental plans include orthodontic coverage, which is usually very costly. Some employer medical insurance plans also cover psychiatric counseling.

## Health-Care Costs

The costs of health-care insurance have escalated at a rate well in excess of inflation for several decades. However, by the mid-1990s, health-care costs had risen to such levels that employers began concerted efforts to control medical premium increases and other health-care related costs. Several approaches to restraining the growth in health-care costs are being used by employers.

One approach to reducing the cost of health care is that a growing number of employers are not offering health-care benefits. One survey of 500 small businesses with 25 or fewer employees found that only 39% of them offer employee health-care benefits, down from 46% in the previous year.[17] These statistics on very small employers reflect the fact that health-care benefits are costs that many firms are not willing or able to incur.

Despite the prevalence of health-care benefit plans in medium and larger employers, the number of workers who have health-care insurance has dropped in the past decade. One study conducted by the AFL-CIO, the union federation, found that fewer U.S. workers have employer-based health insurance than in 1989. Most of the decline of 8 million workers without insurance was attributed to employers dropping health insurance or requiring employees to pay greater percentages of the premiums, which caused some workers to drop health insurance coverage totally.[18] The number of uninsured workers is projected to be 30 million by the year 2005.[19]

A second approach that employers are using to contain health-care costs is to use managed care plans and other cost-control means. Some of the most prevalent ones are discussed next.

## Managed Care

**Managed care**
Approaches that monitor and reduce medical costs using restrictions and market system alternatives.

**Preferred provider organization (PPO)**
A health-care provider that contracts with an employer group to provide health-care services to employees at a competitive rate.

**Health maintenance organization (HMO)**
Managed care plan that provides services for a fixed period on a prepaid basis.

Several types of programs are used to reduce health-care costs paid by employers. **Managed care** consists of approaches that monitor and reduce medical costs using restrictions and market system alternatives. These managed care plans emphasize primary and preventative care, the use of specific providers who will charge lower prices, restrictions on certain kinds of treatment, and prices negotiated with hospitals and physicians. Managed care programs are saving companies billions of dollars by reducing claims, but often such efforts to reduce costs lead to higher costs for employees and a shift in satisfaction with company-provided health plans.

**PREFERRED PROVIDER ORGANIZATIONS (PPOS)** One type of managed care plan is the **preferred provider organization (PPO),** a health-care provider that contracts with an employer or an employer group to provide health-care services to employees at a competitive rate. Employees have the freedom to go to other providers if they want to pay the difference in costs. *Point of service* plans are somewhat similar and offer financial incentives to encourage employees to use designated medical providers.

**HEALTH MAINTENANCE ORGANIZATIONS (HMOS)** A **health maintenance organization (HMO)** provides services for a fixed period on a prepaid basis.

## HR PERSPECTIVE
# Backlash against Managed Care

The expansion of managed care has resulted in a significant backlash from employees who have been forced into health-care plans that restrict their choices and provide little flexibility. Instead of traditional fee-for-service plans through health insurance policies, whereby individuals choose their physicians and decide when to go see them, many HMOs require that individuals have a *primary care physician* who must authorize all treatment and referrals to specialists. This "gatekeeper" role is perceived by many as inflexible, time-consuming, and leading to treatments based on cost control rather than health-care needs.

The following results of a survey published in *US News & World Report* reflect the "image" problem that HMOs have. What is evident is that managed care plans are not viewed by those being treated as positively as traditional fee-for-service plans.

Consequently, federal legislation was discussed in 1999 to place restrictions on what HMOs can do. Also, appeals procedures were identified for those who disagree with HMO treatment and decisions. The provisions of the "patients' rights" bill were being discussed in Congress at the time this book was completed. Further, some employers are having to offer employees health-care choices that include additional fee-for-service options at somewhat similar costs, rather than having HMOs as the only or lowest-cost alternative.[20]

### Consumer Attitudes about Health Maintenance Organizations

| Attitudes differ by health care participants: | Fee for service | Managed care |
| --- | --- | --- |
| Very satisfied with choice of doctor | 78% | 54% |
| Concerned that doctors base treatment decisions on whether they think plans will pay | 21% | 32% |
| Have problems figuring out medical bills | 32% | 25% |
| **Americans are more likely to think things have gotten worse in terms of:** | | |
| Holding down cost of care to families | 65% | 58% |
| Providing health care to everyone | 41% | 36% |

Source: Based on a survey of 3,000 adults, published in *US News & World Report*, March 9, 1998, 48.

The HMO emphasizes prevention as well as correction. An employer contracts with an HMO, which has doctors and medical personnel on its staff, to furnish complete medical care, except for hospitalization. The employer pays a flat rate per enrolled employee or per family. The covered individuals may then go to the HMO for health care as often as they need to. Supplemental policies for hospitalization also are provided.

HMO organizations have experienced a flurry of mergers, alliances, and acquisitions. Critics contend that in some cases, competing HMOs are spending millions of dollars on business matters such as destructive price wars and acquiring other businesses instead of focusing on innovation in health care. Employers in some areas are choosing to negotiate with smaller groups of doctors and hospitals, provide employees with information and vouchers, and let them shop among competing medical groups. But, as the HR Perspective indicates, there has been a backlash against managed care, particularly HMOs.

HMOs and other managed care options have accomplished their purpose—to reduce employer costs. One estimate is that managed care programs saved about $150 billion in health-care costs in six years, for an average of over $200 per employee per year. In California alone, it has been estimated that HMOs saved $770 per family per year.[21] Therefore, it is likely that managed care programs will continue to be the primary means whereby employers provide health-care benefits to employees.

## Other Health-Care Cost Management Tools

Other means used to contain health-care costs include co-payment, utilization reviews, and wellness/communication programs.

**CO-PAYMENT** In the past, many employers offered *first-dollar coverage*. With this type of coverage, all expenses, from the first dollar of health-care costs, were paid by the employee's insurance. Previously, a very small deductible amount was paid by the employee; but many basic coverage plans did not require an employee-paid deductible. Experts say that when first-dollar coverage is included in the basic plan, many employees see a doctor for every slight illness, which results in an escalation of the benefits costs.

As health insurance costs rose, employers shifted some of those costs to employees. The **co-payment** strategy requires employees to pay a portion of the cost of both insurance premiums and medical care. Many employers have raised the deductible per person from $50 to $250 or more.

**UTILIZATION REVIEW** Many employers have found that some of the health care provided by doctors and hospitals is unnecessary, incorrectly billed, or deliberately overcharged. Consequently, both employers and insurance firms are requiring that medical work and charges be audited and reviewed through a **utilization review.** This process may require a second opinion, review of procedures used, and review of charges for procedures done.

**WELLNESS AND COMMUNICATION PROGRAMS** Wellness programs try to encourage employees to have more healthy lifestyles. Included in wellness programs are activities such as smoking cessation classes, diet and nutrition counseling, exercise and physical fitness centers and programs, and health education. Wellness programs are discussed in more detail in Chapter 16.

Employers also are educating employees about health-care costs and how to reduce them. Newsletters, formal classes, and many other approaches are used, all designed to make employees more aware of why health-care costs are increasing and what employees can do to control them.

Finally, some employers are offering financial incentives for improving health habits. These programs reward employees who stop smoking, lose weight, and participate in exercise programs, among other actions.

## Health-Care Legislation

The importance of health-care benefits to employers and employees has led to federal legislation that provides some protection to employees who leave their employers, either voluntarily or involuntarily. The two most important ones, COBRA and HIPAA, are known by the acts in which the provisions are contained.

**COBRA PROVISIONS** Legal requirements in the Consolidated Omnibus Budget Reconciliation Act (COBRA) require that most employers (except churches and

**Co-payment**
Employee's payment of a portion of the cost of both insurance premiums and medical care.

**Utilization review**
An audit and review of the services and costs billed by health-care providers.

the federal government) with 20 or more employees offer *extended health-care coverage* to the following groups:

● Employees who voluntarily quit, except those terminated for "gross misconduct"
● Widowed or divorced spouses and dependent children of former or current employees
● Retirees and their spouses whose health-care coverage ends

Employers must notify eligible employees and/or their spouses and qualified dependents within 60 days after the employees quit, die, get divorced, or otherwise change their status. The coverage must be offered for 18 to 36 months, depending on the qualifying circumstances. The individual no longer employed by the organization must pay the premiums, but the employer may charge this individual no more than 102% of the premium costs to insure a similarly covered employee.

For most employers the COBRA requirements mean additional paperwork and related costs. For example, firms must not only track the former employees but also notify their qualified dependents. The 2% premium addition generally does not cover all relevant costs; the costs often run several percentage points more. Consequently, management efforts to reduce overall health benefits costs have become even more of a concern to employers.

**HIPAA PROVISIONS** The Health Insurance Portability and Accountability Act (HIPAA) of 1996 allows employees to switch their health insurance plan from one company to another to get the new health coverage, regardless of preexisting health conditions. The legislation also prohibits group insurance plans from dropping coverage from a sick employee and requires them to make individual coverage available to people who leave group plans.

# Financial and Other Benefits

Employers may offer workers a wide range of special benefits—financial benefits, insurance benefits (in addition to health-related insurance), educational benefits, social benefits, and recreational benefits. From the point of view of the employer, such benefits can be useful in attracting and retaining employees. Workers like receiving special benefits, which often are not taxed as income.

## Financial Benefits

Financial benefits include a wide variety of items. A *credit union* provides saving and lending services for employees. *Purchase discounts* allow employees to buy goods or services from their employers at reduced rates. For example, a furniture manufacturer may allow employees to buy furniture at wholesale cost plus 10%, or a bank may allow use of a safe deposit box and free checking to its employees.

Employee *thrift, saving,* or *stock-investment plans* may be made available. Some employers match a portion of the employee's contribution. These plans are especially attractive to executive and managerial personnel. To illustrate, in a stock-purchase plan, the corporation provides matching funds equal to the amount invested by the employee to purchase stock in the company. In this way,

*BNA: 2829.10– 2829.70*
**COBRA Continuation Requirements**
The requirements for employers to continue health-care coverage for former employees and others are described in this section. Notice the sample COBRA Election form at 2829.90.10 and compare it to one available from your employer.

*LOGGING ON . . .*
**HIPAA Information**
For a detailed review of the provisions in HIPAA, see the following U.S. government website:

**http://gatekeeper.dol.gov/ dol/pwba/public/pubs/ q&aguide.htm#hipaa**

employees can benefit from the future growth of the corporation. Also, it is hoped that employees will develop a greater loyalty and interest in the organization and its success.

*Financial planning and counseling* are especially valuable to executives, who may need information on investments, tax shelters, and comprehensive financial counseling because of their higher levels of compensation. These financial planning benefits likely will grow as a greater percentage of workers approach retirement age.

Numerous other financial-related benefits may be offered as well. These include the use of a company car and company expense accounts and assistance in buying or selling a house when an employee is transferred.

## Other Insurance Benefits

In addition to health-related insurance, some employers provide other types of insurance. These benefits offer major advantages for employees because many employers pay some or all of the costs. Even when employers do not pay any of the costs, employees still benefit because of the lower rates available through group programs.

**LIFE INSURANCE** It is common for employers to provide *life insurance* for employees. Life insurance is bought as a group policy, and the employer pays all or some of the premiums, but the level of coverage is usually low and is tied to the employee's base pay. A typical level of coverage is one-and-a-half or two times an employee's annual salary. Some executives may get higher coverage as part of executive compensation packages.

**DISABILITY INSURANCE** Other insurance benefits frequently tied to employee pay levels are *short-term* and *long-term disability insurance.* This type of insurance provides continuing income protection for employees who become disabled and unable to work. Long-term disability insurance is much more common because many employers cover short-term disability situations by allowing employees to accrue the sick leave granted annually.

A growing number of employers are integrating their disability insurance programs with efforts to reduce workers' compensation claims. As Figure 15–7 indicates, there are a number of reasons to have *integrated disability management programs.*

**LEGAL INSURANCE** Legal insurance is offered as a benefit through some employers, often as part of cafeteria benefit plans, which let workers choose from many different benefits. Legal insurance plans operate in much the same way health maintenance organizations do. Employees (or employers) pay a flat fee or a set amount each month. In return, they have the right to use the service of a network of lawyers to handle their legal problems.

## Educational Benefits

Another benefit used by employees comes in the form of *educational assistance* to pay for some or all costs associated with formal education courses and degree programs, including the costs of books and laboratory materials. Some employers pay for schooling on a proportional schedule, depending on the grades received; others simply require a passing grade of C or above.

**FIGURE 15–7** *Benefits of Integrated Disability Management**

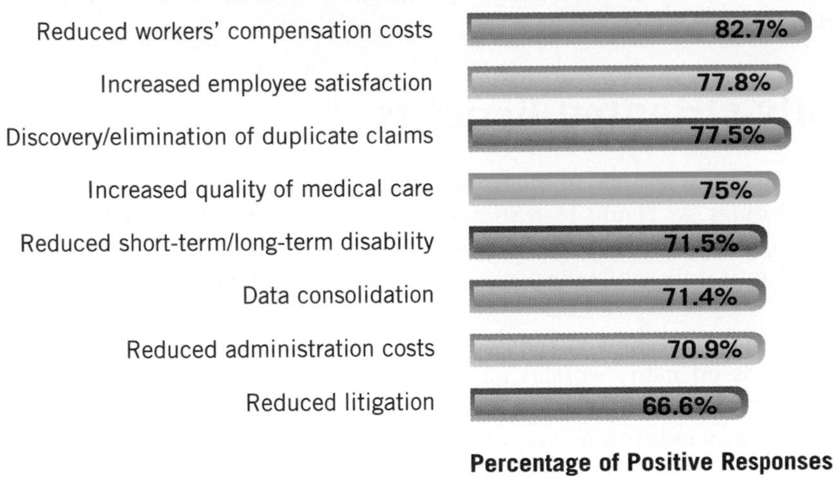

| | |
|---|---|
| Reduced workers' compensation costs | 82.7% |
| Increased employee satisfaction | 77.8% |
| Discovery/elimination of duplicate claims | 77.5% |
| Increased quality of medical care | 75% |
| Reduced short-term/long-term disability | 71.5% |
| Data consolidation | 71.4% |
| Reduced administration costs | 70.9% |
| Reduced litigation | 66.6% |

**Percentage of Positive Responses**

*By percentage of positive responses

SOURCE: Reprinted with permission from *Bulletin to Management (BNA Policy and Practice Series)*, Vol. 49, No. 36, Pp. 285 (Sept. 10, 1998) Copyright 1998 by The Bureau of National Affairs, Inc. (800-372-1033) <http://www.bna.com>

Unless the education paid for by the employer meets certain conditions, the cost of educational aid must be counted as taxable income by employees. To qualify as nontaxable income under Section 127 of the Internal Revenue Code, the education must be:

- *Job-related,* in that it is used to maintain or improve a person's skills for the current job
- *Expressly required,* either to meet specific current job requirements or to maintain required professional standing, such as licenses or continuing education
- *Above minimum standards,* meaning that it is not education necessary for the person to qualify for a job initially

Because of U.S. federal budget deficits, repeated attempts have been made to include all educational benefits as taxable income to employees, thereby raising the taxes to be paid by employees using those benefits. Some proposals have attempted to narrow the criteria for deciding if education is job related and expressly required. As of the writing of this text, those efforts have been unsuccessful, and many employer-provided educational benefits remain nontaxable to employees.

## Social and Recreational Benefits

Some benefits and services are social and recreational in nature, such as bowling leagues, picnics, parties, employer-sponsored athletic teams, organizationally owned recreational lodges, and other sponsored activities and interest groups. As interest in employee wellness has increased, more firms have begun to provide recreational facilities and activities. But employers should retain control of all events associated with their organizations because of possible legal responsibility.

The idea behind social and recreational programs is to promote employee happiness and team spirit. Employees *may* appreciate this type of benefit, but managers should not necessarily expect increased job productivity or job satisfaction as a result. Other such benefits too numerous to detail are made available by various employers as well.

# Family-Oriented Benefits

The composition of families in the United States has changed significantly in the past few decades. As Figure 15–8 shows, the number of traditional families, in which the man went to work and the woman stayed home to raise children, has declined significantly, while the percentage of two-worker families has more than doubled.

The growth in dual-career couples, single-parent households, and increasing work demands on many workers has accelerated the emphasis employers are placing on family-oriented benefits. As mentioned in Chapter 1, balancing family and work demands is a major challenge facing many workers at all levels of

**FIGURE 15–8** *Changing Composition of Families*

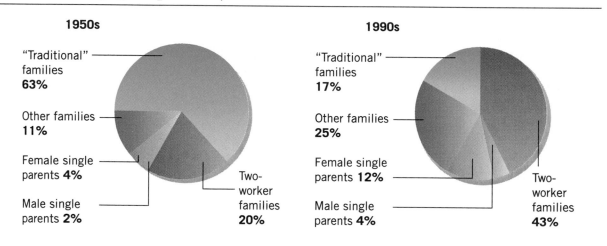

**MOTHERS IN THE WORKFORCE**

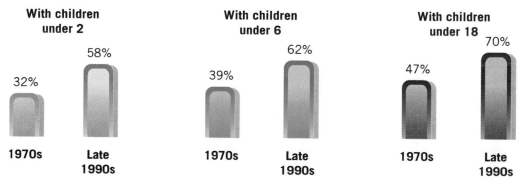

SOURCE: Bureau of Labor Statistics, U.S. Department of Labor, 1999.

organizations. To provide assistance, employers have established a variety of family-oriented benefits.

## Family and Medical Leave Act (FMLA)

Passed in 1993, the Family and Medical Leave Act (FMLA) covers all employers with 50 or more employees who live within 75 miles of the workplace and includes federal, state, and private employers. Only employees who have worked at least 12 months and 1,250 hours in the previous year are eligible for leaves under FMLA.

**FMLA ELIGIBILITY** The law requires that employers allow eligible employees to take a total of 12 weeks' leave during any 12-month period for one or more of the following situations:

● Birth, adoption, or foster-care placement of a child
● Caring for a spouse, child, or parent with a serious health condition
● Serious health condition of the employee

A **serious health condition** is one requiring inpatient, hospital, hospice, or residential medical care or continuing physician care. An employer may require an employee to provide a certificate from a doctor verifying such an illness.
    Regarding taking leaves, FMLA provides for the following:

**Serious health condition**
A health condition requiring inpatient, hospital, hospice, or residential medical care or continuing physician care.

● Employees taking family and medical leave must be able to return to the same job or a job of equivalent status or pay.
● Health benefits must be continued during the leave at the same level and conditions. If, for a reason other than serious health problems, the employee does not return to work, the employer may collect the employer-paid portion of the premiums from the nonreturning employee.
● The leave taken may be intermittent rather than in one block, subject to employee and employer agreements, when birth, adoption, or foster-child care is the cause. For serious health conditions, employer approval is not necessary.
● Employees can be required to use all paid-up vacation and personal leave before taking unpaid leave.
● Employees are required to give 30-day notice, where practical.

**EMPLOYER REACTIONS TO FMLA** Since the passage of the act, several factors have become apparent. First, many employers have not paid enough attention to the law. Some employers are denying leaves or failing to reinstate workers after leaves are completed.[22] Other employers are retaliating against employees by assigning them more difficult workloads or work schedules.
    Employers have had problems with the FMLA. Because of the many different circumstances in which employees may request and use family leave, many employers have difficulty interpreting when and how the provisions are to be applied. Also, the need to arrange work coverage for employees on FMLA leaves can be particularly challenging for smaller employers. This difficulty is compounded because the law requires that workers on these leaves be offered similar jobs at similar levels of pay when they return to work.

*BNA: 625.20*
**Family and Medical Leave Act**
A copy of the required poster on FMLA that must be posted by employers and details on the provisions of the FMLA can be reviewed here.

## Family-Care Benefits

The growing emphasis on family issues is important in many organizations for many workers. But as the HR Perspective indicates, those employees without

## HR PERSPECTIVE

# Benefit "Discrimination" against Childless Workers

With the growing number of employers responding to the family issues faced by workers who have children, one group of employees increasingly is feeling left out: those without children. As more employers stress being family-friendly, to those workers without children at home that increasingly seems to mean being "friendly" only to those workers with children at home.

Silent resentment is growing among the two-thirds of all workers who *do not* have children under age 18. These workers have less opportunity to use certain benefits programs. For instance, employees

without children use significantly fewer of such benefits as telecommuting, floating holidays, and personal days off. Some "childless" employees have been told by their bosses that they must be the ones to travel or put in extra hours, so that employees with families can spend more time with their children. Many childless employees feel that they are "subsidizing" those workers with children through more intense work schedules, heavier travel demands, and using fewer benefits.

Whether this resentment is voiced or stays hidden, there is enough of it that some employers

are having to change some benefits to allow childless workers to use more flexible schedules and allow salaried employees to take additional time off. Of course, if that does not work, one childless worker suggests putting a picture of a small child on his desk and pretending to take off when he wants to in order to care for his "child." Obviously, this particular example raises ethical concerns, but the broader ethical and morale issues of benefits "discrimination" against childless workers will grow in the future, at least until childless workers face eldercare problems.[23]

families are feeling some resentment against those who seem to get special privileges because they have families.

**ADOPTION BENEFITS** Many employers have had maternity and paternity benefits for employees who give birth to children. In the interest of fairness, a growing number of organizations provide benefits for employees who adopt children. In comparison to those giving birth, a relatively small number of employees adopt children, but there is a fairness issue that employers have addressed by providing adoption benefits. For example, Microsoft gives a $5,000 cash benefit and four weeks of paid leave to employees who adopt children. Wendy's provides $4,000 cash payments to cover adoption expenses and up to six weeks of paid leave for employee adoptions.[24]

**CHILD CARE** Balancing work and family responsibilities is a major challenge for many workers. Whether single parents or dual-career couples, these employees often experience difficulty in obtaining high-quality, affordable child care.

Employers are addressing the child-care issue in several ways. Some organizations provide on-site day-care facilities. Relatively few such facilities have been established, primarily because of costs and concerns about liability and attracting sufficient employee use. However for a number of firms, providing on-site child care has had a positive impact on employees who use the service.[25] Having on-site child care also has been an advantage in recruiting workers in tight labor markets.

Other options for child-care assistance include:

- Providing referral services to aid parents in locating child-care providers
- Establishing discounts at day-care centers, which may be subsidized by the employer

**LOGGING ON . . .**
**Work & Family Connection**

This website describes companies that subsidize emergency child care and elder care for their employees. The program is run by the Visiting Nurses Association, and provides care for mildly ill dependents with as little as 2 hours notice.

**http://www.workfamily.com/emergency.htm**

- Arranging with hospitals to offer sick-child programs partially paid for by the employer
- Developing after-school programs for older school-age children, often in conjunction with local public and private school systems

**ELDER CARE** Another family-related issue of growing importance is caring for elderly relatives. Various organizations have surveyed their employees and found that as many as 30% of them have had to miss work to care for an aging relative. The responsibilities associated with caring for elderly family members have resulted in reduced work performance, increased absenteeism, and more personal stress for the affected employees.

One study estimated that lost productivity and absenteeism by workers caring for elders costs employers at least $29 billion per year.[26] Some responses by employers have included conducting needs surveys, providing resources, and giving referrals to elder-care providers. Some employers provide eldercare assistance through contracts with firms that arrange for elder care for employee's relatives located in other geographic locales.

## Benefits for Domestic Partners and Spousal Equivalents

As lifestyles have changed in the United States, employers are being confronted with requests for benefits by employees who are not married but have close personal relationships with others. The employees who are submitting these requests are:

- Gay and lesbian employees requesting benefits for their partners
- Unmarried employees who have living arrangements with individuals of the opposite sex

The terminology most often used to refer to individuals with such living arrangements are *domestic partners* and *spousal equivalents*.

The argument made by these employees is that if an employer provides benefits for the spouses of married employees, then benefits should be provided for employees with alternative lifestyles and relationships as well. This view is reinforced by: (1) the fact that more gays and lesbians are being open about their lifestyles; and (2) data showing that a significant percentage of heterosexual couples live together before or instead of formally marrying.

Some cities, such as San Francisco, have passed laws requiring employers with city contracts to provide domestic partner benefits. The State of Hawaii also has such a law.

Some employers have voluntarily offered benefits to eligible domestic partners. These firms include Lotus Development Corporation, Walt Disney, Levi Strauss & Company, U.S. West, Coors Brewing, and Ben & Jerry's Homemade, Inc. At Lotus, both the employee and the "eligible partner" must sign an "Affidavit of Spousal Equivalence." In this affidavit, the employee and the partner are asked to affirm that:

- Each is the other's only spousal equivalent.
- They are of the same sex and/or not blood relatives.
- They are living together and jointly share responsibility for their common welfare and financial obligations.

Disney's decision to extend benefits to domestic partners has come under attack from certain religious leaders opposed to homosexual lifestyles. However, one interesting facet is that for a number of employers, most of those using the domestic partner benefits are of the opposite sex and are involved in heterosexual relationships.

# Time-Off Benefits

Employers give employees paid time off in a variety of circumstances. Paid lunch breaks and rest periods, holidays, and vacations are the most well known. But leaves are given for a number of other purposes as well. Time-off benefits are estimated to represent from about 5% to 13% of total compensation. Some of the more common time-off benefits include holiday pay, vacation pay, and leaves of absence.

## Holiday Pay

Most, if not all, employers provide pay for a variety of holidays, as Figure 15–9 shows. Other holidays are offered to some employees through laws or union con-

**FIGURE 15–9** *Most Common Paid Holidays in the United States*

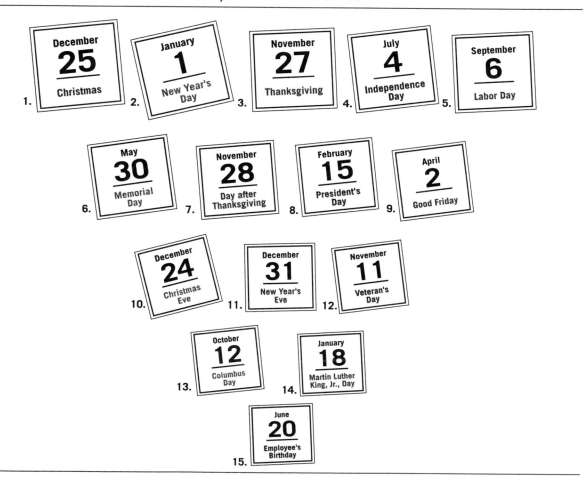

tracts. As an abuse-control measure, employers commonly require employees to work the last scheduled day before a holiday and the first scheduled workday after a holiday to be eligible for holiday pay. Some employers pay time-and-a-half to hourly employees who must work holidays.

## Vacation Pay

Paid vacations are a common benefit. Employers often use graduated vacation-time scales based on employees' length of service. Some organizations allow employees to accumulate unused vacation. A growing number of companies are allowing employees to "buy" additional vacation or let them sell unused vacation back to employers. About 25% of all surveyed firms permit such options.[27] As with holidays, employees often are required to work the day before and the day after a vacation. Figure 15–10 shows the average number of paid vacation days earned in the United States.

## Leaves of Absence

*Leaves of absence,* taken as time off with or without pay, are given for a variety of reasons. All of the leaves discussed here add to employer costs even when they are unpaid, because usually the missing employee's work must be covered, either by other employees working overtime or by temporary employees working under contract.

**FIGURE 15–10** *Average Paid Vacation Days Earned in the United States*

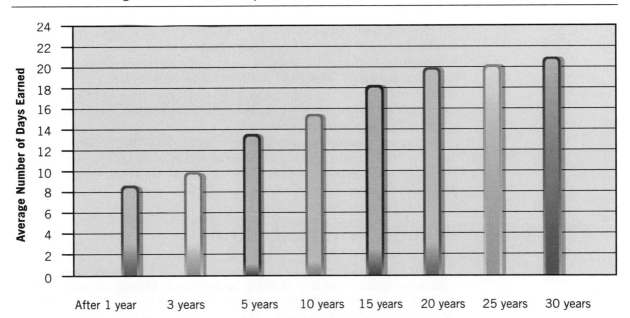

SOURCE: Data from U.S. Department of Labor, U.S. Bureau of Labor Statistics.

**FAMILY LEAVE**  As mentioned earlier in the chapter, the passage of the Family and Medical Leave Act (FMLA) helped clarify the rights of employees and the responsibilities of most employers. Even though *paternity leave* for male workers is available under FMLA, a relatively low percentage of men take it. The primary reason for the low usage is a perception that it is not as socially acceptable for men to stay home for child-related reasons. That view likely will change as a result of the increase in dual-career couples in the workforce.[28]

**MEDICAL AND SICK LEAVE**  Medical and sick leave are closely related. Many employers allow their employees to miss a limited number of days because of illness without losing pay. Some employers allow employees to accumulate unused sick leave, which may be used in case of catastrophic illnesses. Others pay employees for unused sick leave.

**Well-pay**

Extra pay for not taking sick leave.

**Earned-time plan**

Plan that combines all time-off benefits into a total number of hours or days that employees can take off with pay.

Some organizations have shifted emphasis to reward people who do not use sick leave by giving them **well-pay**—extra pay for not taking sick leave. Other employers have made use of the **earned-time plan,** which combines sick leave, vacations, and holidays into a total number of hours or days that employees can take off with pay. One organization found that when it stopped designating a specific number of sick-leave days and an earned-time plan was implemented, absenteeism dropped, time off was scheduled better, and employee acceptance of the leave policy improved.

**PAID TIME-OFF (PTO) PLANS**  Still other firms are using *paid-time off plans,* which lump various time-off-with-pay days together in one package to be used at the employee's discretion. The new programs provide more flexibility in using time off, and some say they add dignity to the process of taking time off. Employers note that they save administrative costs as well.[29]

**OTHER LEAVES**  Other types of leaves are given for a variety of purposes. Some, such as *military leave, election leave,* and *jury leave,* are required by various state and federal laws. Employers commonly pay the difference between the employee's regular pay and the military, election, or jury pay. Some firms grant employees military time off and give them regular pay while the employees also receive military pay. Federal law prohibits taking discriminatory action against military reservists by requiring them to take vacation time to attend summer camp or other training sessions. However, the leave request must be reasonable and truly required by the military.

*Funeral* or *bereavement leave* is another common leave offered. Leave of up to three days for immediate family members is usually given, as specified in many employers' policy manuals and employee handbooks. Some policies also give unpaid time off for the death of more distant relatives or friends.

# Benefits Administration

With the myriad of benefits and regulations, it is easy to see why many organizations must make coordinated efforts to administer benefits programs. Figure 15–11 shows how benefits administration responsibilities can be split between HR specialists and other managers. The greatest role is played by HR specialists, but managers are responsible for some of the communication aspects of benefits administration.

**FIGURE 15–11** *Typical Benefits Administration Responsibilities*

| HR Unit | Managers |
|---|---|
| • Develops and administers benefit systems<br>• Answers employees' technical questions on benefits<br>• Assists employees in filing benefit claims<br>• Coordinates special preretirement programs | • Answer simple questions on benefits<br>• Maintain liaison with HR specialists on benefits<br>• Maintain good communications with employees near retirement |

## Benefits Communication

Employees generally do not know much about the values and costs associated with the benefits they receive from employers. Yet benefits communication and benefits satisfaction are linked. Many employers have instituted special benefits communication systems to inform employees about the value of the benefits they provide.[30]

**BENEFITS STATEMENTS** Employers also give each employee an annual "personal statement of benefits" that translates benefits into dollar amounts. Federal regulations under ERISA require that employees receive an annual pension-reporting statement, which also can be included in the personal statements. By having a personalized statement, each employee can see how much his or her own benefits are worth. Employers hope that by educating employees on benefit costs, they can manage expenditures better and can give employees a better appreciation for the employers' payments.

**HRIS AND BENEFITS COMMUNICATION** The advent of HRIS options linked to intranets provides additional links to communicate benefits to employees. The use of employee self-service kiosks, as mentioned in Chapter 2, allows employees to obtain benefits information on-line. These kiosks and other information technology also allow employees to change their benefits choices, track their benefits balances, and submit questions to HR staff members and external benefits providers. HR professionals are utilizing information systems to communicate benefits information, conduct employee benefit surveys, and provide other benefits communications.

## Flexible Benefits

A **flexible benefits plan,** sometimes called a *flex* or *cafeteria* plan, allows employees to select the benefits they prefer from groups of benefits eatablished by the employer. By making a variety of "dishes," or benefits, available, the organization allows each employee to select an individual combination of benefits within some overall limits. As a result of the changing composition of the workforce, flexible benefits plans have grown in popularity.

**Flexible benefits plan**
One that allows employees to select the benefits they prefer from groups of benefits established by the employer.

As Figure 15–12 indicates, flexible benefits plans are used more by larger employers than by smaller ones. Primarily because benefits vendors require a sufficient number of employees to make providing the choices worthwhile, generally it has been recommended that at least 100 employees are needed before a flexible benefits plan is considered feasible.

These flexible benefits systems recognize that individual employee situations differ because of age, family status, and lifestyles. For instance, individuals in dual-career couples may not want the same benefits from two different employers. Under a flex plan, one of them can forgo some benefits available in the partner's plan and take other benefits instead.

**FLEXIBLE SPENDING ACCOUNTS** Under current tax laws (Section 125 of the Tax Code administered by the Internal Revenue Service), employees can divert some income before taxes into accounts to fund certain benefits. These **flexible spending accounts** allow employees to contribute pretax dollars to buy additional benefits. An example illustrates the advantage of these accounts to employees. Assume an employee earns $3,000 per month and has $100 per month deducted to put into a flexible spending account. That $100 does not count as gross income for tax purposes, so her taxable income is reduced. The employee uses the money in the account to purchase additional benefits.

Under tax law at the time of this writing, the funds in the account can be used only to purchase the following: (1) *additional health care* (including offsetting de-

**Flexible spending account**
Account that allows employees to contribute pretax dollars to buy additional benefits.

**FIGURE 15–12** *Flexible Benefits Plans by Employer Size*

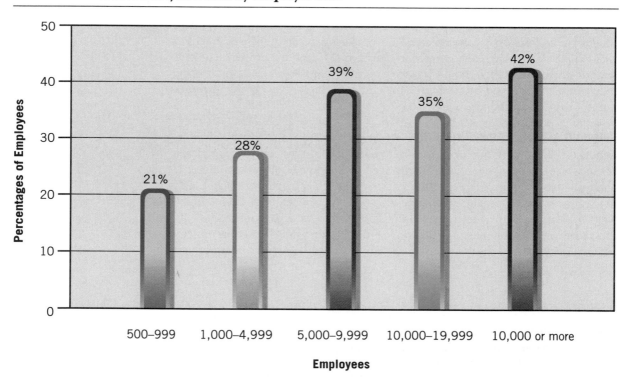

SOURCE: Based on data from KPMG Peat Marwick, as appearing in *1998 Benefits Sourcebook, Employee Benefits News,* 24. Used with permission.

ductibles), (2) *life insurance*, (3) *disability insurance*, and (4) *dependent-care benefits*. Furthermore, tax regulations require that if employees do not spend all of the money in their accounts by the end of the year, they forfeit it. Therefore, it is important that employees estimate very closely the additional benefits they will use.

Flexible spending accounts have grown in popularity as more flexible benefits plans have been adopted by more employers. Of course, such plans and their tax advantages can be changed as Congress passes future health-care and tax-related legislation.

**ADVANTAGES OF FLEXIBLE BENEFITS PLANS** The flexible benefits approach has several advantages. First, this scheme takes into consideration the complexity of people and situations. Because employees in an organization have different desires and needs, they can *tailor benefit packages* to fit their individual life situations within the limits of legal restrictions.

The second advantage, and certainly an important one to most employers, is that flex plans can aid in *benefits cost-control efforts*. Although employers without flex plans can take cost-containment steps, the decision by employers to reduce benefits or increase co-payments is made easier and is more palatable to employees when these measures are integrated into flex plans.

Another advantage of the flexible benefits approach is heightened *employee awareness* of the cost and value of the benefits. Because they must determine what benefits they will receive, employees know what the trade-offs are.[31]

The fourth advantage is that employers with flexible benefits plans can recruit, hire, and retain employees more easily because of the *attractiveness* of flexible plans. If they can tailor benefits to their needs, employees may not be as interested in shifting to other employers with fixed benefits plans.[32]

**DISADVANTAGES OF FLEXIBLE BENEFITS PLANS** The flexible approach to benefits is not without some drawbacks. The major problem is the *complexity* of keeping track of what each individual chooses, especially if there are a large number of employees. Sophisticated computer software is now available to manage these complexities. Also, the *increase in benefits communications costs* is a concern. As more benefits are made available, employees may be less able to understand the options because the benefits structure and its provisions may become quite complicated.

A third problem is that an *inappropriate benefits package* may be chosen by an employee. A young construction worker may not choose a disability benefit; however, if he or she is injured, the family may suffer financial hardship. Part of this problem can be overcome by requiring employees to select a core set of benefits (life, health, and disability insurance) and then offering options on other benefits.

A final problem can be **adverse selection,** whereby only higher-risk employees select and use certain benefits. Because many insurance plans are based on a group rate, the employer may face higher rates if insufficient numbers of employees select an insurance option.

Despite these disadvantages, it is likely that flex plans will continue to grow in popularity. The ability to match benefits to differing employee needs, while also controlling some costs, is so attractive that employers will try to find ways to overcome the disadvantages while attuning all of their benefits plans to the 21st century.

**Adverse selection**
Situation in which only higher-risk employees select and use certain benefits.

# Summary

- Benefits provide additional compensation to employees as a reward for having organizational membership.
- Because benefits generally are not taxed, they are highly desired by employees. The average employee now receives an amount equal to about 40% of his/her pay in benefit compensation.
- Strategic reasons for offering benefits include attracting and retaining employees, improving the company's image, and enhancing job satisfaction.
- The general types of benefits include security, retirement, health-care, financial, social and recreational, family-oriented, and time-off.
- An important distinction is made between mandated and voluntary benefits. Mandatory benefits are required by law.
- Three prominent security benefits are workers' compensation, unemployment compensation, and severance pay.
- Organizations that provide retirement-related benefits should develop policies on how to integrate Social Security benefits into employees' benefit plans.
- The pension area is a complex one, and it is governed by the Employee Retirement Income Security Act (ERISA) and other laws.

- Individual retirement accounts (IRAs), 401(k) plans, and Keogh plans are important individual options available for supplementing retirement benefits.
- Health-care benefits are the most costly insurance-related benefits. Employers have become more aggressive in managing their health-care costs.
- Various types of insurance, financial planning assistance, tuition aid, and other benefits that employers may offer enhance the appeal of benefits to employees.
- Family-related benefits include complying with the Family and Medical Leave Act (FMLA) of 1993 and offering both child-care and elder-care assistance.
- Holiday pay, vacation pay, and various leaves of absence are means of providing time-off benefits to employees.
- Because of the variety of benefit options available and the costs involved, employers need to develop systems to communicate these options and costs to their employees.
- Flexible benefits systems, which can be tailored to individual needs and situations, have grown in popularity.

# Review and Discussion Questions

1. Why have benefits grown in strategic importance to employers?
2. Discuss the following statement: "Employers should expect that more benefits will become mandatory and that voluntary benefits will become more varied."
3. Why are workers' compensation, unemployment compensation, and severance pay appropriately classified as security-oriented benefits?
4. Define the following terms: (a) *contributory plan,* (b) *defined-benefit plan,* (c) *portability,* (d) *vesting.*

5. Discuss the following statement: "Health-care costs are out of control in the United States, and it is up to employers to put pressure on the medical system to reduce costs."
6. Some experts have forecasted that family-oriented and time-off benefits will expand in the future. Why?
7. Why are benefits communications and flexible benefits systems so intertwined?

# Terms to Know

# Using the Internet

## OWBPA and Early Retirement Plans

As the HR manager of your organization, you are in charge of all benefits and compliance with the laws. Senior management is considering offering a voluntary early retirement plan for employees who are age 55 or older and have at least 10 years of service. Before making the final decision to proceed with the early retirement option, the managers have asked you to investigate and report back about the effects of the Older Workers Benefit Protection Act (OWBPA) and the conditions that must be met. Using the following website from the Employment Law Resource Center, write your report.

**http://www.ahipubs.com/FAQ/benefits/
older.html**

# CASE

## Don't Cut My Benefits

Organizational mergers and acquisitions have been numerous during the last decade, and the trend shows little evidence of easing. Such combinations often are driven by the attraction of economies of scale and increased market share. The joined companies usually want to combine their benefit plans to reduce administrative costs and to provide the same benefits for all the employees. But often unnoticed in the atmosphere surrounding the merger or takeover are the difficulties and potential costs of merging benefits programs.

The difficulties are seen when Federal Mogul acquired Fel-Pro. Although both firms are auto parts manufacturers, they are very different in corporate culture. Federal Mogul, with 13,000 employees, has numerous unionized workers represented by the United Auto Workers and United Steel Workers. However, Fel-Pro, with 2,700 employees, had no unionized workers. The difference in culture and employee relations resulted in each firm having significantly different benefit plans.

Fel-Pro, as a family-owned firm based in Chicago, had established a broad range of highly employee-oriented benefits. For example, Fel-Pro had a company-owned summer camp for employees' children and funded college scholarships now worth $3,500 per child in grants for employees' children. As a result, Fel-Pro had employee loyalty, low employee turnover, and a highly team-oriented environment.

Federal Mogul's culture and benefits program did not include many of the Fel-Pro benefits. Instead, having a union-dominated environment, the benefits plan for Federal-Mogul employees had been gained through years of union-management negotiation and bargaining. Therefore, its benefits program contained few of the family-friendly and flexible benefits offered by Fel-Pro.

The acquisition of Fel-Pro made strategic sense for Federal Mogul. But executives at Federal Mogul had to confront two worries: (a) that Federal Mogul employees might want to add the Fel-Pro benefits; and (b) that the Fel-Pro employees would react very negatively if some benefits were discontinued, thus affecting productivity and morale.

To address these issues, Richard Snell, chairman of Federal Mogul, had to reassure Fel-Pro employees that the combined companies would continue to provide good benefits. But he stated that the scholarships would continue for five years and might be discon-tinued after that. Also, it was decided that the summer camp would operate for two more years. But the Fel-Pro employees have recognized that the organizational culture and job security, as special benefits they had, are likely to be diminished as a result of the acquisition. There is real concern that the benefits changes may diminish the success of the acquired firm.[33]

## Questions

1. Why should evaluating benefits programs be a crucial part of any planning for mergers and acquisitions?
2. What could be done to meld the different benefits plans in ways that balance both employer costs and employee morale considerations?

# Notes

1. Anna M. Rappaport, "The New Employment Contract and Employee Benefits: A Road Map for the Future," *ACA Journal,* Summer 1997, 6–15; Stephanie Armour, "Fringe Benefits On the Rise," *USA Today,* October 8, 1997, 1B–2B; David Albertson, "Non-Traditional Benefits Targeted for Expansion," *Employee Benefit News,* June 1998, 23; and Stephanie Armour, "Bonanza of Job Benefits," *USA Today,* August 3, 1998, 2B.
2. "Employee Benefit Costs Declined in 1996, Survey Reveals," *Bulletin to Management,* January 29, 1998, 29.
3. Mary Ann Crowley and Virginia M. Olson, "Developing a Global Benefits Strategy," *ACA News,* January 1999, 28–30; and Ken Dychtwald, "The Impact of Demographic Trends on Benefits and the Work Force," *ACA Journal,* Summer 1997, 16–22.
4. Rodd Zolkos, "Employers' Simple Steps Are Key to Reducing Comp Costs," *Business Insurance,* April 21, 1997, 24–26.
5. Elaine McShulskis, "Severance Pay Drops, Benefits Rise," *HR Magazine,* February 1998, 29.
6. "Early Retirement Rates Remain Stable," *Working Age,* July/August, 1998, 4.
7. *Public Employees Retirement System of Ohio v. Betts,* 109 S. Ct. 256 (1989).
8. Frances A. McMorris, "AARP Seeks High Court Review of Ruling on Health-Care Benefits," *The Wall Street Journal,* June 1, 1998, B2; and "Companies Betray Retirees by Reneging on Health Care," *USA Today,* June 11, 1998, 16A.
9. "Retiree Health Plans Dwindle," *Bulletin to Management,* September 3, 1998, 273.
10. For technical details on Social Security, see *1998 Social Security Summary* (Philadelphia: Hay Group, Inc., 1998).
11. Dallas L. Salisbury, "The Future of Social Security," *ACA Journal,* Summer 1997, 24–31.
12. R. Evan Inglis, "Deferred Benefit Plans Still Measure Up," *HR Magazine,* June 1997, 123–128.
13. Phil Peterson, "Defined Benefit vs. Defined Contribution: Which Is Better?" *Benefits & Compensation Solutions,* March 1997, 29–30.
14. Kerry Hannon, "Companies Switching to Portable Cash Pensions," *USA Today,* July 20, 1998, 1B.
15. *Arizona Governing Committee v. Norris,* 103 S. Ct. 3492, 32FEP Cases 233 (1983).
16. Mary Vanac, "401(k) Plans High on Employees' Wish List," *Omaha World-Herald,* October 11, 1998, 25G.
17. Rodney Ho, "Fewer Small Businesses Are Offering Health Care and Retirement Benefits," *The Wall Street Journal,* June 2, 1998, B2.
18. *Paying More and Losing Ground: Employer Cost Shifting Is Eroding Health Coverage of Working Families* (Washington DC: AFL-CIO, 1998).
19. Jay Greene, "Too Big a Blanket?" *HR Magazine,* March 1998, 90–94.
20. Dennis J. Nirtant, "Despite Many Hurdles, Managed Care Is Here to Stay,"; and Marie R. Dufresne, "Managed Care: Promising Future or Backlash?" in "Multiple Perspectives: A Series of Essays About Managed Care," *ACA Journal,* Autumn 1997, 28–37.
21. Susan Brink, "HMOs Were the Right Rx," *U.S. News & World Report,* March 9, 1998, 47.
22. "Family Leave," *The Wall Street Journal,* March 7, 1998, A1.
23. Adapted from Del Jones, "Child-Free Workers Silent Revolt," *USA Today,* November 12, 1997, 1A–2A.
24. Tina Kelley, "In Adoption, New Help from Employers," *New York Times,* November 16, 1997, 11.

25. Stephanie Armour, "School Bells at the Work Site," *USA Today,* August 26, 1998, 1B–2B.

26. "DOL Offers Advice on Elder-Care Programs," *HR Policies & Practices Update,* May 30, 1998, 3.

27. Del Jones, "Vacation as a Commodity: Sell It or Buy More," *USA Today,* July 17, 1998, 1B.

28. Keith H. Hammonds, "The Daddy Trap," *Business Week,* September 21, 1998, 56–64.

29. M. Michael Markowich, "PTO Banks: Changing the Roles from Entitlement to Shared Accountability," *ACA News,* January 1999, 24–26.

30. Craig Gunsauley, "So Long 'Communications,' Hello Marketing," *Employee Benefit News,* June 1998, 37–39.

31. S. Cauldwell, et al., "A Flex Plan for Your Organization," *Journal of Compensation & Benefits,* January/February 1998, 46–47.

32. For a discussion of some facets of using flex plans, see Melissa W. Barringer and George T. Milkovich, "A Theoretical Exploration of the Adoption of Flexible Benefit Plans," *Academy of Management Review* 23 (1998), 305–324.

33. Based on Richard A. Melcher, "Warm and Fuzzy, Meet Rough and Tumble," *Business Week,* January 26, 1998, 38.

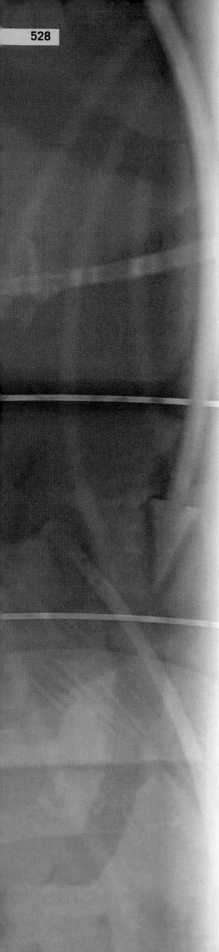

# CHAPTER 16

# Health, Safety, and Security

*After you have read this chapter, you should be able to:*

- Define *health*, *safety*, and *security* and explain their importance in organizations.

- Explain how workers' compensation and child labor laws are related to health and safety.

- Identify the basic provisions of the Occupational Safety and Health Act of 1970.

- Describe the Occupational Safety and Health Administration (OSHA) inspection and record-keeping requirements.

- Identify and briefly discuss three different approaches to safety that comprise effective safety management.

- Discuss three different health problems and how employers are responding to them.

- Discuss workplace violence as a security issue and describe some components of an effective security program.

## HR TRANSITIONS

# Companies Develop Best Safety Practices with Voluntary Protection Programs

Companies with Voluntary Protection Programs (VPP) are ones that choose to go beyond regulations with exemplary safety and health practices at work. Most participating companies are award winners, with safety records that are two-thirds better than industry averages. Following are some recent programs these companies have implemented to establish "best practices" benchmarks in safety and health.

### Lee Company

The Lee Company in Springfield, Missouri, operates 24 hours a day, seven days a week. Its 135-member workforce, which is mostly female, had some special problems related to workforce violence. After two employees were assaulted in the parking lot, the company initiated a policy for workplace violence. First, employees attended a free training session on avoiding violence, presented jointly by local police and an association for battered women. Further, the company now screens all telephone calls to employees. Video surveillance cameras also were installed in the parking lot and screens are monitored continuously. The cameras have been helpful in protecting several employees from violence right from the start.

### Titleist and Foot-Joy Worldwide

Golf supplies manufacturer Titleist and Foot-Joy Worldwide classifies jobs based on required strength levels in order to avoid people getting injured

who are not strong enough to do a given job. The job classifications range from level 1 for office workers to level 6, for which employees must routinely lift 80 lbs. Classifying jobs in this manner allows Titleist to hire for each job level based on individuals' physical abilities to do work at that level without straining themselves. Further, the company had problems with carpal tunnel syndrome for "winders," who each make 8,500 golf-ball centers daily. Videotaping the motions used and then giving the winders training using the videos helped reduce the incidence of repetitive stress injuries.

### AG Communications Systems

Safety training—in the form of a respiratory training course—saved the lives of two workers at AG Communications Systems in Genoa, Illinois. While the two employees were working underground in a confined space, carbon monoxide gases seeped into the workspace. Fortunately, as part of their training, the workers had learned to use a portable atmospheric testing machine. The industrial hygienist at the company attributed the two employees' successful rescue to

proper training in the use of up-to-date equipment.

### Tropicana Dole Beverages

Tropicana Dole Beverages of Bradenton, Florida, has discovered that a poor safety program on the part of their subcontract suppliers can affect Tropicana's own workers' compensation costs. To offset the problem, the company requires subcontractors' employees at Tropicana sites to attend monthly safety meetings, which are also required for Tropicana employees. When subcontractor employees have completed the training, they receive

*Voluntary Protection Program companies meet annually to share ideas and approaches that have improved health, safety, and security in their workplaces.*

an electronic card that gives them admittance to Tropicana's facilities.

Voluntary Protection Program companies meet annually to share ideas and approaches that have improved health, safety, and security in their workplaces. They do so, not because the law requires it, but because they are committed to providing healthy and safe workplaces for employees. It is obvious that VPP companies are the leaders in continuous improvement of employee health, safety, and security.[1]

> 66 *If only it weren't for the people always getting tangled up with the machinery . . . Earth would be an engineer's paradise.* 99
>
> KURT VONNEGUT

Today employers are obligated to give their employees safe, healthy, and secure work environments. But meeting that general goal is not easy; nor can all situations affecting employee health, safety, and security always be anticipated. Nevertheless, both operating managers and HR specialists have responsibilities for the health, safety, and security issues of their organizations. Requiring employees to work with unsafe equipment or in areas where hazards are uncontrolled is a highly questionable practice that has led to the passage of workplace safety and health laws. Managers also must ensure that employees are safety conscious and are not subjected to conditions causing poor health.

Failure to provide a safe place to work can result in major fines and even criminal convictions for managers. For example, two agricultural employers faced fines of over a million dollars each. DeBruce Grain faced fines of $1.72 million for an explosion that killed seven workers, and Archer-Daniels Midland Company faced fines of $1.6 million for violating the Occupational Safety and Health Administration (OSHA) "confined space" standard at a rail car repair facility.[2] Further, individual managers can be held personally responsible. Thomas E. Bowley, Chief Executive of Tewksbury Industries Inc., was indicted on manslaughter charges after two company workers were killed in accidents. Mr. Bowley allegedly failed to repair safety hazards that had been identified by OSHA. If convicted, he could face up to 20 years in prison.[3] In another case, the U.S. Supreme Court held that criminal penalties on top of civil fines do *not* constitute double jeopardy. For that case, in which three workers were killed, the employer was charged $750,000 in criminal fines and later $680,000 more in civil penalties.[4]

The attitude of society toward an employer's responsibility to provide a safe workplace has changed a great deal over the years. This chapter examines that responsibility in a legal sense and considers what can be done to establish and maintain good health, safety, and security at work.

# Health, Safety, and Security

**Health**
A general state of physical, mental, and emotional well-being.

**Safety**
Condition in which the physical well-being of people is protected.

**Security**
Protection of employer facilities and equipment from unauthorized access and protection of employees while on work premises or work assignments.

The terms *health, safety,* and *security* are closely related. The broader and somewhat more nebulous term is **health,** which refers to a general state of physical, mental, and emotional well-being. A healthy person is one who is free of illness, injury, or mental and emotional problems that impair normal human activity. However, the question of exactly what is healthy or normal behavior is open to interpretation. Health management practices in organizations strive to maintain the overall well-being of individuals.

Typically, **safety** refers to protecting the physical well-being of people. The main purpose of effective safety programs in organizations is to prevent work-related injuries and accidents.

The purpose of **security** is to protect employer facilities and equipment from unauthorized access and to protect employees while they are on work premises or work assignments. Certainly, preventing unauthorized persons from having access to organizational premises and internal systems such as computer systems is part of protecting employees. Also, security may include providing emergency assistance programs to employees who encounter health problems while traveling on business internationally. With the growth of workplace violence, security at work has become an even greater concern for employers and employees alike.

## Health, Safety, and Security Responsibilities

As Figure 16–1 indicates, the primary health, safety, and security responsibilities in an organization usually fall on supervisors and managers. An HR manager or safety specialist can help coordinate health and safety programs, investigate accidents, produce safety program materials, and conduct formal safety training. However, department supervisors and managers play key roles in maintaining safe working conditions and a healthy workforce. For example, a supervisor in a ball-bearing plant has several health and safety responsibilities: reminding employees to wear safety glasses; checking on the cleanliness of the work area; observing employees for any alcohol, drug, or emotional problems that may affect their work behavior; and recommending equipment changes (such as screens, railings, or other safety devices) to specialists in the organization.

Regarding security, HR managers and specialists must coordinate their efforts with those in other operating areas to develop access restrictions and employee identification procedures, contract or manage organizational security services such as guards, and train all managers and supervisors to handle potentially explosive situations. Managers and supervisors must observe work premises to identify potential security problems and communicate with employees exhibiting signs of stress that could lead to workplace violence.

## Legal Requirements for Safety and Health

Complying with a variety of federal and state laws is fundamental for employers developing a healthy, safe, and secure workforce and working environment. A look at some major legal areas follows next.

**LOGGING ON . . .**
**Health, Safety, and Security Buyer's Guide**
The SHRM organization provides a directory of companies assisting employers with health, safety, security, ergonomics, and wellness programs.

**http://www.shrm.org/buyers/ safety.htm#search**

**FIGURE 16–1** *Typical Health, Safety, and Security Responsibilities*

| HR Unit | Managers |
|---|---|
| • Coordinates health and safety programs<br>• Develops safety reporting system<br>• Provides accident investigation expertise<br>• Provides technical expertise on accident prevention<br>• Develops restricted-access procedures and employee identification systems<br>• Trains managers to recognize and handle difficult employee situations | • Monitor health and safety of employees daily<br>• Coach employees to be safety conscious<br>• Investigate accidents<br>• Observe health and safety behavior of employees<br>• Monitor workplace for security problems<br>• Communicate with employees to identify potentially difficult employees<br>• Follow security procedures and recommend changes as needed. |

**WORKERS' COMPENSATION** Currently, all states have workers' compensation laws in some form. Under these laws, employers contribute to an insurance fund to compensate employees for injuries received while on the job. Premiums paid reflect the accident rates at each employer. Also, these laws usually provide payments for lost wages, for medical bills, and for retraining if the worker cannot go back to the old job.

Before the passage of workers' compensation laws, an employee might not recover damages for an injury, even if it was caused by hazards of the job or through the negligence of a fellow worker. Workers who died or became disabled as a result of occupational injury or disease received no financial guarantees for their families. Employers (and society) assumed that safety was the employee's responsibility.

Employers once viewed accidents and occupational diseases as unavoidable by-products of work. This idea was replaced with the concept of using prevention and control to minimize or eliminate health and safety risks in the workplace.

Workers' compensation coverage has been expanded in many states to include emotional impairment that may have resulted from physical injury, as well as job-related strain, stress, anxiety, and pressure. Some cases of suicide also have been ruled to be job-related, with payments due under workers' compensation. However, the most common injuries are back problems, broken bones, cuts, and carpal tunnel syndrome. The most common illnesses are stress and allergies. Vehicle accidents are the number one cause of death on the job, with around 22,000 deaths occurring per year.[5] These are examples of injuries and illnesses typically covered by workers' compensation.

A new twist on workers' compensation coverage is the increasing use of telecommuting by employees. It is not widely known that in most situations while working at home for an employer, individuals are covered under workers' compensation laws. Therefore, if an employee is injured while doing employer-related work at home, the employer is liable for the injury. Some employers, including Merrill Lynch, inspect home offices and give telecommuters a two-week training course.[6]

Workers' compensation costs have increased dramatically in the past and have become a major issue in many states. These costs represent from 2% to 10% of payroll for most employers. Only recently has there been a small decline as workplaces have become safer and management has begun to manage workers' compensation programs to hold costs down.[7]

Employers must continually monitor their workers' compensation expenditures. To reduce accidents and workers' compensation costs, an employer should have a well-managed health and safety program. These programs typically result in:

- A reduction of insurance premiums
- Savings on litigation costs
- Less money paid to injured workers for lost work time
- Lowered expenses for training new workers
- Decreased overtime
- Increased productivity

Efforts to reduce workplace injuries and illnesses can reduce workers' compensation premiums and claims costs. Many of the safety and health management suggestions discussed later in this chapter can be part of an effort to reduce workers' compensation costs.

**FIGURE 16–2** *Child Labor and Hazardous Occupations (18 is minimum age in these occupations)*

1. Manufacturing or storing explosives
2. Driving a motor vehicle and being an outside helper
3. Coal mining
4. Logging and sawmilling
5. Using power-driven woodworking machines*
6. Exposure to radioactive substances and to ionizing radiations
7. Operating power-driven hoisting apparatus
8. Operating power-driven, metal-forming, punching, and shearing machines*
9. Mining, other than coal mining
10. Slaughtering, or meat packing, processing, or rendering*
11. Using power-driven bakery machines
12. Operating power-driven paper products machines*
13. Manufacturing brick, tile, and related products
14. Using power-driven circular saws, and guillotine shears*
15. Wrecking, demolition, and ship-breaking operations
16. Roofing operations*
17. Excavation operations*

*In certain cases, the law provides exemptions for apprentices and student learners in these occupations

SOURCE: Employment Standards Administration, Wage and Hour Division, U.S. Department of Labor, *Child Labor Requirements in Nonagricultural Occupations*, WH Publication no. 1330 (Washington, DC: U.S. Government Printing Office).

## Child Labor Laws

Another area of safety concern is reflected in restrictions affecting younger workers, especially those under the age of 18. Child labor laws, found in Section XII of the Fair Labor Standards Act (FLSA), set the minimum age for most employment at 16 years. For "hazardous" occupations, 18 years is the minimum. Figure 16–2 lists 17 occupations that the federal government considers hazardous for children who work while attending school.

Age can be an issue with workers at the other end of the spectrum as well. The HR Perspective on the next page examines ethical issues in dealing with older workers.

In addition to complying with workers' compensation, ADA, and child labor laws, most employers must comply with the Occupational Health and Safety Act of 1970. This act has had a tremendous impact on the workplace. Therefore, any person interested in HR management must develop a knowledge of the provisions and implications of the act, which is administered by the Occupational Safety and Health Administration (OSHA).

## Americans with Disabilities Act and Safety

The Americans with Disabilities Act (ADA) is an entirely new form of regulation for health and safety. The ADA has created some problems for employers. For

## HR PERSPECTIVE
### Ethical Gray Area?

People 65 and older who are still at work have half as many accidents at work as their younger (perhaps more reckless) colleagues. This is good news, because federal legislation has essentially eliminated mandatory retirement ages except for police, firefighters, and pilots.

But those figures hide a problem. While it is true that older workers have only half as many accidents, they are four times as likely as younger people to die from those accidents. Further, as a group the older employees take twice as long to mend from injuries due to accidents.

Older workers face many impediments to being hired or staying hired because of their age, and a spokesperson for the American Association of Retired Persons (AARP) warns that pointing out these problems may lead to "rein-forcing the negative images held by employers."[8] The ethical dilemma is whether older employees should be treated differently in job assignments, during required training, or regarding other job issues in an attempt to overcome safety issues—and whether this treatment makes it more difficult for older employees to find and keep jobs.

example, employers sometimes try to return injured workers to "light-duty" work in order to reduce workers' compensation costs. However, under the ADA, in making accommodations for injured employees through light-duty work, employers may be undercutting what really are *essential job functions*. Making such accommodations for injured employees for extended periods of time may require an employer to make accommodations for job applicants with disabilities.

Health and safety record-keeping practices have been affected by the following provision in the ADA:

> Information from all medical examinations and inquiries must be kept apart from general personnel files as a separate confidential medical record available only under limited conditions specified in the ADA.

As interpreted by attorneys and HR practitioners, this provision requires that all medical-related information be maintained separately from all other confidential files. Also, specific access restrictions and security procedures must be adopted for medical records of all types, including employee medical benefit claims and treatment records.

# Occupational Safety and Health Act

The Occupational Safety and Health Act of 1970 was passed "to assure so far as possible every working man or woman in the Nation safe and healthful working conditions and to preserve our human resources." Every employer engaged in commerce who has one or more employees is covered by the act. Farmers having fewer than 10 employees are exempt. Employers in specific industries, such as coal mining, are covered under other health and safety acts. Federal, state, and local government employees also are covered by separate provisions or statutes.

The Occupational Health and Safety Act of 1970 established the Occupational Safety and Health Administration, known as OSHA, to administer its provisions.

The act also established the National Institute of Occupational Safety and Health (NIOSH) as a supporting body to do research and develop standards. In addition, the Occupational Safety and Health Review Commission (OSHRC) has been established to review OSHA enforcement actions and address disputes between OSHA and employers who have been cited by OSHA inspectors.

## Current Mission/Priorities of OSHA

OSHA has fewer than a thousand inspectors for the entire country. With over six million workplaces to visit, some kind of priority system must be established. Inspection is aimed most frequently at sites that have higher-than-industry average injury and illness records.[9] OSHA recently proposed a controversial CCP (Cooperative Compliance Program) through which employers could avoid an OSHA inspection in exchange for agreeing to establish a comprehensive safety and health program that would exceed the legal requirements of existing OSHA standards. However, the CCP idea has met with some resistance by employers.

Two recent legislative actions have been taken that affect OSHA. One law codifies the existing "consultation" programs, in which employers may voluntarily—and without penalty—request OSHA consultations to identify hazards and violations so that the problems can be corrected. The other law prohibits OSHA from basing evaluations for inspectors on the number of citations they issue.[10] Figure 16–3 on the next page shows some areas commonly considered during a safety inspection.

**LOGGING ON . . .**
**Occupational Safety and Health Administration**
This website is the OSHA home page. Access to the OSHA library, regulations for compliance, newsroom, and much more can be found here.

**http://www.osha.gov/**

*The OSHA-Safe Skier*

© Mike Keefe, The Denver Post 1998

**FIGURE 16–3** *Some Areas to Audit for OSHA Safety/Health Compliance*

- Is there a written safety/health program?

- Can safety and health training be documented?

- Is a hazards communication program in place?

- Are employees knowledgeable about hazardous materials?

- Are employees trained in first aid/CPR?

- Are employees trained in using personal protective equipment?

- Have accident investigators been trained?

- Can the firm show OSHA a good-faith effort to provide a safe and healthy workplace?

SOURCE: U.S. Department of Labor, Occupational Safety and Health Administration.

## Major OSHA Provisions Affecting Employers

The Occupational Health and Safety Act requires that in areas in which no standards have been adopted, the employer has a *general duty* to provide safe and healthy working conditions. Employers who know of, or who should reasonably know of, unsafe or unhealthy conditions can be cited for violating the general duty clause. Also, employers are responsible for knowing about and informing their employees of safety and health standards established by OSHA, and for displaying OSHA posters in prominent places. In addition, employers are required to enforce the use of personal protective equipment and to provide communications to make employees aware of safety considerations. The act also states that employees who report safety violations to OSHA cannot be punished or discharged by their employers.

**REFUSING UNSAFE WORK** Union as well as nonunion workers have refused to work when they considered the work unsafe. Although such actions may appear to be insubordination, in many cases they are not. The following are current legal conditions for refusing work because of safety concerns:

- The employee's fear is objectively reasonable.
- The employee has tried to have the dangerous condition corrected.
- Using normal procedures to solve the problem has not worked.

**WORK ASSIGNMENTS AND REPRODUCTIVE HEALTH** Related to unsafe work is the issue of assigning employees to work in areas where their ability to have children may be affected by exposure to chemical hazards. Women who are able to bear children or who are pregnant have presented the primary concerns, but in some situations, the possibility that men might become sterile also has been a concern.

In a court case involving reproductive health, the Supreme Court held that Johnson Controls' policy of keeping women of childbearing capacity out of jobs that might involve lead exposure violated the Civil Rights Act and the Pregnancy Discrimination Act. To protect unborn children from the toxic effects of lead, Johnson Controls (which made lead batteries) barred women from jobs working around the lead. The Court said, "Decisions about the welfare of future children must be left to the parents who conceive, bear, support, and raise them rather than to the employers who hire those parents."[11]

There is very little research on reproductive health hazards. Yet employers need to protect themselves from liability for the effects of workers' exposure to threats to reproductive health. To do so, the following actions are suggested:

- Maintain a safe workplace for all by seeking the safest methods.
- Comply with all state and federal safety laws.
- Inform employees of any known risks.
- Document employee acceptance of any risks.

However, it should be noted that there is no *absolute* protection from liability for employers.[12]

**ENFORCEMENT STANDARDS**  To implement OSHA, specific standards were established regulating equipment and working environments. National standards developed by engineering and quality control groups are often used. Figure 16–4 on the next page shows the OSHA standard for personal protective equipment (PPE) as an illustration. OSHA rules and standards often are very complicated and technical. Small-business owners and managers who do not have specialists on their staffs may find the standards difficult to read and understand. In addition, the presence of many minor standards has hurt OSHA's credibility.

**HAZARD COMMUNICATION**  OSHA also has enforcement responsibilities for the federal Hazard Communication Standard, which requires manufacturers, importers, distributors, and users of hazardous chemicals to evaluate, classify, and label these substances. Employers also must make available—to employees, their representatives, and health professionals—information about hazardous substances. This information is contained in *material safety data sheets* (MSDSs), which must be kept readily accessible to those who work with chemicals and other substances. The MSDSs also indicate antidotes or actions to be taken should someone come in contact with the substances.

**PERSONAL PROTECTIVE EQUIPMENT (PPE)**  One goal of OSHA has been to develop standards for personal protective equipment (refer again to Figure 16–4). These standards require that employers conduct analyses of job hazards, provide adequate PPE to employees in those jobs, and train employees in the use of PPE.

**BLOODBORNE PATHOGENS**  OSHA issued a standard "to eliminate or minimize occupational exposure to hepatitis B virus (HBV), human immunodeficiency virus (HIV), and other bloodborne pathogens." This regulation was developed to

*BNA: 3405.10*
**Chemical Safety and Hazard Communication**
The details of complying with the OSHA hazard communication standards are explained here. After reading, check with your current employer for the availability of the material safety data sheets (MSDS).

FIGURE 16–4 *OSHA Personal Protective Equipment (PPE) Standard*

**OSHA standard 1910.132, General Requirements for *Personal Protective Equipment* for General Industry, requires employers to**

- Perform a hazard assessment and equipment selection.
- Inform all affected employees of the hazards and the type of equipment that will be used to protect them.
- Ensure that each employee is properly fitted.
- Verify that the required workplace hazard assessment has been performed through a written certification that identifies the workplace and the person certifying that the evaluation has been performed.
- Mandate that defective or damaged PPE shall not be used and determine the extent of applicable "defect or damage."
- Train each employee to know, at a minimum, the following: when PPE is necessary: what PPE is necessary; how to properly don, doff, adjust, and wear PPE; PPE's limitations; and proper care, maintenance, life, and disposal of PPE.
- Test employees or otherwise ensure that employees can demonstrate understanding of the training covered and the ability to use the PPE properly before being allowed to perform work requiring the use of PPE. The employer must first define the learning objectives of the training required.
- Retrain an employee when there is reason to believe that an affected employee who has undergone training does not have the understanding and skill required.
- Verify that each affected employee has received and understands the required training through a written certification bearing the name of each employee trained and the subjects of certification.

SOURCE: General Industry Standards. USDOL Pamphlet OSHA No. 2206, OSHA Safety & Health STDS (29 CFR1910).

protect employees from AIDS who regularly are exposed to blood and other such substances. Obviously, health-care laboratory workers, nurses, and medical technicians are at greatest risk. However, all employers covered by OSHA regulations must be prepared in workplaces where cuts and abrasions are common. Employers with the most pronounced risks are required to have written control and response plans and to train workers in following the proper procedures.

## OSHA Inspections

The Occupational Safety and Health Act provides for on-the-spot inspections by OSHA representatives, called *compliance officers* or *inspectors*. Under the original act, an employer could not refuse entry to an OSHA inspector. Further, the original act prohibited a compliance officer from notifying an organization before an inspection. Instead of allowing an employer to "tidy up," this *no-knock provision* permits inspection of normal operations. The provision was challenged in numerous court suits. Finally, in 1978, the U.S. Supreme Court ruled on the issue in the case of *Marshall v. Barlow's, Inc.* In that case, an Idaho plumbing and air conditioning firm, Barlow's, refused entry to an OSHA inspector. The government argued that the no-knock provision was necessary for enforcement of the act, and that the Fourth Amendment did not apply to a business situation in which employees and customers have access to the firm.

The Supreme Court rejected the government's arguments, holding that safety inspectors must produce a search warrant if an employer refuses to allow an inspector into the plant voluntarily. However, the Court ruled that an inspector does not have to show probable cause to obtain a search warrant. A warrant can easily be obtained if a search is part of a general enforcement plan.[13]

**DEALING WITH AN INSPECTION** When an OSHA compliance officer arrives, managers should ask to see the inspector's credentials. Next, the HR representative for the employer should insist on an opening conference with the compliance officer. The compliance officer may request that a union representative, an employee, and a company representative be present while the inspection is conducted. In the inspection, the officer checks organizational records to see if they are being maintained and to determine the number of accidents that have occurred. Following this review of the safety records, the officer conducts an on-the-spot inspection and may use a wide variety of equipment to test compliance with standards. After the inspection, the compliance officer can issue citations for any violations of standards and provisions of the act.

**CITATIONS AND VIOLATIONS** While OSHA inspectors can issue citations for violations of the provisions of the act, whether a citation is issued depends on the severity and extent of the problems, and on the employer's knowledge of them. In addition, depending on the nature and number of violations, penalties can be assessed against employers. The nature and extent of the penalties depend on the type and severity of the violations as determined by OSHA officials. Figure 16–5 shows sample OSHA proposed penalties and violations for a recent year.

There are five types of violations, ranging from severe to minimal, including a special category for repeated violations:

● *Imminent danger:* When there is reasonable certainty that the condition will cause death or serious physical harm if it is not corrected immediately, an imminent-danger citation is issued and a notice posted by an inspector. Imminent-danger situations are handled on the highest-priority basis. They are reviewed by a regional OSHA director and must be corrected immedi-

**FIGURE 16–5** *Examples of OSHA-Proposed Penalties for a Recent Year*

| Company | Proposed Penalty | Alleged Violations |
| --- | --- | --- |
| Wyman-Gordon Forgings | $1.8 million | Lockout/tagout |
| Cagle's Inc. | $1.3 million | Lockout/tagout |
| CF & I Steel | $1.3 million | Fall Protection |
| AgriGeneral Co. | $1 million | Fire Electrical, Sanitation |
| American Rockwood Inc. | $824,600 | Confined Space |
| Landis Plastics Inc. | $720,700 | Record keeping, Machine Guards, Ergonomics |

SOURCE: The U.S. Department of Labor, Occupational Safety and Health Administration

ately. If the condition is serious enough and the employer does not cooperate, a representative of OSHA may go to a federal judge and obtain an injunction to close the company until the condition is corrected. The absence of guard railings to prevent employees from falling into heavy machinery is one example.

- *Serious:* When a condition could probably cause death or serious physical harm, and the employer should know of the condition, a serious-violation citation is issued. Examples are the absence of a protective screen on a lathe or the lack of a blade guard on an electric saw.
- *Other than serious:* Other-than-serious violations could have an impact on employees' health or safety but probably would not cause death or serious harm. Having loose ropes in a work area might be classified as an other-than-serious violation.
- *De minimis:* A *de minimis* condition is one that is not directly and immediately related to employees' safety or health. No citation is issued, but the condition is mentioned to the employer. Lack of doors on toilet stalls is a common example of a *de minimis* violation.
- *Willful and repeated:* Citations for willful and repeated violations are issued to employers who have been previously cited for violations. If an employer knows about a safety violation or has been warned of a violation and does not correct the problem, a second citation is issued. The penalty for a willful and repeated violation can be very high. If death results from an accident that involves such a safety violation, a jail term of six months can be imposed on responsible executives or managers.

## Record-Keeping Requirements

*BNA: 3405.40*
**OSHA Record Keeping and Reporting**
The various records and reports required by OSHA are detailed here. Check with your current employer about the posting requirements and the most recent OSHA 200 form.

OSHA has established a standard national system for recording occupational injuries, accidents, and fatalities. Employers are generally required to maintain a detailed annual record of the various types of accidents for inspection by OSHA representatives and for submission to the agency. Employers that have had good safety records in previous years and that have fewer than 10 employees are not required to keep detailed records. However, many organizations must complete OSHA form 200, a portion of which is shown in Figure 16–6. Those organizations required to complete OSHA 200 reports are:

- Firms having frequent hospitalizations, injuries, or illnesses
- Firms having work-related deaths
- Firms included in OSHA's annual labor statistics survey

No one knows how many industrial accidents go unreported. It may be many more than anyone suspects, despite the fact that OSHA has increased its surveillance of accident-reporting records. OSHA guidelines state that facilities whose accident record is below the national average rarely need inspecting.

**ACCIDENT FREQUENCY RATE** Accident frequency and severity rates must be calculated. Regulations from OSHA require organizations to calculate injury frequency rates per 100 full-time employees on an annual basis. Employers compute accident severity rates by figuring the number of lost-time cases, the number of lost workdays, and the number of deaths. These figures are then related to total work hours per 100 full-time employees and compared with industry-wide rates and other employers' rates.

**FIGURE 16–6** *OSHA Form 200*

| | | | | | | | | | | | | | | | | | | | | |
|---|---|---|---|---|---|---|---|---|---|---|---|---|---|---|---|---|---|---|---|---|

**U.S. Department of Labor**

For Calendar Year 19__      Page___of___

| Company Name | Form Approved |
|---|---|
| Establishment Name | O.MB No. 1220-0029 |
| Establishment Address | |

| Extent of and Outcome of INJURY | | | | | | Type, Extent of, and Outcome of ILLNESS | | | | | | |
|---|---|---|---|---|---|---|---|---|---|---|---|---|
| Fatalities | Nonfatal Injures | | | | | Type of illness | Fatalities | Nonfatal illnesses | | | | |
| Injury Related | Injures With Lost Workdays | | | | Injures Without Lost Workdays | CHECK Only one Column for Each Illness *(See other side of form for terminations or permanent transfers.)* | Injury Related | Injures With Lost Workdays | | | | Illness Without Lost Workdays |
| Enter DATE of death  Mo./day/yr.  (1) | Enter a CHECK if injury involves days away from work, or days of restricted work activity, or both.  (2) | Enter a CHECK if injury involves days away from work.  (3) | Enter number of DAYS *away from work.*  (4) | Enter number of DAYS of *restricted work activity.*  (5) | Enter a CHECK if no entry was made in columns 1 or 2 but the injury is recordable as defined above.  (6) | (a) Occupational skin diseases or disorders / (b) Dust diseases of the lungs / (c) Respiratory conditions due to toxic agents / (d) Poisoning (systemic effects of toxic materials) / (e) Disorders due to physical agents / (f) Disorders associated with repeated trauma / (g) All other occupational illnesses  (7) | Enter DATE of death  Mo./day/yr.  (8) | Enter a CHECK if illness involves days away from work, or days of restricted work activity, or both.  (9) | Enter a CHECK if illness involves days away from work.  (10) | Enter number of DAYS *away from work.*  (11) | Enter number of DAYS of *restricted work activity.*  (12) | Enter a CHECK if no entry was made in columns 8 or 9.  (13) |

**REPORTING INJURIES AND ILLNESSES** Four types of injuries or illnesses have been defined by the Occupational Safety and Health Act of 1970:

● *Injury- or illness-related deaths*
● *Lost-time or disability injuries:* These include job-related injuries or disabling occurrences that cause an employee to miss his or her regularly scheduled work on the day following the accident.
● *Medical care injuries:* These injuries require treatment by a physician but do not cause an employee to miss a regularly scheduled work turn.
● *Minor injuries:* These injuries require first-aid treatment and do not cause an employee to miss the next regularly scheduled work turn.

The record-keeping requirements for these injuries and illnesses are summarized in Figure 16–7 on the next page. Notice that only minor injuries do not have to be recorded for OSHA. Managers may attempt to avoid reporting lost-time or medical care injuries. For example, if several managers are trained in first aid, some minor injuries can be treated at the worksite.

## Evaluating Effects of OSHA

By making employers and employees more aware of safety and health considerations, OSHA has had a significant impact on organizations. But how effective the act has been is not clear. It does appear that OSHA regulations have been able to reduce the number of accidents and injuries in some cases. But while some studies have shown that OSHA has had a positive impact, others have shown that OSHA has had no impact.

**FIGURE 16–7** *Guide to Recordability of Cases Under the Occupational Safety and Health Act*

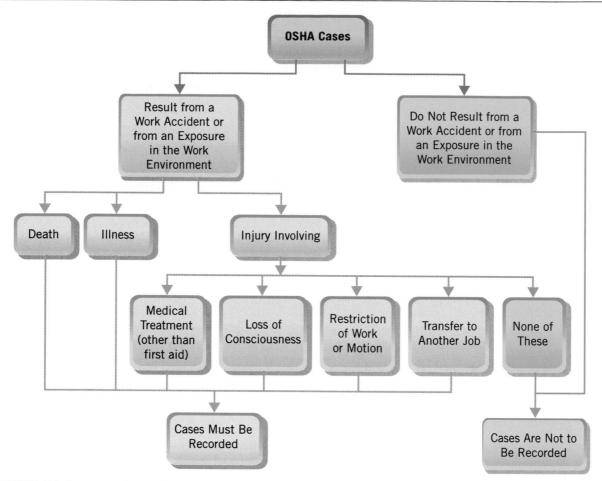

SOURCE: U.S. Department of Labor Statistics, *What Every Employee Needs to Know About OSHA Record Keeping* (Washington, DC: U.S. Government Printing Office).

OSHA has been criticized on several fronts. Because the agency has so many worksites to inspect, many employers have only a relatively small chance of being inspected. Some suggest that many employers pay little attention to OSHA enforcement efforts for this reason. Labor unions and others have criticized OSHA and Congress for not providing enough inspectors. For instance, it is common to find that many of the worksites at which workers suffered severe injuries or deaths had not been inspected in the previous five years.

Employers, especially smaller ones, continue to complain about the complexity of complying with OSHA standards and the costs associated with penalties and with making changes required to remedy problem areas. Small employers point out that according to statistics from OSHA, their businesses already have significantly lower work-related injury and illness rates than larger ones. For larger firms, the costs of penalties and required changes may be larger, but incurring such costs does not appear to significantly affect the way outsiders—such as investors—view the firms.

# Safety Management

Effective safety management requires an organizational commitment to safe working conditions. But more importantly, well designed and managed safety programs can pay dividends in reduced accidents and the associated costs, such as workers' compensation and possible fines. Further, accidents and other safety concerns do respond to management efforts emphasizing safety. The difference between firms with good safety performance and those OSHA has targeted as being well below the industry average often is an effective safety management program.

## An Effective Safety Management Program

An effective safety management program usually entails the following:

- Organizational commitment and responsibility
- Safety policies and discipline
- Safety training and communications
- Safety committees
- Inspection, accident investigation, and research
- Evaluation of safety efforts

**ORGANIZATIONAL COMMITMENT AND RESPONSIBILITY** At the heart of safety management is an organizational commitment to a comprehensive safety effort. This effort should be coordinated from the top level of management to include all members of the organization. It also should be reflected in managerial actions. If the president of a small electrical manufacturing firm does not wear a hard hat in the manufacturing shop, he can hardly expect to enforce a requirement that all employees wear hard hats in the shop. Unfortunately, sincere support by top management often is missing from safety programs. However, the importance of a real commitment to safety is strongly demonstrated by some public and private organizations, which choose to reject contract bids from firms with poor safety records.

Once a commitment is made to safety, planning efforts must be coordinated with duties assigned to supervisors, managers, safety specialists, and HR specialists.[14] Naturally, duties vary according to the size of the organization and the industry.

There are three different approaches that an employer might choose in managing safety. Successful programs may use *all three* in dealing with safety issues. Figure 16–8 on the next page shows the organizational, engineering, and individual approaches and their components.

The focus of any systematic approach to safety is the continued diligence of workers, managers, and others. Employees who are not reminded of safety violations, who are not encouraged to be safety conscious, or who violate company safety rules and policies are not likely to be safe.

**SAFETY POLICIES AND DISCIPLINE** Designing safety policies and rules and disciplining violators, are important components of safety efforts. Frequently reinforcing the need for safe behavior and supplying feedback on positive safety practices also are extremely effective in improving worker safety.

Consistent enforcement has been used by employers as a defense against OSHA citations. In one situation, a utility foreman was electrocuted while

FIGURE 16–8 *Approaches to Effective Safety Management*

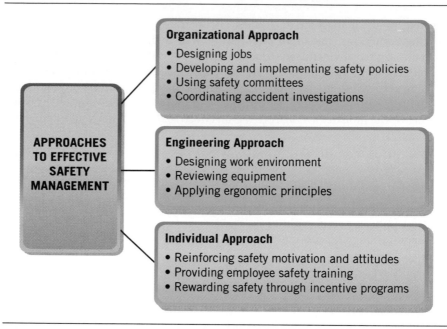

operating an overhead crane. However, the company was exonerated because it had consistently enforced safety rules and penalized violators. The employee who was killed had violated a safety rule for grounding equipment even though the company had given him regular safety training, had posted signs prominently, and had warned all employees about grounding equipment. The OSHA district director ruled that the employee's action was an isolated incident and management was not to blame.

**SAFETY TRAINING AND COMMUNICATIONS** One way to encourage employee safety is to involve all employees at various times in safety training sessions and committee meetings and to have these meetings frequently. In addition to safety training, continuous communication to develop safety consciousness is necessary. Merely sending safety memos is not enough. Posting safety policies and rules is part of this effort. Contests, incentives, and posters are all ways to heighten safety awareness. Changing safety posters, continually updating bulletin boards, and posting safety information in visible areas also are recommended. Safety films and videotapes are additional ways to communicate safety ideas.

**SAFETY COMMITTEES** Workers frequently are involved in safety planning through safety committees, often composed of workers from a variety of levels and departments. A safety committee generally has regularly scheduled meetings, has specific responsibilities for conducting safety reviews, and makes recommendations for changes necessary to avoid future accidents.[15] Usually, at least one member of the committee is from the HR unit.

Care must be taken that managers do not compose a majority on a safety committee. Otherwise, the employer may be in violation of some provisions of the National Labor Relations Act. That act, as explained in detail in Chapter 18, prohibits employers from dominating a *labor organization*. Some safety committees have been ruled to be labor organizations because they deal with working conditions.

In approximately 32 states, all but the smallest employers may be required to establish safety committees. From time to time, legislation has been introduced at the federal level to require joint management/employee safety committees. But as yet, no federal provisions have been enacted. Figure 16–9 shows a job description for a safety committee.

**INSPECTION, ACCIDENT INVESTIGATION, AND RESEARCH** It is not necessary to wait for an OSHA inspector to inspect the work area for safety hazards. Inspections may be done by a safety committee or by a safety coordinator. They should be done on a regular basis, because OSHA may inspect organizations with above-average lost workday rates more frequently.

When accidents occur, they should be investigated by the employer's safety committee or safety coordinator. In investigating the *scene* of an accident, it is important to determine the physical and environmental conditions that contributed to the accident. Poor lighting, poor ventilation, and wet floors are some possible contributors.[16] Investigation at the scene should be done as soon as possible after an accident to ensure that the conditions under which the accident occurred have not changed significantly. One way to obtain an accurate view of the accident scene is with photographs or videotapes.

The second phase of the investigation is the *interview* of the injured employee, his or her supervisor, and witnesses to the accident. The interviewer attempts to

**FIGURE 16–9** *Job Description for a Safety Committee*

**SAFETY COMMITTEE**

**Commitment:** *To eliminate workplace hazards that are capable of causing significant injury or illness.*

**Mission:** *To foster a spirit of open communication and cooperation in resolving all issues that pertain to employee safety and health.*

**Responsibilities:** The safety committee shall:
1. Review the results of workplace safety inspections to identify and analyze hazards.
2. Review accident and injury reports (including close calls) to identify and analyze hazards.
3. Review and act upon safety and health concerns, suggestions, and needs communicated by employees and supervisors.
4. Review workplace hazard assessments.
5. Conduct semiannual walk-through safety inspections.
6. Identify and communicate specific safety and health related needs and improvements to the employer, supervisors, and employees.
7. Perform an annual audit of the safety and health program.

SOURCE: Dennis Zimet, "A Comprehensive Safety and Health Program for the Small Employer," *Occupational Health & Safety*, October 1997, 129. Used with permission.

determine what happened and how the accident was caused. These interviews may also generate some suggestions on how to prevent similar accidents in the future. In the third phase, based on observations of the scene and interviews, investigators complete an *accident investigation report*. This report form provides the data required by OSHA.

Finally, *recommendations* should be made on how the accident could have been prevented, and on what changes are needed to avoid similar accidents. Identifying why an accident occurred is useful, but taking steps to prevent similar accidents from occurring also is important.

Closely related to accident investigation is *research* to determine ways of preventing accidents. Employing safety engineers or having outside experts evaluate the safety of working conditions is useful. If many similar accidents seem to occur in an organizational unit, a safety education training program may be necessary to emphasize safe working practices. As an example, a publishing company reported a greater-than-average number of back injuries among employees who lifted heavy boxes. Safety training on the proper way to lift heavy objects was initiated to reduce the number of back injuries.

**EVALUATION OF SAFETY EFFORTS** Organizations should monitor and evaluate their safety efforts. Just as organizational accounting records are audited, a firm's safety efforts should be audited periodically as well. Accident and injury statistics should be compared with previous accident patterns to identify any significant changes. This analysis should be designed to measure progress in safety management. A manager at a hospital might measure its safety efforts by comparing the hospital's accident rate with hospital industry figures and with rates at other hospitals of the same size in the area.

## Engineering Issues in Safety and Health

Logic and reason suggest that both work design and human work behaviors contribute to safety. Yet some approaches to reducing accidents focus on one or the other exclusively. Both approaches as part of a well-organized safety effort are valuable, so they tend to be most effective when considered jointly.

**PHYSICAL SETTING OF WORK** Designing jobs properly requires consideration of the physical setting of a job. The way the work space surrounding a job is utilized can influence the worker's performance of the job itself. Several job-setting factors have been identified, including: size of work area, kinds of materials used, sensory conditions, distance between work areas, and interference from noise and traffic flow. Temperature, noise, and light levels are sensory conditions that affect job performance. For example, noise decreases performance on complex mental tasks, tasks requiring speed, and tasks requiring high levels of perceptual capacity. "Personal space" is another factor to be considered. Some people need more space than others, and space needs vary from culture to culture. Violation of space requirements makes people feel either isolated or crowded. Both reactions may cause stress and related safety and health problems.

**SICK BUILDING SYNDROME** The Environmental Protection Agency (EPA) defines *sick building syndrome* as a situation in which occupants experience acute health problems and discomfort that appear to be linked to time spent in a building. As an example, judges, lawyers, jurors, and employees who stayed in the Suffolk

County Courthouse in Boston for any length of time complained of headaches, dizziness, sore throats, and other illnesses. After extensive study, the problems were traced to a waterproof coating used when the building was renovated. The problems were so severe that approximately 200 workers had to be relocated for several years while various solutions were tried. Unfortunately, this building is not the only example of such problems.

One cause of sick buildings is poor air quality, which arises in "sealed" buildings where windows cannot be opened. Inadequate ventilation, as well as airborne contamination from carpets, molds, copy machines, adhesives, and fungi, can cause sick buildings. Also, problems may result when the air flow and circulation controls are too sophisticated for the people who maintain them, or when operators try to cut corners to save energy.

**ERGONOMICS AND SAFETY** **Ergonomics** is the proper design of the work environment to address the physical demands experienced by people. The term comes from the Greek *ergon,* meaning "work," and the suffix *-omics,* meaning "management of." An ergonomist studies physiological, psychological, and engineering design aspects of a job, including such factors as fatigue, lighting, tools, equipment layout, and placement of controls. Human factors engineering is a related field.

Most recently, attention has focused on the application of ergonomic principles to the design of workstations where computer operators work with personal computers (PCs) and video display terminals (VDTs) for periods of time. Figure 16–10 shows an ergonomically correct PC/VDT workstation. Notice that the level of the table, vision line of the screen, and chair height are all designed ergonomically. Workstations, tools, and jobs must "fit" a person just as a pair of shoes

**Ergonomics**
The proper design of the work environment to address the physical demands experienced by people.

**FIGURE 16–10** *An Ergonomically Correct Workstation*

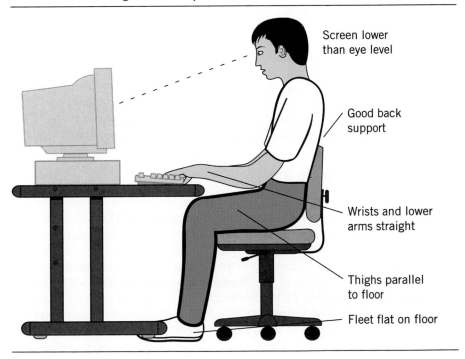

Screen lower than eye level

Good back support

Wrists and lower arms straight

Thighs parallel to floor

Fleet flat on floor

**LOGGING ON . . .**
**NexGen Ergonomics**
This website provides recommended links to organizations and associations that offer information on ergonomic development and trends.

**http://www.nexergo.com/ sites.htm**

**Cumulative trauma disorders (CTDs)**
Muscle and skeletal injuries that occur when workers repetitively use the same muscles to perform tasks.

must fit, or injuries can occur. Many eyestrain problems are related to glare and poor lighting or poor screen resolution. Ergonomically correct workstations focus on chair adjustments and support, VDT area and quality, station height, lighting, glare, noise levels, document placement, and screen flicker; rest breaks and employee training are also emphasized.[17]

**ENGINEERING OF WORK EQUIPMENT AND MATERIALS** Employers can prevent some accidents by designing machines, equipment, and work areas so that workers who daydream periodically or who perform potentially dangerous jobs cannot injure themselves and others. Providing safety equipment and guards on machinery and installing emergency switches often forestall accidents. To prevent a punch-press operator from mashing her finger, a safety guard is attached to a machine so her hand cannot accidentally slip into the machine. Actions such as installing safety rails, keeping aisles clear, and installing adequate ventilation, lighting, heating, and air conditioning can all help make work environments safer.

**CUMULATIVE TRAUMA AND REPETITIVE STRESS** Repetitive stress injuries, repetitive motion injuries, cumulative trauma disorders, carpal tunnel syndrome, ergonomic hazards—this listing of serious-sounding problems applies to many workplaces. **Cumulative trauma disorders (CTDs)** occur when workers repetitively use the same muscles to perform tasks, resulting in muscle and skeletal injuries. These problems are occurring in a variety of work settings. The meatpacking industry has the highest level of CTDs. But office workers increasingly are experiencing CTDs, primarily from extensive typing and data entry on computers and computer-related equipment. Grocery cashiers also have experienced CTDs from repetitively twisting their wrists when they scan bar codes on canned goods.

Carpal tunnel syndrome, one of the most common cumulative trauma disorders, has existed for years. Figure 16–11 shows lost-time injuries caused by carpal tunnel syndrome. It is an injury common to people who put their hands through repetitive motions such as typing, playing certain musical instruments, cutting, or sewing. The motion irritates the tendons in the "carpal tunnel" area of the wrist. As the tendons swell, they squeeze the median nerve. The result is pain and numbness in the thumb, index finger, and middle finger. The hands of victims become clumsy and weak. Pain at night increases, and at advanced stages not even surgery can cure the problem. Victims eventually lose feeling in their hands if they do not receive timely treatment.

## Individual Approach to Safety

Engineers approach safety from the perspective of redesigning the machinery or the work area. Industrial psychologists see safety differently. They are concerned with the proper match of individuals to jobs and emphasize employee training in safety methods, fatigue reduction, and health awareness.

Industrial psychologists have conducted numerous field studies with thousands of employees, looking at the "human factors" in accidents. The results show a definite relationship between emotional factors, such as stress, and accidents. Other studies point to the importance of individual differences, motivation, attitudes, and learning as key factors in controlling the human element in safety.

**FIGURE 16–11** *Lost Time to Carpal Tunnel Syndrome, by Industry*

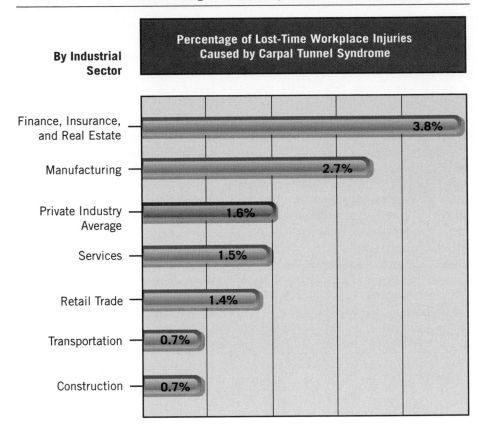

SOURCE: U.S. Department of Labor, Bureau of Labor Statistics

Individual-based safety attempts to identify and modify behaviors that can lead to accidents.[18] It may use "coaches" or "observers" to identify dangerous behavior.

**ACCIDENT RATES AND INDIVIDUALS** Attitudinal variables are among the individual factors that affect accident rates. Attitudes toward working conditions, accidents, and safe work practices can be important, because more problems are caused by careless employees than by machines or employer negligence. At one time, workers who were dissatisfied with their jobs were thought to have higher accident rates. However, this assumption has been questioned in recent years. Although employees' personalities, attitudes, and individual characteristics apparently have some influence on accidents, exact cause-and-effect relationships are difficult to establish.

**ACCIDENT RATES AND WORK SCHEDULES** Work schedules can be another cause for accidents. The relationship between work schedules and accidents can be explained as follows: Fatigue based on physical exertion rarely exists in today's industrial workplace. But fatigue defined as boredom, which occurs when a person is required to do the same tasks for a long period of time, is rather common. As

## HR PERSPECTIVE

# Working on the Railroad

For more than 130 years, napping on the job would get you fired at the Union Pacific Railroad. The huge carrier is the nation's largest railroad, serving the western two-thirds of the country with its 36,000 miles of track. But following a year in which 11 Union Pacific employees died on the job, it was clear that some changes were needed. The accidents led to an investigation by the Federal Railroad Administration, which concluded that Union Pacific had suffered a "fundamental breakdown" in safety. Employee fatigue was identified as one of the main problems.

Traditionally, railroads have called engineers and conductors to work whenever they are needed to move trains. That practice made for unpredictable lifestyles for train crews and their families. Even though federal law requires that crew members take 8 to 10 hours off between trips, it has been difficult for many crew members to get rest on such a schedule.

Union Pacific hired Alertness Solutions, a California firm that studies worker fatigue. The company helped Union Pacific develop test programs that give workers at least 2 days off in a row on a set schedule. Schedules might include 5 days on and 2 off, or 8 on and 3 off. Fur-

ther, "napping programs" allow one of two members of a typical train crew to nap while the other is awake, but only when the train is stopped. Based on research by the California firm and others, napping has been found to make workers 34% more effective at their jobs and 100% more alert.

Union Pacific will monitor results on the test programs developed with Alertness Solutions before deciding whether to use them throughout the company. But already the changes have caused culture shock as a result of worker rescheduling for the sake of safety.[19]

fatigue of this kind increases, motivation is reduced; along with decreased motivation, workers' attention wanders, and the likelihood of accidents increases.

A particular area of concern in work scheduling is overtime. Overtime work has been consistently related to accident incidence. Further, the more overtime worked, the more severe accidents appeared to be.

Another area of concern is the relationship of accident rates to different shifts, particularly late-night shifts. Many employees who work late-night shifts experience sleeplessness during the day, so that they arrive back at work tired and not as alert. Also, because there tend to be fewer supervisors and managers working the "graveyard" shifts, workers tend to receive less training and supervision. Both of these factors lead to higher accident rates; see the HR Perspective for an example.

**EMPLOYEE SAFETY MOTIVATION AND INCENTIVES** Convincing employees to keep safety standards continuously in mind while performing their jobs is difficult. Often, employees think that safety measures are bothersome and unnecessary until an injury occurs. For example, it may be necessary for employees to wear safety glasses in a laboratory most of the time. But if the glasses are awkward, employees may resist using them, even when they know they should have protection. Also some employees, who may have worked for years without wearing the glasses, may think this requirement is a nuisance. Because of such problems, safety training and communication efforts must address safety issues, so that employees view safety as important and are motivated to follow safe work practices.

To encourage employees to work safely, many organizations have used safety contests and have given employees incentives for safe work behavior.

Jewelry, clocks, watches, and even vacation trips have been given as rewards for good safety records. For example, safe driving awards for drivers in trucking firms have been quite successful in generating safety consciousness. Belt buckles and lapel pins are especially popular with the drivers. Unfortunately, there is some evidence that incentives tend to reinforce underreporting and "creative" classifying of accidents. In the last few days of a big safety contest, most people will think long and hard before they cost their team the prize by reporting an accident.[20]

# Health

Employee health problems are varied—and somewhat inevitable. They can range from minor illnesses such as colds to serious illnesses related to the jobs performed. Some employees have emotional health problems; others have alcohol or drug problems. Some problems are chronic; others are transitory. But all may affect organizational operations and individual employee productivity. A look at some common health problems at work follows next.

## AIDS and Other Life-Threatening Illnesses

Employers are increasingly confronted by problems associated with employees who have AIDS or other life-threatening illnesses such as cancer. First, there is eventual decline in productivity and attendance brought on by progressive deterioration. Then, with AIDS specifically, there are the problems associated with coworker anxiety in the workplace. However, with new treatments for HIV and AIDS, more HIV-positive employees are able to participate in the workforce longer. The Centers for Disease Control estimates that there are between 650,000 and 900,000 people with HIV or AIDS in the United States, with 40,000 added each year.[21] Of those, 85% are male, 35% are African American, 18% are Hispanic American, and 46% are white.[22]

Some firms have policies to deal with AIDS and other life-threatening illnesses. Firms that have lost an employee to one of these diseases are more likely to have

Dilbert reprinted by permission of United Feature Syndicate, Inc.

a policy than those that have not. But estimates are that only 25% of the larger employers in the United States have a policy on life-threatening illness.

It appears that many companies deem it unnecessary to adopt specific policies that deal solely with AIDS and other life-threatening illnesses because they do not want to draw attention to them and unnecessarily alarm employees. No matter what information the experts might offer to assuage the fear of other employees, a co-worker with AIDS, whether on the shop floor or in the executive offices, creates feelings of anxiety and unease among other employees, suppliers, and customers. To meet this problem, and yet address the needs of afflicted employees, some companies are electing to continue to pay the employees full salary, medical, and retirement benefits on the stipulation that they not return to work. In a different approach, other employers have instituted education and training programs to educate employees about AIDS and other life-threatening illnesses.

## Smoking at Work

Arguments and rebuttals characterize the smoking-at-work controversy, and statistics are rampant. A multitude of state and local laws have been passed that deal with smoking in the workplace and public places. Passage of these laws has been viewed by many employers positively, because they relieve employers of the responsibility for making decisions on smoking issues. But many courts, unlike state legislatures, have been hesitant to address the smoking-at-work issue. They clearly prefer to let employers and employees resolve their differences rather than prohibiting or supporting the right to smoke.

As a result of health studies, complaints by nonsmokers, and state laws, many employers have established no-smoking policies throughout their workplaces. Although employees who smoke tend to complain initially when a smoking ban is instituted, they seem to have little difficulty adjusting within a few weeks, and many quit smoking or reduce the number of cigarettes they use each workday. Employers have also offered smoking cessation workshops and even cash incentives to employees who quit smoking, and these measures do seem to reduce smoking by employees.

## Substance Abuse

**Substance abuse**

The use of illicit substances or the misuse of controlled substances, alcohol, or other drugs.

**Substance abuse** is defined as the use of illicit substances or the misuse of controlled substances, alcohol, or other drugs. There are millions of substance abusers in the workforce, and they cost the United States billions of dollars annually. The incidence of substance abuse is greatest among white men aged 19 to 23. At work it is higher among men than women and higher among whites than other groups. Also, blue-collar workers are more likely than white-collar workers to abuse substances.

Drug tests are used by many employers, and the number of positive test results are dropping. These results may mean that fewer employees are using drugs, or that drug users have learned to avoid analysis, or both. If an employee tests positive, 22% of employers terminate that worker immediately, 21% take disciplinary actions, and 63% refer the worker to counseling and treatment.[23] More information on drug testing is contained in Chapter 17.

Alcohol testing is on the rise as well; about a third of businesses test for alcohol use.[24] Most such testing follows an accident or is done for reasonable cause, such as failing a fitness-for-duty test.[25]

**FITNESS-FOR-DUTY TESTS** Everyone experiences day-to-day variations in their ability to perform their work-related duties. These variations are usually small and of little consequence. However, alcohol or drugs can cause significant changes. Fitness-for-duty tests are an attempt to detect such impairment *before* putting a person behind dangerous equipment. As an example, when a crew of delivery-truck drivers comes to work, they are asked to "play" a video game—with serious consequences. Unless the machine presents a receipt saying they passed the test, they are not allowed to drive their trucks that day. These video games measure whether employees have the hand-eye coordination to perform their jobs on a given day. The computer has already established a baseline for each employee. Subsequent testing measures the employees against these baselines. Interestingly, most test failures are *not* drug- or alcohol-related. Initial results suggest that fatigue, illness, and personal problems more frequently render a person unfit to perform a sensitive job.

Not everyone likes fitness-for-duty testing. One federal drug official questions the reliability of such tests in detecting impairment. And a union official opposes the tests on the principle that management could come in and establish a company baseline designed to eliminate older employees. But another union president notes that fitness-for-duty tests are less invasive than drug tests overall and the results from them are often available sooner. Indeed, as a common saying goes in some dangerous jobs, urinalysis results arrive just in time for the funeral.[26]

**SUBSTANCE ABUSE AND THE ADA** The Americans with Disabilities Act (ADA) determines how management can handle substance-abuse cases. The practicing illegal drug abuser is specifically excluded from the definition of *disabled* under the act. However, those addicted to legal substances (alcohol, for example) are *not* excluded. Previous legislation and various government agencies have defined *disabled* differently, but members of the medical community seem to agree that both alcohol and drug abuse are mental disorders. Therefore, addiction is generally regarded as a disease, similar to mental disorders. Further, regulations developed to administer the ADA define as disabilities both alcoholism and drug addiction that have been treated. Therefore, the prudent employer considers recovering substance abusers as disabled under the ADA and proceeds accordingly in considering them for employment and making accommodations for them to receive treatment.

**SUBSTANCE ABUSE AND MANAGERIAL RESPONSIBILITY** Employers are concerned about substance abuse because it alters work behaviors. The effects may be subtle, such as tardiness, increased absenteeism, slower work pace, higher rate of mistakes, and less time spent at the workstation. Substance abuse also can cause altered behaviors at work, so that more withdrawal (physical and psychological) and antagonistic behaviors occur. Also, the organization may be held liable for injuries to others if its managers should have been aware that an employee's drug use was a problem. Figure 16–12 on the next page shows common signs of substance abuse. However, not all signs are present in any one case. A pattern that includes some of these behaviors should be a reason to play closer attention.

To encourage employees to seek help for their substance-abuse problems, a *firm-choice* option is usually recommended and has been endorsed legally. In this procedure, the employee is privately confronted by a supervisor or manager about unsatisfactory work-related behaviors. Then, in keeping with the disciplinary system, he or she is offered a choice between help, possibly through an

**FIGURE 16–12** *Common Signs of Substance Abuse*

- Fatigue
- Slurred speech
- Flushed cheeks
- Difficulties walking
- Many unscheduled absences, especially on Mondays and Fridays
- Inconsistency
- Difficulty remembering details
- Misses deadlines
- Depression
- Irritability
- Emotional
- Overreacts
- Exhibits violence
- Borrows money frequently
- Argues

employee assistance program (discussed later in this chapter), and discipline. Treatment options and consequences of further unsatisfactory performance are *clearly* discussed, including what the employer will do. Confidentiality and follow-up are critical when employers use the firm-choice option.

## Stress

The pressures of modern life, coupled with the demands of a job, can lead to emotional imbalances that are collectively labeled *stress*. Not all stress is unpleasant. To be alive means to respond to the stress of achievement and the excitement of a challenge. In fact, there is evidence that people *need* a certain amount of stimulation, and that monotony can bring on some of the same problems as overwork. The term *stress* usually refers to excessive stress.

Evidence of stress can be seen everywhere, from the 35-year-old executive who suddenly dies of a heart attack to the dependable worker who unexpectedly commits suicide. Several studies indicate that some people who abuse alcohol and/or drugs do so to help reduce stress.[27]

When an emotional problem (stress-related or otherwise) becomes so severe that it disrupts an employee's ability to function normally, the employee should be directed to appropriate professionals for help. Because emotional problems are difficult to diagnose, supervisors and managers should not become involved in the diagnosis. For example, if a worker is emotionally upset because of marital difficulties, a supervisor should not give advice. Instead, the employee should be referred to a program staffed by professionals.

Stress, long considered an American phenomenon, is showing up in other places as well. For example, in France, a survey found that 57% of respondents said they work in stressful conditions. The main causes were time pressure, fear of losing a job, deadlines, and fragmented work.[28]

## Managing Health Issues at Work

Employers who are concerned about maintaining a healthy workforce must move beyond simply providing healthy working conditions and begin to address employee health and wellness in other ways. Some major ways employers are attempting to deal with employee health issues are described next.

## Wellness Programs

Employers' desires to improve productivity, decrease absenteeism, and control health-care costs have come together in the "wellness" movement. **Wellness programs** are designed to maintain or improve employee health before problems arise. Wellness programs encourage self-directed lifestyle changes. Early wellness programs were aimed primarily at reducing the cost and risk of disease. Newer programs emphasize healthy lifestyles and environment. Typical programs may include the following:

- Screenings (risk factors, blood pressures, cardiovascular disease, etc.)
- Exercise programs (endurance, aerobics, strength, etc.)
- Education and awareness programs (stress reduction, weight control, prevention of back pain, etc.)
- Skills programs (CPR, first aid, etc.)

Organizations have entered the "wellness business," not just because they have suddenly developed a higher social conscience, but because each year, employers spend billions of dollars on group life and health insurance premiums. Much of that money goes to finance care after emergencies (such as heart attacks) that are, at least to some degree, preventable.[29]

There are a number of ways to assess the effectiveness of wellness programs. Participation rates by employees is one way. The participation rates vary by type of activity, but generally 20% to 40% of employees participate in the different activities in a wellness program. Although more participation would be beneficial, the programs have resulted in healthier lifestyles for more employees. Cost/benefit analyses tend to support the continuation of wellness programs as well.[30]

**Wellness programs**
Programs designed to maintain or improve employee health before problems arise.

## Employee Assistance Programs (EAPs)

One method that organizations are using as a broad-based response to health issues is the **employee assistance program (EAP),** which provides counseling and other help to employees having emotional, physical, or other personal problems. In such a program, an employer establishes a liaison with a social service counseling agency. Employees who have problems may then contact the agency, either voluntarily or by employer referral, for assistance with a broad range of problems. Counseling costs are paid for by the employer, either in total or up to a preestablished limit.

EAPs are attempts to help employees with a variety of problems. Some HR managers feel that EAPs make their other HR programs more effective.[31] For example, in one large company, the Vice President of Human Resources found that much of his department's time was being consumed by such problems as employee anxiety reactions, suicide attempts, alcohol- and drug-related absences, and family disturbances. Further, the medical department was not able to provide accurate information on whether affected employees could successfully return to work. The vice president decided an EAP might save a great deal of time and money and was able to convince the president of the firm to fund the costs of the EAP.

It is especially important to have such programs available when dealing with a potentially violent employee or one involved with substance abuse. Also, those with life-threatening illnesses or suffering from extreme stress can be referred to EAPs. Figure 16–13 shows the areas addressed by a typical EAP.

**Employee assistance program (EAP)**
Program that provides counseling and other help to employees having emotional, physical, or other personal problems.

***LOGGING ON . . .***
**Assistance Services**
This website describes employee assistance services, such as counseling, crisis debriefing, and others.

**http://www.neas.com/ htsqml.cgi/sections**

FIGURE 16–13 *Typical Areas Addressed by Employee Assistance Programs (EAPs)*

Unfortunately, it is hard to find an objective assessment of how effective EAPs have been. On the one hand, the Employee Assistance Professionals Association contends that for every dollar employers invest in EAPs, they recover an estimated three to five dollars in reduction of other costs or increased productivity. On the other side of the issue are those who contend that EAPs cause health-care costs to go up, not down, because of difficulty in measuring effectiveness. Further, there are many areas of potential liability arising out of EAPs for employers that must be considered before establishing them.[32]

# Security

Traditionally, when employers have addressed worker health, safety, and security, they have been concerned about reducing workplace accidents, improving workers' safety practices, and reducing health hazards at work. However, a shocking statistic is that *homicide* (meaning murder) is the second leading cause of workplace fatalities in the United States, following only transportation-related deaths.

During the last few years, workplace homicide has been the number one cause of job deaths in several states. Nationally, in one year, approximately one thousand individuals were killed at work, and an additional two million people were attacked at work. About 70% of the workplace fatalities involved armed robberies. (See Figure 16–14.)

Workers such as police officers, taxi drivers, and convenience store clerks are more likely to be murdered on the job than employees in many other occupations. Often, these deaths occur during armed robbery attempts. But what has shocked many employers in a variety of industries has been the number of disgruntled employees or former employees who have resorted to homicide in the workplace to deal with their anger and grievances.

Security in workplaces is increasing in importance as an HR issue. Vandalism of organization property, theft of company equipment and employees' personal property, and unauthorized "hacking" of organization computers are all examples of major security concerns today.

## Workplace Violence

The violence committeed at work against employees by coworkers and former coworkers is a growing concern for employers.[33] Also, employers have faced legal action by employees or their survivors for failing to protect workers from violence at work by disgruntled spouses, boyfriends, or girlfriends.

These concerns have led many employers to conduct training for supervisors and managers on how to recognize the signs of a potentially violent employee and what to do when violence occurs. During training at many firms, supervisors learn the typical profile of potentially violent employees. They are trained to notify the HR department and to refer employees to outside counseling

**FIGURE 16–14 *Workplace Violence***

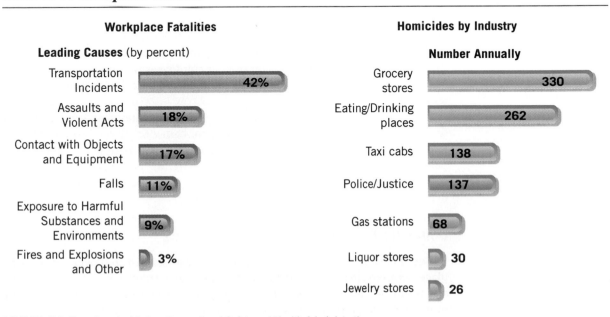

SOURCE: U.S. Department of Labor, Occupational Safety and Health Administration

**FIGURE 16–15** *Profile of a Potentially Violent Employee*

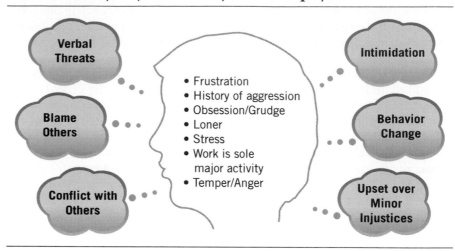

professionals, whose services are covered by employee assistance programs that are offered by employers.

Figure 16–15 shows the warning signs and characteristics of a potentially violent person at work. Research on individuals who have committed the most violent acts shows the relatively common profile depicted in Figure 16–15. A person with some of these problems may cope for years until a trauma pushes him or her over the edge. A profound humiliation or rejection, the end of a marriage, or the loss of a lawsuit or job may make a difficult employee take a distinct turn for the worse.

Some experts recommend that supervisors talk with employees who make threats in order to allow the employees to vent some of their hostility and anger. Also, supervisors should try to get HR professionals involved. Often, an HR staff member can arrange for an upset employee to talk with the trained professionals available through employee assistance programs.[34] Another approach is to establish a violence response team, composed of employees trained to handle violent individuals. Members of this team can discuss and/or deal with potentially violent employees and customers.[35]

However, employers must be careful, because they may face legal action for discrimination if they discharge employees for behaviors that often precede violent acts. For example, in several cases, employees who were terminated or suspended for making threats or even engaging in physical actions against coworkers have sued their employees, claiming they had mental disabilities under the Americans with Disabilities Act (ADA).

## Domestic Causes of Workplace Violence

Violence that begins at home with family or "friends" can spill over to the workplace. Women are much more likely than men to experience violence committed as a result of a personal relationship. The same is true in the workplace. On the other hand, men are more likely to be attacked by a stranger. Close to 1 in 5 homicides for women at work are current or former husbands or boyfriends.

***LOGGING ON . . .***
**OSHA—Workplace Violence Initiative**
This OSHA site provides guidelines for preventing workplace violence, along with additional recommendations and information.

**http://www.osha-slc.gov/ NewInit/WorkplaceViolence/ index.html.**

About 75% of battered women report frequently being harassed by abusing partners at work, by telephone, or in person.[36]

Many employers are unaware of domestic violence and its effects on employees. As the problem gets more recognition, employers are taking some of the following actions to combat the problems:

- Classes in prevention
- Recommending counseling services for victims
- Domestic violence training
- Inclusion of victims in EAPs

## Security Audit

Conducting a comprehensive analysis of the vulnerability of organizational security is the purpose of a **security audit.** Often, such an audit uses managers inside the organization—such as the HR manager and facilities manager—and outsiders, such as security consultants, police officers, fire officials, and computer security experts.[37]

Typically, a security audit begins with a survey of the area around the facility. Such factors as lighting in parking lots, traffic flow, location of emergency response services, crime in the surrounding neighborhood, and the layout of the buildings and grounds are evaluated. Also included is an audit of the security available within the firm, including the capabilities of guards and others involved with security.

Another part of the security audit is a review of *disaster plans,* which address how to deal with natural disasters such as floods, fires, and civil disturbances. The most commonly used preventative measures for enhancing workplace security are:

- Workshops/training
- Security cameras/doors, etc.
- Security guards
- ID badges
- Discipline/termination of offenders
- Threat assessment

**Security audit**
A review of the security vulnerability in an organization.

## Controlled Access

A key part of security is controlling access to the physical facilities of the organization. As mentioned earlier, many workplace homicides occur during robberies. Therefore, those employees most vulnerable, such as taxi drivers and convenience store clerks, must be provided secure areas to which access is limited. For instance, providing plexiglass partitions and requiring use of cash trays have reduced deaths in some convenience store/gasoline station locations.

Many organizations limit access to facilities and work areas by using electronic access or keycard systems. While not foolproof, these systems can make it more difficult for an unauthorized person, such as an estranged husband or a disgruntled ex-employee, to enter the premises. Access controls also can be used in elevators and stairwells to prevent unauthorized persons from entering certain areas within a facility.

Yet another part of security is controlling access to computer systems. With so many transactions and records being handled by computers, it is crucial that

*BNA: 3455.50–
3455.60*
**Workplace Violence**
Following an overview on workplace violence, review the pointers on violence prevention policies and compare them to policies at an employer.

adequate security provisions be in place to prevent unauthorized access to computer systems, including human resource information systems (HRIS).

## Employee Screening and Selection

A key facet of providing security is to screen job applicants. As discussed in Chapter 9, there are legal limits on what can be done, particularly regarding the use of psychological tests and checking of references. However, firms that do not screen employees adequately may be subject to liability if an employee commits crimes later. For instance, an individual with a criminal record for assault was hired by a firm to perform interior maintenance of sound equipment. The employee used a passkey to enter a home and assault the owner, and the employer was ruled liable. Of course, employers must be careful when selecting employees to use only valid, job-related screening means and to avoid violating federal EEO laws and the Americans with Disabilities Act.

## Security Personnel

Having sufficient security personnel who are adequately trained is a critical part of security management. Many employers contract for this service with firms specializing in security. If employees are to be used, they must be selected and trained to handle a variety of workplace security problems, ranging from dealing with violent behavior by an employee to taking charge in natural disasters.

# Summary

- Health is a general state of physical, mental, and emotional well-being.
- Safety involves protecting the physical well-being of people.
- Security involves protection of employer facilities and equipment from unauthorized access and protection of employees while on work premises or work assignments.
- Workers' compensation coverage is provided by employers to protect employees who suffer job-related injuries and illnesses. The costs are paid by employers, who must make efforts to control them.
- The Fair Labor Standards Act (FLSA) limits the types of work that employees under the age of 18 can perform.
- The Occupational Safety and Health Act states that employers have a general duty to provide safe and healthy working conditions, and enforcement standards have been established to aid in that process.
- The Occupational Safety and Health Administration (OSHA) conducts inspections of workplaces

- and can issue citations for several different levels of violations. Also, OSHA requires employers to keep records on occupational illnesses and injuries.
- Effective safety management requires integrating three different approaches: organizational, engineering, and individual.
- Among the organizational approaches to safety management, key elements include organizational commitment, safety policies and discipline, safety training and communications, safety committees, safety inspections and accident investigations, accident research, and evaluation of safety efforts.
- Accident prevention should be approached from both engineering and individual perspectives.
- Some work environments pose health problems, such as sick building syndrome. Fetal protection concerns may also arise in some environments.
- The engineering approach to safety and health considers the physical setting of work, work equipment and materials, and ergonomics to address problems such as cumulative trauma disorder (CTD).

- Accidents and industrial health concerns are major problems, both from cost and personal standpoints. Worker attitudes play a major role in accidents and accident prevention.
- Various health issues have grown in importance for organizations and employees. AIDS, smoking at work, substance abuse, and job stress are among the most prevalent.
- Employers have responded to health problems by establishing and supporting wellness programs and employee assistance programs (EAPs).

- Security of workplaces has grown in importance, particularly in light of the increasing frequency in which workplace violence occurs.
- Employers can enhance security by conducting a security audit, controlling access to workplaces and computer systems, screening employees adequately, and providing security personnel.

# Review and Discussion Questions

1. Identify the purpose of health, safety, and security as HR activities and discuss how they are interrelated.
2. Discuss how controlling workers' compensation costs is related to effective health, safety, and security practices.
3. Describe the Occupational Safety and Health Act and some of its key provisions, including current issues and standards.
4. What should an employer do when faced with an OSHA inspection, and what records should be available?

5. Why must safety management address organizational, engineering, and individual perspectives to be effective?
6. Discuss the following statement by a supervisor: "I feel it is my duty to get involved with my employees and their personal problems to show that I truly care about them."
7. Consider an organization where you have worked and describe some of the security issues discussed in the chapter as they might be identified during a security audit.

# Terms to Know

cumulative trauma disorders
   (CTDs)   548
employee assistance program
   (EAP)   555

ergonomics   547
health   530
safety   530
security   530

security audit   559
substance abuse   552
wellness programs   555

# Using the Internet

# Conducting a Job Safety Analysis

As the HR manager of your organization, safety is one of your responsibilities. You have decided to conduct a safety analysis of some jobs. Before the analysis can be completed, it must be approved by the CEO. She has asked you to explain what a job safety analysis is,

tell her why she should approve it, and describe the basic steps involved in the process. Use the following website to assist you.

**http://www.ncci.com/html/ncfom5.htm**

# CASE

## Improving Safety and Health at Oneida Silversmiths

Oneida Silversmiths is a manufacturer of silver flatware and utensils located in Oneida, New York. In the early 1990s, Oneida was experiencing 137 lost-time incidents per year; these were cases in which a work-related injury or illness caused an Oneida worker to miss at least one scheduled workday. Also, Oneida was experiencing 7.3 lost-time accidents per 100 full-time workers. While both of these statistics were below national averages, they were still too high for Oneida. The firm's management knew that occupational injuries and illnesses affected productivity and insurance costs. But being concerned about their employees, Oneida's management also recognized that having workers miss work disrupted work-team activities and results and caused problems for employees and their families.

Oneida's management decided a multifaceted effort was needed to reduce occupational illnesses and injuries. A key manager in this effort was Dr. Scott Treatman, Oneida's medical director. Oneida's approach used both reactive and proactive efforts.

Reactive efforts included actions taken after injuries and illnesses had occurred to (1) prevent them from occurring again and (2) reduce the associated costs. A more thorough injury investigation process was instituted, with the manager of the department where the injured employee worked playing a key role. Part of this process involved identifying how and understanding why the accident occurred and what changes were needed to prevent future accidents. Because back injuries were common at Oneida (and throughout the flatware industry), particular attention was given to reducing the number and severity of back injuries. Now, in addition to having medical assessments of their back disabilities, employees who lose work time due to a back injury must attend "back school training" before returning to their jobs. The focus of this training is to teach workers how to lift objects and move correctly in order to prevent back injuries. Additionally, the firm began monitoring its workers' compensation costs and claims more closely.

Proactively, Oneida began an ergonomics review of jobs in the firm, particularly those in which the greatest number of occupational illnesses and injuries occurred. Under the direction of a coordinator, departmental ergonomics teams now assess ergonomic hazards, identify potential solutions, and monitor changes after they are made. Regular team meetings are held, and the coordinator reviews the team's activities with senior managers every six months.

An on-site exercise program was started as well. Employees are shown stretching exercises and other movements that will help reduce fatigue and muscle tension. A wellness program builds on this program and focuses on employee health more broadly.

As a result of all of these efforts, over a four-year period, the number of lost-time incidents decreased to fewer than 50, and the number of accidents per 100 full-time workers declined from 7.3 to 1.0. In summary, safety management clearly paid off for Oneida and its workers.[38]

## Questions

1. Discuss how the organizational approach to safety management contributed to the changes at Oneida.
2. Oneida integrated the engineering and individual approaches to safety management. Identify some examples, and discuss why you believe they were successful.

# Notes

1. Jean M. Patterson, "VPP Companies' Best Practices," *Occupational Health & Safety,* January 1997, 60–61.
2. "Million-Dollar Fines Proposed for Willful Safety Violations," *Bulletin to Management,* December 17, 1998, 396.
3. "Workplace Accidents," *The Wall Street Journal,* February 4, 1997, A1.
4. "Fines Can Follow Conviction," *Bulletin to Management,* March 26, 1998, 89.
5. "Back to Driving School as On-the-Job Accidents Rise in U.S.," *Manpower Argus,* August 1997, 7.
6. Stephanie Armour, "Working at Home Raises Job Site Safety Issues," *USA Today,* January 28, 1998, B1.

7. Kristin Grimsley, "Workers' Compensation Costs, Payments Down," *The Washington Post,* December 19, 1997, G3.
8. Based on Michael Moss, "Gray Area," *The Wall Street Journal,* June 17, 1997, 1A.
9. "Lead Report—Safety and Health," *Human Resources Report,* April 21, 1998, 397.
10. "OSH Act Is Changed to Emphasize Cooperation," *HR News,* September 1998, 14.
11. *United Autoworkers v. Johnson Controls, Inc.,* 111 S. Ct. 1196 (1991).
12. Mary Anne O'Neal, "Warning Signs," *Occupational Health & Safety,* December 1997, 42–48.
13. *Marshall v. Barlow's Inc.,* 98 S. Ct. 1816 (1978).
14. Keith E. Barenklau, "Doing the Right Things Right," *Occupational Health & Safety,* March 1999, 20–21; and Craig S. Philson, "Workplace Safety Accountability," *Occupational Health & Safety,* April 1998, 20–24.
15. "Team Efforts Help Employees Reduce Workplace Injuries," *Bulletin to Management,* October 29, 1998, 340.
16. David C. Breeding, "Surveying Office Illumination," *Workplace Ergonomics,* October/November 1997, 23–24.
17. Linda F. Johnson, "The Unbridled Joy of a Good Chair," *Occupational Health & Safety,* January 1999, 80–81.
18. E. Scott Geller, "Behavior-Based Safety: Confusion, Controversy, and Clarification," *Occupational Health & Safety,* January 1999, 40–49.
19. Jim Rasmussen, "UP Safety Review Leads to Crew Naps," *Omaha World-Herald,* September 27, 1998, 1A.
20. Tom Krause and Stan Hodson, "A Close Look at Safety Incentives," *Occupational Health & Safety,* January 1998, 28.
21. "New Treatments for HIV, Aids Raise Questions for Employers," *Bulletin to Management,* December 10, 1998.
22. Sandy Hunter, "Your Infection Control Program," *Occupational Health & Safety,* August 1998, 78.
23. Jane Bahls, "Drugs in the Workplace," *HR Magazine,* February 1998, 81–87.
24. Ron Winslow, "Productivity Data Indict Casual Drinking," *The Wall Street Journal,* December 22, 1998, B1.
25. "Employee Alcohol Testing on the Rise," *Bulletin to Management,* August 20, 1998, 261.
26. Robert G. Perry, "Fitness for Duty Testing," *Occupational Health & Safety,* April 1998, 41–44.
27. Richard S. DeFrank and John M. Ivancevich, "Stress of the Job: An Executive Update," *Academy of Management Executive,* August 1998, 55–66.
28. "New Technology Causes Stress for French Workers," *Manpower Argus,* August 1998, 6.
29. "Employers Adopting Wellness Programs," *Bulletin to Management,* November 5, 1998, 345.
30. Darrell L. Browning, "Integrated Solutions," *Human Resource Executive,* September 1998, 52–56.
31. Jodi Arthur, "Gaining Trust," *Human Resource Executive,* January 1998, 64–66.
32. Jane Easter Bahls, "Handle with Care," *HR Magazine,* March 1999, 60–67; and Joan Szabo, "Rusty Gatekeepers," *Employee Benefits News,* May 1997, 37–38.
33. James W. Fenton, Jr., et al., "Employer Legal Liability for Employee Workplace Violence," *SAM Advanced Management Journal,* Fall 1997, 44–47.
34. Julie Cook, "Walking Time Bombs," *Human Resource Executive,* February 1999, 34–36.
35. Makom P. Coco, Jr., "The New War Zone: The Workplace," *SAM Advanced Management Journal,* Winter 1998, 15–20.
36. "Managed Care Plans Are Cited for Domestic Violence Programs," *Human Resource Executive,* Feburary 1999, 22; and "Domestic Violence: A Workplace Issue," *Womenews* (Nebraska Commission on the Status of Women), September/October 1997, 1–2.
37. Tim Schelldardt, "A Former High-Tech Thief Shares Tricks of the Trade," *The Wall Street Journal,* November 12, 1997, B1.
38. Based on Scott L. Treatman, "The Shotgun Approach," *Occupational Health & Safety,* August 1995, 65–70.

# CHAPTER 17
# Employee Rights and Discipline

*After you have read this chapter, you should be able to:*

- Explain the difference between statutory rights and contractual rights.

- Define employment-at-will and identify three exceptions to it.

- Describe what due process is and explain some means of alternative dispute resolution.

- Identify employee rights concerns associated with access to employee records and free speech.

- Discuss issues associated with workplace monitoring, surveillance, investigations, and drug testing.

- List elements to consider when developing an employee handbook.

- Differentiate between the positive approach and progressive approach to discipline.

## HR TRANSITIONS

# Employment Practices Liability Insurance (EPLI)

There is a growing recognition by employers in the United States that employee rights issues are creating significant liabilities. For instance, disciplining or discharging employees may lead to lawsuits.

Another illustration of the legal exposure employers face is that the number of sexual harassment claims doubled in six years, and monetary damages in federal sexual harassment suits were over $50 million. For sexual harassment and other employment-related claims, the average award to individuals is $1.5 million, which ultimately is paid by employers. Just as employers have insured "risks" on their facilities and equipment, they are recognizing that they need to insure their employment-related risks.

Beginning in 1992, some insurance companies offered employers a new type of insurance coverage—employment practices liability insurance (EPLI). In seven years the number of insurance carriers offering EPLI has grown to more than 70, and additional insurance carriers are entering the market each year. Because general company insurance policies do not include employment-related areas in their coverage, EPLI provides another means to insure organizational risks.

EPLI is purchased by employers for amounts ranging from $5,000 to hundreds of thousands of dollars, depending on the industry of the employer and the size of an employer's workforce. The EPLI policies typically cover employer costs for legal fees, settle-

ments, and judgments associated with employment-related actions. Insurance carriers provide coverage for some or all of the following employment-related actions:

- Discrimination
- Sexual harassment
- Wrongful termination
- Breach of employment contract
- Negligent evaluation
- Failure to employ or promote
- Wrongful discipline
- Deprivation of career opportunity
- Infliction of emotional distress
- Improper management of employee benefits

Employers use EPLI when faced with lawsuits from current or former employees, applicants, or other parties. Coverage of costs up to $100 million can be purchased, obviously with significantly higher premiums being charged by the insurance carriers. However, most EPLI policies exclude employment claims based on retaliatory actions by employers against employees who allege violations in legally protected areas.

To determine the level of risk and premiums to be charged to employers

wanting EPLI, most insurance carriers conduct reviews of employers' HR policies and practices. Included in this review is a detailed look at an employer's HR policy manuals, employee handbooks, employment forms, and other items. Also, the employer's history of employment-related charges and complaints over the past 3–5 years is reviewed. For multisite organizations, reviews may be done in several locations outside of corporate headquarters in order to ensure that consistency of HR policies and practices exists throughout the organization.

Viewing the growth of EPLI opti-

*By taking positive steps to ensure that their HR policies and practices are conducted legally and that all employees are treated appropriately, employers will be better protected in the litigious world they face.*

mistically, it may indicate that more and more employers are recognizing that their employment-related policies and practices create liabilities. By taking positive steps to ensure that their HR policies and practices are conducted legally and that all employees are treated appropriately, employers will be better protected in the litigious world they face.[1]

> ❝ *The right to be left alone—the most comprehensive of rights and the most valued by civilized men.* ❞
>
> LOUIS BRANDEIS

This chapter considers three related and important issues in managing human resources: employee rights, HR policies and rules, and discipline. These areas may seem separate, but they definitely are not. The policies and rules that an organization enacts define employee rights at work to a certain extent, and they also constrain those rights (sometimes inappropriately or illegally). Similarly, discipline for those who fail to follow policies and rules often is seen as a fundamental right of employers. Employees who feel that employer actions have been taken inappropriately can challenge those actions—both inside and outside the organization—using the legal system. As the opening discussion of employment practices liability insurance (EPLI) indicates, the costs to employers of those challenges can be substantial.

Employees come to organizations with certain rights that have been established by the U.S. Constitution. Some of those rights include *freedom of speech, due process, unreasonable search and seizure,* and others. Although the U.S. Constitution grants these and other rights to citizens, over the years laws and court decisions have identified limits on those rights in the workplaces. For example, an employee who voices threats against other employees may face disciplinary action by the employer without the employee's freedom of speech being threatened. Indeed, the right of management to run organizations as it chooses was at one time so strong that employee rights were practically nonexistent. However, today management rights have been restrained to some degree as employee rights have been expanded.

# Employee Rights and Responsibilities

**Rights**
That which belongs to a person by law, nature, or tradition.

Generally, rights do not exist in the abstract. They exist only when someone is successful in demanding their practical applications. **Rights** belong to a person by law, nature, or tradition. Of course, there is considerable potential for disagreement as to what really is a right. Pressures placed by employers on employees with "different" lifestyles illustrate one area in which conflicts can occur. Moreover, *legal* rights may or may not correspond to certain *moral* rights, and the reverse is true as well.

**Employee responsibilities**
Obligations to be accountable for actions.

Rights are offset by **employee responsibilities,** which are obligations to be accountable for actions. Employment is a reciprocal relationship (both sides have rights and obligations). For example, if an employee has the right to a safe working environment, the employer has an obligation to provide a safe workplace. Because rights and responsibilities are reciprocal, the employer also has a right to expect uninterrupted, high-quality work from the employee, meaning that the worker has the responsibility to be on the job and meet job performance standards. The reciprocal nature of rights and responsibilities suggests that each party to an employment relationship should regard the other as having equal rights and should treat the other with respect.

## Statutory Rights

**Statutory rights**
Rights based on laws.

Employees' **statutory rights** are the result of specific laws passed by federal, state, or local governments. Federal, state, and local laws that granted employees certain rights at work, such as equal employment opportunity, collective bargaining, and safety have changed traditional management prerogatives. These laws and their interpretations have been the subjects of a considerable number of court cases. For instance, in a 12-month period, over 23,000 employment discrimination claims were filed in federal trial courts. During the same time frame, over 78,000 employment-related discrimination complaints were filed with the federal Equal Employment Opportunity Commission (EEOC).[2]

## Contractual Rights

An employee's **contractual rights** are based on a specific contractual agreement with an employer. For instance, a union and an employer may agree on a labor contract that specifies certain terms, conditions, and rights that employees have with the employer.

Contracts are used when a formalized relationship is needed. For instance, if someone is being hired as an independent contractor or consultant, then a contract spells out the work to be performed, expected time lines, parameters, and costs and fees to be incurred by the hiring firm. Another situation in which formal contracts are used is in a **separation agreement.** In this agreement, an employee who is being terminated agrees not to sue the employer in exchange for specified benefits, such as additional severance pay or other considerations. Contractual rights can be spelled out formally in written employment contracts or implied in employer handbooks and policies disseminated to employees.

**EMPLOYMENT CONTRACTS** Details of an employment agreement are often spelled out in a formal **employment contract.** These contracts are written and often very detailed. Traditionally, employment contracts have been used mostly for executives and senior managers. However, the use of employment contracts is filtering down the organization to include scarce-skilled, highly specialized professionals and technical employees. Even flexible staffing firms providing temporary help services are using contracts for employees with specialized skills. Employers who hire individuals from a staffing service after a short-term temporary assignment often are obligated to pay the staffing service a "placement fee" that can run as high as 30% of the employee's annual base salary at the new company.[3]

Employment contracts typically contain several provisions relating to a number of different areas. Following an identification section listing the parties to the contract, the nature of employment is specified. The employment contract may note whether the employment relationship is to be for an indeterminate time, or whether it can be renewed automatically after a specified period of time. Typically, employment contracts indicate that employment can be terminated at the will of either the employer or employee, or for just cause. Also typically identified is the general nature of the employee's job duties.[4] The level of compensation and types of benefits often are addressed next, including any special compensation, benefits, incentives, or perquisites to be provided by the employer.

Common in employment contracts are nonpiracy and noncompete provisions. A **nonpiracy agreement** contains provisions stating that if the individual leaves the organization, existing customers and clients cannot be solicited for business for a specified period of time, usually one year. **Noncompete covenants** are even more restrictive and prohibit an individual who leaves the organization from competing with the employer in the same line of business for

**Contractual rights**
Rights based on a specific contractual agreement between employer and employee.

**Separation agreement**
Agreement in which an employee who is being terminated agrees not to sue the employer in exchange for specified benefits.

**Employment contract**
Agreement that formally spells out the details of employment.

**Nonpiracy agreement**
Provisions stating that if the individual leaves the organization, existing customers and clients cannot be solicited for business for a specified period of time.

**Noncompete covenants**
Agreement that prohibits an individual who leaves the organization from competing with the employer in the same line of business for a specified period of time.

**FIGURE 17–1** *Typical Employment Contract Provisions*

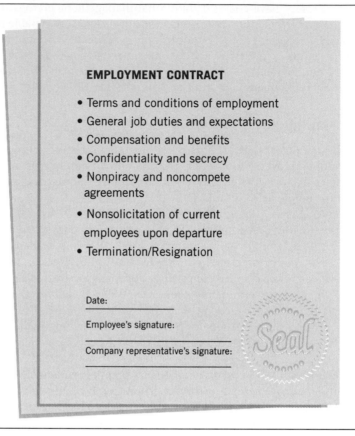

**EMPLOYMENT CONTRACT**

- Terms and conditions of employment
- General job duties and expectations
- Compensation and benefits
- Confidentiality and secrecy
- Nonpiracy and noncompete agreements
- Nonsolicitation of current employees upon departure
- Termination/Resignation

Date: _____

Employee's signature:
_____

Company representative's signature:
_____

**LOGGING ON . . .**

**Employment Contracts**

This site describes a firm that specializes in providing employers with employment contracts. A directory of the jobs they write contracts for can be reviewed here.

**http://www.espros.com/ contract_info.html**

a specified period of time. These agreements may be overly restrictive, so that they prohibit an individual from earning a living, and that affects how enforceable they are in state courts.[5] In a related area, employment contracts also may place limitations on an individual to prevent that person from soliciting the firm's employees for employment with another company. As the HR Perspective indicates, employment contracts also are used to protect organizational secrets. Employment contracts also can restrict what employees may disclose to another employer.[6]

Finally, Figure 17–1 identifies typical employment provisions. Employment contracts identify the nature and conditions under which employees can be terminated from employment, or how they may resign. The contract also may spell out the severance agreement, continuation of benefits, and other factors related to employees leaving the employer.

**IMPLIED CONTRACTS** The idea that a contract (even an implied, unwritten one) exists between workers and their employers affects the employment relationship. Rights and responsibilities of the employee to the employer may be spelled out in a job description, in an employment contract, or in HR policies, but often are not. Employee rights and responsibilities also may exist only as unwritten employer expectations about what is acceptable behavior or performance on the part of the employee. For instance, a number of court decisions have held that if an employer

## HR PERSPECTIVE

# Organizational Secrets and Employment Contracts

A major reason for using employment contracts with nonexecutives is to protect confidentiality and company secrets. Several examples illustrate how the electronic age and technology have made protecting company secrets an important consideration for inclusion in employment contracts.

The best-known battle over company secrets involved General Motors (GM) and Volkswagen. When Volkswagen recruited Jose Ignacio Lopez and seven other GM employees, GM filed suit against Lopez for stealing secrets about production plans and methods. Ultimately, after a year-long court battle in both the United States and Germany, the case was settled by Volkswagen paying GM $1.1 billion.

Even secret ideas have been the subjects of employer disputes. A telecommunications equipment firm, DSC Communications, fired an employee who refused to turn over software details to DSC. After the employee refused, DSC sued the employee because the firm had a signed employment agreement containing an *intellectual-property clause.* This clause, common in the software industry, requires employees who develop new ideas, methods, or patents using company resources to give them to the employer. Now in court, the DSC case illustrates how widespread company secrets can be interpreted to be.

Another example in the software industry involved Novell, the Utah-based network software firm. After three engineers from Novell left to start a new company, Novell sued them, alleging that the engineers stole trade secrets and breached their employment contracts with Novell. Subsequently, Novell won a court order allowing police to search the men's homes and seize personal computers, disks, and other documents that would provide evidence of the secret computer codes for a new type of software that was being developed at Novell.

Concerns about theft of company secrets led to the passage of the Economic Espionage Act of 1996, which made the theft of trade secrets a federal crime punishable by fines up to $500,000 and prison terms up to 15 years. The law is not just used to prevent theft of trade secrets by U.S. firms, but also to prohibit foreign governments and firms from stealing U.S. technological advances. In one case, the Federal Bureau of Investigation (FBI) spent 22 months investigating the theft of information on the anti-cancer drug Taxol from Bristol-Myers Squibb by persons from a Taiwan competitor. The information the men were gathering would have allowed the Taiwan firm to make Taxol. According to the FBI, the men were to be paid $200,000 and a percentage of the profits made by the Taiwan Company on producing and selling Taxol.

This law and these cases illustrate why it is important for employers to have employees—especially those with access to new product and technology secrets—sign employment agreements containing appropriate nonpiracy, nondisclosure, and intellectual-property provisions.[7]

hires someone for an indefinite period or promises job security, the employer has created an implied contract.[8] Such promises establish employee expectations. When the employer fails to follow up on the implied promises, the employee has recourse in court. Numerous federal and state court decisions have held that such implied promises, especially when contained in an employee handbook, constitute a contract between an employer and its employees, even though there is no signed document.

## Rights and Employee-Employer Relations

Workplace litigation has reached epidemic proportions as employees who feel that their rights have been violated sue their employers. As the opening discussion on EPLI indicates, some employers are purchasing insurance to try and cover their risks from numerous lawsuits. Advocates for expanding employee rights warn that management policies abridging free speech, privacy, or due process will lead to further national legislation to regulate the employer-employee relationship. At the same time, HR professionals argue that they must protect management's traditional prerogatives to hire, promote, transfer, or terminate employees as they see fit, or the effectiveness of the organization may be affected.

As employees increasingly regard themselves as free agents in the workplace—and as the power of unions declines—the struggle between employee and employer "rights" is heightening. Employers frequently do not fare very well in court. Further, it is not only the employer that is liable in many cases. Individual managers and supervisors have been found liable when hiring or promotion decisions have been based on discriminatory factors, or when they have had knowledge of such conduct and have not taken steps to stop it. The changing rights associated with employee-employer relationships are an outgrowth of the changing psychological contract between employers and employees that was highlighted in Chapter 3.

# Rights Affecting the Employment Relationship

It can be argued that all employee-rights issues affect the employment relationship. However, several basic issues predominate: employment-at-will, due process, and dismissal for just cause.

## Employment-at-Will (EAW)

**Employment-at-will (EAW)**
A common-law doctrine stating that employers have the right to hire, fire, demote, or promote whomever they choose, unless there is a law or contract to the contrary.

**Employment-at-will (EAW)** is a common-law doctrine stating that employers have the right to hire, fire, demote, or promote whomever they choose, unless there is a law or contract to the contrary. A sample employment-at-will statement is shown in Figure 17–2. Employers often defend EAW based on one or more of the following reasons:

- The right of private ownership of a business guarantees EAW.
- EAW defends employees' right to change jobs, as well as employers' right to hire and fire.
- Interfering with EAW reduces productivity in a firm and in the economy.

In the past three decades an increasing number of state courts have questioned the *fairness* of an employer's decision to fire an employee without just cause and due process. Many suits have stressed that employees have job rights that must be balanced against EAW.

**BNA**

**3610 Employment-at-will**
In this section, see how EAW has been affected by state court rulings on each of the three EAW exceptions.

**EAW AND THE COURTS** Nearly all states have adopted one or more statutes that limit an employer's right to discharge employees. The national restrictions include race, age, sex, national origin, religion, and disabilities. Restrictions on other areas vary from state to state. In general, courts have recognized three different rationales for hearing EAW cases.

- *Public policy exception:* This exception to EAW holds that an employee can sue if he or she was fired for a reason that violates public policy. For example, if an employee refused to commit perjury and was fired, he could sue.

**FIGURE 17–2** *Employment-at-Will Statement*

### Employment-At-Will

On the BNA CD-ROM attached to this text, Section 3605.40.10 contains sample employment-at-will wording on an acknowledgment form that employees sign upon receiving an employee handbook or policy manual. It is reproduced here so that typical at-will language can be reviewed by readers.

## At-Will Acknowledgment Form

I, _____ , acknowledge that my employment with EMPLOYER is an at-will relationship that has no specific duration. This means that I can resign my employment at any time, with or without reason or advance notice, and that EMPLOYER has the right to terminate my employment at any time, with or without reason or advance notic

I also acknowledge that no officer, supervisor, or employee of EMPLOYER, other than the chief executive officer and the vice president of HR, has the authority to promise or agree to any substantive terms of or conditions of employment different from those slated in the written guidelines and policies contained in the employee handbook I received from EMPLOYER. I also understand that any different employment agreement or arrangement entered into by the chief executive officer or vice president of HR must be clearly stated in writing and signed by both of those individuals.

Furthermore, I acknowledge that the employee handbook I received from EMPLOYER is neither a contract of employment nor a legal document, and nothing in the handbook creates an expressed or implied contract of employment. I understand that I should consult my supervisor or a representative of the HR department if I have any questions that are not answered in this handbook.

**Signed:** _____ **Date:** _____

SOURCE: Reprinted with permission from *Employment Guide on CD*, by The Bureau of National Affairs, Inc. (800-372-1033) <http://www.bna.com>

- *Implied employment contract:*  This approach holds that the employee will not be fired as long as he or she does the job. Long service, promises of continued employment, and lack of criticism of job performance imply continuing employment.
- *Good faith and fair dealing:*  This approach suggests that a covenant of good faith and fair dealing exists between the employer and at-will employees. If the employer has broken this covenant by unreasonable behavior, the employee has legal recourse.

**WRONGFUL DISCHARGE** Employers who violate EAW restrictive statutes may be found guilty of **wrongful discharge,** which occurs when an employer terminates an individual's employment for reasons that are illegal or improper. Some state courts have recognized certain nonstatutory grounds for wrongful-discharge suits. Additionally, courts generally have held that unionized workers cannot pursue EAW actions as at-will employees because they are covered by the grievance-arbitration process.

A landmark court case in wrongful discharge is *Fortune v. National Cash Register Company.* The case involved the firing of a salesman (Fortune) who had been with National Cash Register (NCR) for 25 years.[9] Fortune was fired shortly after winning a large order that would have earned him a big commission. From the evidence, the court concluded that he was wrongfully discharged because NCR wanted to avoid paying him the commission, which violated the covenant of good faith and fair dealings.

Wrongful-discharge lawsuits have become a major concern for many firms. According to one study, the median compensatory award for wrongful-termination cases lost by employers was $204,310. The same study found that wrongfully discharged executives won their cases 58% of the time, but general laborers won only 42% of their cases.[10]

The lesson of wrongful-discharge suits is that employers should take care to see that dismissals are handled properly, that all HR management systems are in order, and that due process and fair play are observed. Suggestions for preparing for the defense of any such lawsuits are shown in Figure 17–3.

One often-cited case involving "just cause" examined the right of an employer to terminate an employee following investigation of allegations that a company vice president had sexually harassed two employees. The employee filed suit that he had been terminated without good cause, because the allegations had not been proven. Despite a lower court ruling for the employee, the California Supreme Court ruled that the company had conducted a proper investigation, had not reached its decision arbitrarily, and had a reasonable belief that the employee had engaged in the impermissible conduct.[11] Therefore, this case emphasizes the importance of employers using due process and conducting appropriate investigations when handling employee disciplinary situations.

## Just Cause

What constitutes **just cause** as sufficient justification for employment-related actions such as dismissal usually is spelled out in union contracts, but often is not as clear in at-will situations. While the definition of *just cause* varies, the criteria used by courts have become well-defined. They appear in Figure 17–4.

Related to just cause is the concept of **constructive discharge,** which occurs when an employer deliberately makes conditions intolerable in an attempt

**Wrongful discharge**
Occurs when an employer terminates an individual's employment for reasons that are illegal or improper.

**Just cause**
Sufficient justification for taking employment-related actions.

**Constructive discharge**
Occurs when an employer deliberately makes conditions intolerable in an attempt to get an employee to quit.

**FIGURE 17–3** *Keys for Defense in Wrongful Discharge: The "Paper Trail"*

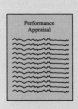 **Performance Appraisal**
Make sure performance appraisals give an accurate picture of the person's performance.

 **Written Records**
Have good written records on behaviors leading to dismissal.

 **Written Warning**
Warn employees in writing before dismissal.

 **Group Involvement**
Involve more than one person in termination decision.

 **Grounds for Dismissal**
Put grounds for dismissal in writing.

to get an employee to quit. Under normal circumstances, an employee who resigns rather than being dismissed cannot later collect damages for violation of legal rights. An exception to this rule occurs when the courts find that the working conditions are so intolerable as to *force* a reasonable employee to resign. Then, the resignation is considered a discharge. For example, an employee had been told he should resign but refused. He was then given lesser assignments, publicly ridiculed by his supervisor, and threatened each day with dismissal. He finally resigned and sued his employer, and the judge held that he had been "constructively discharged." His employer had to pay damages because it had forced him to resign.

**FIGURE 17–4** *Just-Cause Determinants*

**Just-Cause Determinants**

- Was the employee warned of the consequences of the conduct?
- Was the employer's rule reasonable?
- Did management investigate before disciplining?
- Was the investigation fair and impartial?
- Was there evidence of guilt?
- Were the rules and penalties applied in an evenhanded fashion?
- Was the penalty reasonable, given the offense?

## Due Process

**Due process**
In employment settings, the opportunity for individuals to explain and defend their actions against charges of misconduct or other reasons.

**Distributive justice**
Perceived fairness in the distribution of outcomes.

**Procedural justice**
Perceived fairness of the process used to make decisions about employees.

In employment settings, **due process** is the opportunity for individuals to explain and defend their actions against charges of misconduct or other reasons. Figure 17–5 shows some factors that are considered when evaluating whether due process was provided to an individual. These factors usually must be addressed by HR managers and their employers if due process procedures are to be perceived as fair by the courts.

**DISTRIBUTIVE JUSTICE AND PROCEDURAL JUSTICE** Employees' perceptions of fairness or justice in their treatment reflect at least two factors. First, people prefer favorable *outcomes* for themselves. They decide how favorable their outcomes are by comparing them with those of others, given their relative situations. This decision involves the concept of **distributive justice,** which deals with the question: Is the way the outcomes were distributed fair?

**Procedural justice** also is involved in whether an action generally will be viewed as fair by an employee. It focuses on whether the *procedures* that led to an action were appropriate, were clear, and gave appropriate opportunity for input. Procedural justice deals with the question: Was the process used to make the decision fair? Some research has found that if organizations provide procedural justice, employees are more likely to respond to positive behaviors that benefit organizations in return.[12]

**DUE PROCESS AND UNIONIZED EMPLOYEES** For unionized employees, due process usually refers to the right to use the grievance procedure specified in the union contract. Due process may mean including specific steps in the grievance process, imposing time limits, following arbitration procedures, and providing knowledge of disciplinary penalties. More discussion of the grievance process and procedures in unions is contained in Chapter 18.

**NONUNION COMPLAINT PROCESSES** Compared with due process procedures specified in union contracts, procedures for at-will employees are more varied and

**FIGURE 17–5** ***Due Process Considerations***

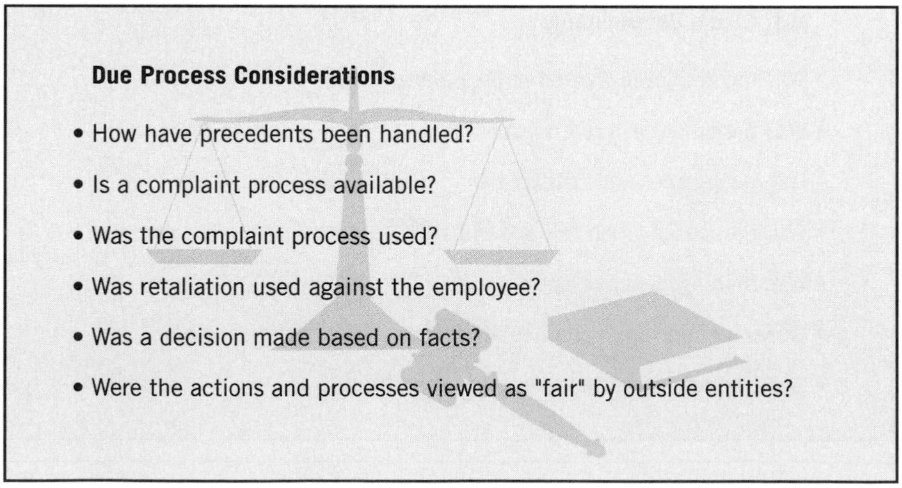
Due Process Considerations
• How have precedents been handled?
• Is a complaint process available?
• Was the complaint process used?
• Was retaliation used against the employee?
• Was a decision made based on facts?
• Were the actions and processes viewed as "fair" by outside entities?

may address a broader range of issues. Nonunion organizations should have formal complaint procedures providing due process for their employees. Just the presence of such a formal complaint mechanism is one indicator that an employee has been given due process. Further, if the due process procedure is seen as fair and available for use, employees with complaints are less likely to sue their employers.

## Due Process and Alternative Dispute Resolutions (ADR)

Alternative means of ensuring that due process occurs in cases involving employee rights are being used with increasing frequency. A major reason for their growth is dissatisfaction with the expense and delays common in the court system when lawsuits are filed.[13] The most common of the alternative dispute resolution (ADR) methods are arbitration, peer review panels, and ombudsmen.

**ARBITRATION** Because employers and employees do not always agree, disagreements often mean lawsuits and big legal bills to determine settlement. One alternative is **arbitration,** which uses a neutral third party to make a decision, thereby making use of the court system unnecessary. While arbitration has been a common feature of union contracts, a growing number of employers are requiring that arbitration be used to settle nonunion employment-related disputes.

**Arbitration**
Process that uses a neutral third party to make a decision.

Many firms have required *compulsory arbitration*. This approach requires employees to sign a preemployment agreement stating that all disputes will be submitted to arbitration, and that employees waive their rights to pursue legal action until arbitration has been completed. However, because the arbitrators often are selected by the employers, and because arbitrators may not be required to issue written decisions and opinions, many critics see the use of arbitration in employment-related situations as unfair.[14] For instance, a female stockbroker was fired and was unable to pursue her sex discrimination claim because she had signed a mandatory arbitration clause when joining the brokerage firm 13 years earlier.[15]

Continuing pressure from state courts, federal employment regulatory commissions, and additional cases have challenged compulsory arbitration as being unfair in some situations. In 1998, the U.S. Supreme Court declined to review a lower-court ruling favorable to employees. As a result, employers cannot force workers to use compulsory arbitration in job-related discrimination cases. Also, it was noted that voluntary arbitration can be agreed to by employees, but blanket mandatory arbitration agreements requiring all employees to waive their rights to pursue legal action were too broad.[16] Consequently, it is recommended that employers eliminate the mandatory arbitration agreements and consider using either individually signed voluntary agreements or other ADR means.[17]

**PEER REVIEW PANELS** Some employers allow employees to appeal disciplinary actions to an internal committee of employees. A **peer review panel** is composed of employees who hear appeals from disciplined employees and make recommendations or decisions. In general, these panels reverse management decisions much less often than might be expected. Such bodies really serve as the last stage of a formal complaint process for nonunion employees. Their use reduces the likelihood of unhappy employees filing lawsuits. Also, if lawsuits are filed, the employer's case is strengthened when a peer group of employees has reviewed the employer's decision and found it to be appropriate.

**Peer review panel**
Alternative dispute resolution method in which a panel of employees hear appeals from disciplined employees and make recommendations or decisions.

**Ombudsman**

Person outside the normal chain of command who acts as a problem solver for management and employees.

**ORGANIZATIONAL OMBUDSMAN** Another means that some organizations use to ensure process fairness is through an **ombudsman,** who is a person outside the normal chain of command who acts as a problem solver for management and employees. Some firms using ombudsmen are Rockwell, Volvo, and Johnson & Johnson, as well as others that are less well known.[18]

# Balancing Employer Security Concerns and Employee Rights

**Right to privacy**

Defined in legal terms for individuals as the freedom from unauthorized and unreasonable intrusion into their personal affairs.

The **right to privacy** that individuals have is defined in legal terms as the freedom from unauthorized and unreasonable intrusion into their personal affairs. Although the right to privacy is not specifically identified in the U.S. Constitution, a number of past Supreme Court cases have established that such a right must be considered. Also, several states have right-to-privacy statutes. Additionally, federal acts related to privacy have been passed, some of which affect HR policies and priorities in organizations.

The growing use of technology in organizations is making it more difficult to balance employer security rights with employee privacy concerns. Although computers, cameras, and telecommunications systems are transforming many workplaces, the usage of these items by employers to monitor employee actions is raising concerns that the privacy rights of employees are being threatened.

On one side, employers have a legitimate need to ensure that employees are performing their jobs properly in a secure environment. On the other side, employees have expectations that the rights to privacy that they have outside of work also exist at work. Although these two views may seem clear, balancing them becomes more difficult when addressing such issues as access to employee records, employees' freedom of speech, workplace performance monitoring and surveillance, employer investigations, and substance abuse and drug testing.

## Rights Issues and Employee Records

As a result of concerns about protecting individual privacy rights, the Privacy Act of 1974 was passed. It includes provisions affecting HR record-keeping systems. This law applies *only* to federal agencies and organizations supplying services to the federal government; but similar state laws, somewhat broader in scope, also have been passed. Regulation of private employers on this issue for the most part is a matter of state rather than federal law. Public-sector employees have greater access to their files in most states than do private-sector employees.

The following legal issues are involved in employee rights to privacy and HR records. These issues include rights to:

● Access personal information
● Respond to unfavorable information
● Correct erroneous information
● Know when information is given to a third party

**AMERICANS WITH DISABILITIES ACT (ADA) AND EMPLOYEE MEDICAL RECORDS**
Record-keeping and retention practices have been affected by the following provision in the Americans with Disabilities Act (ADA):

Information from all medical examinations and inquiries must be kept apart from general personnel files as a separate confidential medical record available only under limited conditions specified in the ADA.[19]

As interpreted by attorneys and HR practitioners, this provision requires that all medical-related information be maintained separately from all other confidential files. As Figure 17–6 shows, the result of all the legal restrictions is that many employers are establishing several separate files on each employee.

**SECURITY OF EMPLOYEE RECORDS** It is important that specific access restrictions and security procedures for employee records be established. These restrictions and procedures are designed to protect both the privacy of employees and employers from potential liability for improper disclosure of personal information. The following guidelines have been offered regarding employer access and storage of employee records:[20]

- Restrict access to records to a limited number of individuals.
- Utilize confidential passwords for accessing employee records in an HRIS database.

**FIGURE 17–6** *Employee Record Files*

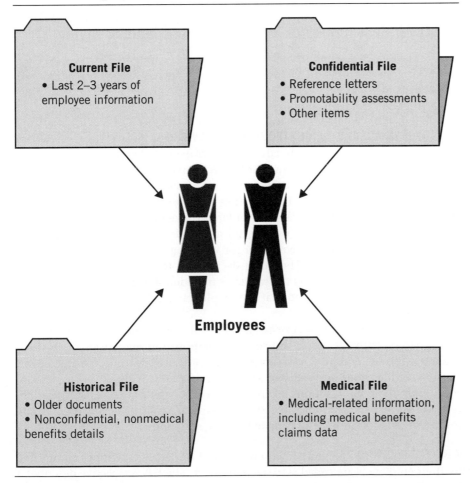

**Current File**
- Last 2–3 years of employee information

**Confidential File**
- Reference letters
- Promotability assessments
- Other items

**Employees**

**Historical File**
- Older documents
- Nonconfidential, nonmedical benefits details

**Medical File**
- Medical-related information, including medical benefits claims data

- Set up separate files and restricted databases for especially sensitive employee information.
- Inform employees of types of data retained.
- Purge employee records of outdated data.
- Release employee information only with employee's consent.

Regarding the last point, employers have run afoul of laws on employee records when other employers have asked for information about former employees. Many lawyers recommend the release of only the most basic employment history, such as job title, dates of employment, and ending salary.

**EMPLOYEE ACCESS TO HR RECORDS** One concern that has been addressed in various court decisions and laws is the right of employees to have access to their own files. Related concerns are the types of information kept in those files and the methods used to acquire that information. In other business-related areas, federal laws have been passed that allow individuals access to their own files, such as credit records and medical records. But only in some states have laws been passed to require employers to give employees access to their HR records, or parts of them. Many of these state laws allow employers to exclude certain types of information from inspection, such as reference letters written by former employers. Some employers in states without access laws nevertheless allow employees access to certain records.

## Employer Restrictions on Employees' Free Speech Rights

The right of individuals to have freedom of speech is protected by the U.S. Constitution. However, that freedom is not an unrestricted one in the workplace. Three areas in which employees' freedom of speech have collided with employers' restrictions are discussed next.

**EMPLOYEE ADVOCACY OF CONTROVERSIAL VIEWS** One area of free speech involves the right of employees to advocate controversial viewpoints at work. One example of an employer restricting free speech involved a woman working at a large telecommunications firm. The woman, an ardent opponent of abortion, wore buttons to work that had pictures of fetuses on them. When other employees complained, the employer ordered the employee to remove the buttons. When she refused, she was disciplined and ultimately terminated. The woman filed suit against the employer for violating her freedom of speech and wrongfully discharging her. The Court decision in this case ruled that the employer had the right to restrict the woman's freedom of expression because of its effect on other employees, and that the employer could have workplace limitations for offensive items.[21]

Numerous other examples can be cited as well. For instance, can an employee of a tobacco company join in antismoking demonstrations outside of work, or can a disgruntled employee at a nonunion employer wear a union badge on his cap at work? In situations such as these, it is important for employers to demonstrate that disciplinary actions taken against employees can be justified for job-related reasons, and that due process procedures are followed. This is especially important when dealing with whistle-blowing situations.

**WHISTLE-BLOWING** Individuals who report real or perceived wrongs committed by their employers are called **whistle-blowers.** The HR Perspective describes a research study on whistle-blowing.

***LOGGING ON . . .***
**Privacy and Employment**
This website is by a non-profit organization. It is a leading resource for information on new and existing business privacy issues.

**http://www.pandab.org/**

**Whistle-blowers**
Individuals who report real or perceived wrongs committed by their employers.

## HR PERSPECTIVE
# Research on Whistle-blowing

As whistle-blowing by employees has become more prevalent, media coverage of the employees doing the whistle-blowing and the employer's actions have become widespread. But for HR professionals and others, it may be important to be familiar with the characteristics of those who report illegal or inappropriate actions.

Sims and Keenan conducted a study on organizational and intrapersonal factors present when external whistle-blowing has occurred. Their study, published in the *Journal of Business Ethics*, focused on external whistle-blowing, which occurs when present or former employees report wrongful actions to individuals or entities outside the organization.

Using both graduate and undergraduate students, the researchers presented three ethical business situations to the research subjects. Three factors were used to analyze the research subjects' responses to the situations: (1) ideal values, which was how the situations should be addressed, including external whistle-blowing; (2) supervisor expectations, which asked subjects to identify how they believed a supervisor would expect them to respond; and (3) organizational commitment, which focused on measuring organizational loyalty.

The study found that external whistle-blowing was more likely to occur when supervisory support and informal policies of external whistle-blowing existed. Interestingly, formal whistle-blowing policies were found to predict the whistle-blowing decision; but evidently, having these policies made external whistle-blowing less likely. The researchers also found that women were less likely to choose external whistle-blowing methods than men were. Even though this research study was conducted using students and hypothetical situations, the researchers suggest that their findings could be used by managers in actual organizations. They believe that organizations would benefit from providing both formal whistle-blowing policies and training of supervisors on handling whistle-blowing situations.[22]

Two key questions in regard to whistle-blowing are (1) When do employees have the right to speak out with protection from retribution? (2) When do employees violate the confidentiality of their jobs by speaking out? Often, the answers are difficult to determine. What is clear is that retaliation against whistle-blowers is not allowed, based on a number of court decisions.[23]

Whistle-blowers are less likely to lose their jobs in public employment than in private employment, because most civil service systems have rules protecting whistle-blowers. However, there is no comprehensive whistle-blowing law that protects the right to free speech of both public and private employees.

Two cases illustrate the consequences of whistle-blowing in the private sector. In one case a scientist, who was the director of toxicology for a major oil company, was awarded almost $7 million. The scientist discovered that a Japanese subsidiary of the oil company was using gasoline containing a high level of benzene, which is carcinogenic. Even though Japanese industry guidelines called for lower levels, no Japanese law was broken. The director complained inside the firm, but was fired. He then filed suit under a New Jersey law protecting whistle-blowers, winning his case and the large monetary settlement.[24]

The other case involved Archer-Daniels Midland (ADM), a large agribusiness firm. A former executive of ADM, Mark Whitacre, blew the whistle on ADM's participation in a price-fixing scheme with other industry competitors throughout the world. ADM ended up pleading guilty and had to pay a $100 million fine. Whitacre, who exposed the scheme, also went to jail when further investigation revealed that he had stolen $9 million through the use of false invoices and foreign bank accounts, and then lied about his involvement.[25]

**MONITORING OF E-MAIL AND VOICE MAIL** Both e-mail and voice-mail systems increasingly are seen by employers as areas where employers have a right to monitor what is said and transmitted. Information and telecommunications technological advances have became a major issue for employers regarding employee privacy. The use of e-mail and voice mail increases every day, also raising each employer's risks of being liable if they monitor or inspect employee electronic communications.[26]

The Electronic Communications Privacy Act (ECPA) has been applied to employer monitoring of e-mail and voice mail. Originally intended for applications by law enforcement officials, the provisions of the ECPA have been extended by court decisions to cover employer "eavesdropping" on e-mail or voice mail. The act requires that at least one party to the electronic communication has provided consent, but that employers can use electronic monitoring as part of the ordinary course of business.

Additionally, the ECPA allows entities that provide electronic communications services to have access to stored electronic communications. This provision has been applied very broadly to employers, because they provide the electronic communications services to employees.

To address the various concerns regarding monitoring of e-mail and voice mail, many employers have established the following policies:

- Voice mail, e-mail, and computer files are provided by the employer and are for business use only.
- Use of these media for personal reasons is restricted and subject to employer review.
- All computer passwords and codes must be available to the employer.
- The employer reserves the right to monitor or search any of the media, without notice, for business purposes.

The most important actions that every employer can take to decrease potential exposure to lawsuits are to: (1) create an *electronic communications policy;* (2) inform employees and have them *sign an acknowledgment;* and (3) *strictly enforce* every portion of the policy and monitor usage for business purposes only. As Figure 17–7 indicates, it is especially important to inform employees that their electric communications may be monitored, and have them acknowledge the policy and sign a consent form. Thus employers can reduce their employees' expectations of privacy, as well as their own potential liabilities. Experts note that due to ECPA considerations, employers should concentrate their monitoring of e-mail and voice mail on stored messages, rather than messages in transit.[27]

**TRACKING EMPLOYEE INTERNET USAGE** Another concern in which employer-employee rights must be balanced is employee usage of employer-provided access to the Internet. As more and more employees access the Internet for business purposes, a major concern is employees' use of the Internet for personal purposes that may be inappropriate. For example, some employees in different organizations have accessed pornographic or other websites which could create problems for employers. If law enforcement investigations were conducted, the employer could be accused of aiding and abetting illegal behavior. Therefore, many employers have purchased software that tracks the websites accessed by employees. Also, some employers use software programs for blocking certain categories and websites that would not be appropriate for business use.

**FIGURE 17–7** *Guidelines for Employer E-mail Monitoring*

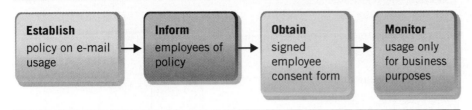

| **Establish** policy on e-mail usage | → | **Inform** employees of policy | → | **Obtain** signed employee consent form | → | **Monitor** usage only for business purposes |

Another concern about Internet usage is composing and/or forwarding personal messages to and from others outside the company. For instance, individuals may receive jokes or other items that clearly are not business related, and then may forward them to coworkers and friends both inside and outside the organization. If the content of the jokes or messages is sexual or otherwise inappropriate, a possibility of sexual harassment may exist. At one financial services firm, some African American employees filed race discrimination charges against their employer because of racist jokes that were forwarded to them and others in the firm. Ultimately the firm resolved the complaint by firing the two executives transmitting the jokes.[28]

A growing number of employers have developed and disseminated Internet usage policies. Communicating these policies to employees, enforcing them by monitoring employee Internet usage, and disciplining offenders are the ways employers ensure that appropriate usage of the Internet access occurs.

## Workplace Performance Monitoring and Surveillance

Federal constitutional rights, such as the right to protection from unreasonable search and seizure, protect an individual only against the activities of the government. Thus, employees of both private-sector and governmental employers can be monitored, observed, and searched at work by representatives of the employer. This principle has been reaffirmed by several court decisions, which have held that both private-sector and government employers may search desks and files without search warrants if they believe that work rules have been violated. Often, workplace searches and surveillance are used as part of employee performance monitoring. Employers also conduct workplace investigations for theft and other illegal behavior. As Figure 17–8 on the next page indicates, various types of monitoring and surveillance means are relatively widespread.

**EMPLOYEE PERFORMANCE MONITORING** Employee performance may be monitored to measure performance, ensure performance quality and customer service, check for theft, or enforce company rules or laws. Performance monitoring occurs with truck drivers, nurses, teleservice customer service representatives, and many other jobs. The common concern in a monitored workplace is usually not whether monitoring should be used, but how it should be conducted, how the information should be used, and how feedback should be communicated to employees.

As a minimum, employers should obtain a signed employee consent form indicating that performance monitoring and taping of phone calls will occur. Also, employers should communicate that monitoring is done and will be done

**FIGURE 17–8** *Employer Monitoring Practices*

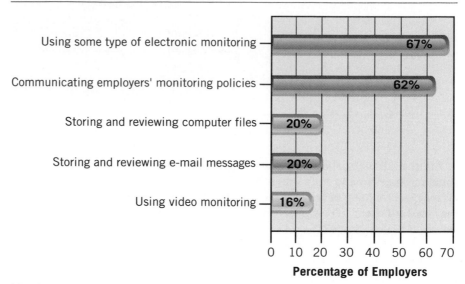

SOURCE: Based on data in American Management Association survey of 1,085 HR managers, reported in "E-mail, Computer Monitoring Is Rising," *Bulletin to Management*, November 26, 1998, 369.

regularly. However, simply stating that employee conversations may be monitored does not eliminate all liability. In one case the employer recorded 22 hours of an employee's personal calls, in order to catch the employee admitting to theft of company property. The court refused to find consent where the employer had indicated that it "might" use monitoring to reduce employee personal phone calls.[29]

Finally, it is recommended that employers publish feedback on monitoring results, to help employees improve their performance or to commend them for good performance. For example, one major catalog retailer allows employees to listen to their customer service calls and rate their own performance. Then the employees meet with their supervisors to discuss both positive and negative performance issues.

**VIDEO SURVEILLANCE AT WORK** Numerous employers have installed video surveillance systems in workplaces. Sometimes these video systems are used to ensure employee security, such as in parking lots, garages, and dimly lighted exterior areas. Other employers have installed them in retail sales floors, production areas, parts and inventory rooms, and lobbies.

But it is when video surveillance is extended into employee restrooms, changing rooms, and other more private areas that employer rights and employee privacy collide. For instance, a small Midwestern firm videotaped women changing in and out of their uniforms. Male managers in the firm later viewed the tapes for entertainment. In this case a court found that the employer had invaded employees' privacy, and that there appeared to be no appropriate business purposes for the taping. In another case involving an electric utility, the use of hidden cameras, even as part of a criminal investigation for drug dealing in a men's locker room, was ruled to be questionable.[30]

As with other forms of surveillance, it is important that employers develop a video surveillance policy, inform employees about it, do it only for legitimate business purposes, and strictly limit those who view the video surveillance results. Also, except in unusual circumstances, employers should not have video surveillance in rest rooms, changing rooms, and other more private areas.

## Employer Investigations

Another area of concern regarding employee rights involves workplace investigations. Public-sector employees are protected by the Constitution in the areas of due process, search and seizure, and privacy. But employees in the private sector are not protected. Whether at work or off the job, unethical employee behavior is becoming an increasingly serious problem for organizatons. On the job, unethical behavior includes theft, illegal drug use, falsification of documents, misuse of company funds, and disclosure of organizational secrets. Workplace investigations are used as well by retailers and other employers, as Figure 17–9 indicates.

## Employee Theft

An increasing problem faced by employers is theft of employer property and vital company secrets. According to one study, workplace theft and fraud have resulted in a 6% increase in the prices charged by employers to consumers.[31] For instance, employee theft is estimated to cost retailers over $10 billion per year. Some major retailers have even joined forces to create a Theftnet database of workers who have confessed to theft, and all job applicants are checked to see if they appear in Theftnet. Any person appearing in Theftnet is not hired.[32]

**POLYGRAPH AND HONESTY TESTING** The theory behind a polygraph is that the act of lying produces stress, which in turn causes observable physical changes. An examiner can thus interpret the physical responses to specific questions and make a judgment as to whether the person being tested is practicing deception. However, the Polygraph Protection Act prohibits the use of

**FIGURE 17–9** *Methods of Workplace Investigations*

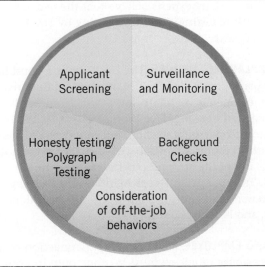

polygraphs for most preemployment screening and for judging a person's honesty while employed.

"Pencil-and-paper" honesty tests have gained popularity recently. They are not restricted by the Polygraph Protection Act nor by the laws of most states. Many organizations are using this alternative to polygraph testing, and over two dozen variations of such tests are being sold.

Honesty tests are developed from test items that differentiate between people known to be honest and those known to be dishonest. (This is similar to the way personality tests are developed.) It is not always easy to determine who is honest for the purpose of validating the tests. In the private sector, honesty tests do not violate any legal rights of employees if employers adhere to state laws. The Fifth Amendment (which protects persons from compulsory self-incrimination) may be a basis for prohibiting such tests in public-sector employment.

**BEHAVIOR OFF THE JOB** It is especially difficult for an employer to establish that there is a "just cause" for disciplining employees for their off-the-job behavior. The premise is that an employer should not control the lives of its employees off the job except when there are clear job-related consequences. However, in general, disciplinary action for off-the-job behavior of employees is unsettling to both employers and employees. Further, the general public is leery of employers' investigating the off-the-job behavior of their workers. Many workers believe that their employers have no right to monitor or question employees' private lives, lifestyles, and off-work activities.

## Employee Substance Abuse and Employer Drug Testing

The issue of substance abuse and drug testing at work has received a great deal of attention. The importance of the problem to HR management is clear. Concern about substance abuse at work also is appropriate, given that accident rates, absenteeism, and worker compensation costs are higher for workers using illegal substances. The extent of substance abuse problems is seen in U.S. Department of Labor estimates that 70% of all users of illegal drugs are employed, totaling over 10 million people.[33] However, among workers, the rate of drug usage has declined from 18% a decade ago to about 5.5% currently, according to data from a major pharmaceutical firm.[34] Many experts believe that the decline is due to increased usage of workplace drug testing, including testing by employers covered by the federal act discussed next.

**DRUG-FREE WORKPLACE ACT OF 1988** The U.S. Supreme Court has ruled that certain drug-testing plans do not violate the Constitution. But private employer programs are governed mainly by state laws, which currently are a confusing hodgepodge. Passage of the Drug-Free Workplace Act in 1988 has required government contractors to take steps to eliminate employee drug usage. Failure to do so can lead to contract termination. Tobacco and alcohol are not considered controlled substances under the act, and off-the-job drug use is not included. Additionally, the U.S. Transportation Department requires testing of truck and bus drivers, train crews, mass-transit employees, airline pilots and mechanics, pipeline workers, and licensed sailors.

**DRUG TESTING AND EMPLOYEE RIGHTS** Disciplinary action of an employee because of substance-abuse problems must be done only in keeping with the due process described in an employer's policy. Unless state or local law prohibits testing, employers have a right to require applicants or employees to submit to a drug test. Random drug testing of current employees may be more controversial, and public agencies must have "probable cause" to conduct drug tests.

However, there are several arguments against drug testing: (1) It violates employees' rights. (2) Drugs may not affect job performance in every case. (3) Employers may abuse the results of tests. (4) Drug tests may be inaccurate, or the results can be misinterpreted.

It is interesting to note that employee attitudes toward drug testing appear to have changed. Apparently, experience with workplace drug problems has made managers and employees less tolerant of drug users. Drug testing appears to be most acceptable to employees when they see the procedures being used as fair, and when characteristics of the job (such as danger to other people) require that the employee be alert and fully functioning. *Procedural justice* appears to be an important issue in perceptions of fairness of drug testing, but drug testing raises less concern about employee rights than it once did.

**TYPES OF TESTS FOR DRUGS**  The most common tests for drug use are urinalysis, radioimmunoassay of hair, and fitness-for-duty testing. Urinalysis is the test most frequently used. It requires a urine sample that must be tested at a lab. There is concern about sample switching, and the test detects drug use only over the past few days. But urinalysis is generally accurate and well accepted.

Hair radioimmunoassay requires a strand of an employee's hair, which is analyzed for traces of illegal substances. These tests are based on scientific studies indicating that a relationship exists between drug dosage and the concentration of drugs detected in the hair. A 1.6-inch hair sample provides a 90-day profile. Sample swapping is more difficult than in urinalysis, and the longer time period covered is advantageous. However, the testing is somewhat controversial, and testing is not recommended following accidents because it does not detect how recent the drug usage has been.[35]

The fitness-for-duty tests discussed in Chapter 16 can be used alone or in conjunction with drug testing. These tests can also distinguish individuals who may have used alcohol or prescription drugs that might impair their abilities to perform their jobs.

**CONDUCTING DRUG TESTS**  Employers who conduct drug tests can do so for both applicants and employees. As mentioned in Chapter 9, preemployment drug testing has become widely used. Its use by more employers is thought to contribute to the decline in employee drug use. It has been reported to employers in some areas that word spreads among applicants about which employers test and which do not test. Therefore, substance abusers do not even apply to employers who conduct preemployment drug tests. The rights of those testing positive who are not yet employed have been ruled to be different from the rights of those who are employees.

If drug testing is done, three different policies are used by employers: (1) random testing of everyone at periodic intervals; (2) testing only when there is probable cause; or (3) testing after accidents. Each method raises its own set of problems.

If testing is done for probable-cause reasons, it is important that managers be trained on how to handle those situations. It is important that managerial action be based on performance-related consequences, not just the substance usage itself. From a policy standpoint, it is most appropriate to test for drugs when the following conditions exist:

- Job consequences of abuse are so severe that they outweigh privacy concerns.
- Accurate test procedures are available.
- Written consent of the employee is obtained.
- Results are treated confidentially, as with any medical record.
- Employers have a complete drug program, including employee assistance for substance users.

# HR Policies, Procedures, and Rules

**Policies**
General guidelines that focus organizational actions

It is useful at this point to consider some guidelines for HR policies, procedures, and rules. They greatly affect employee rights (just discussed) and discipline (discussed next). Where there is a choice among actions, **policies** act as general guidelines that focus organizational actions. Policies are general in nature, while procedures and rules are specific to the situation. The important role of policies in guiding organizational decision making requires that they be reviewed regularly, because obsolete policies can result in poor decisions and poor coordination. Policy proliferation also must be carefully monitored. Failure to review, add to, or delete policies as situations change may lead to problems.

**Procedures**
Customary methods of handling activities.

**Procedures** are customary methods of handling activities and are more specific than policies. For example, a policy may state that employees will be given vacations. Procedures will establish a specific method for authorizing vacation time without disrupting work.

**Rules**
Specific guidelines that regulate and restrict the behavior of individuals.

**Rules** are specific guidelines that regulate and restrict the behavior of individuals. They are similar to procedures in that they guide action and typically allow no discretion in their application. Rules reflect a management decision that action be taken—or not taken—in a given situation, and they provide more specific behavioral guidelines than policies. For example, one computer-repair company has a policy stating that management intends to provide the highest-quality repair service in the area. The rule that repair technicians must have several technical product certifications or they will not be hired promotes this policy, and this constrains HR selection decisions.

## Responsibilities for HR Policy Coordination

For policies, procedures, and rules to be effective, coordination between the HR unit and other managers is vital. As Figure 17–10 shows, managers are the main users and enforcers of rules, procedures, and policies; and they should receive some training and explanation in how to carry them out. The HR unit supports managers, reviews disciplinary rules, and trains managers to use them. It is critical that any conflict between the two entities be resolved so that employees receive appropriate treatment.

## Guidelines for HR Policies and Rules

Well-designed HR policies and rules should be consistent, necessary, applicable, understandable, reasonable, and distributed and communicated. A discussion of each characteristic follows.

FIGURE 17–10 *Typical Responsibilities for HR Policies and Rules*

| HR Unit | Managers |
|---|---|
| • Designs formal mechanisms for coordinating HR policies<br>• Provides advice in development of organizationwide HR policies, procedures, and rules<br>• Provides information on application of HR policies, procedures, and rules<br>• Explains HR rules to managers<br>• Trains managers to administer policies, procedures, and rules | • Help in developing HR policies and rules<br>• Review policies and rules with all employees<br>• Apply HR policies, procedures, and rules<br>• Explain rules and policies to all employees |

**CONSISTENT** Rules should be consistent with organizational policies, and policies should be consistent with organizational goals. The principal intent of policies is to provide written guidelines and to specify actions. If some policies and rules are enforced and others are not, then all tend to lose their effectiveness.

**NECESSARY** HR policies and rules should reflect current organizational philosophy and directions. To this end, managers should confirm the intent and necessity of proposed rules and eliminate obsolete ones. Policies and rules should be reviewed whenever there is a major organizational change. Unfortunately, this review is not always done, and outdated rules are still on the books in many organizations.

**APPLICABLE** Because HR policies are general guidelines for action, they should be applicable to a large group of employees. For policies that are not general, the appropriate areas or people must be identified. For instance, if a sick-leave policy is applicable only to nonexempt employees, that should be specified in the company handbook. Policies and rules that apply only to one unit or type of job should be developed as part of specific guidelines for that unit or job.

**UNDERSTANDABLE** HR policies and rules should be written so employees can clearly understand them. One way to determine if policies and rules are understandable is to ask a cross-section of employees with various positions, education levels, and job responsibilities to explain the intent and meaning of a rule. If the answers are extremely varied, the rule should be rewritten.

**REASONABLE** Ideally, employees should see policies as fair and reasonable. Policies and rules that are perceived as being inflexible or as penalizing individuals unfairly should be reevaluated. For example, a rule forbidding workers to use the company telephone for personal calls may be unreasonable if emergency phone calls are occasionally necessary. Limiting the amount of time the telephone can be used for personal business and the number of calls might be more reasonble.

Some of the most ticklish policies and rules involve employee behavior. Dress codes are frequently controversial, and organizations that have them should be able to justify them to the satisfaction of both employees and outside sources who might question them. Information on policies regarding dress at work in organizations is shown in Figure 17–11.

**DISTRIBUTED AND COMMUNICATED** To be effective, HR policies must be distributed and communicated to employees. It is especially important that any changes in HR policies and rules be communicated to all employees. Employee handbooks can be designed creatively to explain policies and rules, so that employees can refer to them at times when no one is available to answer a question. Supervisors and managers can maintain discipline by reminding their employees about policies and rules. Because employee handbooks are widely used to do so, guidelines for their preparation and use are discussed next.

**FIGURE 17–11** *Dress Policies for Regular Work Days*

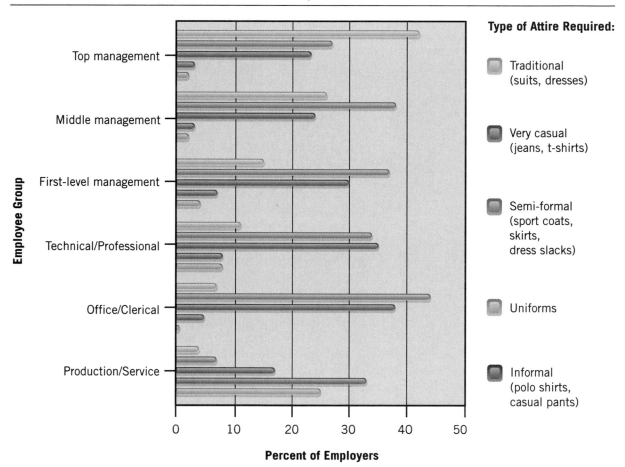

Note: Percentages are based on all 422 responding employers. Percentages in each column may not add to 100 due to rounding or having no response.

SOURCE: *Dress Policies and Casual Dress Days,* Personnel Policies Forum Survey No. 155, (January 1998). Copyright 1998 by The Bureau of National Affairs, Inc. (800-372-1033) <http://www.bna.com>

# Guidelines for an Employee Handbook

An employee handbook gives employees a reference source for company policies and rules and can be a positive tool for effective management of human resources. Even smaller organizations can prepare handbooks relatively easily using computer software. However, management should consider several factors when preparing handbooks.

**LEGAL REVIEW OF LANGUAGE** As mentioned earlier, there is a current legal trend to use employee handbooks against employers in lawsuits charging a broken "implied" contract. But that is no reason to abandon employee handbooks as a way to communicate policies to employees. *Not* having an employee handbook with HR policies spelled out can also leave an organization open to costly litigation and out-of-court settlements.

A more sensible approach is first to develop sound HR policies and employee handbooks to communicate them and then have legal counsel review the language contained in them. Recommendations include the following:

- *Eliminate controversial phrases:* For example, "permanent employee" as a phase often is used to describe those people who have passed a probationary period. This wording can lead to disagreement over what the parties meant by *permanent*. A more appropriate phrase is "regular employee."
- *Use disclaimers:* Contract disclaimers have been upheld in court, but only if they are prominently shown in the handbook.[36] However, there is a trade-off between disclaimers and the image presented by the handbook, so disclaimers should not be overused. A disclaimer also should appear on application forms. A disclaimer in the handbook can read as follows:

  This employee handbook is not intended to be a contract or any part of a contractual agreement between the employer and the employee. The employer reserves the right to modify, delete, or add to any policies set forth herein without notice and reserves the right to terminate an employee at any time with or without cause.

- *Keep the handbook current:* Many employers simply add new material to handbooks rather than deleting old, inapplicable rules. Those old rules can become the bases for new lawsuits. Consequently, handbooks and HR policies should be reviewed periodically and revised every few years.

**READABILITY** The specialists who prepare employee handbooks may not write at the appropriate level. One review of the reading level of some company handbooks revealed that on average they were written at the third-year college level, which is much higher than the typical reading level of employees in most organizations. One solution is to test the readability of the handbook on a sample of employees before it is published.

**USE** Another important factor to be considered in preparing an employee handbook is its method of use. Simply giving an employee a handbook and saying, "Here's all the information you need to know," is not sufficient.

It is important that the HR information be communicated and discussed. A growing number of firms are distributing employee handbooks electronically using an intranet, which enables employees to access policies in employee handbooks at any time.[37] Also, changes in policies in the handbook can be made electronically, rather than having to distribute correction pages and memos that must be filed with every handbook. In addition to distributing policies and rules in an employee handbook, it is important that communication about HR issues, policies, rules, and organizational information be disseminated widely.

## Communicating HR Information

HR communication focuses on the receipt and dissemination of HR data and information throughout the organization. *Downward communication* flows from top management to the rest of the organization and is essential to informing employees about what is and will be happening in the organization, and what top management expectations and goals are. *Upward communication* also is important, so that managers know about the ideas, concerns, and information needs of employees.

**HR PUBLICATIONS AND MEDIA** Organizations communicate with employees through internal publications and media, including newspapers, company magazines, organizational newsletters, videotapes, Internet postings, and computer technology. Whatever the formal means used, managers should make an honest attempt to communicate information employees need to know. Communication should not be solely a public relations tool to build the image of the organization. Bad news, as well as good news, should be reported objectively in readable style. For example, an airline publication distributed to employees has a question-and-answer section in which employees anonymously can submit tough questions to management. Management's answers are printed with the questions in every issue. Because every effort is made to give completely honest answers, this section has been very useful. The same idea fizzled in another large company because the questions were answered with "the company line," and employees soon lost interest in the less-than-candid replies.

Some employers produce *audiotapes* or *videotapes*—explaining benefit programs, corporate reorganizations, and revised HR policies and programs—that are shipped to each organizational branch. At those locations, the tapes are presented to employees in groups and then questions are addressed by a manager or someone from headquarters. The spread of electronic communications has made disseminating HR information more timely and widespread.

**ELECTRONIC COMMUNICATION: E-MAIL AND TELECONFERENCING** As electronic and telecommunications technologies have developed, many employers are adding more technologically based methods of communicating with employees. The growth of information systems in organizations has led to the widespread use of electronic mail. With the advent of e-mail systems, communication through organizations can be almost immediate. E-mail systems can operate worldwide through networks. Replies can be returned at once rather than in a week or more. One feature of e-mail systems is that they often result in the bypassing of formal organizational structure and channels.

Some organizations also communicate through *teleconferencing,* in which satellite technology links facilities and groups in various locations. In this way, the same message can be delivered simultaneously to various audiences.

**Suggestion system**
A formal method of obtaining employee input and upward communication.

**SUGGESTION SYSTEMS** A **suggestion system** is a formal method of obtaining employee input and upward communication. Such programs are becoming even more important as they are integrated with gainsharing or total quality management (TQM) efforts. Giving employees the opportunity to suggest changes or ways in which operations could be improved can encourage loyalty and commitment to the organization. Often, an employee in the work unit knows more about how waste can be eliminated, how hazards can be controlled, or how improvements can be made than do managers, who are not as close to the actual tasks performed. Many suggestion systems give financial rewards to employees for cost-saving suggestions, and often payments to employees are tied to a percentage of savings, up to some maximum level. Often committees of employees and managers are used to review and evaluate suggestions.

# Employee Discipline

Employee rights have been an appropriate introduction to employee discipline, because employee rights are often an issue in disciplinary cases. **Discipline** is a form of training that enforces organizational rules. Those most often affected by the discipline systems in an organization are problem employees. Fortunately, problem employees comprise a small number of employees, but they often are the ones who cause the most disciplinary situations. If employers fail to deal with problem employees, negative effects on other employees and work groups often result. Common disciplinary issues caused by problem employees include absenteeism, tardiness, productivity deficiencies, alcoholism, and insubordination.

Figure 17–12 shows a possible division of responsibilities for discipline between the HR unit and managers. Notice that managers and supervisors are the ones to make disciplinary decisions and administer the discipline. HR specialists often are consulted prior to disciplinary action being instituted, and they may assist managers in administering the disciplinary action.

**Discipline**
A form of training that enforces organizational rules.

## Approaches to Discipline

The disciplinary system (see Figure 17–13) can be viewed as an application of behavior modification for problem or unproductive employees. The best discipline is clearly self-discipline; when most people understand what is required at work, they can usually be counted on to do their jobs effectively. Yet some find that the

**FIGURE 17–12** *Typical Division of Responsibilities for Employee Rights and Discipline*

| HR Unit | Managers |
|---|---|
| • Designs HR procedures that consider employees' rights<br>• Designs progressive discipline process if nonunion<br>• Trains managers on the use of discipline process<br>• Assists managers with administration of discipline | • Are knowledgeable about organizational HR policies and rules<br>• Make disciplinary decisions<br>• Notify employees who violate policies and rules<br>• Discuss discipline follow-up with employees |

**FIGURE 17-13** *The Disciplinary System*

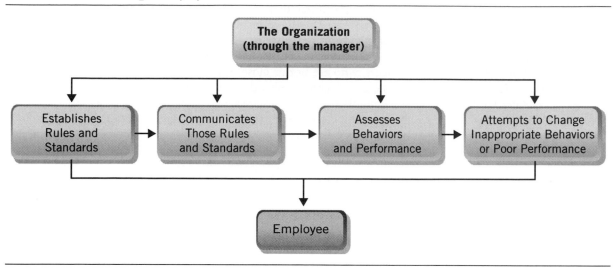

prospect of external discipline helps their self-discipline. This philosophy has led to the development of the positive discipline approach.

**POSITIVE DISCIPLINE APPROACH** The positive discipline approach builds on the philosophy that violations are actions that usually can be constructively corrected without penalty. In this approach, the focus is on fact-finding and guidance to encourage desirable behaviors, instead of on using penalties to discourage undesirable behaviors. There are four steps to positive discipline.

1. *Counseling:* Counseling can be an important part of the discipline process, because it gives a manager or supervisor the opportunity to identify employee work behavior problems and discuss solutions. The goal of this phase is to heighten employee awareness of organizational policies and rules. Knowledge of disciplinary actions may prevent violations. The emphasis is similar to that on preventing accidents. Counseling by a supervisor in the work unit can have positive effects. Often, people simply need to be made aware of rules.
2. *Written documentation:* If employee behavior has not been corrected, then a second conference is held between the supervisor and the employee. Whereas the first stage was done orally, this stage is documented in written form. As part of this phase, the employee and the supervisor develop written solutions to prevent further problems from occurring.
3. *Final warning:* When the employee does not follow the written solutions noted in the second step, a final warning conference is held. In that conference the supervisor emphasizes to the employee the importance of correcting the inappropriate actions. Some firms incorporate a *decision-day off,* in which the employee is given a day off with pay to develop a firm, written action plan to remedy the problem behaviors. The idea is to impress on the offender the seriousness of the problem and the manager's determination to see that the behavior is changed.
4. *Discharge:* If the employee fails to follow the action plan that was developed and further problem behaviors exist, then the supervisor will discharge the employee.

The advantage of this positive approach to discipline is that it focuses on problem solving. Also, because the employee is an active participant throughout the process, employers using this approach are more likely to win wrongful-discharge lawsuits if they are filed. The greatest difficulty with the positive approach to discipline is the extensive amount of training required for supervisors and managers to become effective counselors. Also, the process often takes more supervisory time than the progressive discipline approach discussed next.

**PROGRESSIVE DISCIPLINE APPROACH** Progressive discipline incorporates a sequence of steps into the shaping of employee behaviors. Figure 17–14 shows a typical progressive discipline system. Like the procedures in the figure, most progressive discipline procedures use verbal and written reprimands and suspension before resorting to dismissal. Thus, progressive discipline suggests that actions to modify behavior become progressively more severe as the employee continues to show improper behavior. For example, at one manufacturing firm, failure to call in when an employee is to be absent from work may lead to a suspension after the third offense in a year. Suspension sends a very strong message to an employee that undesirable job behavior must change or termination is likely to follow.[38]

*BNA:*
**1405.10–1405.50**
**Progressive Discipline**
A discussion of progressive discipline, the steps in it, and a model policy and form can be found here.

An employee is given opportunities to correct deficiencies before being dismissed. Following the progressive sequence ensures that both the nature and seriousness of the problem have been clearly communicated to the employee.

Not all steps in the progressive discipline procedure are followed in every case. Certain serious offenses are exempted from the progressive procedure and may result in immediate termination. Typical offenses leading to immediate termination are as follows:

- Intoxication at work
- Possession of weapons
- Alcohol or drug use at work

- Fighting
- Theft
- Falsifying employment application

**FIGURE 17–14** *Progressive Discipline Procedure*

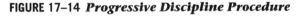

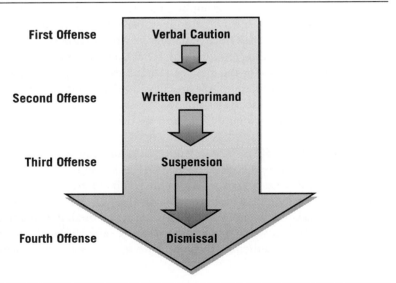

## Reasons Why Discipline Might Not Be Used

Sometimes managers are reluctant to use discipline. There are a number of reasons why discipline may not be used:

- *Organizational culture regarding discipline:* One factor affecting the use of discipline is the culture of the organization and managerial willingness to use discipline. If the organizational "norm" is to avoid penalizing problem employees, then managers are more likely not to use discipline. This reluctance to discipline extends even to dismissal of problem employees.[39]
- *Lack of support:* Many managers do not want to use discipline, because they fear that their decisions will not be supported by higher management. The degree of support also is a function of the organizational culture.
- *Guilt:* Some managers feel that before they become managers, they committed the same violations as their employees, and they cannot discipline others for doing something they used to do.
- *Loss of friendship:* Managers who allow themselves to become too friendly with employees may fear losing those friendships if discipline is used.
- *Time loss:* Discipline, when applied properly, requires considerable time and effort. Sometimes it is easier for managers to avoid taking the time required for disciplining, especially if their actions may be overturned on review by higher management.
- *Fear of lawsuits:* Managers are increasingly concerned about being sued for disciplining someone, particularly for taking the ultimate disciplinary step of dismissal.

## Effective Discipline

Because of legal concerns, managers must understand discipline and know how to administer it properly. Effective discipline should be aimed at the behavior, not at the employee personally, because the reason for discipline is to improve performance.

Discipline can be positively related to performance, which surprises those who feel that discipline can only harm behavior. Employees may resist unjustified discipline from a manager, but actions taken to maintain legitimate standards actually may reinforce productive group norms and result in increased performance and feelings of fairness. A work group may perceive that an inequity has taken place when one individual violates standards. An individual who violates standards may also be violating group norms, so lack of discipline can cause problems for the group as well as for the manager. Distributive and procedural justice suggest that if a manager tolerates this unacceptable behavior, the group may feel it is not fair. Some of the factors leading to effective disciplinary practices in an organization are shown in Figure 17–15 and are discussed next.

**TRAINING OF SUPERVISORS**  Training supervisors and managers on when and how discipline should be used is crucial. Research has found that training supervisors in procedural justice as a basis for discipline results in both their employees and others seeing disciplinary action as more fair than discipline done by untrained supervisors.[40] Regardless of the disciplinary approach used, it is important to provide training on counseling and communicating skills, because supervisors and managers will be using them as they deal with employee performance problems.

**LOGGING ON . . .**
**Effective Discipline**
This site describes assistance with effective disciplinary measures for employers. "Discipline without punishment" is described.

**http://www.grotecon.com/index.html**

**FIGURE 17–15** *Effective Discipline*

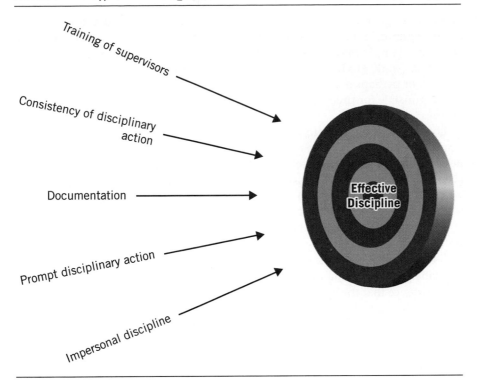

CONSISTENCY OF DISCIPLINARY ACTIONS The manager administering discipline must consider the effect of actions taken by other managers and of other actions taken in the past. Consistent discipline helps to set limits and informs people about what they can and cannot do. Inconsistent discipline leads to confusion and uncertainty.

DOCUMENTATION Effective discipline requires accurate, written record keeping and written notification to the employee. In a number of cases, the lack of written notification has been used to support an employee's argument that he or she "did not know."

PROMPT DISCIPLINARY ACTION Additionally, effective discipline is immediate. The longer the time that transpires between the offense and the disciplinary action, the less effective the discipline will be.

IMPERSONAL DISCIPLINE Finally, effective discipline is handled impersonally. Managers cannot make discipline an enjoyable experience, but they can minimize the unpleasant effects somewhat by presenting it impersonally and by focusing on behaviors, not on the person. Also, managers should limit how emotional they become in disciplinary sessions. Obviously, employees are likely to become angry, upset, or otherwise emotional. But it is important that the supervisor conducting the discipline avoid rising to the same emotional intensity as the employee does.

## Discharge: The Final Disciplinary Step

The final stage in the disciplinary process is termination. A manager may feel guilty when dismissing an employee, and sometimes guilt is justified. If an employee fails, it may be because the manager was not able to create an appropriate work environment. Perhaps the employee was not adequately trained, or perhaps management failed to establish effective policies. Managers are responsible for their employees, and to an extent, they share the blame for failures.

Both the positive and progressive approaches to discipline provide that when dismissal is used, it is clear that employees have been warned about the seriousness of their performance problems. Terminating workers because they do not keep their own promises is more likely to appear equitable and defensible to a jury. Also, such a system seems to reduce the emotional reactions that lead fired workers to sue in the first place.

When dismissal occurs, the reasons for the termination should be clearly stated. Any effort to "sugar-coat" the reason ultimately confuses the employee, and it could undermine the employer's legal case should the termination decision be challenged. Many employers provide a specific letter or memo, which can provide evidence that the employee was notified of the termination decision.

Often, it is valuable to have both an HR representative and the employee's supervisor or manager attend the termination meeting, so that an additional witness exists to what occurred. Also, any severance benefits or other HR-related issues can be described. Some items that are HR related include COBRA notification rights, any continuance of other employee benefits, and payments for unused vacation or sick leave. Finally, throughout the termination discussion it is crucial that the supervisor and others remain professional and calm, rather than becoming emotional or making sarcastic or demeaning remarks.[41]

# Summary

- The employment relationship is a reciprocal one in which both the employers and employees have rights.
- The two primary types of rights are statutory rights and contractual rights.
- Contractual rights can be spelled out in an employment contract or be implied as a result of employer promises.
- Rights affecting the employment relationship include employment-at-will, due process, and dismissal for just cause.
- Employment-at-will allows employers the right to hire or terminate employees with or without notice or cause.
- Employment-at-will relationships are changing in the courts, which have found exceptions for public policy, implied contract, and good-faith/fair-dealing reasons.
- Although due process is not guaranteed for at-will employees, the courts expect to see evidence of due process in employment-related cases.
- Wrongful discharge occurs when an employer terminates an individual's employment for improper or illegal reasons.
- Just cause for employment-related actions should exist. When just cause is absent, constructive discharge may occur, in which the employee is forced to "voluntarily" quit the job.
- Due process is important for both unionized and nonunion employees. In nonunion situations, alternative dispute resolution (ADR) means are growing in use.

- Balancing employer security concerns and employee rights is most often seen when dealing with access to employee records, free speech, workplace monitoring, employer investigations, and employee substance abuse.
- Employers increasingly are facing free speech issues at work, in areas such as whistle-blowing, monitoring of e-mail and voice mail, and Internet usage.
- Drug testing generally is legal and is widely used as employers try to deal with increasing drug problems at work.
- To be effective, HR policies and rules should be consistent, necessary, applicable, understandable, reasonable, and communicated.

- Employee handbooks have been viewed as implied contracts by the courts, which presents few problems as long as the handbook conforms to appropriate standards. Issues to be considered in preparing an employee handbook include reliability, use, and legal review of language.
- Discipline is best thought of as a form of training. Although self-discipline is the goal, sometimes positive or progressive discipline is necessary to encourage self-discipline.
- Managers may fail to discipline when they should, for a variety of reasons. However, effective discipline can have positive effects on the productivity of employees.

# Review and Discussion Questions

1. Assume you had to develop an employment contract for a key research manager. What provisions should be included?
2. Give some examples to illustrate the public policy exception to employment-at-will.
3. Discuss the differences and similarities between the issues of due process and just cause.
4. Discuss the following statement: "Even though employers' efforts to restrict employees' free speech at work may be permissible, such efforts raise troubling questions affecting individual rights."
5. Identify some advantages and disadvantages associated with employers monitoring employee e-mail and work performance using technological and electronic means.
6. Examine an employee handbook from a local employer and identify problems and issues with its content.
7. Why has the positive approach to discipline been useful in reducing employee lawsuits?

# Terms to Know

arbitration  575
constructive discharge  572
contractual rights  567
discipline  591
distributive justice  574
due process  574
employee responsibilities  566
employment-at-will (EAW)  570
employment contract  567

just cause  572
noncompete covenants  567
nonpiracy agreement  567
ombudsman  576
peer review panel  575
policies  586
procedural justice  574
procedures  586
rights  566

right to privacy  576
rules  586
separation agreement  567
statutory rights  566
suggestion system  590
whistle-blowers  578
wrongful discharge  572

# Using the Internet

## Employment Contracts

The president has contacted you, the HR manager, about employment contracts. He would like you to prepare a report identifying the reasons it would be in the best interest of the company to begin using employment contracts for key managers and executives.

He also asked you to identify and discuss what most organizations include in their employment contracts. Use the following website to assist you.
**http://www.careerlinc.com/econtract.htm**

## CASE

# Disciplinary Process at Red Lobster

At the Red Lobster restaurant in Pleasant Hills, Pennsylvania, a waitress was fired for stealing a guest comment card that was critical of her. Having worked for Red Lobster for almost 20 years, the employee naturally was very upset about being terminated for such an infraction.

While situations such as these happen in many organizations, it is the disciplinary due process at Red Lobster that is not common. In disciplinary situations such as these, employees at Red Lobster can request that their situation be reviewed by a panel of other Red Lobster employees. Instead of filing a lawsuit against Red Lobster, which likely would have happened, the discharged employee had her case heard by a peer review panel composed of five employees in the Red Lobster chain, not necessarily from her specific location. The panel was composed of a bartender, food server, hostess, assistant manager, and a general manager. Here are the facts they heard.

According to the manager of the Pleasant Hills restaurant, the waitress was fired because she took a customer comment card from the comment card box. On the customer's card, the customer had called the waitress "uncooperative" and said that the prime rib served had been too rare. The irate customer complained to both the shift supervisor and the restaurant manager about the food and the waitress's service. Through facts not clearly identified, the customer learned that the waitress had retrieved the crit-

ical comment card, which angered the customer more. Based on these facts, and on a policy in the Red Lobster handbook about unauthorized removal of company property, the Pleasant Hill manager terminated the waitress.

The waitress stated her case by noting that the customer had asked for a well-done prime rib. When she received it, the customer explained that it was too rare and that it had too much fat on it. Although the waitress explained that prime rib always has fat on it, the customer was not mollified; so the waitress had the prime rib cooked more. Still unhappy, the customer dumped steak sauce on it and pushed her dinner away. Despite being offered a free dessert by the waitress, the customer demanded the bill, completed a comment card, and dropped it in the locked customer comment box. She then left the restaurant.

Wanting to know what was said, the waitress asked the hostess for the key, unlocked the box, and pocketed the card. Support for the waitress came from the hostess, who stated that other people had requested and received the key to the comment box lock in the past.

After deliberating in the case, the peer review panel ruled that the waitress had not intentionally stolen company property. Further, the panel found that the manager had overreacted with an otherwise satisfactory employee, and a written disciplinary notice would have been more appropriate. In its final decision, the panel decided that the waitress would receive reinstatement to her job; but that she would not receive the three weeks' back wages she had requested. Interviewed several months later, the waitress indicated that the manager treated her professionally and had given her some accommodations when the waitress hurt her back.[42]

## Questions

1. Would you have reached the same decision in this case? Why or why not?
2. Discuss the importance of consistent rule enforcement and due process in disciplinary situations such as this.
3. What do you see as the advantages and disadvantages of using peer review panels?

# Notes

1. Based on Diane Richardson, "Tiptoe through Employment Practices Minefield," *National Underwriter,* February 9, 1998, 21+.
2. U.S. Equal Employment Opportunity Commission, 1997.
3. Bob Calandra, "Workforce Raiders," *Human Resource Executive,* October 19, 1998, 36–39.
4. Michael D. Karpeles, "Employment Contracts Gain Ground in Corporate America," *Workforce,* February 1999, 99–101; and Louis K. Obdyke, "Written Employment Contracts—When, Why, How?" *Legal Report,* Spring 1998, 5–8.
5. Olga Aiken, "Employment Contracts Come into Sharper Focus," *People Management,* May 29, 1997, 39.
6. John J. Myers, et al. "Making the Most of Employment Contracts," *HR Magazine,* August 1998, 106–109.
7. Garry Mathison, "What's in Your Head Can Hurt You," *Fortune,* July 1998, 153; "DSC Sues Ex-Worker Over Software Idea He Has in His Head," *The Wall Street Journal,* May 5, 1997, B7; "Spying for Pills, Not Projectiles," *The Economist,* July 12, 1997, 22–23; and Don Clark, "Novell Suit Says Three Engineers Stole Secrets," *The Wall Street Journal,* May 5, 1997, B7.
8. "Employers: Bite Your Tongue," *Personnel Legal Alert,* June 22, 1998, 1; and *Koepping v. Tri-County Metropolitan Transportation,* 9th Cir., No. 95-36151.
9. *Fortune v. National Cash Register Co.,* 373 Mass. 96, 36NE 2d 1251, 1977.
10. Jay Stiller, "You'll Be Hearing from My Lawyer," *Across the Board,* January 1997, 32–38.
11. *Cotran v. Rollins Hudig Hall International, Inc.,* Calif. Sup.Ct. No. S057098, January 5, 1998.
12. Robert H. Moorman, Gerald L. Blakely, and Biran P. Niehoff, "Does Perceived Organizational Support Mediate the Relationship between Procedural Justice and Organizational Citizenship Behavior?" *Academy of Management Journal* 41 (1998), 351–357.
13. Ira B. Lobel, "Critique of Third-Party Decision-Making in ADR Processes," *Dispute Resolution Journal,* August 1998, 76–80.
14. Stephanie Armour, "Mandatory Arbitration: A Pill Many Are Forced to Swallow," *USA Today,* July 9, 1998, 1A–2A.
15. "Forced into Arbitration? Not Any More," *Business Week,* March 16, 1998, 66–68.
16. Patrick McGeehan, "Supreme Court Lets Stand Ruling on Job-Bias Claims, Arbitration," *The Wall Street Journal,* November 10, 1998, B25.
17. John-Paul Motley, "Compulsory Arbitration Agreements in Employment Contracts from *Gardner-Denver* to *Austin,*" *Vanderbilt Law Review,* April 1998, 687–720.
18. Olaf Isachson, "Do You Need an Ombudsman?" *HR Focus,* September 1998, 6.
19. Americans with Disabilities Act, 1992, Section 102C(3).
20. Michael J. Lotito and Lynn C. Outwater, *Minding Your Business,* (Alexandria, VA: Society for Human Resource Management, 1997), 83–96; and Cynthia J. Guffes and Judy F. West, "Employee Privacy: Legal Implications for Managers," *Labor Law Journal* 47 (1996), 735–745.
21. Sam Jensen, "Omaha Woman's Religious Bias Claim Denied by U.S. Court; Bias Confirmed in Des Moines Case," *Nebraska Employment Law Letter,* November 1995, 3.
22. Randi L. Sims and John P. Keenan, "Predictors of External Whistle-blowing; Organizational and Intrapersonal Variable," *Journal of Business Ethics* 17 (1998), 411–421.
23. Mary Kathryn Zachary, "Whistle-blowers Protected in Varied Settings," *Supervision* March 1998, 17–18.
24. Lynn Atkinson, "Oil Industry Whistle-blower Will Keep $7 Million," *HR Focus,* August 1998, 8.
25. Ronald Henkoff, "ADM's Whitacre Goes to Jail," *Fortune,* March 30, 1998, 17–18.
26. Susan Peticolas and Kerrie R. Heslin, "Electronic Communications in the Workplace," *Legal Report,* Winter 1999, 5–8; and Brenda Paik Sunoo, "What If Your E-mail Ends Up In Court?" *Workforce,* July 1998, 36–41.
27. "Employers Should Define What Privacy Employees Can Expect," *Employment and Labor Law Needs,* April 6, 1998, at http://hr.cch.com/news/labor/.htm.
28. Stephanie Armour, "Offensive E-mail in Office on Increase, Can Endanger Job," *USA Today,* April 5, 1999, B1.

29. *Deal v. Spears d/b/a White Oak Package Store*, CA 8, 1992 (81ER Cases 105).

30. Shirley Sloan Fader, "Privacy at Work," *Family Circle,* March 10, 1998, 130–134.

31. "More Employee Theft, but Less Protection," *Human Resource Executive,* October 1998, 22.

32. "Retailers Track Workers Accused of Theft," *The Wall Street Journal,* April 17, 1997, A1.

33. Carol Patton, "Raising Hairs," *Human Resource Executive,* November 1998, 74–76.

34. Jane Easter Bahls, "Drugs in the Workplace," *HR Magazine,* February 1998, 81–87.

35. Benjamin H. Hoffman, "Caught By a Hair?" *Occupational Health & Safety,* November 1997, 46–49.

36. Maurice Baskin, "Is it Time to Revise Your Employee Handbook?" *Legal Report,* Winter 1998, 1–4.

37. Darrell L. Browning, "By the Book?" *Human Resource Executive,* August 1998, 83–85.

38. Robert D. Ramsey, "Guideline for the Progressive Discipline of Employees," *Supervision,* February 1998, 10–12.

39. Brian S. Klaas and Gregory G. Dell'Omo, "Managerial Use of Dismissal: Organizational-Level Determinants," *Personnel Psychology* 50 (1997), 927–953.

40. Nina D. Cole, "Effects of Training in Procedural Justice on Perceptions of Disciplinary Fairness by Unionized Employees and Disciplinary Subject Matters Experts," *Journal of Applied Psychology* 82 (1997), 699–705.

41. Mark M. Schorr, "Tips on How to Conduct an Employee Termination Meeting," *Nebraska Employment Law Letter* November 1997, 4–5.

42. Adapted from Margaret A. Jacobs, "Red Lobster Tale: Peers Decide Fired Waitress's Fate," *The Wall Street Journal,* January 20, 1998, B1, B16.

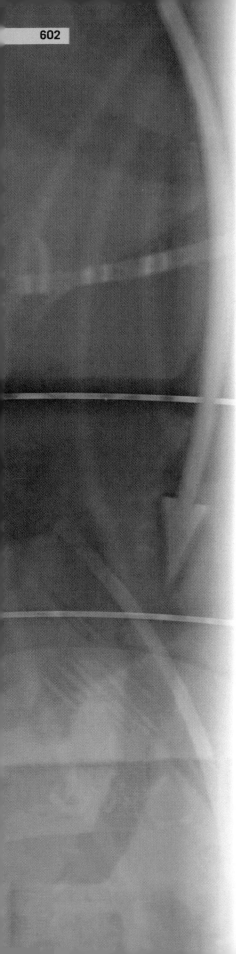

# CHAPTER 18
# Labor/ Management Relations

*After you have read this chapter, you should be able to:*

- Describe what a union is and explain why employees join unions.

- Explain the acts that compose the "National Labor Code."

- Identify and discuss the stages in the process of unionization.

- Describe the typical collective bargaining process.

- Define *grievance* and explain why a grievance procedure is important for every employer.

# HR TRANSITIONS

# General Motors and the United Auto Workers—Labor Conflict

The United Auto Workers (UAW) union, which represents most General Motors (GM) employees, has struck GM several times during the last few years. Typically the strikes have not been against the whole company—only various plants that supply key parts—but the effect has often been to shut down operations across the huge company. Why has the union continued to use labor's ultimate weapon when each shutdown costs members and their employer dearly? The story is one that illustrates clearly the major issues in labor-management relations today.

Competition from Ford Motor Company and global competitors like Daimler-Benz and Toyota has made it clear to GM executives that they *must* close the big gaps in productivity, but their progress to date has been too slow. For years the need to change GM from a "clumsy giant" into a lean global competitor has been obvious. But GM's strategy has been to use attrition to shrink its bloated workforce. As tens of thousands of workers hired in the 1960s retire, the company could restructure itself to operate using significantly fewer employees. But meanwhile at Ford, aggressive cost cutting and an end to a "country-club" approach to competition has led to major successes against GM. To reach Ford's level of productivity, GM would need to cut 50,000 more jobs—not an approach likely to make the UAW happy. At one time, GM had 50% of the huge U.S. market for cars and trucks. Now it is at 31% and falling. Ford and Daimler-Chrysler have already accomplished the streamlining that GM is only beginning.

But even with job cuts, GM cannot be competitive unless the union drops inefficient work rules—for example, a rule allowing some workers to leave with a full day's pay after doing a half-day's work. The average GM worker receives wages and benefits totaling around $44 per hour. For comparison, Mexican workers at GM's Silao plant in Mexico earn $13 per day, which is six times Mexico's minimum wage. Jobs at the GM plant there are much sought after and considered *very good* jobs in Mexico.

Union strikes at GM plants have been very expensive for the company. One 17-day strike cost almost $1 billion, and longer strikes cost even more. GM suppliers are forced to lay off employees and/or shut down during strikes, and the effect ripples through the economy. Further, GM loses sales and customers as its inventory of cars disappears. The UAW struck GM plants nine times in one two-year period. The company estimates that the longer strikes cost about 21,000 customers per day—and those customers buy another brand of vehicle. The result it says, is that the business gets smaller and loses even more jobs.

The string of strikes calls into question GM's HR strategy for dealing with its complex labor and productivity problems. Job outsourcing, closing plants, and moving production outside

> *Job outsourcing, closing plants, and moving production outside the United States will continue to be major issues for GM and the UAW for many years to come.*

the United States will continue to be major issues for GM and the UAW for many years to come. The lack of an easy solution to changes caused by competition, and the resulting need to increase productivity, have been the major reasons for the problems both GM and America's labor unions face.[1]

> 66 *If employees have problems that you aren't addressing—unions* will! 99
>
> MICHAEL SEVERNS

**Union**
A formal association of workers that promotes the interests of its members through collective action.

A **union** is a formal association of workers that promotes the interests of its members through collective action. The state of unions varies among countries depending on the culture and the laws that define union-management relationships. In the United States a complex system of laws, administrative agencies, and precedent is in place to allow workers to join unions when they wish to do so. Although fewer workers choose to do so today than before, the mechanisms remain for a union resurgence if employees feel they need a formal representative to deal with management. This chapter examines why employees may choose to organize a union, how they go about it, and the bargaining and administration of the agreement that union and management reach.

# When Management Faces a Union

Employers usually would rather not have to deal with a union. The wages paid union workers are higher, and unions constrain what managers can and cannot do in a number of HR areas. However, unions *can be* associated with higher productivity, although that may occur when management has to find labor-saving ways of doing work to offset higher wage costs. Some companies pursue a strategy of good relations with the unions. Others may choose an aggressive, adversarial approach, which is especially true among companies that follow a low-cost/low-wage strategy to deal with competition.[2]

## Why Employees Unionize

Whether a union targets a group of employees, or the employees themselves request union assistance, the union still must win sufficient support from the employees if it is to become their legal representative. Research consistently shows that employees join unions for one primary reason: They are dissatisfied with how they are treated by their employers and feel the union can improve the situation. If the employees do not get organizational justice from their employers, they turn to the union to assist them in getting what they believe is equitable. Important factors seem to be *wages and benefits, job security,* and *supervisory treatment.*

The primary determinant of whether employees unionize is management. If management treats employees like valuable human resources, then employees generally feel no need for outside representation. That is why providing good working conditions, fair treatment by supervisors, responsiveness to worker complaints and concerns, and reasonably competitive wages and benefits are all antidotes to unionization efforts. In addition, many workers want more cooperative dealings with management, rather than being autocratically managed.[3] The union's ability to foster commitment from members and to remain as their bargaining agent apparently depends on how well the union succeeds in providing services that its members want.

**LOGGING ON . . .**
**Labor Relations Online**
This website provides links to educational resources, government materials, union-related pages, management details, and other resources.

**http://www.auburn.edu/ ~wilsokc/**

## Targeting Organizations by Unions

Unions may contact employees in industries or occupations where they have a traditional interest, or in new areas where expansion seems possible. For exam-

## HR PERSPECTIVE
# Unions Needed Here?

*Targeting* by unions is very evident today. As unions concentrate their efforts to organize employees, they have identified certain *industries* and one *city* as being ripe for union organizing. For example, Las Vegas, Nevada, has been picked by the largest national labor organization, the AFL-CIO, as a place where employees might see the advantages of union membership. In a sense, Las Vegas may seem an odd place for union organizing. It is a conservative area, but it has been a boom town for some time now, and its core service jobs *cannot* be moved elsewhere by employers. The union is pursuing hotels, hospitals, and construction workers in Las Vegas. Although Las Vegas is a targeted geographical area, certain industries, such as child care and nursing homes, are targeted elsewhere.

Child-care workers are a target in Philadelphia (and elsewhere as well). Child-care workers are often unskilled and receive low pay. For example, in Philadelphia child-care workers make less than $8/hour, 80% have no health insurance, and virtually *none* have employer-paid retirement benefits. Henry Nicholas, President of the National Union of Hospital and Health Care Employees, says, "We are building this movement to put dignity in child care." About 24,000 people are employed in the child-care industry in the Philadelphia area.

Workers in nursing homes dealing with the elderly are a fast-growing segment of the workforce. However, many employees in this industry are relatively dissatisfied. The industry is often noted for its low pay and hard work, and many employees are women who work as nurse's aides, cooks, launderers, and in other low-wage jobs. The Bureau of Labor Statistics lists nursing home workers as among the most susceptible to workplace injuries—from assaults by patients to back injuries from lifting and turning patients. Even in the southern United States, where unions have been notably unsuccessful pre-viously, the employees of nursing homes are organizing. As the vice president of a large nursing-home chain in the South notes, "We prefer to deal with our employees without a union. But if we end up with a union, it's probably because we deserve it in that particular location."

Nursing-home employees earn an average of $6.65 an hour and see unions as a chance for change. Ironically, they are health-care workers— although many of them cannot afford health insurance. Many homes are chronically short staffed, yet each patient must be cared for regularly. Recently, unions won 25 of 37 elections in the South, and three-fourths of their elections nationally.[4]

Unions point out that targeting these areas and industries will help employees increase their wages, benefits, and working conditions. Workers in these industries also represent a source for growth in labor union members to offset declines elsewhere.

ples, see the HR Perspective. The following are some indicators identified by unions to predict when a unionization attempt might be successful in a given organization:

- Dissatisfaction with wages and benefits
- Dissatisfaction with safety or job security
- Boring or demeaning jobs
- Poor supervisory practices, including insufficient communication
- Lack of power to make changes

When these indicators are present, the employees might choose a union to represent them. If employees choose a union to represent them, management and union representatives enter into formal bargaining over certain issues such as pay scales, benefits, and working conditions. Once these issues have been resolved in a labor contract, management and union representatives must work together to manage the contract and deal with grievances, which are formal complaints filed by workers with management. HR professionals may be involved in any or all of the process.

## HR Responsibilities with Unions

Figure 18–1 shows a typical division of responsibilities between the HR unit and operating managers in dealing with unions. This pattern may vary among organizations. In some organizations, HR is not involved with labor relations because operating management handles them. In other organizations, the HR unit is almost completely in charge of labor relations. The typical division of responsibilities shown in Figure 18–1 is a midpoint between these extremes.

# Union Membership Trends

Unionism in the United States has followed a pattern somewhat different from that in other countries. In such countries as Italy, England, and Japan, the union movement has been at the forefront of social policy issues. For the most part, this politicization has not occurred in the United States. Perhaps workers here tend to identify with the American free enterprise system. Further, class consciousness and conflict between the working "class" and the management "class" is less evident in the United States than in many other countries.

## Unions in the United States—and Globally

The union movement in the United States has been characterized by the following approaches, which in some cases are very different from the approaches used in other countries. In the United States the key emphases have been:

● *Focus on economic issues:* Unions typically have focused on improving the "bread and butter" issues for their members—wages, job security, and benefits. In Germany, the workers and their unions have a say in the management of the company, with one or more members on the board of directors of many employers. The German approach is more comprehensive than that used in the United States.

**LOGGING ON . . .**
**International Labor Organization**
Information on global union issues, news, conferences, and research resources can be found here.

**http://www.ilo.org/**

FIGURE 18–1 *Typical Labor Relations Responsibilities*

| HR Unit | Managers |
|---|---|
| ● Deals with union organizing attempts at the company level<br>● Monitors "climate" for unionization and union relationships<br>● Helps negotiate labor agreements<br>● Provides detailed knowledge of labor legislation as needed | ● Promote conditions conducive to positive relationships with employees<br>● Avoid unfair labor practices during organizing efforts<br>● Administer the labor agreement on a daily basis<br>● Resolve grievances and problems between management and employees |

- *Organized by kind of job:*   In the United States, carpenters often belong to the carpenter's union, truck drivers to the Teamsters, and teachers to the American Federation of Teachers or the National Education Association. In Japan, unions are organized on a company-by-company basis or an "enterprise" basis rather than by kind of job.
- *Decentralized bargaining:*   In the United States, bargaining is usually done on a company-by-company basis. In Sweden the government determines wage rates, and in other countries "councils," rather than individual employers, set nationwide rates through bargaining.
- *Collective agreements are "contracts":*   Collective bargaining agreements are referred to as *contracts*. They spell out work rules and conditions of employment for 2 or 3 years or longer. In the United States, the agreements are enforceable after interpretation (if necessary) by an arbitrator. In Great Britain, the agreements are not enforceable; they are similar to a handshake or "gentleman's agreement," and cannot be enforced formally.
- *Adversarial relations:*   U.S. tradition has management and labor as adversaries who must "clash" to reach agreement. In Mexico the employer-employee relationship is more friendly, almost family-like.

**FIGURE 18–2** *Union Membership As a Percentage of U.S. Workforce*

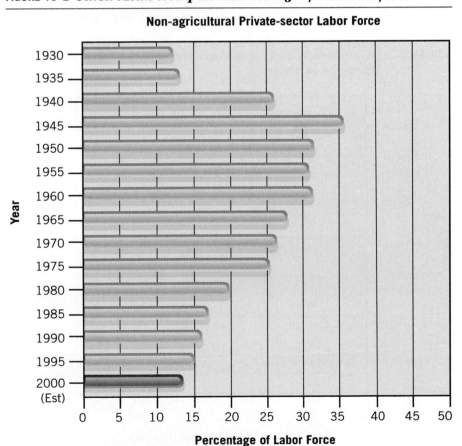

SOURCE: Data from Bureau of Labor Statistics, U.S. Department of Labor.

## Union Decline Worldwide

Over the past several decades, the statistics on union membership have told a disheartening story for organized labor in the United States. As shown in Figure 18–2 on the previous page, unions represented over 30% of the workforce from 1945 through 1960. But by the end of the 1990s, unions in the United States represented less than 14% of all private-sector workers.[5]

As in the United States, unions in other countries are facing declining membership. One factor in the decline of European unions is that European manufacturers have been reducing operations in Europe and moving jobs to the United States, as well as to low-wage countries such as China, Thailand, and the Phillippines. Further, the need to reduce expenditures for social benefits, such as welfare and pensions, has forced European countries to eliminate jobs in their public sectors, which traditionally have been highly unionized. Compounding the problems, many large employers in western European countries are wholly or partially owned by the national government. Figure 18–3 shows the percentage of the labor force that is unionized in different countries. Other reasons for the shifts in union membership in the United States are addressed next.

## Reasons for Union Decline in the U.S.

Economists speculate that several issues have sparked union decline: deregulation, foreign competition, a larger number of people looking for jobs, and a

**FIGURE 18–3** *Union Membership as a Percentage of the Workforce for Selected Countries*

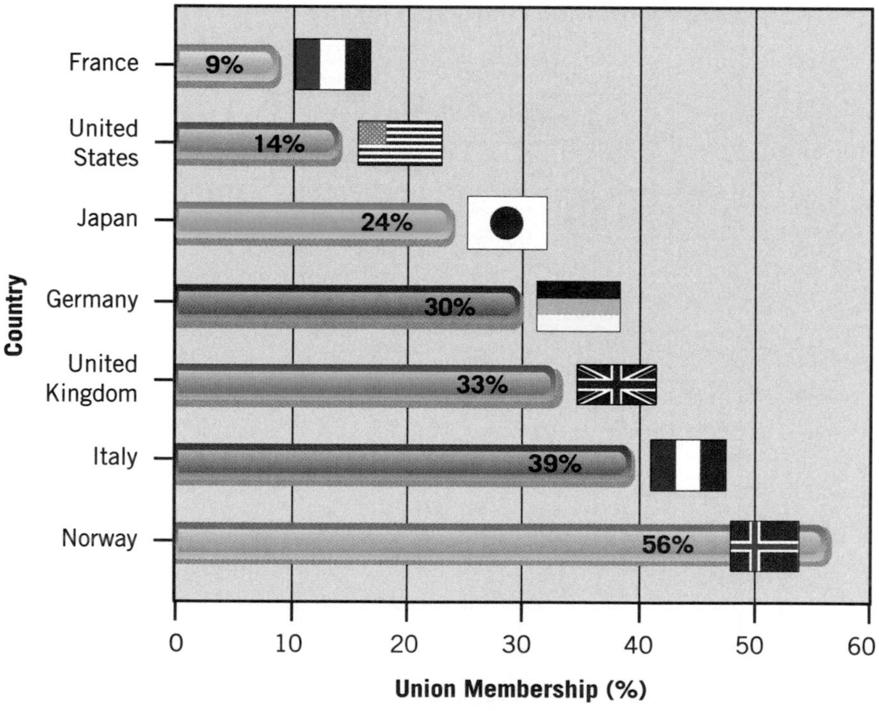

SOURCE: OECD Data from *The Economist*, July 12, 1997, 70.

general perception by firms that dealing with unions is expensive compared with the nonunion alternative. Also, management has taken a much more activist stance against unions than during the previous years of union growth.

Unions have emphasized helping workers obtain higher wages, shorter working hours, job security, and safe working conditions from their employers. Ironically, some believe that one cause for the decline of unions has been their success in getting their important worker issues passed into law for everyone. Therefore, unions are not as necessary for many employees, even though they enjoy the results of past union efforts to influence legislation.

## Geographic Changes

Over the past decade, job growth in the United States has been the greatest in states located in the South, Southwest, and Rocky Mountains. Most of these states have relatively small percentages of unionized workers. This is partly because of "employer-friendly" laws passed to attract new plants, many relocated from northern states, where unions traditionally have been stronger. Foreign competition, automation, and the lack of union traditions are the main barriers to unionization efforts in these areas.

Another issue involves the movement of many lower-skill jobs outside the United States. Primarily because of cheaper labor, many manufacturers such as General Motors have moved a significant number of low-skill jobs to Mexico, the Phillippines, China, Thailand, and other lower-wage countries. Even some white-collar data processing jobs are being moved out of the country. For instance, a major airline has data entry of airline ticket receipts being done by workers on two different Caribbean islands.

A major impetus for moving low-skill, low-wage jobs to Mexico was the passage of the North American Free Trade Agreement (NAFTA). It removed tariffs and restrictions affecting the flow of goods and services among the United States, Canada, and Mexico. Because wage rates are significantly lower in Mexico, a number of jobs that would have been susceptible to unionization are now being moved there. Supporters of NAFTA make the case that jobs are created in the United States as well, but many of those jobs are at higher levels and in areas less likely to be unionized. Thus, the overall result in many situations is that jobs that otherwise could lead to unionization and the growth of unions have been moving out of the reach of U.S. unions.

## Public-Sector Unionism

An area where unions have had some measure of success is with public-sector employees, particularly with state and local government workers. Figure 18–4 on the next page shows that the government sector (federal, state, and local) is the most highly unionized part of the U.S. workforce.

Unionization of state and local government employees presents some unique problems and challenges. First, many unionized local government employees are in critical service areas. Allowing police officers, firefighters, and sanitation workers to strike endangers public health and safety. Consequently, over 30 states have laws prohibiting public employee work stoppages. These laws also identify a variety of ways to resolve negotiation impasses, including arbitration. But unions still give employees in these areas greater security and better ability to influence decisions on wages and benefits.

FIGURE 18–4 *Percentage of Workers in Unions, by Industry*

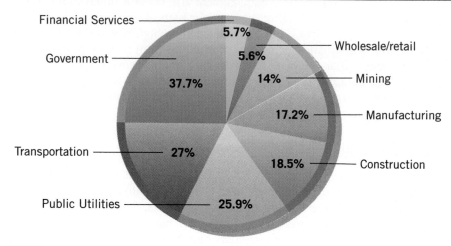

SOURCE: U.S. Department of Labor, Bureau of Labor Statistics.

Although unions in the federal government hold the same basic philosophy as unions in the private sector, they do differ somewhat. Through past Executive Orders and laws, methods of labor/management relations that consider the special circumstances present in the federal government have been established. In the United States, the government sector is the only one in which there has been a recent growth and strengthening of unions.

# The History of American Unions

The evolution of the union movement in the United States began with early collective efforts by employees to address job concerns and counteract management power. As early as 1794, shoemakers organized a union, picketed, and conducted strikes. However, in those days, unions in the United States received very little support from the courts. In 1806, when the shoemaker's union struck for higher wages, a Philadelphia court found union members guilty of engaging in a "criminal conspiracy" to raise wages.

## The AFL-CIO

**LOGGING ON . . .**
**AFL-CIO Home Page**
The AFL-CIO's home page describes unions and Organizing Institute information.

**http://www.aflcio.org/ front.htm**

In 1886, the *American Federation of Labor* (AFL) was formed as a federation of independent national unions. Its aims were to organize skilled craft workers, like carpenters and plumbers, and to emphasize such bread-and-butter issues as wages and working conditions.

The Civil War gave factories a big boost, and factory mass-production methods used semiskilled or unskilled workers. Unions found that they could not control the semiskilled workers entering factory jobs because these workers had no tradition of unionism. It was not until 1938, when the Congress of Industrial Organizations (CIO) was founded, that a labor union organization focused on semiskilled and unskilled workers. Years later, the AFL and the CIO merged to form one coordinating federation, the AFL-CIO.

## Early Labor Legislation

The right to organize workers and engage in collective bargaining is of little value if workers are not free to exercise it. Historical evidence shows that management developed practices calculated to prevent workers from using this right. The federal government has taken action over time to both hamper unions and protect them.

**RAILWAY LABOR ACT** The Railway Labor Act (1926) represented a shift in government regulation of unions. As a result of a joint effort between railroad management and unions to reduce transportation strikes, this act gave railroad employees "the right to organize and bargain collectively through representatives of their own choosing." In 1936, airlines and their employees were added to those covered by the act. Both of these industries are still covered by this act rather than by others passed later.

**NORRIS-LAGUARDIA ACT** The crash of the stock market and the onset of the Great Depression in 1929 led to massive cutbacks by employers. In some industries, resistance by employees led to strikes and violence. Under the laws at that time, employers could go to court and have a federal judge issue injunctions ordering workers to return to work. In 1932, Congress passed the Norris-LaGuardia Act, which guaranteed workers some rights to organize and restricted the issuance of court injunctions in labor disputes.

# Basic Labor Law: "National Labor Code"

The economic crises of the early 1930s and the restrictions on workers' ability to organize into unions led to the passage of landmark labor legislation. Later acts reflected other pressures and issues that had to be addressed legislatively. Together, the following three acts, passed over a period of almost 25 years, comprise what has been labeled the "National Labor Code": (1) the Wagner Act, (2) the Taft-Hartley Act, and (3) the Landrum-Griffin Act. Each act was passed to focus on some facet of the relationships between unions and management. Figure 18–5 on the next page shows each segment of the code and describes the primary focus of each act.

## Wagner Act (National Labor Relations Act)

The *National Labor Relations Act,* more commonly referred to as the Wagner Act, has been called the Magna Carta of labor and is, by anyone's standards, *pro-union*. Passed in 1935, the Wagner Act was an outgrowth of the Great Depression. With employers having to close or cut back their operations, workers were left with little job security. Unions stepped in to provide a feeling of solidarity and strength for many workers. The Wagner Act declared, in effect, that the official policy of the U.S. government was to encourage collective bargaining.

**FIGURE 18–5** *The National Labor Code*

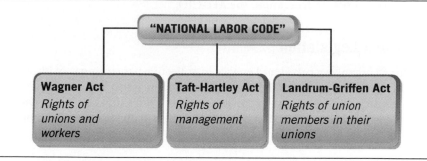

The Wagner Act helped union growth in three ways:

● It established workers' right to organize, unhampered by management interference.
● It defined unfair labor practices on the part of management.
● It established the National Labor Relations Board (NLRB) as an independent entity to enforce the provisions of the Wagner Act.

The Wagner Act established the principle that employees would be protected in their right to form a union and to bargain collectively. To protect union rights, the act prohibited employers from undertaking the following five unfair labor practices:

● Interfering with, restraining, or coercing employees in the exercise of their right to organize or to bargain collectively.
● Dominating or interfering with the formation or administration of any labor organization.
● Encouraging or discouraging membership in any labor organization by discriminating with regard to hiring, tenure, or conditions of employment.
● Discharging or otherwise discriminating against an employee because he or she filed charges or gave testimony under the act.
● Refusing to bargain collectively with representatives of the employees.

The NLRB administers all provisions of the Wagner and subsequent labor relations acts. Although it was set up as an impartial umpire of the organizing process, the NLRB has altered its emphasis depending on which political party is in power to appoint members.

## Taft-Hartley Act (Labor-Management Relations Act)

The passage in 1947 of the *Labor-Management Relations Act,* better known as the Taft-Hartley Act, answered the concerns of many who felt that unions had become too strong. An attempt to balance the collective bargaining equation, this act was designed to offset the pro-union Wagner Act by limiting union actions; therefore, it was considered to be *pro-management.* It became the second part of the National Labor Code.

The new law amended or qualified in some respect all of the major provisions of the Wagner Act and established an entirely new code of conduct for unions. The Taft-Hartley Act forbade unions from a series of unfair labor practices that were very much like those prohibited for management. Coercion, discrimination against nonmembers, refusing to bargain, excessive membership fees, and other practices were forbidden for unions. The Taft-Hartley Act also allows the President of the United States to declare that a strike presents a national emergency. A **national emergency strike** is one that would affect an industry or a major part of it such that the national economy would be significantly affected.

**RIGHT-TO-WORK PROVISION** One specific provision of the Taft-Hartley Act, Section 14(b), deserves special explanation. This "right-to-work" provision affects the **closed shop,** which requires individuals to join a union before they can be hired. Because of concerns that a closed shop allows a union to "control" who may be considered for employment and who must be hired by an employer, Section 14(b) prohibits the closed shop except in construction-related occupations. The act does allow the **union shop,** which requires that an employee join the union, usually 30 to 60 days after being hired. The act also allows the **agency shop,** which requires employees who refuse to join the union to pay amounts equal to union dues and fees in return for the union's representative services.

The Taft-Hartley Act allows states to pass laws that restrict compulsory union membership. Accordingly, some states have passed **right-to-work laws,** which prohibit both the closed shop and the union shop. The laws were so named because they allow a person the right to work without having to join a union. The states that have enacted these laws are shown in Figure 18–6 on the next page.

## Landrum-Griffin Act (Labor-Management Reporting and Disclosure Act)

In 1959 the third segment of the National Labor Code, the *Landrum-Griffin Act,* was passed. A congressional committee investigating the Teamsters union had found corruption in the union. The law was aimed at protecting the rights of individual union members against such practices. Under the Landrum-Griffin Act, unions must have bylaws, financial reports must be made, union members must have a bill of rights, and the Secretary of Labor will act as a watchdog of union conduct. Because a union is supposed to be a democratic institution in which union members vote on and elect officers and approve labor contracts, the Landrum-Griffin Act was passed in part to ensure that the federal government protects those democratic rights.

In a few instances, union officers have attempted to maintain their jobs by physically harassing or attacking individuals who try to oust them from office. In other cases, union officials have "milked" pension fund monies for their own use. Such instances are not typical of most unions, but illustrate the need for legislative oversight to protect individual union members.

## Civil Service Reform Act of 1978

Passed as Title VII of the Civil Service Reform Act of 1978, the Federal Service Labor-Management Relations statute made major changes in how the federal government deals with unions. The act also identified areas that are and are not subject to bargaining. For example, as a result of the law, wages and benefits are not subject to bargaining. Instead, they are set by congressional actions.

The act established the Federal Labor Relations Authority (FLRA) as an independent agency similar to the NLRB. The FLRA was given authority to oversee and

**National emergency strike**
A strike that would affect the national economy significantly.

**Closed shop**
A firm that requires individuals to join a union before they can be hired.

**Union shop**
A firm that requires that an employee join a union, usually 30 to 60 days after being hired.

**Agency shop**
A firm that requires employees who refuse to join the union to pay amounts equal to union dues and fees for the union's representative services.

**Right-to-work laws**
State laws that prohibit both the closed shop and the union shop.

**FIGURE 18–6** *Right-to-Work States*

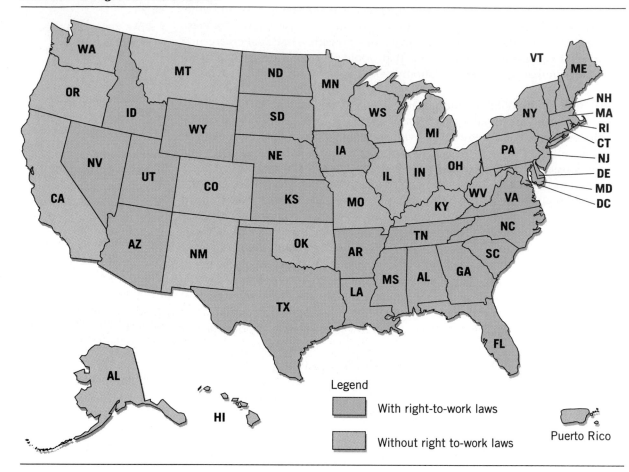

Legend

With right-to-work laws

Without right to-work laws

Puerto Rico

administer union-management relations in the federal government and to investigate unfair practices in union organizing efforts. The FLRA is a three-member body appointed on a bipartisan basis.

# Union Structure

**Craft union**
A union whose members do one type of work, often using specialized skills and training.

**Industrial union**
A union that includes many persons working in the same industry or company, regardless of jobs held.

**Federation**
A group of autonomous national and international unions.

American labor is represented by many different kinds of unions. But regardless of size and geographical scope, two basic types of unions have developed over time. A **craft union** is one whose members do one type of work, often using specialized skills and training. Examples include the International Association of Bridge, Structural, and Ornamental Iron Workers and the American Federation of Television and Radio Artists. An **industrial union** is one that includes many persons working in the same industry or company, regardless of jobs held. Examples are the United Food and Commercial Workers, the United Auto Workers, and the American Federation of State, County, and Municipal Employees.

Labor organizations have developed complex organizational structures with multiple levels. The broadest level is the **federation,** which is a group of autonomous national and international unions. A federation allows individual unions to work together and present a more unified front to the public, legislators, and members. The most prominent federation in the United States is the AFL-CIO, which is a confederation of national and international unions.

## National Unions

National or international unions are not governed by the federation even if they are affiliated with it. They collect dues and have their own boards, specialized publications, and separate constitutions and bylaws. Such national-international unions as the United Steel Workers and the American Federation of State, County, and Municipal Employees determine broad union policy and offer services to local union units. They also help maintain financial records and provide a base from which additional organizing drives may take place. Political infighting and corruption are sometimes problems for national unions, as when the federal government stepped in and overturned an election the Teamsters union had held.[6]

## Local Unions

Local unions may be centered around a particular employer organization or around a particular geographic location. Officers in local unions are elected by the membership and are subject to removal if they do not perform satisfactorily. For this reason, local union officers tend to be concerned with how they are perceived by the union members. They tend to react to situations as politicians do because they, too, are concerned about obtaining votes. In local unions, women generally do not hold offices except when the union has a large percentage of women members.

Local unions typically have business agents and union stewards. A **business agent** is a full-time union official employed by the union to operate the union office and assist union members. The agent runs the local headquarters, helps negotiate contracts with management, and becomes involved in attempts to unionize employees in other organizations. A **union steward** is an employee of a firm or organization who is elected to serve as the first-line representative of unionized workers. Stewards negotiate grievances with supervisors and generally represent employees at the worksite.

# The Process of Unionizing

The process of unionizing an employer may begin in one of two primary ways: (1) union targeting of an industry or company, or (2) employee requests. In the former case, the local or national union identifies a firm or industry in which it believes unionization can succeed. The logic for targeting is that if the union is successful in one firm or a portion of the industry, then many other workers in the industry will be more willing to consider unionizing.

The second impetus for union organizing occurs when individual workers in an organization contact a union and express a desire to unionize. The employees themselves—or the union—then may begin to campaign to win support among the other employees.

Once the unionizing efforts begin, all activities must conform to the requirements established by labor laws and the National Labor Relations Board for private-

**Business agent**
A full-time union official employed by the union to operate the union office and assist union members.

**Union steward**
An employee of a firm or organization who is elected to serve as the first-line representative of unionized workers.

**FIGURE 18–7** *Typical Unionization Process*

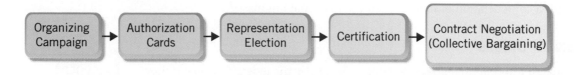

sector employees, or by the appropriate federal or state governmental agency for public-sector employees. Both management and the unions must adhere to those requirements, or the results of the effort can be appealed to the NLRB and overturned. With those requirements in mind, the union can embark on the typical union organizing process, shown in Figure 18–7.

## Organizing Campaign

Like other entities seeking members, a union usually mounts an organized campaign to persuade individuals to support its efforts. This persuasion takes many forms, including personally contacting employees outside of work, mailing materials to employees' homes, inviting employees to attend special meetings away from the company, and publicizing the advantages of union membership.

**HANDBILLING** **Handbilling** is a practice in which unions give written publicity to employees to convince them to sign authorization cards. Brochures, leaflets, and circulars are all handbills. Those items can be passed out to employees as they leave work, mailed to their homes, or even attached to their vehicles, as long as they comply with the rules established by laws and the NLRB.

**"SALTING"** Unions sometimes use paid organizers to infiltrate a targeted employer for the purpose of trying to organize other workers. In this practice, known as **salting,** the unions hire and pay people to apply for jobs at certain companies; when the people are hired, they begin organizing efforts. The U.S. Supreme Court has ruled that refusing to hire otherwise qualified applicants, even if they also are paid by a union, violates the Wagner Act.[7]

## Authorization Cards

A **union authorization card** is signed by an employee to designate a union as his or her collective bargaining agent. At least 30% of the employees in the targeted group must sign authorization cards before an election can be called.

In reality, the fact that an employee signs an authorization card does not mean that the employee is in favor of a union; it means only that he or she would like the opportunity to vote on having one. Employees who do not want a union still might sign authorization cards because they want management to know they are disgruntled.

## Representation Election

An election to determine if a union will represent the employees is supervised by the NLRB for private-sector organizations and by other legal bodies for public-

---

**Handbilling**
Practice in which unions distribute written publicity in order to convince employees to sign authorization cards.

**Salting**
Practice in which unions hire and pay people to apply for jobs at certain companies; when the people are hired, they begin union organizing efforts.

**Union authorization card**
Card signed by an employee to designate a union as his or her collective bargaining agent.

sector organizations. If two unions are attempting to represent employees, the employees will have three choices: union A, union B, or no union.

**BARGAINING UNIT** Before the election is held, the appropriate bargaining unit must be determined. A **bargaining unit** is composed of all employees eligible to select a single union to represent and bargain collectively for them. If management and the union do not agree on who is and who is not included in the unit, the regional office of the NLRB must make a determination.

A major criterion in deciding the composition of a bargaining unit is what the NLRB has called a "community of interest." This concept means that the employees have mutual interests in the following areas:

- Wages, hours, and working conditions
- Traditional industry groupings for bargaining purposes
- Physical location of employees and the amount of interaction and working relationships among employee groups
- Supervision by similar levels of management

**Bargaining unit**
All employees eligible to select a single union to represent and bargain collectively for them.

**UNFAIR LABOR PRACTICES** Employers and unions engage in a number of activities before an election. Both the Wagner Act and the Taft-Hartley Act place restrictions on these activities. Figure 18–8 lists some common tactics that management legally can use and some tactics it cannot use.[8]

**FIGURE18–8** *Legal Do's and Don'ts for Managers during the Unionization Process*

| DO (LEGAL) | DON'T (ILLEGAL) |
|---|---|
| • Tell employees about current wages and benefits and how they compare with those in other firms<br>• Tell employees that the employer opposes unionization<br>• Tell employees the disadvantages of having a union (especially cost of dues, assessments, and requirements of membership)<br>• Show employees articles about unions and relate negative experiences others have had elsewhere<br>• Explain the unionization process to employees accurately<br>• Forbid distribution of union literature during work hours in work areas<br>• Enforce disciplinary policies and rules consistently and appropriately | • Promise employees pay increases or promotions if they vote against the union<br>• Threaten employees with termination or discriminate when disciplining employees<br>• Threaten to close down or move the company if a union is voted in<br>• Spy on or have someone spy on union meetings<br>• Make a speech to employees or groups at work within 24 hours of the election (before that, it is allowed)<br>• Ask employees how they plan to vote or if they have signed authorization cards<br>• Encourage employees to persuade others to vote against the union (such a vote must be initiated solely by the employee) |

Various tactics may be used by management representatives in attempting to defeat a unionization effort. Such tactics often begin when handbills appear, or when authorization cards are being distributed. Some employers hire experts who specialize in combatting unionization efforts. Using these "union busters," as they are called by unions, appears to enhance employers' chances of winning the representation election.

**ELECTION PROCESS** Assuming an election is held, the union need receive only the votes of a *majority of those voting* in the election. For example, if a group of 200 employees is the identified unit, and only 50 people vote, only 50% of the employees voting plus one (in this case, 26) would need to vote yes in order for the union to be named as the representative of all 200 employees.

If either side believes that unfair labor practices have been used by the other side, the election results can be appealed to the NLRB. If the NLRB finds that unfair practices were used, it can order a new election. Assuming that no unfair practices have been used and the union obtains a majority in the election, the union then petitions the NLRB for certification.

Over the years, unions have won representation elections about 45% to 50% of the time. Statistics from the NLRB consistently indicate that the smaller the number of employees in the bargaining unit, the higher the percentage of elections won by the unions. In the past few years, unions have won slightly more elections than they have lost.[9]

## Certification and Decertification

Official certification of a union as the legal representative for employees is given by the NLRB (or by the equivalent body for public-sector organizations). Once certified, the union attempts to negotiate a contract with the employer. The employer *must* bargain, because it is an unfair labor practice to refuse to bargain with a certified union. Negotiation of a labor contract is one of the most important methods that unions use to achieve their major goals.

**Decertification**
A process whereby a union is removed as the representative of a group of employees.

Employees who have a union and no longer wish to be represented by it can use the election process called **decertification.** The decertification process is similar to the unionization process. Employees attempting to oust a union must obtain decertification authorization cards signed by at least 30% of the employees in the bargaining unit before an election may be called. If a majority of those voting in the election want to remove the union, the decertification effort succeeds. Some reasons that employees decide to vote out a union include better treatment by employers, efforts by employers to discredit the union, the inability of some unions to address the changing needs of a firm's workforce, and the declining image of unions. Newly certified unions are given at least a year before decertification can be attempted by workers in the bargaining unit.[10]

**Collective bargaining**
The process whereby representatives of management and workers negotiate over wages, hours, and other terms and conditions of employment.

## Contract Negotiation (Collective Bargaining)

**Collective bargaining,** the last step in unionization, is the process whereby representatives of management and workers negotiate over wages, hours, and other terms and conditions of employment. It is a give-and-take process between representatives of two organizations for the benefit of both. It is also a relationship based on relative power. The power relationship in collective

**FIGURE 18–9** *Collective Bargaining Relationship Continuum*

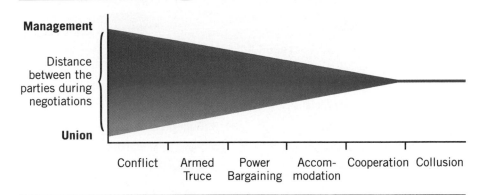

bargaining involves conflict, and the threat of conflict seems necessary to main-tain the relationship. But perhaps the most significant aspect of collective bar-gaining is that it is a continuing relationship that does not end immediately after agreement is reached. Instead, it continues for the life of the labor agree-ment and beyond.[11]

Management-union relationships in collective bargaining can follow one of several patterns. Figure 18–9 shows the relationship as a continuum, ranging from conflict to collusion. On the left side of the continuum, management and union see each other as enemies. On the right side, the two entities join to-gether illegally in collusion. Collusion, relatively rare in U.S. labor history, is against the law. A number of positions fall between these two extremes, as Fig-ure 18–9 illustrates.

*LOGGING ON . . .*
**LABORNET**
This site describes unions, news, legislation, and upcoming union events.

**http://www.igc.org/igc/ labornet**

# Collective Bargaining Issues

Figure 18–10 shows typical items in a formal labor agreement or contract. These items are all legitimate issues for collective bargaining. In addition, although not often listed as such in the contract, management rights and union security are two important issues subject to collective bargaining.

## Management Rights

Virtually all labor contracts include **management rights,** which are those rights reserved to the employer to manage, direct, and control its business. Such a provision often reads as follows:

> The employer retains all rights to manage, direct, and control its business in all particulars, except as such rights are expressly and specifically modified by the terms of this or any subsequent agreement.

By including such a provision, management is attempting to preserve its unilat-eral right to decide to make changes in any areas not identified in a labor con-tract.

**Management rights**
Those rights reserved to the employer to manage, direct, and control its business.

**FIGURE 18–10  *Typical Items in a Labor Agreement***

**LABOR AGREEMENT**

1. Purpose of agreement
2. Nondiscrimination clause
3. Management rights
4. Recognition of the union
5. Wages
6. Incentives
7. Hours of work
8. Vacations
9. Sick leave and leaves of absence
10. Discipline
11. Separation allowance
12. Seniority
13. Bulletin boards
14. Pension and insurance
15. Safety
16. Grievance procedure
17. No-strike or lockout clause
18. Definitions
19. Terms of the contract (dates)
20. Appendices

## Union Security

**Union security provisions**
Contract provisions to aid the union in obtaining and retaining members.

**Dues checkoff**
Provision that union dues will be deducted automatically from payroll checks of union members.

A major concern of union representatives when bargaining is to negotiate **union security provisions,** which are contract provisions to aid the union in obtaining and retaining members. One union security provision is the **dues checkoff,** which provides that union dues will be deducted automatically from the payroll checks of union members. This provision makes it much easier for the union to collect its funds, which it must otherwise collect by billing each member separately.

Another form of security involves *requiring union membership* of all employees, subject to state right-to-work laws. The closed shop is illegal except in limited construction-industry situations. But other types of arrangements can be developed, including *union shops, maintenance-of-membership,* and *agency shops.*

A growing facet of union security in labor contracts is the *no-layoff* policy, or *job security* guarantee. The job security concerns at General Motors, described in the opening discussion, illustrate how important such provisions are to many union workers. This is especially true in light of all the mergers, downsizings, and job reductions taking place in many industries.

## Classification of Bargaining Issues

A number of issues can be addressed during collective bargaining. The NLRB has defined bargaining issues in three ways—mandatory, permissive, and illegal. A discussion of each follows.

**MANDATORY ISSUES** Those issues that are identified specifically by labor laws or court decisions as being subject to bargaining are **mandatory issues**. If either party demands that issues in this category be bargained over, then bargaining must occur. Generally, mandatory issues relate to wages, benefits, nature of jobs, and other work-related subjects.

The following issues have been ruled to be mandatory subjects for bargaining:

- Discharge of employees
- Job security
- Grievances
- Work schedules
- Union security and dues checkoff
- Retirement and pension coverage
- Vacations
- Christmas bonuses
- Rest- and lunch-break rules
- Safety rules
- Profit-sharing plans
- Required physical exams

**Mandatory issues**
Collective bargaining issues that are identified specifically by labor laws or court decisions as being subject to bargaining.

**PERMISSIVE ISSUES** Those issues that are not mandatory but relate to certain jobs are **permissive issues.** For example, the following issues can be bargained over if both parties agree:

- Benefits for retired employees
- Product prices for employees
- Performance bonds

**Permissive issues**
Collective bargaining issues that are not mandatory but relate to certain jobs.

**ILLEGAL ISSUES** A final category, **illegal issues,** includes those issues that would require either party to take illegal action, such as giving preference to individuals who have been union members when hiring employees. If one side wants to bargain over an illegal issue, the other can refuse. The HR Perspective on the next page identifies some current issues.

**Illegal issues**
Collective bargaining issues that would require either party to take illegal action.

# The Bargaining Process

The collective bargaining process is made up of a number of stages: preparation, initial demands, negotiations, settlement, or impasse, and strikes or lockouts.

## Preparation and Initial Demands

Both labor and management representatives spend much time preparing for negotiations. Employer and industry data concerning wages, benefits, working conditions, management and union rights, productivity, and absenteeism are gathered. If the organization argues that it cannot afford to pay what the union is asking, the employer's financial situation and accompanying data are all the more relevant. However, the union must request such information before the employer is obligated to provide it.

Typical bargaining includes initial proposals of expectations by both sides. The amount of rancor or calmness exhibited sets the tone for future negotiations between the parties.

## Continuing Negotiations

After opening positions have been taken, each side attempts to determine what the other values highly so the best bargain can be struck. For example, the union may be asking the employer to pay for dental benefits as part of a package that

## HR PERSPECTIVE
# Important Current Issues in the Labor Movement

For the labor movement nationally the major issues are often related to, but different from, issues confronting a local union and a company. Some of the issues already mentioned are the decline in membership, targeting industries, layoffs, and NAFTA. However, other issues are receiving considerable attention as well:

- *Dues—use and disclosure:* Dues that members pay to the union are used to maintain the union and advance its causes. Recently, union spending has become a topic of debate. For example, the AFL-CIO spent $35 million to back Democrats for Congress despite the fact that nearly 40% of union members routinely vote Republican. The NLRB has ruled that members are entitled to know how union dues money is spent. Further, a Californa voter initiative, which would have allowed workers who did not agree with the union's expenditure of their dues to get the money back, was narrowly defeated in a statewide election.

- *When does cooperation become collusion?* The Supreme Court added another decision to the controversy over employee involvement issues (covered in more detail shortly). It ruled that WEBCOR Packaging, a Michigan-

based cardboard box maker, "created a labor organization" in violation of the NLRA. WEBCOR had argued that it wanted to encourage employee involvement in workplace decisions when it constituted a "plant council." The NLRA, which prohibits company-dominated or "sham" unions, had held that the council was "making recommendations for managements' consideration," relative to terms and conditions of work, and was a "company union."

- *Who is an employee?* Are the independent contractors used by many businesses instead of full-time workers considered "employees" for organizing purposes? Contingent worker growth is a strong trend mentioned earlier. If unions cannot organize this growing group, they will continue to lose potential members.

- *Union mergers:* Like companies, unions find there is strength in size, and several national unions have merged or are considering doing so. However, not all merger attempts succeed. The NEA (National Education Association) recently rejected a plan to merge with the AFT (American Federation of Teachers). The NEA has long cherished its independence from traditional labor unions; and the

AFT, which is affiliated with the AFL-CIO, is a more traditional labor union. The NEA suggests it is more akin to the American Medical Association than to a labor union, and is a "professional" group. However, the issue described next may call that professional orientation into question as a reason *not* to join a traditional labor union.

- *Professionals—in unions?* As the number of physicians who are salaried employees (perhaps of HMOs) increases from less than 25% to almost 50%, these professionals are joining unions. The physicians' most common complaint is that they have lost control of patient care decisions. In another field, teaching assistants (future professors) at several universities such as Harvard and the University of Illinois have tried to start unions. But universities claim assistantships are part of a graduate student's education and not subject to collective bargaining rights.

Dues, cooperation, contractors, mergers, and professionals are all issues forcing change on the union-management relationships. How these issues are addressed by unions and management may be significant in determining future union membership changes.[12]

also includes wage demands and retirement benefits. However, the union may be most interested in the wages and retirement benefits, and may be willing to trade the dental payments for more wages. Management has to determine which the union wants more and decide exactly what to give up.

**GOOD FAITH** Provisions in federal law require that both employer and employee bargaining representatives negotiate in *good faith*. In good-faith negotiations, the parties agree to send negotiators who can bargain and make decisions, rather than people who do not have the authority to commit either group to a decision. Meetings between the parties cannot be scheduled at absurdly inconvenient hours. Some give-and-take discussions also must occur.

## Settlement and Contract Agreement

After an initial agreement has been made, the bargaining parties usually return to their respective constituencies to determine if what they have informally agreed on is acceptable. A particularly crucial stage is **ratification** of the labor agreement, which occurs when union members vote to accept the terms of a negotiated agreement. Prior to the ratification vote, the union negotiating team explains the agreement to the union members and presents it for a vote. If the agreement is approved, it is then formalized into a contract. The agreement also contains language on the duration of the contract.

**Ratification**
Process by which union members vote to accept the terms of a negotiated labor agreement.

## Bargaining Impasse

Regardless of the structure of the bargaining process, labor and management do not always reach agreement on the issues. If impasse occurs, then the disputes can be taken to conciliation, mediation, or arbitration.

**CONCILIATION AND MEDIATION** When an impasse occurs, an outside party may aid the two deadlocked parties to continue negotiations and arrive at a solution. In **conciliation,** the third party attempts to keep union and management negotiators talking so that they can reach a voluntary settlement but makes no proposals for solutions. In **mediation,** the third party assists the negotiators in their discussions and also suggests settlement proposals. In neither conciliation nor mediation does the third party attempt to impose a solution.

**Conciliation**
Process by which a third party attempts to keep union and management negotiators talking so that they can reach a voluntary settlement.

**Mediation**
Process by which a third party assists negotiators in their discussions and also suggests settlement proposals.

**ARBITRATION** The process of **arbitration** is a process that uses a neutral third party to make a decision. It can be conducted by either an individual or a panel of individuals. Arbitration is used to solve bargaining impasses primarily in the public sector. This "interest" arbitration is not frequently used in the private sector, because companies generally do not want an outside party making decisions about their rights, wages, benefits, and other issues. However, grievance, or "rights" arbitration is used extensively in the private sector. Arbitration is discussed in more detail when grievance procedures are described later in this chapter.

**Arbitration**
Process that uses a neutral third party to make a decision.

## Strikes and Lockouts

If a deadlock cannot be resolved, then an employer may revert to a lockout—or a union may revert to a strike. During a **strike,** union members refuse to work in order to put pressure on an employer. Often, the striking union members picket or demonstrate against the employer outside the place of business by carrying placards and signs. In a **lockout,** management shuts down company operations to prevent union members from working. This action may avert possible damage or sabotage to company facilities or injury to employees who continue to work. It also provides leverage to managers.[13]

**Strike**
Work stoppage in which union members refuse to work in order to put pressure on an employer.

**Lockout**
Shutdown of company operations undertaken by management to prevent union members from working.

*LOGGING ON . . .*
**Labor Arbitration and Dispute Resolution Pages**
This website has links to professional arbitration organizations and associations.

**http://www.auburn.edu/ ~wilsokc/arbitration.html**

**TYPES OF STRIKES**  The following types of strikes can occur:

- *Economic strikes* occur when the parties fail to reach agreement during collective bargaining.
- *Unfair labor practice strikes* occur when union members walk away from their jobs over what they feel are illegal employer actions, such as refusal to bargain.
- *Wildcat strikes* occur during the life of the collective bargaining agreement without approval of union leadership and violate a no-strike clause in a labor contract. Strikers can be discharged or disciplined.
- *Jurisdictional strikes* occur when one union's members walk out to force the employer to assign work to them instead of to another union.
- *Sympathy strikes* express one union's support for another union involved in a dispute, even though the first union has no disagreement with the employer.

Workers' rights vary depending on the type of strike that occurs.[14] For example, in an economic strike, an employer is free to replace the striking workers. But with an unfair labor practices strike, workers who want their jobs back at the end of the strike must be reinstated.

Because there has been a decline in union power, work stoppages due to strikes and lockouts are relatively rare. Thus, many unions are reluctant to go on strike because of the financial losses their members would incur, or the fear that the strike would cause the employer to go bankrupt. In addition, management has shown its willingness to hire replacements, and some strikes have ended with union workers losing their jobs.

**REPLACEMENT OF WORKERS ON STRIKE**  Management has always had the ability to simply replace workers who struck, but the option was not widely used. A strike by the United Auto Workers (UAW) against Caterpillar in the 1990s changed that. A contrasting approach to replacing strikers is shown in the United Parcel Service strike, discussed in the HR Perpsective on the next page.

# Management's Choice: Cooperate or Stay Nonunion

The adversarial relationship that naturally exists between unions and management may lead to the conflicts discussed previously. But there is also a growing recognition by many union leaders and employer representatives that cooperation between management and labor unions is sensible if organizations are going to compete in a global economy. An alternative to management cooperating with a union is to try to stay nonunion. The choice between the two is a strategic HR decision that each employer must make.

## Cooperation and Employee Involvement

Companies often cited as examples of successful union-management cooperation include National Steel Corporation, Scott Paper Company, Saturn, and Xerox. All have established cooperative programs of one sort or another that include employee involvement. Some in the labor movement fear that such programs may lead to an undermining of union support by creating a closer identification with the company's concerns and goals.

# Two Very Different Strikes in the '90s

## Caterpillar Beats UAW

One of the most bitter and prolonged strikes in recent times, called by the United Auto Workers, occurred at Caterpillar, Inc. The clear winner was Caterpillar, which used replacement of striking workers as a key part of its management strategy to counterattack UAW efforts.

A partial strike began when the pevious UAW contract expired. Caterpillar responded by locking out UAW members at some Caterpillar plants for several months. Then the UAW began a companywide strike.

Caterpillar threatened to replace strikers permanently by hiring new nonunion workers. The UAW responded by calling off its strike, but began a campaign to increase dramatically the number of grievances that were filed. The UAW members also initiated a number of wildcat strikes over the unresolved grievances.

Finally, the UAW called a national strike. In response, Caterpillar kept production flowing and

plants open by moving salaried office workers, supervisors, and managers into production jobs. Also, Caterpillar hired over 5,000 replacement workers from a huge pool of applicants who wanted the high-paying jobs at the company.

Caterpillar's aggressive approach with the union paid off—with five years of record profits. Ultimately, the UAW caved in and settled with Caterpillar. Some call its bargaining tactics "bad faith," but the result was an improvement of Caterpillar's competitive position globally.[15]

## UPS Teamsters Win

Also during the 1990s, the Teamsters struck United Parcel Service (UPS). The strike lasted only 14 days. The circumstances surrounding this strike were quite different from those of the Caterpillar strike.

UPS is a special case as a company. It is not traded on the stock market, and is thus less inclined to fight for every penny of profit. It is in a strong competitive position, so it can pass costs on to customers

and suffer fewer consequences. Further, the company prides itself on being tolerant of unions. During the strike, management made the decision *not* to hire replacements.

UPS workers received considerable public support. Many people know their UPS driver personally, and the issue of part-time work was one that many could identify with. Management caved in on several of the Teamsters union's demands: pensions, part-time pay, and conversion of part-time jobs to full-time. The biggest victory involved pensions, because the company had wanted to pull out of a union-run pension plan and set up its own.

The outcome was viewed as a union victory. The issues, timing, public relations, and management approach combined to keep the strike short and the outcome favorable for the Teamsters. These circumstances could not have been duplicated in many of the strikes that occur in other industries.[16]

## Employee Involvement and the NLRB

Suggesting that union-management cooperation or involving employees in making suggestions and decisions could be bad seems a little like arguing against motherhood, the flag, and apple pie. Yet some decisions by the National Labor Relations Board appear to have done just that. Some historical perspective is required to understand the issues that surrounded the decisions.

In the 1930s, when the Wagner Act was written, certain employers would form sham "company unions," coercing workers into joining them in order to keep legitimate unions from organizing the employees. As a result, the Wagner Act contained prohibitions against employer-dominated labor organizations. These prohibitions were enforced, and company unions disappeared.

**ELECTROMATION DECISION** Because of the Wagner Act, some or all of the 30,000 employee involvement programs set up in recent years may be illegal, according to an NLRB decision dealing with Electromation, an Elkhart, Indiana, firm. Electromation used teams of employees to solicit other employees' views about such issues as wages and working conditions. The NLRB labeled them as "labor organizations," according to the Wagner Act in 1935. It further found that they were "dominated" by management, which had formed the teams, set their goals, and decided how they would operate. As a result of this and other decisions, many employers have had to rethink and restructure their employee involvement efforts.

**TEAM ACT** Employer opposition to the NLRB decisions led to the drafting of the Teamwork for Employees and Managers Act. This act, called the TEAM Act, tried to amend the Wagner Act to allow nonunion employees in team-based situations to work with management concerning working conditions and workplace situations. Because of strong union opposition, President Clinton vetoed the bill. Nevertheless, the act showed that there was considerable support for overturning the NLRB decisions.

## Union Ownership: The Ultimate Cooperation

Unions have become active participants by encouraging workers to become partial or complete owners of the companies that employ them. These efforts were spurred by concerns that firms were preparing to shut down, or to be merged or bought out by financial investors who the unions feared would cut union jobs.

Unions have been active in assisting members in putting together employee stock ownership plans (ESOPs) to purchase all or part of some firms. One of the best-known purchases is the employee buyout of United Airlines. The unions representing United Airlines employees made a counteroffer after a takeover bid. In conjunction with the top management group at United Airlines, the pilots' union persuaded the unions representing machinists and other employees (excluding the flight attendants) to back the buyout offer.

Some firms also have union representatives on their boards of directors. The best-known example is Daimler-Chrysler Corporation, in which a representative of the United Auto Workers was given a seat on the board in exchange for assistance in getting federal government financial help in the late 1970s. This practice is very common in European countries, where it is called *co-determination*.

## Staying Nonunion

Employees may make a strategic decision to remain nonunion. Such a choice is perfectly rational, but may require some different HR policies and philosophies to accomplish. "Preventative" employee relations may emphasize good morale and loyalty based on concern for employees, competitive wages and benefits, a good system for dealing with employee complaints, and safe working conditions. Other issues may also play a part in employees' decisions to stay nonunion, but if the points just listed are adequately addressed, few workers will feel the need for a union to represent them to management.[17]

# Grievance Management

Unions know that employee dissatisfaction is a potential source of trouble, whether it is expressed or not. Hidden dissatisfaction grows and creates reactions that may be completely out of proportion to the original concerns. Therefore, it is important that dissatisfaction be given an outlet. A **complaint,** which is merely an indication of employee dissatisfaction that has not been submitted in writing, is one outlet.

If the employee is represented by a union, and the employee says, "I should have received the job transfer because I have more seniority, which is what the union contract states," and she submits it in writing, then that complaint is a grievance. A **grievance** is a complaint that has been put in writing and thus made formal. Management should be concerned with both complaints and grievances, because both may be important indicators of potential problems within the workforce. Without a grievance procedure, management may be unable to respond to employee concerns because managers are unaware of them. Therefore, a formal grievance procedure is a valuable communication tool for the organization.[18]

**Complaint**

An indication of employee dissatisfaction that has not been submitted in writing.

**Grievance**

A complaint that has been put in writing and made formal.

## Grievance Responsibilities

Figure 18–11 shows the typical division of responsibilities between the HR unit and line managers for handling grievances. These responsibilities vary considerably from one organization to another, even between unionized firms. But the HR unit usually has more general responsibilities. Managers must accept the grievance procedure as a possible constraint on some of their decisions.[19]

Management should recognize that a grievance is a behavioral expression of some underlying problem. This statement does not mean that every grievance is a symptom of something radically wrong. Employees do file grievances over petty matters as well as over important concerns, and management must be able to differentiate between the two. However, to ignore a repeated problem by taking a legalistic approach to grievance resolution is to miss much of what the grievance procedure can do for management.

**FIGURE 18–11** *Typical Grievance Responsibilities*

| HR Unit | Managers |
| --- | --- |
| • Assists in designing the grievance procedure<br>• Monitors trends in grievance rates for the organization<br>• May assist in preparing grievance cases for arbitration<br>• May have responsibility for settling grievances | • Operate within provisions of the grievance procedure<br>• Attempt to resolve grievances where possible "closest to the problem"<br>• Document grievance cases for the grievance procedure<br>• Engage in grievance prevention efforts |

# Grievance Procedures

**Grievance procedures**
Formal channels of communications used to resolve grievances.

**Grievance procedures** are formal communications channels designed to settle a grievance as soon as possible after the problem arises. First-line supervisors are usually closest to a problem; however, the supervisor is concerned with many other matters besides one employee's grievance, and may even be the subject of an employee's grievance.

Supervisory involvement presents some problems in solving a grievance at this level. For example, William Dunn, a 27-year-old lathe operator at a machine shop, is approached by his supervisor, Joe Bass, one Monday morning and told that his production is lower than his quota. Bass advises Dunn to catch up. Dunn reports that a part of his lathe needs repair. Bass suggests that Dunn should repair it himself to maintain his production because the mechanics are busy. Dunn refuses, and a heated argument ensues; as a result, Bass orders Dunn to go home for the day.

The illustration shows how easily an encounter between an employee and a supervisor can lead to a breakdown in the relationship. This breakdown, or failure to communicate effectively, could be costly to Dunn if he loses his job, a day's wages, or his pride. It also could be costly to Bass, who represents management, and to the owner of the machine shop if production is delayed or halted. Grievance procedures can resolve such conflicts.

In this particular case, the machine shop has a contract with the International Brotherhood of Lathe Operators, of which Dunn is a member. The contract specifically states that company plant mechanics are to repair all manufacturing equipment. Therefore, Bass appears to have violated the union contract. What is Dunn's next step? He may use the grievance procedure provided for him in the contract. The actual grievance procedure is different in each organization. It depends on what the employer and the union have agreed on and what is written in the labor contract.

A unionized employee generally has a right to union representation if he or she is being questioned by management and if discipline may result. If these so-called *Weingarten rights* (named after the court case that established them) are violated and the employee is dismissed, he or she usually will be reinstated with back pay.

**STEPS IN A GRIEVANCE PROCEDURE** Grievance procedures can vary in the number of steps they include. Figure 18–12 shows a typical procedure, which includes the following steps:

1. The employee discusses the grievance with the union steward (the union's representative on the job) and the supervisor.
2. The union steward discusses the grievance with the supervisor's manager.
3. The union grievance committee discusses the grievance with appropriate company managers.
4. The representative of the national union discusses the grievance with designated company executives.
5. The final step may be to use an impartial third party for ultimate disposition of the grievance.

If the grievance remains unsettled, representatives for both sides would continue to meet to resolve the conflict. On rare occasions, a representative from the national union might join the process. Or, a corporate executive from headquar-

**FIGURE 18–12 *Steps in a Grievance Procedure***

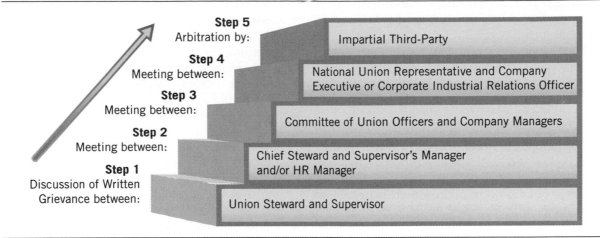

ters (if the firm is a large corporation) might be called in to help resolve the grievance. If not solved at this stage, the grievance goes to arbitration.

Arbitration is flexible and can be applied to almost any kind of controversy except those involving criminal matters. Advisory, or voluntary, arbitration may be used in negotiating agreements or in interpreting clauses in existing agreements. Because labor and management generally agree that disputes over the negotiation of a new contract should not be arbitrated in the private sector, the most important role played by arbitration in labor relations is as the final step in the grievance procedure.[20]

**Grievance arbitration** is a means by which disputes arising from different interpretations of a labor contract are settled by a third party. This should not be confused with contract or issues arbitration, discussed earlier, when arbitration is used to determine how a contract will be written.

Grievance arbitration presents several problems. It has been criticized as being too costly, too legalistic, and too time-consuming. One study found that arbitrators generally treated women more leniently than men in disciplinary grievance situations. In addition, many feel that there are too few qualified and experienced arbitrators. Despite these problems, arbitration has been successful and is currently seen as a potentially superior solution to traditional approaches to resolving union-management problems.[21]

**Grievance arbitration**
A means by which disputes arising from different interpretations of a labor contract are settled by a third party.

# Summary

- A union is a formal association of workers that promotes the interests of its members through collective action.
- Workers join unions primarily because of management's failure to address major job-related concerns.

- Current union membership as a percentage of the workforce is down dramatically from 1960.
- The structural levels of unions include federations, national or international unions, and local unions. Business agents and union stewards work at the local level.

- The "National Labor Code" is composed of three laws that are the legal basis for labor relations today: the Wagner Act, the Taft-Hartley Act, and the Landrum-Griffin Act.
- The Wagner Act was designed to protect unions and workers; the Taft-Hartley Act restored some powers to management; and the Landrum-Griffin Act was passed to protect individual union members.
- The process of organizing includes an organizing campaign, authorization cards, a representation election, NLRB certification, and collective bargaining.
- Collective bargaining occurs when management negotiates with representatives of workers over wages, hours, and working conditions.
- The issues subject to collective bargaining fall into three categories: mandatory, permissive, and illegal.

- The collective bargaining process includes preparation, initial demands, negotiations, and settlement.
- Once an agreement (contract) is signed between labor and management, it becomes the document governing what each party can and cannot do.
- When impasse occurs, work stoppages through strikes or lockouts can be used to pressure the other party.
- Grievances express worker written dissatisfaction or differences in contract interpretations. Grievances follow a formal path to resolution.
- A formal grievance procedure is usually specified in a union contract, but it should exist in most organizations to provide a system for handling problems.
- A grievance procedure begins with the first-level supervisor—and ends (if it is not resolved along the way) with arbitration.

# Review and Discussion Questions

1. Discuss the following statement: "I think anybody who anticipates that unions will reverse their decline in membership during the next 10 years is dreaming."
2. Identify the three parts of the "National Labor Code" and the key elements of each.
3. A coworker has just brought you a union leaflet that urges each employee to sign an authorization card. What events would you expect to occur from this point on?
4. Discuss how union-management cooperation has been affected by NLRB rulings.
5. What steps are followed in a typical grievance process? Why is arbitration, as the final step of a grievance process, important and useful?

# Terms to Know

agency shop   613
arbitration   623
bargaining unit   617
business agent   615
closed shop   613
collective bargaining   618
complaint   627
conciliation   623
craft union   614
decertification   618
dues checkoff   620

federation   614
grievance   627
grievance arbitration   629
grievance procedure   628
handbilling   616
illegal issues   621
industrial union   614
lockout   623
management rights   619
mandatory issues   621
mediation   623

national emergency strike   613
permissive issues   621
ratification   623
right-to-work laws   613
salting   616
strike   623
union   604
union authorization card   616
union security provisions   620
union shop   613
union steward   615

# Using the Internet

## Recognizing Unionization Activity

Some of the supervisors have approached you, the HR manager, about union activity. They have heard some rumors and have asked you to give them a list of activities, behaviors, or actions to look for as they supervise their employees. Their intent is to recognize union activity before the union movement has spread throughout the plant. Use the following website to develop a set of guidelines for the supervisors. **http://www.genelevine.com/Papers/66.htm**

# CASE

## The "Stolen" Orange Juice

Grievances can be filed over large or small matters. The following case represents a grievance that was decided by an arbitrator hired by Greyhound Food Management (Warren, Michigan) and the United Catering, Restaurant, Bar, & Hotel Workers, Local 1064.

The grievance was filed by the union on behalf of Tom, a union member working as a fast-food attendant at a Greyhound-operated cafeteria. The Greyhound Food Service provided food-service management on a contract basis for many firms, including Hydra Matic, a manufacturing company located in Warren, Michigan.

Tom had been working for Greyhound for almost a year and was working the 1 P.M.–8:30 P.M. swing shift at the time of his discharge from the company. The company justified Tom's employment termination by asserting that he had attempted to steal a six-ounce container of orange juice, which normally sold for 58 cents.

Tom's supervisor testified that from his office he had observed Tom attempting to leave the premises with the container of orange juice hidden under his jacket. After stopping Tom, the supervisor had accused him of attempting to steal the orange juice. Then the supervisor had telephoned the assistant manager for instructions. The assistant manager had told the supervisor to document the incident and had stated that he (the assistant manager) would take care of the matter the next morning. The supervisor's written report stated that he had heard the refrigerator door slam, then had heard Tom walking toward the door. The supervisor had asked Tom twice what Tom had in his coat, after which Tom had pulled the juice out of his coat, dropping and spilling it on the floor.

The following morning, the assistant manager called Tom and the union steward into his office and confronted them with the supervisor's written description of the incident. Tom denied that he had attempted to steal the orange juice, saying that the supervisor had just seen some orange juice on the floor. At a meeting later that morning, the assistant manager terminated Tom's employment. Tom filed a grievance, which was immediately denied. Tom and the union then requested arbitration, as was allowed under the company/union labor contract.

The arbitrator reviewed several documents, including statements from the supervisor, the assistant manager, a former employee, and the union steward. Also, he reviewed the relevant sections of the labor contract on management rights, seniority, and the grievance procedure. Finally, the arbitrator reviewed the list of company rules and regulations posted by the time clock, one of which said that disciplinary action ranging from reprimand to immediate discharge could result from rule violation. The first rule prohibited "stealing private, company, or client's property."

### Company Position

The company's position was that Tom had knowledge of the posted work rules, the first of which clearly prohibited theft. The company also had a policy that no company property was to leave the restaurant. The testimony of the supervisor established that Tom had attempted to steal and remove company property. It was not relevant that Tom's impermissible act had not succeeded. The detection by management of the theft before Tom left the premises did not excuse the act. Also, the company said that the size or dollar amount of the theft was immaterial. Therefore, because the company followed the terms of the union contract that provided for dismissal of employees for "just cause," and because Tom knew, or should have known, of the rule against stealing, the arbitrator should rule for the company.

## Union Position

The union's position was that the act of attempting to steal a container of orange juice valued at 58 cents involved moral turpitude and therefore required the ap-plication of a "high degree of proof." The employer carried the burden of convincing the arbitrator beyond a reasonable doubt through the witnesses that Tom had attempted to steal the orange juice. The union contended that even though Tom had been subject to some other minor disciplinary actions in the past, termination was too harsh a penalty and therefore the arbitrator should rule for Tom and the union.[22]

## Questions

1. How important is the value of the item in comparison with the alleged act of stealing?
2. Because Tom never left the company premises with the juice, did he actually steal it?
3. How would you rule in this case? (Your instructor can give you the actual decision of the arbitrator.)

# Notes

1. Based on Gregory L. White, "Stepping on It," *The Wall Street Journal,* June 12, 1998, 1; Rebecca Blumenstein, "Hack-o-Gram Writer Is Sent to Front Line of GM Strike," *The Wall Street Journal,* June 29, 1998, B1; Chriss Woodyard, "Global GM Plants at Strike's Center," *USA Today,* June 19, 1998, 3B; Micheline Maynard, "GM Thinks Globally, Workers Act Locally," *USA Today,* June 12, 1998, B1; Glenn Burkins, "Picket Line's Next Generation Shows UAW Weakness," *The Wall Street Journal,* June 26, 1998, B1; and Rebecca Blumenstein and Fara Warner, "GM Faces a Sales Collapse Due to Strike," *The Wall Street Journal,* July 2, 1998, B3.

2. Adrienne Birecree and Suzanne Konzelmann, "A Comparative Analysis of Conflictual Labor Relations in the Corn Processing, Steel, Paper, and Coal Industries," *Journal of Economic Issues* 29 (1997), 129.

3. William P. Webster, "Maintaining Quality Relationships between Labor and Management," *National Productivity Review,* Spring 1997, 63–69.

4. Based on David Whitford, "Labor's Lost Chance," *Fortune,* September 28, 1999, 177–182; and James Worsham, "Labor's New Assault," *Nation's Business,* June 1997, 16; Pascal Zachary, "AFL-CIO Mounts Organizing Drive in Las Vegas," *The Wall Street Journal,* January 27, 1977, A2; Glenn Burkins, "Small Victories," *The Wall Street Journal,* April 20, 1998, A1; and Glenn Burkins, "Child Care Workers," *The Wall Street Journal,* May 19, 1998, A1.

5. Glenn Burkins, "Labor Unions See Membership Rise Slightly," *The Wall Street Journal,* January 26, 1999, B12.

6. Kevin Galvin, "Political Infighting Wracks Union Headquarters," *Laramie Daily Boomerang,* June 28, 1998, 25.

7. *NLRB v. Town & Country Electric, Inc. and Ameristaff Contractors, Ltd.,* 115 Ct. 450 (1995); and Cory Fine, "Covert Union Organizing," *Workforce,* May 1998, 45–51.

8. James Worsham, "A Course Change at the NLRB," *Nation's Business,* February 1998, 36.

9. Facts and Figures, "Unions Won More Representation Elections than They Lost," *Bulletin to Management,* June 4, 1998, 173; and Kate Bronfenbrenner, "The Role of Union Strategies in NLRB Certification Elections," *Industrial and Labor Relations Review* 49 (1997), 195.

10. Robert W. Schupp, "When Is a Union Not a Union?" *Labor Law Journal* 48 (1997), 359–370.

11. Edward Cohen-Rosenthal, "Sociotechnical Systems and Unions: Nicety or Necessity?" *Human Relations,* May 1997, 585.

12. Adapted from Glenn Burkins, "Unions Are Set Back on Dues Disclosure," *The Wall Street Journal,* January 17, 1997, A2; "Labor-Management Cooperation," *Human Resource Report* (BNA), March 2, 1998, 216; James Worsham, "A Course Change at the NLRB," *Nation's Business,* February 1998, 36; Steven Findley, "Doctors' Hope for Their Ills: Unions," *USA Today,* July 5, 1998, A3; Rene Sanchez, "Teacher's Union Nixes Merger," *Denver Post,* July 6, 1998, 2A; Mary Beth Marklein, "An Advanced Lesson in Labor Relations," *USA Today,* April 1998, A6; and Lisa Jordan, "Deconstructing Contingent Staffing," *Labor Law Journal* 48 (1997), 512–518.

13. Elizabeth M. Goering, "Integration Versus Distribution in Contract Negotiations," *Journal of Business Communications,* October 1997, 383.

14. T. Zane Reeves, "Strikes—Are They Useful Anymore?" *Journal of Collective Negotiations in the Public Sector,* Winter 1997, 65–71.

15. "Not Over Till It's Over," *The Economist,* February 28, 1998, 33–34; Carl Quint Quatanilla, "Caterpillar's Revised Pact Ratified," *The Wall Street Journal,* March 23, 1998, B10; and Clive Gilson, Ellen Dannin, and Terry Wagon, "Collective Bargaining Theory and the Doctrine of Implementation of Final Offers Collide," *Labor Law Journal* 48 (1997), 587–600.

16. Del Jones, "Strike Targets Two-Tier Workforce," *USA Today,* August 5, 1997; and "Labour's Summer Victory," *The Economist,* August 23, 1997, 17–18.

17. Jackson Lewis, *Winning NLRB Elections* (Chicago: CCH Inc., 1997).

18. Robert P. Hebdon and Robert N. Hebdon, "Tradeoffs Among Expressions of Industrial Conflict: Public Sector Strikes Bans and Grievance Arbitrations," *Industrial and Labor Relations Review* 50 (1998), 204–221.

19. Philip Zimmerman, "In-House Dispute Resolution Programs," *CPA Journal,* March 1998, p. 59.

20. Kay O. Wilburn, "Employee Disputes: Solving Them Out of Court," *Management Review,* March 1998, 17–21.

21. "Labor Arbitration Under Fire," *International Labour Review,* Autumn 1997, 435.

22. 89 LA 1138 (1987).

# APPENDIX A

# Content Outline of the HR Body of Knowledge©

©Human Resource Certification Institute

After each of the major functional sub-areas are the weightings for that sub-area. **The first number in the parentheses is the PHR percentage weighting and the second number is the SPHR percentage weighting.** These weightings should help you allocate your time in preparing for each respective examination.

## I. MANAGEMENT PRACTICES (15%, 21%)

**A.** Role of HR in Organizations (2.78%, 3.91%)
1. HR Roles: Advisory/Counselor, Consultant, Service, Control
2. Change Agent Role/Reengineering and Facilitating Both Content & Process
3. HR's Role in Strategic Planning
4. HR Generalist and HR Specialist Roles
5. Effects of Different Organizational Contexts and Industries on HR functions
6. HR Policies and Procedures
7. Integration and Coordination of HR Functions
8. Outsourcing the HR Functions

**B.** Human Resource Planning (2.04%, 2.87%)
1. Environmental Scanning
2. Internal Scanning
3. Human Resources Inventory
4. Human Resource Information Systems
5. Action Plans and Programs
6. Evaluation of Human Resource Planning

**C.** Organizational Design and Development (.65%, .99%)
1. Organizational Structures
2. Organizational Development
3. Diagnosis and Intervention Strategies: Action Research, Sensing, Team Building, Goal Setting, Survey Feedback, Strategic Planning, Visioning, Sensitivity Training (T-groups), Grid Training
4. Role of Organizational Culture in Organizational Development
5. Role of International Culture in Organizational Development
6. Organizational Development in Response to Technological Change

**D.** Budgeting, Controlling, and Measurement (1.08%, 1.56%)
1. HR Budgeting Process
2. HR Control Process
3. Evaluating HR Effectiveness

**E.** Motivation (.59%, .77%)
1. Motivation Theories
2. Applying Motivation Theory in Management

**F.** Leadership (.97%, 1.32%)
1. Leadership Theories
2. Effect of Leadership in Organizatoins
3. Leadership Training

**G.** Quality and Performance Management/TQM (1.82%, 2.41%)
1. Performance Planning: Identifying Goals/Desired Behaviors
2. Setting and Communicating Performance Standards
3. Measuring Results and Providing Feedback
4. Implementing Performance Improvement Strategies
5. Evaluating Results

**H.** Employee Involvement Strategies (2.11%, 2.57%)
1. Work Teams
2. Job Design and Redesign
3. Employee Ownership/ESOPs
4. Employee Suggestion System
5. Participative Management
6. Alternative Work Schedules
7. Role of HR in Employee Involvement Programs

**I.** HR Research (.71%, 1.16%)
1. Research Design and Methodology
2. Quantitative Analysis
3. Qualitative Research

**J.** International HR Management (1.49%, 2.48%)
1. Cultural Differences
2. Legal Aspects of International HR
3. Expatriation and Repatriation
4. Issues of Multinational Corporations
5. Compensation and Benefits for Foreign Nationals and Expatriates
6. The Role of HR in International Business

**K.** Ethics (.77%, .96%)
1. Ethical Issues
2. Establishing Ethical Behavior in the Organization

## II. GENERAL EMPLOYMENT PRACTICES (19%, 17%)

**A.** Legal & Regulatory Factors: Definitions, Requirements, Proscribed Practices, Exemptions, Enforcement, Remedies, & Case Histories (6.38%, 5.29%)

1. Title VII of the Civil Rights Act (1964) as Amended (1972, 1991)
2. Age Discrimination in Employment Act (1967) as Amended
3. Health, Medical, & Rehabilitation Statutes (e.g., Vocational Rehabilitation Act, Pregnancy Discrimination Act, Americans with Disabilities Act, Family & Medical Leave Act, HMO Act, etc.)
4. Vietnam-era Veterans Readjustment Act (1986)
5. Immigration Reform and Control Act (1986) as Amended (1990)
6. Employee Polygraph Protection Act (1988)
7. Uniform Guidelines on Employee Selection Procedures
8. Worker Adjustment and Retraining Notification Act (1988)
9. North American Free Trade Act
10. Common Law Tort Theories
11. Copyright Statutes
12. Compensation Laws and Regulations
13. Consumer Credit Protection Act: Wage Garnishment (1968), Fair Credit Reporting (1970)
14. Social Security/Retirement Legislation (e.g., ERISA)
15. COBRA (Consolidated Omnibus Budget Reconciliation Act (1990)); Omnibus Budget Reconciliation Act (1993)
16. Workers' Compensation and Unemployment Compensation Laws and Regulations
17. Legal and Regulatory Factors Affecting Employee and Labor Relations (e.g., NLRA, Taft-Hartley, Landrum-Griffin, etc.)
18. Federal Health, Safety, and Security Legislation (e.g., OSHA)

**B.** Job Analysis, Job Description, and Job Specification (2.14%, 1.78%)
1. Methods of Job Analysis
2. Types of Data Gathered in a Job Analysis
3. Uses of Job Analysis
4. Job Descriptions
5. Job/Position Specifications
6. Validity & Reliability of Job Analysis, Job Description, & Job Specification

**C.** Individual Employment Rights (1.72%, 1.67%)
1. Employment-At-Will Doctrine
2. Exceptions to Employment-At-Will
3. Common Law Tort Theories
4. Job-As-Property Doctrine
5. Non-Compete Agreements

**D.** Performance Appraisals (5.10%, 4.60%)
1. Performance Measurement—The Criterion
2. Criterion Problems
3. Documenting Employee Performance

4. Category Rating Appraisal Methods
5. Comparative Appraisal Methods
6. Narrative Appraisal Methods
7. Special Appraisal Methods: MBO, BARS, BOS
8. Types of Appraisals
9. Rating Errors
10. Appraisal Interview
11. Linking Appraisals to Employment Decisions
12. Legal Constraints on Performance Appraisal
13. Documentation

**E.** Workplace Behavior Problems (1.90%, 1.55%)
1. Discipline
2. Absenteeism and Tardiness
3. Sexual Harassment
4. Drug and Alcohol Use
5. Off-duty Conduct

**F.** Employee Attitudes, Opinions and Satisfaction (2.01%, 2.11%)
1. Measurement
2. Results Analysis
3. Interpretation
4. Feedback
5. Intervention
6. Confidentiality and Anonymity of Surveys

**III. STAFFING (19%, 15%)**
**A.** Equal Employment Opportunity/Affirmative Action (3.56%, 2.99%)
1. Legal Endorsement of EEO: Supreme Court Decisions
2. Equal Employment Opportunity Programs
3. Affirmative Action Plans
4. Special Programs to Eliminate Discrimination
5. Fairness Issues: Reverse Discrimination, Quota Hiring vs. Merit Hiring

**B.** Recruitment (2.84%, 2.22%)
1. Determining Recruitment Needs and Objectives
2. Identifying Selection Criteria
3. Internal Sourcing
4. External Sourcing
5. Evaluating Recruiting Effectiveness

**C.** Selection (5.94%, 4.39%)
1. Application Process
2. Interviewing
3. Pre-employment Testing
4. Background Investigation
5. Medical Examination
6. Hiring Applicants with Disabilities
7. Illegal Use of Drugs and Alcohol
8. Validation and Evaluation of Selection Process Components

**D.** Career Planning and Development (2.06%, 1.84%)
1. Accommodating Organizational and Individual Needs

2. Mobility Within the Organization
3. Managing Transitions
**E.** Organizational Exit (4.60%, 3.56%)
1. General Issues
2. Layoffs/Reductions-in-Force
3. Constructive Discharge
4. Retaliatory
5. Retirement
6. Employer Defenses Against Litigation

**IV. HUMAN RESOURCE DEVELOPMENT (11%, 12%)**
**A.** HR Training and the Organization (3.06%, 3.72%)
1. The Learning Organization, Linking Training to Organizational Goals, Objectives, and Strategies
2. Human Resources Development as an Organizational Component
3. Funding the Training Function
4. Cost/Benefit Analysis of Training
**B.** Training Needs Analysis (1.52%, 1.52%)
1. Training Needs Analysis Process
2. Methods for Assessing Training Needs
**C.** Training and Development Programs (4.42%, 4.50%)
1. Trainer Selection
2. Design Considerations and Learning Principles
3. Types of Training Programs
4. Instructional Methods and Processes
5. Training Facilities Planning
6. Training Materials
**D.** Evaluation of Training Effectiveness (2.00%, 2.26%)
1. Sources for Evaluation
2. Research Methods for Evaluation
3. Criteria for Evaluating Training

**V. COMPENSATION AND BENEFITS (19%, 15%)**
**A.** Tax & Accounting Treatment of Compensation & Benefit Programs (.57%, .53%)
1. FASB Regulations
2. IRS Regulations
**B.** Economic Factors Affecting Compensation (2.09%, 1.77%)
1. Inflation
2. Interest Rates
3. Industry Competition
4. Foreign Competition
5. Economic Growth
6. Labor Market Trends/Demographics
**C.** Compensation Philosophy, Strategy, and Policy (1.81%, 1.55%)
1. Fitting Strategy & Policy to the External Environment and to an Organization's Culture, Structure, & Objectives
2. Training in and Communication of Compensation Programs

3. Making Compensation Programs Achieve Organizational Objectives
4. Establishing Administrative Controls
**D.** Compensation Programs: Types, Characteristics, and Advantages/Disadvantages (1.71%, 1.20%)
1. Base Pay
2. Differential Pay
3. Incentive Pay
4. Pay Programs for Selected Employees
**E.** Job Evaluation Methods (2.20%, 1.60%)
1. Compensable Factors
2. Ranking Method
3. Classification/Grading Method
4. Factor Comparison Method
5. Point Method
6. Guide Chart-Profile Method (Hay Method)
**F.** Job Pricing, Pay Structures, and Pay Rate Administration (2.14%, 1.49%)
1. Job Pricing and Pay Structures
2. Individual Pay Rate Determination
3. Utilizing Performance Appraisal in Pay Administration
4. Reflecting Market Influences in Pay Structures
5. Wage Surveys
**G.** Employee Benefit Programs: Types, Objectives, Characteristics, and Advantages/Disadvantages (3.42%, 2.17%)
1. Legally Required Programs/Payments
2. Income Replacement
3. Insurance and Income Protection
4. Deferred Pay
5. Pay for Time Not Worked
6. Unpaid Leave
7. Flexible Benefit Plans
8. Recognition and Achievement Awards
**H.** Managing Employee Benefit Programs (3.75%, 3.43%)
1. Employee Benefits Philosophy, Planning, and Strategy
2. Employee Need/Preference Assessment: Surveys
3. Administrative Systems
4. Funding/Investment Responsibilities
5. Coordination with Plan Trustees, Insurers, Health Service Providers and Third-Party Administrators
6. Utilization Review
7. Cost-Benefit Analysis and Cost Management
8. Communicating Benefit Programs/Individual Annual Benefits Reports
9. Monitoring Compensation/Benefits Legal Compliance Programs
**I.** Evaluating Total Compensation Strategy & Program Effectiveness (1.32%, 1.26%)
1. Budgeting

2. Cost Management
3. Assessment of Methods and Processes

## VI. EMPLOYEE AND LABOR RELATIONS (11%, 14%)

A. Union Representation of Employees (1.52%, 1.98%)
   1. Scope of the Labor Management Relations (Taft-Hartley) Act (1947)
   2. Achieving Representative Status
   3. Petitioning for an NLRB Election
   4. Election Campaign
   5. Union Security

B. Employer Unfair Labor Practices (1.68%, 1.91%)
   1. Procedures for Processing Charges of Unfair Labor Practices
   2. Interference, Restraint, and Coercion
   3. Domination and Unlawful Support of Labor Organization
   4. Employee Discrimination to Discourage Union Membership
   5. Retaliation
   6. Remedies

C. Union Unfair Labor Practices, Strikes, and Boycotts (1.96%, 2.60%)
   1. Responsibility for Acts of Union Agents
   2. Union Restraint or Coercion
   3. Duty of Fair Representation
   4. Inducing Unlawful Discrimination by Employer
   5. Excessive or Discriminatory Membership Fees
   6. Strikes and Secondary Boycotts
   7. Strike Preparation

D. Collective Bargaining (2.94%, 4.06%)
   1. Bargaining Issues and Concepts
   2. Negotiation Strategies
   3. Good Faith Requirements
   4. Notice Requirements
   5. Unilateral Changes in Terms of Employment
   6. Duty to Successor Employers or Unions: Buyouts, Mergers, or Bankruptcy
   7. Enforcement Provisions
   8. Injunctions
   9. Mediation and Conciliation
   10. National Emergency Strikes

E. Managing Organization—Union Relations (.88%, 1.16%)
   1. Building and Maintaining Union-Organization Relationships: Cooperative Programs
   2. Grievance Processes and Procedures
   3. Dispute Resolution

F. Maintaining Nonunion Status (.79%, .91%)
   1. Reasons
   2. Strategies

G. Public Sector Labor Relations (1.12%, 1.38%)
   1. Right to Organize
   2. Federal Labor Relations Council
   3. Limitations on Strikes
   4. Mediation and Conciliation

## VII. HEALTH, SAFETY, AND SECURITY (6%, 6%)

A. Health (2.41%, 2.22%)
   1. Employee Assistance Programs
   2. Employee Wellness Programs
   3. Reproductive Health Policies
   4. Chemical Dependency
   5. Communicable Diseases in the Workplace
   6. Employer Liabilities
   7. Stress Management
   8. Smoking Policies
   9. Recordkeeping and Reporting

B. Safety (2.05%, 2.04%)
   1. Areas of Concern
   2. Organization of Safety Program
   3. Safety Promotion
   4. Accident Investigation
   5. Safety Inspections
   6. Human Factors Engineering (Ergonomics)
   7. Special Safety Considerations
   8. Sources of Assistance

C. Security (1.54%, 1.74%)
   1. Organization of Security
   2. Control Systems
   3. Protection of Proprietary Information
   4. Crisis Management and Contingency Planning
   5. Theft and Fraud
   6. Investigations and Preventive Corrections

# APPENDIX B

## Important Organizations in HR Management

### ASSOCIATIONS

**Academy of Management**
P.O. Box 3020
Briarcliff Manor, NY   10510-3020
www.aom.pace.edu/

**AFL-CIO**
815 - 16th Street, NW
Washington, DC   20006
www.afl-cio.org

**American Arbitration Association**
140 W. 51st Street
New York, NY   10020
www.adr.org

**American Compensation Association**
14040 N. Northsight Blvd.
Scottsdale, AZ   85260
www.acaonline.org

**American Management Association**
1601 Broadway
New York, NY   10019-7420
www.amanet.org

**American Payroll Association**
30 East 33rd Street, 5th Floor
New York, NY   10016-5386
www.americanpayroll.org

**American Society for Industrial Security**
1624 Prince Street
Arlington, VA   22314
www.asisonline.org

**American Society for Public Administration**
1120 G Street, NW, Suite 700
Washington, DC   20005
www.aspanet.org

**American Society for Training and Development**
1640 King Street
P.O. Box 1443
Alexandria, VA   22313-2043
www.astd.org

**American Society of Safety Engineers**
1800 East Oakton
Des Plaines, IL   60018
www.asse.org

**Association of Executive Search Consultants, Inc.**
500 Fifth Avenue, Suite 930
New York, NY   10110
www.aesc.org

**College and University Personnel Association**
1233 20th Street, NW, Suite 301
Washington, DC   20036
www.cupa.org

**The Conference Board**
845 Third Avenue
New York, NY   10022-6679
www.conference-board.org

**Employee Benefit Research Institute**
2121 K Street, NW, Suite 600
Washington, DC   20037-1896
www.ebri.org

**Employee Relocation Council**
1720 N Street, NW
Washington, DC   20036-2900
www.erc.org

**ESOP Association**
1726 M St. NW, Suite 501
Washington, DC   20036
www.the-esop-emplowner.org

**Human Resource Certification Institute (HRCI)**
1800 Duke Street
Alexandria, VA   22314
www.shrm.org/hrci

**Human Resource Planning Society**
317 Madison Avenue, Suite 1509
New York, NY   10017
www.hrps.org

**Incentive Manufacturers Representatives Association**
1805 North Mill Street, Suite A
Naperville, IL   60563-1275
(no website)

**Industrial Relations Research Association**
4233 Social Science Building
University of Wisconsin-Madison
1180 Observatory Drive
Madison, WI   53706-1373
www.irra.ssc.wisc.edu

**Institute of Personnel and Development**
IPD House
Camp Road, Wimbledon
London SW   19   4   UX
England
www.ipd.co.uk

**International Association for Human Resource Information Management**
401 North Michigan Avenue
Chicago, IL   60611
www.ihrim.org

**International Foundation of Employee Benefit Plans**
18700 Bluemound Road
Brookfield, WI   53008-0069
www.ifebp.org

**International Personnel Management Association**
1617 Duke Street
Alexandria, VA   22314
www.ipma-hr.org

**National Association for the Advancement of Colored People (NAACP)**
4805 Mt. Hope Drive
Baltimore, MD   21215
www.naacp.org

**National Association of Manufacturers (NAM)**
1331 Pennsylvania Avenue, NW
Washington, DC   20004-1790
www.nam.org

**National Association of Temporary and Staffing Services**
119 South Saint Asaph Street
Alexandria, VA   22314-3119
www.natss.org

**National Employee Services & Recreation Association**
2211 York Road, Suite 207
Oak Brook, IL   60523
www.nesra.org

**Society for Human Resource Management (SHRM)**
1800 Duke Street
Alexandria, VA   22314
www.shrm.org

**U.S. Chamber of Commerce**
1615 H. Street, NW
Washington, DC   20062
www.uschamber.org

**Wellness Councils of America**
Community Health Plaza, Suite 311
7101 Newport Avenue
Omaha, NE   68152
www.welcoa.org

---

# U.S. DEPARTMENT OF LABOR AGENCIES

The following agencies are part of and have the same address as the Department of Labor:

**U.S. Department of Labor**
200 Constitution Ave., NW
Washington, DC   20210
www.dol.gov

**Bureau of Labor Statistics**
www.bls.gov

**Wage and Hour Division**
Employment Standards Administration
www.dol.gov/esa/public/whd-org.htm

**Occupational Safety and Health Administration (OSHA)**
www.osha.gov

**Office of Federal Contract Compliance Programs (OFCCP)**
www.ofccp.gov

# OTHER GOVERNMENT AGENCIES

**Equal Employment Opportunity Commission (EEOC)**
1801 L Street
Washington, DC   20507
www.eeoc.gov

**Federal Mediation and Conciliation Service**
2100 K Street NW
Washington, DC   20427
www.fmcs.gov

**Office of Personnel Management**
1900 E Street NW
Washington, DC   20415-0001
www.opm.gov

**Pension Benefit Guaranty Corporation**
1200 K Street NW
Washington, DC   20005-4026
www.pbgc.gov

# APPENDIX C

# Current Literature in HR Management

Students are expected to be familiar with the professional literature in their fields of study. The professional journals are the most immediate and direct communication link between the researcher and the practicing manager. Three groups of publications are listed below.

## A. RESEARCH-ORIENTED JOURNALS

These journals contain articles that report on original research. Normally these journals contain either sophisticated writing and quantitative verifications of the author's findings or conceptual models and literature reviews of previous research.

ACA Journal
Academy of Management Journal
Academy of Management Review
Administrative Science Quarterly
American Behavioral Scientist
American Journal of Health Promotion
American Journal of Psychology
American Journal of Sociology
American Psychological Measurement
American Psychologist
American Sociological Review
Annual Review of Psychology
Applied Psychology: An International Review
British Journal of Industrial Relations
Decision Sciences
Dispute Resolution Quarterly
Group and Organization Studies
Human Organization
Human Relations
Industrial & Labor Relations Review
Industrial Relations
Interfaces
Journal of Abnormal Psychology
Journal of Applied Behavioral Science
Journal of Applied Business Research
Journal of Applied Psychology
Journal of Business
Journal of Business Communications
Journal of Business and Industrial Marketing
Journal of Business and Psychology
Journal of Business Research
Journal of Communications

Journal of Compensation & Benefits
Journal of Counseling Psychology
Journal of Experimental Social Psychology
Journal of Human Resources
Journal of Industrial Relations
Journal of International Business Studies
Journal of Labor Economics
Journal of Management
Journal of Management Studies
Journal of Managerial Psychology
Journal of Occupational and Organizational Psychology
Journal of Organizational Behavior
Journal of Personality and Social Psychology
Journal of Quality Management
Journal of Quality & Participation
Journal of Social Issues
Journal of Social Policy
Journal of Social Psychology
Journal of Vocational Behavior
Labor History
Labor Relations Yearbook
Management Science
Organizational Behavior and Human Decision Processes
Personnel Psychology
Psychological Bulletin
Psychological Review
Social Forces
Social Science Research
Work and Occupations

## B. MANAGEMENT-ORIENTED JOURNALS

These journals generally cover a wide range of subjects. Articles in these publications normally are aimed at the practitioner and are written to interpret, summarize, or discuss past, present, and future research and administrative applications. Not all the articles in these publications are management-oriented.

ACA News
Academy of Management Executive
Administrative Management
Arbitration Journal
Australian Journal of Management
Benefits and Compensation Solutions
Business Horizons

Business Management
Business Monthly
Business Quarterly
Business and Social Review
California Management Review
Canadian Manager
Columbia Journal of World Business
Compensation and Benefits Management
Compensation and Benefits Review
Directors and Boards
Economist
Employee Benefits News
Employee Relations Law Journal
Employment Practices Decisions
Employment Relations
Employment Relations Today
Entrepreneurship Theory and Practice
Forbes
Fortune
Harvard Business Review
Hospital & Health Services Administration
HR Magazine
Human Resource Executive
Human Resource Management
Human Resource Planning
Human Behavior
IHRIM Link
INC.
Incentive
Industrial Management
Industry Week
International Management
Journal of Business Strategy
Journal of Pension Planning
Journal of Systems Management
Labor Law Journal
Long-Range Planning
Manage
Management Consulting
Management Review
Management Solutions
Management Today
Management World
Managers Magazine
Michigan State University Business Topics
Monthly Labor Review
Nation's Business
Occupational Health & Safety
Organizational Dynamics
Pension World
Personnel Management

Psychology Today
Public Administration Review
Public Manager
Public Opinion Quarterly
Public Personnel Management
Recruiting Today
Reseach Management
SAM Advanced Management Journal
Security Management
Sloan Management Review
Supervision
Supervisory Management
Training
Training and Development
Workforce
Working Woman
Workplace Ergonomics

## C. ABSTRACTS & INDICES

For assistance in locating articles, students should check some of the following indices and abstracts that often contain subjects of interest.

ABI Inform
Applied Science and Technology Index
Applied Social Sciences Index and Abstracts
Business and Industry
Business and Management Practices
Business Periodicals
Compact Disclosure
Dissertation Abstracts
General BusinessFile ASAP
Human Resources Abstracts
Index to Legal Periodicals
Index to Social Sciences and Humanities
Investext
Legaltrac
Management Abstracts
Management Contents
Management Research Abstracts
Psychological Abstracts
Predicasts Prompt
PsychLit
PsycINFO
Reader's Guide to Periodical Literature
Sociological Abstracts
Wilson Business Abstracts
Work-Related Abstracts

# APPENDIX D

# Starting a Career

## STARTING YOUR CAREER

As students reach their Junior and Senior years of college, getting a job after graduation often becomes a major concern. For students who are uncertain about how to approach this process, this appendix provides an outline of the steps to follow, with helpful tips to increase your chance of success in the job market. Many other resources are available to you, and you are encouraged to make use of as many of these as possible.

### Beginning the Job Search

You are looking for the best opportunity and setting in which to begin your career. To identify such an opportunity and setting, you must begin by knowing who you are. The first step is to sit down and determine your abilities, skills, work values, interests, strengths, and weaknesses. Next, go back through your list and determine which of these you would most like to use in your first job. For example, if you are good at understanding and explaining how systems or processes work and like solving problems, you may want to consider jobs that use these skills.

What you are willing and able to do will begin to shape your job search. You will use this information in determining types of positions that are of interest and employers you want to contact, in the construction of your resume and cover letters, and in preparing for your interviews. You must be honest with yourself and know your strengths and weaknesses. Only then will you head down the right path to landing a job that fits you as a person.

Next, you need to investigate the job market. Newspapers and business magazines often carry headlines regarding employment trends and company issues. This is just one source of information. Check with the career center at your school for information particular to the degrees being granted. Campus career fairs featuring employers hiring for different areas provide a wonderful opportunity to collect information on available jobs and preferred skills. Most states publish employment information through their Department of Labor or Commerce. The federal government publishes the *Occupational Outlook Handbook*.

A major source for checking out job opportunities is the Internet. There are many general websites, such as those mentioned in Chapter 8. Also, many professional associations have employment listings for their members. Accessing specific employer websites can provide information on

job possibilities as well. Also, if at all possible, you need to be geographically flexible. A major complaint from employers is that students are not willing to relocate.

Once you have determined who you are and what the job market looks like in your field, you can begin to determine which employers you will pursue. The principles you learned in your marketing class will come into play here. You must have an organized plan for contacting employers. The first part of the plan is to identify those companies in which you are interested. Start with a small list of 10 to 20, which allows you to focus your efforts. This list may include employers that interview on your campus as well as those that don't. The accessibility of the employers will determine how you approach them. For example, if they interview on your campus, your approach will be to sign up for interviews, thoroughly research the employers, and use your resume and interviewing skills to pursue getting a job. If your targeted employers do not interview on your campus, you will use your resume and cover letter to secure an interview on site.

There are many resources available to determine employers in your field. Your college or university career center is a good starting point, because it will have information on employers specifically looking for new college graduates. Membership directories for professional associations can provide member information by field and geographic location. The school or public library may also have company directories and annual reports. The growth of the Internet and World Wide Web has resulted in company home pages that provide information on employment opportunites, as well as several sites available for conducting a job search. Be aware that some of these sites require the user to pay a subscription fee. Campus or regional career fairs provide opportunities to visit in person with employers regarding careers and/or job openings. Many business schools offer free lectures from visiting executives. Attend and take advantage of the information presented in these lectures. Your faculty may also have contacts in various organizations—let them know of your interests.

Once you have determined your list of potential employers, you need to put together your package—your resume, cover letter, interview preparation, and follow-up plans. You also need to purchase a personal day planner and/or large calendar with which to track your job search progress. You may also need to purchase an answering machine. Most employers call you to set up and follow up with interviews. By having an answering machine, you can increase the chance of their reaching you. Make sure you check your initial recording on the machine. It should identify the number called, have a professional greeting, and be easy to understand.

## Your Resume

Many students put off constructing a resume for fear that they don't have enough information to put on the page or because of a lack of personal focus. If you have completed the first step of the job search process, knowing who you are, it will be easier to construct your resume. The resume is a very important document. It is the first impression the employer will have of you as a candidate. IT MUST BE PERFECT! This is the means by which your promote yourself and present your skills. Unfortunately, the employers initially may spend only 20 seconds looking at this document; therefore, you must make it as easy as possible for them to find what they are looking for.

There are some hard and fast rules for resume construction:

**Rule 1—Keep it to one page.** Again, be aware that employers may look at your resume initially for only about 20 seconds. Keep it to the point and on one page. Only those individuals, such as adult students who have significant work experience, should have two-page resumes.

**Rule 2—No mistakes!** This is your presentation of your skills; your lack of attention to the details of your resume will speak a thousand words to the employer. Have three knowledgeable people proofread it, and then correct any mistakes in spelling, punctuation, and grammar.

**Rule 3—No personal information.** The employer can't legally ask about your marital status, weight, health, height, or age, and the resume is not the place to provide this information.

**Rule 4—Provide contact information at the top.** Be sure to include your name, address, phone number, and e-mail address. Use a mailing address that will remain current if you are nearing graduation.

**Rule 5—Keep your resume uncluttered.** Many computer programs allow you to dress up your resume with graphics, but do not distract from your text. In some fields, the use of graphics is more appropriate than others—check with your career center. Many resumes today are being submitted electronically, so be sure yours will be easy to read and will transmit clearly. For printed resumes use a good-quality printer and good-quality bond paper. The additional expense of bond paper is a good investment. The color paper should be conservative and give a professional look. Never print on the back of your resume.

**Rule 6—Place your most important information close to the top.** Include your name, address, phone number, objective, education, skills, and related work experience. Make it easy for the employer to find the things they need.

**Rule 7—Use action verbs, and avoid using "*I*."** Your resume should include incomplete sentences stressing your accomplishments.

**Rule 8—Do not put your references on the resume.** Indicate that references are available upon request. Be sure you compile a list of references should it be requested.

## Resume Format

A variety of resume formats can be used, such as the targeted resume, the functional resume, and the resume letter. Some of them can be seen on career-oriented websites, which allow you to construct your resume using format templates.

For college graduates with limited work experience, the chronological format is used most often. However, for adult students with significant professional experience, either the chronological or functional format may be used. Figure D–1 shows an example of a chronological resume. Notice that the experience listed contains details on accomplishments, not just a listing of tasks performed on the jobs. Figure D–2 is an example of an electronic resume. Notice the inclusion of keywords, which aids in locating your resume in electronic scanning databases. A similar version also can be used for submitting your resume electronically over the Internet or World Wide Web.

## Cover Letter

The cover letter is the most difficult component to write. The purpose of the letter is to tell employers why you are writing, and to persuade them to consider you for an interview if an opening exists, or to consider you for future openings. Submission of electronic resumes may not require a cover letter, depending on the parameters identified by employers. Some employers accept electronic cover letters, while others specify that the resume only should be sent electronically. When submitting printed resumes, you should always send a cover letter.

**FIGURE D–1** *Sample Chronological Resume*

Julie F. Candidate
5866 Jupiter Street
Midvale, KS 67778
Phone: AC-987-6543
e-mail: jcand@abc.com

**Job Objective**
Human resource management position offering professional growth and development

**Education**
**University of Midvale, Bachelor of Science Business Administration, May 2001**
Major: Human Resource Management        Minor: Psychology
- Overall grade point average of 3.7 (A = 4.0)
- Graduated Magna Cum Laude

**Relevant Course work**
- Human Resource Management
- Compensation and Benefits
- Human Resource Seminar
- Industrial Psychology
- Organizational Change
- Management Information Systems

**Special Skills**
- Microsoft Word - Excel - PowerPoint
- Excellent mathematical, writing, and oral communication skills

**Employment History**
10/98 - present   **Payroll Specialist: Financial National Bank, Midvale, KS**
- Prepares biweekly payroll for 150 employees, including payroll taxes and appropriate deductions
- Advises department managers on personnel policies
- Coordinates compliance with Family/Medical Leave Act
- Administers employee bonus incentive plan

4/96 - 10/98   **Human Resources Assistant: Midvale Insurance Company, Midvale, KS**
- Conducted initial interviews for clerical applicants
- Conducted reference checks on applicants
- Maintained employment records in computerized HRIS

9/95 - 3/96   **Compensation and Benefits Intern: Midvale Insurance Co., Midvale, KS**
- Used HRIS to update employee information
- Updated employee compensation
- Completed pay surveys sent to company

**Additional Employment (part-time)**
- Teller, Financial National Bank, Midvale, KS
- Casher, Essex Retail Store, Omaha, NE

Activities   Student Chapter, Society for Human Resource Management (SHRM)
- President, 2000 - 2001
- Program chair, 1999 - 2000
- Member, 1998 - present

**References available upon request**

**FIGURE D–2** *Sample Electronic Resume*

Lee M. Applicant
488 Woodpark Drive
Midvale, KS 67777
Phone: AC-669-6666
e-mail: Lmapp@xyz.com

KEYWORDS

Accounting. Tax Returns. Accounts Payable. Financial Reports. Cost Accounting Systems. Sales Tax Forms. Payroll. Microsoft Office. Excel. Word.

**Education:**  Bachelor of Science, Accounting, University of Midvale, May 2001
GPA 3.4 (A = 4.0)

Related Course Work:

Cost Accounting
Income Tax Accounting
Accounting for Not-for-Profit Organizations
Auditing Principles
Management Information Systems

**Employment:**

9/98-present  Bookkeeper, Holiday - West, Midvale, KS
- Coordinated accounts payable, payroll, preliminary preparation of financial statements, and year-end reports
- Maintained restaurant inventory
- Worked full-time summers; 15-20 hours weekly in school year

5/98-8/98  Camp Counselor, Camp Joy, Rural, KS
- Developed and scheduled water activities and ensured participants' safety
- Created new programs for campers
- Instructed "Working with Others" training for campers

Summers  Lifeguard/Swim Instructor, Midvale Country Club, Midvale, KS
1994-96

**Activities:**  Beta Alpha Psi, Accounting Honorary, 1998-2001
Kappa Kappa Gamma Sorority, President, 2000-2001
Big Brothers, Big Sisters, Volunteer, 1999-2000

**References available upon request**

The cover letter must be specific to the company and demonstrate you know what the firm does and how you might fit into the organization. It should be directed to a specific person or to a title, if a person's name is not available. It is best to send your cover letter and resume to the division or area you are interested in working for rather than the HR department, unless you are otherwise instructed. Because the HR department may receive hundreds of such letters each week, it is more likely that your resume/cover letter will receive the attention you want from the actual department in which you are interested.

The same rules that apply to your resume also apply to your cover letter. It must be error free, one page in length, and printed on a good quality bond paper. It must be specific to the company and to the position of interest. There are two types of cover letters—the letter of inquiry and the letter of application. You use the letter of inquiry to make initial contact with an employer for the purpose of inquiring what positions may be coming open. You may also use it when you have been referred by someone else. For example, a professor suggests you contact a certain person in XYZ corporation that he or she knows. The letter of application indicates that you are writing to apply for a specific position.

In each case, the letter is typically three to four paragraphs in length. The first paragraph details why you are writing (to inquire to apply or at the suggestion of so-and-so). In the second paragraph, you use the information you have gained from prior research of the employer to make comparisons with your qualifications. Do not lie or exaggerate.

In the third paragraph, you refer to your enclosed resume and ask for an interview. You should indicate if you are going to be in the area during a certain time period. Many companies will be happy to visit with you if you are already there. School breaks are a great time to schedule such interviews. You should give them a time frame for responding to your letter, and indicate that you will be back in touch by a certain date. This is where your calendar or daily planner is helpful. Mark the date you are to contact them again. Many employers wait to see if you will follow through and make that second contact. The letter ends with a closing, such as "Sincerely," and signature followed by your typed name. This cover letter should then be sent with your resume. Proofread carefully and make sure you sign it before you put it in the mail.

## Applications

Some employers will ask you to complete an application before being considered for employment. Make sure you are thorough and complete all sections to the best of your ability. On occasion you may run into what may be illegal questions on the application form. Questions can be asked only if they can be shown to concern bona fide occupational qualifications (BFOQ). Therefore questions pertaining to age, gender, marital status, race, national origin, religion, and mental and physical limitations are usually not allowed.

It is best if you, as the applicant, leave these questions blank or put a dash (—) in the blank. Employers asking questions for the purpose of EEO compliance should provide these questions on a separate form or after you have been hired. If possible, type your application—and again, make sure it has no errors.

## Getting the Interview

The purpose of the cover letter and resume is to generate an interview. Once you know you have an interview, you must begin to prepare for it. Because the interview is a conversation with a purpose—finding the best candidate for the job—you can assist the interviewer in this pursuit by being prepared and professional. The key to a successful interview is to know yourself, to know the employer and the position for which you are being interviewed, and to be professional and enthusiastic in your approach.

You should already have done some self-inquiry during the first step of your job search process. The key now is to take, those results and apply them to this employer. To do that, you need to know what the employer does, where the organization is located, and the requirements and description of the positions under consideration. It is highly appropriate to ask the employer for an annual report, job description, or other company information. Your career center may also have this information. Read these, but go beyond that by going to your library and searching for recent information in the news and on the Internet. After reviewing the company information, match your skills and experiences so that you can give specific examples in the interview and show that you have done your homework. It is also recommended that you prepare a list of questions to ask the interviewer. Remember this is a two-way street, and you will also be making a decision on where will be the best place to begin your career. However, it is not appropriate during a screening interview to ask about your salary or benefits.

## Being Prepared for the Interview

It is strongly suggested that you participate in a practice interview prior to the real one. Many career centers offer videotaped practice interviews. By doing this, you will increase your confidence and comfort level. Also take a look at potential interview questions and think of how you would answer each one.

You need to make sure that you present a professional appearance. A suit and tie for men and a skirted suit for women are the most appropriate attire, even if the employer has a "business casual" dress code. You should be conservative with accessories, jewelry, make-up, and cologne or perfume. Your hair should be clean and off the face. This is your first step into the professional world, and you need to look the part. Take the time to make sure everything is clean and pressed, because first impressions last the longest. Also make sure that you reflect enthusiasm about your future.

## During the Interview

On the day of the interview, plan to arrive about 10 to 15 minutes early, which will give you time to locate the proper office. If you are headed to an unfamiliar site, map your route ahead of time and plan for the unexpected. While being lost and having flat tires make funny stories later, your potential employer will not be impressed. Do not smoke before you walk in the door, and remember to get rid of your gum. It is acceptable to have a leather portfolio with extra resumes and a writing portfolio that you take into the interview.

You may initially be greeted by a receptionist or secretary. Be polite and follow their instructions. When the person with whom you will be interviewing comes to get you, stand, smile, and extend your hand. The person is already forming an impression of you based on this initial interaction.

During the interview, sit straight but be comfortable and maintain an acceptable amount of eye contact with the employer. It is important that you listen to each question in its entirety, because it may contain more than one part. Answer the questions to the best of your ability. When appropriate, use an example to personalize your answer, which allows you to demonstrate your research on the company. It is appropriate to ask for clarification if you do not understand a question, but don't do that often. If you should be given the opportunity to ask your questions, ask two or three questions that are focused on the job. At the end of the interview, the interviewer should indicate the next step in the selection process and tell you when that will occur. If the interviewer does not give this information, it is acceptable to ask for it.

The employer may invite you back for a second, more extensive interview. This second interview may include managers, coworkers, and human resource professionals. It also may include meeting with employer representatives at breakfast or lunch. Many students do not think about the meal until it is about to occur. Proper etiquette is very important, especially if you will be placed in situations where you will be dining with clients or customers. Brush up on your dining etiquette before the interview. For example, do not order foods that are difficult to eat or that may spill easily (such as spaghetti), do not order an alcoholic drink even if the employer does, and learn which utensils are appropriate for each course.

## Follow Up

At the conclusion of the interview, shake the interviewer's hand and express thanks for the interview. If it has not already been provided, ask the individual for a business card. When you get home, take a moment to jot down your impression of the interview, what you could have done differently, and your impression of the company. These notes will help you later in preparing for additional interviews and in making your employment decision.

It is important to take time to send a thank-you note. If you interviewed with several people in the company, send a thank-you note to the appropriate individuals. In the note, thank them for their time and again express your interest in the position. If you are no longer interested in the position, send a thank-you note indicating this.

## Accepting a Position

This is the step you hope to get to quickly! Before accepting a position, make sure you have in writing the starting salary and start date, the benefit package, and the location. Once you have accepted a position, you should cease your job search. It is unethical to continue to interview once you have accepted a position, and it could have long-term ramifications for your career.

## Concluding Thoughts

You have worked long and hard to get to this point. With preparation, determination, and persistence, you will be able to reach your goal. The main points are to know yourself and what you are looking for, to know the employer and what they are looking for, and to be able to communicate these things in writing and in person. The easier you can make it for employers to see that the qualications you offer fit what they need, the more successful you will be.

Good luck!

Note: The authors express appreciation to Jo Chytka, the Director of the Career Services Center at the University of Wyoming, for providing the content for this appendix.

# APPENDIX E

# Annual Report Form EEO-1

**Joint Reporting Committee**

- Equal Employment Opportunity Commission
- Office of Federal Contract Compliance Programs (Labor)

## EQUAL EMPLOYMENT OPPORTUNITY

### EMPLOYER INFORMATION REPORT EEO-1

**Standard Form 100**
(Rev. 3/97)

O.M.B. No. 3046-0007
EXPIRES 10/31/99
100-214

---

### Section A — TYPE OF REPORT
Refer to instructions for number and types of reports to be filed

1. Indicate by marking in the appropriate box the type of reporting unit for which this copy of the form is submitted (MARK ONLY ONE BOX).

(1) ☐ Single-establishment Employer Report

Multi-establishment Employer:

(2) ☐ Consolidated Report (Required)

(3) ☐ Headquarters Unit Report (Required)

(4) ☐ Individual Establishment Report (submit one for each establishment with 50 or more employees)

(5) ☐ Special Report

2. Total number of reports being filed by this Company (Answer on Consolidated Report only) _____

---

### Section B — COMPANY IDENTIFICATION (*To be answered by all employers*)

| | OFFICE USE ONLY |
|---|---|
| 1. Parent Company | |
| a. Name of parent company (owns or controls establishment in item 2) omit if same as label | a. |
| Address (Number and street) | b. |
| City or town / State / ZIP code | c. |
| 2. Establishment for which this report is filed. (Omit if same as label) | |
| a. Name of establishment | d. |
| Address (Number and street) / City or town / County / State / ZIP code | e. |
| b. Employer identification No. (IRS 9-DIGIT TAX NUMBER) | f. |

c. Was an EEO-1 report filed for this establishment last year? ☐ Yes ☐ No

---

### Section C — EMPLOYERS WHO ARE REQUIRED TO FILE (*To be answered by all employers*)

☐ Yes ☐ No 1. Does the entire company have at least 100 employees in the payroll period for which you are reporting?

☐ Yes ☐ No 2. Is your company affiliated through common ownership and/or centralized management with other entities in an enterprise with a total employment of 100 or more?

☐ Yes ☐ No 3. Does the company or any of its establishments (a) have 50 or more employees AND (b) is not exempt as provided by 41 CFR 60-1.5. AND either (1) is a prime government contractor or first-tier subcontractor, and has a contract, sub-contract, or purchase order amounting to $50,000 or more, or (2) serves as a depository of Government funds in any amount or is a financial institution which is an issuing and paying agent for U.S. Saving Bonds and Saving Notes?

If the the response to question C-3 is yes, please enter your Dun and Bradstreet identification number (if you have one): ☐☐☐☐☐☐☐☐☐☐

Note: If the answer is yes to questions 1, 2, or 3, complete the entire form, otherwise skip to Section G.

SF 100 Page 2

## Section D — EMPLOYMENT DATA

Employment at this establishment—Report all permanent full-time and part-time employees including apprentices and on-the-job trainees unless specifically excluded as set forth in the instructions. Enter the appropriate figures on all lines and in all columns. Blank spaces will be considered as zeros.

| JOB CATEGORIES | | OVERALL TOTALS (SUM OF COL B THRU K) | NUMBER OF EMPLOYEES | | | | | | | | | |
| --- | --- | --- | --- | --- | --- | --- | --- | --- | --- | --- | --- | --- |
| | | | MALE | | | | | FEMALE | | | | |
| | | | WHITE (NOT OF HISPANIC ORGIN) | BLACK (NOT OF HISPANIC ORGIN) | HISPANIC | ASIAN OR PACIFIC ISLANDER | AMERICAN INDIAN OR ALASKAN NATIVE | WHITE (NOT OF HISPANIC ORGIN) | BLACK (NOT OF HISPANIC ORGIN) | HISPANIC | ASIAN OR PACIFIC ISLANDER | AMERICAN INDIAN OR ALASKAN NATIVE |
| | | A | B | C | D | E | F | G | H | I | J | K |
| Officials and Managers | 1 | | | | | | | | | | | |
| Professionals | 2 | | | | | | | | | | | |
| Technicians | 3 | | | | | | | | | | | |
| Sales Workers | 4 | | | | | | | | | | | |
| Office and Clerical | 5 | | | | | | | | | | | |
| Craft Workers (Skilled) | 6 | | | | | | | | | | | |
| Operatives (Semi-Skilled) | 7 | | | | | | | | | | | |
| Laborers (Unskilled) | 8 | | | | | | | | | | | |
| Service Workers | 9 | | | | | | | | | | | |
| **TOTAL** | 10 | | | | | | | | | | | |
| Total employment reported in previous EEO-1 report | 11 | | | | | | | | | | | |

NOTE: Omit questions 1 and 2 on the Consolidated Report.

1. Date(s) of payroll period used:          2.  Does this establishment employ apprentices?
   1 ☐ Yes    2 ☐ No

## Section E — ESTABLISHMENT INFORMATION *(Omit on the Consolidated Report)*

1. What is the major activity of this establishment? (Be specific, i.e., manufacturing steel castings, retail grocer, wholesale plumbing supplies, title insurance, etc. Include the specific type of product or type of service provided, as well as the principal business or industrial activity.)

OFFICE USE ONLY

g.

## Section F — REMARKS

Use this item to give any identification data appearing on last report which differs from that given above, explain major changes in composition or reporting units, and other pertinent information.

## Section G — CERTIFICATION *(See Instructions G)*

Check one
1 ☐  All reports are accurate and were prepared in accordance with the instructions (check on consolidated only)
2 ☐  This report is accurate and was prepared in accordance with the instructions.

| Name of Certifying Official | Title | Signature | Date |
| --- | --- | --- | --- |
| Name of person to contact regarding this report (Type or print) | Address (Number and Street) | | |
| Title | City and State | ZIP code | Telephone Number (Including Area Code) | Extension |

# Glossary

**4/5ths Rule** Rule stating that discrimination generally is considered to occur if the selection rate for a protected group is less than 80% of the group's representation in the relevant labor market or less than 80% of the selection rate for the majority group.

**401(k) plan** An agreement in which a percentage of an employee's pay is withheld and invested in a tax-deferred account.

**Ability tests** Tests that assess learned skills.

**Active practice** The performance of job-related tasks and duties by trainees during training.

**Adverse selection** Situation in which only higher-risk employees select and use certain benefits.

**Affirmative action** A process in which employers identify problem areas, set goals, and take positive steps to guarantee equal employment opportunities for people in a protected class.

**Agency shop** A firm that requires employees who refuse to join the union to pay amounts equal to union dues and fees for the union's representative services.

**Applicant pool** All persons who are actually evaluated for selection.

**Applicant population** A subset of the labor force population that is available for selection using a particular recruiting approach.

**Aptitude tests** Tests that measure general ability to learn or acquire a skill.

**Arbitration** Process that uses a neutral third party to make a decision.

**Assessment center** A collection of instruments and exercises designed to diagnose a person's development needs.

**Attentional advice** Providing trainees information about the processes and strategies that can lead to training success.

**Attitude survey** A special type of survey that focuses on employees' feelings and beliefs about their jobs and the organization.

**Autonomy** The extent of individual freedom and discretion in the work and its scheduling.

**Availability analysis** An analysis that identifies the number of protected-class members available to work in the appropriate labor markets in given jobs.

**Balance-sheet approach** An approach to international compensation that provides international employees with a compensation package that equalizes cost differences between the international assignment and the same assignment in the home country of the individual or the corporation.

**Bargaining unit** All employees eligible to select a single union to represent and bargain collectively for them.

**Base pay** The basic compensation an employee receives, usually as a wage or salary.

**Behavior modeling** Copying someone else's behavior.

**Behavioral description interview** Interview in which applicants give specific examples of how they have performed or handled problems in the past.

**Behavioral rating approach** Assesses an employee's behaviors instead of other characteristics.

**Behaviorally experienced training** Training methods that deal less with physical skills than with attitudes, perceptions, and interpersonal issues.

**Benchmark job** Job found in many organizations and performed by several individuals who have similar duties that are relatively stable and require similar KSAs.

**Benchmarking** Comparing specific measures of performance against data on those measures in other "best practices" organizations.

**Benefit** An indirect reward given to an employee or group of employees as a part of organizational membership.

**Bona fide occupational qualification (BFOQ)** A characteristic providing a legitimate reason why an employer can exclude persons on otherwise illegal bases of consideration.

**Bonus** A one-time payment that does not become part of the employee's base pay.

**Broadbanding** Practice of using fewer pay grades having broader ranges than traditional compensation systems.

**Business agent** A full-time union official employed by the union to operate the union office and assist union members.

**Business necessity** A practice necessary for safe and efficient organizational operations.

**Career** The sequence of work-related positions a person occupies throughout life.

**Central tendency error** Rating all employees in a narrow band in the middle of the rating scale.

**Checklist** Performance appraisal tool that uses a list of statements or words that are checked by raters.

**Closed shop** A firm that requires individuals to join a union before they can be hired.

**Co-determination** A practice whereby union or worker representatives are given positions on a company's board of directors.

**Co-payment** Employee's payment of a portion of the cost of both insurance premiums and medical care.

**Coaching** Daily training and feedback given to employees by immediate supervisors.

**Collective bargaining** The process whereby representatives of management and workers negotiate over wages, hours, and other terms and conditions of employment.

**Commission** Compensation computed as a percentage of sales in units or dollars.

**Compa-ratio** Pay level divided by the midpoint of the pay range.

**Compensable factor** That used to identify a job value that is commonly present throughout a group of jobs.

**Compensation committee** Usually a subgroup of the board of directors composed of directors who are not officers of the firm.

**Compensatory time off** That given in lieu of payment for extra time worked.

**Competencies** Basic characteristics that can be linked to enhanced performance by individuals or teams.

**Complaint** An indication of employee dissatisfaction that has not been submitted in writing.

**Compressed workweek** Workweek in which a full week's work is accomplished in fewer than five days.

**Conciliation** Process by which a third party attempts to keep union and management negotiators talking so that they can reach a voluntary settlement.

**Concurrent validity** Validity measured when an employer tests current employees and correlates the scores with their performance ratings.

**Construct validity** Validity showing a relationship between an abstract characteristic and job performance.

**Constructive discharge** Occurs when an employer deliberately makes conditions intolerable in an attempt to get an employee to quit.

**Content validity** Validity measured by use of a logical, nonstatistical method to identify the KSAs and other characteristics necessary to perform a job.

**Contractual rights** Rights based on a specific contractual agreement between employer and employee.

**Contrast error** Tendency to rate people relative to other people rather than to performance standards.

**Contributory plan** Pension plan in which the money for pension benefits is paid in by both employees and employers.

**Core competency** A unique capability in the organization that creates high value and that differentiates the organization from its competition.

**Correlation coefficient** An index number giving the relationship between a predictor and a criterion variable.

**Cost/benefit analysis** Compares costs of training with the benefits received.

**Craft union** A union whose members do one type of work, often using specialized skills and training.

**Criterion-related validity** Validity measured by means of a procedure that uses a test as the predictor of how well an individual will perform on the job.

**Culture** The societal forces affecting the values, beliefs, and actions of a distinct group of people.

**Cumulative trauma disorders (CTDs)** Muscle and skeletal injuries that occur when workers repetitively use the same muscles to perform tasks.

**Decertification** A process whereby a union is removed as the representative of a group of employees.

**Defined-benefit plan** Pension plan in which an employee is promised a pension amount based on age and service.

**Defined-contribution plan** Pension plan in which the employer makes an annual payment to an employee's pension account.

**Development** Efforts to improve employees' ability to handle a variety of assignments.

**Differential piece-rate system** Pays employees one piece-rate wage for units produced up to a standard output and a higher piece-rate wage for units produced over the standard.

**Disabled person** Someone who has a physical or mental impairment that substantially limits that person in some major life activities, who has a record of such an impairment, or who is regarded as having such an impairment.

**Discipline** A form of training that enforces organizational rules.

**Disparate impact** Situation that exists when there is a substantial underrepresentation of protected-class members as a result of employment decisions that work to their disadvantage.

**Disparate treatment** Situation that exists when protected-class members are treated differently from others.

**Distributive justice** Perceived fairness in the distribution of outcomes.

**Diversity** Differences among people.

**Downsizing** Reducing the size of an organizational work force.

**Draw** An amount advanced from and repaid to future commissions earned by the employee.

**Due process** In employment settings, the opportunity for individuals to explain and defend their actions against charges of misconduct or other reasons.

**Dues checkoff** Provision that union dues will be deducted automatically from payroll checks of union members.

**Duty** A large work segment composed of several tasks that are performed by an individual.

**Earned-time plan** Plan that combines all time-off benefits into a total number of hours or days that employees can take off with pay.

**Economic value added (EVA)** A firm's net operating profit after the cost of capital is deducted.

**Effectiveness** The extent to which goals have been met.

**Efficiency** The degree to which operations are done in an economical manner.

**Employee assistance program (EAP)** Program that provides counseling and other help to employees having emotional, physical, or other personal problems.

**Employee responsibilities** Obligations to be accountable for actions.

**Employee stock ownership plan (ESOP)** A plan whereby employees gain stock ownership in the organization for which they work.

**Employment contract** Agreement that formally spells out the details of employment.

**Employment-at-will (EAW)** A common-law doctrine stating that employers have the right to hire, fire, demote, or promote whomever they choose, unless there is a law or contract to the contrary.

**Encapsulated development** Situation in which an individual learns new methods and ideas in a development course and returns to a work unit that is still bound by old attitudes and methods.

**Environmental scanning** The process of studying the environment of the organization to pinpoint opportunities and threats.

**Equal employment opportunity (EEO)** The concept that individuals should have equal treatment in all employment-related actions.

**Equity** The perceived fairness of the relation between what a person does (inputs) and what the person receives (outcomes).

**Ergonomics** The proper design of the work environment to address the physical demands experienced by people.

**Essential job functions** The fundamental job duties of the employment position that an individual with a disability holds or desires.

**Executive order** An order issued by the President of the United States to provide direction to government departments on a specific issue or area.

**Exempt employees** Employees to whom employers are not required to pay overtime under the Fair Labor Standards Act.

**Exit interview** An interview in which those leaving the organization are asked to identify the reasons for their departure.

**Expatriate** An employee working in a unit or plant who is not a citizen of the country in which the unit or plant is located, but is a citizen of the country in which the organization is headquartered.

**Experiment** Research to determine how factors respond when changes are made in one or more variables, or conditions.

**Extinction** The absence of an expected response to a situation.

**Extranet** An Internet-linked network that allows employees access to information provided by external entities.

**Federation** A group of autonomous national and international unions.

**Feedback** The amount of information received about how well or how poorly one has performed.

**Flexible benefits plan** One that allows employees to select the benefits they prefer from groups of benefits established by the employer.

**Flexible spending account** Account that allows employees to contribute pretax dollars to buy additional benefits.

**Flexible staffing** Use of recruiting sources and workers who are not employees.

**Flextime** A scheduling arrangement in which employees work a set number of hours per day but vary starting and ending times.

**Forced distribution** Performance appraisal method in which ratings of employees' performance are distributed along a bell-shaped curve.

**Forecasting** Identifying expected future conditions based on information from the past and present.

**Gainsharing** The sharing with employees of greater-than-expected gains in profits and/or productivity.

**Garnishment** A court action in which a portion of an employee's wages is set aside to pay a debt owed a creditor.

**Glass ceiling** Discriminatory practices that have prevented women and other protected-class members from advancing to executive-level jobs.

**Global organization** An organization that has corporate units in a number of countries that are integrated to operate as one organization worldwide.

**Golden parachute** A severance benefit that provides protection and security to executives in the event that they lose their jobs or that their firms are acquired by other firms.

**Graphic rating scale** A scale that allows the rater to mark an employee's performance on a continuum.

**Green-circled employee** An incumbent who is paid below the range set for the job.

**Grievance** A complaint that has been put in writing and made formal.

**Grievance arbitration** A means by which disputes arising from different interpretations of a labor contract are settled by a third party.

**Grievance procedures** Formal channels of communications used to resolve grievances.

**Halo effect** Rating a person high or low on all items because of one characteristic.

**Handbilling** Practice in which unions distribute written publicity in order to convince employees to sign authorization cards.

**Health** A general state of physical, mental, and emotional well-being.

**Health maintenance organization (HMO)** Managed care plan that provides services for a fixed period on a prepaid basis.

**Host-country national** An employee working in a unit or plant who is a citizen of the country in which the unit or plant is located, but where the unit or plant is operated by an organization headquartered in another country.

**HR audit** A formal research effort that evaluates the current state of HR management in an organization.

**HR generalist** A person with responsibility for performing a variety of HR activities.

**HR research** The analysis of data from HR records to determine the effectiveness of past and present HR practices.

**HR specialist** A person with in-depth knowledge and expertise in a limited area of HR.

**HR strategies** The means used to aid the organization in anticipating and managing the supply and demand for human resources.

**Human capital** The total value of human resources to the organization.

**Human Resource (HR) management** The design of formal systems in an organization to ensure the effective and efficient use of human talent to accomplish the organizational goals.

**Human Resource (HR) planning** The process of analyzing and identifying the need for and availability of human resources so that the organization can meet its objectives.

**Human resource information system (HRIS)** An integrated system designed to provide information used in HR decision making.

**Illegal issues** Collective bargaining issues that would require either party to take illegal action.

**Immediate confirmation** The concept that people learn best if reinforcement is given as soon as possible after training.

**Importing and exporting** The phase of international interaction in which an organization begins selling and buying goods and services with organizations in other countries.

**Independent contractors** Workers who perform specific services on a contract basis.

**Individual retirement account (IRA)** A special account in which an employee can set aside funds that will not be taxed until the employee retires.

**Individual-centered career planning** Career planning that focuses on individuals' careers rather than on organizational needs.

**Individualism** Dimension of culture that refers to the extent to which people in a country prefer to act as individuals instead of members of groups.

**Industrial union** A union that includes many persons working in the same industry or company, regardless of jobs held.

**Informal training** Training that occurs internally through interactions and feedback among employees.

**Interfaces** Areas of contact between the HR unit and managers within the organization.

**Intranet** An organizational network that operates over the Internet.

**Job** A grouping of similar positions having common tasks, duties, and responsibilities.

**Job analysis** A systematic way to gather and analyze information about the content and the human requirements of jobs, and the context in which jobs are performed.

**Job criteria** Important elements of a job on which performance is measured.

**Job description** Identification of the tasks, duties, and responsibilities of a job.

**Job design** Organizing tasks, duties, and responsibilities into a productive unit of work.

**Job enlargement** Broadening the scope of a job by expanding the number of different tasks to be performed.

**Job enrichment** Increasing the depth of a job by adding employee responsibility for planning, organizing, controlling, and evaluating the job.

**Job evaluation** The systematic determination of the relative worth of jobs within an organization.

**Job family** A grouping of jobs having similar characteristics.

**Job posting and bidding** A system in which the employer provides notices of job openings within the organization and employees respond by applying for specific openings.

**Job responsibilities** Obligations to perform certain tasks and duties.

**Job rotation** The process of shifting a person from job to job.

**Job satisfaction** A positive emotional state resulting from evaluating one's job experiences.

**Job specifications** List the knowledge, skills, and abilities (KSAs) an individual needs to do the job satisfactorily.

**Just cause** Sufficient justification for taking employment-related actions.

**Keogh plan** A type of individualized pension plan for self-employed individuals.

**Labor force population** All individuals who are available for selection if all possible recruitment strategies are used.

**Labor markets** The external sources from which organizations attract employees.

**Lockout** Shutdown of company operations undertaken by management to prevent union members from working.

**Long-term orientation** Dimension of culture that refers to values people hold that emphasize the future, as opposed to short-term values focusing on the present and the past.

**Lump-sum increase (LSI)** A one-time payment of all or part of a yearly pay increase.

**Managed care** Approaches that monitor and reduce medical costs using restrictions and market system alternatives.

**Management by objectives (MBO)** Specifies the performance goals that an individual hopes to attain within an appropriate length of time.

**Management rights** Those rights reserved to the employer to manage, direct, and control its business.

**Mandated benefits** Those benefits which employers in the United States must provide to employees by law.

**Mandatory issues** Collective bargaining issues that are identified specifically by labor laws or court decisions as being subject to bargaining.

**Marginal functions** Functions that are part of a job but are incidental or ancillary to the purpose and nature of a job.

**Market line** The line on a graph showing the relationship between job value, as determined by job evaluation points, and pay survey rates.

**Market price** Typical wage paid for a job in the immediate labor market.

**Masculinity/Femininity** Dimension of culture that refers to the degree to which "masculine" values prevail over "feminine" values.

**Massed practice** The performance of all of the practice at once.

**Maturity curve** Curve that depicts the relationship between experience and pay rates.

**Mediation** Process by which a third party assists negotiators in their discussions and also suggests settlement proposals.

**Mental ability tests** Tests that measure reasoning capabilities.

**Mentoring** A relationship in which managers at midpoints in their careers aid individuals in the earlier stages of their careers.

**Moonlighting** Work outside a person's regular employment that takes 12 or more additional hours per week.

**Motivation** The desire within a person causing that person to act.

**Multinational enterprise (MNE)** An organization with units located in foreign countries.

**National emergency strike** A strike that would affect the national economy significantly.

**Negative reinforcement** An individual works to avoid an undesirable consequence.

**Nepotism** Practice of allowing relatives to work for the same employer.

**Noncompete covenants** Agreement that prohibits an individual who leaves the organization from competing with the employer in the same line of business for a specified period of time.

**Noncontributory plan** Pension plan in which all the funds for pension benefits are provided by the employer.

**Nondirective interview** Interview that uses general questions, from which other questions are developed.

**Nonexempt employees** Employees who must be paid overtime under the Fair Labor Standards Act.

**Nonpiracy agreement** Provisions stating that if the individual leaves the organization, existing customers and clients cannot be solicited for business for a specified period of time.

**Ombudsman** Person outside the normal chain of command who acts as a problem solver for management and employees.

**Organization chart** A depiction of the relationships among jobs in an organization.

**Organization-centered career planning** Career planning that focuses on jobs and on constructing career paths that provide for the logical progression of people between jobs in an organization.

**Organizational commitment** The degree to which employees believe in and accept organizational goals and desire to remain with the organization.

**Organizational culture** A pattern of shared values and beliefs giving members of an organization meaning and providing them with rules for behavior.

**Orientation** The planned introduction of new employees to their jobs, coworkers, and the organization.

**Outplacement** A group of services provided to displaced employees to give them support and assistance.

**Panel interview** Interview in which several interviewers interview the candidate at the same time.

**Pay compression** Situation in which pay differences among individuals with different levels of experience and performance in the organization becomes small.

**Pay equity** Similarity in pay for jobs requiring comparable levels of knowledge, skills, and ability even where actual job duties differ significantly.

**Pay grade** A grouping of individual jobs having approximately the same job worth.

**Pay survey** A collection of data on existing compensation rates for workers performing similar jobs in other organizations.

**Peer review panel** Alternative dispute resolution method in which a panel of employees hear appeals from disciplined employees and make recommendations or decisions.

**Pension plans** Retirement benefits established and funded by employers and employees.

**Performance appraisal (PA)** The process of evaluating how well employees perform their jobs when compared to a set of standards, and then communicating that information.

**Performance management system** Processes used to identify, encourage, measure, evaluate, improve, and reward employee performance.

**Performance standards** Indicators of what the job accomplishes and how performance is measured; expected levels of performance.

**Permissive issues** Collective bargaining issues that are not mandatory but relate to certain jobs.

**Perquisites (perks)** Special benefits—usually noncash items —for executives.

**Placement** Fitting a person to the right job.

**Policies** General guidelines that focus organizational actions.

**Portability** A pension plan feature that allows employees to move their pension benefits from one employer to another.

**Position** A job performed by one person.

**Positive reinforcement** A person receives a desired reward.

**Power distance** Dimension of culture that refers to the inequality among the people of a nation.

**Predictive validity** Validity measured when test results of applicants are compared with subsequent job performance.

**Predictors** Measurable indicators of selection criteria.

**Preferred provider organization (PPO)** A health-care provider that contracts with an employer group to provide health-care services to employees at a competitive rate.

**Primary research** Research method in which data is gathered firsthand for the specific project being conducted.

**Procedural justice** The perceived fairness of the process and procedures used to make decisions about employees.

**Procedures** Customary methods of handling activities.

**Production cells** Groupings of workers who produce entire products or components of products.

**Productivity** A measure of the quantity and quality of work done, considering the cost of the resources it took to do the work.

**Profit sharing** A system to distribute a portion of the profits of the organization to employees.

**Protected class** Those individuals who fall within a group identified for protection under equal employment laws and regulations.

**Psychological contract** The unwritten expectations that employees and employers have about the nature of their work relationships.

**Punishment** Action taken to repel a person from an undesired action.

**Quality circle** A small group of employees who monitor productivity and quality and suggest solutions to problems.

**Ranking** Listing of all employees from highest to lowest in performance.

**Rater bias** Error that occurs when a rater's values or prejudices distort the rating.

**Ratification** Process by which union members vote to accept the terms of a negotiated labor agreement.

**Realistic job preview (RJP)** The process through which an interviewer provides a job applicant with an accurate picture of a job.

**Reasonable accommodation** A modification or adjustment to a job or work environment that enables a qualified individual with a disability to have equal employment opportunity.

**Recency effect** Error in which the rater gives greater weight to recent events when appraising an individual's performance.

**Reciprocity** A feeling of obligation to "give in return" or reciprocate good treatment.

**Recruiting** The process of generating a pool of qualified applicants for organizational jobs.

**Red-circled employee** An incumbent who is paid above the range set for the job.

**Reengineering** Rethinking and redesigning work to improve cost, service, and speed.

**Reinforcement** A concept that people tend to repeat responses that give them some type of positive reward and avoid actions associated with negative consequences.

**Reliability** The consistency with which a test measures an item.

**Repatriation** The process of bringing expatriates home.

**Retaliation** Punitive actions taken by employers against individuals who exercise their legal rights.

**Return on investment (ROI)** Calculation showing the value of expenditures for HR activities.

**Reverse discrimination** A condition that may exist when a person is denied an opportunity because of preferences given to protected-class individuals who may be less qualified.

**Rights** That which belongs to a person by law, nature, or tradition.

**Right to privacy** Defined in legal terms for individuals as the freedom from unauthorized and unreasonable intrusion into their personal affairs.

**Right-to work laws** State laws that prohibit both the closed shop and the union shop.

**Right-to-sue letter** A letter issued by the EEOC that notifies a complainant that he or she has 90 days in which to file a personal suit in federal court.

**Role playing** A development technique requiring the trainee to assume a role in a given situation and act out behaviors associated with that role.

**Rules** Specific guidelines that regulate and restrict the behavior of individuals.

**Sabbatical leave** Paid time off the job to develop and rejuvenate oneself.

**Safety** Condition in which the physical well-being of people is protected.

**Salaries** Payments that are consistent from period to period despite the number of hours worked.

**Salting** Practice in which unions hire and pay people to apply for jobs at certain companies; when the people are hired, they begin union organizing efforts.

**Secondary research** Research method using data already gathered by others and reported in books, articles in professional journals, or other sources.

**Security** Protection of employer facilities and equipment from unauthorized access and protection of employees while on work premises or work assignments.

**Security audit** A review of the security vulnerability in an organization.

**Selection** The process of choosing individuals who have relevant qualifications to fill jobs in an organization.

**Selection criteria** Characteristics that a person must have to do the job successfully.

**Selection interview** Interview designed to identify information on a candidate and clarify information from other sources.

**Self-directed work team** An organizational team composed of individuals who are assigned a cluster of tasks, duties, and responsibilities to be accomplished.

**Separation agreement** Agreement in which an employee who is being terminated agrees not to sue the employer in exchange for specified benefits.

**Serious health condition** A health condition requiring inpatient, hospital, hospice, or residential medical care or continuing physician care.

**Severance pay** A security benefit voluntarily offered by employers to employees who lose their jobs.

**Sexual harassment** Actions that are sexually directed, are unwanted, and subject the worker to adverse employment conditions or create a hostile work environment.

**Shamrock team** An organizational team composed of a core of members, resource experts who join the team as appropriate, and part-time/temporary members as needed.

**Silver parachute** A severance and benefits plan to protect nonexecutives if their firms are acquired by other firms.

**Simulation** A development technique that requires participants to analyze a situation and decide the best course of action based on the data given.

**Situational interview** A structured interview composed of questions about how applicants might handle specific job situations.

**Skill variety** The extent to which the work requires several different activities for successful completion.

**Spaced practice** Several practice sessions spaced over a period of hours or days.

**Special-purpose team** An organizational team that is formed to address specific problems and may continue to work together to improve work processes or the quality of products and services.

**Statutory rights** Rights based on laws.

**Stock option** A plan that gives an individual the right to buy stock in a company, usually at a fixed price for a period of time.

**Straight piece-rate system** A pay system in which wages are determined by multiplying the number of units produced by the piece rate for one unit.

**Strategic planning** The process of identifying organizational objectives and the actions needed to achieve those objectives.

**Stress interview** Interview designed to create anxiety and put pressure on an applicant to see how the person responds.

**Strike** Work stoppage in which union members refuse to work in order to put pressure on an employer.

**Structured interview** Interview that uses a set standardized questions asked of all job applicants.

**Substance abuse** The use of illicit substances or the misuse of controlled substances, alcohol, or other drugs.

**Suggestion system** A formal method of obtaining employee input and upward communication.

**SWOT analysis** examines the *strengths* and *weaknesses* of the organizations internally and the *opportunities* and *threats* externally.

**Task** A distinct, identifiable work activity composed of motions.

**Task identity** The extent to which the job includes a "whole" identifiable unit of work that is carried out from start to finish and that results in a visible outcome.

**Task significance** The amount of impact the job has on other people.

**Tax equalization plan** Compensation plan used to protect expatriates from negative tax consequences.

**Third-country national** An employee who is a citizen of one country, working in a second country, and employed by an organization headquartered in a third country.

**Total Quality Management (TQM)** A comprehensive management process focusing on the continuous improvement of organizational activities to enhance the quality of the goods and services supplied.

**Training** A process whereby people acquire capabilities to aid in the achievement of organizational goals.

**Transition stay bonus** Extra payment for those employees whose jobs are being eliminated, thereby motivating them to remain with the organization for a period of time.

**Turnover** Process in which employees leave the organization and have to be replaced.

**Uncertainty avoidance** Dimension of culture that refers to the preference of people in a country for structured rather than unstructured situations.

**Undue hardship** Condition created when making a reasonable accommodation for individuals with disabilities that imposes significant difficulty or expense on an employer.

**Union** A formal association of workers that promotes the interests of its members through collective action.

**Union authorization card** Card signed by an employee to designate a union as his or her collective bargaining agent.

**Union security provisions** Contract provisions to aid the union in obtaining and retaining members.

**Union shop** A firm that requires that an employee join a union, usually 30 to 60 days after being hired.

**Union steward** An employee of a firm or organization who is elected to serve as the first-line representative of unionized workers.

**Unit labor cost** The total labor cost per unit of output, which is the average cost of workers divided by their average levels of output.

**Utility analysis** Analysis in which economic or other statistical models are built to identify the costs and benefits associated with specific HR activities.

**Utilization analysis** An analysis that identifies the number of protected-class members employed and the types of jobs they hold in an organization.

**Utilization review** An audit and review of the services and costs billed by health-care providers.

**Validity** The extent to which a test actually measures what it says it measures.

**Validity generalization** The extension of the validity of a test to different groups, similar jobs, or other organizations.

**Variable pay** Compensation linked directly to performance accomplishments; compensation linked to individual, team, and/or organization performance.

**Vestibule training** A type of training which occurs in special facilities that replicate the equipment and work demands of jobs.

**Vesting** The right of employees to receive benefits from their pension plans.

**Wage and salary administration** Activities involved in the development, implementation, and maintenance of a base pay system.

**Wages** Payments directly calculated on the amount of time worked.

**Well-pay** Extra pay for not taking sick leave.

**Wellness programs** Programs designed to maintain or improve employee health before problems arise.

**Whistle-blowers** Individuals who report real or perceived wrongs committed by their employers.

**Work analysis** Studying the workflow, activities, context, and output of a job.

**Work sample tests** Tests that require an applicant to perform a simulated job task.

**Workers' compensation** Benefits provided to persons injured on the job.

**Wrongful discharge** Occurs when an employer terminates an individual's employment for reasons that are illegal or improper.

**Yield ratio** A comparison of the number of applicants at one stage of the recruiting process to the number at the next stage.

# Name Index

# Subject Index